Self-Management and Leadership Development

NEW HORIZONS IN MANAGEMENT

Series Editor: Cary L. Cooper, CBE, *Distinguished Professor of Organizational Psychology and Health, Lancaster University, UK.*

This important series makes a significant contribution to the development of management thought. This field has expanded dramatically in recent years and the series provides an invaluable forum for the publication of high quality work in management science, human resource management, organizational behaviour, marketing, management information systems, operations management, business ethics, strategic management and international management.

The main emphasis of the series is on the development and application of new original ideas. International in its approach, it will include some of the best theoretical and empirical work from both well-established researchers and the new generation of scholars.

Titles in the series include:

Women in Leadership and Management
Edited by Duncan McTavish and Karen Miller

Appreciative Inquiry and Knowledge Management
A Social Constructionist Perspective
Tojo Thatchenkery and Dilpreet Chowdhry

Research Companion to the Dysfunctional Workplace
Management Challenges and Symptoms
Edited by Janice Langan-Fox, Cary L. Cooper and Richard J. Klimoski

Research Companion to Emotion in Organizations
Edited by Neal M. Ashkanasy and Cary L. Cooper

International Terrorism and Threats to Security
Managerial and Organizational Challenges
Edited by Ronald J. Burke and Cary L. Cooper

Women on Corporate Boards of Directors
International Research and Practice
Edited by Susan Vinnicombe, Val Singh, Ronald J. Burke, Diana Bilimoria and Morten Huse

Handbook of Managerial Behavior and Occupational Health
Edited by Alexander-Stamatios G. Antoniou, Cary L. Cooper, George P. Chrousos, Charles D. Spielberger and Michael William Eysenck

Workplace Psychological Health
Current Research and Practice
Paula Brough, Michael O'Driscoll, Thomas Kalliath, Cary L. Cooper and Steven A. Y. Poelmans

Research Companion to Corruption in Organizations
Edited by Ronald J. Burke and Cary L. Cooper

Self-Management and Leadership Development
Edited by Mitchell G. Rothstein and Ronald J. Burke

Self-Management and Leadership Development

Edited by

Mitchell G. Rothstein

Director and Professor, Aubrey Dan Program in Management and Organizational Studies, University of Western Ontario, Canada

Ronald J. Burke

Professor of Organizational Behavior, Schulich School of Business, York University, Canada

NEW HORIZONS IN MANAGEMENT

Edward Elgar

Cheltenham, UK • Northampton, MA, USA

Published by
Edward Elgar Publishing Limited
The Lypiatts
15 Lansdown Road
Cheltenham
Glos GL50 2JA
UK

Edward Elgar Publishing, Inc.
William Pratt House
9 Dewey Court
Northampton
Massachusetts 01060
USA

A catalogue record for this book
is available from the British Library

Library of Congress Control Number: 2009940648

Mixed Sources
Product group from well-managed
forests and other controlled sources
www.fsc.org Cert no. SA-COC-1565
© 1996 Forest Stewardship Council

FSC

ISBN 978 1 84844 323 5

Printed and bound by MPG Books Group, UK

Contents

List of contributors   vii
Acknowledgments   ix

Self-assessment and leadership development: an overview   1
Mitchell G. Rothstein and Ronald J. Burke

PART I   SELF-AWARENESS AND LEADERSHIP
          DEVELOPMENT

1   The role of the individual in self-assessment for leadership
     development   25
     Allan H. Church and Christopher T. Rotolo

2   Inspiring the development of emotional, social and cognitive
     intelligence competencies in managers   62
     Richard E. Boyatzis, Tony Lingham and Angela Passarelli

3   Problems in managing the self-assessment process for
     leaders-to-be   91
     James G.S. Clawson

4   Taking charge: discovering the magic in your psychological
     assessment   108
     Sandra L. Davis

5   Assessing leadership and the leadership gap   129
     Jean Brittain Leslie and Ruohong Wei

6   Emotional intelligence and interpersonal competencies   160
     Ronald E. Riggio

7   How to matter   183
     Stewart Emery

PART II   THE SELF-MANAGEMENT OF COMMON
          LEADERSHIP CHALLENGES

8   Managing your leadership career in hard times   197
     John Blenkinsopp, Yehuda Baruch and Ruth Winden

9   Personal goals for self-directed leaders: traditional and new
    perspectives   226
    Thomas S. Bateman

10 Self-directed work teams: best practices for leadership
    development   251
    *Wendy L. Bedwell, Marissa L. Shuffler, Jessica L. Wildman
    and Eduardo Salas*

11 Work motivations, job behaviors and flourishing in work and
    life   295
    Ronald J. Burke

12 Enlisting others in your development as a leader   336
    Dawn E. Chandler and Kathy E. Kram

13 Resilience and leadership: the self-management of failure   361
    Gillian A. King and Mitchell G. Rothstein

14 The role of developmental social networks in effective leader
    self-learning processes   395
    *Krista Langkamer Ratwani, Stephen J. Zaccaro, Sena Garven
    and David S. Geller*

PART III   SELF-MANAGEMENT AND UNIQUE
           LEADERSHIP CHALLENGES

15 Self-assessment and self-development of global leaders   429
    Paula Caligiuri and Ruchi Sinha

16 Learning from life experiences: a study of female academic
    leaders in Australia   447
    Linley Lord and Susan Vinnicombe

17 Preparing next generation business leaders   464
    Philip Mirvis, Kevin Thompson and Chris Marquis

18 And leadership development for all   487
    Lyndon Rego, David G. Altman and Steadman D. Harrison III

Index   507

Contributors

David G. Altman, Center for Creative Leadership, USA

Yehuda Baruch, University of East Anglia, UK

Thomas S. Bateman, University of Virginia, USA

Wendy L. Bedwell, University of Central Florida, USA

John Blenkinsopp, Teesside University, UK

Richard E. Boyatzis, Case Western Reserve University, USA

Ronald J. Burke, York University, Canada

Paula Caligiuri, Rutgers University, USA

Dawn E. Chandler, California Polytechnic State University, USA

Allan H. Church, PepsiCo Inc., USA

James G.S. Clawson, University of Virginia, USA

Sandra L. Davis, MDA Leadership Consulting, USA

Stewart Emery, Consultant, USA

Sena Garven, US Army Research Institute for the Behavioral and Social Sciences, USA

David S. Geller, George Mason University, USA

Steadman D. Harrison III, Center for Creative Leadership, USA

Gillian A. King, Bloorview Research Institute, Canada

Kathy E. Kram, Boston University, USA

Krista Langkamer Ratwani, Aptima Inc., USA

Jean Brittain Leslie, Center for Creative Leadership, USA

Tony Lingham, Case Western Reserve University, USA

Linley Lord, Curtin University of Technology, Australia

Chris Marquis, Harvard Business School, USA

Philip Mirvis, Center for Corporate Citizenship, USA

Angela Passarelli, Case Western Reserve University, USA

Lyndon Rego, Center for Creative Leadership, USA

Ronald E. Riggio, Claremont McKenna College, USA

Mitchell G. Rothstein, University of Western Ontario, Canada

Christopher T. Rotolo, PepsiCo Inc., USA

Eduardo Salas, University of Central Florida, USA

Marissa L. Shuffler, University of Central Florida, USA

Ruchi Sinha, Rutgers University, USA

Kevin Thompson, IBM, USA

Susan Vinnicombe, Cranfield University, UK

Ruohong Wei, Center for Creative Leadership, Singapore

Jessica L. Wildman, University of Central Florida, USA

Ruth Winden, Careers Enhanced Ltd., UK

Stephen J. Zaccaro, George Mason University, USA

Acknowledgments

My heartfelt thanks to Ron for many years of mentorship, advice and friendship, including your invaluable guidance throughout this project. To our contributors, thanks so much for sharing our vision for the book. The Aubrey Dan Program in Management and Organizational Studies at the University of Western Ontario supported the preparation of this work. And thanks to Gillian for everything you have done.

Mitchell G. Rothstein
London, Canada

I have known and worked with Mitch for almost 20 years. Thanks Mitch for spearheading this initiative. I am also grateful to our contributors for their excellent work. York University contributed to the preparation of my chapters. And finally, thanks to our friends at Edward Elgar for supporting our efforts at every turn in a highly professional and supportive way.

Ronald J. Burke
Toronto, Canada

A very special thanks goes to our assistant, Linda K. Smith, for her diligence and hard work in editing and helping to produce this volume.

Self-assessment and leadership development: an overview

Mitchell G. Rothstein and Ronald J. Burke

This volume fills what we see as a critical gap in the research and writing on leadership and leadership development. The topic of leadership is, arguably, the subject of more research and writing than any other topic in the management literature. A search of the Amazon.com data base reveals that there are currently over 8500 books in print with leadership in the title and over 19 800 books listed on the topic of leadership. In addition, there are hundreds of research articles on leadership published in academic journals. Despite this vast literature, our understanding of leadership and how to develop leaders is still falling short. For example, evidence suggests that a shortage of effective leaders exists (Michaels et al, 2001), that organizations are not doing a satisfactory job at developing future leaders (Fulmer and Conger, 2004), and that between 50 to 75 per cent of individuals in leadership positions are underperforming (Hogan and Hogan, 2001), an estimate borne out by the tenure of individuals holding senior level leadership positions, which has steadily fallen over the past two decades (Burke, 2006; Burke and Cooper, 2006).

Leadership research has been ongoing for decades. Although this research has accumulated a body of knowledge informing us of what leaders do (for example, Yukl, 1998), this work has not generally been useful in contributing to our understanding of how leaders develop. There are several possible explanations for this. First, a considerable amount of this research has focused on what makes leaders successful, in the sense of what they accomplished, rather than on how they developed the expertise to contribute to the success of the work units they lead. Second, organizations have tolerated bad leadership and bad leaders. There was a period during which larger environmental factors (for example, lack of competition, trade barriers, proprietary technology) contributed to making many organizations successful even though their leaders were falling short. In addition, until recently, followers rarely complained about failing leadership (Kellerman, 2004). Third, most research has had a positive and optimistic bias, assuming that leaders were generally successful by virtue of holding leadership positions. Efforts were then made to identify factors associated with their successes. Relatively little research focused on leadership shortcomings, failures or derailments, or the 'dark side' of leadership, with some notable exceptions (for example, Van Velsor and Leslie, 1995). The character and behavioral flaws that limited effectiveness have not received adequate attention until very recently. Fourth, organizational efforts to develop leadership talents have been hit and miss (Fulmer and Conger, 2004). Finally, MBA-level courses that address leadership have been criticized as typically too conceptual and taught by individuals who themselves had never been leaders or demonstrated leadership skills (Mintzberg, 2004).

Despite these many problems in the broad-based leadership literature and common organizational leadership development practices, the theoretical and research-based approaches to the study of leadership have in fact produced a body of knowledge on leadership, albeit often contradictory. In a systematic and thorough review of this literature, Yukl (1998) concludes that even though leadership has been studied with very different approaches, reaching in some cases quite different conclusions, nevertheless, we do know a good deal about what leaders actually do. What we know considerably less about, however, is how leaders got there, what developmental paths led them to their positions of leadership, what experiences and achievements were critical to their development, and what role they themselves took to manage their own development. Although some work has been done to investigate and document organizational practices designed to develop leaders, there is very little work published that systematically focuses on the instrumental role required by leaders to manage their own development. This is the subject of the current volume.

Ironically, not only are individuals not faring well in their leadership roles and organizations are not doing a good job of developing their leadership talent, there is also increasing evidence that many leadership aspirants and those already holding leadership positions are dissatisfied and frustrated (Friedman, 2008a; 2008b; Nash and Stevenson, 2004a; 2004b). Although some of this dissatisfaction clearly must be related to the stress of leading in the turbulent times in which we live (Burke and Cooper, 2004), poor selection, promotion and development practices by organizations must also be considered as major factors contributing to poor leadership performance and leaders who are unhappy in their roles. The authors who have contributed to this volume, however, share in the belief that organizations are not solely to blame for poor leadership development practices, and that the responsibility needs to shift more to aspiring leaders to be instrumental in their own development.

The need for effective leaders grows unabated. For example, one of the biggest challenges faced by business today is coping with rapid and continuous change in markets and competition due to globalization and technological innovations. Many authors, such as Kotter (1996), have highlighted the critical role of leadership in managing these change issues. The sheer volume of research and writing on the subject of leadership underscores the importance of this topic and the value put on increasing our understanding of leadership effectiveness by academics, organizations, and individuals aspiring to be leaders. The need to understand how leaders develop, therefore, remains a subject of critical interest in the business and management literature.

In response to this need, business schools around the world have strengthened their focus on leadership development in both degree programs and executive education programs. In addition to traditional knowledge-based curricula and strategic analysis and decision making, business education has increasingly emphasized leadership skill development. Texts, such as that authored by Whetten and Cameron (1998), that provide skill practice guidelines and exercises have been very popular. Yet there continues to be criticism of business school curricula, in particular with regard to the poor preparation of graduates for assuming leadership roles. In addition, we are constantly made aware of the failures of leaders through research and the popular press. Whether through the pioneering work of the Center for Creative Leadership (for example, Van Velsor and Leslie, 1995) on the factors that lead to the derailment of leaders' careers, or through the frequent news reports of unethical behavior and poor performance of business leaders, it has been made clear that leaders still fail at a rather alarming rate. Moreover, as the population ages and more people retire, the need for effective leadership throughout all levels of an organization will increase what has been termed the 'war for talent' (Michaels et al., 2001). It seems to us, therefore, that despite the immense literature on leadership, and all the efforts to develop leaders by organizations and business schools, the critical need for more effective leaders requires continuing efforts to determine the critical factors that contribute to leadership development.

The present volume addresses this need by taking a perspective that has received little systematic attention by researchers and authors on leadership. Although several books have been published on the topic of leadership development, including an excellent volume produced by the Center for Creative Leadership (McCauley and Van Velsor, 2004), all of the books we are aware of are almost exclusively focused on leadership development practices from the perspective of organizations, training institutions and managers in their role of developing their subordinates. What is clearly missing in this body of work is the important role of the individual in self-managing his/her own development as an aspiring leader. What are the responsibilities and requirements of aspiring leaders to influence and manage their own development process? How does the critical role of self-awareness impact the self-management process? How does the individual cope with the multitude of challenges faced during the development process? What are the ways and means open to individuals interested in self-managing their own leadership development? What does this self-management process contribute to our understanding of leadership generally, as well as our understanding of how leadership develops most effectively? These and other related questions are critical for individuals to understand in order that they may assume responsibility and take an instrumental role in their own development as a leader.

The need for individuals to take direct personal responsibility for their development has never been greater. Increasingly, as organizations downsize, outsource, and cut costs to deal with fierce competition, globalization, and demands from shareholders to maintain profits, there is little commitment given to leadership development activities at the organizational level. Organizations are no longer willing to commit resources to leadership development because of other short-term needs and the belief that if individuals want to develop, it is up to them to figure out how to do it (Moses, 1997).

OBJECTIVES AND SCOPE OF THIS VOLUME

The goal of this volume is to bring together contributions from leading scholars and practitioners in the leadership development field in a collection that will document current research and practice regarding the self-management of leadership development. Although this topic has been broached by a number of authors previously, it has typically been on an ad hoc basis and most often discussed as tangential to some other topic. For example, there is considerable literature on the critical role of mentors and networks in the career development of leaders, but relatively little discussion of how individuals should manage these important relationships. Similarly, a great deal of research has been conducted on the value of performance feedback as well as how to evaluate performance and provide appropriate personal feedback (cf. Murphy and Cleveland, 1995), but relatively little has been written on how an individual can effectively manage the process of obtaining good feedback and applying it to his/her own leadership development. In general, the role of assessment of leadership skills, values and personality is well recognized at the organizational level to identify and develop leadership talent, but the responsibility of an individual to engage in self-assessment and develop self-awareness has received very little attention. This volume is the first comprehensive treatment of what is known from research and best practice on the self-management of leadership development.

Our view of leadership development in this volume is deliberately broad and integrated with consideration of challenges faced in the course of adult development. We share the views of Friedman (2008a; 2008b) and Nash and Stevenson (2004a; 2004b) that individuals flourish (or not) in both work and personal life domains and that experiences in one domain are influenced by and in turn influence experiences in most other domains. Friedman's (2008a; 2008b) concept of 'total leadership development' emphasizes becoming successful in all domains of one's life: private life, family, work and community. According to Friedman, individuals need to value 'winning' in all these domains rather than believing that trade-offs are necessary in order to succeed in the work domain. Further, individuals who fail to meet their leadership potential at work often do so because they are falling short in other domains of their life. Similarly, Nash and Stevenson (2004a; 2004b) found in their research that successful leaders integrated four spheres of their lives: happiness (satisfaction with one's life), achievement (accomplishments that compare favorably with those of others), significance (having a positive impact on people you care about), and legacy (helping others achieve their success). Leaders in the Nash and Stevenson study defined success as obtaining 'just enough' in each of the four spheres, rather than maximizing all four or any one of the spheres. Consistent with Friedman, Nash and Stevenson argue that when leaders make trade-offs across these spheres it detracts from their overall feelings of success. The self-management of leadership development must, therefore, attend to and engage activity in all these domains or spheres of life to achieve one's leadership potential.

THE FOUNDATION OF LEADERSHIP DEVELOPMENT: SELF-ASSESSMENT AND SELF-AWARENESS

We believe there is a growing consensus among scholars of leadership that self-awareness is the foundation of leadership development and therefore the core of self-management efforts. Self-awareness provides a basis for introspection, choice, priority setting, change and development. Numerous leadership researchers and authors have discussed the critical element of self-awareness in leadership performance. Drucker (1999) advises that success as a leader comes to those who know themselves – their strengths, their values, and how they best perform. Tichy (1997) refers to a leader's ability to tell 'who I am' stories as essential to their effectiveness. Kotter (1996) discusses the importance of honest and humble self-reflection as one of the critical mental habits of lifelong learning as a leader. The first leadership principle in Useem's *The Leadership Moment* (1998) is know yourself. Whetten and Cameron's (1998) textbook, widely used for leadership development in MBA programs, titled *Developing Management Skills*, provides self-assessment exercises in almost every chapter, giving the reader an opportunity to evaluate their current skills and approaches to various leadership challenges (for example, conflict management). These authors, and others, are all emphasizing self-awareness as an essential component of leadership effectiveness. The critical issue of how self-awareness is achieved is, however, most often not articulated.

Attempts to increase self-awareness to guide leadership development are not new. An underlying assumption of many organizationally driven assessment and evaluation systems is that the data derived from these systems will enhance self-awareness and thereby provide focus and motivation to improve in those areas identified as weaknesses. Performance appraisal systems, 360-degree feedback, assessment centers, psychological assessments, formal mentoring, and executive coaching all provide, with various degrees of accuracy and value, information to aspiring leaders on their performance and development needs (Fulmer and Conger, 2004). Some of these systems provide very unique functions in enhancing self-awareness: 360-degree feedback systems broaden the range of information available to leaders to help them see themselves as others see them; performance appraisals and assessment centers tend to focus on skills and performance areas that need immediate improvement or are necessary for promotion; mentoring and executive coaching typically emphasize advice and support regarding behavior and attitude change. There is no question that all of these approaches to increasing self-awareness and thereby performance, if done well, provide value to leadership development. Unfortunately, however, cost controls and short-term goals drive today's organizations, and individuals are expected to take control of their own leadership development (Moses, 1997). Moreover, assessment provided by organizational systems must focus on what the organization needs, which may or may not be congruent with the development goals of an individual. The individual aspiring leader must take ownership of the assessment process and use the resulting information and insight to meet his/her own needs and development goals. The individual must take direct personal responsibility for his/her own development because no one else will, or is able to, manage the process to achieve the goals the individual truly wants. Self-assessment, therefore, fills a critical need in the leadership development process.

Self-assessment is the means by which self-awareness is achieved, and both the process of self-assessment and the resulting increase in self-awareness are central to the themes of self-management and leadership development in the current volume. Chapter authors repeatedly reinforce these themes throughout the volume, arguing for the contribution of self-awareness to leadership effectiveness and development, and providing specific advice and techniques for self-assessment. For the purposes of this volume, our operational definition of self-assessment and its relationship to leadership development is as follows: self-assessment involves the use of self-knowledge and introspection in a structured and guided format, the generation of information and data about oneself, and the use of this data to enrich understanding of important personal issues (for example, job/career/life satisfaction; defining success; identifying strengths, shortcomings, and areas of potential concern) in order to commit to developmental initiatives that will enrich one's work, self, family and community.

APPROACHES TO SELF-ASSESSMENT IN LEADERSHIP DEVELOPMENT

As discussed previously, numerous researchers and authors have promoted the value of self-awareness in leadership effectiveness, although for the most part these authors have provided little, if any, detailed advice on conducting a self-assessment process. However, there are a few examples of specific self-assessment techniques that have been published previously, and these are noteworthy. One of the earliest and most thorough approaches to self-assessment was published by Clawson et al., (1992). These authors primarily focused on applications to career development and provided a program rich in detail and with interpretive guidelines intended to assist individuals in making appropriate job and career choices. Although the objectives of the self-assessment process these authors recommended were specifically focused on career development, Clawson et al. provided an excellent model of how self-assessment should be approached, and many of their exercises and techniques could be easily adapted to the purpose of leadership development.

There are several other examples of previously published self-assessment methods that have focused more specifically on leadership development, although the rationale for these approaches is primarily based on promoting self-awareness as a critical leadership competency, rather than as a core component of a broader self-management program for leadership development, which is presented in the current volume. Nevertheless, these approaches to self-assessment complement the approaches and techniques recommended by authors in the current volume and are worthy of note for the interested reader. For example, previously we discussed Friedman's (2008a; 2008b) perspective on 'total leadership development', which includes becoming successful in all domains of one's life, not just the work domain. Friedman also developed a self-assessment program to facilitate the development of what he termed 'Total Leadership'. The program begins with individuals assessing what is important to them, what they want, and what they can contribute to, now and in the future, in each of the four domains of life: private self, family, work and community. Past life events are considered to determine their impact on how individuals currently define who they are today, their chosen direction, their core values, and their leadership vision and aspirations. Discussions with key stakeholders in each domain of the individual's life are also carried out to determine their expectations of the individual. This is followed by creating and enacting small 'experiments' to change behavior to better meet individual and stakeholder needs and expectations in each of the four domains. Continuous self-reflection is a key ingredient in this program, and individuals are encouraged to record their activities, thoughts and feelings during their experiments. Friedman studied hundreds of participants in his Total Leadership Program and reported improvements in their job satisfaction, relationships with both customers and co-workers, and job performance.

Another approach to self-assessment, focusing on 'strengths', has been developed by individuals associated with the Gallup Organization (Buckingham, 2007; Buckingham and Clifton, 2001). Based on their research showing that only 17 per cent of the workforce report using all of their strengths on the job, and that those who do use their strengths report working in more productive teams with lower turnover and higher customer satisfaction, Buckingham and Clifton (2001) argue that individuals should focus more on their strengths to enhance performance rather than attempting to improve their weaknesses. In other words, they argue that focusing on what is working rather than what is broken is a better strategy for leadership development. Unfortunately, they find that most people still believe that fixing weaknesses is the best way to improve performance. To facilitate a greater commitment to focusing on strengths, Buckingham and Clifton (2001) developed an inventory of strengths related to leadership and managerial performance and obtained responses from a nationally represented sample of workers in the United States. Individuals taking the inventory are able to compare themselves against this normative sample and determine their own relative strengths and weaknesses. On the basis of this self-assessment, individuals are encouraged to strive to do things that play to their strengths and to avoid activities requiring their weaknesses.

Another self-assessment methodology has been developed by Kaplan and his colleagues (Kaplan, 2006; Kaplan and Kaiser, 2006; 2009) to address what they regard as one of the significant challenges of leadership, the tendency to overreact or underreact to various situations, which results in a negative impact on their performance. According to Kaplan and Kaiser (2006), leaders bring certain 'baggage' with them to their leadership roles. This baggage creates sensitivities to circumstances such as fatigue, illness and stress, or feelings of vulnerability, threat, or inadequacy, all of which may help explain why they over- or underreact to various situations, which leads to poor performance. Kaplan (2006) has developed an approach to assess the extent to which a leader exhibits a variety of these reactions. Through self-assessment and feedback from others such as co-workers, leaders come to recognize their over- and underreactions, better understand their behavior, and learn more effective coping responses.

We see therefore, from this discussion, that self-assessment has been recommended for leadership development by a number of authors previously, although not in the context of a broader approach to self-management as presented in the current volume. Nevertheless, these approaches reinforce the value of self-awareness as a core leadership competency and we recommend them as complementary to the methods presented in this text. Authors contributing to this volume address the broader issue of self-management as it applies to numerous responsibilities and challenges faced by leaders and aspiring leaders. Within each of these contributions, the importance of self-awareness as the foundation to self-management will be made clear, and many of our authors will, in addition, provide practical self-assessment tools that contribute to the self-management of leadership development with respect to the specific issue or challenge that is the focus of each chapter.

SELF-MANAGEMENT OF LEADERSHIP DEVELOPMENT: SOME UNIQUE CONTEXTS

The principles and practices of self-management for leadership development discussed in this volume are for the most part focused on the mythical 'average' or typical leader or aspiring leader. We fully acknowledge that there are diverse groups of individuals and unique contexts in which leadership development will face challenges and require solutions that differ from those discussed here. Some of these unique contexts are touched on by our contributors, but the full extent of the diversity of issues cannot be adequately dealt with in this volume. Where possible, we refer the interested reader to some additional literature regarding several unique contexts in the following paragraphs.

There is increasing evidence that women may bring slightly different skills and strengths to their managerial and professional jobs than men do. In addition, women face different work, family and career realities than men (Burke and Mattis, 2005; Barreto et al., 2009). As a consequence their career landscape is different (Mainiero and Sullivan, 2005; 2006). Readers interested in some aspects of the use of self-assessment for women and the unique nature of women's careers would find useful information in Ruderman and Ohlott (2002), Vinnicombe and Bank (2003), and Eagly and Carli (2007).

Differences in career stage will undoubtedly create differences in the role and value of self-assessment in the lives of mid-career men and women. These individuals have a lot more experience to process, more data to inform their self-assessments, more information on their successes and failures, and a different array of possibilities and choices than do women and men just beginning their careers.

Self-assessment in mid-career can help individuals break out of unsatisfying routines. Managers often are in denial about their circumstances and feelings, and may believe that changing their job/career/organization would be disloyal and difficult, or that their investment in their current position to date makes it difficult to contemplate something different (Drummond and Chell, 2000). These beliefs and feelings can create a sense of being trapped that in turn creates a kind of 'psychic prison' of the individual's own making. Engaging in self-assessment is an effective way to deal with these beliefs and feelings, and enables the individual to identify potential new opportunities that would be more rewarding.

Korman and Korman (1980) studied mid-career issues and coined the term 'career success and personal failure' to capture a syndrome that afflicts managers that have the external trappings of career success (high-level jobs, good salaries) but when pressed, admit feelings of estrangement from their work, organizations and families. This syndrome emerges in mid-life since some degree of career success is required, before these individuals start to become aware of aspects of decline (for example, health, goals that will not be reached, feelings of obsolescence). Korman and Korman (1980) identified four 'cognitive realizations' that serve as potential contributing factors to career success and personal failure: loss of affiliative satisfactions from work colleagues and family members; a sense of being controlled by external factors (one's manager and organization, one's family) in one's work and career decision making; an appreciation that some things one had expected to happen would not; and a realization that many of the life and work goals that were pursued were contradictory (for example, meeting organizational demands and having time for family). Korman and Korman (1980) suggest that organizational programs supporting self-assessment, life and career planning, and career change would address the sources of this debilitating syndrome.

Another unique context for leadership development that deserves brief mention is the situation in which models of leadership may vary, for example as a function of operating within a public sector or not-for-profit organization. Self-management strategies may vary in this context to some degree, although we are unable to explore this possibility in detail here. However, Rego and his colleagues discuss an innovative approach to leadership development with youth in the developing world in the current volume. Much more deserves to be said about self-management and leadership development in these unique contexts, and we hope that the current volume will encourage others to conduct research on this topic in these special circumstances.

HOW TO USE THIS BOOK

We believe that this book should be of interest to a wide variety of readers, including students of leadership, researchers interested in leadership development, and practitioners such as consultants, trainers, human resource professionals, and managers at all levels who are involved with leadership development. The primary focus of this book is, however, on the *self-management* of leadership development, and therefore we hope that this volume will be especially useful to aspiring leaders. The contents of this collection will provide considerable 'food for thought' for all those who aspire to progress in leadership positions throughout their careers. Most importantly, the role of self-awareness in leadership development is reinforced repeatedly by the authors in this volume. Self-awareness provides aspiring leaders with essential knowledge on what they can do themselves to own and manage their development. It helps leaders understand what they need to change and how to integrate their development plans with their opportunities, as well as providing a basis for priority setting and choice of development activities. And perhaps more fundamentally, self-awareness enhances motivation to shift the responsibility for development to the individual leader, a shift that is critical to the long-term career success of all leaders (Useem, 2006).

To obtain full value from this collection, we encourage readers who wish to take a more active role in their own leadership development to allow the material they encounter to stimulate their thinking about how to enhance their self-awareness. We encourage you to reflect on your experiences in various life roles including work, take stock of your current circumstances, consider reprioritizing some activities, and begin to set some concrete goals for development in one or more life domains. We also encourage you to think about your satisfaction and performance in various domains, as well as your own psychological and physical well-being. You might also find it helpful to solicit support from your spouse or partner, your co-workers, or a valued and trusted peer or mentor in your efforts.

Numerous self-assessment instruments have been included in the various chapters, and in most cases scores from normative samples have been provided (for example, business students, managers, various professional groups). These scores are typically mean values, so a reader can see how they compare with the mean value of a particular normative group. A general rule of thumb when comparing scores with an appropriate normative group is to focus on 'extreme' scores, that is, those scores that are considerably higher or lower than the norm. Individuals with extreme scores, again assuming the normative comparison group is appropriate, should more likely expend their energy and resources developing these characteristics or behaviors, as the potential implications of these extreme scores in terms of future satisfaction and effectiveness may be profound.

Once the characteristics or behaviors that you wish to change have been identified, action planning may begin. For example, the following simple process may be followed:

1. Identify five things you want to start doing more of, starting today (be specific). What actions will you undertake? How will you evaluate progress in your efforts? How will you know that you have been successful? What supports do you have in place that will help you in your efforts?
2. Identify five things you want to stop doing or do less of, starting today (be specific). What actions will you undertake? How will you evaluate progress in your efforts? How will you know that you have been successful? What supports do you have in place that will help you in your efforts?

You may also wish to consult the goal-setting and action-planning recommendations of Buckingham (2007) regarding developing your strengths. Whichever method you choose, remember that although the past cannot be changed, the future can be managed.

We believe that leaders and leadership play critical roles in the success of any society. The emphasis on self-awareness and self-assessment in leadership development will have a positive impact on the success of leaders and the effectiveness of their leadership development activities. As this is borne out, we see value for individuals and their families, for their employing organizations, and for the wider society as a whole. Healthy individuals, healthy families, and healthy organizations all contribute to healthy communities.

AN INTRODUCTION TO THE CONTENTS OF THE CURRENT VOLUME

Each chapter in this collection focuses on a unique aspect of self-management as it relates to leadership development. These contributions are grouped into three broad categories: the role of self-awareness and self-assessment in leadership development, the contribution of self-management to common leadership challenges, and unique challenges to self-management related to changes in the global environment of business.

The first part of this volume brings additional perspective to the importance of self-awareness in leadership development. Chapters in this part focus on the critical role of self-assessment to achieve self-awareness, the importance of taking the responsibility to self-assess, and the need to take ownership of the process and data obtained from various sources of developmental feedback. Some general self-assessment techniques are provided, and the value of some specific types of data to leadership development is discussed. The unique perspective of this section is the focus on how the individual takes responsibility and manages these assessment methods, rather than how organizations use these methods.

- Allan Church and Christopher Rotolo (Chapter 1) address the role of the individual learner in self-assessment and leadership development. They position their writing squarely in the organizational context incorporating their work with PepsiCo. They first identify three moderators of effective use of self-assessment and development: organizational culture, supporting tools and processes, and individual characteristics. Individual characteristics that are important include willingness to learn, openness to change, and motivation and ambition to advance. Church and Rotolo offer a typology of 'leader learners' based on their organizational practice. A five-phase individual feedback, development and change model is proposed with detailed treatment of the role of the individual learner in the process. Questions are posed for the reader at each stage and helpful responses are identified. In addition, each stage is fleshed out with individual and organizational examples. They also identify individual obstacles to change and offer suggestions on how these might be addressed.

- Richard Boyatzis, Tony Lingham and Angela Passarelli (Chapter 2) address the questions regarding what competencies make leaders effective and how individuals can be inspired to develop them. Outstanding leaders display cognitive, emotional and social intelligences. The authors use Intentional Change Theory (ICT) to capture the key elements and processes that support sustained and desired changes in behaviors, thoughts, feelings and perceptions. Initial phases of ICT involve self-assessment of real and desired selves. Using data from 22 years of longitudinal assessment, they convincingly show that MBAs can develop competencies associated with effective leadership and management.

- James Clawson (Chapter 3) asserts, like many of the authors in this volume, that leaders must continuously learn, grow and adapt if they are to remain successful, including learning about themselves. The problem Clawson focuses on in this chapter is that so many leaders find it difficult to self-assess and then deal effectively with the findings. This chapter provides an understanding of why leaders do not engage in self-assessment and offers some very positive recommendations on how leaders should overcome this reluctance to engage in a critical component of their development and success. The reluctance to self-assess and use this information effectively to develop stems from a variety of factors including a failure to understand its importance and value (in some cases this is open distain), an assumption among some that they know all there is to know about themselves already, an inability and/or lack of concern for understanding how their behavior and motives affect others, a belief and drive to do whatever they have to regardless of personal consequences, and a number of other reasons detailed in this chapter. Clawson recommends a variety of ways for leaders to break out of their reluctance to develop better self-awareness such as utilizing 360 feedback to help them see how others see them, developing listening skills, relying less on the power of their positions and more on understanding, and a variety of other helpful suggestions.

- Sandra Davis (Chapter 4) examines one of the most important sources of information potentially available to increase self-awareness, a psychological assessment. Davis begins by describing some common reactions to this source of information by leaders and emerging leaders – they avoid it, minimize its usefulness, and/or just plain ignore it. But Davis provides a convincing rationale for the value of these data to leadership development, especially if leaders actively engage this information to inform their development activity. To this end, a detailed, step-by-step process is described for how to work effectively with a psychologist to get the most out of feedback from the assessment and use it to guide leadership development. Davis emphasizes the importance of being an active participant in the feedback process. This means engaging the psychologist in a dialogue concerning the feedback, asking questions, and challenging interpretations, not defensively, but in the spirit of gaining clarity. Common assessment tools are then described including what the data means (and does not mean) and how to approach the feedback constructively. Sample questions are provided for probing the meaning of the data with the psychologist. Worksheets are also provided for guiding the process of engaging other stakeholders (boss, peers, direct reports) in the leader's development.

- Jean Leslie and Ruohong Wei, from the Center for Creative Leadership (CCL), examine the 'leadership gap' – the shortfall between current and forecasted leadership capacity (Chapter 5). Using an extensive data base from CCL, they first provide evidence for the leadership gap between present skills of leaders and what they report needing to be more effective now and in the future. The authors argue that these data support an overwhelming need for leadership development. They then focus on the individual and their responsibility for understanding what they need to learn and what they need to do to close their own leadership gaps. An exercise, based on the rich history of CCL leadership research, is provided for readers to self-assess their development needs. Leslie and Wei complete their chapter by providing very specific and helpful recommendations, again based on CCL research, on strategies individuals can employ to close their own leadership gap and manage their own development.

- The self-development of emotional intelligence (EQ) and its contribution to leadership development is the topic discussed in Chapter 6 by Ronald Riggio. He begins by distinguishing between the two models of EQ, the abilities model and the mixed model. This is an important distinction, as the trait component of the mixed model will be more difficult to self-manage. Riggio provides an excellent summary of the controversies in EQ research, the conceptual problems, and the measurement challenges, but despite these difficulties, he makes a good case for the importance of EQ to leadership. Riggio then summarizes the best practices in self-development of EQ and leadership competencies, and he briefly reviews published resources available for use in self-development.

- Stewart Emery (Chapter 7) tackles some deep soul-searching leadership questions – do you matter? Are you, as an individual, a positive force in other people's lives? From these, additional questions follow: who are you? What do you provide? Why does it matter? What are your core values? What do you bring to others? Each of these questions begins with a journey of self-assessment leading to self-awareness. Emery then encourages an exploration of 'how' to matter, using actual people as examples. Learning what you do emerges as a central theme here. Individuals can grow to be great by doing work they believe is great, that is, by loving what they do. Deliberate practice is a vital step on this path. Goal-setting and feedback are crucial. He concludes with some questions supportive of deliberate practice. Emery extends the use of self-assessment and self-awareness to some very personal issues that are critical for leaders to consider.

The second part of the book focuses on the contribution of a self-management perspective to numerous challenges faced by leaders during the course of their development and careers. Topics include personal goal-setting, managing your career, managing team performance, resilience, stress and work addiction, and working constructively with mentors and networks. Again, the emphasis here is not the organizational or managerial perspective on how to manage these problems; rather, our contributors focus on how individuals take personal responsibility to manage through these critical leadership issues, how self-reflection and self-awareness aids in the response to these challenges, and how these experiences contribute to leadership development.

- John Blenkinsopp, Yehuda Baruch and Ruth Winden (Chapter 8) consider career management in times of economic downturn. The career landscape has changed over the past two decades in significant ways. While individuals have a responsibility for their careers, a surprisingly large number of managers still fail to exercise it. Organizational support for careers is also important, and these authors review a number of organizational career practices including assessment, training and development, and varied experiences. Their use of individual case examples captures current career and organizational realities and illustrates how meshing self-knowledge and organizational needs can foster career and leadership development.
- Thomas S. Bateman (Chapter 9) emphasizes goals and feedback in his vision of Self-Directed Leadership (SDL). SDL involves the setting of specific goals. He identifies a variety of personal goals

that support leadership development. SDL requires making choices, setting specific goals, taking action, and minimizing self-sabotage. Prominent leadership theories are used to identify potential goals that SDL might pursue. Proactive behavior, including both self-assessment and the assessment of others, is central to success in development and the managerial role. He concludes with tangible suggestions regarding moving goals into action.

- Wendy Bedwell, Marissa Shuffler, Jessica Wildman and Eduardo Salas (Chapter 10) using a competency-based approach to learning, propose that work teams provided a rich context for self-assessment and leadership development, that is, individuals are provided with opportunities to learn within the context of work teams. Bedwell et al. begin with a review of self-directed work teams (SDWTs) and leadership functions. Their discussion illustrates how leadership functions and team member functions overlap, how leadership development within SDWTs emphasizes self-management, and how self-management is facilitated by self-observation. Best practices are described that allow emerging leaders to take charge of their learning and practice effective leadership skills as well as improving the effectiveness of their SDWT, phases of team development, and team competencies. These best practices include self-criticism, seeking feedback, and providing feedback to others. These processes reinforce the themes seen throughout the chapters in this collection, but they are positioned here in a work team context.
- Ronald Burke (Chapter 11) examines the issue of flourishing in leadership and life generally. He provides a practical guide on the self-assessment of factors related to flourishing to determine those that may be risks for the developing leader and that need to be changed to increase leadership and life effectiveness. Specifically, 12 factors that contribute to our understanding of why leaders work so hard are discussed in detail including the consequences (positive and negative) of these different sources of motivation. Available theory and research on each factor is reviewed and a self-assessment exercise is provided in which readers may gain insight into their own motivation for leadership. Implications for flourishing as a leader, in terms of effectiveness as well as well-being, are discussed for each concept and measure provided.
- Dawn Chandler and Kathy Kram (Chapter 12) emphasize the role other people play in one's leadership development. Leadership is essentially a relational process, so it should come as no surprise that other people can be central to its development. Others can support leadership development through mentoring, providing 360-degree

feedback, and the benefits of developmental networks. Chandler and Kram indicate how managers can proactively use relationships to guide their development as leaders. Self-awareness is a critical catalyst in their model. When one is clear about one's motivations it can lead to the identification of relevant job- and career-related knowledge and career contacts and networks. They offer specific questions one needs to ask to address one's developmental needs.

- Managers are likely to face failure, disappointment, disillusion-ment, career setbacks and adversity at points in their lives. Gillian King and Mitchell Rothstein (Chapter 13) discuss the importance of personal resilience at these critical times. Learning from such experiences is vital. Failure offers opportunities for significant per-sonal and career choices with resilience-related processes opening up more directions. Resilience involves 'bouncing back'. Resilience is a capability and like all capabilities can be strengthened. Their model of resilience in the workplace includes feeling, thought and action components. Each of these is defined, expanded upon and illustrated using management and organization examples. They conclude with suggestions on strengthening resilience.

- Krista Langkamer Ratwani, Stephen Zaccaro, Sena Garven and David Geller (Chapter 14) emphasize self-development on the premise that leaders need to be engaged in continuous learning. Leader self-development requires self-appraisal, self-regulation, and the development of self-learning activities and opportunities, as well as an inventory of available learning resources, and clear definitions of important leadership competencies. Supportive activities include learning tools tied to self-development goals, assessments of learn-ing progress, and ways to stay motivated towards self-development. Langkamer et al. integrate these preparatory and supportive activi-ties into a 'self-instructional system' consistent with traditional training models. Social networks (for example, mentors, advisors, coaches, bosses, peers) perform a significant role in both prepara-tory and supportive initiatives. Developmental social networks expand the range of resources available to emerging leaders. The authors examine the processes of leadership development and the role of developmental social networks, and why these have value, in considerable detail.

In the third part of the book, the topic areas focus on some unique chal-lenges to self-management faced by leaders in the rapidly changing global business context. Topics in this part include challenges faced by women leaders in academia, the next generation of leaders, and global leaders.

- Paula Caligiuri and Ruchi Sinha (Chapter 15) apply concepts of self-assessment and self-development to potential global leaders. They begin by outlining tasks or activities among those holding global leadership roles. Cultural agility, the ability of individuals 'to move quickly and successfully from one cultural context to another', lies at the heart of their thinking. Individuals can develop global leadership competencies through self-initiated activities and organization-initiated development programs. Individual differences and the self-assessment of these differences are discussed in considerable depth. Self-assessments address knowledge, skills, abilities and personality characteristics necessary for success in other countries and cultures. Tools for supporting such self-assessments are indicated in their chapter.

- Linley Lord and Susan Vinnicombe (Chapter 16) discuss the importance of self-management techniques in the context of how they can be used to address a very specific applied problem – the lack of leadership opportunities for women in Australian universities. The authors describe a study they conducted to examine this problem using a qualitative research design. Their purpose was to identify what women in leadership positions, or aspiring to these positions, can do to develop their leadership potential. First, they describe the nature of the problem in Australian universities. Factors such as negative role models, lack of preparation for leadership roles, lack of acceptance or support, and many other components contributing to this problem are identified. The authors then provide recommendations, based on their research, on self-management techniques for women seeking development in these leadership positions. The reader will recognize some of these techniques as they are discussed by several other authors in the current volume, providing support for their general value to leadership development in many organizational contexts (for example, seeking out mentors, developing social networks). One unique self-management technique found in this context, however, was to use negative role models to identify how *not* to act. Subjects in this study reported this approach was born out of necessity when there were few positive role models to emulate, but that it was a useful and helpful addition to their efforts to self-manage.

- Philip Mirvis, Kevin Thompson and Chris Marquis (Chapter 17) examine the question of what leadership skills will be required of the next generation regarding business leaders. They begin by describing the economic and social changes that are already underway, which will add to the complexity of the next generation of leaders' work.

Just one example of the effect on leaders' behavior is the demand for more transparency, sustainable business practices, and responsible leadership. Mirvis et al. focus on four domains of developing the next generation of leadership: self-leadership, leading others, leading systems, and leading enterprises. For each domain, they then provide a 'developmental agenda' – a detailed analysis of the competencies for next generation leaders. For example, in the domain of self-leadership, they describe the importance of competencies such as self-awareness, reflection, cognitive complexity, tolerance for ambiguity, adaptability, and emotional resilience. Optimal development experiences are next outlined for these competencies, followed by a detailed case example of how IBM's Corporate Service Corps has incorporated these experiences to develop the next generation of leadership competencies.

- Lyndon Rego, David Altman and Steadman Harrison (Chapter 18) 'democratize' leadership development beyond large organizations and extend it to young men and women in the developing world. In their case, leadership development emphasizes building self-awareness and individual skills to be more effective in working with others (that is, soft skills). Their model, Assessment, Challenge and Support (ACS) involves understanding of self and others, identifying growth experiences that lead to development, and providing support and help in reaching growth goals. They provide interesting case examples of how ACS has been used in several developing countries to improve the quality of people's lives and to build their communities.

SOME CONCLUDING THOUGHTS

There is a growing body of literature in the areas of person–job fit and person–organizational fit showing clearly that individuals who achieve a better fit with their jobs and workplaces are more satisfied and healthy (Leiter and Maslach, 2005). Self-management provides individuals with the opportunity to take responsibility to achieve greater levels of fit with their jobs and careers. The current worldwide economic downturn is forcing many university graduates to reconsider their career options, at least in the short term. Most business school graduates have in the past decade or more gravitated to financial services, consulting and accounting careers, motivated by the high salaries given to individuals working in these areas. The current recession has resulted in significantly fewer firms in these sectors hiring university graduates, and those fortunate enough to get jobs often take lower salaries. Those without jobs are exploring careers in very different sectors including health care, social services, non-profit organizations, and small businesses. A by-product of these events is that aspiring leaders must learn to self-manage more effectively to thrive in this environment, but by doing so, they may in fact achieve greater levels of person–job and person–organization fit and thereby greater levels of personal satisfaction with their jobs and careers.

REFERENCES

Barreto, M., Ryan, M.K. and Schmitt, M.T. (2009) *The Glass Ceiling in the 21st Century: Understanding Barriers to Gender Equality*, Washington, DC: American Psychological Association.

Buckingham, M. (2007), *Go Put Your Strengths to Work,* New York: The Free Press.

Buckingham, M. and Clifton, D.O. (2001), *Now Discover Your Strengths*, New York: The Free Press.

Burke, R.J. (2006). 'Why leaders fail: exploring the dark side', in R.J. Burke and C.L. Cooper (eds), *Inspiring Leaders*, London: Routledge, pp. 237–46.

Burke, R.J. and Cooper, C.L. (2004), *Leading in Turbulent Times: Managing in the New World of Work*, Oxford, UK: Blackwell Publishing.

Burke, R.J. and Cooper, C.L. (2006), *Inspiring Leaders*, London: Routledge.

Burke, R.J. and Mattis, M.C. (2005), *Supporting Women's Career Advancement: Challenges and Opportunities*, Cheltenham, UK and Northampton, MA, USA: Edward Elgar.

Clawson, J.G., Kotter, J.P., Faux, V.A. and McArthur, C.C. (1992), *Self-assessment and Career Development*, Englewood Cliffs, NJ: Prentice Hall.

Drucker, P. (1999), *Management Challenges for the 21st Century*, New York: HarperCollins.

Drummond, H. and Chell, E. (2000), 'Life's chances and choices: a study of entrapment in career decisions with reference to Becker's side bets theory', *Personnel Review*, **30**, 186–202.

Eagly, A.H. and Carli, L.L. (2007), *Through the Labyrinth: The Truth about how Women Become Leaders*, Boston, MA: Harvard Business School Press.

Friedman, S.D. (2008a), 'Be a better leader, have a richer life', *Harvard Business Review*, April, 112–18.

Friedman, S.D. (2008b), *Be a Better Leader, have a Richer Life*, Boston, MA: Harvard Business School Press.

Fulmer, R.M. and Conger, J.A. (2004), *Growing your Company's Leaders*, New York: AMACOM.

Hogan, R. and Hogan, J. (2001), 'Assessing leadership: a view of the dark side', *International Journal of Evaluation and Assessment*, **9**, 40–51.

Kaplan, R.E. (2006), 'Lopsidedness in leaders: strategies for assessing it and correcting it', in R.J. Burke and C.L. Cooper (eds), *Inspiring Leaders*, London: Routledge, pp. 293–304.

Kaplan, R.E. and Kaiser, R.B. (2006), *The Versatile Leader: Making the Most of your Strengths – Without Overdoing it*, San Diego, CA: Pfeiffer.

Kaplan, R.E., and Kaiser, R.B. (2009), 'Stop overdoing your strengths', *Harvard Business Review*, February, 100–103.

Kellerman, B. (2004), *Bad Leadership*, Boston, MA: Harvard Business School Press.

Korman, A.K. and Korman, R.W. (1980), *Career Success/Personal Failure*, Englewood Cliffs, NJ: Prentice-Hall.

Kotter, J.P. (1996), *Leading Change*, Boston, MA: Harvard Business School Press.

Leiter, M.P. and Maslach, C. (2005), *Banishing Burnout: Six Strategies for Improving your Relationship with Work*, San Francisco, CA: Jossey-Bass.

Mainiero, L.A. and Sullivan, S.E. (2005), 'Kaleidoscope careers: an alternative explanation for the "opt-out" revolution', *Academy of Management Executive*, **19**, 106–23.

Mainiero, L.A. and Sullivan, S.E. (2006), *The Opt-out Revolt: Why People are Leaving Companies to Create Kaleidoscope Careers*, Mountain View, CA: Davies-Black Publishing.

McCauley, C.D. and Van Velsor, E. (2004), *Handbook of Leadership Development*, San Francisco, CA: Jossey-Bass.

Michaels, E., Handfield-Jones, H., and Axelrod, B. (2001), *The War for Talent*, Boston, MA: Harvard Business School Press.

Mintzberg, H. (2004), *Managers not MBAs: A Hard Look at the Soft Practice of Managing and Management Development*, San Francisco, CA: Berrett-Koehler.

Moses, B. (1997), *Career Intelligence*, Toronto, Canada: Stoddart.

Murphy, K.R. and Cleveland, J.N. (1995), *Understanding Performance Appraisal: Social, Organizational, and Goal-Based Perspectives*, Thousand Oaks, CA: Sage Publications.

Nash, L. and Stevenson, H. (2004a), 'Success that lasts', *Harvard Business Review*, February, 103–109.

Nash, L. and Stevenson, H. (2004b), *Just Enough. Tools for Creating Success in your Work and Life*, New York: John Wiley.

Ruderman, M.N. and Ohlott, P.J. (2002), *Standing at the Crossroads: Next Steps for High Achieving Women*, San Francisco, CA: Jossey-Bass.

Tichy, N.M. (1997), *The Leadership Engine: How Winning Companies Build Leaders at Every Level*, New York: HarperCollins.

Useem, M. (1998), *The Leadership Moment: Nine True Stories of Triumph and Disaster and their Lessons for us all*, New York: Three Rivers Press.

Useem, M. (2006), *The Go Point: When it is Time to Decide – Knowing What to Do and When to Do it*, New York: Three Rivers Press.

Van Velsor, E. and Leslie, J.B. (1995), 'Why executives derail: perspectives across time and cultures', *Academy of Management Executive*, **9**(4), 62–72.

Vinnicombe, S. and Bank, J. (2003). *Women with Attitude: Lessons for Career Management*, London: Routledge.

Whetten, D.A. and Cameron, K.S. (1998), *Developing Management Skills*, Reading, MA: Addison-Wesley.

Yukl, G. (1998), *Leadership in Organizations*, Upper Saddle River, NJ: Prentice-Hall.

PART I

Self-Awareness and Leadership Development

1. The role of the individual in self-assessment for leadership development[1]

Allan H. Church and Christopher T. Rotolo

Much has been written over the last hundred years about the study of leadership and the practice of leadership development. The field has seen everything from different taxonomies and typologies proposed of leadership as a construct (e.g. Antonakis et al., 2004; Bass, 1990; Burke, 1982), to more focused applications regarding the development of leadership skills and capabilities through development interventions and planned experiences (e.g., Byham et al., 2002; Conger and Benjamin, 1999; Fulmer and Conger, 2004; McCall, 1998). There has even been a popular emphasis in recent years on the concept of differentiated stages and developmental needs for leaders as they progress in their careers, popularized by the Leadership Pipeline (Charan et al., 2001).

While these approaches are all very important to the field, they often assume that leaders are fully engaged in the learning and development agenda that is being offered or applied. It is difficult to imagine that a well constructed leadership development program or a developmental move to a new leadership role in an emerging market will have a significant impact on the individual's development if he or she does not possess certain key individual characteristics such as a willingness to learn, an openness to change, and the motivation and ambition to succeed in the future. These approaches also often assume that what is being offered from a tools, intervention or curriculum perspective is accurately filling the leader's specific developmental needs. That said, it is interesting to note that very few treatments of leadership development focus on the important role that the individual leader (or learner) plays him or herself in this process.

Self-assessment, or the use of multiple sources of data about the individual to help him or her identify areas of strength and development, has played an important role in leadership development (Jeanneret and Silzer, 1998). When included strategically in a larger leadership development effort (or as the development effort itself), it can not only increase the leader's engagement and motivation to develop, but also helps to pinpoint the *right* areas for development. Self-assessment for development, therefore, serves to increase the efficiency and effectiveness of the development effort. In addition, the ability to recognize one's strengths, development areas, and overall effectiveness is important before a leader can make appropriate decisions to change his or her behavior in the future (Ashford, 1989).

While considerable theory and applied research have been done on the related subjects of self-awareness as part of a 360-degree feedback process (e.g., Antonioni, 1996; Bracken et al., 2001; Church, 1997; London and Beatty, 1993), understanding the role career-development-related self-management behaviors (e.g., Chiaburu et al., 2006; Kossek et al., 1998), feedback-seeking behaviors (e.g., Ashford, 1986; Janssen and Prins, 2007), and empowered self-development (e.g., London and Smither, 1999), few practitioner efforts in these areas explicitly describe in depth the elements of a self-assessment and development process *from the individual's perspective,* nor do they discuss the key moderators to successful self-development efforts. The few that do venture into this area tend to be relatively short chapters or tips and tactics in development resource guides such as *The Leadership Machine* (Lombardo and Eichinger, 2002) or the *Successful Manager's Handbook* (Personnel Decisions International Corporation, 2004). Typically, however, the emphasis in these types of books is on providing a 'mini coaching session' versus an exploration of the underlying stages of development or the factors involved.

The purpose of this chapter is to contribute to the literature in this area by focusing on the role of self-assessment in leadership development efforts. Our emphasis here is on the process by which individual leaders use assessments and feedback from a variety of sources to create insights, develop action plans, take action to manage their own development, and assess the results of their efforts. We will begin by describing three key moderators to effective self-assessment and development (i.e., organizational cultural orientation, supporting tools and processes, and individual characteristics) that are applicable at different phases in the change model. Next we will introduce a five-phase individual feedback development and change model which is grounded in existing theory and practice in the area of Organization Development (OD). Each phase of the model will be discussed in detail with an emphasis on the role of the individual in the assessment and development process. Examples from PepsiCo will be included where relevant and appropriate. Finally, the chapter will conclude with some key questions regarding the area of self-assessment for development.

KEY MODERATORS TO EFFECTIVE SELF-ASSESSMENT AND DEVELOPMENT

Before moving into the process for self-assessment and development it is important to have a clear understanding of the potential moderators or contextual factors that can have a significant impact on the success or failure of these types of efforts. While these factors are also important to consider when planning any sort of leadership program, they are critically important to the success of self-directed development.

Organizational Cultural Orientation

The first factor to consider is the organizational cultural orientation, particularly as it relates to the perceived value of leadership development efforts. By cultural orientation we are referring to a number of facets. One of these is the belief structure of senior leadership (which is one of the most powerful ways that a culture is created and therefore a reflection of what is valued in that organization). Individual learners are unlikely to want to engage in development activities if their senior leadership does not support their efforts via funding for assessment measures, time away from work for their own development, or simply lacks an expressed interest in development. Sponsorship for development from the top of the organization is critical in ensuring a learning and supportive culture, as is the case with most OD and culture change interventions (Burke, 1994). Similarly, the extent to which senior leaders model behaviors that support their own personal continued development will impact the motivation levels of lower-level leaders to embrace development themselves.

Supporting Tools and Processes

The second moderating factor, which is somewhat related to the leadership and culture/environment they create, is the availability and number of supporting tools and processes for development. While there are many types of self-assessment tools and learning and development programs (as will be discussed later), the extent to which the organization provides access to these (either internally through formal programs or externally through various vendor relationships) can make a significant difference in how much development an individual learner can engage in successfully. For example, if an organization only offers two 40-person attendee leadership programs in a given year, even the most ambitious leader will have difficulty advancing their case for attendance if the target population for that program is all 400 middle managers. It could take as long as five years before an individual will be able to attend. In a situation such as this, self-directed development behavior will require other means.

As noted above, organizations vary considerably in how much emphasis they place on leadership development, and as a result, the philosophical stance they take regarding providing access to tools and resources. In our experience there is a continuum here between companies that emphasize individual accountability for development (for example, we will provide the tools but you must be the initiator and drive your own development), and those that are quite prescriptive in nature (for example, you must progress through these programs, experiences and assessments before being allowed to move to a new role or level in the hierarchy). Some researchers have suggested that the trend swung towards more self-management of careers as much as a decade ago given the downsizing efforts and other changes that occurred in the employment contract during the 1980s and 1990s (Kossek et al., 1998). This is probably a positive shift in direction (although providing no formal development programs at all would be a serious concern to us) given that it allows those individuals with a clear desire and motivation to develop the opportunities and tools to do so themselves. Clearly, it can be more difficult for individuals to engage in developmental experiences if the only ones offered are through formal prescriptive channels. Regardless of where an organization is on the continuum, the tools and resources available to a leader clearly have an impact on his or her ability to develop. This is why companies selected for inclusion in the 'Top companies for leaders' lists (e.g., Fortune, 2007) usually have a multi-platform approach to development (for example, classroom, distance learning, web-based, coaching and mentoring programs). At PepsiCo the philosophy is a shared one between the employee, the manager, and the organization, that is, somewhere in the middle of the continuum (see Figure 1.1).

Individual Characteristics

The final and perhaps most important moderating variable in self-assessment and development are the individual characteristics of the leader in question. These characteristics essentially break down into three separate areas: (a) the personality disposition and motivation to develop; (b) the level of learning ability and cognitive capacity to develop; and (c) the degree of career aspirations to develop and advance. For self-development to occur in a leadership context the individual needs to be moderate to high on all three of these areas. In short, the psychological make-up of the individual will directly impact on his or her ability to learn from assessment tools, motivation to seek assessment and development

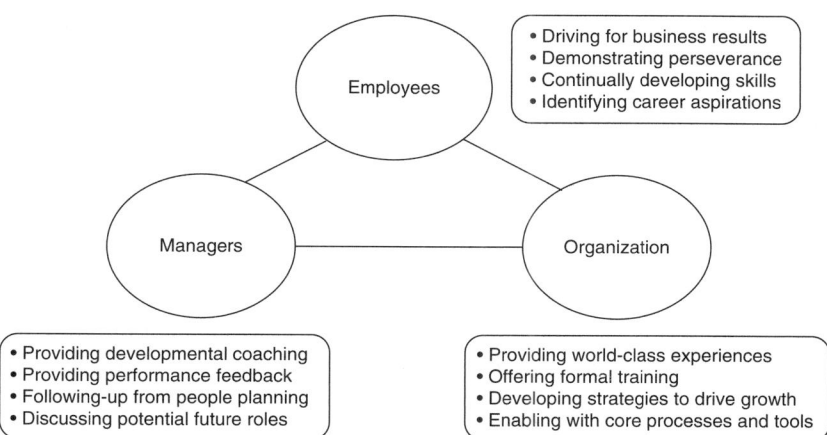

Figure 1.1   PepsiCo career development partnership model

efforts, and level of personal engagement in the process. This can affect all phases of assessment-development.

Let us take some simple examples using concepts from various personality theories and measures (e.g., Burke and Noumair, 2002; Costa and McCrae, 1991; Hogan Assessment Systems, 2009; Hogan and Shelton, 1998). Individuals with a low learning ability or orientation will be far less likely to want to seek development opportunities on their own, let alone attend offerings provided by an organization. Leaders with lower than average levels of ambition or motivation to enhance their standing or develop in their career would also be less likely to exhibit interest in initiating a self-assessment and development process. Introverts or individuals with low affiliation needs may be less willing to share their feedback with others or work with a coach on a development plan. From a social motive perspective (McClelland, 1961), individuals may engage in self-assessment and development for different reasons. Those high in a need for achievement, for example, may seek opportunities to improve their performance or achieve their career goals. On the other hand, those high in need for power may see the exercise as critical to moving up the corporate ladder. Lastly, those high in a need for affiliation may engage in these activities simply because they are opportunities to meet new people or better understand their colleagues. Even if an individual does have the motivation to complete an assessment tool, the initial feedback they receive may be completely denied or overly anxiety provoking to the point of paralysis if they are low in adjustment. Individuals low in conscientiousness are less likely to follow through with their action plan.

As noted above, however, personality is not the only factor as other types of skill sets and capabilities can also impact self-assessment-related behavior. The degree to which an individual has the cognitive capacity and learning ability to recognize new information from developmental activities and integrate and synthesize those learnings is also a critical component. Someone with a lower than average IQ is much less likely to be able to process new information from a leadership styles assessment tool and make effective use of the insights identified than someone with a higher cognitive ability. Constructs such as learning agility (Lombardo and Eichinger, 2000) and feedback-seeking behavior (e.g., Ashford, 1986; Janssen and Prins, 2007) are also relevant here. Even existing levels of self-awareness can also play an important moderating role in whether the individual initiates or gains any further insights from their developmental actions at all (e.g., Bracken et al., 2001).

Finally, the third area of individual characteristics, the level of career aspirations that someone may have, is also important to consider from a self-development perspective, and is particularly important when considering development from an organizational context. Although related to motivation and ambition, these concepts are not synonymous. An individual may be very motivated to succeed in his or her career, for example, but not at all interested in attaining any of the existing roles that are higher in his or her specific organization (for example, perhaps because of the managers of those roles, their geographical location, or simply because of the elements of the jobs themselves). Conversely, we have seen many individuals who have very high career aspirations but who are unwilling or unmotivated to engage in the assessment and development efforts that would be required to attain them (for example, perhaps they are unwilling to move to Asia for several years to obtain the critical experience of leading in an emerging market). From an individual perspective, then, it is critical to truly understand your own motivational levels, but also your own career aspiration levels, and what you would be willing to put up with to attain those roles (for example, level of geographic mobility, learning a new set of language skills, changing to a new function and having to step back on the career ladder temporarily in order to learn new capabilities). Of course organizations desire an accurate assessment of this information as well for development and succession planning purposes (Silzer and Church, forthcoming).

A TYPOLOGY OF LEADER LEARNERS

In our experience of working with different types of leaders on development efforts we have identified six distinct types of individuals that in many ways combine some of the individual factors discussed above. As will be evident from the descriptions below, the degree to which each of these would be willing to initiate self-directed development efforts will differ considerably. The six types are as follows:

1. 'First timers' are individuals who have not yet experienced formal developmental assessments and action planning efforts. Once they have experienced the process for the first time they are reclassified into one of the other categories.
2. 'Feedback junkies' are individuals who take advantage of every opportunity for developmental feedback that they can, and regularly seek it of their own accord. These are the most likely types of leaders to engage in self-assessments.
3. 'Good soldiers' are individuals who willingly comply with a development program, process or mandate without overly complaining, regardless of their internal opinion of the effort. These types will engage in self-directed development if instructed to do so as part of their formal responsibilities.
4. 'Begrudging adopters' are individuals who will also comply with mandated development efforts but who are outwardly dissatisfied with some aspects or elements of the process. They will also be likely to engage in self-development if required to do so. Sometimes these individuals become more positive following a successful feedback and action planning process.
5. 'Resisters' are individuals who are completely negative and will probably be resistive or even refuse to engage in the process at all. Mandates may work, but self-directed development is less likely to occur among this group unless there is truly something perceived to be in it for them.
6. 'Renegades' are individuals who intentionally attempt to understand and then game the system (for example, inflate self-assessment ratings, invite only friends or family members to rate them on assessments, bully direct reports into proving positive ratings) to their own advantage for personal gain. These individuals will utilize the self-development process but in a potentially unethical manner.

We will refer back to these types of leaders from time to time as we discuss the process phases of self-assessment and development in more detail. Next we will discuss the foundation for the feedback development process and its philosophical grounding in the field of OD and change.

THE CONTEXT OF ORGANIZATION DEVELOPMENT

While many would be likely to agree that the field of leadership development and OD are different areas of research and practice, the fact remains that there is considerable overlap between the two. From an OD perspective leadership development reflects a targeted practice area, that is, focusing on leaders as a lever for change versus an emphasis on mission, culture, strategy, climate, systems or other factors (see Burke and Litwin, 1992 for a comprehensive model). Thus, leadership development is one of many possible interventions or approaches to driving organizational change, whether it is in the form of action learning (e.g., Marquardt, 1999; Marsick et al., 2002), a formal leadership curriculum such as the ones used at Johnson and Johnson (Fulmer, 2001) or PepsiCo (Conger and Benjamin, 1999), or using 360 feedback for leaders to drive cultural integration at SmithKline Beecham (Burke and Jackson, 1991; Church et al., 2001). From a leadership development perspective, however, OD is more on the periphery since the primary emphasis is often on building leadership capability (for example, learning new skills or building self-awareness to support development planning), and improving the quality of the talent for the organization's bench for more senior roles. That said, when any form of individual assessment or self-assessment component is added to a leadership development effort it is essentially adding a critical component of OD to the process. Although few practitioners would consider individual assessment as being an OD intervention per se, the manner in which the assessment information is processed and utilized by the leader to drive development change is very consistent with an OD approach.

One of the core tenets of OD is that change and improvement, whether at the individual or organizational level, are facilitated through a data-based process (Waclawski and Church, 2002). Based on the early work of Kurt Lewin (1946) and later adapted to the popular change model of Beckhard and Harris (1987), data provides the means for (a) unfreezing the individual from the current state; (b) helping them create a plan for movement, development or change; and (c) achieving that desired future state. This approach also forms the basis for the seven-phase OD consulting model (Church et al., 2001). The phases are as follows:

1. Entry
2. Contracting
3. Data gathering
4. Data analysis
5. Data feedback

6. Intervention
7. Evaluation.

Both Lewin's original change model and the consulting model remain quite popular in the OD field today, and are the underlying principles behind tools and processes such as organizational culture surveys, 360 feedback programs, focus groups and interviews, action learning programs, and so on (Waclawski and Church, 2002). Over the years, however, many practitioners have observed that the pace of change in organizations has dramatically increased, such as Peter Vaill with his classic description of the term 'permanent whitewater' back in 1989. We would argue further that this rate has only increased exponentially since then with examples such as the fall of Enron in 2001, industry consolidation in different sectors, and the collapse of the financial sector in 2008. The result of such change is that the desired future state is often not achieved before more change is needed. From an individual leadership development perspective, however, enhancing one's unique skills and abilities is definitely achievable (for a given learning or development objective) through data-based interventions if the appropriate conditions are present. As a result, we can quite easily adapt the OD consulting model to the process of leadership development particularly when some form of assessment (for example, self or other) is the primary impetus for change.

FIVE-PHASE INDIVIDUAL FEEDBACK DEVELOPMENT AND CHANGE MODEL

Although not quite a one-to-one translation, the process for using self-assessment in development efforts is quite consistent with the OD model. The differences are more in the subtleties between how certain phases come together in the self-assessment process. The idea here is that there is some form of data that unfreezes the individual from their current state, then drives insights and understanding about some aspect of their development needs, and then ultimately results in the selection of an intervention of some sort (for example, an action plan). In addition, the orientation in our model is from the individual's perspective rather than from that of the client to whom the consulting effort is being directed. Similar to how OD practitioners see themselves as instruments of change (e.g., Burke, 1982; Cheung-Judge, 2001; Seashore et al., 2004), in our model the self essentially becomes the instrument of one's own change. From our perspective there are five distinct phases to the self-assessment and development process. We use the term *phases* here, not steps, because some overlap can occur at times throughout the process of development. The five phases are:

I.   Initiation (a combination of entry and essentially self-contracting for the development process)
II.   Assessment and feedback (this combines the data gathering and feedback phases)
III.   Planning for development (this reflects parts of the analysis phase and parts of the intervention phase)
IV.   Taking action (essentially the intervention phase, and the types of developmental actions can range as widely as those in OD)
V.   Measuring change (the evaluation phase, although rather than evaluating the intervention the individual is measuring progress against their development plan).

Next we will discuss the application, process, contextual factors, and potential challenges for self-directed development through each of these five phases of the model.

Phase I: Initiation

The first phase in the model, initiation, is the process of an individual leader electing or deciding to engage in some individual development work. A very significant part of the self-development equation, literally this is the process of someone saying to themselves 'I need some development' to achieve a specific end in mind. While this is unlikely to occur with first timers, resisters or renegades, clearly this is the purview of feedback junkies and perhaps good soldiers or even begrudging adopters, depending on their point of view and level of self-awareness, ambition, career aspiration and introspection. Regardless of the type of learner, there are four important aspects to initiation that need to be considered during this phase largely because these can both impact and be impacted by the three moderating variables discussed earlier. These are described below.

Impetus for development
The first aspect or question to consider is where exactly does the desire for self-development come from? What is the origin or impetus? Other than feedback junkies, relatively few individuals, except perhaps Millennials as some have suggested (e.g., Dychtwald et al., 2006; Hankin, 2005; Zemke et al., 2000), are probably consciously and constantly seeking their own development regardless of the context. Here we have several options, and this is where the moderating variable of individual characteristics plays

a role. Individuals high in career aspiration, motivation to succeed, or learning orientation are going to be much more driven to engage in self-development and therefore initiate a developmental process. Someone that truly wants to obtain a promotion or reach the highest level position in marketing (for example, Chief Marketing Officer) in an organization is likely to seek out any and all developmental opportunities in whatever form they may exist. Similarly, someone who is a voracious learner will read as many books and articles and Google as many constructs as they can to continue to stimulate their thinking and expand their knowledge base. Some individuals proactively elect to change careers, and with that decision comes the need for the development of new skills and knowledge.

These are perhaps the simplest of cases and the easiest to understand why they would initiate a developmental experience. On the opposite side of the equation are those individuals who lack the self-awareness and/ or interest in engaging in any sort of development (and if coerced by the system to engage will become at best begrudging adopters and at worst resisters or renegades). In other cases, however, where these characteristics are perhaps at a more moderate level in the leader, the impetus is likely to have originated from some form of data from another individual, source or process. For example, one-on-one feedback from a manager regarding development needs to sustain current performance in a role is a common reason for individuals pursuing some form of development. Coaching from a Human Resources (HR) professional regarding career progression and the lack of certain skills required to advance is another very common driver of development activity. One-on-one engagements with a professional external coach are also an increasingly popular source of development ideas (e.g., Valerio and Lee, 2005). In addition, many formal leadership development programs include a component of assessment and follow-up development planning (e.g., Seldman, 2008) and in some cases action learning projects (e.g., Conger and Benjamin, 1999; Tichy and DeRose, 1996) that essentially require an individual to engage in a self-directed development experience. In some organizations continuous individual development is simply expected and supported as part of the culture such as at Google (Mills, 2007) and the senior most leaders reinforce it. As noted earlier, the number of hours a CEO spends in succession planning, talent reviews and/or actively engaged in leadership programs is often a criterion of the best companies for developing leader lists (e.g., Fortune, 2007). In comparison, in other companies continuous development is integrated into a formal process such as performance management or career development. At PepsiCo, for example, leaders are required to have a Career Development Action Plan (CDAP) that includes annual developmental objectives focused on helping them achieve their long-term career goals. Church et al. (2002b) provide an overview of the role of technology in integrating the PepsiCo career development tools. The bottom line here is that how the self-development process is initiated will have an impact on how well the development agenda is executed and the long-term growth of the individual.

Purpose of development

The second consideration regarding the initiation phase is for the individual to answer the question regarding what exactly is being developed and why? Let us start with the why. While we discussed the why as an impetus above for the initiation itself, in this context the why is more about the answer to the question, *to what end*? Regardless of the source or need for development, leaders deciding to engage in a developmental assessment process need to fully understand and embrace the purpose of that effort. Otherwise given the pressure on everyone's time, they will engage in some other activity. For a vast majority of individuals (exceptions noted earlier), development must have a purpose. This could be to obtain a promotion, enhance their current performance, change to another functional area, switch to a new career, or simply broaden their general knowledge base and mindset. So the end state goal is an important one and also one that impacts a leader's level of motivation to engage in particular.

Switching to *the what* that is being developed is another consideration. Often this is clearly identified by some influential individual in an organization (for example, manager, senior leader, coach or mentor, or HR professional), process feedback or program (for example, performance management, a talent review where a clear gap in capability or competency has been identified, or a CEO-led leadership program where future needs are identified), or even an individual's self-selected need for a functional or career change. It may even be the result of a prior assessment tool (for example, conflict management is identified as an outage based on a broader measure of leadership skills resulting in the search for a more in-depth assessment and development plan targeted at this competency). In other cases the initiative for self-development may be more diffuse. Under what conditions do leaders simply decide to engage in a leadership styles assessment or participate in an assessment center on their own? How do they select the right tools, programs, processes? Again this brings us back to the moderating variable of individual characteristics.

Assessment options

The third major aspect of initiation, and related to the idea of what needs to be developed, is the identification and selection of a development assessment, tool or instrument. Since our focus here is on self-directed

Personality measures	Leadership competencies
Functional competencies	Targeted areas/special skills

Figure 1.2   Types of assessments

assessment for development (versus just deciding to engage in any type of developmental activity) this is a critical area for the individual to consider. The leadership development field (as well as the realm of Industrial-Organizational (I/O) Psychology and even the broader area of Human Resource Management) is replete with assessments tools, measures, scorecards and checklists which focus on all sorts of constructs ranging from the broadest leadership orientation to the most minute skill sets in areas such as presentation skills, to an increasingly wide range of personality variables (some of which are well validated and psychometrically sound, and others which are entirely without any merit whatsoever). In fact, a Google search on the term 'self-assessment leadership' in June 2009 resulted in over 2 600 000 hits. Clearly, anyone and everyone can create an assessment tool, just not necessarily one that is psychometrically grounded. Thus it is critical that leaders consult the appropriate content experts (for example, I/O, OD or HR professionals) when selecting a tool or measure for assessment as part of their development plan.

In terms of the options for assessment in this area, when initiating a new development agenda there are generally four broad categories of measures for individuals to choose from. These consist of the following (see Figure 1.2):

1. *Personality measures.* Usually grounded in psychological theory, these are generally self-only assessments that provide feedback on an individual's level of a given attribute, type, dimension, factor or other element of personality based on the given framework of the instrument. These get at the underlying reasons why an individual leader behaves the way they do. Personality has been a commonly used assessment tool for many years (Jeanneret and Silzer, 1998) and is often integrated with other more behaviorally oriented assessment tools such as 360-degree feedback for assessment and development purposes (e.g., Burke and Noumair, 2002). The challenge with these

measures, however, is that personality as a construct is difficult to change and thus development planning can be challenging. The emphasis here is often on mitigating the effects of a given personality profile and/or a focus on what is commonly referred to as derailers (e.g., Dotlich and Cairo, 2003; Hogan Assessment Systems, 2009).

2. *Leadership competencies.* Perhaps the most common form of assessment in the current leadership development marketplace, measures of leadership competencies (or skills, styles, behaviors, and so on) form the basis of both many individual assessment tools as well as the core of the majority of 360-degree feedback programs (Bracken et al., 2001; Church and Waclawski, 1998; Gentry and Leslie, 2007). Since these are generally conceptualized as skills, the prevailing wisdom is that they can be developed through experiences on the job, coaching and mentoring, and formal training. Most of the popular development resource guides noted earlier focus on these types of leadership competencies as targeted development areas for individuals, and provide a wealth of ideas and suggestions for improvement.

3. *Functional competencies.* Not surprisingly, the use of assessment tools that direct individuals in how to develop functional skills is probably one of the longest established practices. Dating back to the concept of the apprentice in the middle ages and more recently characterized by the notion of an internship, there are an abundance of tools and models that focus on helping individuals determine their strengths and development areas regarding functional knowledge (for an example of an HR competency model applied to a developmental career framework, see Church and Herena, 2003). From an individual leadership development perspective these are most useful to focus on for more junior individuals in the early stages of their careers, or for those electing to move across functions to broaden their perspective, or those that have decided to switch careers entirely. At PepsiCo, for example, implicit in our Career Growth Model (a developmental framework for all employees), functional competence is required earlier in one's career and then, as leaders progress to higher levels, leadership capability becomes more important in the mix (Church and Waclawski, forthcoming).

4. *Targeted areas/special skills.* The fourth and final area of individual developmental focus is typically around special skill sets or more specific targeted competencies. Examples of self-assessments and development resources here include social skills, conflict management, group facilitation, presentation acumen, time management, candidate interview techniques, stress management, PowerPoint tips and tricks, and even managing one's own executive presence and stamina

(Seldman and Seldman, 2008). The selection of one of these areas is generally driven by personalized feedback from some other source or process or at the suggestion of a coach or mentor. The offerings in this area also range from the very well grounded to the entirely ethereal in their content. Again the leader searching for the right assessment and supporting tools is best advised to consult a subject matter expert (SME) before moving forward. Also, many of the resource guides noted earlier have great suggestions for development in many of these areas.

Critical nature of self-assessment

The fourth and final aspect of the initiation phase is, on the one hand, the most obvious, and on the other, the most often overlooked. That is, the inclusion of a self-assessment component to any planned assessment and development learning intervention. As individual leaders select their development tools it is critical that they choose those that also have a self-assessment component. Based on the extensive literature around 360-degree feedback (e.g., Antonioni, 1996; Bracken et al., 2001; Church and Waclawski, 1998; Lepsinger and Lucia, 1997; London, 1997) and even at the heart of the principles from our perspective of some types of clinical psychology including psychoanalysis, the inclusion of self-assessments provides a perspective (when compared with views from other co-workers, managers, external clients, peers, second-level managers, and so on), that is invaluable to helping the individual leader understand exactly where they stand relative to their own perspective versus the more grounded behaviorally based observations of other co-workers. Going back to the Lewin and Beckhard change models, it is imperative that the individual has the opportunity to see the difference between behavioral observations that is afforded by having a self versus other comparison in an assessment process. More specifically, this comparison and the cognitive processing outcome as a result is what creates the need for change (again the concept of unfreezing from the present state) in an individual and therefore the *raison d'être* for engaging in development activities. Church et al. (2002a) outline a model for how this process occurs at multiple levels in the organization. While some practitioners focus on only assessment from others (and we agree these are valuable inputs in and of themselves), from our perspective it is critical that the self-assessment be included in any type of leadership development effort that is intended to have a significant impact. It is the cognitive dissonance (Festinger, 1957) between a leader's own perceptions and those of others that will create the burning platform for change – that is, to create a development plan and act on it (as will be discussed in greater detail).

Phase II: Assessment and Feedback

Moving next into the second phase in the individual feedback develop-ment and change model is the concept of the assessment process and the feedback results that follow. This is the phase that combines both the ele-ments of conducting the actual assessment itself (for example, including responding to various assessment tools and measures, or being observed in an assessment center, or working with an executive coach), along with the data that is provided from the assessment process (for example, the 360-degree feedback report, normative comparisons, personality profile, narrative summary of strengths and development areas). Once again in this phase there are several different elements for the leader and individual self-learner to consider. In general these consist of (a) how the assessment is conducted and the type of data collected; (b) the modalities by which the feedback will be delivered; and (c) the natural reactions individuals have to any type of data-based feedback on their behavior (that is, good or bad). Each of these will be described below.

Types of assessments
Once an individual has decided to proceed with a development initiative (and the question of what is being developed has been answered), the next consideration is what type of assessment tool should be utilized. While in some instances the nature of the development area may in fact dictate the tool selected, more often than not the leader will have a variety of options available to him or her. As noted above, these range across a variety of content areas and include everything from individual self-initiated (and self-only) assessment tools (for example, online personality measures, adjective checklists, or behavioral items and rating scales), to multi-rater assessments of skills, behaviors or capabilities such as 360-degree feed-back, which is one of the more commonly used tools in organizations today (Bracken et al., 2001), to more in-depth observation based assessment processes such as participating in an assessment center or being shadowed by an executive coach during the course of a working day, week or month. Of course each of these assessment approaches has a cost associated with it both in terms of time and resources required. These can range from hardly nothing at all (for example, to complete a free conflict management assess-ment online) to extremely expensive and intensive (for example, being observed by a coach for a month or more). Below are some high-level examples of costs associated with various external development options.

- Reading a series of business books or journal articles and taking some sort of knowledge test (free to about $250).

- Personality assessment online (free to about $300 depending on model, vendor, and level of rigor associated with the test).
- 360-degree feedback assessment online (free to about $500 depending on content, vendor, level of oversight by manager or the HR function when selecting raters, and so on).
- Engaging in an online learning course or distance learning program with an assessment component at the end ($100 to $1000 or more depending on content and length of learning – these can run even higher for online executive MBA programs).
- Full-scale individual assessment, which usually entails personality instruments, 360-degree feedback assessment, and an in-depth interview ($600 to about $10 000 depending on methodology, leadership level being assessed, and so on).
- Single executive coaching session where the coach provides some form of developmental feedback either during or after the session ($200 to $10 000 depending on coach, tools, process used).
- Attending a formal assessment center ($4000 to $30 000 per individual depending on how extensive the approach is, leadership level being assessed, and so on).
- Full-scale coaching engagement ($10 000 to $100 000 or more depending on the coach, length of engagement and level of the individual leader being coached – for example, CEO-level coaches are quite expensive).

Of course these are not the only types of development experiences available to leaders (others might include job rotations, participation in special task forces or teams, international assignments, secondment programs with other organizations, and so on); however, they are generally the ones that an individual can self-initiate and that include some form of assessment component. It should also be noted, however, that even if the motivation to develop oneself is present, there is still the issue of the costs involved (and whether these are carried by the organization or the individual him or herself). This is where cultural and resource moderators are important. In organizations where the leadership and culture are supportive of development and tools and support mechanisms are provided, the cost factor is often less of an issue. When the individual is not supported, however, the confluence of motivation and career aspirations will dictate how much the individual is willing to spend of his or her own resources to engage in development activities.

Feedback delivery mechanisms
The next factor to consider in the assessment process is the nature of the results themselves and the method or mechanism by which they will

need to be delivered. As might be expected from the range of assessments described above, there is a high degree of variability in this area as well. Some personality assessments, for example, require the completion of a formal certification process (on the part of the feedback provider, not the individual leader taking the test) before the results can be delivered. This can make the process more complex (for example, if the leader has to find someone with the appropriate certification for a given tool) and costly, depending on the method selected. Similarly, assessment centers are much more expensive because of the high degree of rigor involved in the process (for example, usually having trained observers involved, physical space to run the simulations, and custom development and/ or assessment summaries written up about the results). There is also a time component as well, for example, some tools can be administered and scored immediately following completion, while other approaches require time for synthesis and integration (particularly in the cases where multiple measures are employed at the same time such as combining a personality assessment with a 360 feedback measurement). The quality and quantity of the assessment feedback provided will vary based on these variables.

The other aspect of feedback delivery to consider is the importance of having a formally trained or certified feedback provider. While most assessment tools will provide a report of some sort that highlights strengths and development areas for the individual, in our experience few leaders have been trained to be able to interpret these types of results effectively. Although this is particularly true with personality measures (hence the certification requirement by many test vendors to even be able to sell the assessments), it is also true with managers receiving 360 feedback reports and other behavioral assessments. Being able to interpret a 360 feedback report and understand the nuances between the self-ratings and ratings from peers, direct reports, managers and sometimes even clients is not always easy (Church and Waclawski, 1998). It requires experience with these types of tools to be able to make the best use of the results. Although having an individual provide the leader with the feedback results increases the overall cost of the assessment process, it is absolutely worth the additional investment from a developmental standpoint. Even peer to peer results sharing is often more engaging and results in better insights being generated than just an individual reviewing his or her results alone. However, this typically requires a more formal leadership development program or setting to ensure the appropriate context and guardrails are in place. It is unlikely that many individuals who self-initiate an assessment will want to share their own results with a colleague who is not engaged in the same process.

Reactions to feedback

The third and final aspect to consider in the assessment and feedback phase is the nature of individual reactions to feedback. One of the most fundamental aspects of effective assessment and feedback is the psychological and interpersonal processes by which individuals come to understand, accept and ultimately use the assessment results for their personal growth and development (Church et al., 2002a). Even if self-initiated (and for development only versus decision making as in some organizations), the very process of being assessed can produce fear and anxiety in the mind of the individual. This aspect needs to be recognized and addressed for the results to be used for meaningful development planning. In general, and regardless of the content of the assessment or the method of delivery of the results, most individuals process feedback results according to the simple SARAH model. Based on the classic Kubler-Ross (1969) model of the five stages of grieving, SARAH is defined as the cycling through of:

- Shock – at the results themselves and what they might reveal (particularly with personality measures which can be some of the most unsettling of assessment measures).
- Anger – at being assessed in the first place and the implications of the results (for the self-directed assessment this can be a case of 'be careful what you wish for').
- Rejection – that the data is not accurate or the test is invalid (many people never get past this stage, particularly without a trained feedback provider, coach or development program setting).
- Acceptance – this means coming to terms with the results and what they indicate about strengths and more importantly development areas (this is often linked to the level of executive maturity in a leader and is critical for development planning).
- Hope – that future efforts and actions can be done to drive positive change, growth and development.

Although many people are naturally intuitive and self-aware, and therefore can make effective use of the assessment results, there is a large percentage of leaders and managers who are less adept in this area and who may require assistance to work through these stages. Again this is where the nature of the assessment and the delivery mechanism intersect to ensure a quality development process. From a self-directed individual perspective, then, it is important that the right assessment measure be selected and the appropriate feedback process be included as part of the process. Begrudging adopters, resisters, renegades and first timers all may have a particularly difficult time working through these issues (given their disposition or total lack of knowledge). Feedback junkies, on the other hand, are the least likely to have issues, probably because feedback seeking and feedback acceptance are related constructs.

The other consideration here relative to reactions to feedback is how the results of the assessment will be used by the organization (if at all). In the 360 feedback literature there is a long history of what has been termed 'the great debate' between using that type of data for development only versus decision making (e.g., London, 2001). From the context of the individual electing to have an assessment conducted, there will be very real and significant differences in the type of tool identified and the process used (for example, external versus leveraging an existing internal process if one is provided by the organization) based on who will have access to the results delivered and how they will be used. Although assessment centers have been largely decision-making vehicles since their inception (Thornton and Byham, 1982), tools such as 360 feedback and personality measures began as developmental assessments and have only recently entered the decision-making arena in organizations (Bracken et al., 2001). Thus, it is important that the individual initiating the assessment process be crystal clear as to how widely the results will be shared, with whom, and under what circumstances. Often a simple indicator here is who gets to see the feedback report – for example, the recipient only or others as well. Even then, though, you can't be too certain. Many organizations, for example, use 360 feedback in succession planning discussions (Silzer and Church, 2010) so in those situations it might be more prudent for an individual to use an external vendor for their own development assessment (unless they want to have their data shared). This is one of the potential downsides to utilizing tools and processes offered by organizations as sometimes they are not for developmental purposes only. Similarly, many formal leadership programs in corporations serve the dual purpose of providing development, but also allowing senior leadership to make an assessment and determination of the future potential of each of the attendees. Even individual coaching engagements need to be carefully contracted up front regarding the sharing of insights and the outcome of the observations and assessment made by the coach.

Phase III: Planning for Development

The third phase of the individual feedback development and change model is comprised of the actual planning for development. As the demand for a leader's time and attention continues to increase, leaders too often perceive that participating in a self-assessment and development opportunity may take away valuable time from their daily job duties. Certainly, the tasks of communicating to and inviting raters (as in the 360 feedback process), completing self-assessment inventories (particularly those with 300 or more questions), attending training to understand the results, and so on can take time, not to mention time that might be required to register for a program, seek funding approval for the program, and so forth. It is no wonder then that for many leaders, receiving the feedback report is the end of the road – that is, the final deliverable in the (perceived) 'long' process of invitations, deadlines and surveys. In actuality, however, receiving feedback is just the beginning of the development journey.

Once an individual receives his or her feedback and understands how to interpret it, the next phase in the process is to integrate the disparate pieces of data to gain valuable insights for development, and turning those insights into action plans. This is one of the most critical and complex phases in the process. If not done, and done well, meaningful change rarely occurs.

From data to insights to action

Assessment vendors and providers recognize the importance of turning data into action. No longer is it a business differentiator as it was in the 1990s to merely have web-based assessment instruments and automated feedback reports. Providers that lead today's assessment and development industry are those that have resources to aid the leader in identifying insights into the data, and help identify specific targeted actions to take from the feedback. Some vendors use complex algorithms in their feedback reports to identify strengths and areas of opportunity. Still others use trained or certified specialists to write each feedback report manually, usually in instances where results from multiple measures need to be synthesized to tell a holistic story.

The main advantages of providing the leader with insights into the data are that it helps jumpstart the individual's analysis of the feedback and provides an 'outsider's' opinion of the results, which is particularly helpful when multiple assessment measures are used. It can also accelerate the action planning process, as many leaders easily get seduced into 'analysis paralysis' of the data without some direction of how to move forward (Church and Waclawski, 2001).

However, we believe that leaders should be cautious about assessment processes that over-prescribe the insights and actions for the feedback recipient. There are three advantages to requiring the individual to at least somewhat review, reflect on, and analyze their own data: (a) it helps them hone their analytical skills; (b) it helps develop their self-awareness if they have done the actual introspective work; and (c) it creates ownership and accountability for their results (which is critical for actually doing something with them). We also believe that an organization's strategy towards leadership development should be one of enablement, that is, *teach leaders to fish* versus *giving them the fish.* When it comes to assessment, the balance between providing 'the answers' versus letting them 'fish' for them is a delicate one, given the leaders' demand for time. If taken to the extremes, it can become either a fishing expedition or shooting in a barrel. Neither option builds capability or ownership.

Resources to the rescue

While organizations attempt to measure a variety of aspects of a leader's behavior and performance, leaders participating in self-assessment and development opportunities find themselves overwhelmed with a variety of disparate assessment feedback. The variety of assessment tools and options described earlier is all too often part of a growing suite of instruments of which individuals are being asked to partake. While advantageous to measure a broad range of the leader's behavior and performance, it all too often comes across as an overwhelming amount of feedback, with no underlying framework to tie the disparate pieces together. From an individual development perspective more data is indeed better, but more data is also more complex. The bundling of a 360 feedback measure along with a cognitive abilities test, a motives and values measure, and a personality assessment suite is a classic example of this type of practice. It results in radically different types of data with little integration points on its own. In these cases, individuals are left to rely on their cognitive capacity and learning ability to make sense of the data. Typically first timers don't have the knowledge to proceed, and begrudging adopters, resisters and renegades don't have the motivation to even try. Again, only feedback junkies and good soldiers will get value from the data in this context.

In response to these concerns, some organizations (typically, those with a feedback and development orientated culture) provide a variety of tools and resources to help individuals gain insights into their data. We typically see three broad categories of assistance: (1) integration frameworks – to help leaders conceptualize how all the different data components fit together; (2) tools for insights – to help them gain meaningful insights into their results; and (3) resources for development planning – to help them delve deeper into their insights and determine what to do about them. We will describe each of these in more detail below.

1. Integration frameworks While organizations often craft their own internal frameworks that fit their own culture and strategy, there are two integrating models that are particularly useful and have been adapted widely. The first is the employee–customer–profit chain model (Rucci et al., 1998). Originally, the model was used to demonstrate how employee

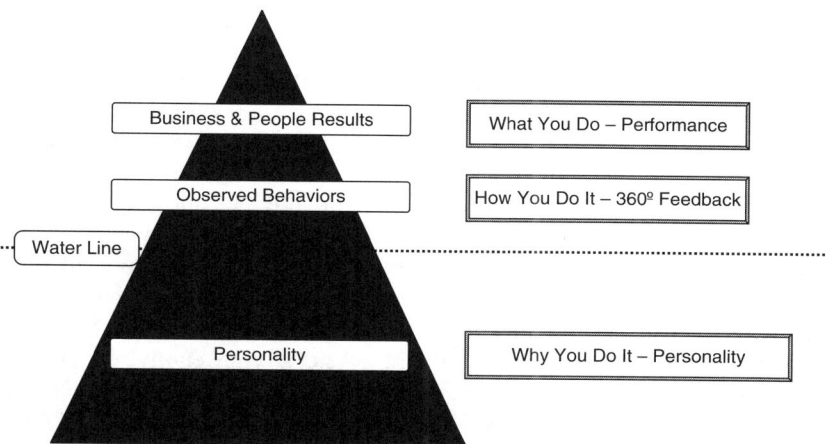

Figure 1.3   Sample iceberg model of personality

attitudes impact customer attitudes, which in turn impact business performance. Over the last decade a number of organizations have extended the model to include leadership behavior; that is, to show how a leader's behaviors (via competencies, derailment factors, personality traits, and so on) influence his or her workgroup's behavior and levels of employee engagement (via climate and engagement surveys), which in turn impact customer and business outcomes. The advantage of using a model such as this for interpreting individual assessment results is that it provides leaders with an understanding of how their behavior has direct and indirect influence on the business performance of the group. It also helps individuals understand how each piece of feedback relates to another, which in turn helps them begin to integrate the data in a more holistic manner.

The other model widely used for integrating different data sets is an adaptation of Freud's iceberg model of personality structure (Hall, 1961, p. 54; Lucia and Lepsinger, 1999). This model is particularly helpful in describing how assessments that measure a leader's more deep-seated dispositions, values and motives have an influence (or drive) the leader's behaviors (that is, things 'above the water line'). At PepsiCo this model is used as part of a certification workshop for feedback facilitators that helps integrate the use of the Hogan Assessment Suite along with an internally developed 360 feedback process (see Figure 1.3).

2. Tools for insights   After frameworks for understanding data come tools that help deliver important insights from the data. Tools can take a variety of forms, and the most progressive companies offer a variety to account for the variance in individual capability and learning styles to turn data into action. Probably the most popular and least costly tool is group session-based training – which entails the HR specialist taking a group of leaders through the feedback report(s) to ensure understanding and proper interpretation, how to analyze their data, and how to plan for action. The advantage to a training approach is that leaders can get their specific questions answered in real time, and HR can monitor who has gone through the training and who hasn't. The potential downside to this approach is that individuals are not given unique attention to their own specific results (unless that's formalized as part of the process). This is why some companies use either internal or external one-on-one feedback sessions with leaders and certified facilitators or even executive coaches to truly get to insights and action plans. Of course these are more costly and time-intensive interventions than group sessions or other methods.

Some companies have taken this concept online as well, providing a self-paced or self-directed learning approach. PepsiCo, for example, has developed an online module for gaining insights out of organizational survey data and action planning, using the acronym THINK:

● The *T*ask is to understand your report
● Create *H*ypotheses based on what you need to know
● Identify the *I*nsights (test your hypotheses)
● Develop *N*ew Ideas for communicating and action planning
● Make sure you have the right *K*ey Performance Indicators.

Other types of tools available focus on the action planning process itself. The simplest of these are action planning templates that require the leader to think through the specifics of actions to be taken – for example, steps to be taken, resources involved, key milestones, required funding/approval, and success indicators. Of course for those leaders who are engaging in development initiatives outside an organizational context (or where there is limited internal support and resources) the degree to which an assessment vendor or provider can provide these types of tools and online resources is critical to consider when making a selection.

3. Resources for development planning   In addition to tools to help structure the data, insights and action planning process, there are a variety of internal and external resources available to help the leader identify areas for intervention and guide them through the necessary steps. As noted above, and often the only source of support for self-funded individuals, development resource guides such as *The Leadership Machine* (Lombardo and Eichinger, 2002) the *Successful Manager's Handbook* (Personnel

Decisions International Corporation, 2004) and *For Your Improvement* (Lombardo and Eichinger, 1998) provide on-the-job 'active learning' tips, lists of relevant books and articles, and external development program offerings centered around specific competencies or development areas. Many organizations have also internalized this concept, providing a similar suite of resources around their own specific competency models, and incorporating their own internal leadership development offerings, development tools, action planning templates and e-learning modules.

The role of the coach

As noted earlier, coaches are another useful resource that is potentially available to assist leaders going through an assessment process. Some organizations provide and pay for coaches as part of their leadership development program while in other cases, coaches must be identified outside the formal system (particularly given the nature of the data inherent in the assessment process). Organizations such as IBM, Bank of America, and PepsiCo have formalized the use of coaches as an instrumental part of the process in helping the leader prepare for and execute development plans. Given the relatively high cost of utilizing external coaches, however, and the resource intensiveness required of leveraging internal coaches instead, this option is usually reserved for the most senior of executives or high potential talent pools. However, coaches can serve five critical roles in the leadership development process:

1. assist the leader in interpreting and gaining insights from the assessment data
2. work with the leader to identify the critical insights coming out of the feedback
3. ensure that the leader creates an appropriate action plan
4. coach and guide the leader through development challenges
5. hold the leader accountable for making timely progress towards his or her development goals.

Organizations are recognizing the importance of coaching in this process and implementing what we would call 'smart coaching' – that is, the surgical application of coaching when and where it's most needed (Valerio and Lee, 2005).

Phase IV: Taking Action

As critical as the planning for action phase is, even the most insightful analysis of feedback and carefully crafted action plans are pointless if they don't result in meaningful positive change in leader behavior. This next major phase in the individual feedback development and change model is all about taking action from the insights and plans prepared in the previous phase. If some leaders fall short in the previous (preparation) phase, others fall even shorter in this (execution) phase.

Unfortunately, many leaders who go through a self-assessment and development effort fail to realize that the mere act of going through a self-assessment process sets expectations among others (particularly those that have provided feedback) for meaningful behavior change. In other words, the simple act of asking questions (or collecting feedback) alone from anyone (including the self) raises the expectations that some action will be taken. As a result, not acting on or visibly demonstrating the action taken from such a process can have detrimental effects on subsequent perceptions of the individual, and of future development efforts for that individual. Church and Oliver (2006), for example, demonstrated that taking action yields more favorable perceptions of employee satisfaction in subsequent surveys than not taking action at all, or sharing results but doing nothing with them.

What does taking action look like?

The term 'action' here stems from the Latin term *agere* which means 'to do'. Taking action means doing something as a result of the assessment feedback. This can translate into several concepts including: (a) doing more of something effective; (b) doing less of something ineffective; or (c) doing something different from before.

The critical component of the taking action phase of the model is defining specifically what this action will be. This is why the action plan format as discussed in the previous phase is integral to success in any change effort. A good action plan should answer the following questions:

- What specific action will be taken (for example, 'Communicate better' is too vague; 'Meeting with my direct reports each week to discuss sales targets' is better)?
- By whom should the action be taken (for example, the leader is typically assumed to be the focal person here, but quite often others may need to be involved, as described below)?
- When/how often should the action be expected (for example, 'each week for one hour')?
- What are the expected results of the action (for example, 'increased clarity among the team regarding sales targets and sales strategy')?
- What are the supporting (and restraining) forces that will help (and hinder) the intended action (for example, restraining forces include

client meetings and leadership team meetings that take precedence; supporting forces include inviting my manager to the meetings to help create awareness and support)?

As with the other phases of the model described above, individuals vary greatly in their ability to succeed effectively in this phase. Generally, leaders must have all three individual characteristics described previously to succeed in this phase – personality disposition, learning ability and career aspirations. However, we have found that personality dispositions and motivation to develop oneself quite often are the main determinants of success. Traits such as conscientiousness, openness to experience, and courage (see also Siebert et al.'s, 1999, concept of proactive personality) all play a role in a leader's ability to guide themselves successfully through a change effort. One can easily see the linkages between these dispositions and taking action when examining what change entails – namely, publicly sharing one's intent to change, and then attempting new ways of doing things. Of course it goes without saying that feedback junkies are more likely to be effective at this phase than others, though there are individuals who perpetually want the feedback but continue to do nothing with it.

Tools and processes that support taking action

While individual characteristics are a critical determinant of success, organizations typically employ tools and processes to embed hard and soft support and accountability mechanisms into the design of the assessment and development process as well. These mechanisms help ensure the individual accomplishes his or her individually identified development goals. Soft mechanisms include the support of the individual's manager, team, and perhaps his or her HR practitioner. Manager support is critical to allow the individual time to develop a new repertoire of behavior. Manager support is also sometimes required to provide the individual with stretch assignments or new job duties to help develop a specific capability. Team support is also needed to give the individual the flexibility that one needs to develop a new capability. HR support can be helpful in ensuring that 'old tapes' following development and behavior change are not being played by the organization (that is, that others look beyond past experiences).

Hard mechanisms include linking the assessment and development process, and action planning follow-through efforts, to internal systems such as performance management and individual development plans (IDPs). As mentioned in Phase I, the individual going through the assessment should know up front if the results will be hard linked to any performance management or formal IDP systems. In many organizations, the extent to which one ties assessment results to hard mechanisms is still a manual process rather than a formal, automated one. Still, merging the results of the assessment and intended action plans into systems such as the formal IDP (or as noted earlier, the CDAP at PepsiCo) helps to create accountability and a sense of urgency to take action.

The good news for individuals self-initiating assessment and development initiatives is that these mechanisms are relatively easy to implement even if the organization doesn't have the formal tools and processes in place or if the culture does not support taking action. Most contemporary performance management systems involve some opportunity for the individual to list their goals for the year – either performance-based or developmental in nature. This provides the individual with an opportunity to include the actions and goals listed in their action plan, and 'formalizes' them by getting manager alignment and approval. In some systems, HR is also involved in the process as is the manager at the next level up. In short, the greater the level of accountability for taking action in this phase (and the more integrated the approach), the more likely is it that action will be taken.

Phase V: Measuring Change

Leaders who have gone through all of the previously described phases, that is, electing to engage in development, conducting the assessment and receiving the feedback, planning for development, and taking action – should feel pretty good about overcoming a variety of individual and organization obstacles. With that said, how does one know if the change effort has been successful? This last phase in the feedback and development model focuses on measuring change to determine if the leader's development goals have actually been achieved.

Resistance to change

It goes without saying that change does not come easily. Just as anyone who has had a New Year's resolution or tried a fad diet can attest, the intent or motivation to change doesn't necessarily mean that change will indeed occur (even if the action plan was well executed). In a similar vein, a leader who religiously implements an action plan is *likely* to meet his or her change goals, but results may not be as fast or as apparent as expected. There are a variety of individual and cultural forces that pull for the status quo (Kotter and Schlesinger, 1979). Individually, humans possess a strong natural bias in favor of perpetuating the status quo (Saad, 2007). It evolved as a survival tactic and is a powerful force hindering behavioral change – even if it is a positive one. Culturally, organizations that do not have an orientation for development will hinder a leader's efforts to change. As mentioned in the beginning of the chapter, even when development support is espoused by senior leadership, it may not be an underlying belief that drives systems, policies and processes. For example, some of the large consultancies espouse the importance of personal development, but then set utilization targets so high that development is prohibitive (that is, the ratio of the percentage of time an individual must spend during the work week on 'billable hours' to a client on a project versus working on other internally focused activities such as time and experience reports, knowledge management sharing, training, or even employee appraisals). No wonder the book *Consulting Demons* (Pinault, 2000) was so intriguing to many practitioners upon its release.

Methods for measuring change
In general, there are a variety of ways that a leader can determine if their intended change has occurred. Borrowing from Kirkpatrick's (1959; 1994) four levels of training evaluation, these can be summarized as follows:

- Level 1 – Reaction. This entails the leader simply asking him or herself if they think development has occurred. The advantages to this approach are that it is immediate – that is, if the leader thinks change has occurred, then quite often he or she could be right. However, this assumes that the leader is focusing on the right cues in his or her environment, and drawing the correct inferences from those cues. As you can imagine, first timers, begrudging adopters, resistors and renegades typically find this approach challenging at best and useless at worst.
- Level 2 – Learning. This typically entails re-testing on some of the same instruments initially used in the assessment, or similar instruments that measure the same construct so that change can be demonstrated quantitatively (although this has some challenges, as discussed below). Another, less commonly used approach is to go through a simulation to determine if the desired capability has been developed sufficiently. The advantage to this approach is that precise change over time can be seen since the same measure is being used in both instances. The disadvantage is that it does not provide an indication as to whether the change in the instrument scores actually yielded a positive impact in the leader's job performance. Typically, this approach is used for assessments measuring personality, cognitive ability, or functional/technical proficiency (for example, financial acumen).

- Level 3 – Transfer. This entails measuring if the desired change is actually exhibited behaviorally on the job. This can mean conducting a 360-degree assessment focused on the development areas (or resurveying if a 360-degree measure was used in the initial assessment process), or less commonly but just as effective is to have a trained observer (often a coach) shadow the individual and assess their on-the-job behavior. The advantages to this approach are that it is rigorous and ensures that the desired changes are positively impacting behavior at work. The disadvantage is that no matter what the method chosen (for example, surveys or observation), it can be rather disruptive to those involved in the process.
- Level 4 – Results. This last and most sophisticated approach to evaluation entails determining if specific business outcomes have been positively affected by the development effort. These vary by the nature and level of the role but can include sales revenue, quality measures, staff turnover, customer satisfaction ratings, employee engagement and/or climate ratings, and so on. The disadvantage of this approach is that it is often a challenge to link such measures to an individual's change efforts (in fact, the less control an individual has over the measure, the less likelihood of influencing it). However, the positive here is that such a linkage is not only of the utmost interest to the leader (typically this is why they are interested in changing in the first place), but it also helps to justify the business value of the time and resource investment in the assessment process.

Potential issues in measuring change

Measuring individual development and change is a complex effort. In general, there are a variety of potential issues or considerations that one should be mindful of when measuring change:

1. Change is easier to observe for some areas than others. For example, personality is considered relatively stable and thus more difficult to change; conversely, functional knowledge or skill is more easily acquired. Therefore, one should consider what is being targeted for the change effort when determining how to measure progress.
2. Time interval to expect results varies. It is often a challenge to know when to follow up to see if an individual's development and change efforts have been successful. The answer is determined not only by the area being developed (per above), but also by other factors such as the pace of change in the individual's job, the individual's tenure with the company, and so on.

3. The change may not be solely or even partially due to the individual's efforts. Depending on what indicators are being used to measure change, sometimes change measures are influenced by extraneous factors. For example, a leader using his workgroup's employee engagement survey scores as a measure of his ability to motivate his team may find that engagement scores increase or decrease simply because the economy has shifted.

Just as some (for example, resistors and renegades) believe that merely receiving the feedback is the end of the road, even the most well-intended leaders (for example, good soldiers and feedback junkies) fail to consider this last phase of measuring change. However, it plays the vital role of a continuous feedback loop in much the same way as any other OD intervention needs to evaluate its efforts to ensure it reaches the desired goal state. Unfortunately, the evaluation phase is often a challenge in the field of OD as well (for example, Church, 2003; Martineau and Preskill, 2002).

QUESTIONS THAT REMAIN

Throughout this chapter we have attempted to define the process by which individuals initiate, assess and receive feedback, develop targeted action plans, take action on the results, and assess the outcomes of their efforts in the interest of their own development. Whether reinforced and formally supported by an organization's leaders and internal processes and programs, or completely self-directed and funded at the individual leader level, the process by which assessments are conducted, feedback is used for planning purposes and action is taken (or not) is the same. That said, there remain a few important questions regarding self-assessment and leadership development.

First, *how much can an individual truly change and develop on their own?* While we have attempted to straddle the line in this chapter between self-directed development and organizational and management mandated agendas, or at a minimum simply the provision of tools and resources, what is the true individual capacity for change? Unique levels of motivation, cognitive and learning capability, and career aspirations will certainly be a moderating component in answering this question (that is, there is a contingent of individuals, and at this point in time many would say Millennials fall into this category, that will stop at nothing to continue broadening their own horizons), but in the end how much is the average leader willing to go above and beyond for their own development at the broadest of levels? One of the tenets of Western culture is mandated education for a fixed number of years. Students go to school and learn because it is a requirement. Similarly, organizations that have very formal and complex leadership development agendas select their high potentials and require them to follow a prescriptive learning path. What about the rest of the leaders in an organization? If high potentials make up only 10 percent of a given talent pool (e.g., Silzer and Church, forthcoming) what are the opportunities for the remaining 90 percent to develop? If it is all self-directed and self-funded then that would suggest a real breakdown in the development agenda for most corporations and perhaps for Western society in general. We would like to see research directed at how much and how far individuals can go on their own.

Second, based on our experience, there are many leaders who simply don't understand the need for feedback and development. That is, they do not have the foresight to see the need for increasing their own personal self-awareness and capabilities. In short, they don't know what they don't know, and they don't know that they should know. The question here is *how to get the clueless to realize they are indeed so clueless*? Leaders who are high in feedback-seeking behaviors are not the problem – research has shown that they will engage in assessment and development efforts, and are likely to benefit from them depending on their goal orientation (Janssen and Prins, 2007). Even the good soldiers and begrudging adopters are fine here. These most troubling individuals are usually the resisters and the renegades in the leadership development arena. We truly wonder whether it is ever possible to break through to these individuals and show them the need, value and utility of assessment and development.

Finally, our third question is more individualistic in nature. Having seen many leaders and managers engage in assessment and development activities, the question often is *how accurate is my own self-assessment of my behavior*? While the comparison between self ratings and those of other co-workers is a cornerstone of 360 feedback programs, often individuals have a tendency to want to believe their own internal assessments over other perspectives. This is part of the SARAH model described above, and as noted, many leaders end at the rejection phase and do not move forward to development planning. While some self-assessment tools such as personality measures have been designed to reduce or eliminate self-ratings bias, it is almost impossible to do so in behaviorally-based assessments such as 360 measures. We would like to see more research into the process of self-ratings and the acceptance of those ratings. We'd also like to see more research on the accuracy of self versus other ratings. It is assumed that others' ratings of a leader are unbiased, and the self, if different from other's ratings, are in fact the biased assessments. However, is this always true? Are there certain capabilities or situations where the self actually knows thyself the best?

SUMMARY

The field of leadership development is both broad and deep. With this chapter we have attempted to contribute to the literature by focusing on the individual's perspective to initiating and engaging in a data-based assessment and development journey. Rather than focus on models of leadership or singular methods for development we have taken the reverse route, that is, to explore an OD-based process by which data and feedback (from whatever source) is used to unfreeze a leader from his or her current state and drive positive development, growth and change. We have also highlighted the importance of individual characteristics, the tools and resources available, and the cultural and leadership-based moderating variables in the process of individuals seeking development, as well as the wide range of development options available. In the end, a leader's selection of a developmental assessment and action planning program must be made with clear attention and self reflection to what is being developed, to what end, with what assessment tool(s), within what context of the data being used, via what delivery mechanism, and fundamentally with what accountability for change. This is never, and should never be, a quick and easy decision, but one based on thoughtful planning, reflection and with an eye to the future.

NOTE

1. The authors would like to acknowledge the contributions of David H. Oliver and Erica I. Desrosiers to the framework described in this chapter.

REFERENCES

Antonakis, J., Cianciolo, A.T. and Sternberg, R.J. (eds) (2004), *The Nature of Leadership*, Thousand Oaks, CA: Sage.
Antonioni, D. (1996), 'Designing an effective 360-degree appraisal feedback process', *Organizational Dynamics*, **25**(2), 24–38.
Ashford, S.J. (1986), 'Feedback seeking in individual adaptation: a resource perspective', *Academy of Management Journal*, **29**, 465–87.
Ashford, S.J. (1989), 'Self-assessments in organizations: a literature review and integrative model', in B.M. Staw and L.L. Cummings (eds), *Research in Organizational Behavior*, Vol. 11, Greenwich, CT: JAI Press, pp. 133–74.
Bass, B.M. (1990), *Bass and Stogdill's Handbook of Leadership: Theory, Research, and Managerial Applications*, 3rd edn, New York: The Free Press.
Beckhard, R., and Harris, R.T. (1987), *Organizational Transitions: Managing Complex Change*, 2nd edn, Reading, MA: Addison-Wesley.

Bracken, D.W., Timmreck, CW., and Church, A.H. (eds) (2001), *The Handbook of Multisource Feedback: The Comprehensive Resource for Designing and Implementing MSF Processes*, San Francisco, CA: Jossey-Bass.

Burke, W.W. (1982), *Organization Development: Principles and Practices*, Glenview, IL: Scott, Foresman.

Burke, W.W. (1994), *Organization Development: A Process of Learning and Changing*, 2nd edn, Reading, MA: Addison-Wesley.

Burke, W.W. and Jackson, P. (1991), 'Making the SmithKline Beecham merger work', *Human Resource Management*, **30**, 69–87.

Burke, W.W. and Litwin, G.H. (1992), 'A causal model of organizational performance and change', *Journal of Management*, **18**, 523–45.

Burke, W.W. and Noumair, D.A. (2002), 'The role of personality assessment in organization development', in J. Waclawski, and A.H. Church (eds), *Organization Development: A data-driven approach to organizational change*, San Francisco, CA: Jossey-Bass, pp. 55–77.

Byham, W.C., Smith, A.B. and Paese, M.J. (2002), *Grow your Own Leaders*, Pittsburg, PA: DDI Press.

Charan, R., Drotter, S. and Noel, J. (2001), *The Leadership Pipeline: How to Build the Leadership Powered Company*, San Francisco, CA: Jossey-Bass Inc.

Cheung-Judge, M. (2001), 'The self as an instrument: a cornerstone for the future of OD', *OD Practitioner*, **33**(3), 11–16.

Chiaburu, D.S., Baker, V.L., and Pitariu, A.H. (2006), 'Beyond being proactive: What (else) matters for career self-management behaviors', *Career Development International*, **11**(7), 619–32.

Church, A.H. (1997), 'Managerial self-awareness in high performing individuals in organizations', *Journal of Applied Psychology*, **82**(2), 281–92.

Church, A.H. (2003), 'Organization development', in J.E. Edwards, J.C. Scott and N.S. Raju (eds), *The Human Resources Program-Evaluation Handbook*, Thousand Oaks, CA: Sage, pp. 322–42.

Church, A.H. and Herena, M.R. (2003), 'The PepsiCo HR career framework: a data-driven approach to career development', *Organization Development Practitioner*, **35**(4), 27–33.

Church, A.H. and Oliver, D.H. (2006), 'The importance of taking action, not just sharing survey feedback', in A. Kraut (ed.), *Getting Action from Organizational Surveys: New Concepts, Technologies and Applications*, San Francisco, CA: Jossey-Bass, pp. 102–130.

Church, A.H. and Waclawski, J. (1998), 'Making multirater feedback systems work', *Quality Progress*, **31**(4), 81–9.

Church, A.H. and Waclawski, J. (2001), *Designing and Using Organizational Surveys: A Seven Step Process*, San Francisco, CA: Jossey-Bass.

Church, A.H. and Waclawski, J. (forthcoming), 'Take the Pepsi challenge: talent development at PepsiCo', in R.F. Silzer and B.E. Dowell (eds), *Strategy-Driven Talent management: A Leadership Imperative*, San Francisco, CA: Jossey-Bass.

Church, A.H., Waclawski, J. and Burke, W.W. (2001), 'Multisource feedback for organization development and change', in D.W. Bracken, C.W. Timmreck and A.H. Church (eds), *The Handbook of Multisource Feedback: The Comprehensive Resource for Designing and Implementing MSF Processes*, San Francisco, CA: Jossey-Bass pp. 301–17.

Church, A.H., Walker, A.G. and Brockner, J. (2002a), 'Multisource feedback for organization development and change,' in J. Waclawski, and A.H. Church (eds),

Organization Development: A Data-Driven Approach to Organizational Change, San Francisco, CA: Jossey-Bass, pp. 27–54.

Church, A.H., Gilbert, M., Oliver, D.H., Paquet, K. and Surface, C. (2002b), 'The role of technology in organization development and change', *Advances in Human Resource Development*, **4**(4), 493–511.

Conger, J.A. and Benjamin, B. (1999), *Building Leaders: How Successful Companies Develop the Next Generation*, San Francisco, CA: Jossey-Bass.

Costa, P.T. and McCrae, R.R. (1991), *Revised NEO personality inventory (NEO PI-R)*, Odessa, FL: Psychological Assessment Resources.

Dotlich, D. and Cairo, P.C. (2003), *Why CEO's Fail: The 11 Behaviors that can Derail your Climb to the Top and how to Manage Them*, San Francisco, CA: Jossey-Bass.

Dychtwald, K., Erickson, T.J. and Morison, R. (2006), *Workforce crisis: How to Beat the Coming Shortage of Skills and Talent*, Boston, MA: Harvard Business School Press.

Festinger, L. (1957), *A Theory of Cognitive Dissonance*, Evanston, IL: Row-Peterson.

Fortune (2007), *The Top Companies for Leaders 2007*, available at http://money.cnn.com/magazines/fortune/leadership/2007/global/.

Fulmer, R.M., (2001), 'Johnson and Johnson: Frameworks for leadership', *Organizational Dynamics*, **29**(1), 211–20.

Fulmer, R.M., and Conger, J.A. (2004), *Growing your Company's Leaders: How Great Organizations Use Succession Management to Sustain Competitive Advantage*. New York: AMACOM.

Gentry, W.A., and Leslie, J.B. (2007), 'Competences for leadership development: what's hot and what's not when assessing leadership-implications for organization development', *Organization Development Journal*, **25**(1), 37–46.

Hall, C.S. (1961), *A Primer of Freudian Psychology*, New York: New American Library.

Hankin, H. (2005), *The New Workforce: Five Sweeping Trends that will Shape your Company's Future*, New York: AMACOM.

Hogan, R. and Shelton, D. (1998), 'A socioanalytic perspective on job performance', *Human Performance*, **11**(2/3), 129–44.

Hogan Assessment Systems Inc. (2009), *The Hogan Development survey: Overview Guide*, Tulsa, OK: Hogan Assessment Systems, available at www.hoganassessments.com.

Janssen, O. and Prins, J. (2007), 'Goal orientations and the seeking of different types of feedback information', *Journal of Occupational and Organizational Psychology*, **80**, 235–49.

Jeanneret, R. and Silzer, R. (eds) (1998), *Individual Psychological Assessment: Predicting Behavior in Organizational Settings*, San Francisco, CA: Jossey-Bass.

Kirkpatrick, D.L. (1959), 'Techniques for evaluating training programs', *Journal of ASTD*, **13**, 3–9.

Kirkpatrick, D.L. (1994), *Evaluating Training Programs: The Four Levels*, San Francisco, CA: Berrett-Koehler.

Kossek, E.E., Roberts, K., Fisher, S. and DeMarr, B. (1998), 'Career self-management: a quasi-experimental assessment of the effects of a training intervention', *Personnel Psychology*, **51**, 935–62.

Kotter, J.P. and Schlesinger, LA. (1979), 'Choosing strategies for change', *Harvard Business Review*, March–April, 106–14.

Kubler-Ross, E. (1969). *On Death and Dying*, New York: Macmillan.

Lepsinger, R. and Lucia, AD. (1997), *The Art and Science of 360° Feedback*, San Francisco, CA: Pfeiffer/Jossey-Bass.

Lewin, K. (1946), 'Action research and minority problems', *Journal of Social Issues*, **2**, 34–46.

Lombardo, M.M. and Eichinger, R.W. (1998), *For your Improvement: A Development and Coaching Guide*, Minneapolis, MN: Lominger Limited.

Lombardo, M.M. and Eichinger, R.W. (2000), 'High potentials as high learners', *Human Resource Management*, **39**(4), 321–9.

Lombardo, M.M. and Eichinger, R.W. (2002), *The Leadership Machine*, Minneapolis, MN: Lominger Limited.

London, M. (1997), *Job Feedback: Giving, Seeking and Using Feedback for Performance Improvement*, Mahwah, NJ: Lawrence Erlbaum.

London, M. (2001), 'The great debate: Should 360 be used for administration or development only?', in D.W. Bracken, C.W. Timmreck and A.H. Church (eds), *The Handbook of Multisource Feedback*, San Francisco, CA: Jossey-Bass, pp. 368–85.

London, M. and Beatty, R.W. (1993), '360-degree feedback as a competitive advantage', *Human Resource Management*, **32**(2&3), 353–72.

London, M. and Smither, J.W. (1999), 'Career-related continuous learning: defining the construct and mapping the process', in G.R. Ferris (ed.), *Research in Personnel and Human Resource Management*, Vol. 17, San Diego, CA: JAI Press, pp. 81–121.

Lucia, A.D. and Lepsinger, R. (1999), *The Art and Science of Competency Models: Pinpointing Critical Success Factors in Organizations*, San Francisco, CA: Jossey Bass.

Marquardt, M.J. (1999), *Action Learning in Action: Transforming World Problems and People for World-class Organizational Learning*, Palo Alto, CA: Davies-Black.

Marsick, V.J., O'Neil, J. and Watkins, K.E. (2002), 'Action learning' in J. Waclawski and A.H. Church (eds), *Organization Development: A Data Driven Approach to Organizational Change*, San Francisco, CA: Jossey-Bass, pp. 177–202.

Martineau, J.W. and Preskill, H. (2002), 'Evaluating the impact of organization development interventions', in J. Waclawski and A.H. Church (eds), *Organization Development: A Data-driven Approach to Organizational Change*, San Francisco, CA: Jossey-Bass, pp. 286–301.

McCall, M.W., Jr., (1998), *High Flyers: Developing the Next Generation of Leaders*, Boston, MA: Harvard Business School Press.

McClelland, D. (1961), *The Achieving Society*, Princeton, NJ: D. Van Nostrand.

Mills, E. (2007), 'Meet Google's new culture zar', *CNET News*, available at http://news.cnet.com/Meet-Googles-culture-czar/2008-1023_3-6179897.html.

Personnel Decisions International Corporation (2004), *Successful Manager's Handbook*, 7th edn, Minneapolis, MN: Personnel Decisions International Corporation.

Pinault, L. (2000), *Consulting Demons: Inside the Unscrupulous World of Global Corporate Consulting*, New York: HarperBusiness.

Rucci, A.J., Kirn, S.P. and Quinn, R.T. (1998), 'The employee–customer profit chain at Sears', *Harvard Business Review*, **76**(1), 83–97.

Saad, G. (2007), *The Evolutionary Bases of Consumption*, Mahwah, NJ: Psychology Press.

Seashore, C.N., Shawver, M.N., Thompson, G. and Mattare, M. (2004), 'Doing good by knowing who you are: the instrumental self as an agent of change', *OD Practitioner*, **36**(3), 55–60.

Seibert, S., Crant, J. and Kraimer, M. (1999), 'Proactive personality and career success', *Journal of Applied Psychology*, **84**(3), 416–27.

Seldman, M. (2008), 'Elevating aspirations at PepsiCo', *Training and Development*, **62**(6) 36–8.

Seldman, M. and Seldman, J. (2008), *Executive Stamina: How to Optimize Time, Energy, and Productivity to Achieve Peak Performance*, Hoboken, NJ: John Wiley and Sons.

Silzer, R.F. and Church, A.H. (forthcoming), 'Identifying and assessing high potential talent: Current organizational practices', in R.F. Silzer and B.E. Dowell (eds), *Strategy-driven Talent Management: A Leadership Imperative*, San Francisco, CA: Jossey Bass.

Thornton, G.C. and Byham, W.C. (1982), *Assessment Centers and Managerial Performance*, New York: Academic Press.

Tichy, N.M. and DeRose, C. (1996), 'The Pepsi challenge: building a leader-driven organization', *Training and Development*, **50**(5), 58–66.

Vaill, PB. (1989), *Managing as a Performing Art: New Ideas for a World of Chaotic Change*, San Francisco, CA: Jossey Bass.

Valerio A.M. and Lee, R.J. (2005), *Executive Coaching: A Guide for the HR Professional*, San Francisco, CA: John Wiley and Sons.

Waclawski, J. and Church, A.H. (eds) (2002), *Organization Development: A Data Driven Approach to Organizational Change*, San Francisco, CA: Jossey-Bass.

Zemke, R., Raines, C. and Filipczak, B. (2000), *Generations at Work: Managing the Clash of Veterans, Boomers, Xers, and Nexters in your Workplace*, New York: American Management Association.

2. Inspiring the development of emotional, social and cognitive intelligence competencies in managers

Richard E. Boyatzis, Tony Lingham and Angela Passarelli

Leadership educators must ask themselves two fundamental questions when designing developmental programs. First, what competencies make leaders effective (that is, what do we want our students to learn)? Second, how can we inspire students to develop them? Successful leadership development courses in management education need to address these two questions in a way that promotes shared responsibility between educators and students. Such courses need to be designed around theoretical frameworks that lead to meaningful and sustained adult change and development.

The first segment of this chapter discusses the competencies that distinguish outstanding leaders from average leaders, managers and professionals – answering the *what* question above. Intentional Change Theory (ICT) is explained in the second segment, as the central theoretical framework to inspire self-development in MBAs through the Leadership Assessment and Development Course (LEAD). Specific examples of *how* these competencies are developed within the MBA program are then described. In the third segment, results from 22 years of longitudinal assessment of learning outcomes related to competency development in a full-time MBA program show that MBAs can change in ways that are essential to effective leadership and management.

COMPETENCIES AS THE FOCUS OF SELF-MANAGED DEVELOPMENT

It could be said that developing human talent breaks down into three categories: acquiring knowledge, learning to use that knowledge effectively, and discovering why one is driven to use one's knowledge and competencies. Leaders on a journey of self-development must undergo all three.

Knowledge. Acquiring knowledge means developing the functional, declarative, procedural and meta-cognitive knowledge needed to perform. Examples of these types of knowledge are, respectively, market segmentation for a new product, the time it takes a polymer to set, calculating the present value of a capital acquisition, and ethical principles as applied in international business transactions. These forms of knowledge are necessary but not sufficient for the leader, manager, or professional to add value to organizations. In this sense, knowledge bases are threshold talents (Boyatzis, 1982; 2008; Spencer and Spencer, 1993; Goleman, 1998).

Competencies. To be an effective leader, manager or professional, a person needs the ability to use knowledge and to make things happen. These abilities can be called competencies, which Boyatzis (1982) defined as, 'the underlying characteristics of a person that lead to or cause effective and outstanding performance'. A set of competencies have been shown empirically to cause or predict outstanding leader, manager, or professional performance in the literature (Bray et al., 1974; Boyatzis, 1982; 2008; in press; Kotter, 1982; Thornton and Byham, 1982; Luthans et al., 1988; Howard and Bray, 1988; Druskat et al., 2005; special issue of the *Journal of Management Development* in February, 2008 on 'Competencies in the 21st Century', and the special issue of the *Journal of Management Development* in April, 2009 on 'Competencies in the EU'). Conceptual syntheses have also shown this relationship to effectiveness (Campbell et al., 1970; Spencer and Spencer, 1993; Goleman, 1998). Compiling these findings and summaries, it can be said that the important competencies fall into three clusters: (1) Cognitive intelligence competencies, such as systems thinking or pattern recognition; (2) Emotional intelligence competencies, such as adaptability, emotional self-control, emotional self-awareness, positive outlook, and achievement orientation; and (3) Social intelligence competencies, such as empathy, organizational awareness, inspirational leadership, influence, coaching and mentoring, conflict management, and teamwork. In addition, there are several cognitive capabilities that appear to be threshold competencies from the research cited above. That is, they are needed to be adequate in performance, but using more of them does not necessarily lead to outstanding or effective performance. Given research to date, these would include: knowledge (technical and functional); deductive reasoning; and quantitative reasoning.

Drive. Beyond knowledge and competencies, the additional ingredient necessary to outstanding performance appears to be the desire to use one's talent. This seems driven by a person's values, philosophy, sense of calling or mission, unconscious motives and traits (Boyatzis and Sala,

2004; Boyatzis, 2006). The motives and traits affect the way a person sees the world, especially the perception of opportunities and challenges they perceive in the environment (McClelland, 1985). But they are also persistent and generalized drivers. They arouse dispositional ways a person responds to his/her environment and create a focus for a person's behavior (McClelland, 1985).

These three domains of capability or talent (knowledge, competencies and motivational drivers) help us to understand *what* a person can do (knowledge), *how* a person can do it (competencies), and *why* a person feels the need to do it (values, motives, and unconscious dispositions). Our role in management education is to help people add value on each of these domains, to help them take charge of their own development toward greater effectiveness in their future jobs and careers.

INTENTIONAL CHANGE THEORY AS A MODEL FOR SELF-DIRECTED COMPETENCY DEVELOPMENT

What the studies referred to above have shown is that adults learn what they want to learn. Other things, even if acquired temporarily (for example, for a test), are soon forgotten (Specht and Sandlin, 1991). Students, children, patients, clients and subordinates may act as if they care about learning something, go through the motions, but they proceed to disregard it or forget it unless it is something that they want to learn. In this way, it appears that most, if not all, sustainable behavioral change is intentional. Intentional change is a desired change in an aspect of who you are (the Real) or who you want to be (the Ideal), or both. The process of intentional change is shown graphically in Figure 2.1 (Boyatzis and McKee, 2005; Boyatzis, 2006).

Change is a discontinuous process for most people. That is, it goes through 'fits and starts' or surprises. While these are often experienced as a conscious revelation or epiphany, we can call them discoveries. In complexity theory, these moments are called experiences of emergence.

Intentional Change Theory (ICT) describes the essential components and processes that encourage sustained, desired change to occur in a person's behaviors, thoughts, feelings and/or perceptions (Boyatzis, 2006). The theory includes five phases or discontinuities, called 'discoveries' (Boyatzis, 2006; Goleman et al., 2002). The five phases include: (1) the Ideal Self, or Personal Vision; (2) the Real Self, or Personal Balance Sheet; (3) creation of a Learning Agenda and Plan; (4) Experimentation and Practice with new behaviors, thoughts or feelings outlined in the Learning

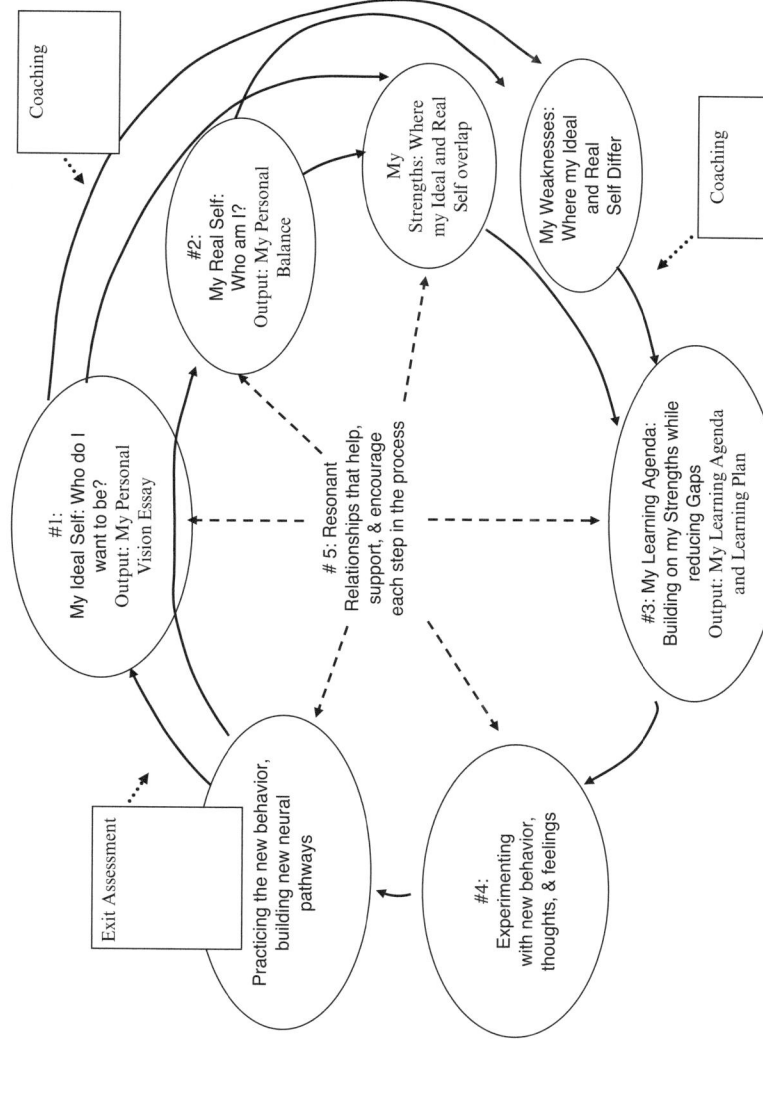

Figure 2.1   How Intentional Change Theory is incorporated into the LEAD course

65

Plan, and (5) Trusting Relationships that support a person's development experience.

The first discovery and potential starting point for the process of personal development is the discovery of an individual's deepest aspirations for his or her life. This is his/her image of their Ideal Self. Three major components comprise the development of this image: (1) an image of a desired future; (2) hope that one can attain it; and (3) inclusion of one's core identity, which serves as a foundation upon which to build the desired image (Boyatzis and Akrivou, 2006). The Ideal Self emerges from our ego ideal, dreams and aspirations. This is quite different from the 'ought self' in which others around the person impose their image of what the ideal should be (Boyatzis, 2006).

The last twenty years have revealed literature supporting the power of positive imaging or visioning in sports psychology, meditation and biofeedback research, and other psycho-physiological research. It is believed that the potency of focusing one's thoughts on the desired end state or condition is driven by the emotional components of the brain (Goleman, 1995; Boyatzis and McKee, 2005). This research indicates that we can access and engage deep emotional commitment, arousing neurogenesis and endocrine processes that allow for learning and openness to new experiences, people and feelings.

A person's awareness of their current self is often elusive. The Real Self, which is addressed by the Second Discovery, is the person that others see and with whom they interact. This discontinuity involves assessing one's strengths and weaknesses and creating a Personal Balance Sheet as an outcome. Coming to grips with who we are (strengths and weaknesses) indicates a readiness to make the necessary changes to become the person we want to be.

For normal reasons, the human psyche protects itself from the automatic 'intake' and conscious realization of all information about ourselves. These ego-defense mechanisms serve to protect us. They also conspire to delude us into an image of who we are that may feed on itself, become self-perpetuating, and possibly dysfunctional (Goleman, 1985).

For a person to truly consider changing a part of him or herself, he or she should have a clear sense of what they value and want to keep. These areas in which the Real Self and Ideal Self are consistent or congruent can be considered Strengths. Likewise, to consider what you want to preserve about yourself involves admitting aspects of yourself that you wish to change or adjust in some manner. Areas where your Real Self and Ideal Self are inconsistent may be considered Gaps (that is, aspects considered weaknesses or things we wish to change). Self-assessment and 360-degree assessment instruments are examples of resources available and commonly used by coaches to stimulate reflection and encourage mindfulness as a person develops awareness of their current capabilities and limitations.

All too often, people explore growth or development by focusing on the 'gaps' or deficiencies. Organization-based leadership training programs and managers conducting annual reviews often make the same mistake. There is an assumption that we can 'leave well enough alone' and get to the areas that need work. It is no wonder that many programs or procedures intended to help a person develop often result in the individual feeling battered, beleaguered and bruised, not helped, encouraged, motivated or guided.

The third discontinuity in intentional change is development of a learning agenda, which encompasses the individual's personal vision, learning goals and actions in support of those goals. It provides a framework to document a person's desired future as well as the steps he or she chooses to take to create that desired future through the articulation of clear goals.

A learning agenda is unique in that it places the focus more on the development process itself and less on discrete outcomes such as improved performance or greater fulfillment at work. It differs from a traditional *development plan* in that it ideally embodies a *learning orientation* rather than a *performance orientation*. A learning orientation arouses a positive belief in one's capability and the hope of improvement. This encourages people to set personal standards of performance, rather than 'normative' standards that mimic what others have done or serve to meet an imposed goal. Contrary to a learning orientation, a performance orientation often evokes anxiety and doubts about whether or not change is possible or even desired (Chen et al., 2000).

The fourth discovery includes experimentation and practice with desired changes. The essence of this stage is really about implementing the goals and action steps articulated in the prior discovery and taking risks to develop new behavioral 'habits'. These behaviors become habits by practicing them beyond the point of comfort to the point of mastery.

Experimentation and practice is most effective when it occurs in conditions in which the person feels safe (Kolb and Boyatzis, 1970). This sense of psychological safety creates an atmosphere in which the person can try new behaviors, perceptions and thoughts with relatively less risk of shame, embarrassment, or serious consequences of failure.

It is often helpful if a person can find ways to leverage learning from current, or on-going experiences happening in their professional and/or personal life vs. creating an elaborate, new application. That is, the experimentation and practice can but usually does not need to involve formal learning such as attending training courses or creating a new project assignment. The process of translating practice into effective learning and developmental growth occurs by trying something new in the context of everyday work and life, extracting the best of what worked from the experience through reflection and committing to further experimentation. During this part of the process, intentional change looks and feels like a 'continuous improvement' process.

The impact of experimentation and practice on development of one's capabilities was empirically proven by Dreyfus (2008). She studied managers of scientists and engineers who were considered superior performers. After observing that the managers used considerably more of certain abilities than their less effective counterparts, she investigated how they developed some of those abilities. One of the distinguishing abilities was Group Management, also called Team Building. She found that many of these middle-aged managers had first experimented with team building skills in high school and college, in sports, clubs, and living groups. Later, when they became 'bench scientists and engineers' working on problems in relative isolation, they still pursued use and practicing of this ability in activities outside work. They practiced team building and group management in social and community organizations, such as community-based clubs to help youth, and professional associations in planning conferences and such.

Our relationships are an essential part of our environment. The most crucial relationships often exist in groups that have particular importance to us. These relationships and groups give us a sense of identity, guide us as to what is appropriate and 'good' behavior, and provide feedback on our behavior. In sociology, they are called reference groups. These relationships create a 'context' within which we interpret our progress on desired changes, the utility of new learning, and even contribute significant input to formulation of the Ideal (Kram, 1996).

Based on social identity groups, and now relational theories, our relationships both meditate and moderate our sense of who we are and who we want to be. We develop or elaborate on our Ideal Self from these contexts. We label and interpret our Real Self from these contexts. We interpret and value Strengths (that is, aspects considered our core that we wish to preserve) from these contexts. We also interpret and value Gaps (that is, aspects considered weaknesses or things we wish to change) from these contexts.

In this sense, our relationships are mediators, moderators, interpreters, sources of feedback, sources of support and permission for the change and learning we seek. They may also be the most important source of protection from relapses or returning to our earlier forms of behavior. Wheeler (2008) analyzed the extent to which the MBA graduates worked on their goals in multiple 'life spheres' (that is, work, family, recreational groups, and so on). In a two-year follow-up study of two graduating classes of part-time MBA students, she found those who worked on their goals and plans in multiple sets of relationships improved the most and to a greater degree than those working on goals in only one setting, such as work or within one relationship.

The process of experiencing sustained desired change is an iterative, cyclical process of ongoing development for most people most of the time. Using complexity theory, the process of development engages, in this case, the cycle of individual change, or the lack of it through two self-organizing properties of the human organism. Two attractors are the Positive Emotional Attractor (PEA) and the Negative Emotional Attractor (NEA), determining the context of the self-organizing process and whether it is an adaptation to existing conditions or an adaptation to new, emergent conditions.

Intentional Change Theory offers an explanation as to how the disequilibrium occurs and suggests forces to drive new self-organizing systems. An attractor becomes the destabilizing force. We call this the Positive Emotional Attractor. It pulls the person toward their Ideal Self. In the process of focusing the person on future possibilities and filling them with hope, it arouses the Parasympathetic Nervous System (PSNS) (Boyatzis et al., 2006). Once the PSNS is aroused, the person has access to more of their neural circuits, finds themselves in a calmer, if not elated state in which their immune system is functioning well and their body is sustained. They are able, in this state, to experience neurogenesis (that is, the conversion of hippocampal stem cells into new neurons) and the new degrees and extent of learning that becomes possible. It is even suggested that formation of learning goals or learning oriented goals works from this attractor and results in more successful change (Boyatzis, 2006).

But another attractor is also at play in the system – the Negative Emotional Attractor. In an analogous manner, it aroused the Sympathetic Nervous System (SNS) which helps the human to deal with stress and threat and protect itself. Within the threatened environment and state, the NEA pulls a person toward defensive protection. In this arousal, the body shunts blood to the large muscle groups, closes down non-essential neural circuits, suspends the immune system, and produces cortisol – important for protection under threat (Boyatzis et al., 2006). But cortisol inhibits or even stops neurogenesis and overexcites older neurons, rendering them useless (Boyatzis et al., 2006).

If a person's adaptation is self-organizing, then desired change not already part of this system is only possible when it is intentional. We would add because of the difficulty in sustaining the effort, it also must be driven by a powerful force. This is where the image of the Ideal Self activates the energy of the PEA, and the two attractors become 'a limit cycle' for the person. This also helps us to understand why there is a need for more positivity than negativity in change efforts (Fredrickson and Losada, 2005).

In the studies of the impact of the year-long executive development program, Ballou et al. (1999) found that the program increased self-confidence amongst doctors, lawyers, professors, engineers and other professionals. The finding was interesting because these professionals appeared, on the surface, to have high self-confidence already. How could any program increase it? The best explanation came from follow-up questions to the graduates of the program. The increase in self-confidence seemed to occur because the graduates had greater trust in their ability to change. Their existing reference groups (that is, family, groups at work, professional groups, community groups) all had an investment in them staying the same, whereas the person wanted to change. The Professional Fellows Program allowed them to develop a new reference group that created more 'psychological space' for change.

COMPETENCY DEVELOPMENT THROUGH INTENTIONAL CHANGE IN AN MBA PROGRAM

At the Weatherhead School of Management, a leadership course was focused on developing the 'whole person' and was based on the underlying philosophy that adult sustainable behavioral change has to be intentional. The Leadership Assessment and Development (LEAD) course in the MBA curriculum is designed on the basis of Intentional Change Theory (ICT). The course has four benchmarks or outcomes: (1) a persona vision; (2) a personal balance sheet; (3) a coaching session with a specially trained professional coach; and (4) a learning agenda, as shown in Figure 2.1. For the first 18 years, the LEAD course was a semester long (15 weeks) to align with all other courses in the MBA curriculum. Rhee (2008) showed that in the first semester MBAs were preoccupied with learning accounting and finance. Their first mid-term exams were almost always traumatic. As a result, the LEAD course was split into two major components of six-week sessions, one at the beginning of the Autumn and one at the beginning of the Spring semester. The new design was launched in Autumn 2008.

In this new design, the first component was devoted to helping the MBA develop his/her Personal Vision, including the search for the most meaningful and appropriate job and career for them. In the second half of the course (at the beginning of the Spring semester), the ESCI-U 360 is collected to enable students to know each other well before assessing each other. In the second component, competency development is based on their personal vision with students bringing in their printed reports from the 360-degree feedback and signing up for a one-hour coaching session with a specially trained, professional coach. The coaching session focuses on identifying and preserving their strengths while looking at a few of their gaps close to the tipping point to help each student make progress toward their personal vision. This results in a type of audit or personal balance sheet. On the basis of the personal vision and personal balance sheet, they create a learning agenda. This document highlights competencies they would like to develop over the course of their MBA program. To assess the development of competencies and value-added of the MBA program, an Exit Assessment is required in which students take the ESCI-U 360-degree feedback in their last semester prior to graduation. In the Exit Assessment seminar, students evaluate their development of competencies, review their learning agenda, and engage in discussions of their internship or work experiences. They use this to decide what work environment they would most prefer.

The Leadership Assessment and Development leads a student through assessments and activities about their dreams and aspirations, current behavior, strengths and gaps as a manager and leader, and culminates in the writing of a learning plan. Students pursue the learning plan through the remainder of the program and afterward. We also assess their competency development in the MBA program through the Exit Assessment seminar conducted toward the end of their final semester.

ASSESSING COMPETENCY DEVELOPMENT OUTCOMES

Even before the humbling Porter and McKibbin (1988) report showed that MBA graduates were not fulfilling the needs of employers or the promise of the schools, the Association to Advance Collegiate Schools of Business (AACSB) started a series of outcome assessment studies in 1978. They showed faculty to be effective in producing significant improvement of students with regard to some abilities (Boyatzis and Sokol, 1982; Development Dimensions International-DDI, 1985). Boyatzis and Sokol (1982) showed that students had significantly increased on 40 percent to 50 percent of the competencies assessed in two MBA programs, while DDI (1985) reported that students in the two MBA programs in their sample had significantly increased on 44 percent of the variables assessed.

But, they also decreased significantly on 10 percent of the variables in the Boyatzis and Sokol study. When the overall degree of improvement in these abilities was calculated (Goleman et al., 2002), these studies showed about a 2 percent increase in emotional and social intelligence competencies in the one to two years students were in the MBA programs.

To address program impact, as of the early 1990s, only a few management schools had conducted student-change outcome studies which compared their graduates to their students at the time of entry into the program (Albanese et al., 1990). Today, many schools have conducted other types of outcome studies, namely studies of their alumni or studies with employers and prospective employers. Some schools have examined the student-change from specific courses (Bigelow, 1991; Specht and Sandlin, 1991). Student-change outcome studies have been a focus in undergraduate programs (Astin, 1993; Pascarella and Terenzini, 1991; Mentkowski and Associates, 2000; Winter et al., 1981), but still relatively little has been documented about the effects of graduate programs.

METHODS

Since 1990, entering data have been collected during the LEAD course (for a detailed description of the course and the longitudinal study, see Boyatzis, 1994; Boyatzis et al., 2002). The longitudinal study focuses on the impact of the MBA program on the development of cognitive, social and emotional intelligence competencies. The information included in this chapter is an update of earlier published studies. It continues and builds on the earlier studies (Boyatzis et al., 2002; Boyatzis et al., 1996; Boyatzis et al., 1995; Boyatzis and Saatcioglu, 2008) using a combination of cross-sectional and longitudinal, time series data collected as part of a 50-year longitudinal study of multiple cohorts of MBA students at the Weatherhead School of Management (WSOM), Case Western Reserve University.

Data collected during the years of 1987–89 reflect the results of students' development prior to revisions in the MBA program and are considered baseline samples. Many of the results of the 1987–96 studies have been reported in conference presentations, books and journal articles. Boyatzis et al. (2002) summarized all of these 12 prior studies and added results for 2000 and 2001. Boyatzis and Saatcioglu (2008) added results from 2004, 2005 and 2006. This chapter adds results from 2008. The result is a set of data from 13 cross-sectional and longitudinal studies of the full-time MBAs and six of the part-time MBAs.

The samples used in the earlier studies, as well as the additional samples first reported here, are described in Table 2.1. For clarification of sampling in each of the earlier years, see Boyatzis et al. (2002).

Table 2.1   Description of the samples and populations for the cohorts in this study

Cohort	No. MBAs entering	No. tested	No. graduating	Students tested	% female	ave. age	US news	FT ranking
1987 FT[a]	100	72	61	27[b]	31	26		
1988 FT[a]	89	70	71	17[b]	31	26		
1990–92 FT	124	108	96[c]	71	37	27		
1991–93 FT	105	83	71[c]	58	30	27		
1992–94 FT	137	104	127[c]	58	45	27		
1993–95 FT	140	125	146	77	35	27		
1998–2000 FT	186	89	191	56[d]	25	29	31	
1999–2001 FT	171	142	169	80[d]	35	27	44	39
2000–2002 FT	202	–	–	–	32	28	34	56
2002–2004 FT	162	164	108	–	36	27	51	77
2003–2005 FT	130	113	104	–	28	27	63	64
2004–2006 FT	109	136	104	–	38	28	56	84
2006–2008 FT	63	64	62	36	36	26	58	63

Notes:

a Assessment was considered voluntary, but not everyone appeared at the orientation program for the full-time students. For the randomly selected samples, participation was voluntary, so all assessed had given their permission.

b All randomly selected samples were comparable to the populations from which they were drawn as to age, gender, GMAT, undergraduate GPA and percentage international students.

c Some entering students did not graduate due to working toward a joint degree (e.g., MBA/JD) or transferring to the part-time program. Of those that permitted their data to be included in the study, some students were dropped from the final sample due to various unforeseen circumstances (e.g., incomplete assessments).

d Samples for those graduating in 1997, 1998 and 1999 were lost due to a series of computer crashes. The 2003 graduating sample was lost due to data entering errors. Consent was not garnered from 2007 sample. In 1997, participation in exit assessment near graduation became a required part of the program for full-time students. Part-time students were not approached for exit assessment.

INSTRUMENTS

All of the instruments used in these studies assessed competencies. In the earlier studies, five instruments were used: (1) the Learning Skills Profile (LSP) (Boyatzis and Kolb, 1991); (2) the Critical Incident Interview (CII), which is a one-hour, audiotaped interview (Flanagan, 1954; Boyatzis, 1982; Spencer and Spencer, 1993) coded for the competencies (Boyatzis,

1998); (3) the Group Discussion Exercise (GDE) is a 45-minute, videotaped simulation, coded for the competencies (Boyatzis, 1998); (4) the Presentation Exercise (PE) is an assessment of an individual's Oral Communication ability, also coded for the competencies (Boyatzis, 1998); and (5) a 360° informant-based assessment (the SAQ/EAQ and later the ECI-U and ESCI-U). For all of the data coded from qualitative sources, two or three people independently coded the interviews and videotapes. In this research, the coders averaged 89–90 percent inter-rater reliability on 16 of the competencies.

The Self-Assessment Questionnaire (SAQ) is a 73-item questionnaire in which the participants are asked to assess the frequency with which they demonstrate each behavior. The External Assessment Questionnaire (EAQ) is the informant, or 360, variation of the SAQ. In 2002, five of the cognitive competencies included in these two instruments were dropped because they did not predict effectiveness in management, leadership or professional jobs. They were threshold competencies, predicting average from poor performance (Boyatzis, 2008).

In the late 1990s, the SAQ and EAQ were expanded and adapted to assess emotional and social intelligence competencies more directly (Boyatzis and Sala, 2004). The new test was called the ECI. A special version of it, called the ECI-U, WSOM Version was used in the new outcome studies. The ECI-U, WSOM Version assessed several of the cognitive competencies most directly linked to effectiveness in leadership, management, and professional jobs. The ECI-U, and its base test, the ECI, and ECI-2 showed reliability and validity in numerous studies (summarized in Boyatzis and Sala, 2004).

The ECI-U, WSOM Version had 71 percent of items that were the same or very close in wording to the original SAQ/EAQ. All of the 17 scales in the SAQ/EAQ were included in the ECI-U. Eight new scales were added. The scales that were the same on the SAQ/EAQ and ECI-U WSOM version were: Achievement Orientation (earlier called Efficiency Orientation, Planning was folded into Achievement Orientation); Adaptability (earlier called Flexibility); Emotional Self-Control (earlier Self-Control); Self-confidence; Empathy; Conscientiousness (earlier called Attention to Detail); Initiative; Conflict Management (earlier called Negotiating); Communication; Developing Others; Influence (earlier called Persuasiveness); Building Bonds (earlier called Networking); Teamwork (earlier called Group Management); Cultural Awareness (earlier called Social Objectivity); Systems Thinking; and Pattern Recognition. The following scales were added in the ECI-U: Emotional Self-Awareness; Accurate Self-Assessment; Trustworthiness; Optimism; Organizational Awareness; Service Orientation; Inspirational Leadership; and Change Catalyst. For the latest revision refined to increase reliability and discriminant validity, the ESCI-U (Boyatzis, in press; Wolff, 2007), adjustments to some of the scales were made to maintain the total number of items at 70 while increasing number of items per scale: Accurate Self-Assessment was merged into Emotional Self-awareness; Initiative was merged into Achievement Orientation; Self-Confidence, Conscientiousness, Trustworthiness and Communications were dropped; Optimism was renamed Positive Outlook; Cultural Awareness was merged into Empathy, Building Bonds was merged into Teamwork, and Developing Others was renamed Coach & Mentor.

All full-time students were assessed using the ESCI-U in both the first and fourth semesters of the MBA program. In each assessment, they were asked to solicit feedback from at least 12 raters in the categories of supervisor, direct report, client, significant other, siblings, friends and classmates. Each student also completed a self-evaluation using the same instrument. T-tests were conducted on self and other competency ratings to identify significant changes from the beginning to the end of program.

RESULTS

Findings reported in Boyatzis et al. (2002) showed that full-time MBAs strongly (multiple measures with multiple cadres), significantly increased on Goal Setting, Action, Initiative, Leadership, Helping, Sense Making, Information Gathering, skills and competencies from entry to graduation as compared to comparison groups of full-time MBAs from the times series classes of 1987 to 1990. They significantly increased on Relationship skills as well. They maintained the significantly value-added, as in the comparison time series cohorts on Self-confidence, Information Analysis, Theory Building, Quantitative Analysis and Use of Technology. Similar and even more dramatic increases in value-added were found in studies of the part-time MBAs as compared to the comparison groups.

Boyatzis et al. (2002) showed that full-time MBAs significantly improved statistically on each of the 21 competencies as viewed by others with the EAQ in the 2001 sample and all 16 competencies assessed in the 2004 sample. Using the Self-Assessment Questionnaire, students significantly or near significantly improved on 15 of the 21 competencies in the 2001 sample and improved on all 16 in the 2004 sample.

Boyatzis and Saatcioglu (2008) reported on the full-time MBA cohorts of 2003–05 and 2004–06 as assessed using the ECI-U. They showed that full-time MBAs significantly improved on the following competencies in both years, as viewed by others: Accurate Self-Assessment, Initiative, Adaptability, Emotional Self-Control, Achievement Orientation,

Optimism, Empathy, Cultural Awareness, Communications, Conflict Management, Influence, Building Bonds, Systems Thinking and Pattern Recognition. They did not improve, as viewed by others in either year on: Self-Confidence, Organizational Awareness, Inspirational Leadership, Change Catalyst, Developing Others and Teamwork. They improved in their own eyes from 2003 to 2005 but not in 2004 to 2006 in: Emotional Self-Awareness, Trustworthiness, Conscientiousness and Service Orientation. Building Bonds was the only competency others saw their improvement in 2003–05 but not in 2004–06. In these two cohorts they saw themselves improving in most of the competencies. They did not improve in either cohort in Emotional Self-Awareness and Teamwork. They improved in 2003–05 but not in 2004–06 in: Achievement Orientation and Conscientiousness. They did not improve in 2003–05 but saw themselves improving in 2004–06 in: Optimism, Empathy, Organizational Awareness and Cultural Awareness.

Due to staff transition, informed consent was not gathered for the 2005–07 cohort. As indicated by the blank spaces in Table 2.2, the 2006–08 cohort used the newest version of the assessment instrument, the ESCI-U. In both their own opinion and in the view of others, these students significantly improved on the following competencies: Emotional Self-Awareness, Emotional Self-Control, Achievement Orientation, Adaptability, Positive Outlook, Empathy, Inspirational Leadership, Influence, Systems Thinking, and Pattern Recognition. They improved on Conflict Management and Teamwork in the eyes of others, but not in their own opinion. Their self-assessment showed improvement in Organizational Awareness, but this was not the case for others' reports. Finally, Coach and Mentor was the only competency for which no significant improvement was found in either of the two measures, self and other.

As compared to the proceeding cohorts, this data suggests that there was an increase in two Emotional Intelligence competencies: Emotional Self-Awareness, as reported by both self and others, and Achievement Orientation, as reported by others. They also showed significant increases in two Social Intelligence competencies: Inspirational Leadership and Teamwork, both reported by others. Numerous competencies remained the same as present or absent. Two Social Intelligence competencies decreased in the self-assessment: Conflict Management and Coach & Mentor.

Table 2.2   Comparison of full-time entering and graduating MBA students scores on the ECIU and ESCIU

Cluster	Scale	OTHER 2003–05 n = 104	OTHER 2004–06 n = 104	OTHER 2006–08 n = 36	SELF 2003–05 n = 92	SELF 2004–06 n = 74	SELF 2006–08 n = 29
Self-Awareness	Emotional Self-Awareness	4.0–4.1[a] t = −1.9**	4.0–4.0 t = −1.2	3.9–4.0 t = −1.3**	3.9–4.0 t = −0.6	3.9–4.0 t = −1.1	3.9–4.0 t = −0.8+
	Accurate Self-Assessment[b]	4.1–4.2 t = −1.4+	4.1–4.2 t = −2.4**		4.0–4.2 t = −2.6*	3.9–4.1 t = −2.4**	3.8–4.1
	Self-Confidence	4.1–4.1 t = −0.8	4.2–4.2 t = −0.9		3.8–3.9 t = −2.1*	3.8–4.0 t = −1.8*	
Self-Management	Emotional Self-Control	4.0–4.1 t = −3.6***	4.0–4.1 t = −2.8**	4.0–4.1 t = −1.1*	3.7–3.9 t = −2.6*	3.7–3.9 t = −3.4***	3.7–3.9 t = −0.9*
	Achievement Orientation	3.9–4.0 t = −3.5***	4.0–4.0 t = −2.7**	4.1–4.2 t = −2.1***	3.7–3.8 t = −2.0*	3.7–3.8 t = −1.3	3.8–4.1 t = −1.9***
	Initiative	3.7–3.9 t = −7.3***	3.6–3.8 t = −6.3***		3.4–3.7 t = −4.1***	3.4–3.5 t = −1.8*	
	Trustworthiness	4.0–4.1 t = −1.4+	4.1–4.1 t = −1.2		3.8–3.9 t = −1.4+	3.7–3.8 t = −1.8*	
	Conscientiousness	4.3–4.4 t = −1.9*	4.4–4.4 t = −0.7		4.0–4.2 t = −2.3*	4.1–4.2 t = −1.0	
	Adaptability	4.0–4.1 t = −4.5***	4.0–4.1 t = −2.8**	4.0=4.1 t = −0.8+	3.7–3.9 t = −2.4**	3.6–3.9 t = −3.04***	3.8–4.1 t = −1.1*
	Positive Outlook	4.2–4.3 t = −1.9*	4.2–4.3 t = −1.7*	4.1–4.1 t = −0.8+	4.0–4.0 t = −0.1	4.0–4.2 t = −1.5+	3.7–3.9 t = −1.0*

77

Table 2.2 (continued)

Cluster	Scale	OTHER 2003–05 n = 104	OTHER 2004–06 n = 104	OTHER 2006–08 n = 36	SELF 2003–05 n = 92	SELF 2004–06 n = 74	SELF 2006–08 n = 29
Social-Awareness	Empathy	4.0–4.1 t = −2.3**	4.0–4.0 t = −1.8*	4.0–4.1 t = −0.9*	3.9–4.0 t = −1.3	3.9–4.0 t = −1.8*	3.9–4.0 t = −0.8+
	Service Orientation	4.2–4.3 t = −1.4+	4.2–4.2 t = −0.6		4.0–4.2 t = −2.4**	3.9–4.1 t = −2.0*	
	Organizational Awareness	4.2–4.2 t = −0.7	4.2–4.2 t = −1.1	4.2–4.2 t = −0.01	3.8–3.9 t = −1.1	3.9–4.0 t = −1.6+	3.9–4.1 t = −0.7+
	Cultural Awareness	4.1–4.1 t = −1.9*	4.1–4.2 t = −2.0**		3.9–4.0 t = −0.6	3.9–4.0 t = −1.4+	
Relationship Mgmt	Inspirational Leadership	3.9–3.9 t = −0.7	3.9–3.9 t = −0.7	3.7–3.9 t = −1.0*	3.5–3.7 t = −2.7**	3.6–3.8 t = −2.8**	3.4–3.7 t = −0.9*
	Communication	3.9–4.0 t = −2.9**	3.9–4.0 t = −3.0**		3.5–3.9 t = −4.2***	3.6–3.8 t = −2.4**	
	Conflict Management	3.7–3.8 t = −3.9***	3.6–3.7 t = −1.8*	3.8–3.9 t = −0.9*	3.5–3.7 t = −2.3*	3.4–3.6 t = −2.1*	3.7–3.8 t = −0.3
	Change Catalyst	3.8–3.9 t = −1.2	3.8–3.8 t = −0.1		3.5–3.7 t = −2.0*	3.5–3.7 t = −2.1*	
	Influence	3.8–4.0 t = −4.0***	3.9–4.0 t = −2.9**	3.8–4.0 t = −2.0***	3.7–3.9 t = −2.4**	3.7–3.8 t = −1.5+	3.7–3.9 t = −0.7+
	Coach & Mentor	3.9–3.9 t = −0.4	3.9–3.9 t = −1.0	3.9–3.8 t = 0.3	3.7–3.9 t = −2.5**	3.7–3.8 t = −1.7*	3.5–3.5 t = −0.1
	Building Bonds	4.1–4.2 t = −1.0	4.1–4.2 t = −3.4***		3.8–3.9 t = −1.4+	3.8–4.0 t = −3.3***	

	Teamwork	4.3–4.3 t = −0.4	4.2–4.3 t = −1.18	4.1–4.2 t = −0.8+	4.0–4.1 t = −1.3	4.1–4.2 t = −1.3	4.0–4.0 t = −0.2
Cognitive	Systems Thinking	3.8–3.9 t = −2.5**	3.8–3.9 t = −1.9*	3.8–4.0 t = −2.5***	3.5–3.7 t = −3.9***	3.4–3.6 t = −2.3*	3.4–4.0 t = −2.1***
	Pattern Recognition	3.8–4.0 t = −5.4***	3.9–3.9 t = −2.4**	3.8–4.0 t = −2.4***	3.8–4.0 t = −3.3***	3.6–3.7 t = −2.2*	3.6–3.9 t = −1.2*

Notes:

Matched-pair t-tests were run with the 't' reported because a longitudinal design was used. Significance levels are one-tailed: + p < .10; * p < .05; ** p < .01; *** p < .001.

a Entering and graduating scores were rounded to one decimal point. This created visual anomalies in significance reported.

b Competency labels reflect those measured by the ESCI-U. Competencies for which no data is reported are from the ECI-U version and have been integrated into other competencies as follows: Items from 'Initiative' and 'Change Catalyst' scales were integrated into 'Achievement Orientation'. Items from 'Service Orientation' were integrated into the 'Organizational Awareness' scale. Items from 'Cultural Awareness' were integrated into the 'Influence' scale. Items from 'Building Bonds' were integrated into the 'Teamwork' scale.

DISCUSSION

To aid in the comparison, results of the assessment of learning outcomes in terms of competency development as value-added, or not, are shown in Table 2.3 for 1987 to 2008 for full-time MBAs at WSOM. The figure is organized in terms of the competencies measured in the most recent version of the assessment instrument. But to summarize the findings from this study in the context of the Boyatzis et al. (2002) and Boyatzis and Saatcioglu (2008), the full-time MBAs improved strongly (that is, statistical significance on multiple measures for multiple cohorts) on the following percentage of all of the competencies measured in those years:

1987–1990 baseline	1990–2001	2002–2006	2006–2008[1]
38 percent	92 percent	75 percent	86 percent

Using an even more conservative measure of improvement on the competencies, analysis of only behavioral measures (that is, coded work samples from Critical Incident Interviews, coded videotapes of group simulations and the presentation exercise, and informants' views from 360-degree measures) which were not available for the baseline years but thereafter, showed the following statistically significant percentage improvement (again for multiple measures with multiple cohorts except for the 2006–2008 study in which only one cohort was assessed): 1990–2001, 59 percent; 2002–2006, 75 percent, 2006–2008, 86 percent.

Overall, the 2006–2008 data suggests that students' development through the MBA program adds value in most EI, SI and CI competencies. As in the past, both CI competencies have consistent value-added. Emotional Intelligence competencies showed a slight improvement in impact in Emotional Self-Awareness (reported by both self and others) and Achievement Orientation (self), as compared to previous years. All other EI competencies remained steady as showing positive change. There was also a slight improvement in value-added with regard to the Social Intelligence competencies of Inspirational Leadership (self) and Teamwork (others). However, two SI competencies, Conflict Management and Coach & Mentor, also decreased from 2004–06 to 2006–08 based on students' self reports. All others remained consistent with the previous year.

Two consistencies in SI competencies are of note. First, informant reports showed no significant change in the Coach & Mentor competency during the MBA program. This has been a trend since the 2003–05 cohort. This trend, coupled with 2006–08 students' weaker self-rating, suggests that this needs programmatic review. Interestingly, a group of MBAs created a self-directed study group on coaching and learning in response

Table 2.3   *Summary of competency improvement from 1987 to 2006 in full-time MBAs*

Cluster	Competency[a]	Behavioral through other (360 Informant)						Self-Assessment						
		90–96	99–01	02–04	03–05	04–06	06–08	Pre 90	90–96	99–01	02–04	03–05	04–06	06–08
Emotional Intelligence	Emotional Self-Awareness	na	na	na	✓		✓	na	na	na	na			✓
	Emotional Self-Control	✓	✓	✓	✓	✓	✓	~	na	✓	✓	✓	✓	✓
	Achievement Orientation	✓	✓	✓	✓	✓	✓		✓	✓	✓	✓	✓	✓
	Adaptability	na	✓	✓	✓	✓	✓	na	na	✓	✓	✓	✓	✓
	Positive Outlook	na	na	na	✓	✓	✓	na	na	na	na		✓	✓
Social Intelligence	Empathy	✓	✓	✓	✓	✓	✓	na	~	✓	✓	✓	✓	✓
	Organizational Awareness	na	na	na				na	na	na	na		✓	✓
	Inspirational Leadership	na	na	na			✓		✓	na	na	✓	✓	✓
	Conflict Management	~	✓	✓	✓	✓	✓	na	na	✓	✓	✓	✓	✓
	Influence	~	✓	✓	✓	✓	✓	na	na	✓	✓	✓	✓	✓
	Coach & Mentor	~	✓	✓					✓		✓	✓	✓	✓
	Teamwork	✓	✓	✓	✓	✓	✓	na	na		✓		✓	✓
Cognitive Intelligence	Systems Thinking	✓	✓	✓	✓	✓	✓	✓	✓	✓	✓	✓	✓	✓
	Pattern Recognition	✓	✓	✓	✓	✓	✓	~	✓	✓	✓	✓	✓	✓

Notes:

na = not assessed.

~ = some evidence among that assessed.

" " = significant or near significant evidence on all or most of the measures assessed for that competency.

a   Competency labels reflect those measured by the ESCI-U.

81

to a perception of this missing component to their experience, without seeing the formal data analysis presented here. Second, 2006–08 students' self reports of Conflict Management dropped from 2004–06 to showing no change during the program. This is ironic given that others reported a statistically significant change in Conflict Management during the same period of time.

The paradox of a decrease in self-rating of Conflict Management with a simultaneous increase in other-rating of the same competency could be explained by the increase in Emotional Self-Awareness as reported by self and others. An increase in ESA means higher sensitization to one's own feelings as well as being critical and discerning in self-assessment. Having the awareness to be in tune with one's own emotional reaction to conflict might increase one's ability to manage conflict externally; hence, improvement in informant rating. However, this same level of internal awareness may cause an individual to be more self-critical, thus lowering their self-reported scores.

Although the full-time MBAs showed a dramatic improvement over the comparison group baseline years (that is, 1990–96 versus 1987–90), there was a decrease in impact on the MBAs in overall assessments, but there was a decrease in the years 2002–06. Boyatzis and Saatcioglu (2008) attributed that to the disruption caused by rapidly changing Deans, Provosts and University Presidents and the resulting loss of social capital among the faculty, staff and students. This was accompanied by a dramatic drop in the full-time MBA program rankings. But with a new administration in place and the climate of the school and university improving, the latest assessment showed an increase in impact on the competencies. When examining only the most conservative behavioral measures (that is, excluding self-assessments), the percentage of competencies improved has actually increased to a new high.

The differences between the impact of the program shown in Table 2.3 reveal some variation between self-report and changes behaviorally observed by others. This could be the result of different standards, perceptions or developmental progress. For example, it is possible that a person feels he/she has changed a great deal, but the change is too small to be apparent to others. In addition, some competencies are easier to observe than others.

Another possibility is that the person senses a change in himself/herself before he/she shows this in behavior, or shows it consistently enough for others to notice. Rhee (2008) interpreted this as a sensitization effect. He studied 22 of the full-time graduates of the 1995 cohort by interviewing and testing them about every six weeks throughout their two-year program. His sample showed dramatic improvement on all of the scales in the Learning Skills Profile and direct behavioral results slightly less than the overall 1995 sample, which were considerably less dramatic than the self-report results.

The disparity could have been the result of the Hawthorne Effect, or the result of cognitive dissonance reduction. An MBA might say to himself/herself, 'I have spent all this time and money, I must have changed.' But that would cause a self-justifying distortion in the self-report data, not the direct behavioral data. Regardless of the causes of the observed differences, the multi-method, multi-cohort results provide increased confidence when we observe results from both self-report and measures directly assessing behavior demonstrated in audiotapes of work samples and videotapes of their behavior in simulations.

There may also be cohort effects. For example, the class graduating in 2005 appeared to improve on fewer of the competencies than the 2006 cohort in their own view. But in the view of others, they improved more than the 2006 cohort.

Another source of confusion in monitoring impact over the twenty years is the occasional change in tests. Although this results from a desire to improve tests and evolution of methods, it makes comparisons across many years more difficult. As was described earlier, the shift to a 360 was a dramatic change in method to one considerably less labor-intensive. The shift from the SAQ/EAQ to the ECI-U was a slight shift in the items, with eight scales added. The change to the revised ESCI-U was another slight shift, but a change nonetheless.

The increased impact of the program shown in the time series results may have been the result of factors other than the curriculum change. A review of the full-time faculty teaching in the school showed that from 1988–89 to 1993–95, 67 percent of the faculty were the same. Although the program did not change its admissions procedures and criteria during this period, as the new program became known it resulted in applications and enrollment by students with higher scores on measures like GMAT, undergraduate GPA, the percentage of females in the program, and higher scores on some of the competency measures used across the cohorts in the time series. Even with this increase in entering ability, the improvements noted after the program changed were significant and dramatic. So these aspects of the school and program did not appear to have an impact on competency improvement up to 1996.

What caused these dramatic improvements in cognitive and emotional intelligence competencies from the MBA program of the 1980s? Unfortunately, there was no research design in place to make specific attributions. But the components of the MBA program that were changed from the earlier program included: (1) an explicit philosophy of education and pedagogy (Boyatzis et al., 1995); (2) a course on Leadership Assessment and Development using Intentional Change Theory as the basis for its design (Boyatzis, 1994; Goleman et al., 2002; Boyatzis, 2008); (3) a focus on specific competencies in selected courses while addressing course material, such as the marketing course that assessed students on the presentation skills or the operations management course using group projects assessing their group process competencies; (4) a dramatic increase in the percentage of courses requiring field projects in companies, group work and student collaboration; and (5) opportunities to participate in voluntary activities, such as a chapter for Habitat for Humanity and functional clubs, like the marketing club (which the part-time students did not have the time or inclination to participate in).

In response to these trends, changes have been made to the MBA curriculum, as described earlier. Rather than being taught over the course of one full semester, LEAD is taught during the first six weeks of the Autumn and Spring semesters. The students craft their vision and values in the first half of the course. They receive ESCI-U feedback, have a one-on-one coaching session, and complete a learning agenda in the second semester. This expands the focus of self-development across the entire first year and avoids them getting lost in the demands of mid-term and final exams.

In addition to structural change, the curriculum has been shifted to focus on learning and teamwork early in the course. The lack of teamwork skills in our MBA graduates was highlighted from results in a survey given to recruiters in 2006. As part of the MBA curriculum redesign for the academic year 2009–10, students will go through four 3-hour sessions in the orientation week that will focus on learning and teamwork.

PERSONAL RESPONSIBILITY FOR LEADERSHIP DEVELOPMENT

Although educators typically assume responsibility for the design and delivery of courses like LEAD, students share responsibility for their own leadership development. With intentional change theory in mind, students take charge of their own development in the program and beyond, and it becomes a shared responsibility.

One way to create this shared responsibility for development is the creation of their personal vision. The MBA spends 3–6 weeks working on reflective exercises, discussions with others and their faculty member and coach. The result is a holistic depiction of their Ideal Self and life (McKee et al., 2008). This personal vision statement is the basis for creating the actionable Learning Agenda and Plan at the end of the LEAD course. Part of the document is a section on goals, sub-goals and action steps that relate to their personal and professional spheres, and another on developing specific competencies in their MBA program, which has been shown to predict significant change on those competencies targeted in their learning plan as compared to others not targeted (Leonard, 2008). An example is taken from a student's actual learning plan which shows the desire to become an inspirational leader and taking on personal responsibility to develop this competency. Although this was one part of his learning plan, it is illustrative:

> Based on the results of my vision and 360-degree feedback, the competency goal I am going to focus on [is]becoming a more inspirational leader . . . If I can't successful[ly] inspire employees or appear to be unsympathetic, I will fail to guide my team/department to reach its' [*sic*] full potential. To improve my inspirational leadership abilities, I have developed the following sub-goals which will allow me to become a more effective manager if successfully achieved.
>
> The first sub-goal is to become [a] better listener/communicator . . . By implementing the methods to improve my 'observation mode' and communication skills I will become a better listener/communicator which will help me to become a more inspirational leader.
>
> My second sub-goal is to increase my faith in my team members to complete their tasks in the project . . . Trusting my team members to do their parts by the deadline and not reminding them about the deadlines will improve my ability to trust. However, in the spirit of making myself a more valuable team member I am still synthesizing the work into one document. This is one way I make sure that I am being [a] valuable team member.
>
> A third sub-goal is to improve my ability to give effective feedback. Offering meaningful feedback will allow me to become a more inspirational leader because employees will know what is expected. I can develop my feedback skills in my learning team and other group projects by discussing the work with team members . . .
>
> The final sub-goal is to develop my relationships building skills. By taking the time to understand and learn about the people on my team it should build a cohesiveness that makes the team stronger. Every time I work with someone new in a team setting I can develop this ability . . .

Another student presents a more succinct segment of his learning plan for developing Emotional Self-Control but includes a monitoring system to ensure the development of this competency:

- Goal: Through demonstrating more emotional self-control beginning immediately I will be more respected and viewed as more mature through my 3-month transition phase.
- Action Step 1: Consciously make an effort to think before I speak.
- Action Step 2: Remind myself of the following responses/questions:
  - Wait to answer
  - Ask the question: 'What is the seed of truth in what they are saying?'
  - Remind myself of my career or life goal.

- Action Step 3: Use techniques such as meditation, yoga, and Pilates.
- Action Step 4: Listen to classical music.
- Monitoring: The best way to monitor this is to write down daily the ways I overreacted or did not express emotional self-control. Hopefully the list will continue to get shorter and shorter. It takes 3 months to break a habit, as with active monitoring, I should begin to exhibit this competency within 3 months . . .

A final example is a student who identified Coaching and Mentoring as a competency she wanted to develop and indicates criteria for success in developing this competency:

- Goal: I will improve my ability to effectively coach and mentor others over the next 8 months.
- Action Step 1: I will work with my new manager to set this as one of the goals in my performance evaluation at work.
- Action Step 2: I will start a new job that will require me to coach and mentor others as my primary activity by January 1.
- Action Step 3: I will proactively seek feedback for improvement monthly from my peers and reassess what additional improvement activities I need to be taking.
- Action Step 4: I will log the techniques I use to reinforce my learning for the next 8 months.
- Success Criteria: I will be starting a new role at work on the first of the year. It will be critical to my success in this role to have this skill . . . If I do well on my mid-year performance review for this category I will be successful.

It may seem that these three 'typical' components of full-time MBAs learning agenda and plans are things that anybody could have identified. They are. But the dramatic difference is that in this program, they actually work on them and accomplish many of the changes desired. It is the deep commitment and desire evident in their personal vision essays and thorough, but compassionate, coaching they receive that helps to insure that the learning agenda and plans are truly things they want to do and are excited about doing. In this sense, the course and program help to focus the MBA's attention, to increase his/her mindfulness, which not only helps them to maintain a physiological sustainable arousal (Boyatzis et al., 2006; Boyatzis and McKee, 2005), but helps them to keep their focus on what they are really trying to accomplish through the MBA program.

The impact of promoting intentional change and responsibility for development in the LEAD course has recently caused two consequences to emerge: (1) building on the coaching in the course, student-driven peer coaching sessions; and (2) changes in career plans to align with the vision component in LEAD. The first started as a discussion by a group of students in one of the LEAD classes in Autumn 2008. This group approached the faculty member teaching LEAD that they wanted more sessions to dive deeper into content and practice to develop coaching skills. The faculty member felt that such initiatives were critical to innovation in education and decided to support the students by teaching extra three-hour sessions for them every other week in the Autumn and Spring semesters and did it as a free service. As coaching and mentoring was one of the competencies lacking in the outcome studies discussed earlier, such initiatives should indicate drive, and it is believed that there should be a significant increase in coaching and mentoring skills for this cohort forward.

The second consequence demonstrates the significance of ICT in the LEAD course. Some students, upon completing the Values and Vision Essay, discovered they were in the wrong field or career and took active steps to redirect their futures. One example was a student who had a Ph.D. in chemistry and worked as a researcher but realized he was not happy with his work and that unhappiness caused him to clam up and lose much of his joy. After the coaching session, he decided to apply for a position in an organization where his expertise would be valued and where he could work in a managerial capacity. He included it in his learning plan and over the course of a few months landed a job in a large organization. He emailed his instructor (who was also his coach) two years later stating that the LEAD course had changed his life significantly and now he has a much happier professional and personal life. He mentioned that his wife was also glad that he had taken the LEAD course. Such stories are indicators that leadership development courses that focus on knowledge, competencies and drive can have sustained change beyond the classroom and MBA program.

NOTE

1. This assessment was on one cohort, with one measure being used.

REFERENCES

Albanese, R. (chair), Bernardin, H.J., Connor, P.E., Dobbins, G.H., Ford, R.C., Harris, M.M., Licata, B.J., Miceli, M.P., Porter, L.W., and Ulrich, D.O. (1990), 'Outcome measurement and management education: An Academy of Management Task Force Report', presentation at the Annual Academy of Management Meeting, San Francisco.
Astin, A.W. (1993), *What Matters in College? Four Critical Years*, San Francisco, CA: Jossey-Bass.

Ballou, R., Bowers, D., Boyatzis, R.E. and Kolb, D.A. (1999), 'Fellowship in life-long learning: an executive development program for advanced professionals', *Journal of Management Education*, **23**(4), 338–54.

Bigelow, J.D. (ed.) (1991), *Managerial Skills: Explorations in Practical Knowledge*, Newbury Park, CA: Sage.

Boyatzis, R.E. (1982), *The Competent Manager: A Model for Effective Performance*, New York: John Wiley & Sons.

Boyatzis, R.E. (1994), 'Stimulating self-directed change: a required MBA course called Managerial Assessment and Development', *Journal of Management Education*, **18**(3), 304–23.

Boyatzis, R.E. (1998), *Transforming Qualitative Information: Thematic Analysis and Code Development*, Thousand Oaks, CA: Sage.

Boyatzis, R.E. (2006), 'Intentional change theory from a complexity perspective', *Journal of Management Development*, **25**(7), 607–23.

Boyatzis, R.E. (2008), 'Competencies in the 21st century', *Journal of Management Development*, **27**(3), 5–12.

Boyatzis, R.E. (in press), 'A behavioral approach to emotional intelligence', *Journal of Management Development*.

Boyatzis, R.E. and Akrivou, K. (2006), 'The ideal self as a driver of change', *Journal of Management Development*, **25**(7), 624–42.

Boyatzis, R.E. and Kolb, D.A. (1991), 'Assessing individuality in learning: the learning skills profile', *Educational Psychology*, **11**(3 and 4), 279–95.

Boyatzis, R. and McKee, A. (2005), *Resonant Leadership: Renewing Yourself and Connecting with Others Through Mindfulness, Hope and Compassion.* Boston, MA: Harvard Business School Press.

Boyatzis, R.E. and Saatcioglu, A. (2008), 'A twenty-year view of trying to develop emotional, social and cognitive intelligence competencies in graduate management education', *Journal of Management Development*, **27**(3), 92–108.

Boyatzis, R.E. and Sala, F. (2004), 'Assessing emotional intelligence competencies', in G. Geher (ed.), *The Measurement of Emotional Intelligence*, Hauppauge, NY: Novas Science Publishers, pp. 147–80.

Boyatzis, R.E. and Sokol, M. (1982), *A Pilot Project to Assess the Feasibility of Assessing Skills and Personal Characteristics of Students in Collegiate Business Programs*, Report to the AACSB, St. Louis, MO.

Boyatzis, R.E., Baker, A., Leonard, D., Rhee, K. and Thompson, L. (1995), 'Will it make a difference? Assessing a value-based, outcome oriented, competency-based professional program', in R.E. Boyatzis, S.S. Cowen and D.A. Kolb (eds), *Innovating in Professional Education: Steps on a Journey from Teaching to Learning*, San Francisco, CA: Jossey-Bass, pp. 167–202.

Boyatzis, R.E., Cowen, S.S. and Kolb, D.A. (1995), *Innovation in Professional Education: Steps on a Journey from Teaching to Learning*, San Francisco, CA: Jossey-Bass.

Boyatzis, R.E., Leonard, D., Rhee, K. and Wheeler, J.V. (1996), 'Competencies can be developed, but not the way we thought', *Capability*, **2**(2), 25–41.

Boyatzis, R.E., Smith, M. and Blaize, N. (2006), 'Sustaining leadership effectiveness through coaching and compassion: It's not what you think', *Academy of Management Learning and Education*, **5**(1), 8–24.

Boyatzis, R.E., Stubbs, E.C. and Taylor, S.N. (2002), 'Learning cognitive and emotional intelligence competencies through graduate management education', *Academy of Management Journal on Learning and Education*, **1**(2), 150–62.

Bray, D.W., Campbell, R.J. and Grant, D.L. (1974), *Formative Years in Business: A Long Term AT&T Study of Managerial Lives*, New York: John Wiley & Sons.

Campbell, J.P., Dunnette, M.D., Lawler, E.E., III and Weick, K.E. (1970), *Managerial Behavior, Performance, and Effectiveness*, New York: McGraw Hill.

Chen, G., Gully, S.M., Whiteman, J.A. and Kilcullen, R.N. (2000), 'Examination of relationships among trait-like individual differences, state-like individual differences, and learning performance', *Journal of Applied Psychology*, **85**(6), 835–47.

Development Dimensions International (DDI) (1985), *Final Report: Phase III. Report to the AACSB*, St. Louis, MO.

Dreyfus, C. (2008), 'Identifying competencies that predict effectiveness of R and D Managers', *Journal of Management Development*, **27**(1), 76–91.

Druskat, V., Mount, G. and Sala, F. (eds) (2005), *Emotional Intelligence and Work Performance*, Mahwah, NJ: Lawrence Erlbaum.

Flanagan, J.C. (1954), 'The critical incident technique', *Psychological Bulletin*, **51**, 327–35.

Fredrickson, B.L. and Losada, M.K. (2005), 'Positive affect and the complex dynamics of human flourishing', *American Psychologist*, **60**, 678–86.

Goleman, D. (1985), *Vital Lies, Simple Truths: The Psychology of Self-deception*, New York: Simon and Schuster.

Goleman, D. (1995), *Emotional Intelligence*, New York: Bantam Books.

Goleman, D. (1998), *Working with Emotional Intelligence*, New York: Bantam Books.

Goleman, D., Boyatzis, R.E. and McKee, A. (2002), *Primal Leadership: Realizing the Power of Emotional Intelligence*, Boston, MA: Harvard Business School Press.

Howard, A. and Bray, D. (1988), *Managerial Lives in Transition: Advancing Age and Changing Times*, New York: Guilford Press.

Kolb, D.A. and Boyatzis, R.E. (1970), 'Goal-setting and self-directed behavior change', *Human Relations*, **23**, 439–57.

Kotter, J.P. (1982), *The General Managers*, New York: Free Press.

Kram, K.E. (1996), 'A relational approach to careers', in D.T. Hall (ed.), *The Career is Dead: Long Live the Career*, San Francisco, CA: Jossey-Bass, pp. 132–57.

Leonard, D. (2008), 'The impact of learning goals on emotional, social and cognitive competency development', *Journal of Management Development*, **27**(1), 109–28.

Luthans, F., Hodgetts, R.M. and Rosenkrantz, S.A. (1988), *Real Managers*, Cambridge, MA: Ballinger Press.

McClelland, D.C. (1985), *Human Motivation*, Glenview, IL: Scott, Foresman.

McKee, A., Boyatzis, R.E. and Johnston, F. (2008), *Becoming a Resonant Leader: Develop your Emotional Intelligence, Renew your Relationships, Sustain your Effectiveness*, Boston, MA: Harvard Business School Press.

Mentkowski, M. and associates (2000), *Learning that Lasts: Integrating Learning, Development, and Performance in College and Beyond*, San Francisco, CA: Jossey-Bass.

Pascarella, E.T. and Terenzini, P.T. (1991), *How College Affects Students: Findings and Insights from Twenty Years of Research*, San Francisco, CA: Jossey-Bass.

Porter, L. and McKibbin, L. (1988), *Management Education and Development: Drift or Thrust into the 21st century?*, New York: McGraw-Hill.

Rhee, K. (2008), 'The beat and rhythm of competency development over two years', *Journal of Management Development*, **12**(1), 146–60.

Specht, L. and Sandlin, P. (1991), 'The differential effects of experiential learning activities and traditional lecture classes in accounting', *Simulations and Gaming*, **22**(2), 196–210.

Spencer, L.M., Jr. and Spencer, S.M. (1993), *Competence at Work: Models for Superior Performance*, New York: John Wiley & Sons.

Thornton, G.C., III and Byham, W.C. (1982), *Assessment Centers and Managerial Performance*, New York: Academic Press.

Wheeler, J.V. (2008), 'The impact of social environments on emotional, social, and cognitive competency development', *Journal of Management Development*, **27**(1), 129–45.

Winter, D.G., McClelland, D.C. and Stewart, A.J. (1981), *A New Case for the Liberal Arts: Assessing Institutional Goals and Student Development*, San Francisco, CA: Jossey-Bass.

Wolff, S.B. (2007), *Emotional and Social Competency Inventory: Technical Manual Up-dated ESCI Research Titles and Abstracts*, Boston, MA: The Hay Group.

3. Problems in managing the self-assessment process for leaders-to-be

James G.S. Clawson

These days what managers desperately need is to stop and think, to step back and reflect thoughtfully on their experiences. Indeed, in his book *Rules for Radicals*, Saul Alinsky makes the interesting point that events, or 'happenings,' become experience only after they have been reflected upon, thoughtfully: 'Most people do not accumulate a body of experience. Most people go through life undergoing a series of happenings, which pass through their systems undigested. Happenings become experiences when they are digested, when they are reflected on, related to general patterns, and synthesized.'

(Gosling and Mintzberg, 2003)

Self-knowledge leads to wonder, and wonder to curiosity and investigation, so that nothing interests people more than people, even if only one's own person. Every intelligent individual wants to know what makes him tick, and yet is at once fascinated and frustrated by the fact that one's self is the most difficult of all things to know.

(Watts, 1966)

The unexamined life is not worth living.

(Socrates)

If people in leadership positions aren't learning, growing and adapting, they are falling behind. They fall behind in a number of ways. The skills they learned earlier in life may no longer be relevant. Their followers may have changed as new cohorts come through and are no longer responsive to the old methods. The challenges that their competitors present may become overwhelming. More profoundly, their assumptions about the way the world works may become inaccurate. Technology may outpace them.[1] Without belaboring the point, it seems obvious that leaders must learn not just about the world around them, but also about the world within them, or become obsolete and ineffective.

There's a problem with that premise and its effectuation, though. A series of problems actually, which I propose to introduce here with the intent of helping those who are leader/managers and those who are studying manager/leaders. Henry Mintzberg (Gosling and Mintzberg, 2003) asserts that reflection or self-awareness is a critical leadership skill. Charles

Manz (Neck and Manz, 2006) surely agrees. The problems listed below are intended to begin a discussion of why so many leader/managers find it difficult to reflect, to introspect, to self-assess – and then deal with the findings.

LACK OF DESIRE TO BE SELF-AWARE

Many people are disdainful of self-assessment as unproductive navel gazing. In teaching career management courses that include a significant portion of self-assessments for over thirty years, I have found that about one in five students will sign up for courses designed to help them learn more about who they are. That means that roughly four out of five 30-year-olds are not very interested in knowing much about what makes them tick. They assume that they know themselves well. Perhaps they do. They assert self-knowledge and focus their efforts on doing. But there is a significant potential problem with this smugness.

INVISIBLE SELF-DECEPTION

People often do not see themselves as others do. The popular and now dated-but-true Johari's Window, is a 2 × 2 model that invites us to consider what we see or know about ourselves, what we see or know about others and vice versa (Luft and Ingham, 1955). The see–see cell is public information that we'd both agree on. The Self see/Others not-see cell we could call private or secret information. We'll ignore the not-see/not-see cell for now. In the Self not-see/Others see cell we have 'blind spots', things that others see in us that we don't see. Over time we might hope and/or expect that a person would become more and more aware of his or her blind spots and learn to manage them. This might be a good measure of maturity or wisdom. Yet we all know people who, as they age, merely become, as one colleague said, 'more so'.

When I ask students and participants how many of them have blind spots, everyone raises their hand. It's a cheap joke to then ask, 'How do you know?' The answer of course is that our significant others tend to remind us of our foibles. In the workplace, this may – or probably happens less frequently.

The problem remains, though, how do you know for sure if your self-image is an accurate one? Are your social antennae tuned enough to read what others think of you? Are people 'smart' enough to question their self-images?

TOO MUCH OF THE WRONG KIND OF INTELLIGENCE

Smart people, it seems, tend to assume that their self-image is accurate. Chris Argyris at Harvard has raised the question of how to teach smart people to learn (Argyris, 2002). Ironically, they might not be the best learners, especially when they assume they know more than they do – even about self. Eric Hoffer once wrote that 'the learners shall inherit the earth while the learned shall find themselves increasingly suited for a world that no longer exists' (Hoffer, 2006). The point being, of course, how do you know if you really know something? At 61 and epistemological studies aside, I'll be the first to say that many things I once thought I knew well have not turned out to be so accurate after all. Hoffer's quote above points out that the 'learned', that is those who 'know' things, are likely to be less interested in learning and hence more and more obsolete in our rapidly changing world. Mick McGill also pointed this out in a nice article defining varying habitual patterns of learnedness (McGill and Slocum, 1993).

Daniel Goleman's work noted how our usual interpretation of intelligence, intellectual horsepower, may not be the best precursor for management success. He cites a study of valedictorians who years later tend to be working for their classmates (Goleman, 2006). Social intelligence, he suggests, tends to be more important in a social science-like business. Social intelligence includes, he says, self-knowledge (Goleman, 2007).

INATTENTION TO HABITUALITY

Self-assessment would not be so important in the study of leadership if people did not behave in characteristic ways. In fact, though, it seems that humans tend to be creatures of habit. If they were not, we could not recognize them by their behavior. By 'habitual' I mean 'unthinkingly repetitive'. Consider three levels of human behavior:

1. *Visible Behavior*: the things that you can capture on film that people say and do.
2. *Conscious Thought*: the things that we think but do not emote or reveal intentionally at Level 1.
3. *Semi-Conscious Values, Assumptions, Beliefs and Expectations about the way the world is or should be*: I refer to these as 'VABEs' for short. They include our pre-conscious beliefs about the way the world is or should be.

I've asked over 1500 senior managers (country managers, functional managers, program managers) worldwide in places like Bangkok, Rio de Janeiro, San Jose, Johannesburg, Cairo, Athens, Istanbul, London, Berlin, and many American cities what their assessment is of the people they've met thus far in life. On average they say their acquaintances tend to behave habitually 75 percent, 85 percent, and 95 percent+ at levels 1, 2 and 3 respectively. There is evidence of this repetitive behavior in virtually every corner of the world: Northern Ireland, Central Africa, the Middle East, the Balkans, the USA.

To the extent that people do exhibit characteristically patterned behavior, they present a challenge to teachers and leaders. That is, can people change their habits? If so, how many actually *will* change their habits? How can leaders get others to change their habits? How could leaders who can't change their own habits get others to change theirs?

The collection of our habits (from wherever they come) defines our personalities. Because we behave or think or believe in repetitive ways, we have a profile or a personality. Knowing those habits is essential in order to make good decisions on so many fronts: careers, life style, relationships, and so forth. If we charge ahead oblivious to our own characteristics we either waste a lot of time in trial and error trying to find a good fit or we bulldoze over others – who may not respond well thereafter. So the issue of sensitivity to others comes to the fore.

TOO MUCH OUTSIDE-IN-NESS

One big part of the issue of leadership self-assessment is the concept of living inside-out or outside-in. If you consider the two worlds, the outside world and the inside world, we might wonder about the degree to which we live dynamically toward one or the other. Those who tend to live outside-in tend to consider what the world will say or think before they act. Conforming to the expectations of the world around you is living outside-in. Society and civilization depend on most people living in large part outside-in. Unless they did, we couldn't expect people to obey laws, to drive on the proper side of the road, and to respect the rights of others.

One of the main reasons that people tend to live outside-in is the fear of rejection. Whether this is an evolutionarily developed social concept or not (was it not easier to survive if you tended to hang together?), most people tend to adjust their behavior in order to fit in.

At the same time, if a person lives too much outside-in, they are not likely to be influencing for change, that is, leading. Rather, on balance, they will tend to protect yesterday.

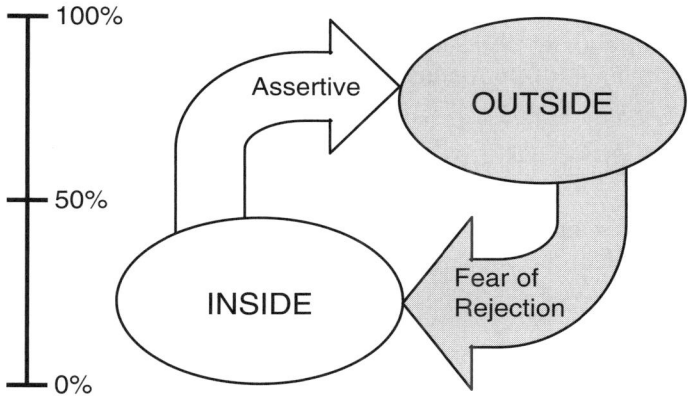

Figure 3.1   Living inside-out or outside-in

Consider a scale of inside-out-ness ranging from zero to 100 percent (see Figure 3.1). At the bottom of the scale we'd have people who don't do anything without assessing first whether the behavior will fit in or not. We might call these people doormats or wishy-washy or devoid of personal opinion. James Joyce wrote a wonderful short story about a young Dubliner woman who had no opinions of her own. Whichever group she was with, she molded her thoughts and opinions to fit (Joyce, 2006).

At the other end of the scale, near 100 percent, we'd have egocentric, narcissistic, self-centered dictators. These would be people who care little to nothing about the views and opinions of others, even of society, but tend to do what they want, how they want, when they want. Clearly there tend to be more of the latter type in leadership positions than the former type. But living too much inside-out can have serious consequences for the would-be leader. Many followers are disenchanted with dictatorial egocentric leaders. For such people, the dictatorial leader would be unlikely to generate any energy for following.

From this scale at least two questions arise. The first is, 'How much of your life do you live outside-in?' In other words, what percentage of the time do you censor, modify, or change what you'd like to do because of your concerns about what others might think? My observations lead me to conclude that most people vastly underestimate the degree to which they live outside-in.

The second question would be, 'Where on this scale would we be likely to find effective leaders?' Most people conclude in the discussions I've been a part of that the third quartile between 50 and 75 percent is a good range for leaders. They are more inside-out than outside-in; that is, on average they have learned how to assert over time rather than to conform. This habitual pattern and the inside-out scale lead us to another dimension on which a person's self-knowledge might lead to greater effectiveness.

OBLIGATION OVER CHOICE

Consider the image of a continental divide. On the one side is the Land of Choice and on the other side is the Land of Obligation. When a person goes from the Land of Choice to the Land of Obligation, what happens? What happens to energy? Productivity? Engagement? Innovation?

Virtually every business manager I've worked with will say that when people go from choice to obligation bad things happen. All of the dimensions above would show declines rather than flat or upticks.

The implication is that depending on how one attempts to lead or influence others, one is likely to get a variety of responses based on the methods that one uses; that is, followers as well as leaders experience a difference in motivation when they go from choice to obligation. This variance in responsiveness we might call after the common parlance the 'buy-in' scale. When one attempts to influence others, one could get any one of the following responses:

1. *Passion*: what you ask me to do is the number one thing in my life and I will sacrifice health, family relationships, and other preferences to make sure this happens.
2. *Engagement*: I *want* to do what you ask me to do and will do it energetically, yet I will maintain time and energy for my health, relationships and other interests.
3. *Agreement*: I agree to do what you ask me to do and will fit it into the portfolio of my competing interests.
4. *Compliance*: I will do what you ask me to do but I will be looking for loopholes the whole time.
5. *Apathy*: I don't really care what you ask me to do; it won't affect what I do or don't do.
6. *Passive Resistance*: I don't like what you ask me to do but I have to respond so I'm going to go slow, make mistakes, drop an occasional wrench in the works, and generally drag my feet.
7. *Active Resistance*: I think what you're asking me to do is the wrong thing and I'm going to fight you on this as best I can.

I argue that leadership occurs when you have a *voluntary* response. If you don't have a voluntary response it may be the use of power, but it's not leadership – in other words, given a choice, people would not follow your suggestions. Getting a Level 1 begrudging response (the body moves but the head and heart do not) from threat or intimidation is not leadership. Power then is the ability to get people to do what you want them to do (at Level 1). Dictators may have power at Level 1, but they seldom do at Level 2 or Level 3. Professors typically seek to influence Level 2, the way people think. Prophets tend to have power at all three levels.

Another of the things that leaders should, therefore, be self-aware about is their own reasons for wanting to lead, and the kinds of habitual responses their style of leading tends to engender. Ignorance of these issues would mean that a leader was groping around in the dark. Creating a visible behavior (at the extreme consider a forced confession) is no indication of leadership or of followership.

UNDERESTIMATION OF ENERGY AND FEEL

The concept of buy-in relates to energy, the energy that followers bring to their work. Energy in the form of engagement over the last fifty years, perhaps much longer, has been overlooked as a management/leadership concept. Energy relates to the concept of choice versus obligation because when one *has* to do something one tends to have less energy to do it than when one *chooses* to do something. Energy is a big issue under another name – motivation. Clearly the motivation level or the energy level varies widely as one moves up and down the buy-in scale above.

Further, motivation and energy are closely related to feel. If you ask a room full of executives anywhere in the world 'Does how you feel affect your performance?' *every* hand in the room goes up. If you then ask, 'How many times in your career has your boss asked you how you wanted to feel?' they start laughing. They think that is an absurd question. Yet a moment before they all acknowledged that feel affects performance. The third question, 'How do you want to feel?' is mind-boggling for most people. Most people have never been asked that question nor have they considered it. I've only met one person, my dean, who could answer that question immediately.

The day my friend, colleague and co-author, Doug Newburg, first asked me that question, I couldn't sleep that night. No one had *ever* asked me that before. Not my mother, not my father, none of my teachers or clergy or anyone. It took me dozens of drafts, hours of reflections and eighteen months of chronological time to answer that question. Note that 'happy' or 'productive' are too broad to be of use. Jeff Rouse, Olympic gold medalist and former world record holder in the 100 meter backstroke, calls it 'easy speed', the feeling he gets when at 80 percent effort he gets

100 percent speed because of the harmony of his movements with the water. For me it turned out to be at age 52, 'light, unhurried, and engaged' (Clawson and Newburg, 2009).

If a leader doesn't know how he or she wants to feel, he or she may end up as an anecdote in books like *Must Success Cost So Much*? (Evans and Bartolome, 1981) or *The Failure of Success* (Marrow, 1972) or *Career Success, Personal Failure* (Korman and Korman, 1980) or *The Overworked American* (Schor, 1993). Each of these is filled with anecdotes of people who focused on their professional success at the expense of their emotional/feeling side and woke up one day ruing their lives. This phenomenon was well understood by Erik Erikson when he described the difference between despair and integrity as the final dilemma in life (Erikson, 1963).

The problem is that most managers seem to hold a common assumption (a semi- or pre-conscious VABE) that 'professionals will do what they have to do regardless of how they feel'. Many parents and managers seem to assume that this assumption is the central core of maturation and professionalism. I say this assumption is a leadership formula for mediocrity. People in leadership positions who follow it will be likely to get responses of apathy and compliance on the buy-in scale above, and maybe agreement from their followers, but what are the odds they'll get engagement and passion? How can a team or an organization compete with apathetic levels of buy-in?

Can one lead effectively if one doesn't know how one wants to feel, or much less, how one's own behavior is driven by obligation and its resulting lower levels of energy? Yet this is a common occurrence. How many people in leadership or pre-leadership positions approach their day with the common thought, 'What do I *have* to do today?' That typically unexamined thought is a self-imposed habit of outside-in thinking that puts one in an obligatory mindset, drains energy, and leads over time to mediocrity.

TOO MANY TYPE I AND NOT ENOUGH TYPE II LEADERS

The motivation to lead raises some interesting issues and potential pitfalls as well. I have observed two categories of leaders. The first, who I call 'Type I Leaders', want to lead because they want the benefits of leadership and power. The perquisites, the cars, the offices, the parting of the crowd when they arrive, the adulation, and the ability to make things happen. I don't trust these people as far as I can throw them because in the end, Type I Leadership is about serving the self. Type I Leaders who learn sophisticated ways of creating instruments and garnering fees from those who actually serve and produce can, and, we could argue, *did*, become so powerful as to bring the global financial structure to its knees. One pundit, Bill O'Reilly, put it this way, 'People I really don't have any respect for are the people that feel they're entitled to all kinds of things and everybody else can go take a flying leap. These are the people who push to the head of the line, people demand special services, and people who accumulate an enormous amount of wealth and buy 18 houses. I have no use for these people. I'm much more in tune with people who realize we are here for a very short time, and we should try to use our talents and skills for the benefit of as many people as possible' (2003).

Type II Leaders are those who couldn't care less about the benefits of positions of power but who want to create something. They have a vision and a purpose, and personal aggrandizement is not a part of that vision. Power, the ancients said, corrupts. It is, in my experience, a heady thing. Having been the CEO of a non-profit organization with 3000 people in eight different units for more than seven years, I'm aware of how the respect that people give your position and perhaps the way you handle your position can seep into one's psyche almost undetected. Type II Leaders are those who not only resist this temptation (to enjoy power) but are so focused on their creative vision that nothing else, including personal well-being, tends to matter. You may think this an extreme view; if so, I'd love to discuss it with you at some time.

We might ask if people actually choose to become leaders. Clearly some do; what about the rest of us? Nigel Nicholson asserts that there may be a gene for leadership, that is, that those who possess this gene may be driven to be in charge. Being in charge may or may not be the defining factor in leadership. Dictators may be driven to be in charge. Is that drive genetic? The History Channel has aired an interesting comparison between Hitler and Stalin. Among the similarities in their lives is the fact that both were beaten to within an inch of their lives by their fathers. Both later beat and nearly murdered paramours. Whether the drive to lead is genetic, based on non-nurturing or nurturing history, based on a need for power or posh life-style or a vision that demands creation, it seems to me that the leader-to-be ought to be reflective enough to know this. But is self-awareness enough?

OVERESTIMATION OF THE CONCEPT OF CHARACTER

The distinction between Type I and Type II leaders suggests that we should rethink society's obsession with character. Since I was a small child, I've heard thousands of talks, sermons, discussions, and read a similar number of books, articles and declarations about the value of character in leaders. Capitalism, it has been said, depends on leaders of high character.

Yet what captain of industry would stand up and admit to being a person of questionable character? Wouldn't every organizational leader, from President of the United States to the CEO of Enron, to the Governor of Illinois, claim to have high character? What does that even mean – to have high character? Does it mean that you tell the truth *all* the time? I posed this question, 'Can you, should you, tell the truth in business?' once to a group of executives from one company who had been arranged in a U-shaped configuration for our discussions. To my amazement, during that conversation a heated argument broke out. On one side of the room these colonels of industry were arguing that if you didn't tell the truth, people couldn't trust you and you'd go out of business. On the other side of the room, people were arguing that if you told the truth, others would take advantage of you and you'd go out of business. The debate got so hot, no kidding, that one of the vice presidents was standing on his chair, shaking his finger at the other side and shouting. Wow.

Could you assess your *own* character? Would you use the common 'headline' test? 'If you'd be embarrassed to have it in the newspaper the next morning, don't do it.' Hmm, can I go to the bathroom? Can I nuzzle my wife? Clearly these are normal, 'ethical' things that I would not want on the front page of the newspaper.

In my experience people tend to be so intent on thinking well of themselves that they justify most of what they themselves do as either moral, ethical, the right thing to do, necessary, or justified by the outcomes – imagined or yet-to-be-realized.

So, I have come to believe and argue that character is a vastly overrated concept. If someone says, 'Trust me', you should run for the hills.

That's not to say that character is not to be admired and sought after. It's only to say that no one in any position in any organization should be trusted blindly. Only transparency and oversight should be trusted. If you don't have the raw data and you don't have someone else providing transparent oversight and a strong system of checks and balances, beware. The character in the driver's seat will soon show his or her lack of character. The deal on the table is usually not the real deal.

FOCUS ON PROBLEM SOLVING RATHER THAN CREATION

'Problem solving' ability is often mentioned in the list of leadership characteristics that companies spend millions developing. Candidates are screened and assessed for their problem-solving ability. Having seen a number of these leadership characteristics lists, I can say that the lists are not so unique as the clients would like to believe. Hal Leavitt at Stanford noted that leadership often includes problem identification and problem solving and that it should include more and more problem *creation* as leaders attempt to get followers habituated to old ways of doing things to change their behavior (Leavitt, 1986). If a problem is defined as a want-got gap for somebody, then the question is whether the leader can create problems for people who want to do things in the same old ways. Does a leader tend to focus on problem solving?

There's another problem with problem solving. Robert Fritz long ago made a very powerful distinction between problem solving and the creative process. He argued that those who focus on problem solving tend to get caught up in an oscillating pattern that does not move forward. If you've ever seen an organization move from a centralized structure to a decentralized one and then back again, you've observed this oscillation. At some point, employees, like the Swiss shepherd boy's family, become inured to cries for the need to change ('Wolf!'). A focus on problem solving reinforces a focus on problem solving. As one begins to solve the problem its symptoms decline. This decline leads to less focus on the problem, which leads to its resurgence. An oscillating pattern emerges.

Better, Fritz argues, is to take the creative person's mindset. Rather than thinking reactively, better to think creatively. 'What do you want to create with your time in office?' 'What do you want to create in the next ten years?' 'What do you want to create next year?' (Fritz, 1989).

Fritz, like Nohria and Lawrence (2002), asserts that humans have an innate drive to create and that if we would focus more on nurturing and unleashing that natural tendency, we'd see more productivity and accomplishment. If indeed, all humans have a drive to create, perhaps we should focus on that in our leadership efforts. Do leaders have a sense of their creative abilities? Of their habitual ways of thinking? Of, perhaps, how they have learned to focus on problem solving and along the way suppressed and allowed to atrophy their natural childhood creativity and vision?

IGNORANCE OF CAREER CONCEPTS

Peter and Hull's best-selling *The Peter Principle* long ago brought attention to what seems to be an on-going phenomenon: that people get promoted to their level of incompetency (Peter and Hull, 1969). The notion makes sense. A person does well and is recognized. They get promoted and if they do well they get recognized. And so on, until at some level, their abilities are not up to the job. It's hard, of course, to demote people, so there they stay – stuck one level above their abilities.

The problem with this line of reasoning as pointed out by Mike Driver and Ken Brousseau at USC is that not everyone has a linear career concept (Driver, 1979). A career concept to them is a natural internal motivation toward one of four major kinds of career tracks: the upwardly mobile, the horizontal craftsman, the spiraling learner, and the oscillations of the part-time worker. Linear Types, they argued, those who want to be promoted, are only one kind of *naturally* occurring career motivation. Yet society has fixated on this one approach, rising to the top. The media are filled with the air currents of the linear model – they permeate our culture.

But some, many, millions of people have little or no desire to be in charge. They just want to do a good job, be recognized for it and continue to polish their skill. Malcolm Gladwell argues in *Outliers* that this usually takes about 10 000 hours – to become an artisan, an expert (2008). And experts don't want to be promoted. Given the choice, they will spend the rest of their careers doing the same thing over and over again while polishing their skills. You can see this in the professions, in the skilled trades, and in fact in many parts of society. If you ask managers, as I have, 'How many of you have ever seen a steady state expert ruined by promotion into management?' every hand in the room goes up.

Why would a person who wants to be a steady state expert accept a promotion into management? It's expected of them. They're told that if they say no, they may not get 'another chance'. The implication being 'it's the American Dream' and that everyone *should* want to be promoted: 'What's wrong with you?' The reason should be clear by now: they don't know themselves well *and* they're living too much outside-in. Pressured by the organization and society, they take jobs that don't suit them, fail, and everyone (employee, boss, co-workers, company, customers) bear the consequences.

I met a man recently in a leadership development program who told me privately that he'd left his last company six months before because they kept trying to get him into management and sending him to leadership development programs. He had told them he didn't want that, but they persisted, so he left. It bothered him so much that he quit his job. He came to my client, told them the same thing, and the next thing he knew he was in a leadership development program that I was teaching. 'Why won't they listen?' he asked. This gentleman knew himself. Even his courage in conveying his self-knowledge did not deter the Linear Types above him who assumed that since he was talented at his job, he'd be talented at management – and that he'd *want* to join the leadership fraternity.

SELF-ASSESSMENT AND LEADERSHIP

So. Would you hire as a high potential leader-to-be the following kind of person? One who:

1. Is not interested in knowing him or herself better.
2. Doesn't see him or herself the way that others do.
3. Is too smart to learn.
4. Is unaware of his or her habits in behavior, thinking and believing.
5. Is living predominantly outside-in.
6. Manages self and others by obligation rather than choice.
7. Doesn't know how he or she wants to feel or how others want to feel or the relationship between feel and performance.
8. Focuses on personal rewards instead of organizational or societal outcomes.
9. Believes him or herself to be a person of character above reproach and supervision.
10. Is an expert on problem identification and solving, but weak on creativity and the creative process.
11. Doesn't know what a 'career concept' is, either for self or for those around.

Of course not. Would you put yourself forward as a leadership candidate with a similar profile? Maybe. Because we all want to think well of ourselves – and immediately we fall into the second trap, self-deception.

Again, Henry Mintzberg made the case well in his articles and books on the difference between managers and leaders, and in particular between MBA graduates and leaders. His notion of the five essential mindsets of a successful manager includes, right up front, reflection and self-awareness.

Today's generations are impatient. They want answers in a moment. Their lives of 30-minute television shows, text messaging, worldwide web access, personal communicators and data devices, and the pressures learned early in school to compete to win sooner rather than later, and more, have all combined to make them impatient. How long are you willing to spend learning who you are? Who needs it? Who cares? If you've read this far, I hope you do. Most MBAs won't give it one semester, much less a lifetime of introspection and learning.

The Millennial response of course demands a quick-and-dirty self-assessment tool that promises an answer to what you should be after 15 minutes of ticking of 'yes' or 'no' while on a flight to the next client site. My mentors at the Harvard Business School, particularly a man I greatly admired, Tony Athos, said, and I believe, 'no single instrument is accurate enough or comprehensive enough to give you a true picture of yourself'. Perhaps this is part of the reason why so many people don't believe in self-assessment instruments. They've been toying around with the weak ones and become cynical.

Science, though, operates in a different way. Every 'discovery' must be duplicated and made available to others for confirmation. Transparency and oversight. While some data might suggest a possible pattern or principle in the natural world, scientists never trust those early tentative patterns until and unless they can repeat and verify. They often use different tools and instruments to examine their data.

Those using self-assessment or assessment tools should do the same. I cringe when I see participants in various assessment programs walking around wearing their name badges with various categories on them. 'Hi. My name is Jim. I'm an ENTJ.' 'Hi, Jim'. It's like being in an AA meeting and in my view utterly inappropriate for professional public settings. First, remember that no single instrument is accurate enough or comprehensive enough to define who one is or what their leadership style and skills might be. The implication of course is that one should use multiple instruments looking for the patterns that emerge *across* those data pools as descriptions of an individual. *Leaders and the Leadership Process* by Jon Pierce and John Newstrom (2007) is an example of a volume that offers multiple self-assessment tools and strong research-based concepts and therefore encourages readers and students to take an empirical, pattern-based approach. Yet, for the reasons I have outlined above, many, if not most leaders and leaders-to-be are not willing to do this.

CONCLUSION

Most managers today have learned to think deductively. They have rules or principles in mind that they apply in their attempts to influence others. They do this often semi- or sub-consciously. They assume naturally that they are correct in doing so. When others don't respond the way they want them to, they are perplexed and assume that the followers have a motivation problem. Then they come to people like me and say, 'Will you develop a leadership development program that will teach people how to motivate others?' My answer is that we can do that but it would be a lot more effective and efficient if you would just start asking them different questions, like 'What do you think we should do, and why?' Typically, these senior people will respond, 'No, no, you don't understand. *We're* not the problem. *They* are the problem. You need to help them get more backbone and more energy to push their ideas.' Listening to these conversations, I infer that these leaders do not see themselves clearly. They are, in their own minds, learned. They know what they know. And hence are too smart to learn.

Leaders and leaders-to-be will be more effective and have a longer leadership influence if they are self-aware and use that self-awareness to develop stronger personal characteristics. Self-assessment tools can help burgeoning and existing leaders to learn more carefully who they are. In self-assessment or in the assessment of others, we will reach much better conclusions if we use multiple sources of data (data pools or databases), if we understand the logic of each of those sources, and like good inductive scientists we learn to look for the patterns (habits) in the data.

Inductive thinkers would gather data, let the data do the talking, look for patterns, draw tentative inferences based on those patterns, and finally, when necessary make (high stakes) decisions and live with the consequences – which would provide more data. This kind of an iterative mental habit in an individual would augur well for continued growth and the development of ever stronger leadership capability.

If one determines to become more self-aware, one would be well served to note that self-assessment data can and should come from multiple sources: projective tests, objective tests, behavioral instruments, 360-degree instruments that solicit the views of others, performance reviews, diaries, and much more. For each pool of data, one should know something about the quality of the data. What did the author purport to assess and how? Is the approach reasonable? Theoretically sound? Statistically sound? How many different kinds of pools of data are you looking at? After all, before you buy a company you would gather data from accounting, consultants, newspapers, your network, lawyers, television and more and then look for patterns. Do the same in your self-assessment. Gather data from multiple kinds of sources. Understand the quality of the data. Look for patterns across the pools of data (databases). When you're *comfortable* (having informed your regular and your enteric brains – the 100 000 000 neurons that comprise your fourth brain in your alimentary canal (Furness, 2006; Gershon, 1998)), make a decision based both on data *and* gut feel. Reflect on whether you're making your decisions based on good data or impulse, or outside-in pressures or underlying assumptions that are no longer true or functional. Then, and here's another hallmark of a good leader, *live* with the consequences. Learn from the consequences. They are your own data and should inform your experience rather than passing through your system as an undigested happening.

All of this is not so easy. Maybe that's why we continue to look for more leaders. A good leader, I will say, is in large part a person who is willing – nay, who has the *courage* – to look inward with the intent of clarifying *who* he or she is. Self-assessment or the lack of it need not be an extreme obsessive effort: on the one hand, self-defeating endless navel-gazing or on the other hand the product of a ten-minute airline magazine survey. Effective leaders realize that knowledge of who they are is the most important leadership tool they have and that if they cannot use that tool and polish it, they can never achieve greatness. Effective leaders see the importance of embarking on a life-long process of *clarifying and creating* who they are. They realize that while the story may never be finished, avoiding its writing only leads to confusion and embarrassment.

Self-assessment and leadership? How can one lead without leading self first? How can one lead well without knowing one's tendencies, habits and biases? How can you lead well without knowing how your early life has shaped you – for better or worse? What great leader faced with life and death issues for millions has not plumbed the depths of his or her own soul in a desperate attempt to know the right thing to do and whether they can pull it off? Why then should today's pretenders be so chary of the very thing that can make them more than who they are?

NOTE

1. I once had a colleague who wrote a book entitled *Real Managers Don't Use Computers*. His point perhaps was a good one, that it takes face-to-face interaction to influence others, but can you imagine an executive today who is not current with and actively using the latest technology?

REFERENCES

Argyris, C. (2002), 'Teaching smart people to learn', *Reflections: The SoL Journal*, **4**(12), 4–16.
Clawson, J.G.S. and Newburg, D. (2009), *Powered by Feel: How Individuals, Teams, and Companies Excel*, Hackensack, NJ: World Scientific.
Driver, M.J. (1979), 'Career concepts and career management in organizations', in C.L. Cooper (ed.), *Behavioral Problems in Organizations*, Englewood Cliffs, NJ: Prentice-Hall, pp. 79–139.
Erikson, E. (1963), *Childhood and Society*, 2nd edn, New York: Norton.
Evans, P. and Bartolome, F. (1981), *Must Success Cost so Much?* New York: Basic Books.
Fritz, R. (1989), *The Path of Least Resistance*, New York: Ballantine.
Furness, J.B. (2006), *The Enteric Nervous System*, Malden, MA: Blackwell.
Gershon, M. (1998), *The Second Brain: Your Gut has a Mind of its Own*, New York: Harper.
Gladwell, M. (2008), *Outliers: The Story of Success*, New York: Little, Brown & Company.

Goleman, D. (2006), *Emotional Intelligence*, New York: Bantam.

Goleman, D. (2007), *Social Intelligence*, New York: Bantam.

Gosling, J. and Mintzberg, H. (2003), 'The five minds of a manager', *Harvard Business Review*, **81**(11), November, 54–63.

Hoffer, E. (2006), *The Ordeal of Change*, Crossville, TN: Hopewell Publishing.

Joyce, J. (2006), 'Clay', in *Dubliners*, Clayton, DE: Prestwick House, pp.79–84.

Korman, A.K. and Korman, R.W. (1980), *Career Success and Personal Failure*, Englewood Cliffs, NJ: Prentice-Hall.

Leavitt, H. (1986), *Corporate Pathfinders*, Homewood, IL: Dow Jones-Irwin.

Luft, J. and Ingham, H. (1955), *The Johari Window: A Graphic Model of Interpersonal Awareness*, University of California Western Training Laboratory.

Marrow, Alfred J. (1972), *The Failure of Success*, New York: AMACOM.

McGill, M. and Slocum, J. (1993), 'Unlearning the organization', *Organizational Dynamics*, **22**, 67–79.

Neck, C. and Manz, C. (2006), *Mastering Self-leadership*, Upper Saddle River, NJ: Prentice-Hall.

Nohria, N. and Lawrence, P. (2002), *Driven: How Human Nature Drives our Choices*, San Francisco, CA: Jossey-Bass.

O'Reilly, B. (2003), *Saturday Evening Post*, Jan/Feb., p. 68.

Peter, L.J. and Hull, R. (1969), *The Peter Principle: Why Things Always go Wrong*, New York: Morrow.

Pierce, J. and Newstrom, J. (2007), *Leaders & the Leadership Process*, 5th edn, New York: McGraw Hill.

Schor, J. (1993), *The Overworked American*, New York: Basic Books.

Watts, A. (1966 [1989]), *The Book: On The Taboo Against Knowing Who You Are*, New York: Vintage.

4. Taking charge: discovering the magic in your psychological assessment

Sandra L. Davis

People travel to wonder at the height of mountains, at the huge waves of the sea, at the long courses of rivers, at the vast compass of the ocean, at the circular motion of the stars; and they pass by themselves without wondering.

(St Augustine)

Sam drove away from the psychologist's office relieved to be done with all the multiple choice tests, interviews and simulations. Dr Thompson seemed savvy enough, but Sam knew that the leadership assessment was an important part of the selection process for the company he was interviewing with. While people kept telling him that this was not a 'pass/fail' process, his experience taking all of those tests told him otherwise. 'OK,' he thought, 'I'm done with that and I'll just keep my fingers crossed.' A week later the recruiter called to tell him he was getting a job offer. Excited, Sam promptly forgot about Dr Thompson's offer of feedback. Even when the head of Human Resources suggested that he make an appointment for feedback, Sam expressed his thanks, but did nothing. He got the job, he thought, why should he bother?

Can you identify with this story? Individual leaders have many reasons for choosing not to take advantage of feedback following a leadership assessment. Some simply are skeptical about tests and psychologists in general. Some have good intentions, but let procrastination win until the feedback seems too old or irrelevant. Others get so wrapped up in their real work that assessment results fall to last place on the priority list. The set of reasons or excuses is long; even if you are curious, other things can get in the way.

This chapter educates you about how to get the most out of your assessment feedback. An informed participant can gain a great deal from the process and the psychologist. You'll find some practical tips for how to approach feedback from your psychological assessment, how to prepare for the feedback so it serves your needs and how to use it later to inform your development. Rather than being a passive participant, you will have the tools you need to shape the feedback session to you. Literally, the more active you are, the harder psychologists work to make sure your needs are met!

A MODEL FOR DRIVING PERSONAL GROWTH: AWAKEN, ALIGN, ACCELERATE

There are three phases to using your information from an assessment. It is not just the conversation itself, but what you ultimately do with it that matters. We like to think of a three-phase model: Awaken, Align, Accelerate. *Awaken* means learning about yourself, your leadership style and the impact you have on others. *Align* means discovering from your company, your manager, your direct reports or your peers what is important to them and to the role you play. *Accelerate* speaks to jump-starting your development so you can become more effective as a leader. If you can think of this feedback conversation as part of a journey, you will listen with clear intentions.

Awaken: Feedback – Why Do We Bother?

> There are three things extremely hard: steel, a diamond and to know one's self.
> (Benjamin Franklin)

Let's be honest. How many of us can really agree with this statement, 'I get all the feedback I want about my leadership impact'? If you are like most leaders, feedback arrives in spurts, small clues or not at all. Leaders often tell me they receive feedback about one or two aspects of their impact, but that they rarely have a chance to hear the whole story. Or, they tell me that the 360 feedback process they participated in provided great data, but they wondered how much of it was really only specific to their current circumstances. Was the information really about them or about how they behave in the culture of their organization?

Many individual leaders do take advantage of the debrief or feedback process. Whether they participated in a psychological leadership assessment as part of a hiring or promotion decision or as part of a leadership development effort, they have multiple reasons for coming to get feedback.

In true Letterman style, look through this list of the top 10 reasons people come to a feedback session. Which two or three are most applicable to you?

Check all that apply	Reason for choosing to get feedback
	Because I would like more quality feedback
	Because I put in the time to take all of those tests
	Because I expect to learn something useful
	Because the psychologist is objective and has no other agenda
	Because the psychologist could have useful information about who succeeds in my company
	Because I am curious about why I was not hired (or promoted)
	Because I want to learn and grow as a leader
	Because my manager or human resources told me to go
	Because others told me they learned something from their feedback
	Because I'm having trouble adjusting to my new role or new company

Logic certainly says that anyone who participates in feedback has a reason. Start the feedback session by giving your reason(s); let the assessor or psychologist in on the secret. Even if you're motivated to be there simply because your manager said you should go, that's a great starting place. Hidden agendas don't do either of us any good and while you might suspect that the psychologist can read your mind, it's not true.

Preparing for getting feedback. Finding out what you'll get feedback about
Unfortunately, there is great variation among psychologists as to how much information they reveal about how you performed in the assessment process. Therefore, be active in setting the stage so you can gauge the depth and breadth of your questions. For example, if you completed three inventories for the evaluation, then it is reasonable to expect specific feedback on each of those measures. Don't always expect hard copies of those profiles; sometimes there is a narrative version you can take away, but it is not unusual for the psychologist to just show you the profile and *talk* with you about the implications. If there is also 360 data available, you can expect full disclosure of those results and themes (but not who said what!)

Confirm the ground rules for confidentiality. Sometimes the feedback session is simply a private and confidential conversation between you and the psychologist. This is often the case when a job candidate who was not hired returns for feedback from the assessment process. Sometimes the person providing your feedback will also be communicating back to your organization. Find out what that communication link is. What will or won't the psychologist convey back? In most cases, the psychologist simply lets human resources or the individual's manager know that the feedback session happened. That is a key action in development planning. It lets others know they should schedule follow-up conversations with you so development planning can move forward within your own organization.

Help the psychologist plan your time together well. A general rule of thumb is to spend about two-thirds of your time together hearing from the psychologist and asking questions about specific results. Work toward spending one-third of the time on the 'so what' of the results. What are the implications for your learning, your success and your growth as a leader?

Take notes! Even if you get to take away materials from the assessment feedback, don't assume that the written report will be a good reflection of what you talked about or even what implications occurred to you at the time. Not all elements of your conversation will have been written down in advance. Remember, you are shaping the feedback by how you participate in it.

Be prepared emotionally. Not all feedback is easy to digest and you will have many different emotions based on what you expect to hear, the size of your own blind spots, how open others have been with you about your impact on them and the degree to which you work in an organization that emphasizes feedback and development. Table 4.1 is a useful tool for categorizing the kind of feedback you will receive and the emotions you might experience.

If you can, express your emotional reaction to the feedback in the moment. The dialogue can be much richer when you trust enough to be yourself. Don't be surprised when the psychologist asks you how you feel about what you have just heard. We know feedback is not emotionally neutral. During the feedback conversation, feel free to agree and disagree. If something doesn't ring true for you, say so and do it in a way that engenders further dialogue. Rejecting a result out of hand is too easy. Try being curious instead of dismissive. The person who says, 'That just doesn't sound like me; what else can you tell me about that result?' will foster a lively dialogue.

Be ready to listen beyond the psychologist's style. We know that feedback is more welcomed when it comes from a credible source. An individual's style can interfere with your willingness to consider him/her as a credible source. The chemistry between you and the psychologist may click really well or hardly at all. Even if you don't have a strong personal connection, the information you take away can still be valuable. Just remember that the content of the feedback – the information, the tools, the tests and inventories have credibility on their own.

Table 4.1   Feedback and your self perceptions

	Your Perceived Strengths	Your Perceived Development Needs
Assessment Revealed Strength	*Confirmed Strength* Emotionally positive: 'great to know that I was accurate'; good feelings about having a strength confirmed.	*Hidden Strength* Emotional surprise but a pleasant one. 'I had not thought of that before.'
Assessment Revealed Development Need	*Blind Spot(s)* Emotionally surprised, disappointed, defensive or angry. 'These results must be wrong' or 'how could someone say that about me?'	*Confirmed Development Need* Emotional acceptance, but some embarrassment. 'Now someone else knows this too.'

Ask for the specifics. Feedback can be delivered at several different levels. An adaptation of The Ladder of Inference (created initially by Chris Argyris) provides a visual reminder (Figure 4.1) of how to make feedback understandable and actionable. As human beings we find short-cuts for communicating with each other – ways to translate meaning and summarize what occurred without having to 'run the videotape' of what happened. So the dialogue from that meeting is replaced by a statement like 'he argued with every point that was brought up'. Then at a higher level of abstraction, he is described by adjectives such as 'argumentative and difficult'. Finally, at the highest step on the ladder he is stereotyped as a jerk. If you get feedback that either stereotypes you or is only provided through adjectives, you have to *infer meaning* to understand it. Instead of inferring what the psychologist means from adjectives or descriptors about you, ask for behaviors. What does that mean I might do at work? What do you know about how I behaved in the assessment? What do you mean and what might others mean when they describe me as aggressive?

Consider cultural and ethnic differences. You and the psychologist from whom you receive feedback may or may not come from similar backgrounds. There are cultural differences within a country that can influence meaning, just as there are variations across cultures and countries about what behaviors are accepted or expected. It is certainly fair to ask about the psychologist's personal biases, cultural assumptions and experience working with individuals from other cultures. You may want to have a discussion about the validity of the feedback for you in different kinds of settings.

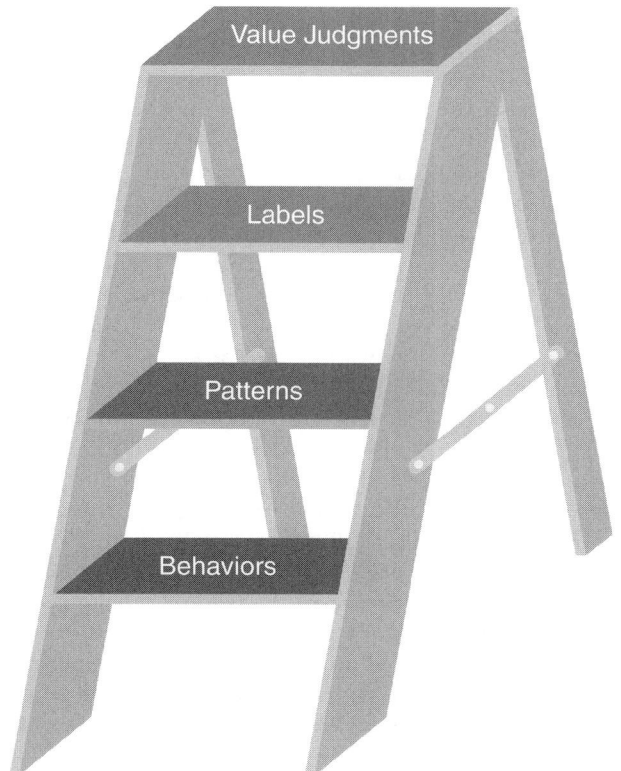

Figure 4.1 Ladder of judgment

Understanding psychological inventories
Psychological evaluations routinely include tests of personality, motivation, interests, style and values. There are aspects of personality that are core to who you are and that rarely change over time, and there are other aspects that change with time, deliberate development actions or environment. Some elements of your personality are malleable and others are very difficult to change. Therefore, as you embark on this journey of learning about yourself through the lens of a standardized inventory, be aware that not everything is set in stone but that some aspects of who you are will be difficult to change. For more on this topic peruse the book by Seligman, *What you can Change and What you Can't* (1993).

Here is an example of a hard-wired personality trait. Recently Anita, who is a general manager of a business unit inside a large corporation, came for her development feedback session. She had completed a 360 survey, psychological inventories, simulations and an in-depth workstyle interview. Each of the personality inventories she completed revealed her to be introverted, reserved and even distant with people. The 360 feedback from her peers and direct reports provided context; they wanted her to communicate more, include them in her planning on major business initiatives and spend more time with them. Changing from being an introvert to becoming an extravert would be an unnecessary and insurmountable task. She is hard-wired. However, Anita can recognize the impact she has as a leader and learn to behave differently in some settings. She can learn to include others in decision making and she can change her routine so that she does more management by walking around.

Preferences, interests and motivational variables also tend to solidify into stable patterns once you reach adulthood. If you love change and being creative, that is unlikely to change. If you thrive on competing with others and keeping score, that won't shift even if you move to a new work setting. Those personality traits clearly affect how you lead. In fact, according to Hogan and Kaiser (2005), personality predicts leadership.

Turning to specific inventories that you completed, it is often helpful to gear your questions toward what the inventory really measures. You answered numerous questions in completing the inventories, but don't expect to see how you answered any of those questions specifically. Most inventories base a profile on your answers to multiple and sometimes interlocking questions. It is the patterns in inventories that have meaning, not the individual answers to any single question.

As you probably realize, if you were to complete the same set of 60 to 434 questions a second time, you would answer some items differently. Just recall how quickly you could answer some of the items and how much you had to pause and think on others. As psychologists we work hard to develop and use inventories that generate reliable patterns over time, so that those few changes you make in your answers from one time to the next don't make a difference in what the resulting profile says about you.

Table 4.2 lists some of the most popular assessment inventories, what they measure and the kind of questions that could yield the best insights for you.

Tying the assessment results to your company or industry

If the psychologist has had a long-standing relationship with your company and your industry, you can bet he/she has a wealth of knowledge about how things work, who succeeds, how your results fit with others in similar positions and what you can do to be more effective. Ask early

Table 4.2   Common assessment inventories

Inventory	What it measures	Questions to ask about your profile
Myers Briggs Type Indicator	Personal preferences around communication patterns, people orientation, decision making and thinking style	• What does it say about how I make decisions? • With whom will I have the 'easiest' relationship because we are similar? • With whom will I struggle the most? • What are my greatest gifts that I need to make sure I play to?
Hogan Motives, Values and Preferences	Your patterns of interests that underlie what you want out of your life and out of a job in general	• How am I similar or different from the prevailing culture in my company and what difference does that make? • What do I need to be most satisfied in my work and my life? • As a leader, what will I emphasize and what might I overlook?
Hogan Development Survey	The ways in which your personal characteristics can 'get you into trouble' with others when you are under stress	• What do I need to watch out for? • How are my high scores also an asset for me? • What are others most likely to criticize me for as a manager?
Hogan Personality Inventory	Several primary elements of personality that are relevant to the work world	• What kinds of roles will fit my style best? • What aspects of how I score would you call 'hard-wired'? • How do I compare with others in my field? • What do the results suggest about my development as a leader?
16 PF Inventory	Multiple elements of personality that relate to how you deal with emotions, your general stance toward others,	• What stands out from this inventory about my approach to work? • What can you tell me is hard-wired?

Table 4.2   (continued)

Inventory	What it measures	Questions to ask about your profile
	your primary interests and your openness to learning	• How quickly do I form relationships with others; what are my interpersonal strengths? • What do you see about how well I express or deal with emotions? • What kinds of interpersonal demands will be most difficult for me to handle?
California Psychological Inventory	Multiple scales that describe your typical interpersonal behavior, how you relate to society in general, your personal achievement drive and your current level of life satisfaction	• How would you describe my leadership style based on this test? • How are others likely to experience me? • What kind of work environment will I be most satisfied in? • What would you point to as my primary development needs? • What aspect of my results could change over time?
Strong Interest Inventory	Patterns of interest that are related to occupational preferences and fit; comparisons of individual results to those of individuals in specific fields	• What are my primary interests that need an outlet on or off the job? • What does the pattern say about my leadership style? • What kinds of companies or occupations are most congruent with my interests?
NEO Personality Inventory	Five major dimensions of personality, including multiple facets that underlie them.	• What can you tell me about my core personality traits that are not highly amenable to change? • What do these results say about my leadership style? • What might I need to work on or watch out for? • How do my results compare to other leaders at my level?
OPQ (Occupational	Provides an indication of an individual's preferred behavioral style at work	• Since this inventory describes my self-perceptions, how do I

Table 4.2 (continued)

Inventory	What it measures	Questions to ask about your profile
Personality Questionnaire)		verify that others actually see me this way?
		• What do the results suggest about the roles that I will be most satisfied in?
		• What patterns do you most often see in effective leaders in my company?

on in your conversation about how much work he/she has done in your company and what he/she knows about who succeeds. If the answer is that the psychologist has just begun working with your organization or is not familiar with your industry, then don't expect context-specific wisdom. However, you should expect that he/she knows quite a bit about the reason for the assessment, what will be important to success in the role *you were assessed for* and how the hiring manager or others talked about what they expect the position to deliver.

Here are specific questions you might ask:

- What do you know about the traits of the most successful leaders in my company?
- In what ways am I similar to or different from those leaders?
- What is something I should consider changing to achieve greater impact in this company?
- Who is most connected to my success? What relationships will be critical for me to have?
- To what extent did the hiring manager or human resources outline specific deliverables for the role, and what were they?
- How involved is my company in development and using the assessment results to help individual leaders plan for growth?

Don't expect to hear about other individuals or other candidates' results or about why you were chosen rather than someone else. Nor will you get much insight from questions about how your manager scores on any of these measures. Psychologists have ethical guidelines about what they can specifically tell you about other people. Of course, if your manager has told the psychologist to share his/her results, then ask away.

Deriving themes: making sense of all your feedback

If you have participated in an assessment that includes many components such as intellectual inventories, personality measures, motivation indexes, simulations and interviews, you can expect to be almost overwhelmed by the amount of information coming your way. Think of each of these individual components as a window or a lens. By viewing you through the lens of various inventories or tests, the psychologist has a picture of you from several angles. Each lens provides certain kinds of information; no single inventory or measure tells the whole and complete story about you. It is also true that these inventories are a snapshot or a cross-section of you at a certain moment in time.

Think about this: what do you know about your own personal circumstances at the time you completed the assessment that might have affected the results? Had something significant just happened in your personal or work life? If you completed the assessment when you were in a period of great stress, the results are likely to reflect that. You and the psychologist will have the task of sorting through which results might be situational and which are more stable and true for you over time and across numerous contexts.

Here are several questions you can ask to understand the feedback from each element:

- What does this component say about my leadership style?
- What does it reveal about my strengths or development needs?
- Is there anything here that I should be concerned about?
- How do I compare to other successful leaders at my level?
- How does my profile 'matter' in terms of my performance?
- What themes here are the most relevant and important?

After you have talked through the results of all the pieces of the assessment, pause and ask the psychologist this question, 'What are the themes you see?' Don't leave the conversation until you have heard that summary. Just listen and take notes at this point as you want to hear what sense he or she makes of the data for you.

Align: Determining the 'So What?' of your Feedback Information

> Everyone thinks of changing the world, but no one thinks of changing himself.
> (Leo Tolstoy)

Getting to this step is critical to get real value from the assessment. People frequently enjoy the feedback session because it really is 'all about me'. Now your job is to take the feedback into the 'so what' stage. Feedback is not an event; if you use it well, it is a springboard to reflection and to action. In the end, it is the meaning *you* make from what you have heard and the importance of the feedback for your work that has the most value.

Personal reflection

As a first step, schedule some time for yourself following the feedback. Take your notes and the report (if you have one) and come up with themes for your strengths and themes for your development needs. What did you hear; what made sense to you; what are you still wondering about; what questions do you still have? Use or modify Worksheet 4.1 for your work.

Worksheet 4.1   Reflecting on your feedback

My confirmed strengths:

●

My confirmed development needs:

●

A hidden talent I did not realize I have:

●

Possible blind spot(s) for me:

●

What I wonder about – is this true for me; do others see this in me at work?

●

What I would like to find out more about from my manager, peers, direct reports or family:

●

What other questions do I still have from the feedback?

●

Consider sending the themes that you come up with to the psychologist who provided you with feedback. If you let him/her know what your takeaways are, you can find out whether you have missed anything important. Most psychologists will welcome this request. In many cases, when individuals leave a feedback session, we don't really know what they do with what was said or what they learned.

Exploring context

Before digging further into the 'so what' of your feedback data, take a moment to reflect on the opportunities and challenges you face as a leader in your organization. The way you use your strengths or decide to approach development will depend a great deal on context. Context matters, and you need a strategic context within which to review and understand the implications from your feedback. Use the following questions to help you summarize your circumstances:

What are the most critical results you and your team need to produce for the organization in the next three to six months?
What would you like to accomplish in the next three to six months that would make you most proud of your contribution to your organization's success?
What obstacles and challenges do you see or anticipate that may get in the way of your and your team's success?
Who, other than your team members, are most important to your success?

Once you have answers to these questions, you can begin to make some choices about what will be most important for you to focus on developmentally. You can use your strengths to produce results and use the framework of your deliverables to have development happen in real time.

Engaging your manager

Once you have clarity about what you have learned and what additional questions you have, take it to the next step. That next step means learning what importance others you work with place on the feedback. They may rely heavily on some of your strengths, they may wish you would work on development and change some of your behavior, or they may have additional insights about your blind spots. Through the conversations you have, you will discover the importance of the feedback you received.

Meet with your manager. Bring your summary of what you have learned, what you believe your development needs are and what you are still curious about. Your purpose is to reach agreement about what strengths you should rely on and what areas you should focus on for development. This is not just about development for development's sake; you want to know what to focus on that will have the most impact on your job responsibilities. Here are questions that will help you zero in on the 'so what' of development:

- What strength should I be using even more than I am now to produce superior results?
- Which development needs are most critical to my doing an outstanding job in this role?
- Six months from now, what would you like to say I have made progress on?
- What should I work on (whether it is on my list or not) that will help prepare me for the next level of leadership?
- If you think of my primary accountabilities, what is most critical for me to do well?
- What do you know about my relationships with my peers and my direct reports? Is there anything you think I need to do differently?
- How could I do a better job of helping you to succeed – what do you need from me?
- If you agree that I need to work on—, then it would be great if you could help me by—
- How will you measure my progress?

These questions give you and your manager the best chance for getting aligned about your development. Some managers are natural coaches; most are not. By being active in bringing your plans and ideas to your manager, you can nudge even a rather uninterested manager to be helpful to your growth as a leader. There are no excuses. While you can blame your lack of development and learning on your manager, it still primarily rests with you.

Engaging your peers

These conversations are clearly different in character from the dialogue you have with your manager. Your manager will expect to talk with you about your development, but your peers may need a reason for engaging with you. If you work in a matrixed organization, success demands interdependence, and these conversations will seem natural. If you work in a more traditional independent business unit setting, there may be more silos than collaborative efforts. The setting influences who and how many individuals you connect with. You might choose only one peer to talk with or you may choose several. One criterion for choosing is: whose results does my performance have the most impact on and vice versa? Secondarily, you can ask yourself who you trust and who seems most open to talking about learning or leadership.

Once you decide who among your peers would be a good confidante or sounding board, *ask* each whether she/he would be willing to talk with you about what you learned from your feedback and what difference it makes to your work. Always ask. Peers don't have to engage with you. Some will be interested if you are willing to reciprocate and help them with their development.

Start with a conversation about alignment in general. What do our two areas have to do with each other's success? Then proceed to specifics. Talk about one or two strengths you believe you need to play to. Describe one or two of your development needs and what you believe is most important to your working together well. Ask for confirmation. Find out whether you and your peer are in alignment about what is most important.

Here are other questions you might pose:

- I learned this about myself – how do you see that play out here?
- What do you wish I would do more of or less of in the way I lead my area?
- What are others expecting of me in this company that I might not be aware of?
- Which of my development needs that I have articulated do you believe is most relevant to our work together?
- What do you or your team members wish I would do differently?
- How could I or the area I lead be more effective?

After Sam got his feedback from Dr Thompson, he chose to bring his results to one of his peers. Through that conversation, he learned that his predecessor had routinely made unilateral decisions that often had a negative impact on others' areas. His peers were 'waiting' to see whether he would operate similarly or more collaboratively. That information was news to Sam, and he quickly realized that his highly independent nature was a strength and also a potential development need. As a result of that dialogue, Sam and his peer agreed to take on one specific project together and involve other peers in it as well. That is a perfect example of achieving alignment.

Engaging your direct reports

There is no other group with more hopes and expectations about your performance or even your development than your direct reports. Day in and day out they experience your leadership. Whether they have told you or not, they know what makes a difference for them individually and collectively. Your job is to engage them in how you lead and to discover their priorities and ideas for development action planning.

Many leaders choose silence when they are working on development. It's a misguided choice because changing behavior is visible and not at all silent. There is such power in a leader openly talking about her strengths and one or two things she has decided to change. For example, when Marlene talked to her team after getting her assessment feedback, she said, 'I learned that in my enthusiasm to move ahead with a plan, I tend to interrupt and not even give you a chance to share your ideas, cautions or concerns. So, I am going to work on asking more questions, listening more attentively and not interrupting. What I need you to do is let me know when I do that well and when I slip back into my old behavior.' Her openness and specific actions made it easy for her team members to respond positively.

You'll need to decide what and how much to share. Even sharing just one development goal can be enough. Some choose to reveal a great deal. One leader took his assessment data (test profiles and all), put them into a PowerPoint presentation and talked to his team about what he had learned. They were startled at first, but later they stated his willingness to be vulnerable sent a powerful message to them. That level of openness won't work for all or in all circumstances, but it fit for him in terms of the level of candor he wanted to continue to foster within his team.

When you bring a development need to your team and ask for their help, don't ask them to confirm that you are working on the right behavior. To the extent they like and respect you, they might feel compelled to downplay the development need. If you need confirmation, seek out one individual on your team in advance whom you know will give you a straight answer. When you get together with the entire team, know what you want to do and tell them about it.

Remember that changing your behavior means that others have to change theirs. Work teams have an uncanny ability to 'train' a leader back to her 'old' behavior if they don't agree with the goal. Gain a commitment from your team members either collectively or individually to help you change and you will see faster results.

Accelerate: Setting Goals and Practicing

There are numerous ways to approach development, which are covered in other chapters in this book. Use those ideas and never underestimate the value of planning. Even writing down one or two goals that you will work on over the next several months will help you stay focused on your learning. Worksheet 4.2 gives you a sample development plan format that you may find helpful.

Think of the implications for leadership. Recent articles about practice and becoming a master at anything (sports, the arts, leadership) suggest that to be truly outstanding you must practice (Ericcson et al., 2007). Practicing means trying something, experimenting with a new behavior, evaluating how it worked and trying it again until it becomes part of your repertoire. While your first attempts may feel awkward, the more you work to make the new behavior a habit, the less you will need to be intentional about it.

PUTTING IT ALL TOGETHER: A CASE STUDY

Gloria had just started in her new role as Vice President of Marketing for the Software Division of ABC Corporation. When her new boss, the President of the Division, encouraged her to go for feedback he said explicitly, 'I think you'll find this helpful; the psychologist knows me and the rest of your peers pretty well'. Gloria figured it couldn't hurt; the psychologist had also suggested that she make an appointment for feedback in the first month of her new role. As soon as that was done, Gloria received an email with a brief two-page article called 'how to get the most out of your feedback session'. She skimmed it the night before, thought a little bit about what she might learn and showed up curious and a little skeptical.

Immediately the psychologist asked her what she wanted to get out of the session and then started talking about context for the feedback. 'Your new role is a first for you; you have never been a member of a senior

Worksheet 4.2   Development Action Plan

Company Name:	Date:
Participant Name:	E-mail:
Manager Name:	E-mail:
Coach (if applicable) Name:	E-mail:

Summary of strengths:

●

Summary of development areas:

●

Summary of action plan focus:

●

Goals:

Goal #1: ●

Goal #2: ●

Goal #3: ●

Development action plan – Goal 1

Over the next six months I will: {describe what you will achieve}

●

Desired results: {describe the benefit or pay-off for yourself and for the team}

●

Activities:	Timeline:
1.	1.
2.	2.
3.	3.
4.	4.

Worksheet 4.2   (continued)

Activities:	Timeline:
5.	5.
6.	6.
7.	7.
8.	8.
Support needed:	
1.	
2.	
Indicators of my success: {evident to others}	
1.	
2.	
3.	
4.	

Source: © Copyright MDA Leadership Consulting 2009.

leadership team. Believe me, what it took to be successful one level below is different from what it will take to be successful at this level. So, let's start by talking about your new role, your key deliverables and what you believe your manager expects of you.'

Then they talked through all the data – the California Psychological Inventory, the Hogan Development Survey, the Hogan Motives, Values and Preferences Inventory and the simulations. Some of the personality inventory results seemed uncannily accurate to Gloria and she felt just a little exposed. Yet, they talked and Gloria and the psychologist filled in the chart shown in Table 4.3. Gloria was actually surprised and pleased to see strategic thinking skills as a strength. She expected to hear that she needed to bolster her financial understanding, so she did not expect to see strategic thinking skills as an asset. That was a pleasant surprise.

Then, she was really taken aback when the psychologist told her the conclusions about execution and priority setting. She wondered aloud, 'how could that be? I always move projects ahead and get them done on time.' In response, the psychologist talked about how execution and priority setting at the executive level differ from the same skills at a director level. 'It is about giving others clarity on their deliverables and your expectations; it is about making decisions about what can and cannot get done.' This rang true to her, however, that she was likely to try to do it all and by herself.

The notion that she could be aloof initially struck her as wrong. No one

Table 4.3   Charting overall feedback conclusions

	Self-perceived strength	Self-perceived development need
Assessment strength	*Confirmed strengths* Collaborative leadership style Intellectual ability Decision-making skills Executive presence Achievement driver	*Hidden talents* Strategic thinking skills Learning agility – capacity to learn from experience
Assessment development need	*Blind spots* Execution and priority setting Initially comes across as aloof	*Confirmed development needs* Financial acumen Understanding organizational dynamics

had ever given her that feedback before and she told the psychologist as much. The answer was, 'Here is why I said that. You have always taken a while to trust other people even though you ultimately develop solid relationships. It could even be a derailer for you. I don't expect you to agree or disagree right now; why don't you take this bit of feedback as something to think about?'

Gloria also asked what the psychologist knew about her peers and her boss. Apparently they were not only serious about being a solid team, but they also all loved debate. Gloria was told, 'You have the intellectual talent and the strategic skills to keep up with everyone else on that team. Make sure you enter into debates, add in your opinions, and don't get surprised by how lively their debates become. They expect you to be part of that.'

After the feedback, Gloria filled in Worksheet 4.2 and then reluctantly asked a couple of people she trusted about being aloof. To her chagrin, they had experienced that distance in the first few months of their relationship. 'It was like you were judging me and deciding whether I was worthy or not.' Eventually, Gloria confirmed her feedback themes with the psychologist and then took what she had learned to her boss. He agreed that she needed to work on higher-level execution skills and told her that while financial acumen was a development need, it could wait to be addressed until later. Together they planned what she could do to be a great team member and what two things she could do developmentally. They agreed she should leverage her strategic thinking skills with her new peers in real time in team meetings. Gloria also emailed the psychologist and asked what she might do to come across as being more personable and open.

Gloria later said that had she not received the feedback about being aloof and having good strategic thinking skills, she never would have been as confident and quick to participate in the senior team. In response to her engagement, they initiated conversations about their expectations for marketing. This is a great example of taking the feedback and moving it back into the work setting. Like Gloria, you will find the feedback data to be valid and valuable; yet it is what you do with the feedback that will help you learn and grow as a leader.

CONCLUSIONS

There is much to be gained and learned from a psychological assessment. Prepare, be an active participant and use the feedback to enhance your knowledge of yourself and jump-start your development. As Albert Camus said, 'To know oneself, one should assert oneself. Psychology is action, not thinking about oneself. We continue to shape our personality all our life.'

REFERENCES

Ericsson, K.A., Prietula, M.J. & Cokely, E.T. (2007), 'Making of an expert', *Harvard Business Review*, (July/August) 114–21.
Hogan, R., & Kaiser, R.B. (2005), 'What we know about leadership', *Review of General Psychology*, **9**(2), 169–80.
Seligman, M.E. (1993), *What You Can Change and What You Can't: The Complete Guide to Successful Self-Improvement*, New York: Alfred A. Knopf.
Senge, P. (1990), *The Fifth Discipline: The Art and Practice of the Learning Organization*, New York: Doubleday.
Senge, P.M., Kleiner, A., Roberts, C. & Ross, R. (1994), *The Fifth Discipline Fieldbook*, London: Nicholas Brealey Publishing.

5. Assessing leadership and the leadership gap

Jean Brittain Leslie and Ruohong Wei

There is little doubt that leadership is one of the most salient aspects of organizational life. Yet, there seems to be an undeniable sentiment that there is a shortage of leaders. These opinions are often driven by the media. The popular press is inundated with articles surfacing concerns that leaders lack the 'right' skills necessary to meet organizations' current and future needs. Additionally, news of a pending leadership crisis has been looming in the literature since 2001. At the heart of these articles are arguments that there is a lack of talent, a lack of capabilities in the leadership pipeline, and a lack of good organizational selection and development practices.

Concerns about the shortage of talented leaders exist not only in North America, but in Asian countries as well. A survey conducted by Development Dimensions International, Inc. identified essential leadership skills for Chinese managers, such as motivating others, building trust, retaining talent, and leading high-performance teams. However, the demonstrated levels of these critical skills were considered weak among one quarter of the business leaders in China (Bernthal et al., 2006). A recent survey with 249 Indian managers also indicated leadership gaps in the area of coaching and mentoring, speed in decision making, and the ability to learn (Gaur, 2006).

THE LEADERSHIP GAP

We use the term 'leadership gap' similarly to the definition provided by Weiss and Molinaro (2005) in their book, *The Leadership Gap*. It refers to a shortfall between current and forecasted leadership capacity. Even though the phrase 'leadership gap' has been part of the business vernacular, scholars are still struggling to identify what aspects of leadership are most critical to develop and why (to what end)?

A 2002 Conference Board survey indicated that confidence in leadership benchstrength went down from 1997 to 2001. Roughly 50 percent of respondents to the earlier survey indicated their organizations' leadership strength was either excellent or good, while in 2001, this figure was only about 33 percent (Barrett and Beeson, 2002). The American Society for Training and Development published a survey-based report in which 45 percent of respondents indicated a leadership skills gap, making it a top concern among talent management professionals (ASTD, 2006). Similarly, another large-scale survey found leadership team capability to be the number one human capital issue (Weiss and Finn, 2005).

In the wake of today's pressing economic challenges and concerns about keeping jobs, a leadership gap may not seem like a burning issue. It's true that organizations can't control the economy but they can select and help develop top leaders. Furthermore, research indicates a clear link between an organization's leadership, employee motivation and performance, as well as corporate results (Kaiser et al., 2008). With good leadership comes engaged employees, employee retention, productivity, customer satisfaction and profitability (Macey and Schneider, 2008; Buckingham and Coffman, 1999; Harter et al., 2002). These linkages make the leadership gap an urgent concern.

TRENDS CONTRIBUTING TO A SHORTAGE OF LEADERS

Several critical forces are shaping future leadership requirements, resulting in a forecasted leadership gap (Barrett and Beeson, 2002). These factors include but are not limited to: changes in workforce demographics; intensified competition brought by globalization; flattening organizational structures; use of advanced technology; and changes in the general nature of work.

Organizations worldwide are facing challenges of aging personnel and increasing numbers of retirees, resulting in fewer available workers to fill the voids. In India and Singapore, the number of workers over 60 years of age will increase 38 percent and 92 percent respectively by the year 2015 (http://data.un.org/Browse.aspx?d=POP). Nowhere, however, is the aging demographic shift more obvious than in the US, where the Western workforce is aging in record numbers. With more baby-boomers approaching retirement age and fewer younger workers waiting to fill the void, the result is a predicted shortage in talent (Bernhart, 2006; Rappaport et al., 2003). Although the general consensus is that companies should begin to strategize now for this demographic shift, studies indicate that the majority of companies have no goals or strategies either in place or in preparation

(Schramm, 2006). Clearly, companies need to identify which leadership capacities will be lacking.

In addition to a shortage of workers in general, competition for skilled workers is being experienced worldwide. The demand for skilled leaders has countries working hard to develop policies that will attract talent, retain talent, and in some countries, like India, reverse talent migration. A recent survey of nearly 43 000 employers in 33 countries reveals that 31 percent of employers worldwide are struggling to locate qualified candidates (Manpower, 2008). The survey found the shortage most prevalent in Singapore, where 57 percent of employers report difficulty, followed by the US, with 22 percent of employers reporting difficulty.

The flattening of organizational structures is another trend impacting leadership and contributing to the leadership gap. As organizational structures flatten, decision making becomes decentralized. This change has led to blurred divisions of labor and increased emphasis on distributed teamwork (Friedman, 2005). The trend towards flattening organizational structures is preventing managers from having the career opportunities which they may have had in the past that allow them to develop their skills and capabilities (Weiss and Molinaro, 2005). Weiss and Malinero are suggesting that career paths which naturally resulted in hierarchical organizations are missing in flatter ones. With this loss has come less formal training and development.

The very nature of work has changed greatly too. Globalization and advances in communication technologies have concurrently enabled information from distant localities to spread far and quickly in ways that make local concerns global and global concerns local in the blink of an eye (Zacharakis, 1996). Employees now must compete globally for jobs and career advancement. This means that a critical criterion for success in a global environment requires managers to manage across boundaries (Freidman, 2005; Dalton et al., 2002). Managing across boundaries implies setting and implementing direction across functions, work teams, organizations and cultures. In such an environment, competencies such as perspective-taking and cross-cultural adaptation become hallmarks of effective leaders (Dalton et al., 2002).

Finally, even though the above-mentioned trends have triggered profound changes in the workplace, organizations have generally lacked effective talent management practices to deal with them. Organizations must be vigilant in their development of future leaders as the changing nature of work leads to the changing nature of leadership for managers. Managers, too, have a greater responsibility for their own leadership development.

What trend is impacting your organization's leadership? To assess the above-mentioned trends on your organization's leadership, complete Exercise 5.1.

EXERCISE 5.1   TRENDS CONTRIBUTING TO THE SHORTAGE OF LEADERS

Please read each statement below thinking about the specifics of your organization. Check all that apply:

Aging Workforce

1. The majority of managers in my organiza-
    tion are reaching retirement.   _____
2. We are experiencing low morale among
    employees because retirees are finan-
    cially unable to retire.   _____
3. There is resentment among younger
    workers because they perceive blocked
    career paths/opportunities.   _____
4. There is concern that important intellec-
    tual capital that resided with older workers
    will be lost.   _____
5. There are fewer workers available to fill
    the voids created by retirees.   _____

Competition for Skilled Workers

6. There is scarce supply and high demand
    for some skill sets.   _____
7. My organization has a hard time attracting
    talent.   _____
8. My organization has a hard time retaining
    talented individuals.   _____
9. The country where I work is developing
    policies to reverse talent migration.   _____

Flattening Organizational Structures

10. The structure of my organization has
    decreased my visibility with senior
    management.   _____

11. The structure of my organization is preventing managers from developing their skills and capabilities. _____

12. The structure of my organization is preventing managers from having career opportunities. _____

Nature of the Work

13. In my organization employees now must compete globally for jobs and career advancement. _____

14. There are increasing concerns that my organization is not training employees for the future (e.g. technical and professional skills). _____

15. The number of highly skilled, specialized jobs needed for the future success of my organization is increasing. _____

Lack of Talent Management

16. Senior executives in my organization have identified leadership capacity as a strategic issue. _____

17. Human Resources conducts a regular leadership capacity audit in my organization. _____

18. My organization uses a talent review process that includes a frank and honest discussion. _____

19. My organization has a well-developed talent retention and measurement process in place. _____

WHAT THE DATA SAY

In this chapter, we explore gaps between current and desired levels of leadership. This information addresses basic questions about the current state of leadership and offers suggestions for development. How widespread is the gap between the strengths leaders possess and the strengths needed for their organizations to succeed? Is this strictly a US-based problem – or is it also a problem in other countries? What does our data suggest managers focus on to enhance corporate performance?

To address these questions, we analyzed data gathered as part of a research study[1] among 2200 managers working in 12 financial services and IT companies across three countries (USA, Singapore and India). These data were collected between December 2006 and April 2008. The sample is largely male (69 percent) and the average age is 42. The managers' organizational levels include 5 percent top executive (responsible for entire business; for example, CXO, CFO, COO, CIO); 12 percent senior executive (oversee multiple departments/units, or highest level); 33 percent upper-middle manager (heads of functions or departments); and 50 percent middle (have groups reporting to me, but I report to a function head).

For our measure, we relied upon previous research on competency-based approaches to leadership effectiveness. Competencies are defined as persistent characteristics, skills or behaviors that are causally related to effective performance in a job or role (Boyatzis, 1982; Meger, 1996; Spencer and Spencer, 1993). The most generalizable competencies for understanding leadership effectiveness are those that cut across many leadership jobs, roles and functions. These leadership competencies were selected because the measurement and structural equivalence of Benchmarks®, a 360-degree tool that assesses the skills and characteristics of successful managers has been examined across a broad range of managerial levels, organizational settings and cultures (Raju et al., 1999; Lee and Ang, 2003; Braddy, 2007). See Table 5.1 for the list of competencies and definitions. The 20 leadership competencies we examined in this research are from a modified version of Benchmarks® (Lombardo et al., 1999). Modifications to Benchmarks® included reducing the number of items and including additional leadership competencies from other sources that we deemed relevant to the context of global managers. The assessment was also modified from a 360-degree assessment to one that requested that respondents rate managers, in general, at a specific level (their own) rather than individual managers.

To expose potential gaps between managerial strengths and organizational needs, we compared the relative *importance* managers attributed to leadership competencies with their *skill levels*. To determine what leadership competencies are critical for success, we examined how managers rated the

Table 5.1 Definitions of leadership competencies

Competency	Definition
Balancing personal life and work	Balancing work priorities with personal life so that neither is neglected
Being a quick learner	Quickly learning new technical or business knowledge
Building and mending relationships	Responding to co-workers and external parties diplomatically
Compassion and sensitivity	Showing understanding of human needs
Composed	Remaining calm during difficult times
Confronting people	Acting resolutely when dealing with problems
Culturally adaptable	Adjusting to ethnic/regional expectations regarding Human Resource practices and effective team process
Decisiveness	Preferring doing or acting over thinking about the situation
Doing whatever it takes	Persevering under adverse conditions
Employee development	Coaching and encouraging employees to develop in their career
Inspiring commitment	Recognizing and rewarding employees' achievements
Leading people	Directing and motivating people
Managing change	Using effective strategies to facilitate organizational change
Managing one's career	Using professional relationships (such as networking, coaching and mentoring) to promote one's career
Participative management	Involving others (such as listening, communicating, informing) in critical initiatives
Putting people at ease	Displaying warmth and using humor appropriately
Resourcefulness	Working effectively with top management
Respecting individuals' differences	Effectively working with and treating people of varying backgrounds (culture, gender, age, educational background) and perspectives fairly
Self-awareness	Recognizing personal limits and strengths
Strategic planning	Translating vision into realistic business strategies including long-term objectives

*Table 5.2   Highest percentage of managers who rated the competency
critical for success in their organization (n=2200)*

Critical now		Critical five years from now	
Leading people	73%	Leading people	89%
Strategic planning	64%	Strategic planning	86%
Managing change	63%	Inspiring commitment	86%
Resourcefulness	64%	Managing change	82%
Doing whatever it takes	64%	Resourcefulness	82%
Inspiring commitment	62%	Participative management	81%
Being a quick learner	60%	Being a quick learner	79%

competencies in terms of how *important* they were for success in the organization right now and how important each will become for success over the next five years. Each leadership competency was rated on a seven-point scale with the following anchors: 1 = Not at all important, 4 = Moderately important, and 7 = Critically important. The column in Table 5.2 labeled 'Critical now', presents the highest percentage of managers who rated the competency critical (6 or 7). Similarly, the second column in Table 5.2 presents the competencies most needed for organizations to succeed in the future.

These data reveal managers *strongly agree* on which skills are essential for effective leadership. Managers in Singapore, India and the US consider *leading people* (directing and motivating people), *strategic planning* (translating vision into realistic business strategies including long-term objectives), *inspiring commitment* (recognizing and rewarding employees' achievements), *managing change* (using effective strategies to facilitate organizational change), *resourcefulness* (working effectively with top management), and *being a quick learner* (quickly learning new technical or business knowledge) to be competencies that are important now and in the future.

In addition, managers rated the increased importance of *participative management* (involving others in early stages of critical initiatives), *employee development* (coaching and encouraging employees to develop in their careers), and *balancing personal life and work* (balancing work priorities with personal life so that neither is neglected) as necessary skills for the future.

Next we examined the extent to which managers perceive they are meeting these needs. Each competency was rated on a nine-point scale (1 = extremely small amount, 5 = moderate amount, and 9 = extremely large amount) from two different perspectives: 'what is the overall amount of skill managers at my level are currently demonstrating?' and 'what do we need to demonstrate to be maximally effective?' Table 5.3 presents the results.

Table 5.3 Comparison of managers' top 10 current strengths with their top 10 development needs (n=2200)

Top 10 current strengths		Top 10 needed strengths	
Doing whatever it takes	28%	Inspiring commitment	60%
Respecting individuals' differences	30%	Strategic planning	59%
		Leading people	58%
Culturally adaptable	23%	Resourcefulness	58%
Composed	23%	Employee development	55%
Compassion and sensitivity	23%	Managing change	55%
Being a quick learner	22%	Participative management	54%
Resourcefulness	22%	Composed	54%
Building and mending relationships	17%	Doing whatever it takes	53%
		Building and mending relationships	51%
Participative management	16%		
Self-awareness	15%		

When we compared the amount of skill leaders report demonstrating to what they report they need to be effective, we uncovered a surprising challenge – an overwhelming lack of preparedness. Table 5.3 shows the 10 skills that leaders consider current strengths and the top 10 competencies they perceive to be lacking. Only 28 percent of managers surveyed, for example, report demonstrating large amount of the skill *doing whatever it takes*, while 53 percent of them report that they need a large amount of this skill to be effective.

In other words, managers reported an overwhelming need for leadership development. Statistically significant differences between leaders' *current* strengths and *needed* strengths were found across all countries, industries and levels.

Next, we looked for potential leadership gaps by comparing the competencies managers reported to be strengths with organizational competency needs. For example, Table 5.2 reports that 89 percent of managers consider *leading people* to be of critical importance five years from now, while Table 5.3 does not show *leading people* as a current strength. Examinations of the skills leaders considered critical for success in the future with perceptions of their current strengths revealed the presence of a universal leadership gap. The most notable leadership gaps from a statistical standpoint are *leading people* (directing and motivating people), *strategic planning* (translating vision into realistic business strategies including long-term objectives), *managing change* (using effective strategies to facilitate organizational change) *employee development* (coaching and encouraging employees to develop in their career), *inspiring commitment* (recognizing and rewarding employees' achievements), *balancing personal life and work* (balancing work priorities with personal life so that neither is neglected), and *decisiveness* (preferring doing or acting over thinking about the situation). These skills are perceived to be critical to success and also the weakest in terms of current strength. In other words, these are the biggest leadership gaps.

WHAT DOES THIS ALL MEAN?

The managers in this study have expressed that they don't think the leadership in their organizations is prepared for the future – a stunning and somewhat troubling finding. For researchers at The Center for Creative Leadership, however, it provides strong evidence to support the need for leadership development. There is no doubt these managers are working in highly unpredictable business environments and, with the looming global financial crisis upon us, it seems that these circumstances will not get better any time soon. In fact, training dollars are often the first to be cut when organizations start to see financial downturns. Taking responsibility for your own career development is now imperative!

WHAT YOU CAN DO TO CLOSE THE LEADERSHIP GAP

This section of the chapter describes what an individual can do to shape his or her own leadership development. The material is organized around two questions: (1) What do you need to learn? and (2) How can you close the leadership gap? The first question, 'what do you need to learn?' invites the reader to do a self-assessment of his or her own leadership gap and choose a developmental goal.

The second question, 'how can you close the leadership gap?' allows the reader to target specific experiences and tactics that he or she can employ to close their own leadership gaps.

What do you Need to Learn?

An assumption of this book is that you, the reader, are already a reasonably skilled manager, but you can't be perfect at everything. We invite you to test this assumption by rating yourself on the key leadership gaps identified by our research. Exercise 5.2 asks you to rate yourself on the key leadership gap identified by our research. Please read each statement and respond

EXERCISE 5.2   KEY LEADERSHIP GAPS

Please read each statement below and think about your performance over time as well as feedback you have received from bosses, peers, colleagues or external stakeholders such as vendors and customers. Rate your current level of skill from 1 to 5 using the following anchors. If you are not sure how others might rate you, ask them.

This statement describes:
1) One of my greatest strengths.
2) Something I am good at.
3) Something I can do but I need to improve a little.
4) Something I can do but I need to improve a lot.
5) Something I am really not able to do.

1. Balancing personal life and work – balancing work priorities with personal life so that neither is neglected.   1 2 3 4 5

2. Managing change – using effective strategies to facilitate organizational change.   1 2 3 4 5

3. Decisiveness – preferring doing or acting over thinking about the situation.   1 2 3 4 5

4. Leading people – directing and motivating people.   1 2 3 4 5

5. Employee development – coaching and encouraging employees to develop in their career.   1 2 3 4 5

6. Strategic planning – translating vision into realistic business strategies including long-term objectives.   1 2 3 4 5

7. Inspiring commitment – recognizing and rewarding employees' achievements.   1 2 3 4 5

If your score on any item is a 3 or greater, this is a competency you might consider for development.

from your perspective. Look at your ratings and decide which of the seven competencies you most need to develop. This should become your developmental goal. Remember a competency is a set of characteristics, skills and behaviors. Development planning for competency can take a longer time than simple behavior change, and it requires multiple tactics.

Now that you have completed Exercise 5.2 and have some understanding of your own development needs, let's focus on the first tactic towards accomplishing a competency goal: learn about the competency.

Strategic Planning
Consider your own score on Strategic Planning. Managers having high competence in this area typically:

- Articulate long-term objectives and strategies.
- Develop plans that balance long-term goals with immediate needs.
- Update plans to reflect changing circumstances.
- Develop plans that contain contingencies for future changes.

Employee Development
Please note your own score on Employee Development. Individuals skilled in the area of employee development usually:

- Coach employees to improve performance.
- Provide employees with guidance.
- Encourage employees to develop careers.
- Make sure employees understand their roles.

Managing Change
Please note your score on the competency of Managing Change. Individuals who can manage change well use effective strategies to facilitate organizational change. Such managers:

- View change positively.
- Adapt plans as necessary.
- Manage others' resistance to change.
- Adapt to the changing external pressures facing the organization.
- Involve others in the design and implementation of change.

Inspiring Commitment
Turn to your score on Inspiring Commitment. People with competence in this area are more likely to recognize and reward employees' achievements and are able to inspire commitment from his/her subordinates. Such managers:

- Publicly praise others for their performance.
- Understand what motivates other people to perform at their best.
- Provide tangible rewards for significant organizational achievements.

Leading People

Note your score in Leading People. Managers who lead people effectively:

- Are willing to delegate important tasks, not just things he/she doesn't want to do.
- Provide prompt feedback, both positive and negative.
- Push decision making to the lowest appropriate level and develop employees' confidence in their ability to make those decisions.
- Act fairly and do not play favorites.
- Use his/her knowledge base to broaden the range of problem-solving options for direct reports to take.
- Interact with staff in a way that results in the staff feeling motivated.
- Actively promote their direct reports to senior management.
- Develop employees by providing challenge and opportunity.
- Set a challenging climate to encourage individual growth.
- Reward hard work and dedication to excellence.

Balancing Personal Life and Work

Please note your own score on Balancing Personal Life and Work. Managers with adequate work–life balance are able to balance work priorities with personal life so that neither is neglected. Such managers:

- Act in ways that give the impression that there is more to life than having a career.
- Participate in activities outside of work.
- Don't let job demands cause family problems.
- Don't take careers so seriously that personal life suffers.
- Are not workaholics.

Decisiveness

Finally, look at your scores on Decisiveness. A decisive manager prefers doing or acting over thinking about the situation. Such a manager:

- Does not hesitate when making decisions.
- Does not become overwhelmed when action is needed.
- Is action oriented.

Please note that we do believe that all of these competencies can be learned through some combination of modeling, practice and feedback.

In the next section we discuss how to integrate the knowledge of what you need to learn and what you can do about it.

How can you close the leadership gap?

This section of the chapter describes ways to close the gaps you identified through the self-assessment tool. In the first part we step back and present core principles of leadership development. In the second part we discuss specific strategies and tools that you can use to bridge your leadership gaps.

Principles of development

Over the past three decades, researchers at the Center for Creative Leadership (CCL) have been studying the ways managers learn from experience. Seeking answers to questions like the ones below have been the subject of the continuing stream of research we labeled 'The Lessons of Experience'.

- What does it take to be an effective leader?
- How do successful executives develop important leadership skills?
- Do certain critical experiences matter?
- Do these experiences teach specific and valuable lessons?

The first study, conducted in the US in the early 1980s, included structured in-depth interviews with 79 successful executives in three Fortune 100 corporations (Lindsey et al., 1987). Follow-up studies using both quantitative and qualitative methodologies were carried out with women, African-Americans, Hispanics and Asian-Americans, as the workforce and leadership pool became more diversified across the US (McCall et al., 1988; Morrison et al., 1987; Douglas, 2003; McCall, 1998; McCall and Hollenbeck, 2002). In 2003, the Lessons of Experience research expanded globally. Data were collected from over 500 senior leaders in 47 country-based organizations across seven industry sectors in the US, India, Singapore and China (Wei and Yip, 2008a; Wilson, 2008; Yip and Wilson, 2008; Zhang and Wei, 2008).

The assumptions underlying all these investigations have been that managers develop over their careers, and this development is driven by major experiences. All executives who participated in these studies reflected on critical experiences in their careers and what they learned from their experiences:

When you think about your career as a manager, certain events or episodes probably stand out in your mind – things that led to a lasting change in your

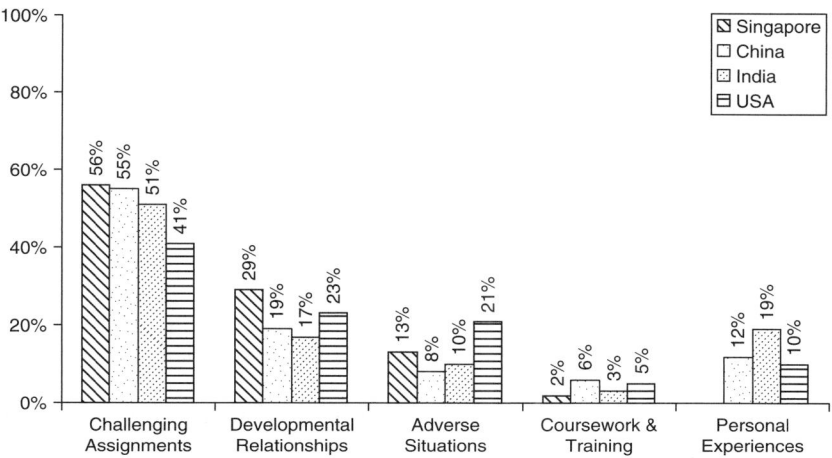

Figure 5.1 Event clusters: a four-country comparison

approach to management. Please identify at least three 'key events' in your career – things that made a difference in the way you manage now. When we meet with you, we'll ask you about each event: (1) What happened? (2) What did you learn from it (for better or worse)?

The findings from these studies have overwhelmingly revealed that the most critical and meaningful events that facilitate learning involve either challenging assignments, important relationships, learning from adverse situations, training courses, or personal experience. Figure 5.1 shows the breakdown of events that teach lessons of leadership from the 2003 study.

Grounded in this research are three often misunderstood principles of leadership development.

Principle 1: Development is a process Today's business world, characterized by dynamic change and bottom-line orientation, has created a sense of urgency to produce short-term results and hence short-term solutions. However, the fact remains that development, by its nature, is a process not an event or a quick fix. CCL's research (Van Velsor et al., 2004) has confirmed that no single developmental event is powerful enough to create lasting change in an individual's approach to the tasks of leadership. Rather, leadership development is a lifelong and ongoing process.

Principle 2: Experience drives development Many individuals believe that classroom-based training is the sole method to develop leadership, and off-site workshops or seminars are best to improve certain skills. CCL research has demonstrated, however, that training is only one component of the development process. Formal training actually makes up less than 20 percent of the events that teach important lessons of leadership (Berke et al., 2008). Richer sources of leadership development come from day-to-day work or on-the-job experience. Managers report becoming better leaders through experiences such as adding responsibilities to jobs, transferring between functions and divisions, observing their bosses' behaviors, introspection resulting from mistakes and career setbacks, and significant changes in their personal life (McCall et al., 1988). Thus, development does not mean taking people away from their work. Instead, it means helping them learn from their work (Van Velsor et al., 2004).

Principle 3: You are responsible   The decay of the paternalistic organization and the increasing complexity of modern life are calling for a qualitatively different mind-set about work and leadership. People are not only held accountable for their work and performance, but also are responsible for their own career development. The shift in responsibility from the organization to the individual requires people to define themselves instead of relying on the organization to tell them who they are (Van Velsor and Drath, 2004). In addition, every employee is encouraged to take on leadership responsibilities. Leadership is not the exclusive ownership of a few top managers. As a result, employees need to actively assess their own leadership strengths and areas for improvement, seek developmental opportunities, and secure support and resources to enhance their leadership capacities.

Strategies and tools to close leadership gaps

With these general principles in mind, we recommend you employ two or three of the following strategies to close your leadership gaps. The strategies are organized around CCL Lessons of Experience research. More specifically, this research has shown that across the globe, leadership skills can be acquired through challenging assignments at work, through people both inside and outside the organization, through adverse situations and failures, through personal experience, and course work. Effective executives and managers are those who know how to maximize the learning from their daily work and life. To further enhance your ability to learn, tools for self reflection are also provided.

Strategy 1: Seek challenging assignments   Several studies suggest that significantly more leadership lessons are learned from job assignments compared to other event categories (Yip and Wilson, in press). A job assignment can refer to an entire job, such as starting up a new business branch or redesigning a system. It can also be an aspect of a job, such as dealing with problematic subordinates or working on a task force. The key factor that makes a job assignment developmental is the challenge.

> Essentially it must be something that stretches people, pushes them out of their comfort zone, and requires them to think differently. It may involve roles that are not well-defined, and it usually contains some elements that are new to the person. These assignments place people in challenging situations full of problems to solve, dilemmas to resolve, obstacles to overcome, and choices to make under conditions of risk and uncertainty (Ohlott, 2004: p. 154).

There are five broad sources of challenge related to learning: (1) increase in job scope; (2) creating change; (3) job rotation and transitions; (4) boundary spanning; and (5) working in a different culture (McCauley et al., 1994; McCauley et al., 1999; Ohlott, 2004). To enable you to access and use this complex knowledge easily and quickly, Table 5.4 gives descriptions and examples of these sources of challenges and leadership lessons learned from each type (see Table 5.4; Yip and Wilson, in press).

Challenging assignments exist in organizations, but it is not always accessible to every individual. A practical strategy to get learning and development under your control is to seek out new challenges in the context of your current job, and to expose yourself to a wide variety of experiences (McCauley, 2006). There are several ways to do this: (1) reshape your job and add new responsibilities; (2) work on temporary assignments such as projects, task forces, and one-time events which provide you with new responsibilities bound by time; and (3) seek challenges and leadership responsibilities outside the workplace such as in community and volunteer work, in religious, social and professional organizations, as well as in your family.

Diversity in the types of assignments you select is critical to growth, as different assignments lead to distinct leadership lessons. For example, managers in fix-it assignments learned the skill of interpersonal flexibility – being tough but fair while addressing a difficult issue. Managers in start-up assignments learned the skill of doing whatever it takes – forging ahead and getting others to commit and participate in an uncertain enterprise. Managers with task force assignments learned how to influence without authority. Managers who took a huge leap in scope or scale learned who to trust and how to delegate.

Meanwhile, it is also important to have a focused plan and clear purpose when you seek out challenging assignments. It will work best if you add challenges that target the development of a particular leadership skill (McCauley, 2006). Table 5.5 provides specific types of assignments

Table 5.4 Challenging assignments: examples of events and lessons learned

Event type / context	Description	Examples of events	Examples of lessons learned
Increase in scope Occurs as a part of normal career progression	Responsibilities and pressures are assumed that are broader and different from before. With that comes more decision-making power, influence and visible success or failure.	A new employee is promoted and has to manage a team of direct reports for the first time, including former peers. A high potential manager is appointed as general manager of several functions and experiences job overload, pressures, scrutiny and public accountability.	Managing and motivating subordinates Managing direct reports Functional expertise
Creating change Triggered by regional or global growth and inducements to improve productivity	Decisions and actions are required under business, political or social conditions that are neither clear nor predictable.	New initiatives present opportunities to create or launch new products, adopt new technologies, or build a plant or unit from scratch in another region or new country. Change, or a turnaround, must be effected to fix problems left behind by previous managers. An underperforming or failing business operation must be stabilized, sometimes by restructuring or downsizing.	Confidence Build trust Influence
Job rotation and transitions Aimed at providing holistic perspective on	New knowledge and expertise is needed that the manager does not possess, but is required for proving him or herself. Previously	A variety of transfers are possible. The transfer can be self or company initiated, one or several, and in either direction. ● From line management to a staff role; ● From policy work to field work;	Self-awareness Client focus Managing stakeholders

the organization's structure, operations, strategy and culture.	effective behaviors, work processes and mental models are inadequate.	• From administration to operations; • From headquarters to a regional office; • From an urban to semi-urban or rural setting; and • From private to public or the non-profit or educational sector.	
Boundary spanning Proliferating due to globalization and changes in the structure of organizations.	Leadership influence must be exercised, but with little or no formal authority. Two or more competing points of view must be reconciled.	Negotiations with potential clients, vendors and government officials are necessary to move forward on a technology transfer; tensions result from the process not proceeding per expectations. Two organizations undertake a collaborative venture with initial enthusiasm; unexpected differences in how decisions are made and information is shared cause complications that stall the work.	Network mindset Managing trade-offs Managing stakeholders
Work in a different culture Becoming pervasive due to the global aspirations of organizations	Leadership tasks involve regular, direct contact with co-workers whose values, language, motivations, life routines and cultural customs are different. Even beliefs about leadership, and the practice of leadership, are dissimilar.	While remaining in his or her country of origin, the manager is accountable for global operations of a function, product line or business. Business objectives must be met under political, legal, and economic conditions that are unlike what the manager has previously experienced; hazardous and even life-threatening situations may be features of the overall expatriate assignment.	Self-awareness Cultural adaptability Managing teams

Source: Used with permission and copyright © 2009 Center for Creative Leadership.

Table 5.5   Bridging leadership gaps by using challenging assignments

Leadership skill gap	Potential challenging assignments
Balancing personal life and work	Look for experiences where you can practice setting priorities, managing stress, and keep balance. • Manage something with which you are unfamiliar (e.g., a function, market, product, technology or group of people). • Take a temporary assignment in another function of the organization. • Chair a professional conference.
Managing change	Look for experiences where you can set new directions or fix problems. • Be responsible for a new project or a new process in your group. • Deal with a business crisis. • Lead a task force to fix a problem.
Decisiveness	Look for experiences that provide opportunities to work on ill-defined/recurring problems, or make decisions that require broad input from across the organization. • Lead a quality improvement initiative in a non-profit or professional organization. • Represent your group on a task force that prioritizes projects across groups. • Improve the metrics used to assess your group's effectiveness.
Leading people	Look for experiences where you must motivate and develop employees. • Delegate one of your job responsibilities to a direct report. • Hire and develop an employee who shows promise but doesn't have the needed experience for the job. • Work to retain a valued employee who is thinking about leaving the organization.
Employee development	Look for experiences where you coach employees to improve performance. • Develop succession plans for direct reports. • Manage the training of new employees in your group. • Fire an employee who has not met performance standards despite coaching and support.

Table 5.5 (continued)

Leadership skill gap	Potential challenging assignments
Strategic planning	Look for experiences that allow you to think about the future and craft strategies for aligning people and systems to achieve long-term objectives. • Develop five-year business scenarios for your unit. • Join a project team that is plowing new ground in your organization. • Take a temporary assignment in new product development.
Inspiring commitment	Look for experiences where you must inspire employees. • Organize an event to celebrate and share successes. • Push tasks and decision making down to direct reports. • Coach a sports team.

that can enhance the seven leadership skill gaps identified in the previous section.

Strategy 2: Establish developmental relationship Another important source for leadership development is other people. Managers reported events where people had a significant impact on how they led (McCall et al., 1988). These 'significant' others were people who either worked with the managers in the same organization as superiors, peers and subordinates, or were people outside of the workplace (such as family members and friends).

Significant others can provide a crucial substitute for direct experience and teach lessons missed in challenging assignments (McCall et al., 1988). In addition, lessons learned from other people can bring balance to the lessons learned from challenging assignments. Many successful executives, for example, are aggressive adults who are highly capable of getting other people to go the extra mile to help them achieve their goals. The potential damage of the insensitivity bred by this instrumental use of others can be offset by the values and virtues that these executives learned from other people (McCall et al., 1988).

There are various types of roles or developmental relationships people can play in developing your leadership skill (McCauley and Douglas, 2004). Table 5.6 summarizes these roles and the functions that each role provides in leader development. In the table, you will also find questions

Table 5.6   Roles played by others in developmental relationships and guidelines to seek development relationships

Role	Function	Who can provide this role
Feedback provider	Provides ongoing feedback as the person works to learn and improve.	• Someone who is in the position of observing you practice new behaviors • Someone who is good at observing and assessing the impact of your behaviors • Someone you trust to be straightforward and honest
Sounding board	Evaluates developmental strategies before they are implemented.	• Someone who is good at thinking out loud and considering alternatives • Someone who has already faced these same sorts of choices • Someone who you are willing to share your uncertainties with
Comparison point	Provides standards for evaluating your skill or performance level.	• Someone who would be a relevant comparison point • Someone who would be willing to share their progress with you • Someone whose successes would be easy for you to see
Feedback interpreter	Assists in integrating or making sense of feedback from others.	• Someone who is good at making sense of complex data • Someone who you are comfortable sharing your feedback with • Someone who others trust as a gatherer of feedback for you
Dialogue partner	Provides perspectives or points of view different from your own.	• Someone who has a perspective different from your own • Someone who is good at engaging in dialogue, at examining underlying assumptions • Someone who is good in the role of devil's advocate

Assignment broker	Provides access to challenging assignments (new jobs or additions to current ones).	• Someone who can sponsor you when certain jobs become available • Someone who can help you add needed challenge to your job • Someone who can help you find stretch opportunities outside the workplace
Account	Provides pressure to fulfill development goals.	• Someone who holds you accountable for achieving your goals • Others who want you to achieve your goal
Role model	Serves as an example of high (or low) competence in areas being developed.	• Someone who you should watch or talk to for more specifics • Someone whose ability in this area has always been an inspiration to you
Counselor	Examines what is making learning and development difficult.	• Someone who can be your confidante as you struggle with your goals • Someone who can be both empathetic and objective • Someone who understands you enough to see through your excuses and procrastinations
Cheerleader	Boosts the belief that success is possible.	• Someone who is usually able to make you feel competent • Someone you can share your small successes with • Someone who is in the position to reward you for success
Reinforcer	Provides formal rewards for progress toward goals.	• Someone who is usually able to make you feel competent • Someone you can share your successes with • Someone who is in the position to reward you for success
Companion	Provides a sense that you are not alone in your struggles and that if others can achieve your goals, you can too.	• Someone who understands what you are going through • Peers in the same situation • Someone who would be 'good company' for this journey

Source: Adapted from McCauley and Douglas (2004), pp. 96–8.

EXERCISE 5.3   EXAMPLES OF EXPERIENCES
FOR YOUR ACTIVE INQUIRY

Ask others to describe experiences where they:

- Started something from scratch such as setting up a new function or branch.
- Managed a business turnaround.
- Moved from one function to another within their organization.
- Made business mistakes.
- Dealt with a subordinate's performance problems.
- Changed from a technical to a supervisory role.
- Dealt with prejudice or discrimination.
- Managed conflicts with their peers.
- Managed conflicts with their boss.
- Dealt with downsizing and resulting emotions.
- Handled an international assignment.
- Managed from a distance.

to help you identify the appropriate person to play these developmental relationships.

A tip to help you fully utilize your developmental relationship network is to ask others about their past experiences (Wei and Yip, 2008b). This strategy enables you to learn from other people's experience simply by asking questions of those that you carefully select. In practice, many people need to and want to consult others for dialogue and multiple perspectives. However, they are unsure about how to do it in a way that can elicit rich learning yet is non-intrusive. The following exercises provide examples of experiences that you can ask others about (Exercise 5.3) along with the lessons learned from these experiences (Exercise 5.4).

Strategy 3: Enhance your ability to learn from experience   Over the years, CCL research has demonstrated that failure to learn in the face of transitions and new environments is one of the most frequent causes of executive derailment (Leslie and Van Velsor, 1996). Managers who continue to be effective over time are those who learn from their own experience as well as those of others, and apply what they learn (Van Velsor et al., 2004). Thus, it is critical for you to consider how you can improve your ability to learn from experience.

EXERCISE 5.4   QUESTIONS TO ASK FOR EACH EVENT

Ask questions from all four categories.

What happened?
- What was the history of the situation?
- What was the main goal (objective, intention) of the event?
- When did it happen?
- Where did it happen?
- What exactly happened?
- Who was involved?
- What was your role?
- What did you hope to achieve?

How did you feel?
- What were the highs? Lows? How did they make you feel?
- What was your biggest concern?
- Where did you feel most challenged?
- Where did the work go easily for you?
- What surprised you most?
- What did others like (or dislike) about the situation?
- What significance did you attach to the situation?

What did you learn, and how?
- What did you learn from the experience? What were your major insights? Why?
- What would you do differently? Why?
- What did you think was really going on? What were the implications? What might be some underlying issues?
- What prompted you to. . .?
- What might have happened if you had. . .?
- What might have happened if you hadn't. . .?
- What advice would you give others who may go through the same experience?

What conclusions did you draw, and what actions did you take?
- What decision was required? What action was needed?
- What were your priorities? What did you do?

- What could you do to address the concerns of key stakeholders?
- What could you do to make the problem or situation different?
- What resources (people, financial, etc.) did you use?
- What additional resources were needed?

You can learn the most from experience if you employ a variety of learning tactics (Dalton, 1998). There are four basic types: (1) *feeling tactics*; (2) *action tactics*; (3) *thinking tactics*; and (4) *accessing-others tactics*. *Feeling tactics* describe behaviors that individuals use to manage feelings of anxiety or discomfort when new situations arise. *Action tactics* are characteristics of learning-by-doing and experiencing the effects. *Thinking tactics* describe behaviors that are solitary. Individuals who prefer thinking tactics work scenarios out by themselves through a comparison of past experiences, contrasting situations, drawing parallels, rehearsing and generating possibilities. Finally, *accessing others tactics* are learning behaviors that are observational. These include behaviors like modeling, seeking advice, support and formal training.

To assist you in becoming a versatile learner, we provide the following descriptions of the four learning tactics. Use this list to identify your preferred method of learning especially when you are faced with new challenges. Think about the tactics you use least often and decide if you would like to flex your preferred learning style in the future by trying new tactics.

1. Feeling tactics:
   - I carefully consider how I feel.
   - I carefully consider how others might feel.
   - I trust my feelings.
   - I acknowledge the impact of my feelings on my decisions.
2. Action tactics:
   - I allow my own experience to be my guide.
   - I immerse myself in situations to figure them out quickly.
   - I don't allow the lack of information or input to keep me from taking action.
   - I commit myself to making something happen.
3. Thinking tactics:
   - I regularly access magazine articles, books, or the internet to gain knowledge or information.
   - I ask myself, 'How is this similar to other things I know?'

- I imagine how different options might play out.
- I try to mentally rehearse my actions before entering the situation.
4. Accessing others tactics:
   - I often seek the advice of those around me.
   - I look for role models, and I try to emulate the behavior of these people.
   - I find people who can give me feedback about my performance.
   - I look for experienced role models.

Strategy 4: Reflect on your experience   Reflection can enhance one's ability to extract wisdom from experiences (Van Velsor et al., 2004; Wei and Yip, 2008b). Here we present two types of self-reflection – surface and deep. Surface reflection is characterized by a set of questions focused on specific behaviors and actions. The questions require that you step back from the experience, reflect on your actions, and begin to see the situation from others' perspectives. Deep reflection is characterized by a set of questions focused on the assumptions and values which underpin your actions. By considering the perceptions and lenses through which you interpret your experiences, these questions can help you learn from past experiences and better handle future ones. Below is a list for surface and deep reflection questions to help you reflect on your experiences.

a. Questions for surface reflection
    - What was the experience that led to your learning?
    - What happened?
    - What actions were taken?
    - What was the response of others?
    - What were the consequences?
    - What could or should you have done to make it better?
    - What would you do now if you were in a similar situation?
    - How can you apply this learning?
b. Questions for deep reflection
    - What did you learn about yourself through this experience?
    - What was good or bad about the experience? Why?
    - What are some beliefs that impact the way you view this experience?
    - What other knowledge can you bring to the situation?
    - What broader issues arise from the situation?
    - What seem to be the root causes of the issue or problem addressed?

- What are broader issues that need to be considered if this action is to be successful?
- What might you do differently?

Strategy 5: Solicit ongoing feedback   The final tactic to consider when working towards competency goal attainment is to seek ongoing feedback. Sources of support can include family members, friends, church members, co-workers, neighbors and community affiliates. The kind of support you can receive from involving others ranges from informational (for example, a good book to read or 360-degree feedback) to emotional (for example, coaching). When deciding who to engage for support and feedback consider: who will notice when you achieve your goals? What difference will they notice? How will they be impacted? And how often should you ask for feedback? Whoever you choose to support your developmental efforts, remember the objective is to discuss your progress so that you can confirm your perceptions, ask for specific feedback and keep the dialogue going so that you can look for opportunities to try out your new behavior.

CONCLUSION

It is our hope this chapter will serve as a tool for anyone who is eager to learn about leadership and wants to take responsibility for developing their skills through experience. The chapter began with research describing a survey of 2200 managers from the USA, India and Singapore. The results showed critical importance both now and in the future for all leaders to be effective in: *leading people, strategic planning, managing change, employee development, inspiring commitment, balancing personal life and work* and *decisiveness.*

The second part of the chapter focuses on tools, techniques and strategies individuals can use in order to increase the likelihood that they can learn to develop through their experiences. More specifically, this section of the chapter provides strategies and tools to help close leadership gaps, gives advice about who to seek help from during this developmental phase, and allows each person to begin to craft their own development plan.

NOTE

1.   The Center for Creative Leadership gratefully acknowledges the Singapore Economic Development Board for their support of this research.

REFERENCES

American Society for Training and Development (ASTD) Public Policy Counsel (2006) *Bridging the Skills Gap: How the Skills Shortage Threatens Growth and Competitiveness. . .and What to Do About It.* Alexandria, VA: ASTD Publications Department.

Barrett, A. and Beeson, J. (2002), *Developing Business Leaders for 2010*, New York: The Conference Board.

Berke, D., Kossler, M.E. and Wakefield, M. (2008), *Developing Leadership Talent*, San Francisco, MA: Pfeiffer.

Bernhart, M. (2006), 'Preparing for a skills shortage, work intensification', *Employee Benefit News*, November.

Bernthal, P.R., Bondra, J. and Wei, W. (2006), *Leadership in China: Keeping Pace with a Growing Economy*, Pittsburgh, PA: Developmental Dimensions International, Inc. (DDI).

Boyatzis, R. (1982). *The Competent Manager: A Model for Effective Performance*, New York: John Wiley.

Braddy, P. (2007), 'A psychometric analysis of benchmarks', unpublished report prepared by the Center for Creative Leadership.

Buckingham, M. and Coffman, C. (1999), *First Break all the Rules: What the World's Greatest Managers do Differently*, New York: Simon and Schuster.

Dalton, M.A. (1998), *Becoming a More Versatile Learner*, Greensboro, NC: Center for Creative Leadership.

Dalton, M.A., Ernst, C., Deal, J.J. and Leslie, J. (2002), *Success for the New Global Manager: How to Work across Distances, Countries, and Cultures*, San Francisco, CA Jossey-Bass.

Douglas, C.A. (2003), *Key Events and Lessons for Managers in a Diverse Workforce: A Report on Research and Findings*, Greensboro, NC: Center for Creative Leadership.

Friedman, T.L. (2005), 'It's a flat world, after all', New York Times, 3 April.

Gaur, A.S. (2006,), 'Changing demands of the leadership in the new economy: a survey of Indian managers', *IMB Management Review*, June 149–58.

Harter, J.K., Schmidt, F.L., and Hayes, T.L. (2002), 'Business-unit-level relationship between employee satisfaction, employee engagement, and business outcomes: a meta-analysis', *Journal of Applied Psychology*, **87**, 268–79.

Kaiser, R.B., Hogan, R. and Craig, S.B. (2008), 'Leadership and the fate of organizations', *American Psychologist*, **63**, 96–110.

Lee, C.H. and Ang, S. (2003), 'Assessing the measurement equivalence of benchmarks between United States and Singapore', unpublished report prepared by the Center for Cultural Intelligence Division of Strategy, Management and Organization, Nanyang Business School, Nanyang Technological University.

Leslie, J.B., and Van Velsor, E. (1996), *A Look at Derailment Today: North America and Europe*, Greensboro, NC: Center for Creative Leadership.

Lindsey, E.H., Homes, V. and McCall, M.W., Jr. (1987), *Key Events in Executives' Lives*, Greensboro, NC: Center for Creative Leadership.

Lombardo, M.M., McCauley, C.D., McDonald-Mann, D. and Leslie, J.B. (1999), *Benchmarks® Developmental Reference Points*, Greensboro, NC: Center for Creative Leadership.

Macey, W.H. and Schneider, B. (2008), 'The meaning of employee engagement', *Industrial and Organizational Psychology: Perspectives on Science and Practice*, **1**, 3–30.

Manpower (2008), *Talent shortage survey 2008 global results* (research report), Milwaukee, WI: Manpower Inc.

McCall, M.W., Jr (1998), *High Flyers: Developing the Next Generation of Leaders*, Boston, MA: Harvard Business School Press.

McCall, M.W., Jr and Hollenbeck, G.P. (2002), *Developing Global Executives: The Lessons of International Experience*, Boston, MA: Harvard Business School Press.

McCall, M.W., Jr, Lombardo, M.M., and Morrison, A.M. (1988), *The Lessons of Experience: How Successful Executives Develop on the Job*, San Francisco, CA: New Lexington Press.

McCauley, C.D. (2006), *Developmental Assignments: Creating Learning Experiences Without Changing Jobs*, Greensboro, NC: Center for Creative Leadership.

McCauley, C.D. and Douglas, C.A. (2004), 'Developmental relationships', in C.D. McCauley and E. Van Velsor (eds), *The Center for Creative Leadership Handbook of Leadership Development*. San Francisco, CA: Jossey-Bass, pp. 85–115.

McCauley, C.D., Ruderman, M.N. and Ohlott, P.J. (1999), *Job Challenges Profile: Facilitator's Guide*, San Francisco, CA: Jossey-Bass.

McCauley, C.D., Ruderman, M.N., Ohlott, P.J., and Morrow, J.E. (1994), 'Assessing the developmental components of managerial jobs', *Journal of Applied Psychology*, **79**(4), 544–60.

Meger, B. (1996), 'A critical review of competency-based systems', *The Human Resource Professional*, **9**(1), 22–5.

Morrison, A.M., White, R.P. and Van Velsor, E. (1987), *Breaking the Glass Ceiling: Can Women Reach the Top of America's Largest Corporations?* Reading, MA: Addison-Wesley.

Ohlott, P.J. (2004), 'Job assignments', in C.D. McCauley and E. Van Velsor (eds), *The Center for Creative Leadership Handbook of Leadership Development*, 2nd edn., San Francisco, CA: Jossey-Bass, pp. 151–82.

Raju, N., Leslie, J., McDonald-Mann, D. and Craig, B. (1999), 'IRT-based evaluation of 360-degree assessments: The Benchmarks story', paper presented at the 14th annual meeting of the Society for Industrial and Organizational Psychology, Atlanta, GA.

Rappaport, A., Bancroft, E. and Okum, L. (2003), 'The aging workforce raises new talent management issues for employers', *Journal of Organizational Excellence*, **23**(1), 55–66.

Schramm, J. (2006). *Human Resource Management 2006 Workplace Forecast*, Alexandria, VA: Society for Human Resource Management (SHRM).

Spencer, L.M. and Spencer, S.M. (1993), *Competence at Work: Models for Superior Performance*, New York: John Wiley.

United Nations (2006), 'World population prospects: the 2006 revision', United Nations Population Division, available from UN Data website, http://data.un.org/Browse.aspx?d=POP.

Van Velsor, E. and Drath, W. (2004), 'A lifelong developmental perspective on leader development', in C.D. McCauley and E. Van Velsor (eds), *The Center for Creative Leadership Handbook of Leadership Development*, 2nd edn, San Francisco, CA: Jossey-Bass, pp. 234–67.

Van Velsor, E., Moxley, R.S. and Bunker, K.A. (2004), 'The leader development process', in C.D. McCauley and E. Van Velsor (eds), *The Center for Creative Leadership Handbook of Leadership Development*, 2nd edn, San Francisco, CA: Jossey-Bass, pp. 204–33.

Wei, R., and Yip, J. (2008a), 'Self awareness and its triggering events of Chinese business leaders', presented at the International Association for Chinese Management Research Symposium, Guangzhou, China, June.

Wei, R. and Yip, J. (2008b), *Leadership Wisdom: Discovering the Lessons of Experience*, Greensboro, NC: Center for Creative Leadership.

Weiss, D. and Finn, R. (2005), 'HR metrics that count', *Human Resources Planning*, February/March.

Weiss, D. and Molinaro, D. (2005), *The Leadership Gap: Bridging Leadership Capability for Competitive Advantage*, Mississauga, ON: John Wiley.

Wilson, M. (2008), 'Developing future leaders for high-growth Indian companies', technical report, Greensboro, NC: Center for Creative Leadership.

Yip, J. and Wilson, M. (2008), 'Developing public service leaders in Singapore', technical report, Greensboro, NC: Center for Creative Leadership.

Yip, J., and Wilson, M. (in press), 'Learning from experience', In C.D. McCauley and E. Van Velsor (eds), *The Center for Creative Leadership Handbook of Leadership Development*, 3rd edn, San Francisco, CA: Jossey-Bass. (Used with Permission and Copyright ©2009 Center for Creative Leadership.)

Zacharakis, A. (1996), 'The double whammy of globalization: differing country and foreign partner cultures', *Academy of Management Executive*, **10**(4), 109–10.

Zhang, Y. and Wei, R. (2008), 'Chinese leaders tackle global challenges', *Leadership in Action*, **28**(1), 20–22.

6. Emotional intelligence and interpersonal competencies

Ronald E. Riggio

Daniel Goleman's 1995 book, *Emotional Intelligence*, became a bestseller and a must-read for managers and leaders. As a result, the term 'emotional intelligence' (or EQ, as opposed to IQ) became part of the everyday language of management. While emotional intelligence is still a relatively new construct, there are historical roots and justification for the importance of emotions in effective leadership. For example, leader emotional expressiveness has long been viewed as a key component for charismatic leadership (Bass, 1990; Riggio and Riggio, 2008). More recently, ability to recognize emotions in others has also been related to charismatic/transformational leadership (Rubin et al., 2005). Perhaps more important than emotional skills/intelligence, however, is the impact of interpersonal skills and competencies in effective management. For instance, nearly every leadership scholar or practicing leader on the planet will stress the importance of 'people skills' in effective leadership. There are a number of terms used to describe these people skills, but they are most commonly referred to as: 'interpersonal skills' or 'interpersonal competencies'. For leaders, interpersonal skills are used in interacting with followers, peers, clients and others, and they are very important in developing and maintaining relationships. In this chapter, we will look at the emotional and interpersonal skills that are so critical to leader success and focus on the development of these competencies. First, however, it is important to understand the constructs and the research behind them.

EMOTIONAL INTELLIGENCE AND LEADERSHIP: THE EMOTIONAL COMPETENCIES OF LEADERS

The concept of emotional intelligence was first introduced by Salovey and Mayer (1990) and was conceptualized as a set of abilities to know and understand emotions and emotional processes in oneself and others. It was viewed as analogous to verbal/academic intelligence, and much of the early work by Salovey, Mayer and their colleagues focused on substantiating emotional intelligence as a *true* form of intelligence (Mayer et al., 1999; Mayer and Salovey, 1993). Portions of emotional intelligence, particularly the ability to communicate and regulate emotions – the elements that are so critical to leadership – had earlier roots in research on emotional skills (e.g., Rosenthal, 1979) and emotional regulatory processes (Frijda, 1986; Izard, 1990; see Gross, 2007 for a review). Emotional skills are more focused on particular abilities, such as skill in expressing emotions in reading, or 'decoding', the emotional states of others, or skill in regulating emotions and emotional expression. Emotional intelligence is a broader construct that typically subsumes basic emotional skills. Some of this research on basic emotional communication will inform the development of leaders' emotional skills and will be addressed later.

It is important to note that there is a schism in theory and research on emotional intelligence. The original Salovey and Mayer (1990) model and subsequent work is referred to as the 'abilities model', and focuses on four sets of skills: (1) managing emotions in order to attain specific goals; (2) understanding emotions; (3) using emotions to facilitate thinking; and (4) perceiving and interpreting emotions accurately in oneself and others (Mayer and Salovey, 1997). The other approach to emotional intelligence is referred to as the 'mixed model' because it mixes together emotional abilities with traditional personality traits, such as empathy, optimism, self-esteem, stress tolerance/hardiness, as well as elements of interpersonal skill, such as assertiveness. The mixed model is represented in the popular press (e.g., Goleman, 1995; 1998), and by measurement instruments and research by Bar-On (1997) and others (e.g., Boyatzis and McKee, 2006).

In addition to research on emotion, emotional intelligence has been closely related to conceptions of social intelligence, with some viewing emotional intelligence as a subset of social intelligence, and other scholars arguing for multiple types of intelligence, which includes intelligences related to understanding oneself and understanding others in interpersonal relationships (e.g., Gardner, 1983; Guilford, 1967). Indeed, there has been research exploring the multiple forms of intelligence and their role in leadership (Riggio et al., 2002), and there is growing interest specifically in studying emotional intelligence and leadership, with many dozens of articles and dissertations in just the past few years. These studies range from examining the emotional intelligence in gifted adolescent leaders (Lee and Olszewski-Kubilius, 2006), to emotional intelligence and performance of members of school district boards (Hopkins et al., 2007), to the relationship between leadership and emotional intelligence in senior female managers (Downey et al., 2006).

The question of the two models of emotional intelligence, abilities vs.

mixed, has generated quite a bit of discussion and controversy in the academic literature (see Mayer et al., 2008, for a good overview), but for purposes of leaders' development and our discussion, the distinction may not be too important. Specifically, in developing leaders' emotional and interpersonal competencies, we want to develop the emotional abilities associated with emotional intelligence, but the personality-like constructs of the mixed model of EQ, such as empathy, self-awareness, resiliency and the like, are also related to leader effectiveness. To the extent that qualities such as empathy, self-awareness, stress tolerance and other related constructs, can be developed, they are part of the emotional and interpersonal competencies 'package' that would be targeted for leader development. The real question is 'how effective are programs designed to increase leaders' emotional intelligence, regardless of the theoretical orientation of the EQ program?'

Although there has been a great deal of research devoted to the role of emotions and emotional intelligence in leadership, there has been little systematic, research-based work in developing leaders' EQ. Instead, a variety of trainers and leadership coaches have used conceptions of emotional intelligence as a basis for providing training workshops and programs. However, there has been very little research evaluating the effectiveness of these emotional intelligence development efforts.

A recent scholarly review located 12 published studies of emotional intelligence training, with the majority, but not all, focused on training the emotional intelligence of managers/leaders (McEnrue et al., 2009). This review noted that most of these studies suffered from serious methodological flaws and concerns, such as a lack of a control/comparison group, experimental demand characteristics, questionable measurement of outcomes – problems that make it difficult to draw clear conclusions about the effectiveness of these training efforts (McEnrue et al., 2009).

These same authors (Groves et al., 2008) conducted an 11-week emotional intelligence training program for employed MBA students that attempted to correct the shortcomings of many of the previous training evaluations. It is important to emphasize that this program relied on the Mayer and Salovey (1997) abilities model to guide the training program. Their results suggested that emotional intelligence can indeed be enhanced through training/developmental efforts, but bear in mind that gains from even the best programs designed to develop emotional intelligence, are typically small, but significant (Boyatzis, 2007a). We will further analyze EQ training programs and evaluation research of these programs to extract developmental best practices later in this chapter.

It is also important to emphasize that well-controlled efforts to develop emotional skills and abilities have had some success. For example, training designed to enhance emotional/nonverbal sensitivity (similar to EQs 'interpreting emotions accurately in others') has found that this specific emotional skill can be developed and enhanced over time with practice (e.g., Costanzo, 1992; Elfenbein, 2006; Ickes et al., 1997). In addition, there is clear evidence that ability to communicate emotions effectively can be enhanced through practice and training, particularly the ability to pose or enact emotions, or the aforementioned ability to read the emotional expressions of others, and this has been the focus of development efforts with medical doctors (Satterfield and Hughes, 2007), in families (Gottman et al., 1997) and in clinical populations (e.g., Silver et al., 2004).

While much attention in emotional communication is focused on abilities to express emotions and read emotions in others, emotional self-awareness and emotional regulation are equally, if not more, important aspects of emotional intelligence for most leaders. Emotionally intelligent/competent leaders need to be aware of the emotions they are experiencing, and whether these emotions are being conveyed to followers and others. Persons lacking ability to control the expression of their emotions may not be viewed as effective leaders or as potential leaders because they are unable to maintain composure in emotionally-charged situations, such as during a crisis (Gross, 1998). Similarly, inability to control emotions may lead to extreme expressions of negative emotions, such as anger, that may alienate or offend followers and others.

Emotional regulation in particular, and emotional intelligence, more generally, are important in leader impression management (Kellett et al., 2002). Tiedens (2000), for example, suggests that it is acceptable for leaders to express strong, felt emotions to peers, but not to followers. Moreover, leaders may use their ability to control emotions in a strategic way, exaggerating or feigning particular emotions, such as exaggerating positive emotions to praise followers, inspire them, or to raise their spirits following a failure or setback (George, 2000; Dasborough and Ashkanasy, 2002). Of course, regulation of strong, felt emotions, through suppressing them or faking positive emotions, may come with some costs to the leader, such as causing feelings of stress, job dissatisfaction, and withdrawal – what has been termed 'emotional labor' (Ashforth and Humphrey, 1993; Brotheridge and Lee, 2002; Gross, 1998).

One model that has been suggested as a simple, nonverbal communication-based framework for emotional skill development focuses on assessing skills in expressing emotions, receiving and 'decoding' others' emotions, and regulating/controlling emotional expressions (Riggio, 2006a). This is part of a broader framework that also focuses on corresponding social/verbal skills – ability to express oneself in social interaction, ability to 'read' others and social situations, and skill in social role-playing (Riggio, 1986). Using a self-report measure, the Social Skills Inventory (Riggio, 2005), assessment is made of an individual's possession of both basic emotional communication skills and more complex social and interpersonal abilities.

There has been considerably more work on developing emotional intelligence/competencies using the mixed model of emotional intelligence – focusing on developing emotional skills, but also certain personality-like competencies, such as empathy, resilience and optimism. A great deal of this work has been done by Boyatzis and his colleagues, and by Bar-On and associates. The Bar-On (1997) emotional intelligence measure, the EQi, measures emotional self-awareness, self-esteem, assertiveness, interpersonal skills (for example, empathy), stress management and adaptability, and mood (optimism, happiness). It is typically a self-report instrument, but can also be used as a multi-rater instrument or an interview. Using the EQi, Bar-On reports a 'moderate to high relationship between EI and leadership [performance] based on the respective predictive validity coefficients of .39 (n=536), .49 (n=940) and .82 (n-236)' (Bar-On, 2007: p. 8). Bar-On (2007) also reports some small-scale programs that found increases in managers' EQi scores from pre- to post-training (see also Dulewicz et al., 2003). It is important to emphasize, however, that some of the constructs measured by the EQi go well beyond the more focused abilities model of emotional intelligence used by Salovey, Mayer and colleagues (e.g., Mayer et al., 2000).

Boyatzis and colleagues (Boyatzis, 2007b; Boyatzis et al., 2002) report on programs designed to improve a broad range of emotional and interpersonal competencies that fit under the mixed model of emotional intelligence. Boyatzis (2007b) argues that, to be effective, leaders need to possess knowledge of emotions and emotional processes, have emotional and interpersonal competencies, and have the motivation to develop and use these knowledge bases and competencies. Boyatzis et al. (2002) report on a program to improve emotional intelligence of MBA students at the Weatherhead School of Management at Case Western Reserve University. This program, which is encompassed in a 'leadership assessment and development course', uses assessment instruments and exercises with extensive feedback and coaching, coupled with self-development plans and goal-setting to help students improve their emotional and interpersonal competencies. The results suggest that there are significant, although sometimes modest, improvements in emotional and social competencies that seem to hold up in follow-up investigations even several years post-graduation (Boyatzis and Saatcioglu, 2007; Boyatzis et al., 2002).

It is apparent that programs designed to improve emotional competencies via the mixed model of emotional intelligence go beyond merely improving emotional intelligence and cross over into the domain of interpersonal and social competencies. In actuality, it is often difficult to separate the two and focus only on emotions or only on social skills/ competencies. Before returning to the development of emotional and interpersonal competencies, we will review the theory and research on interpersonal skills and competencies and their relevance to leadership.

INTERPERSONAL COMPETENCIES: THE PEOPLE SKILLS OF LEADERS

Many early theories of leadership focused primarily on the technical skills of leaders, such as leaders' abilities to make good decisions (Vroom and Yetton, 1973). It has long been known, however, that effective leadership requires both technical (e.g., analytical and decision-making skills) and 'people' skills. It was the Ohio State and University of Michigan studies that first highlighted the need for both; *initiating structure*, or *task-oriented*, leader behaviors, and *showing consideration*, or *relationship-oriented*, behaviors were both deemed important by these post-World War II researchers (see Bass, 2008, chapters 19 and 20; Riggio, 2006b, for reviews). More recent theories of leadership, such as transformational leadership theory and leader–member exchange (LMX), have placed a greater emphasis on interpersonal skills, while still acknowledging the importance of technical leader skills. It is interesting to note that even though this distinction between technical and interpersonal skills was made more than 60 years ago, recent research still demonstrates that this dichotomy exists and that both are important for effective leadership (Judge et al., 2004).

In terms of the development of interpersonal skills for the business world, perhaps the most impressive early work was done by Dale Carnegie with his skill training seminars and the publication of *Public Speaking and Influencing Men in Business* in 1913, and the best-selling *How to Win Friends and Influence People* in 1937. Indeed, Dale Carnegie training courses are still popular today, and include training interpersonal skills for effective leadership (and for employees more generally). Of course, Carnegie was not an academic and there has been no published evaluation of his training seminars' effectiveness, yet it is surprising how many of the 'common sense' ideas Carnegie incorporated, such as the importance of positive reinforcement for workers' efforts, and exhibiting positive affect, have shown to be effective in subsequent leadership research.

A critical issue is, what constitutes 'interpersonal skills' for managers/ leaders? While Carnegie and others may focus on ability to engage others in quality interactions, providing positive feedback, and effective speaking and listening, a good portion of interpersonal skills development for managers has considered more complex abilities, such as negotiation skill and conflict management. The latter can be seen as more strategic interpersonal skills, rather than the more simplistic abilities to communicate information effectively to others (for example, speaking and listening). In short, the domain of interpersonal skills is large, varied, and consists of both simpler and more complex abilities.

A review of the literature makes it quite clear that the best research on developing interpersonal skills has not been done in the business world, but in therapeutic settings. Social skill training has been used in various clinical settings since before the 1960s (Bellack, 2004; Mueser and Bellack, 2007, Trower et al., 1978). Many psychological disorders, ranging from schizophrenia to shyness, are exacerbated because of poor interpersonal and social skills. Indeed, the use of role-playing strategies that are common in interpersonal skill training programs of all sorts began in clinical settings, and has been quite successful. It is also interesting to note that there has been far more work published on development of the interpersonal skills of doctors and medical personnel, than on developing managers, leaders', and/or employees' social skills. Although there may not be a direct connection, many of the methods for training social skills in clinical populations, such as role-playing, experiential exercises (such as simulated social situations; 'homework' assignments requiring participation in social gatherings), and video-recorded rehearsing, have been used to develop interpersonal skills for employees and managers.

Despite the fact that many business schools purport to develop leader/manager interpersonal skills, most business schools have placed little emphasis on developing students' interpersonal skills, focusing primarily on the technical skills needed by managers and leaders. Porter and McKibbin (1988) and Mintzberg (2004) noted this omission in well-known critiques of MBA programs. It is only very recently that business schools have been placing greater emphasis on the development of interpersonal skills, although much of the development of these skills is done outside the regular coursework, or embedded in courses that teach more theoretical and/or technical content (the Weatherhead program to develop emotional competencies described earlier is a notable exception). As a result, development of interpersonal skills for managers and leaders is still very much an area that requires self-development and personal initiative.

There is also a variety of programs designed to develop employees' and leaders' interpersonal skills. Yet there has been very little systematic evaluation of these programs. In what is perhaps one of the best evaluation studies of interpersonal skill training, Hunt and Baruch (2003) evaluated the effects of a concentrated, five-day workshop designed to improve executives' managerial skills, with a large part of the program focusing on interpersonal skills involved in providing feedback, coaching, motivation and team building. The program utilized role-playing, team and individual exercises, and extensive feedback from other participants and expert facilitators. Participants were 252 executives from 48 different organizations in 22 different countries. The measure of evaluation was the executives' subordinates' ratings of the executives' interpersonal skills six weeks before and six months after the training. The results suggested that the training program was effective, leading to subsequent enhancements of managerial interpersonal skills, but, as the authors state, the gains were 'modest' (Hunt and Baruch, 2003). There are important reasons why such mass training programs lead to only 'modest' improvements. First, is the variation in participants' motivation and willingness to learn. Second, and related, individuals may vary in their potential to improve. Some may be too set in their ways (average age of participants in the Hunt and Baruch study, for example, was about 43 years). Others may have already reached their maximum level of interpersonal skill development. Finally, a single training program – even an intense multi-day program – is simply not enough time to expect dramatic improvements in skills as complex as interpersonal competencies (perhaps this is an even greater issue for developing more 'elusive' emotional competencies).

WHY IS THERE SUCH A BIG GAP BETWEEN RESEARCH AND TRAINING?

Any scholar who is familiar with research on emotional intelligence and interpersonal competencies knows that there is a very large gap between research on emotional intelligence and the claims of popularizers of the construct and of persons offering emotional intelligence training. Good academic research on emotional intelligence, for example, is rare (but growing), but there are numerous training programs being offered each and every day. For instance, on consecutive days, I received a brochure for a one-day seminar on 'managing emotions' and another the following day for an 'intensive two-day workshop' on 'communicating with tact and finesse'. Clearly there is a demand (and supply) for training these critical 'people skills' to managers/leaders. As we have seen, however, there are rarely evaluations of the efficacy of these programs.

It is very clear that when it comes to emotional and social intelligence the practitioner 'cart' has gotten way out in front of the research 'horse'. That is, practitioners, who tout enormous claims about the importance of emotional and social intelligence (for example, the back cover of Goleman's (1998) *Working with Emotional Intelligence* book claims that 'emotional intelligence is almost 90 percent of what sets stars apart from the mediocre'), are capitalizing on the popularity of these constructs, and because they involve common sense ideas, practitioners believe they are relatively easy to train. Academics, on the other hand, are still carefully trying to define the constructs, substantiate emotional intelligence as a *true* intelligence, and differentiate emotional, social, and academic/verbal intelligence from one another (see, for example, Murphy, 2006).

There are three things that are clearly needed in the area of developing emotional and interpersonal competencies. First, are theoretical models to guide research and practice. There are already the two competing models for emotional intelligence, the abilities and the mixed models, and those have been used to some extent to guide the development of emotional intelligence. There is, however, no agreed-upon theoretical framework for developing interpersonal competencies. The general emotional and social skill framework mentioned earlier (Riggio, 1986; Riggio and Carney, 2003) divides both emotional and social/verbal skills into three general categories: sending or expression (both emotional and verbal/social expressiveness), sensitivity (both the ability to read emotions, but also ability to read and interpret social situations, norms and social scripts), and management/control of emotional and interpersonal behavior. This is merely a very general sort of framework for emotional and interpersonal skills. What is needed, particularly on the interpersonal skill side, is a very detailed and comprehensive model that takes into account the vast array of interpersonal skills and abilities.

Second, there needs to be much more research on the techniques used to train emotional and interpersonal skills. For example, many emotional intelligence development programs have participants practice decoding facial expressions of emotions in order to become more skilled at recognizing emotions in others. Yet, it is not clear that merely improving recognition of basic emotional expressions (and often these are posed expressions of basic facial expressions, such as happiness, anger, and so on) will actually enhance the ability to uncover the often more subtle emotions that are displayed in actual interactions. Moreover, because people often feign certain emotions to cover up their true feelings, perhaps such exercises lead to immediate 'acceptance' of the portrayed emotion as representing the person's true feelings, thus actually inhibiting accurate 'reading' of true emotions.

Finally, there should be more evaluation research of existing programs, to determine which are more effective in improving emotional and interpersonal competencies. Do the EQ training programs offered by many consulting organizations actually lead to improving EQ? Do programs, such as the Dale Carnegie courses, actually work? In addition, what is the cost–benefit trade-off associated with programs designed to develop emotional and interpersonal skills? Clearly, there is much to be learned.

THE DEVELOPMENT OF EMOTIONAL AND INTERPERSONAL COMPETENCIES: BEST PRACTICES

David Day (2000) made a very important distinction between *leader* development, and *leadership* development. Leader development is the more well-known and traditional approach of training individual leaders and increasing their leadership skills and capacity. Leadership development focuses more on the group or organizational level and refers to improving the shared leadership capacity of the unit. It is important to note that traditional development programs in work organizations have always focused on individual leader development, and companies typically took on the primary responsibility of providing training for their leaders – sending them to training sessions, workshops, retreats and the like. Many organizations have shifted to a focus on increasing the shared leadership capacity of the organization – the leadership development approach. As a result of this shift in emphasis, the current bleak economic picture, and increased employee mobility and the fact that employees' average tenure with an organization has decreased, employers are giving less attention to individual leader development. Therefore, individuals need to take more responsibility for their personal leader development. This is particularly true when it comes to developing emotional and interpersonal competencies, which are often given less training attention in comparison to more technical training. The bottom line is that most leaders today need to take individual responsibility for developing emotional and interpersonal competencies, and a great deal of research suggests that the success of any developmental efforts are dependent, in large part, on the motivation and commitment of the person undergoing development, whether it be company-sponsored training or self-development.

The Center for Creative Leadership (CCL) promotes a process model for leader development (Van Velsor et al., 2004). This model suggests that leader development is a long-term process, and one that incorporates experience-based learning (either primarily, or in conjunction with classroom-based training). CCL also emphasizes that experiential exercises should be integrated with actual (rather than simulated) work, for example, advocating on-site coaching and action learning methodologies. This is consistent with action learning strategies that have proven useful in many organizations (e.g., Conger and Toegel, 2003; Dotlich and Noel, 1998). CCL also stresses that leader development is complex, requiring that learning experiences should be well planned and connected to one another (Van Velsor et al., 2004).

In an effort to provide guidance for self-development of emotional and interpersonal competencies, we will extract best practices from the general leadership training/development literature, and from the specific programs targeting emotional and interpersonal skill development.

Developmental Readiness and Motivation

The training literature consistently emphasizes the notion of trainee, or developmental, *readiness* to learn, and this is important in leader development as well (Avolio and Hannah, 2008). In the instance of company-sponsored development programs, there may be initial resistance if leaders are encouraged to attend an emotional intelligence or interpersonal skills training program ('What do you mean I'm not emotionally intelligent/interpersonally skilled?'). In self-development, motivation to develop is critically important. Developing emotional and interpersonal competencies is a long-term process that requires long-term commitment. Acquisition of emotional and interpersonal skills is incremental, and rarely involves dramatic changes. Over time, however, as one develops better emotional and social communication skills, persons respond more favorably and social interactions become more positive and rewarding.

Provide a Supportive Environment for Development

All too often, company-sponsored leadership development programs fail because when trainees return to the work setting there is a lack of support, and sometimes even active resistance, to the new leadership techniques/ styles. In self-development, it is important to involve others in the development process. Feedback (see below) from others in the work setting and at home is important in continuing growth and development. Creating a supportive relationship for self-development, such as a mentor or coach, or partnering with another developing leader to share the developmental process and experiences is a good strategy.

Creating Development Plans: Setting Goals

In order to sustain motivation to continue developmental efforts, it is imperative to create a development plan for improving emotional and interpersonal skills, and to have concrete goals or milestones. There are two general approaches to development: The first, and more traditional approach, is to focus on areas of weakness and work to strengthen those. For example, if an individual has a tendency to 'fly off the handle' emotionally, working to regulate emotional reactions and control the expression of emotions might be part of the development plan. The second is the strengths-based approach that is often associated with the Gallup Organization (Clifton and Nelson, 1992). The strengths-based approach focuses on capitalizing on existing strengths and further developing those competencies. A good strategy is to combine the two approaches, exercising and expanding on strengths and targeting deficiencies for strategic improvement.

Developmental goal-setting is also a best practice. Goals should be challenging, yet attainable (see Locke and Latham, 1984). Goals should focus on specific, 'real-world' outcomes for the developing leader, such as 'improving the frequency and quality of interactions with supervisees', by scheduling one-on-one time, actively listening and responding to concerns and feelings, and providing positive reinforcement. These should, of course, be associated with measurable outcomes and means to evaluate if development goals are being achieved.

The Critical Role of Assessment and Feedback

Many leadership development programs make use of standardized assessments and/or feedback from others. Standardized assessments include the measures of emotional intelligence associated with the different models of EQ. The aforementioned EQi is a self-report measure of the mixed model of emotional intelligence and can be used for initial assessment of areas of strength and weakness. The Emotional Competence Inventory (ECI) is another mixed model self-report instrument that has been used by Boyatzis and Goleman in their research and in programs to improve emotional intelligence (Boyatzis et al., 2000). The *Mayer-Salovey-Caruso Emotional Intelligence Test* (*MSCEIT*) (Mayer et al., 2003) is a performance-based test of the abilities model of emotional intelligence, and, unlike the other instruments, measures whether respondents are able to accurately recognize emotions and understand emotional situations.

Although there are no widely-accepted measures of interpersonal competencies, the Social Skills Inventory (SSI) (Riggio and Carney, 2003) measures both emotional skills and social skills, following the model of basic emotional/social communication presented earlier. This self-report measure can be used to assess skills associated with both emotional and social competence and can be a useful starting point for discussing both emotional intelligence/competencies, and broader social competencies. Other sorts of assessments, such as checklists of social behaviors and leadership/management situations that trainees find particularly difficult or problematic, can also help provide some baseline indications of areas that require attention.

In addition to standardized measures, ratings by subordinates, peers, supervisors, or others can help provide some initial assessment of possession of emotional and interpersonal competencies and areas that can be targeted for development. The use of 360-degree ratings is commonplace in many organizations, so these can be easily incorporated into a leader development program. Moreover, these ratings can be obtained over time to provide feedback about areas of improvement.

Increasing Self-Awareness and Introspection

Most leader development programs emphasize the importance of leaders' self-awareness. This is critically important for developing emotional and interpersonal skills. Obviously, assessments and feedback are critical for gaining self-awareness, but it is the development of self-awareness and insight that will foster continual leader development over time.

Bruce Avolio (2005) emphasizes the importance of reflecting on leader development experiences and doing an 'after action review' that focuses on lessons learned. He also stresses the critical role that 'trigger events' – particular leadership challenges – play in providing key lessons for ongoing leader development. Many programs recommend keeping a journal of critical events for later self-reflection.

Experiential Learning

The use of experiential strategies, such as role-playing exercises and engaging in tasks that promote emotional and interpersonal skill development, is a hallmark of successful programs to promote emotional and interpersonal skill development. In training emotional skills/competencies, for instance, trainees will participate in exercises to try to recognize specific emotions (happiness, sadness, irritation) through facial expressions, tone of voice, and other cues. They may role-play emotionally-charged workplace situations (for example, dealing with an angry supervisee), or simply practice expressing emotions. At the same time, there are efforts to assign 'homework' to get participants to practice the techniques they are learning in their actual worksites.

Combining Formal Training and Experiential Development

While experiential learning is important for honing emotional and interpersonal competencies, it is a combination of 'learning about' and 'learning to do' that will be successful in developing these elusive and abstract competencies. The Mayer and Salovey abilities model represents this combination of learning about emotions and learning to perform (for example, being able to 'read' or decode emotional expressions). When it comes to developing emotional and interpersonal competencies it is important to know what to do as well as having the skills to perform the appropriate leader behavior.

Resources for Self-Development of Emotional and Interpersonal Competencies

In this final section, we will review books that focus on leadership development, with at least some emphasis on developing emotional and interpersonal competencies. This is not meant to be an exhaustive review, but is intended to be a starting point for leader development. Some of the books focus on leadership development more broadly, others are specific to emotional intelligence/competencies. Some are guides for trainers/facilitators, and others are meant for individual self-development.

General leader development guides
McCauley, C.D. and Van Velsor, E. (eds) (2004), *The Center for Creative Leadership Handbook of Leadership Development*, 2nd edn, San Francisco, CA: Jossey-Bass.

The Center for Creative Leadership's (CCL) comprehensive, edited handbook of leadership development (McCauley and Van Velsor, 2004), which will soon be released in its third edition, is a good resource for trainers, but also contains material of interest for anyone who is seriously interested in leadership development. CCL is one of the most respected sources for leadership development activities, because it grounds its programs and tools in scholarly research. The *Handbook* contains general information about areas of leadership development, but also covers specific programs and best practices.

Avolio, B.J. (2005), *Leadership Development in Balance: Made/Born*, Mahwah, NJ: Lawrence Erlbaum.

Written by one of the top leadership scholars, Avolio's guide to personal leadership development is strongly grounded in research, but written in a conversational tone. The author provides both examples of his personal leader development and his work with leadership development in organizations. Although only a portion focuses specifically on the development of emotional and interpersonal competencies, this is a comprehensive guidebook that can help in structuring a personal leadership development program and understanding the process.

Guides for developing emotional intelligence

Ciarrochi, J. and Mayer, J.D. (eds) (2007), *Applying Emotional Intelligence: A Practitioner's Guide*, New York: Psychology Press.

This brief, edited book focuses more broadly on emotional intelligence for various groups, including teachers, students and leaders. There are chapters that focus on developing emotional intelligence based on the abilities model, the mixed model (Boyatzis, 2007a), and an attempt to look for commonalities across the various models of emotional intelligence. The chapters are written by the leading scholars in each area. Although intended as a trainer/practitioner guide, the material is accessible and can be used for personal leader development.

Hughes, M., Patterson, L.B. and Terrell, J.B. (2005), *Emotional Intelligence in Action: Training and Coaching Activities for Leaders and Managers*, San Francisco, CA: Pfeiffer.

This is essentially a book of exercises for developing emotional competencies from a very broad, mixed-model approach. There is an attempt to connect the exercises to the various models of emotional intelligence, and there is a CD-ROM that contains handouts and materials for each exercise. It is primarily a guide for trainers, but could also be used in personal leader development. Because the authors are practitioners, not scholars, it is unclear whether there has been any research on the efficacy of the various training exercises, although many are relatively straightforward and the connections to the broad range of competencies are readily apparent. The authors have also published some additional tools for developing emotional intelligence, including measures of team emotional and social intelligence, all available from the same publisher.

Shankman, M.L. and Allen, S.J. (2008), *Emotionally Intelligent Leadership: A Guide for College Students*, San Francisco, CA: Jossey-Bass.

This book is designed as a sort of workbook for college students that would be incorporated into a leadership development class. It could also be used as a self-development guide, and is noteworthy because it is grounded in research on emotional intelligence.

Bar-On, R., Maree, J.G. and Elias, M.J. (eds) (2007), *Educating People to be Emotionally Intelligent*, Westport, CT: Praeger.

This book is more of a review of emotional intelligence interventions, with only a portion focusing on leadership and/or the workplace. It does contain descriptions of several programs, so may be useful to trainers and to persons trying to find out more about the breadth of work on developing emotional intelligence.

Developing Interpersonal Competencies

In contrast to emotional intelligence, there are surprisingly few guides for leaders to help develop the broader range of interpersonal skills and competencies. In some ways, the Dale Carnegie guides, and their many imitators, are just as good as the few interpersonal skill guidebooks for leader development. The modern best-selling version is Stephen Covey's (1989) *The 7 Habits of Highly Effective People*. In addition, there are a few textbooks designed to help develop leaders' and employees' interpersonal skills at work. We will note some examples of these. There are scholarly books on interpersonal skill development, with some applications to leadership, and these may be useful in becoming more informed. Finally, there are a number of 'pocket guides' related to interpersonal skill development. These will not be reviewed, although some offer good self-development tips.

Interpersonal skill development textbooks

De Janasz, S.C., Dowd, K.O. and Schneider, B. (2008), *Interpersonal Skills in Organizations*, 3rd edn. New York: McGraw-Hill.

Fritz, S.M., Lunde, J.P., Brown, W. and Banset, E.A. (2004), *Interpersonal Skills for Leadership*, 2nd edn, Upper Saddle River, NJ: Prentice-Hall.

Robbins, S.P. and Hunsaker, P.L. (2008), *Training in Interpersonal Skill*, 5th edn, Upper Saddle River, NJ: Prentice-Hall.

These books are most often used in courses in business schools, leadership programs and other professional programs to develop students' communication and interpersonal skills. They contain both a review of research and theory on communication and interpersonal interaction, but also practical exercises for improving leadership and organizational communication, useful in self-development. In addition, there are a number of textbooks on basic interpersonal communication that are typically taught in university schools of communication.

Research and theory in interpersonal competencies
Greene, J.O. and Burleson, B.R. (eds) (2003), *Handbook of Communication and Social Interaction Skills*, Mahwah, NJ: Lawrence Erlbaum.

This book represents a more scholarly guide to interpersonal and social interaction skills. Chapters include a review of social skills training and development, ways to assess interpersonal skills, specific skills such as persuasion and negotiation, and the like. Surprisingly, there is scant attention to developing interpersonal skills for leaders, but this is a good source for understanding the basics of interpersonal communication.

SUMMARY AND CONCLUSIONS

Despite the popularity of the construct of emotional intelligence, and the decades-long assertion that interpersonal skills are crucial for leadership success, research and development of emotional and interpersonal competencies are still in the nascent stage. There are a number of programs available to develop emotional intelligence and interpersonal skills for leaders/managers (and employees more generally), but there has been very little sound, systematic evaluation of the effectiveness of these programs. Although this is troubling from a research perspective, many of the elements of training emotional and interpersonal skills have a sort of 'face validity'. In other words, they are the sorts of exercises that common sense tells us would increase emotional and interpersonal skills. For example, becoming more aware of one's own emotions and being more attentive to the emotional communications of others would no doubt have some positive effect on emotional competency (the research question is whether it has a significant effect). On the interpersonal side, exercising conversational skills, or developing one's assertiveness, is likely to be beneficial despite the fact that there has been no good evaluation of whether these sorts of development programs actually enhance leadership effectiveness.

There are clearly some important issues that need to be resolved. For emotional intelligence, the ongoing debate is over the abilities versus the mixed models of emotional intelligence. Although this may not be such a major issue for the development of the broad range of abilities that constitute the domain of emotional intelligence, the fact that the mixed models often include personality, motivation and elements that go quite beyond mere emotional competencies, means that what is being represented as 'emotional intelligence' may, in some instances, have little to do with emotions. Perhaps a greater concern is understanding exactly how emotions and emotional communication play out in the context of leadership. For example, it is clear from decades of research that emotional expressiveness and particularly the expression of positive affect is related to a host of positive social outcomes, ranging from making people appear more attractive, honest/trustworthy, to actually influencing the moods of others (see Riggio, 1987, for a review of early research). So, leaders could be trained to be expressive and to portray positive emotions more frequently. Yet would this constitute emotional intelligence, and would this lead to positive outcomes? Perhaps this would only lead to surface-level change that followers and others might perceive as phony or inauthentic. In short, there is a great deal of research that needs to be done to better understand the connections between emotional competencies and effective leadership, in all their complexities. When we have reached this better understanding, then it will be easier to develop programs that actually develop the emotional competencies that enhance leader effectiveness. On a more positive note, however, becoming more aware of emotions and emotional communication is likely a good thing and it is unlikely that programs designed to enhance emotional competencies do any real harm.

While emotional intelligence is a relatively new construct, interpersonal competencies – the people skills of leaders – have been discussed in the management and leadership literature for nearly a hundred years. Experience and common sense both drive programs to develop leaders' interpersonal skills. It is amazing, however, that there is no general model or framework to guide interpersonal skill development. A general framework is badly needed to guide development efforts as well as assisting efforts to evaluate the impact and effectiveness of developing specific interpersonal skills.

Finally, emotional and interpersonal competencies are interrelated, so it may make sense to consider them together (Riggio and Lee, 2007). In some ways, the mixed model of emotional intelligence is doing this – moving beyond a focus on emotional competencies and including elements of interpersonal skill, but also personality traits and other constructs, but this is done in a somewhat haphazard manner. What is needed is a comprehensive framework that outlines both emotional and interpersonal competencies and demonstrates how they are different, but also how they are interrelated. Such a framework would be a significant advancement for guiding research and development efforts in these crucial skills that are so very important for leader effectiveness.

REFERENCES

Ashforth, B.E. and Humphrey, R.H. (1993), 'Emotional labor in service roles: the influence of identity', *Academy of Management Review*, **18**(1), 88–115.

Avolio, B.J. (2005), *Leadership Development in Balance: Made/Born*, Mahwah, NJ: Lawrence Erlbaum.

Avolio, B.J., and Hannah, S.T. (2008), 'Developmental readiness: accelerating leader development', *Consulting Psychology Journal: Practice and Research*, **60**(4), 331–47.

Bar-On, R. (1997), *BarOn Emotional Quotient Inventory: Technical manual*, Toronto: Multi-Health Systems.

Bar-On, R. (2007), 'How important is it to educate people to be emotionally intelligent, and can it be done?', in R. Bar-On, J.G. Maree and M.J. Elias (eds), *Educating People to be Emotionally Intelligent*, Westport, CT: Praeger, pp. 1–14.

Bar-On, R., Maree, J.G. and Elias, M.J. (eds) (2007), *Educating People to be Emotionally Intelligent*, Westport, CT: Praeger.

Bass, B.M. (1990), *Bass and Stogdill's Handbook of Leadership: Theory, Research, and Managerial Applications*, 3rd edn, New York: Free Press.

Bass, B.M. (2008), *The Bass Handbook of Leadership: Theory, Research, and Managerial Applications*, 4th edn, New York: Free Press.

Bellack, A.S. (2004), 'Skills training for people with severe mental illness', *Psychiatric Rehabilitation Journal*, **27**, 375–91.

Boyatzis, R.E. (2007a), 'Developing emotional intelligence competencies', in J. Ciarrochi and J.D. Mayer (eds), *Applying Emotional Intelligence: A Practitioner's Guide*, New York: Psychology Press, pp. 28–52.

Boyatzis, R.E. (2007b), 'Developing emotional intelligence through coaching for leadership, professional and occupational excellence', in R. Bar-On, J.G. Maree and M.J. Elias (eds), *Educating People to be Emotionally Intelligent*, Westport, CT: Praeger, pp. 155–68.

Boyatzis, R.E. and McKee, A. (2006), *Resonant Leadership: Renewing Yourself and Connecting with Others Through Mindfulness, Hope and Compassion*, Boston, MA: Harvard Business School Press.

Boyatzis, R.E. and Saatcioglu, A. (2007), 'A 20-year view of trying to develop emotional, social and cognitive intelligence competencies in graduate management education', *Journal of Management Development*, **27**(1), 92–108.

Boyatzis, R.E., Goleman, D. and Rhee, K. (2000), 'Clustering competence in emotional intelligence: Insights from the Emotional Competence Inventory (ECI)', in R. Bar-on and J.D. Parker (eds), *Handbook of Emotional Intelligence*, San Francisco, CA: Jossey-Bass, pp. 343–62.

Boyatzis, R.E., Stubbs, E.C., and Taylor, S.N. (2002), 'Learning cognitive and emotional intelligence competencies through graduate management education', *Academy of Management Learning and Education*, **1**(2), 150–62.

Brotheridge, C.M. and Lee, R.T. (2002), 'Testing a conservation of resources model of the dynamics of emotional labor', *Journal of Occupational Health Psychology*, **7**(1), 57–67.

Carnegie, D. (1913), *Public Speaking and Influencing Men in Business*, New York: Association Press.

Carnegie, D. (1937), *How to Win Friends and Influence people*, New York: Simon and Schuster.

Ciarrochi, J. and Mayer, J.D. (eds) (2007), *Applying Emotional Intelligence: A Practitioner's Guide*, New York: Psychology Press.

Clifton, D.O. and Nelson, P. (1992), *Soar with your Strengths*, New York: Delacorte.

Conger, J.A. and Toegel, G. (2003), 'Action learning and multi-rater feedback: pathways to leadership development?', in S.E. Murphy and R.E. Riggio (eds), *The Future of Leadership Development*, Mahwah, NJ: Lawrence Erlbaum Associates, pp. 107–25.

Costanzo, M. (1992), 'Training students to decode verbal and nonverbal cues: effects on confidence and performance', *Journal of Educational Psychology*, **84**(3), 308–13.

Covey, S.R. (1989), *The 7 Habits of Highly Effective People*, New York: Simon and Schuster.

Dasborough, M.T. and Ashkanasy, N.M. (2002), 'Emotion and attribution of intentionality in leader–member relationships', *The Leadership Quarterly*, **13**(5), 615–34.

Day, D.V. (2000), 'Leadership development: a review in context', *The Leadership Quarterly*, **11**, 581–613.

De Janasz, S.C., Dowd, K.O. and Schneider, B. (2008), *Interpersonal Skills in Organizations*, 3rd edn, New York: McGraw-Hill.

Dotlich, D.L. and Noel, J.L. (1998), *Action Learning*, San Francisco, CA: Jossey-Bass.

Downey, L.A., Papageorgiou, V. and Stough, C. (2006), 'Examining the relationship between leadership, emotional intelligence and intuition in senior female managers', *Leadership and Organization Development Journal*, **27**(4), 250–64.

Dulewicz, V., Higgs, M. and Slaski, M. (2003), 'Measuring emotional intelligence: content, construct and criterion-related validity', *Journal of Managerial Psychology*, **18**(5), 405–20.

Elfenbein, H.A. (2006), 'Learning in emotion judgments: training and the cross-cultural understanding of facial expressions', *Journal of Nonverbal Behavior*, **30**, 21–36.

Frijda, N.H. (1986), *The Emotions*, Cambridge, UK: Cambridge University Press.

Fritz, S.M., Lunde, J.P., Brown, W. and Banset, E.A. (2004), *Interpersonal Skills for Leadership*, 2nd edn, Upper Saddle River, NJ: Prentice-Hall.

Gardner, H. (1983), *Frames of Mind: The Theory of Multiple Intelligences*, New York: Basic Books.

George, J.M. (2000), 'Emotions and leadership: the role of emotional intelligence', *Human Relations*, **53**, 1027–55.

Goleman, D. (1995), *Emotional Intelligence: Why it can Matter More than IQ*, New York: Bantam.

Goleman, D. (1998), *Working with Emotional Intelligence*, New York: Bantam.

Gottman, J.M., Katz, L.F. and Hooven, C. (1997), *Meta-emotion: How Families Communicate Emotionally*, Hillsdale, NJ: Lawrence Erlbaum.

Greene, J.O., and Burleson, B.R. (eds) (2003), *Handbook of Communication and Social Interaction Skills*, Mahwah, NJ: Lawrence Erlbaum.

Gross, J.J. (1998), 'Sharpening the focus: emotion regulation, arousal, and social competence', *Psychological Inquiry*, **9**, 287–90.

Gross, J.J. (ed.) (2007), *Handbook of Emotion Regulation*, New York: Guilford Press.

Groves, K.S., McEnrue, M.P. and Shen, W. (2008), 'Developing and measuring the emotional intelligence of leaders', *Journal of Management Development*, **27**(2), 225–50.

Guilford, J.P. (1967), *The Nature of Human Intelligence*, New York: McGraw-Hill.

Hopkins, M.M., O'Neil, D.A. and Williams, H.W. (2007), 'Emotional intelligence and board governance: leadership lessons from the public sector', *Journal of Managerial Psychology*, **22**(7), 683–700.

Hughes, M., Patterson, L.B. and Terrell, J.B. (2005), *Emotional Intelligence in Action: Training and Coaching Activities for Leaders and Managers*, San Francisco, CA: Pfeiffer.

Hunt, J.W. and Baruch, Y. (2003), 'Developing top managers: the impact of interpersonal skills training', *Journal of Management Development*, **22**(8), 729–52.

Ickes, W., Marangoni, C. and Garcia, S. (1997), 'Studying empathic accuracy in a clinically relevant context', in W. Ickes (ed.), *Empathic Accuracy*, New York: Guilford Press, pp. 282–310.

Izard, C. (1990), 'Facial expressions and the regulation of emotions', *Journal of Personality and Social Psychology*, **58**, 487–98.

Judge, T.A., Piccolo, R.F. and Ilies, R. (2004), 'The forgotten ones? The validity of consideration and initiating structure in leadership research', *Journal of Applied Psychology*, **89**(1), 36–51.

Kellett, J.B., Humphrey, R.H. and Sleeth, R.G. (2002), 'Empathy and complex task performance: two routes to leadership', *The Leadership Quarterly*, **13**(5), 523–44.

Lee, S. and Olszewski-Kubilius, P. (2006), 'The emotional intelligence, moral judgment, and leadership of academically gifted adolescents', *Journal for the Education of the Gifted*, **30**(1), 29–67.

Locke, E.A. and Latham, G.P. (1984), *Goal Setting: A Motivational Technique that Works*, Englewood Cliffs, NJ: Prentice-Hall.

Mayer, J.D. and Salovey, P. (1993), 'The intelligence of emotional intelligence', *Intelligence*, **17**, 433–42.

Mayer, J D. and Salovey, P. (1997), 'What is emotional intelligence?', in P. Salovey and D. Sluyter (eds), *Emotional Development and Emotional Intelligence: Implications for Educators*, New York: Basic Books, pp. 3–31.

Mayer, J.D., Caruso, D.R. and Salovey, P. (1999), 'Emotional intelligence meets traditional standards for an intelligence', *Intelligence*, **27**, 267–98.

Mayer, J.D., Salovey, P. and Caruso, D.R. (2000), 'Models of emotional intelligence', in R.J. Sternberg (ed.), *The Handbook of Intelligence*, New York: Cambridge University Press, pp. 396–420.

Mayer, J.D., Salovey, P. and Caruso, D.R. (2008), 'Emotional intelligence: new ability or eclectic traits', *American Psychologist*, **63**(6), 503–17.

Mayer, J., Salovey, P., Caruso, D.R. and Sitarenios, G. (2003), 'Measuring emotional intelligence with the MSCEIT V2.0', *Emotion*, **3**(1), 97–105.

McCauley, C.D. and Van Velsor, E. (eds) (2004), *The Center for Creative Leadership Handbook of Leadership Development*, 2nd edn, San Francisco, CA: Jossey-Bass.

McEnrue, M.P., Groves, K.S., and Shen, W. (2009), 'Emotional intelligence training: evidence regarding its efficacy for developing leaders', unpublished manuscript, California State University, Los Angeles.

Mintzberg, H. (2004), *Managers not MBAs: A Hard Look at the Soft Practice of Managing and Management Development*, New York: Prentice-Hall.

Mueser, K.T. and Bellack, A.S. (2007), 'Social skills training: alive and well?', *Journal of Mental Health*, **16**(5), 549–52.

Murphy, K.R. (ed.) (2006), *Critique of Emotional Intelligence: What are the Problems, and How Can they be Fixed?*, Mahwah, NJ: Lawrence Erlbaum.

Porter, L.W. and McKibbin, L.E. (1988), *Management Education and Development: Drift or Thrust into the 21st Century*, New York: McGraw-Hill.

Reichard, R.J. and Riggio, R.E. (2008), 'An interactive, process model of emotions and leadership', in N.M. Ashkanasy and C.L. Cooper (eds), *Research Companion to Emotions in Organizations*, Cheltenham, UK and Northampton, MA, USA: Edward Elgar, pp. 512–27.

Riggio, R.E. (1986), 'Assessment of basic social skills', *Journal of Personality and Social Psychology*, **51**, 649–60.

Riggio, R.E. (1987), *The Charisma Quotient*, New York: Dodd Mead.

Riggio, R.E. (2005), 'The Social Skills Inventory (SSI): measuring nonverbal and social skills', in V. Manusov (ed.), *The Sourcebook of Nonverbal Measures: Going Beyond Words*, Mahwah, NJ: Lawrence Erlbaum, pp. 25–33.

Riggio, R.E. (2006a), 'Nonverbal skills and abilities', in V. Manusov and M. Patterson (eds), *The SAGE Handbook of Nonverbal Communication*, Thousand Oaks, CA: Sage, pp. 79-95.

Riggio, R.E. (2006b), 'Behavioral approach to leadership', in S. Rogelberg (ed.), *Encyclopedia of Industrial/organizational Psychology*, Thousand Oaks, CA: Sage, pp. 48–50.

Riggio, R.E., and Carney, D.O. (2003), *Manual for the Social Skills Inventory*, 2nd edn, Redwood City, CA: MindGarden.

Riggio, R.E. and Lee, J. (2007), 'Emotional and interpersonal competencies and leader development', *Human Resources Management Review*, **17**(4), 418–26.

Riggio, R.E., and Riggio, H.R. (2008), 'Social psychology and charismatic leadership', in D.R. Forsyth, C. Hoyt and G. Goethals (eds), *Leadership at the Crossroads: Social Psychology and Leadership*, Westport, CT: Praeger Press, pp. 30–44.

Riggio, R.E., Murphy, S.E. and Pirozzolo, F.J. (eds), (2002), *Multiple Intelligences and Leadership*, Mahwah, NJ: Lawrence Erlbaum Associates.

Robbins, S.P. and Hunsaker, P.L. (2008), *Training in Interpersonal Skills*, 5th edn, Upper Saddle River, NJ: Prentice-Hall.

Rosenthal, R. (ed.) (1979), *Skill in Nonverbal Communication*, Boston, MA: Oelgeschlager, Gunn, and Hain.

Rubin, R.S., Munz, D.C. and Bommer, W.H. (2005), 'Leading from within: the effects of emotion recognition and personality on transformational leadership behavior', *Academy of Management Journal*, **48**, 845–58.

Salovey, P. and Mayer, J.D. (1990), 'Emotional intelligence', *Imagination, Cognition, and Personality*, **9**, 185–211.

Satterfield, J.M. and Hughes, E. (2007), 'Emotion skills training for medical students: a systematic review', *Medical Education*, **41**, 935–41.

Shankman, M.L. and Allen, S.J. (2008), *'Emotionally Intelligent Leadership: A Guide for College Students*, San Francisco, CA: Jossey-Bass.

Silver, H., Goodman, C. Knoll, G., and Isakov, V. (2004), 'Brief emotion training improves recognition of facial emotions in chronic schizophrenia: a pilot study', *Psychiatry Research*, **128**, 147–54.

Tiedens, L.Z. (2000), 'Powerful emotions: the vicious cycle of social status positions and emotions', in N.M. Ashkanasy, C.E. Hartel and W.J. Zerbe (eds), *Emotions in the Workplace: Research, Theory, and Practice*, Westport, CT: Greenwood, pp. 72–81.

Trower, P., Bryant, B. and Argyle, M. (1978), *Social Skills and Mental Health*, London: Methuen.

Van Velsor, E., Moxley, R.S. and Bunker, K.A. (2004), 'The leader development process', in C.D. McCauley and E. Van Velsor (eds), *The Center for Creative Leadership Handbook of Leadership Development*, 2nd edn, San Francisco, CA: Jossey-Bass, pp. 204–33.
Vroom, V.H. and Yetton, P.W. (1973), *Leadership and Decision-making*, Pittsburgh, PA: University of Pittsburgh Press.

7. How to matter

Stewart Emery

Today, if someone took a poll of your customers, constituents, followers – whatever – and asked if you matter to them, how do you think you would come out? If you ceased to exist tomorrow, do you think anyone would *really* care? In other words, has your product, service, or brand established an emotional connection with your customers to the extent that they are invested in your enduring success?

This is the deep soul-searching question we want you to ask yourself. Really, honestly, answer this. Are you a positive force in people's lives? If you disappeared, would their lives be diminished in some way?

DO YOU, IN FACT, MATTER?

This is a question we ask senior managers to answer about their brand or business. The question takes on an added dimension when asked as a personal question. As a leader, as a manager, as an individual contributor, ask yourself three questions:

Who are you? Think about this. At a very deep level this question probes to the core of what you stand for – your core values as a person and what deeply matters to you. This is a question that is not served by a series of rapid responses, but rather by a period of contemplative inquiry. You might be certain that you know the answer; however, ask some people you trust, who see you in action, what they think matters to you – what you're about based on the way you act in daily personal and professional life.

What do you provide? As a leader, as a manager, as contributor in life? Here again it is worth asking other people what they count on you for, the value they see you bring to situations and opportunities. Be prepared to be surprised – some people will see in you qualities they that you have perhaps taken for granted and that they value highly. Quality answers to this question enable you to further develop yourself. In a world in which lifetime employment is an idea whose time has passed, what is next is the idea of lifetime employability.

Why does it matter? The answer is a two-part thing. Of course you have to know why it matters to you. I spend a significant amount of time interviewing people who are world class at what they do. Part of being world class at something is being totally clear about the answer to this question. Again, no rapid responses on this one. Contemplation is required. Hold the question in your mind until an answer that you can trust arises in consciousness. Then you can hear the answer of why what you're about matters to other people – people you lead and/or manage along with customers and stakeholders.

Why do you matter? Well, you will be closing in on the answer to this question by now along with the answer to the next one:

Do you, in fact, matter? While you are contemplating this (it is more a question to keep lastingly in mind rather than to find your final answer for) I would like to propose a somewhat non-traditional view of leadership. The traditional view assumes the existence of followers in an organized hierarchical structure. There is another space of leadership living at a level beyond titles.

HOW TO MATTER

Most of us can remember conversations that leave a lasting imprint and may forever change us for the better. The dialogue in the story that follows redefined for me the way I think about leadership. Perhaps it will also impact on you in a good way.

Although an exceptionally successful entrepreneur and leader, Ed Penhoet is not a naturally charismatic man, at least until he starts talking about something that matters to him. When he does, a passionate intensity drives a simple eloquence that commands attention. At the time of this interview, Ed was providing leadership to the Gordon and Betty Moore foundation, one of the largest private foundations in the world.

In the 1970s, Ed was a faculty member of the Biochemistry Department of UC Berkeley. In 1981, he co-founded Chiron Corporation and served as its Chief Executive Officer until 1998. Beginning with the sequencing of the HIV genome in 1984 and discovery of the Hepatitis C genome in 1987, Chiron has been a consistent leader in making groundbreaking discoveries in the field of medical research. Since he knows a thing or two about enduring success, Mark Thompson and I were there to interview him for our book *Success Built to Last: Creating a Life That Matters* (Porras et al., 2006).

Towards the end of the dialogue, I asked Ed what advice he could offer freshly minted college students about to start a career in what passes for the real world. He lit up and said, 'I'm so glad you asked!' To my astonishment (he's a scientist remember) he proclaimed through a mischievous grin 'I'm a big believer in fortune cookies! When I was a professor at Berkeley, I once got one that said, "Whatever you are, be a good one". And to me that's the only [business] advice I can give anybody.'

'When you are good at one thing, doors open up in front of you. People want to work with you, so people provide opportunities to you. You don't have to go looking for them. Usually, they come to find you,' he said.

'Success is always built on doing well the job that's in front of you today, not being resentful that you don't have a CEO job yet,' Penhoet said. 'In fact, it's an amazing phenomenon. I see it in MBAs in particular. They all think because they have an MBA, they ought to be at least a senior vice president [by] the next week. But what they need to do is prove that they can actually do something well,' Penhoet insisted.

'In my own life, I found that people who are always worried about the next move in the chess game of their life never quite get at that move. Don't think that way because, if you're always worrying about the next step, it will compromise your ability to do your current job well,' Penhoet said.

'People get to know you as the person who does a good job or the one who does a bad job. You won't be remembered as having done that job badly – you'll be remembered as a person who does a bad job.' Ed thinks that your determination to become good at what you do – for its own sake – is an essential key to success. 'After all, if you find it's impossible to go deep, then you've found out something valuable – you shouldn't be doing it – it's not your calling,' he said.

Opportunity comes from expertise, not just luck, talent and passion. If you find yourself striving for excellence that is unreachable, joyless, or precipitates the kind of misery you find in a Stephen King horror movie, take this as a message to move on to something else. For the pursuit of becoming a good one to transform your life, it must reach into your heart in a personal way to unlock all you have to give.

A week or two later, I was interviewing Alice Waters at her restaurant, Chez Panisse, in Berkeley. The restaurant was named Best Restaurant in America by *Gourmet* magazine in 2001. *Cuisine et Vins de France* listed Alice as one of the ten best chefs in the world in 1986.

I asked Alice how she defined success for herself. She simply replied that she had never thought about becoming successful, she had simply always focused on becoming very good at what really matters to her.

I then headed back to the room in which I write and began to revisit many of the interviews that were a part of the Success Built to Last project to find out how often this idea of being a good one was a refrain. Very often as it turned out. I suspect it would have been often to the point of being universal if Mark and I had specifically gone searching for the idea when we did the original interviews.

The people we talked with who did bring up the theme of being a good one would always go on to talk about the transformational power of becoming good at something that matters to you, something you love to do. These people would light up as they talked about how learning to become good at something is literally life changing. Alice Waters evangelized with shining eyes how important it was to get this message out to young people in high schools and colleges.

I remembered back to my report cards from high school that noted, 'he excels at anything that he is interested in and pretty much ignores everything else'. At the time I interpreted this commentary as an indictment – only to find out too many years later this was a trait shared by successful people.

At my father-in-law's 85th birthday dinner in Beverly Hills, with many of the invited guests around the same age, I noticed that the most alive people present were those still committed to being good at things that mattered to them. At the other end of the spectrum, we have all been touched by toddlers filled with wonder at the discovery that they can get better at doing the things that capture their imagination!

Consider this. If you are really, really good at doing something you love, you'll be at the leading edge of the bell curve and you will therefore be a leader. And you will matter.

Actor Sally Field got excited in a dialog about leadership and exclaimed,

> Be excellent at something you love, that's the only way you can be a leader. Who wakes up one day and asks, 'shall I go to school or shall I be a leader? Let's see, what shall I do today? I think I'm going to go out and lead.' It's a non-thing – it's a non-thing. That [leadership] happens – by accident. After you've pursued and struggled and kicked yourself around the block four hundred gazillion times – and one day you look up and say 'OK, I've done that and I've done that' and people are turning to you and saying 'lead us.'

The implicit assertion here is that your leadership journey begins with getting clear about what you love to do and learning how to get really, really good at it. We agree. Totally.

Love It or Lose

Much is said today about the importance of loving what you do, but most people simply pay lip service to the idea. Sure, it would be nice to do what you love, but as a practical matter, most people don't feel they can afford such a luxury. For many, doing something that really matters to them would be a sentimental fantasy based on wishful thinking.

It's dangerous not to do what you love. You may hear this as really bad news. The harsh reality is that if you don't love what you're doing, you'll lose to someone who does! For every person who is half-hearted about their work or relationships, there is someone else who loves what they're half-hearted about. This person will work harder and longer. They will outrun you. Although it might feel safer to hang onto an old role, you'll find your energy is depleted and, guess what, you'll be the first in line for the layoffs when they come. And they are coming. Will be for a while.

'You can survive without loving it, but you will be second-rate', said Brigadier General Clara Adams-Ender, ret. 'To spend any part of your career not knowing why you're there will take your power away.' It's dangerous not to be fully engaged. If you want to have success that outlasts any job you have, then only love will find the way.

Warren Buffett loved his work long before he had two pennies to rub together. Today, he is one of the richest men on earth. 'I always worry about people who say, "you know, I'm going to do this for ten years. I really don't like it very well, but I'll do ten more years of this and then . . ." I mean, that's a little like saving up sex for your old age. Not a very good idea', Buffett laughed.

'The only way to be truly satisfied is to do what you believe is great work', said Apple co-founder and CEO, Steve Jobs, in his now famous and intimate 2005 commencement speech at Stanford University.

> And the only way to do great work is to love what you do. If you haven't found it yet, keep looking. And that is as true for your work as it is for your lovers. As with all matters of the heart, you'll know when you find it. And, like any great relationship, it just gets better and better as the years roll on. So keep looking until you find it. Don't settle

he insisted.

Check in with yourself and ask, 'Self, am I really doing something I love?' Another way of getting at the answer is to ask, 'At work, do I have the opportunity to do what I do best every day?' If your answer is yes, move on to the next section, as they say in the quick start guides. If no, then you have some work to do.

Assuming a 'yes' to the above question, here is the next question: 'Do you actually know how to get really, really good at doing something that you love?' This is perhaps the most essential skill you need to develop to achieve lifelong employability in the global marketplace. Surprisingly, even people who have achieved pre-eminence in a field often cannot accurately articulate how they did it – they just did it. Sometimes with the best of intentions they will be happy to tell how they did it, except what they tell you won't be it! Not that they would be trying to lead you astray. They are simply not aware of the precise details of the process they used to achieve excellence.

Around three years ago, Geoffrey Colvin (*Fortune* Magazine) posed the question, what makes Tiger Woods great? What made Berkshire Hathaway Chairman Warren Buffett the world's premier investor? We think we know: each was a natural who came into the world with a gift for doing exactly what he ended up doing. As Buffett told *Fortune* not so long ago, he was 'wired at birth to allocate capital'. Well, with all due respect Warren, you would be wrong about that.

The notion that a lucky few win the game of conception roulette and are born with talent into a world of opportunity is mythic and toxic nonsense. The best definition I ever heard of a myth was from a boy in grade school who said 'A myth is something that is true on the inside but not true on the outside'. In other words, a myth is something that lives inside you as a belief, as a building block of your internal construction of reality, but is at odds with external reality.

This myth is toxic because if you believe it, you will rob yourself of power and consign yourself to a life of squandered possibilities. People hate abandoning the notion that they would coast to fame and fortune if they could only find their talent. But this view is tragically toxic, because it will keep people on the yellow brick road looking for the Wizard in all the wrong places. When they stumble on the inevitable loose bricks, they conclude that they just aren't gifted and give up.

Let's set the record straight. From a body of research published in 1996, edited by K. Anders Ericsson, and being made famous by Malcolm Gladwell in *Outliers* (2008) as *The 10,000 Hour-Rule*, you will learn you were not born to be 'a butcher, a baker, or a candlestick maker' or an exceptional manager, a great leader, or a world class anything. You do not possess a natural gift for a certain vocation, because targeted natural gifts don't exist.

This is not a popular idea because it is a good news/bad news kind of deal. First the bad. If you really grasp this, you are left with nowhere to hide. Now the good news. If you really grasp this, you are left with nowhere to hide. If you have ever hesitated to pursue your passion because you doubted that you had the talent for it, rejoice. Your lack of a natural gift is irrelevant – this has little or nothing to do with greatness. You can, if you want to, make yourself into any number of things, and you can even make yourself great. You can get to be really good at anything you love to do if you grasp the true nature of the 10 000 hour-rule, which basically asserts that if you put in 10 000 hours of work over a 10-year period you can get world class at anything (you love to do), and talent has nothing to do with it.

Unfortunately for the world of readers keeping *Outliers* on the New York Times Best Sellers List for more than half a year, Gladwell does not emphasize the Meta message of the rule. You can put in 10 000 hours doing something and not get to be world class at it or even really good. Been on a golf course lately? Enough said. To become really good at doing something you have to adopt a discipline that Ericsson calls *Deliberate Practice*. Simply put, an activity becomes a deliberate practice when you do what you do with an intention of becoming progressively, measurably better at doing it. This takes disciplined self-management and a highly developed awareness of process.

Back to golf for a moment. Simply going out and hitting a bucket of balls on a semi-regular schedule is not deliberate practice, which is why most golfers don't get much better. Hitting an 8 iron 300 times with a goal of leaving the ball within 20 feet of the pin 80 percent of the time, continually observing results and making appropriate adjustments, and doing that for hours every day – that's deliberate practice. The best people in any field are those who devote the most hours to deliberate practice. This requires that you design activity that's explicitly intended to improve your performance that has you reaching for objectives just beyond your current level of competence, activity that provides feedback on results and involves high levels of conscious repetition.

Obviously this takes a great deal of self-management. It also takes high levels of awareness that must be developed along the way. Here's why. In our conversations with highly successful people, we find that they are able to make extraordinarily fine distinctions about the various elements comprising their field of passion that the rest of us cannot make. I am on the advisory board of Equator Estate Coffees & Teas. Run by two exceptional women, they supply roasted coffee to some of the best restaurants on earth, notably Thomas Keller's *French Laundry* and restaurant group. Here is a *brief* description of one of my favorites, their organic espresso; 'Oaky base notes are topped off with accents of spice (nutmeg) and unsweetened cocoa. Smooth mouth-feel and finish' and a more detailed description by Kenneth Davids (the Robert Parker of Coffee) of their Aleta Wondo from Western Ethiopia, 'Pungent fir, nut-toned chocolate in the aroma. Rich acidity, lightly syrupy mouthfeel. A spicy lemon dominates in the cup, supported by continued nut and chocolate notes. Long, deep-toned finish, fading to a very slight astringency.'

Can you make these distinctions in your morning cup of Joe? That would probably be a no. It has taken me five years to develop my palette and the levels of awareness to cup coffee (the coffee equivalent of wine tasting) at Equator. And I will never be a Kenneth Davids.

The level of awareness required to be able to make fine distinctions is key to Tiger's golf game and Buffet's performance at Berkshire Hathaway. You will have to develop the awareness required for your desired levels of achievement in any field of human endeavor that matters to you. This awareness is developed in the disciplined process of deep and deliberate practice. It is not easy. If it were, then, as they say, 'everybody would do it'.

In the spirit of the idea that you are not born to be great but you can grow to be great, talent is being defined as any recurring pattern of thinking, feeling or behavior that can be productively applied. This definition is not traditional. World-class performance in any role requires that you develop world-class talent. While you may still be holding on to the belief that talent is a quality reserved for the special few, almost all of us have patterns of thinking, feeling and behavior that can be productively applied or we can surely develop them. Doing so represents one of the secrets to true success in life.

The evidence, scientific as well as anecdotal, seems overwhelmingly in favor of deliberate practice as the way talent is developed to source great performance. In *The Talent Code*, a wonderfully written book by Daniel Coyle (2009), you will find an elegant and practical exposition on exactly how to go about growing to be great. Coyle has coined the term 'Deep Practice' as an alternative to Ericsson's Deliberate Practice. In many ways the term 'Deep Practice' is more descriptive of the nature of the discipline and self-management involved. Enduringly successful people develop amazing depths of knowledge and skill in the endeavors that matter to them.

So how do you develop a deep and deliberate practice for business? Many elements of business, in fact, lend themselves to deep and deliberate practice. Presenting, negotiating, delivering evaluations, and deciphering financial statements – you can practice them all. While not the essence of great managerial or leadership performance, they are none the less skills that matter. Great management and leadership performance requires making judgments and decisions with imperfect information in an uncertain world, interacting with people, and the possession of well rounded so-called 'soft' skills. Can you practice these things too? You can, though not in the way you would practice a Bach partita.

Instead, it's all about refining how you go about doing what you're already doing to create your work as a deliberate practice. Make the following critical change. Start going about every task with an additional goal. Instead of merely doing it to get it done, intend to get better at it. Preparing a special report involves finding information, analysis, integration and presentation – each step requiring the productive application of patterns of thinking and behavior. These steps all involve improvable skills.

Anything that anyone does at work, from the lowliest task to the most elevated, involves an improvable skill. To improve, self-manage yourself out of your Comfort Zone and into the Performance Zone where you are operating just beyond what you think are your limits. As a manager and leader, arguably your most important job is to develop talent and turn talent into performance. You do this with yourself, you do this with others, and you do this with teams.

Mindset matters
Armed with a mindset of deep and deliberate practice, people engage in work in a new way. Research shows they will process information more deeply and retain it longer. They seek more information on what they're doing and explore other perspectives. They adopt a longer-term point of view. In each activity this mindset is present. You aren't just doing the job; you're also explicitly trying to get better at it in measurable ways.

Again, research shows that this difference in mindset is vital. By way of example, when amateur dancers take lessons and practice, they report that they experience dancing as fun, and a release of tension. For professional dancers, it is different. They enter into a state of deep concentration and focus on improving their performance during the lessons and during practice. They have worked out a system technically known as a feedback loop to track their improvement. Some days, progress seems painful or nonexistent. This is another reason you have to love what you do. Only loving it will get you through the pain of gain. To the casual observer the amateur and the professional appear to be engaged in the same activity. However, the mindset and therefore the outcomes are radically different.

THE SECRET LIFE OF GOALS

Feedback is crucial, and in professional sports feedback is in your face on a play-by-play, stroke-by-stroke basis. You made the basket or you didn't. You sank the putt or you didn't. In business and in life feedback matters just as much, and getting it should be no problem. Yet most people don't go looking for it and may go out of their way to avoid getting it. What to do? Now the self-managing process of setting goals becomes truly useful – vital actually. Many of us have been exhorted to set goals. We have been told this is the secret of success. Ask why, however, and you'll get mostly not-useful answers.

But goals do matter. Learn to set small goals that measure incremental improvement in the direction of the big goal. This is a little-understood purpose of goals. They are the metrics of deep and deliberate practice. There is something profoundly satisfying about discovering tomorrow that you are more effective than you thought you were yesterday. Deep and deliberate practice tracked by the achievement of incremental goals will give you this. People consistently tell us that once they make the commitment to a deep and deliberate practice for excellence in a field that they love, their life immediately becomes a richer experience. Scientists and performance psychologists really have cracked the code for human achievement and satisfaction.

Many people protest that they feel work is already hard enough and they simply don't have the energy to push harder. On further probing we inevitably discover that these souls are not nurtured because they are not in fact doing something that they love and that deeply matters to them. This said, I am not an advocate of a relentless push to greatness for all people. I'm tempted to propose that good is the new great. As an idea this may get howled down, but really, we all need to make a life and not just a living. In any event, following your passion, finding out what really matters to you, and committing to a deliberate practice for getting good at it will enrich your life.

Go forth and matter!

Try this Practical Approach to Deep and Deliberate Practice

1. Go about each activity that matters with an explicit goal of getting better at it.
2. Develop a series of achievable 'mini goals' to measure your progress.
3. As you engage in an activity, be aware of what's happening and why you're doing what you're doing the way you are. Welcome your mistakes, back up and find a better way forward.
4. During and after the activity, get feedback on your performance from multiple sources. Make changes in your actions as necessary.
5. Continually develop your ability to make fine distinctions as you build mental models of your industry, your company and your career. Expand models to include more detailed distinctions.
6. Do these steps regularly, not intermittently. Sporadic practice does not work.
7. Seek out and keep the company of others who are engaged in deep and deliberate practice on their journey to excellence in a field that matters to them.

SUGGESTED READING

Brunner, R. and Emery, S. (with Hall, R.) (2009), *Do you Matter?: How Great Design will Make People Love your Company*, Upper Saddle River, NJ: Pearson Education.

Colvin, G. (2006), 'What it takes to be great', *Fortune*, **154** (9), 30 October.

Coyle, D. (2009), *The Talent Code: Greatness isn't Born. It's Grown. Here's How*, New York: Bantam Dell.

Ericsson, K.A. (ed.) (1996), *The Road to Excellence: The Acquisition of Expert Performance in the Arts and Sciences, Sports and Games*, Mahwah, NJ: Lawrence Erlbaum.

Gladwell, M. (2008), *Outliers: The Story of Success*, New York: Little, Brown and Company.

Jobs, S. (2005), '"You've got to find what you love." Jobs says', *Stanford Report*, 14 June.

Porras, J., Emery, S. and Thompson, M. (2006), *Success Built to Last: Creating a Life that Matters*, Upper Saddle River, NJ: Pearson Education.

PART II

The Self-Management of Common
Leadership Challenges

8.   Managing your leadership career in hard times

**John Blenkinsopp, Yehuda Baruch and
Ruth Winden**

INTRODUCTION

In this chapter we seek to blend an overview of theory and research with a discussion of the practical implications of this work for your own career. Those who take on leadership roles in organizations are often perceived to be highly careerist and therefore, it is assumed, active in managing their own careers. In our experience such individuals are often a good deal less careerist than one might imagine and may lack career management skills. The original title of this chapter was 'Managing your leadership career', and we thought long and hard before adding 'in hard times' to give it a focus on the current economic situation. However, we felt we couldn't ignore it – recession is likely to have a major effect on leadership careers, derailing some and enhancing others. Perhaps the most vivid recent example is the way in which the financial meltdown of September 2008 proved to be the pivotal moment in the careers of two well-known senators, testing their leadership credentials in ways that led one to victory and the White House, and the other to defeat. Though focusing on hard times might seem to make the chapter rather specific, career management approaches which work in recession will also work in times of growth. More importantly, while it is possible to have a successful career in a time of growth without engaging in effective career management, the same is not true in a time of recession.

THE CHANGING CONTEXT OF CAREERS

Collin and Watts (1996) suggest that significant structural changes within most Western countries have led to changes in the nature of career – see Sullivan and Baruch (2009) for a recent review. This proposition is widely cited though still controversial (Currie et al., 2006; Dany et al., 2003).

These 'contemporary careers' (Arthur, 2008) – conceptualized variously as the intelligent (DeFillippi and Arthur, 1994), protean (Hall, 1976; 1996), boundaryless (Arthur and Rousseau, 1996) or post-corporate career (Peiperl and Baruch, 1997) – have two broad elements. The first is the argument that careers are increasingly pursued across various boundaries, in particular organizational boundaries (Arthur and Rousseau, 1996), the second that careers are to be understood in terms of personal learning and growth (Hall, 1996). Mark Twain drily noted that the reports of his death had been exaggerated, and the same is true of the demise of the organizational career (Baruch, 2006; Lips-Wiersma and Hall, 2007). For example, there *is* some evidence of a reduction in the average length of time people stay in post, but it's not a radical reduction. One UK estimate suggests the average is down to five years, where previously it was seven years, and for the US it is suggested to be down to four years – undoubtedly a significant change, but still showing a trend for the 'average' person to stay in the same organization doing the same job for quite a while (see Cascio, 2000).

Nevertheless, it is clear that our perceptions of the nature of career have shifted considerably. Hall suggests career management will be increasingly driven by the individual, not the organization, that individuals will measure their own career success in terms of psychological fulfillment rather than promotional progression, and will make rapid and potentially radical shifts in career, re-inventing themselves many times, rather than entering an occupation in their twenties and retiring decades later having progressed in that occupation as far as talent and luck allowed. He terms this the protean career, after the mythical figure of Proteus, who could change shape at will (Hall, 1996). Collin and Watts (1996) suggest contemporary careers are increasingly viewed through the lens of what Hughes termed the subjective career, 'the moving perspective in which the person sees his life as a whole and interprets the meaning of his various attributes, actions, and the things that happen to him' (Hughes, 1937: p. 413). This conception of career links to Weick's work on sensemaking as identity construction (Weick, 1995; Weick et al., 2005). Career can be seen as a significant element of many individuals' identities, but is likely to be particularly central for managers.

There is an important caveat to this discussion of changes to the nature of career. The last decade or so has seen sustained economic growth in most countries, and with it has come a much tighter labor market. Whilst the structural changes have not been undone by this period of growth, many individuals have experienced a degree of insulation from these changes. When people with the right competencies are hard to recruit and retain, organizations become more willing to engage in career management, and individuals are more able to take advantage. This has created the impression of a career environment 'more like it used to be'. For many it was a welcomed change to the contemporary careers paradigm which promised greater freedom but also greater risk and uncertainty. However, as the credit crunch and subsequent recession have shown, the underlying changes which changed the nature of careers (a more competitive environment, different organizational structures, shifting demographics) remained firmly in place even during the 'NICE' era.[1] There is therefore a sense of 'back to the future' for the career – the new career patterns predicted by researchers in the 1990s are now re-emerging. We will return to the implications of this in the conclusion.

LEADERSHIP CAREERS OR MANAGERIAL CAREERS?

The careers literature to date has tended to talk in terms of managers rather than leaders, perhaps because 'manager' is by far the commoner job title. Despite longstanding debates on the difference between managers and leaders, in career terms they will encounter rather similar issues. The key difference is likely to be the basis on which they are judged, by the individual and others, echoing Bennis's dictum that 'managers do things right, leaders do the right things'. Since researchers find it difficult to shift away from discussion of managerial careers even in work explicitly focused on leadership careers (e.g., Hirsh, 2004; Sturges, 2004), we will treat managerial and leadership careers as broadly interchangeable.

Managerial careers are hugely significant for organizations. Gunz (1989) describes them as 'the process by which organizations renew themselves' and suggests that managerial career systems will have an impact on the strategic direction of organizations (Gunz and Jalland, 1996). Managers traditionally pursued their careers within a single organization, as management knowledge was viewed as something specific and local – executives didn't know 'how to manage,' they knew 'how to manage *here*'. This view was challenged by the development of management as a quasi-profession, and the associated belief that it involves skills and knowledge which can be applied in a range of settings. In the aftermath of the structural changes noted above, many organizations engaged in de-layering and downsizing, breaking up many of the traditional career ladders for managers. Pursuing a career within a single organization became a less reliable basis for accruing career capital, reducing the transaction costs involved in changing organization. Managers are now as likely as other occupations to pursue their careers across organizational boundaries, consistent with the memorable description of modern careers as 'just sex, not marriage' (Mirvis and Hall, 1994: p. 377).

This change in career patterns may appear to make managerial careers more similar to other occupations, but there are occupational constraints on managers which arise from their close identification with the organization. Chatman et al. (1986) suggest that managers are affected by the identity of the organization: they in part create that identity and have their own identity shaped by it (see also Ibarra, 2003). This has important implications for their career stories, and the career decisions they take. Take the example of a corporate scandal: the manager can choose to defend or criticize the organization, to quit or go down with the ship, blow the whistle or assist in a cover-up. Lavelle (2003) suggests the actions of Sherron Watkins in blowing the whistle on Enron were partly influenced by career concerns, as her first email to Kenneth Lay suggests:

> I am incredibly nervous that we will implode in a wave of accounting scandals. My eight years of Enron work history will be worth nothing on my résumé.

Her concerns reflect the reality that, despite greater mobility between organizations, managerial careers remain relatively tightly-coupled situations: the organization's trials and tribulations are a more pressing concern for managers than for other employees.

Watson and Harris (1999) note that despite the emotion-laden activities required of managers, they are expected to manage their emotions and behave always in a professional manner, not only to their staff and their own managers, but also to their managerial peers, with whom they jockey for position in the career 'tournament' (Rosenbaum, 1984). Managers have to be conscious of appearance in their careers, notably in their career history – they understand the considerable importance of a career history which shows an appropriate balance between stability and change. Career volatility might be forgivable in a specialist, but not for a potential steward of the organization. Perhaps this ought to apply less to leadership careers, as one might argue that leaders have less need to be seen as predictable – in many cases it would be appropriate for them to be mavericks who can stimulate change. However, a distinctly non-maverick career path is usually required to get to a position of influence from which one could enact such change – Mikhail Gorbachev stands out as a striking example of someone whose impeccably conventional but highly competent leadership career allowed him to achieve a position of power from which he could then drive radical change.

ORGANIZATIONAL SUPPORT FOR CAREER DEVELOPMENT

As writing on contemporary careers has tended to emphasize the individual perspective, the role of the organization has been downplayed or even ignored. At times employers have been only too happy to subscribe to this view – when mass layoffs seem more likely than recruitment drives, it is easier to work with a 'career deal' that is not based on job security and developing a career within a single organization. Yet adopting this stance has considerable drawbacks for the organization. Many elements of HRM which have been shown to be effective in attracting and retaining staff, and engendering their commitment, are to varying degrees forms of career management, and are implicitly based on the idea of some sort of career deal. In the next section we will examine the idea of the self-managed career in more detail, but here we want to outline some of the approaches to career management which can be adopted by organizations. Understanding these approaches is important for individuals – we need to recognize a career management opportunity when we see one! Researchers have identified a range of career practices that organizations may employ to plan and manage careers (e.g., Gutteridge et al., 1993; Baruch and Peiperl, 2000), and despite the changes to career, recent studies show that organizations are still a crucial partner in managing careers. Though they may delegate more responsibility to the individual, this has not led to an abandoning of career management (Baruch, 2006). Baruch (1999; 2004a) and Baruch and Peiperl (2000) provided a comprehensive review of the variety of career practices and their role in HRM.

Internal Recruitment

Whenever a position needs to be filled, the organization can look to recruit either internally or externally. The choice depends on the level and type of position and the norms of its practice in career management. Many organizations have a policy that requires internal job posting before any external search is conducted, which signals to employees that the organization prefers internal promotion to recruiting from outside. The firm may even decide they wish to have a specific employee apply, and give explicit or implicit signals to that person. However, it remains the responsibility of individual employees to keep track of the opportunities on offer, and apply when appropriate.

Induction

Induction is often experienced by individuals as a rather practical process of introducing you to your new organization. It is, however, a key career management practice, being the starting point for newcomers to learn the behaviors and attitudes necessary for assuming roles in an organization (Van Maanen, 1977). Whilst newcomers don't always value it, the benefits can be significant in providing a rapid orientation to the organization. The proactive newcomer should therefore make sure she or he gains a thorough induction program to reduce the 'shocks and surprises' which can trip up a new start, but also because, if the organization proves to be rather different from the organization you thought you were joining, it is useful to know that as early as possible (Blenkinsopp and Zdunczyk, 2005).

Assessment and Development Centers

These centers have gained a great deal of interest from academics and practitioners as a reliable and valid tool for career development. Assessment centers can be used as a selection tool for high-potential recruitment, and as an indicator of leadership potential. The proactive individual developing a self-managed career should aim to be nominated for such a process, and attend well-prepared, learning to anticipate what to expect under such evaluation.

Education and Training

The tendency to cut training budgets in hard times is so widespread that it has even made it into a Dilbert cartoon. Organizations are likely to retain job-specific training required to ensure individuals can perform their current roles, but may be more reluctant to support the more formal training or education programs which might form part of a career development path. However, even job-specific training can be of considerable value, and since more developmental education and training routes are rarely formally closed down it is useful to consider how you might make a pitch to get organizational support for such programs.

Lateral Moves to Create Cross-Functional Experience

Lateral moves can provide you with the cross-functional experience which is often an essential requirement for moving into more senior leadership roles (Hirsh, 2004), but which can also improve your employability by spreading the risk – a degree of specialization is necessary in all careers, but it is valuable to have sufficient experience to turn to alternative career pathways if demand for your field of expertise lessens. Currie et al. (2006) note that in times of uncertainty managers who moved into management from another profession (for example, finance, marketing, engineering) may opt to 'go back to their roots' if they think these occupations are a safer bet. Another reason to engage in cross-functional transfer is that many organizations now have much flatter structures, so the traditional model of 'X years in role A, then step up to role B' is much harder to achieve, and movement at the same level is a way to develop a unique set of competencies by gaining multi-role knowledge across the firm, in different operational areas. These may be at the same level as their former position, but will be viewed as a sign of progress and can generate 'promotability' potential.

Secondments

These are temporary assignments to another area within the organization, and sometimes even to another associated organization (such as a customer or supplier). The impetus for secondment can come from the individual, or their manager, mentor, or HR. Secondments need long-term HR planning and a degree of mutuality to be effective, thus making them a viable career management strategy only for large or well established corporations. There is a risk of losing successful executives, either if they opt to stay away, or if their return is transformed into a bumpy road. International management offers a good illustration of the latter, with expatriate managers often complaining that they are sent on assignment with promises of career development, and return to find the firm has little to offer them.

Career Information

This can take several forms – specific information on career opportunities within the organization, information on career development and management support, and self-managed career support (for example, career aptitude and preference tests, career workbooks). Traditionally available as leaflets or workbooks, this material is increasingly presented online via organizational intranets. They highlight what is on offer from the organization in terms of career opportunities, perhaps providing detailed information on career paths, the competencies required for each position on the path, the conditions set for career development (for example, minimal time in a certain position before promotion), and so on. One advantage of this type of career development support is that individuals can engage with it without the organization needing to be aware. With so many organizations cutting jobs, people may not want to be seen to be exploring career options, lest this be seen as evidence of a lack of commitment or loyalty, so it is appealing to be able to explore career options for yourself before committing to any discussion with HR or your boss.

Mentoring, Coaching and Counseling

The principal aim of mentoring is to bring together a person with significant leadership potential (who may already be in a management role) and an experienced senior manager, generally not his or her immediate manager, to provide advice, tutoring and support. This practice has proved positive within organizations (for example, Baugh et al., 1996), with both mentor and protégé benefiting (Kram, 1985). Individuals can be active in looking for and securing agreement of the right mentor for themselves, and indeed research suggests that informal mentoring relationships are often more effective and long-lived (Ragins and Cotton, 1999). Mentoring relationships vary with respect to the number and quality of the mentoring functions provided (Ragins et al., 2000; Fletcher and Ragins, 2007), and individuals may have one or many mentoring relationships (or none) in the course of their careers (Kirchmeyer, 2005). Mentoring relationships and network ties are manifestation of social capital (Bozionelos, 2003; Seibert et al., 2001). Finding and 'exploiting' the right mentor, and moving forward to new mentorship settings would be an asset to the self-managed career. A key challenge, for individuals and organizations, is the availability of appropriate mentors, as there may be few managers with the relevant skills and experience to serve as mentors. Limited numbers of skilled mentors is one of the factors which led to a growth in career coaching as a key element of organizational career management (Feldman, 2001). Using external coaches allows the firm to select from a broader range of individuals with the right experience to provide effective coaching. Career counseling offers a similar opportunity, and there are a great number of experienced and qualified career counselors. In time of transition, coaching or counseling can be an effective way to support executives in entering new roles and with coping with the issues that emerge, both managerial and personal.

Career Workshops

Career workshops are short-term workshops focusing on specific aspect(s) of career management and which aim to provide managers with relevant knowledge, skills and experience. Participating in career workshops can contribute to the effectiveness of the employee (Sweeney et al., 1987). Career workshops usually focus on specific aspects such as identifying future opportunities, and in some cases can be directed towards preparing executives for specific assignments (for example, working internationally). The impetus for sending people to these workshops can come from their manager, mentor or the HR counseling system, but self-managed career employees who are aware of the availability of a workshop can opt to nominate themselves for participation.

Performance Appraisal

There is a close connection between performance appraisal and career development. Formally, the appraisal is your opportunity to gain clear, unequivocal feedback about the way your performance is viewed. It provides a forum to discuss the implications of this for your future career development. As such it can be the ideal opportunity for you to signal your aspirations to your manager and the organization. Note, however, that appraisal can have something of an 'ask not what your country can do for you, but what you can do for your country' feel to it, so you need to think through not just what you are looking for, but how the organization's support for your career development will be of benefit to the bottom line. Information from the performance appraisal process also feeds into decision-making processes on promotion, succession planning, identification of training and development needs and also, highly relevant in the current climate, to decisions as to who will be retained and who will get pink slips.

Special Programs for High Flyers

Whilst all employees, as the prime asset of the organization, deserve the investment in their career by their organization, those identified as 'high flyers' are perceived as a special asset, capable of making a unique contribution to the future of the organization. Derr et al., (1988) view high flyers as a scarce resource, and because of the demographic reduction in workforce numbers, including managerial layers, suggest that organizations will look for more varied ways of developing future leaders. Getting oneself identified as a member of this elite group, and enrolled on a special program for high flyers would be an aim of an aspiring leader, and this requires both that your talents and your desire to progress are recognized – seek advice on how these individuals are identified and selected, and consider ways in which you could make the list (in some cases self-nomination is an option!).

Common Career Paths

A career path is the preferred/recommended route for the career advancement of a manager in the organization – it may be quite formally laid out, or it may take the form of some simple rules (for example, 'the CEO in this place always comes from Finance' or 'no one ever got to Board level without spending at least a year in our Paris office'). Career paths can lead people through various departments and units within the organization, as in the case of future top-level managers in multinational companies who are expected at some point to take a managerial role in an overseas subsidiary. As traditional hierarchical structures become replaced by flatter structures or boundaryless and virtual organizations, the importance of career paths seems likely to decline. Yet, for the aspiring employee it would be important to learn what the routes were for gaining top positions in the organization (Hirsh, 2004), and aim to be appointed to 'springboard' rather than 'dead-end' positions.

WHO OWNS AND MANAGES YOUR CAREER?

As promising young scientist, Mary had joined a large pharmaceutical company straight after her Ph.D. from a top university. Attracted by the state-of the-art research facilities, the global projects and the excellent prospects for career progression, she dedicated herself fully to her career, quickly rising through the ranks. Her promotion to Head of Cancer Research was the pinnacle of her career – a demanding, rewarding and prestigious position. Two years later, her situation could not be more different. Following an internal review, her research projects were axed and her department reorganized, so Mary now finds herself 'surplus to requirements' and looking for work for the first time in over two decades. After the initial shock, she begins to question her long-standing focus on climbing the ladder within a single organization. She comes to the painful realization that this has left her in a difficult situation: the internal company networks she built to drive her research management career are practically useless overnight; the prospects of finding a similarly challenging senior role elsewhere are severely limited, given the drive to outsource and a general downturn in the industry. Her confidence to sell herself to another employer is low – she has not had a 'proper' interview for 25 years, and her résumé is so strongly embedded in a single organization that she has doubts how effective she would be working elsewhere. She wonders whether prospective employers would regard her as 'institutionalized'?

To what extent can this individual be said to have owned and managed her career? And how do we explain the apparent paradox that an ambitious, careerist individual actually engaged in little or no career management? Academic debates are typically of limited interest to practitioners, but the discussion within the careers literature about the nature of the modern career and who might be said to own and manage it goes to the heart of issues of paramount concern to people at work. The essence of the debate is as follows – is a career something owned and managed by the individual, or is it a product of processes of workforce development and succession planning, and thus 'owned' by the organization? Since most individuals nowadays will be employed by several different organizations over the course of their working lives, individuals clearly own their careers. However, we need to recognize that organizations have a key influence on them. We might therefore think of ourselves as following self-managed careers which can be enabled, or constrained, by the organizations which employ us.

Within personality psychology, a distinction is made between whether a situation is 'strong' or 'weak' (Mischel, 1969). In 'strong' situations, we know what behavior is expected (indeed, we might almost say there is a script) and we would expect to see only limited variation due to personality. 'Weak' situations are much less structured, we perceive greater choice, and personality differences are much more likely to predict behavior. To take an extended example, people traveling through airports show behavior which is in many ways quite similar, as indeed it needs to be if we are to be appropriately processed by the various departments. However, when a flight is considerably delayed, the range of behavior is more diverse – some people become very anxious, others get angry, some sit and wait for news, others go off to find out, whilst the rest head to the nearest bar. We can see why it is advisable for airlines to continue to provide up-to-date information in such situations, in an effort to create a 'strong' situation in which the scripted behavior is 'stay here and wait patiently'. Arthur et al. (1999) suggest careers are nowadays pursued in the context of increasingly weak situations – situations in which there are fewer obvious and necessary steps or routes, situations in which there may not even be clear destinations. They suggest employers have a vested interest in creating 'strong' career situations (or at least the appearance of them) in order to make things more manageable, whereas individuals have an interest in creating 'weak' career situations in order to give themselves greater choice and opportunity.

Sturges et al. (2002) suggest individuals can engage in two forms of career self-management activities – those calculated to further a career with their current organization, and those aimed at furthering a career they anticipate pursuing outside that organization. We suggest it is useful to take stock of which strategy you appear to be adopting, and to consider whether it remains the most appropriate one. Activities focused on your current organization, for example internal networking, seeking career advice and mentoring, publicizing your achievements, all serve to signal your commitment to the organization and mark you out as someone seeking to develop your career within it. However, these activities may have little impact on enhancing your résumé in the eyes of another employer. Think in terms of hard and soft currencies – brownie points earned with your current employer are a soft currency, not readily convertible on the wider labor market. Whilst it is wise to consider what is career-enhancing in your current organization, it is equally important to keep an eye on what is required to maintain your attractiveness to future employers.

HUMAN AND SOCIAL CAPITAL AND SUCCESSFUL SELF-MANAGED CAREERS

Tom considers himself a conscientious, hard-working, loyal and effective employee and an expert in his particular field in the telecommunications industry. He has been told he is regarded as 'high potential', and his latest move to his current organization as a senior technology consultant reflects his professional standing. Tom has his eyes firmly set on becoming a divisional director within the next three years. Yet lately Tom has started to doubt his progress: he notices that more junior colleagues are given the high caliber assignments that he considers as 'his' and that he is no longer put forward for professional development opportunities. Tom is starting to feel short changed. When he raises his concerns with his boss, he is shocked to hear that senior management are having doubts about his suitability for a director role. Tom's boss recommends an external mentor to help him get his career back on track. With the help of his mentor, Tom quickly realizes that being excellent at his job is not enough any longer. He has fallen into the trap of neglecting his internal and external contacts for too long, lacking visibility across the organization. Reluctantly, Tom begins to see the need to raise his profile, quickly and widely, whilst continuing to deliver results. He agrees to spend more time answering queries from senior colleagues, contributing his expansive knowledge to new projects, and volunteering his time for strategic company initiatives. In addition, he is seeking opportunities to represent his employer on regional committees of the telecommunications industry. All these extra responsibilities feel like a real burden, coming on top of his already demanding day job. But after six months, Tom is starting to see first results. When he is asked to become the lead consultant for a multi-million pound project, Tom realizes he is firmly back on senior management's radar.

Individuals are increasingly taking the lead in planning and managing their career, many through choice, but others because they are forced to do so as more employers cease to view career management as their responsibility (Gutteridge et al., 1993; Baruch, 1999). Individuals managing their own careers need to recognize they have an intangible worth through their knowledge, skills and experience (their competencies), which Becker (1964) termed 'human capital'. The human capital view posits that societal or organizational rewards (such as hierarchical progression and increased income) are distributed according to relevant competencies, thus rewarding those competencies that contribute to organizational performance or to the functioning of society. These competencies can be acquired in various ways, including education, training, general and job-specific work experience, and tenure (either within an organization or profession). In terms of career and career mobility, the human capital theory fits the tournament view of career progress (Rosenbaum, 1979). Individuals compete for a limited amount of organizational rewards in open and fair contests, being judged on the basis of their credentials and contributions (Turner, 1960), and their relevance for achieving high performance.

DeFillippi and Arthur (1994) built upon the human capital view to identify specific career competencies, which they framed in terms of knowing-why, knowing-how and knowing-whom. They suggest these three competencies are required for developing what they term an 'intelligent career'. Knowing-why concerns the attitudes, internal needs, and identity that relate to aspirations and underpinning values, including ethical values (or lack of them). Knowing-how is the skills, abilities and technical competencies that enable people to perform well. Knowing-whom is the networking, connections, relationships, which relates to the contacts and relationship that people develop with others. Their claim that these competencies would form a basis for career success was empirically tested by Eby et al. (2003). For knowing-why they measured career insight (the extent to which one has realistic career expectations, knowledge of one's strengths and weaknesses, and specific career goals), proactive personality, and openness to experience. Knowing-whom was measured in terms of experience in a mentoring relationship, and the extensiveness of networks within and outside the organization. They found strong support for the impact of these competencies on career success. Jones and DeFillippi (1996) subsequently elaborated the intelligent career framework by anchoring a person's career in its context. Knowing why, how and whom are primarily individual career competencies, crucial for the self-managed career. Yet individual careers evolve in specific contexts, which have spatial, temporal and historical dimensions. Knowing 'where', 'when', and 'what' were added as important in placing careers in their geographic, temporal and historical contexts. Such a framework can be instrumental for individuals in realizing the rules of the game in managing careers.

The social capital perspective (Seibert et al., 2001) demonstrates that factors beyond structure and human capital must be considered in order to develop an exhaustive account of what determines career success. Social capital signifies resources (that is, information, influence, solidarity) that may be available to the individual via relationship ties within a particular social structure, such as the organization, the profession, or society in general (Adler and Kwon, 2002), and is a major ingredient of career success (Baruch et al., 2005). The social capital view suggests that informal interpersonal processes play an important role in career success. Research provides support for the link between social capital and objective career success, as it appears to assist in both career entry and later career stages. For example, the social capital of university students in their final year was related to the likelihood of them having a full-time job commensurate with their educational credentials six months later (Jokisaari and Nurmi, 2005). Similarly, Seibert et al. (2001) found a positive relationship between social capital and both objective and subjective career success amongst MBA alumni.

The self-managed careerist cannot rely only on organizational support mechanisms. Proactivity may mean a variety of alternative ways to gain knowledge on possible opportunities and to acquire different ways to progress a career (Seibert et al., 2001). Networking is such one proven way, for example it is instrumental for many in developing a successful second career both in traditional labor markets like the defense industry (Baruch and Quick, 2007) or in a highly dynamic and volatile industry like bio-chemistry (Higgins, 2005). Higgins uses the term 'career eco-system' to describe how networks of people, all former employees of a certain firm (Baxter), were able to develop networks of relationships and a culture of initiation that led to a significant number of them becoming leaders of new ventures in the industry.

MANAGING YOURSELF: COPING WITH CAREERS

Adam's desire has always been to become a business leader. Following in his father's footsteps, he chose to become an engineer. Graduating from a good university, he gained a place on the graduate development scheme of a multi-national energy firm, and was quickly identified as future talent. Yet only three years into his career, Adam started to feel he wasn't being sufficiently challenged – he wanted a customer-facing role, and international travel. When an internal opportunity came up, he didn't hesitate to apply. Though his boss was supportive of his application, senior management decided he was not experienced enough. Frustrated by the lack of progress, Adam accepted a European assignment with a competitor instead. Initially full of enthusiasm and ready to conquer the world, Adam quickly found his new employer also placed great emphasis on age and experience. Within a year or two with that firm he had become frustrated again – convinced he could do a better job than his boss, and keen to move into a leadership role, he applied unsuccessfully for promotion, only to be told that he needed at least three more years in his job to gain relevant experience. For a while, Adam lost interest in his career and focused more on his family, putting just enough into his job to keep his employer satisfied. But the frustration built up – he increasingly wondered whether he would ever become the leader he wants to be. Then, to his surprise, his employer offered him a move to Asia: a similar role but a new challenge, and the opportunity to live and work in a different culture. His wife was against the move, worried about the impact on their family, but his employer warned that he'd better not ignore this opportunity. Frustrated by the lack of alternatives, Adam decided to move on again. This time, he is convinced that his third employer within a decade will finally offer him the chance to prove himself, despite his relatively young age.

To the modern reader, Adam's career story is not an unusual one, but it isn't that long ago that moves between organizations for people in leadership and management roles were rare – and even today in some countries, notably France and Japan, they remain relatively uncommon. The freedom to move more readily between organizations provides individuals with considerable opportunities, but it also poses a hidden problem, vividly illustrated by Adam's case – our freedom to move can lead us to make moves on the basis of emotion (in this case, frustration) which are poorly timed or badly thought out. Adam's first employer clearly rates him highly, but also places great value on age and experience as a basis for promotion. Frustrated by this limitation to his progress, he makes a switch to another corporation which he hopes will provide him with greater opportunity, but which in fact has the same attitude towards leadership 'career timetables' as his previous employer. Blenkinsopp (2007) suggests that the relatively open labor market in leadership and management careers means that emotion can play a greater role in our decision making, and this requires leaders to engage in greater emotional self-management and coping.

Grey (1994) noted that individuals' self-discipline in furtherance of their careers produces for the organization a highly desired set of behaviors, behaviors it would be costly and difficult to produce through direct control. Being aware of this in one's own career can be exceptionally useful – a realization that you are only following a particular course of action out of career considerations can allow you to evaluate whether it is worth it.[2] But why are career considerations so influential on our behavior? Career is a key element of identity for most individuals, and as such, it shapes the meanings we ascribe to a range of life events, work-related or otherwise. The sensemaking involved in the career is thus tightly bound up with identity construction, and this sensemaking produces a career narrative (Bujold, 2004), a story we tell to ourselves and others in order to account for events.

When we plan prospective career paths and attempt to follow them, we are seeing whether we can 'pull off' the prospective identity we have projected for ourselves: this is seen most vividly in interviews, where we present our 'best' identity (which may be more potential than actual at that point). The identity construction in a leadership career narrative is aspirational and ambitious: whilst not everyone aspires to be Chief Executive, almost everyone will aspire to progress, and some will inevitably be disappointed. The narrative is therefore chronically fragile, we will encounter hassles or setbacks which appear to have the potential to disrupt our career project, decelerating progress and thus disconfirming a positive career narrative and identity. Events which disrupt our career narrative stimulate sensemaking in order to 'repair the breach' (Weick et al., 2005). The revised narrative forms the basis for subsequent action ('enactment') by the individual. This process is represented diagrammatically in Figure 8.1.

The volatility of narratives arising out of the sensemaking process is noted by Glanz, who suggests that 'apparently random moments of revelation can overturn well established belief and behavior in a very short time frame and as a result of an infinite number of variables' (Glanz, 2003: p. 262). Marshall suggests stories 'undergo changes and reformulations as relatively routine life processes' (Marshall, 2000: p. 206). Yet, as we have seen, leaders and managers are conscious of the need to present themselves in a 'careerist' manner which conforms to expectations and may choose to mask any volatility in their career thinking, including at times masking it from themselves.

The process shown in Figure 8.1 might appear to lead to repeated rewrites of the career story, but it is important to stress that the cycle may equally lead to escalation or entrapment. Our early commitment to a particular interpretation makes it more difficult to change that interpretation (Drummond and Chell, 2001), and we may therefore subtly rewrite our career narrative in ways that don't significantly alter our overall career commitments. Feldman suggests sensemaking often leads not to action but to an understanding 'that an action should not be taken or that a better understanding of the event or situation is needed' (Feldman, 1989, p. 20). Whilst this may mean sensibly biding one's time waiting for the

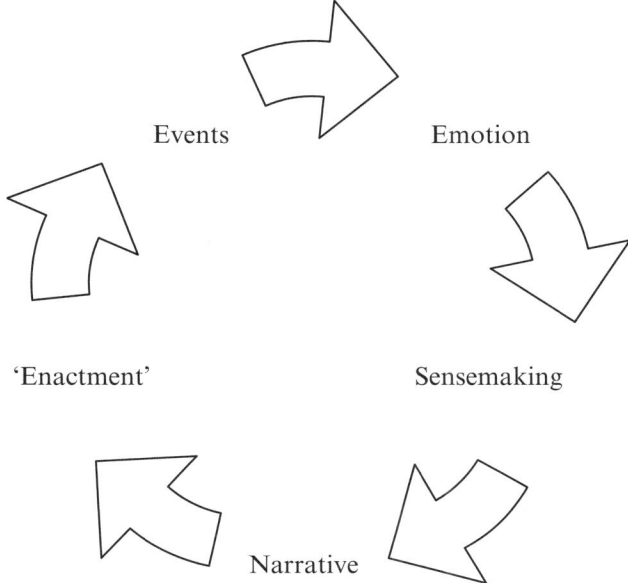

*Figure 8.1   A process model of the impact of emotion in careers
(Blenkinsopp, 2007)*

right moment, the rejection of action as an available option means that we will remain in a work situation which we would prefer to exit, sometimes for an extended period. Dealing with this will require us to engage in various coping strategies.

The literature on coping draws a distinction between problem-focused and emotion-focused coping (Lazarus and Folkman, 1984), though Lazarus (2006) suggests individuals can and do deploy both strategies simultaneously. Emotion-focused coping is concerned with dealing with the emotion stimulated by a situation, problem-focused coping with taking action to address that situation. Emotion-focused coping strategies are generally perceived as less effective since they do not deal with the problem (Ashkanasy et al. 2004), however in situations where the problem cannot be changed, emotion-focused strategies are more appropriate (Sears, Unizar, and Garrett, 2000). In some career situations a problem may be appraised as unchangeable because the change required is seen as too drastic. Alternatively, the change may be seen as possible but not immediately available, for example, the individual decides to leave, but only when she or he has found another job to go to. In either case, the individual will be forced to engage in emotion-focused coping over an extended period. In leadership careers, very minor events may disrupt the career identity project, causing us to 'surface' from our immersion in the project, and thus forcing repeated rewrites of the career story. Coping with this is one of the major challenges in a leadership career.

UNEMPLOYMENT AND THE LEADERSHIP CAREER

Thus far we have not discussed one of the biggest coping challenges for any leadership career, and one which becomes more likely in hard times – losing your job. Long identified as one of the most stressful life events, the loss of work in recession can be especially stressful as the state of the labor market can make it more difficult to get back into work rapidly. The financial pressures too can be acute, especially with a recession like the present one, which arrived so unexpectedly.[3] In good times there is a tendency to live just a little beyond our means, as finance is relatively easy to obtain and we anticipate our income will grow in the coming years, so a sudden onset of recession can throw our financial planning into disarray.

HR professionals use the term 'golden handcuffs' to describe financial incentives designed to retain employees, but we can create our own golden handcuffs by managing our personal finances in a way that leaves us unable to take risks in our career moves. It is hard to switch our personal finances to a 'war footing' overnight, but it clearly makes sense for us all to have some contingency plans.

Sonnenfeld and Ward (2008) examined how high-profile business leaders recovered from 'career disasters'. The examples they offer are largely of apparent failures or corporate scandals, rather than simply losing one's job as the result of cost-cutting, but of the five steps they propose for recovering from these setbacks, three seem equally relevant to coping with the aftermath of job loss:

> Fight not flight (facing up to the issue); Recruiting others into battle (seeking opportunities through social networks. . .); Proving your mettle (rebuilding trust and credibility through getting back in the game) (Sonnenfeld and Ward, 2008).

The issue of networking, already discussed, becomes much more important in such situations. Obviously the number of vacancies in a recession goes down, but the proportion of vacancies which get advertised goes down even more sharply, as employers look to save costs by recruiting via more informal means. As a result, those seeking work often end up sending out their résumé on an unsolicited basis – a necessary course of action, but one which inevitably has a lower strike rate than applying for advertised

Source: Reproduced by kind permission of Charles Peattie and Russell Taylor. Alex appears in the Daily Telegraph and can also be found at www.alexcartoon.com.

Figure 8.2   Planning for the future the Alex way

posts. Effective networking can provide the middle way between these two options, allowing you to submit your résumé in response either to advice from someone that opportunities exist at their firm or, even better, an actual invitation to send your details or to come in for a meeting.

Another key element of coping with a period of unemployment is, though we hesitate to say it, that old chestnut that 'you have to keep yourself busy'. There are three elements to this. First, participating in activities which offer opportunities for personal development (for example, training and education, or volunteering) can add value to your résumé. Second, employers are perennially nervous about gaps in employment – the old argument was that unexplained gaps might mean a time in jail! However, organizations are usually more concerned at the length of time since you last had to 'punch the clock', and whether you're still ready for work. Finally, though we view work as stressful, lack of work is even more stressful, as it robs us of structure and rhythm to our days, week and months. All told, we recommend any and all activities which contribute to keeping us active, being seen to be productive and engaged, and filling the time on a résumé in ways which might add value.

The last point we want to note about the impact of job loss on a leadership career is that it is an externally imposed time to review and reflect. Though you may conclude that you wish to continue with your existing career path, it is clearly appropriate to reflect on these issues – different roles and sectors have been hit differently, and you may need to explore whether you're swimming against the tide in trying to get back into exactly the same line of work. For many executives an obvious alternative to unemployment is self-employment or business start-up, or to be entrepreneurial in a broader sense, and it is to this issue that we now turn.

ME PLC: BEING A CAREER ENTREPRENEUR

The management guru Tom Peters coined the term 'Me plc' to describe the way in which individuals needed to think of their own career as if they were a business trying to survive and prosper. In this analogy individuals who are employed full-time by one employer become like those firms which supply a single main customer. Such firms have to focus on meeting that customer's needs, but at the same time need to be alive to possible alternative customers, and to the vulnerability of their situation if demand from that customer dries up. One might equally compare the situation to a marriage,[4] though we recognize that tips for a successful marriage would not normally include advice to be constantly on the lookout for a better partner and to prepare for the day your spouse leaves! This shift, from the metaphorical marriage to conditional attachment was discussed earlier by Baruch (2004b: pp. 165–6). We might, however, follow the advice of Paul Newman, who attributed the success of his long marriage to Joanne Woodward to the fact that 'we fight with equal-sized clubs'. In the context of Me plc, this means striving to ensure that you have something of value to offer an employer which matches the things of value an employer can offer you. This requires us to pay attention to developing our competencies, but also invites us to consider how we might contribute to value creation – in other words, to be more entrepreneurial.

There has been a rapid growth of interest in entrepreneurship, stemming from the recognition that as economic environments become more competitive, complex and unpredictable, this creates challenges for large corporations but also opportunities for entrepreneurs. Western governments began to recognize that their continued economic strength would not come from supporting their largest corporations to defend a market position against increasingly aggressive foreign entrants, but from creating conditions under which entrepreneurial activity could flourish. Entrepreneurs are often seen as risk takers, but this label can be misleading; though entrepreneurs may make a decision to take a chance which non-entrepreneurs would not, this seems to be more because they are optimists than because they are risk takers (Chell, 2008). A more defining characteristic is that entrepreneurs are skilled in recognizing opportunities and exploiting these opportunities to create new ventures. In the context of career, entrepreneurial can be taken to mean three things. Dyer (1994) uses the term 'entrepreneurial career' to mean simply the careers of individuals who start up businesses. Kanter (1989) uses it to refer to careers which are built on a logic of advancement through wealth creation, and therefore includes what are sometimes termed *intra*preneurs, that is, individuals who create 'new' ventures from within existing organizations. In this chapter, we suggest there is a third way to look at the idea of entrepreneurship and careers, which is that some individuals can be seen to act entrepreneurially towards their own careers – they are skilled in recognizing opportunities, exploiting those opportunities, and creating value.

Of course, it could be argued that our definition of entrepreneurial careers merely describes people who engage in adroit career management, but we have in mind something subtly different from this. A useful analogy can be made with the difference between soccer and American football. American football, like many other team sports, has a strong element of formal turn taking and interruptions to play, and this allows coaches to develop clear game plans and to amend these plans as the game progresses. In this sense this makes the game more like traditional careers – not actually predictable, but having enough predictability to allow a degree of planning. Soccer is much more fluid; play can move back and forth very rapidly indeed and coaches have little direct influence on matters once the game is underway. Teams therefore prize players who are quick to spot opportunities over those who 'merely' execute the tactics set by the coach (though they are also valuable). An excellent example of this is the young David Beckham, who was propelled to instant fame by a goal he scored from a distance of 55 yards, after he spotted the goalkeeper had come a long way up the pitch, and decided to try an audacious chip over his head. This is a classic analogy for career entrepreneurship – his actions created value for his employer, which was in itself of benefit to his career, but the manner and timing of his actions meant they were especially career-enhancing. The goal made a huge difference to his profile – it was replayed repeatedly on TV, and he was called up into the national team just two weeks later. Given that Beckham went on to become almost a textbook example of effective management of his own 'brand', it is difficult not to read into his triumphal expression after scoring a sense that he knew *exactly* the career significance of what he'd just done.

It is clearly difficult to give advice on how individuals can act entrepre-neurially towards their own careers – opportunity recognition and exploi-tation lie at the heart of this, and other than 'look out for opportunities and be ready to exploit them', what can we say? A couple of examples may help, however. The first is very brief – the first author, in his former life as an HR professional, noticed that relatively few HR specialists were comfortable with IT, and even fewer with numerical data. Volunteering to become the lead person in running the HR system proved an adroit move in securing a permanent position at a time when the organization was putting staff on short-term contracts. The second example, below, is more detailed, and also usefully illustrates the role of networking and social capital.

David had been pursuing a management career within the same bulk chemi-cals company for over 15 years when, in the mid-1980s, he was offered an assignment to run the joint venture they had formed with a state-owned enterprise in China. The joint venture was reasonably successful – there were numerous teething problems, but these were seen as inevitable, and David was acknowledged to have performed well. The return on investment was not, however, especially high, and the board of the parent company were not interested in David's plans to expand operations. They felt the 'experiment' had shown that China was not yet sufficiently developed economically to be a major player, and favored investing more in their Malaysian operations. David was dismayed by their analysis, and for a while contemplated propos-ing a management buy-out, but felt this was too great a risk. However, this train of thought led him to think in more businesslike terms about himself and what he had to offer. Few Western executives had his level of experience of doing business in China, and even fewer could point to a successful track record as CEO of a joint venture. He contacted executive search agencies to alert them of his interest in finding a new position, but they reported no openings – many other companies were as uncertain as his own board about developing business in China. David began to think the role he sought, in essence a CEO position for a larger firm, would only come along if he created it. He worked his networks, both in China and back at home, and also built links with government agencies involved in promoting trade. He started to offer his services as a guest speaker for business dinners on his favorite topic, 'doing business in China', and was regularly invited to dine with trade delegations visiting the province. David's enthusiasm for China, and his obvious skills and experience as a business leader, persuaded several firms to upgrade their speculative interest in China to a full-blown business evaluation, and in all cases the boards had David penciled in as their first choice for CEO if the venture proceeded. The final outcome of his efforts was as surprising as it was welcome – his assiduous work in persuading other firms of the opportunities offered by China had an indirect impact on his own board, who couldn't help noticing how many other firms were now seriously looking to invest in China. Anxious not to lose the benefit of having been an early entrant, they asked David to prepare a business plan for doubling the size of the operations within the next 18 months, and told him that the expanded joint venture would become a listed company, giving him greater prestige and autonomy.

This vignette illustrates entrepreneurial career behavior in three ways. First, David demonstrates a yen for autonomy and control. Second, he skillfully spots an opportunity. Third, he develops a strategy to exploit that opportunity. Finally, he perseveres with his strategy – it takes a good while for this to pay off, but when it does, the benefits are substantial. This doggedness is another trait associated with entrepreneurship, though it is important that you temper this by seeking advice – you need to know when you are flogging a dead horse!

EMERGING TRENDS

We noted earlier that for an extended period the 'contemporary career' patterns didn't become quite the norm that researchers had expected because of the extended period of economic growth. Our research, and work with clients, suggests the expected changes to career are becoming increasingly visible as a result of the recession, and we note five trends of particular relevance to leaders managing their careers (Sullivan and Baruch, 2009). The first is one we have already mentioned, the continuing decline of recognizable career paths. Career progression from following a clear-cut career path is increasingly rare, even in professions with previously clear pathways. Although individuals are often aware of this, there is a real reluctance to accept it. Many feel overwhelmed by the notion of having to carve out a career path themselves, and they lack the knowledge on how to make the 'right' career decisions, choosing from amongst the many different options. The second trend is the disappearance of career discussions at work, apparently replaced by discussion of talent management. This has important implications, since talent management is inevitably more focused on individuals' contributions to the organization, and whilst most individuals want to make a contribution, they also have concerns about their career prospects.

The third trend is the rapid reorientation to the credit crunch, which is particularly striking for two segments of the workforce. The younger generation, a few years into their career, are beginning to realize that many of the promises (implicit or explicit) that employers made to them are not going to be delivered because of the recession. Some are being laid off, while many of those who have retained their jobs nevertheless feel 'messed about' as they are shifted round organizations in response to changed priorities. Among the older generation, typically 55-plus, many have put retirement plans on hold and indeed in some cases come back to work after retirement, as a result of the impact of the financial crisis on their retirement savings and investments. They experience an emotional challenge in attempting to gear up for a potentially significant extension to their working lives, whilst also having to face a labor market which practices age discrimination.

The fourth trend is a challenge to the shift in work values and expectations which ten years of a booming economy and plentiful job opportunities have created. We regularly encounter individuals who have the following expectations: a) a high salary; b) challenging work with no routine and plenty of potential for development and promotion; plus c) an excellent work–life balance. Adam's story in the section on coping with careers epitomizes these values, and also the much greater willingness to go elsewhere if expectations are not met. Whilst we applaud such aspirations, it doesn't take a cynic to see that there is a degree of tension to these three elements. For example, the most highly paid jobs are rarely conducive to work–life balance, whilst progressing to higher-level jobs usually requires an individual to endure a formative period which includes significant routine.

Finally, the impact of technology on career management has been significant, but many individuals appear utterly bewildered by it. The use of social networking sites has rapidly grown from 'teens talking to teens' to be a powerful vehicle for building social capital, but individuals are often ignorant of how to utilize this, and/or naive about the possible detrimental sides (for example, risks of identity theft, publicizing one's job search to your current employer). Individuals who do use the internet for career management often do very simplistic things like posting a résumé on a jobs site and waiting for the offers to come in. The rapid pace of change can so overwhelm people that they opt to do nothing at all, thereby missing out.

CONCLUSION

The career landscape has changed enormously, and established axioms about the nature and notion of career are being challenged. A whole system of careers was shattered when the basic building blocks of its existence crumbled. Clear structures, stability, a sound and growing economy, and high levels of predictability have diminished, and with this a dawning realization that a new world of careers has emerged. At the organizational level, former commitments and values proved unsustainable, in particular the old psychological contract of security and continuation. At the individual level we note a growing trend of individualization. A dynamic and risky labor market followed multi-level changes – in society, industry and organizations that caused more people to take their fate in their own hands, with a multidirectional rather than linear career system (Baruch, 2004a). The theoretical developments in career studies reflect those changes. An unstable economy, blurring of organizational structure, escalation of technological development and globalization have all contributed to a new era of career systems. The trend towards individualism was coupled with a collapse of the traditional set of norms and beliefs about the nature of progress, and the meaning of career success – internal and external dimensions of such success.

The challenge is to balance the needs of the individual and the demands of the organization, a challenge felt especially acutely by leaders who represent and direct the organization and yet who may also sometimes see their long-term career interests lie elsewhere. In the new system, different kinds of career competencies become important. Having an intelligent career, employability and career resilience all proved crucial for surviving and flourishing in a boundaryless, post-corporate industry. Career attitudes like those of the protean career have helped shift the focus and burden of planning and management of careers from the organization as the primary player, into a mutual responsibility and shared planning and management of careers with the employees, sometimes passing this role in full to individuals. The self-managed leadership career is increasingly a reality.

NOTES

1. NICE = Non-Inflationary Constant Expansion, a term coined by Mervyn King, the Governor of the Bank of England, to describe the immediate pre-credit crunch era.
2. Re-evaluation of career aspirations often occurs in the aftermath of major life events, both positive (for example, becoming a parent) and negative (for example, a health scare). We suggest it can be good to re-evaluate without such prompts and the associated pressures and urgency they bring.
3. Although the number of commentators who claim they 'saw this coming' appears to grow by the day, there can be few people who went to bed on New Year's Eve 2007 expecting that by the end of 2008 the global economy would have come to the very brink of meltdown.
4. The first author is grateful to Tanya Greenwell for pointing out this useful non-business analogy.

REFERENCES

Adler, P. and Kwon, S. (2002), 'Social capital: prospects for a new concept', *Academy of Management Review*, **27**(1), 17–40.

Arthur, M.B. (2008), 'Examining contemporary careers: a call for interdisciplinary inquiry', *Human Relations*, **61**(2), 163–86.

Arthur, M.B., and Rousseau, D. (1996), 'Introduction: the boundaryless career as a new employment principle', in M. Arthur and D. Rousseau (eds), *The Boundaryless Career*, New York: Oxford University Press, pp. 3–20.

Arthur, M.B., Inkson, K. and Pringle, J.K. (1999), *The New Careers: Individual Action and Economic Change*, London: Sage.

Ashkanasy, N.M., Ashton-James, C.E. and Jordan, P.J. (2004), 'Performance impacts of appraisal and coping with stress in workplace settings: the role of affect and emotional intelligence', in P.L. Perrewe and D.C. Ganster (eds), *Research in Occupational Stress and Well Being*, Vol. 3, London: Elsevier, pp. 1–43.

Baruch, Y. (1999), 'Integrated career systems for the 2000s', *International Journal of Manpower*, **20**(7), 432–57.

Baruch, Y. (2004a), 'Transforming careers: from linear to multidirectional career paths: Organizational and individual perspective', *Career Development International*, **9**(1), 58–73.

Baruch, Y. (2004b), *Managing Careers: Theory and Practice*, Harlow, UK: FT-Prentice Hall/Pearson.

Baruch, Y. (2006), 'Career development in organizations and beyond: balancing traditional and contemporary viewpoints', *Human Resource Management Review*, **16**(2), 125–38.

Baruch, Y. and Peiperl, M.A. (2000), 'Career management practices: an empirical survey and theoretical implications', *Human Resource Management*, **39**(4), 347–66.

Baruch, Y. and Quick, J.C. (2007), 'Understanding second careers: lessons from a study of US navy admirals', *Human Resource Management*, **46**(4), 471–91.

Baruch, Y., Bell, M. and Gray, D. (2005), 'Generalist and specialist graduate business degrees: tangible and intangible value', *Journal of Vocational Behavior*, **67**(1), 51–68.

Baugh, S.G., Lankau, M.J. and Scandura, T.A. (1996), 'An investigation of the effects of protégé gender on responses to mentoring', *Journal of Vocational Behavior*, **49**(3), 309–23.

Becker, G.S. (1964), *Human Capital*, 1st edn, New York: Columbia University Press.

Blenkinsopp, J. (2007), 'Emotion in managerial careers', *paper presented to the Academy of Management annual meeting*, Philadelphia.

Blenkinsopp, J. and Zdunczyk, K. (2005), 'Making sense of mistakes in managerial careers', *Career Development International*, **10**(5), 359–74.

Bozionelos, N. (2003), 'Intra-organizational network resources: relation to career success and personality', *International Journal of Organizational Analysis*, **11**, 41–66.

Bujold, C. (2004), 'Constructing career through narrative', *Journal of Vocational Behavior*, **64**, 470–84.

Cascio, W.F. (2000), 'New workplaces', in J.M. Kummerow (ed.), *New Directions in Career Planning and the Workplace*, 2nd edn, Palo Alto, CA: Davies-Black Publishing.

Chatman, J., Bell, N. and Staw, B. (1986), 'The managed thought: the role of self justification and impression management in organizational settings', in D. Gioia and H. Sims (eds), *The Thinking Organization: Dynamics of Social Cognition*, San Francisco: Jossey-Bass, pp. 191–214.

Chell, E. (2008), *The Entrepreneurial Personality: A Social Construction*, London: The Psychology Press/Routledge.

Collin, A. and Watts, A.G. (1996), 'The death and transfiguration of career – and of career guidance?', *British Journal of Guidance and Counselling*, **24**, 385–98.

Currie, G., Tempest, S. and Starkey, K. (2006), 'New careers for old? Organizational and individual responses to changing boundaries', *International Journal of Human Resource Management*, **17**, 744–55.

Dany, F., Mallon, M. and Arthur, M.B. (2003), 'The odyssey of career and the opportunity for international comparison', *International Journal of Human Resource Management*, **14**(5), 705–12.

DeFillippi, R.J. and Arthur, M.B. (1994). 'The boundaryless career: a competency-based prospective', *Journal of Organizational Behavior*, **15**(4), 307–24.

Derr, C., Jones, C. and Toomey, E. (1988), 'Managing high potential employees: current practices in thirty-three US corporations', *Human Resource Management*, **27**(3), 273–90.

Drummond, H. and Chell, E. (2001), 'Life's chances and choices – A study of entrapment in career decisions with reference to Becker's side bets theory', *Personnel Review*, **30**, 186–202.

Dyer, W.G. (1994), 'Toward a theory of entrepreneurial careers', *Entrepreneurship Theory and Practice*, **19**(2), 7–21.

Eby, L.T., Butts, M. and Lockwood, A. (2003), 'Predictors of success in the era of the boundaryless career', *Journal of Organizational Behavior*, **24**, 689–708.

Feldman, D.C. (2001), 'Executive coaching: a review and agenda for future research', *Journal of Management*, **31**(6), 829–48.

Feldman, M.S. (1989), *Order without Design*, Stanford CA: Stanford University Press.

Fletcher, J.K. and Ragins, B.R. (2007), 'Stone Center relational cultural theory', in B. Ragins and K. Kram (eds), *The Handbook of Mentoring at Work: Research, Theory, and Practice*, Thousand Oaks, CA: Sage, pp. 373–99.

Glanz, L. (2003), 'Expatriate stories: a vehicle of professional development abroad?', *Journal of Managerial Psychology*, **18**, 259–74.

Grey, C. (1994), 'Career as a project of the self and the labor process discipline', *Sociology*, **28**, 479–98.

Gunz, H.P. (1989), 'The dual meaning of managerial careers: organizational and individual levels of analysis', *Journal of Management Studies*, **26**, 225–49.

Gunz, H.P., and Jalland, R.M. (1996), 'Managerial careers and business strategies', *Academy of Management Review*, **21**, 718–56.

Gutteridge, T.G., Leibowitz, Z.B. and Shore, J.E. (1993), *Organizational Career Development*, San Francisco, CA: Jossey-Bass.

Hall, D.T. (1976), *Careers in Organizations*, Glenview, IL: Scott, Foresman.

Hall, D.T. (1996), *The Career is Dead – Long Live the Career: A Relational Approach to Careers*, San Francisco, CA: Jossey-Bass.

Higgins, M. (2005), *Career Imprints: Creating Leaders Across an Industry*, San Francisco, CA: Jossey-Bass.

Hirsh, W. (2004), 'Positive career development for leaders and managers', in J. Storey (ed.), *Leadership in Organizations: Current Issues and Key Trends*, London: Routledge.

Hughes, E.C. (1937), 'Institutional office and the person', *American Journal of Sociology*, **43**, 404–13.

Ibarra, H. (2003), *Working Identity: Unconventional Strategies for Reinventing your Career*, Boston, MA: Harvard Business School Press.

Jokisaari, M. and Nurmi, J.-E. (2005), 'Company matters: goal-related social capital in the transition to working life', *Journal of Vocational Behavior*, **67**, 413–28.

Jones, C. and DeFillippi, R.J. (1996), 'Back to the future in film: combining industry and self-knowledge to meet the career challenges of the 21st century', *Academy Management Executive*, **10**(4), 89–103.

Kanter, R.M. (1989), 'Careers and the wealth of nations: a macro-perspective on the structure and implications of careers', in M. Arthur, D.T. Hall and B. Lawrence (eds), *A Handbook of Career Theory*, Cambridge, UK: Cambridge University Press.

Kirchmeyer, C. (2005), 'The effects of mentoring on academic careers over time: testing performance and political perspectives', *Human Relations*, **58**, 637–60.

Kram, K.E. (1985), *Mentoring at Work: Developmental Relationships in Organizational Life*, Glenview, IL: Scott Foresman and Company.

Lavelle, M. (2003), 'Enron end run', *Washington Monthly*, May.

Lazarus, R.S. (2006), 'Emotions and interpersonal relationships: toward a person-centered conceptualization of emotions and coping', *Journal of Personality*, **74**, 9–46.

Lazarus, R.S. and Folkman, S. (1984) *Stress, Appraisal, and Coping*, New York: Springer.

Lips-Wiersma, M. and Hall, D.T. (2007), 'Organizational career development is not dead: a case study on managing the new career during organizational change', *Journal of Organizational Behavior*, **28**, 771–92.

Marshall, J. (2000), 'Living lives of change: examining facets of women managers' career stories', in M. Peiperl, M. Arthur, T. Morris and R. Goffee (eds), *Conversations in Career Theory: Insights and Trends*, Oxford, UK: Oxford University Press, pp. 202–27.

Mirvis, P.H. and Hall, D.T. (1994), 'Psychological success and the boundaryless career', *Journal of Organizational Behaviour*, **15**, 365–80.

Mischel, W. (1969), 'Continuity and change in personality', *American Psychologist*, **24**, 1012–18.

Peiperl, M. and Baruch, Y. (1997), 'Back to square zero: the post-corporate career', *Organization Dynamics*, **25**, 7–22.

Ragins, B.R. and Cotton, J.L. (1999), 'Mentor functions and outcomes: a comparison of men and women in formal and informal mentoring relationships', *Journal of Applied Psychology*, **84** (4), 529–50.

Ragins, B.R., Cotton, J.L. and Miller, J.S. (2000), 'Marginal mentoring: the effects of type of mentor, quality of relationship, and program design on work and career attitudes', *Academy of Management Journal*, **43** (6), 1177–94.

Rosenbaum, J.E. (1979), 'Tournament mobility: career patterns in a corporation', *Administrative Science Quarterly*, **24**, 221–41.

Rosenbaum, J.E. (1984), *Career Mobility in a Corporate Hierarchy*, London: Academic Press.

Sears, S.F., Unizar, G.G. and Garrett, D.E. (2000), 'Examining a stress coping model of burnout and depression in extension agents', *Journal of Occupational Health Psychology*, **5**, 56–62.

Seibert, S.E., Kraimer, M.L. and Liden, R.C. (2001), 'A social capital theory of career success', *Academy of Management Journal*, **44**, 219–37.

Sonnenfeld, J. and Ward, A. (2008), 'How great leaders rebound after career disasters', *Organizational Dynamics*, **37**(1), 1–20.

Sturges, J. (2004), 'The individualisation of the career and its implications for management and leadership development', in J. Storey (ed.), *Leadership in Organizations: Current Issues and Key Trends*, London: Routledge.

Sturges, J., Guest, D., Conway, N. and Mackenzie Davey, K. (2002), 'A longitudinal study of the relationship between career management and organizational commitment among graduates in the first ten years at work', *Journal of Organizational Behavior*, **23**(6): 731–48.

Sullivan, S.N. and Baruch, Y. (2009), 'Advances in career theory and research: critical review and agenda for future exploration', *Journal of Management*, **35**(6), 1452–571.

Sweeney, D.S., Haller, D. and Sale, F. (1987), 'Individually controlled career counseling', *Training and Development Journal*, **41**(8), 58–61.

Turner, R.H. (1960), 'Sponsored and contest mobility and the school system', *American Sociological Review*, **25**(6), 855–62.

Van Maanen, J. (1977), 'Experiencing organizations: notes on the meaning of careers and socialization', in J. Van Maanen (ed.), *Organizational Careers: Some New Perspectives* New York: Wiley, pp. 15–45.

Watson, T.J. and Harris, P. (1999) *The Emergent Manager: Becoming a Manager in the Modern Work Organization*, London: Sage.

Weick, K.E. (1995), *Sensemaking in Organizations*, London: Sage.

Weick, K.E., Sutcliffe, K.M. and Obstfeld, D. (2005), 'Organizing and the process of sensemaking', *Organization Science*, **16**, 409–21.

9. Personal goals for self-directed leaders: traditional and new perspectives

Thomas S. Bateman

All my life I've always wanted to be somebody. But I see now that I should have been more specific.

(Fictional character who never quite got her act together, played by Lily Tomlin, from *Searching for Signs of Intelligent Life in the Universe*, Wagner, 1985)

And you may ask yourself . . . same as it ever was?

(With apologies to David Byrne)

If you care enough about a result, you will almost certainly attain it.

(William James)

Self-management is of course exceedingly complex, but at its core are personal goals and feedback (Latham and Locke, 1991). Other chapters in this volume focus on feedback, and offer many useful perspectives on this vital construct. This chapter focuses on the other core construct: personal goals.

Your motivation can come from many sources, but the most powerful driver is your personal goals. Goals motivate us in all important aspects of our lives, and leadership development is no exception. This chapter offers a variety of personal goals that are potentially helpful toward developing into a better leader.

Goals direct people's attention, energize and change behavior, and inspire accomplishment and higher performance (Locke and Latham, 1990). Specific goals are more effective at these things than vague goals. 'I want to be an awesome person' and 'I want to be a successful businessperson' are worthy aspirations, but they are pretty vague. 'I want to become a better leader' is arguably a bit more specific, especially when used as a stepping stone toward personal greatness and business success. Goals concerning *what to change* about your leadership can be more specific yet.

For example, having clear intentions to become a better leader by improving one's strategic thinking and developing stronger people skills are more specific goals than 'becoming a better leader'. Developing a viable vision within the next month and motivating people by using new and more powerful approaches are more specific yet. This chapter is intended to provide you with a set of potentially-useful options from which to choose.

The specific goals you choose to pursue are completely up to you, of course, but it is better to choose valid, high-leverage goals than goals that won't make much difference. Thankfully, at least a half century of management research and theorizing have made clear the aspects of leadership that really do have an impact on a leader's performance and effectiveness. This chapter will identify a variety of useful goals that have appeared in mainstream leadership theories, and will also offer some new perspectives. From this array of options, the self-directed leader can pick and choose goals that are most personally relevant and useful.

The self-directed leader (SDL) is one who makes valid, useful decisions and takes appropriate action in the pursuit of personal development in the domain of leadership. Self-directed leadership requires making choices mindfully rather than mindlessly. It also requires taking high-leverage actions, rather than acting in the ways that are simply the easiest and most natural. Self-directed leadership begins with selecting personal goals and making conscious choices about what dimensions of leadership to learn and what strategies and tactics to implement. This description of the self-directed leader contrasts with the too-common mindless approach to one's own leadership, and with merely hoping for improvement, which are easy but tend to result in no development at all. The point is, whatever goals you decide to pursue, wishing and hoping to achieve them won't make it happen; making a decision to take specific action is the key to moving from the worthy ideas that can be found in this volume to an actual result.

I will use the term *self-sabotage* to refer to undermining one's own self-development efforts or leadership effectiveness by failing to act on things under one's control, or by acting in suboptimal ways. Dubrin (1992) defined self-sabotage as doing things against your best interests, even though you probably could do otherwise. Thus, knowing that one needs to improve one's leadership effectiveness by improving 'people skills', but failing to take decisive action in that regard, is self-sabotage. So is choosing a self-development goal that is not as important as one that goes ignored; so is choosing an important goal but not pursuing it or progressing as far as one could. I will sometimes use *self-command* to suggest appropriate goal selection and the application of appropriate strategies and tactics that counteract the tendency to self-sabotage and enable progress toward greater leadership effectiveness.

GOAL CHOICE

Before you attain your leadership development goals, you must first engage in the tasks of appropriately choosing and then effectively pursuing them. Traditional leadership theories that have been validated with evidence, as well as recent perspectives that have potential impact on leader effectiveness, can identify the most important goals for personal leadership development. Specifics about how to implement these ideas are readily found in training sessions, manuals, and some of the cited references; therefore the chapter is more strategic than tactical.

How people choose their goals has been the subject of surprisingly little study. But criteria that you can apply in making goal choices include the potential value of the goals in question, their importance compared with other options, your confidence regarding your ability to pursue and achieve them (or at least make progress), and what your thoughts and emotions seem to indicate that you should pursue (Klein et al., 2008). Thoughts and emotions have potential diagnostic value in indicating the potential value you place on achieving the goal. Then, once you've chosen your goals, it becomes time to commit to the chosen goal(s), and enter the volitional control phase of self-regulation, which consists of focusing attention on the chosen goal, executing strategies to attain it, and monitoring performance (Zimmerman, 2000).

For academics, this entire domain of goal choice and pursuit is a wide-open field for research inquiry, particularly in the domain of leadership. For practitioners, unless and until you have feedback or other data that indicate which goals you most need to pursue, you can use the criteria listed above on an intuitive basis. Most of this chapter is dedicated to providing a wide-ranging set of goal options from which to choose, and it includes relevant references for diving deeper into topics of particular interest.

GOAL PURSUIT

People often hold certain beliefs, or feel that they know what they should do, but don't act in ways that are consistent with what they think. Pfeffer and Sutton (2000) described the 'knowing–doing gap': the often-large discrepancy between what people know they *should* do, and what they in fact do. Argyris (1993) described the difference between espoused theories and theories-in-use: people say the right things, but don't act commensurately. To illustrate this point, pick a well-known and useful concept such as 'world-class customer service' or 'employee empowerment'. We all 'know' these things, but do we use them to their full potential? To think about how we fall short of realizing the full impact of important ideas, consider this metaphorical ladder:

The first level of (pseudo-) knowledge is characterized by mere awareness. We sometimes erroneously assume that we are applying concepts simply because we are familiar with them, and perhaps because they seem commonsensical or like old news. Imagine sitting in a classroom, hearing the instructor bring up a popular management term, dismissively thinking 'sure, I've heard of that. There's nothing new here', and failing to hear the rest of the message which may include new perspective, depth, nuance, or creative application.

At the second level, you progress from recognizing a shallow buzzword to actually knowing what it means. Take 'empowerment', for example: can you articulate what it means psychologically, what it means in fact, the common misperceptions surrounding it (including what it is not), and what is required for its effective implementation? The same questions pertain to all important leadership concepts.

At the next level, you move beyond the intellectual understanding of a concept to also appreciating its potential importance and impact. At this level, you embrace the concept, and agree that (done properly) it is potentially worth implementing.

The levels of knowledge just described increase progressively in terms of depth of understanding and commitment to execution. But all are cognitive, not behavioral, and all still sit on the cognitive side of the knowing–doing gap. All, even at the top level of complexity and commitment, remain espoused theories rather than theories-in-use. Therefore, the self-directed leader needs to move to higher, more behaviorally-oriented rungs of the ladder. At these levels of use, climbing the ladder becomes potentially more impactful, although, of course, the ladder must be leaning against the right wall; some goals are not as helpful as others. The aspiring leader who starts pursuing an important goal behaviorally rather than merely in her head can:

- Try it once, but perhaps without adequate persistence, and perhaps never again.
- Do it sometimes, when it is easily remembered or attempted.
- Live it, consistently and over time, as appropriate.

It is, of course, this final rung that represents true development in a leadership competency. As an aside to researchers: espoused vs. enacted theories, and what psychologists call implicit theories (in this context, of leadership effectiveness) have not been adequately studied in managerial populations, and offer valuable opportunity for future theorizing and empiricism.

PERSONAL GOALS AND MAINSTREAM LEADERSHIP THEORIES

Choosing goals represents the 'what' to focus on in self-management and leadership development. Other chapters focus on the *how*, such as how to be resilient in the wake of failure and how to cope with stress. Leadership theories and research, not to mention readers' intuitions, make clear the *why*. It is up to the reader, perhaps with reference to sources that describe the theories in full detail, to identify and act upon the *where* and *when*.

The theories and new concepts summarized below identify many important dimensions of leadership that are most likely to have a positive impact and enhance leader effectiveness. They offer many possible destinations for the self-directed leader, all of which are potentially valid and useful. The *choice* of destinations, though, is up to the reader, and should be based on what s/he deems most personally important (and perhaps most urgent).

Attending to People and to Task Performance

Pioneering studies done more than half a century ago investigated two fundamental types of leader behavior: consideration or relations-oriented behavior, and initiating structure or task-oriented behavior (Yukl, 2006). The former concerns supportive, helpful behavior toward people, in particular subordinates, and the latter concerns task accomplishment by subordinates, including setting performance goals, planning and scheduling, and providing resources.

These are broad, important, and enduring categories of leader behavior (Judge et al., 2004). Some leaders are effective on both dimensions. Many, it seems, focus on one to the neglect of the other. Some seem ineffectual at both.

Because acquiring and attending to feedback, as discussed in other chapters, is a fundamental component of effective self-management and personal development, the straightforward implication of these leader behaviors is to collect feedback on effectiveness at dealing with people and with making sure their work gets done properly. Assuming room for improvement in one or both of these two leadership capacities, and substantial upside such that a concerted effort is worthwhile, the self-directed leader mindfully sets goals to practice and further develop the relevant competencies.

A common form of self-sabotage is to engage in actions that are easiest or most enjoyable. Some manager/leaders prefer to deal with task issues and wish the human element of work would just go away. Some enjoy working with people and don't want to deal with performance problems. Leader self-command derives from applying a different criterion in choosing what dimensions to tackle: those most important to one's personal leadership development and effectiveness.

Participative Leadership

In addition to attending properly to both people and to task performance, a third fundamental dimension of leadership is the extent to which leaders involve others in decision making (Tannenbaum and Schmidt, 1958). Leaders can make decisions autocratically, engage the group in decision making, consult others and then decide, or delegate decisions altogether. Of course, a leader may make use of all of these approaches, depending on the task at hand, as well as on other considerations, such as followers' interests and expertise. Often, however, leaders have personal preferences and tendencies that over time constitute a single personal style.

Common self-sabotage tendencies are to be overly autocratic and not engage others in decision making; to routinely engage others in decision making even when it is unnecessary and time-consuming; and, associated with each of these tendencies, to employ a single approach inflexibly rather than applying a contingency analysis to determine when it is most and least appropriate to involve the group. As with all aspects of leadership, self-appraisal and feedback can inform leaders as to their personal tendencies. As a consequence of such feedback, leaders can choose goals in the form of (a) more extensive use of underutilized styles; and (b) practicing and developing the requisite skills, including situational analysis, that inform when (and when not) to use each style. Thus the leader who learns that he is too autocratic can set goals both to make more joint decisions with the group and to practice the skills that enhance group decision-making effectiveness. He also can set a goal to learn to diagnose the features of situations that are best for making the decision as a group – for example, the members are able to contribute and need to be committed to executing the decision – as well as retaining his habitual autocratic style when the decision must be made immediately or group members have nothing to contribute and don't care to be involved.

One solution is to consult the Vroom and Jago (1988) model to learn how situational features – including characteristics of the team, the problem and circumstances – affect the need for team-based decision making. Another is to apply the tactic of consensus with qualification (Eisenhardt, 1989): when appropriate, work with the team to achieve consensus, but when time runs short and/or consensus appears impossible, conclude the effort and make the decision autocratically.

Transactional Leadership

Transactional leadership is based on the leader's authority to tell direct reports what to do and on the use of rewards (and punishments) to get them to comply (Bass, 1985). This approach to leadership can be effective because people are more likely to do things that result in rewards, and less likely to do things that result in punishment (at minimum, they may repeat the punishable offense but do it in a way that makes them less likely to get caught). Rewards – including not just money but also intangibles such as compliments – do motivate people. The challenge is to allocate rewards properly.

The leader interested in improving her transactional leadership skills could make a point of carefully contemplating or seeking feedback about how pay is distributed, about whether she plays favorites in terms of job assignments and giving praise, and how thoughtfully and fairly she applies disciplinary action. Upon finding indications of doing a poor job in any of these regards, or of doing an adequate job but not realizing the full potential of reward systems as motivators, she could set a goal for herself to motivate people more effectively via rewards. This could include subgoals of making sure that rewards are based on performance and desirable behaviors, and that rewards are allocated fairly and/or transparently.

A common trap for leaders was described in an important article titled 'On the folly of rewarding A while hoping for B' (Kerr, 1975). For example, business leaders sometimes want colleagues to cooperate but create competitive reward structures, cut budgets for those who keep spending down and increase funding for those who go over budget, and ask for long-term thinking and action, but reward and punish on the basis of short-term results.

A second common trap is to unwittingly deliver rewards and administer punishments unfairly. Employees often think that they are unfairly treated compared to someone else, sometimes due to perceived favoritism and bias. Leaders can set a goal for themselves of achieving fairness in the workplace. Subgoals could include making sure the top performers receive significantly higher rewards than lower performers, creating greater transparency so that people know what criteria are being used, or becoming better at appraising performance and giving appropriate feedback, in part so that people can improve their performance and earn higher rewards in the future.

A more specific self-sabotage trap is being more likely to give compliments than criticism, or vice versa, sometimes for reasons that aren't valid. It is not uncommon to be off the mark in these regards. For example, the well-known Myers–Briggs Type Inventory includes the dimension Thinking vs. Feeling. Thinking types are more likely to criticize than to compliment; feeling types are more likely to compliment than to criticize. A leader who wants to do better in giving valid positive and negative feedback can set personal goals – regardless of 'type' – to give both praise and constructive criticism rather than over-rely on one or the other, and to give such feedback only when it's truly deserved.

Charismatic Leadership

Many leaders and aspiring leaders wish they had charisma. The good news is that theory and research have identified concrete actions that leaders can take to make it more likely that others will view them as charismatic. Charisma is thus not something that only a select few are born with and that others missed out on. In fact, people can 'work on' their charisma and noticeably enhance it.

Charisma (e.g., Conger and Kanungo, 1998; House and Shamir, 1993; cf. Miner, 2005) is defined in part by its impact on followers, including its appeal to their emotions and values in ways that inspire intrinsic motivation. Charismatic leadership is defined also by the leaders' actions, which impress followers and enhance perceptions of charisma. These perspectives suggest to the self-directed leader the possible need to display emotion as appropriate (at least, passion for the cause); to consider followers' ethics and values in communications, decisions and actions; and to appeal to intrinsic sources of motivation. Compared with the extrinsic motivators highlighted in transactional leadership, intrinsic motivation derives from the work itself, as the individual engages in it and performs. Charisma-conferring behaviors include communicating a compelling vision for the future, showing self-confidence, expressing confidence in others, and sacrificing on behalf of the team. The self-directed leader who wants to increase his personal charisma would assess his behavior on those dimensions and set personal goals to display them more often and clearly.

Two common traps are thinking that charisma is the single key to effective leadership, and misunderstanding the meaning of charisma.

Related to both of these is thinking that charisma is mostly about style and personality. Perhaps this is true in the colloquial sense, but this is not the way that leadership scholars or self-directed leaders think about charisma. Avoid these traps by understanding what charisma really means, as described above. Work on those specific behaviors, such as communicating the vision and showing confidence in followers, rather than on your 'personality' or image. Also make sure that you supplement charismatic behaviors with the substance and sheer competence that will impress people, deliver results, and sustain your leadership over the long run. This will be discussed in greater detail later in the chapter.

Thus the leader can set goals of increasing her displays of passion for the mission, creating a culture that is based more strongly on values and ethics, or reducing an over-reliance on extrinsic rewards and increasing the intrinsic rewards of people's work. The latter can be done by, for instance, enhancing and conveying the importance and significance of their work to customers both outside and inside the organization, and providing direct feedback to people about the impact and importance of their work.

Transformational Leadership

There is much overlap and potential synergy between charisma and transformational leadership. Yukl (2006) offers a thorough discussion of the similarities, differences and sources of conceptual confusion. Transformational leadership is that which inspires followers to perform beyond expectations and transcend their own self-interest for the good of the team or organization (Bass, 1985). Transformational leadership activates people's higher-order needs such as self-actualization, and includes the values-based, charismatic behaviors described above. It further includes giving personalized attention to individuals, stimulating team members intellectually, and conveying expectations of superior performance beyond the norm. For example, the self-directed leader interested in developing and strengthening her skills as a transformational leader will make a concerted effort to develop and communicate in inspiring fashion not only a compelling vision of the future but also followers' roles in helping to attain that future. She also will provide more individualized attention through personal coaching and mentoring, assigning tasks and goals that challenge people and develop their skills, and allowing people to express their personal interests and strengths.

Leadership effectiveness can be defined by leaders' achievement of their own goals, but a more useful definition considers the achievement of team and organizational goals. A common trap and source of self-sabotage in the domain of charismatic and transformational leadership is to develop and pursue a vision that is personally appealing to the leader but to others is unethical, inappropriate, or strategically mistaken. The leader who is effective at transforming people and organizations can as easily transform them for the worse as for the better. One important antidote to this trap is to involve others in formulating and evaluating the vision – and an important tactic is to inject intellectual stimulation into the process by inviting others' ideas and constructive dissent. A second antidote is to revisit the vision periodically, again with team involvement and intellectual stimulation. Some elements of the vision, particularly those involving high ethical standards, should remain permanent features. Other aspects, particularly at the tactical and sometimes strategic levels, may need to change as circumstances change.

NEW DIRECTIONS AND IMPLICATIONS FOR SELF-DIRECTED LEADERS

The discussion above used prominent leadership theories to identify an array of important goals that self-directed leaders can choose to pursue. Next, I draw from a variety of (mostly) recent ideas from the academic literature that leaders may also find interesting and useful as sources of additional developmental opportunities. Some are not new topics in and of themselves, but have not been fully integrated into the leadership literature or become standard topics in leadership development. Others are very new to the literature, in some cases not explicitly linked to leadership but still opening potentially important avenues toward further theorizing, empiricism and leader development.

Ethics

You don't have to be an outstanding leader, or attend leadership workshops, to understand that the things done by Ken Lay, Bernie Madoff and some of the culprits behind the economic meltdown were unethical. Most people can't imagine themselves doing the heinous things that make the news. But most people are not as ethical as they think they are, in part because they make so many decisions on the basis of unconscious biases (Banaji et al., 2003). Making ethical decisions takes moral awareness (recognizing that the issue has ethical implications), moral judgment (discerning which actions are morally defensible), and moral character – the courage and persistence to act in accordance with your ethics, despite the challenges (Trevino and Brown, 2004).

Moreover, there is a difference between being an ethical person and being an ethical leader (Trevino and Brown, 2004). Whereas ethical people make decisions and behave ethically, they often do so invisibly or silently or on their own. An ethical leader is a role model, visibly setting the standard, communicating openly to others, and creating and strengthening a culture of ethical behavior. A self-directed leader can set a goal of being not just an ethical person but also an ethical leader.

A common self-sabotaging trap is to simply not realize that biases often drive decisions; another is to recognize the factors driving a decision but not realize that they constitute biases. Different people take contrary but principled stands: people are responsible for their own fates vs. people are victims of circumstances; war is bad vs. war is sometimes necessary; government is the solution vs. government is the problem; the markets work vs. the markets need some regulating. Whatever side leaders take on these and other philosophical debates, traps can occur when decisions are driven by an ideology or belief system based in preconceived bias that one party considers ethical and another, unethical.

One potential solution to these quandaries is to apply the ethics system of consequentialism. In contrast to making decisions intuitively, or unknowingly applying personal biases, consequentialism means deciding and acting on the basis not of the leader's predilections, but of the best consequences for pertinent stakeholders (Baron, 1998). This requires a thorough forecasting of consequences, considering for all relevant stakeholders the tangible outcomes, short- and long-term impact, and so on. Applying this ethical system helps to ensure that leaders are vigilant in the pursuit of rational problem-solving and thus take fewer actions that ignore the consequences for some important constituencies.

Leadership Self-Efficacy

One of the most powerful psychological predictors of behavior and performance is self-efficacy: believing in your ability to organize and execute the courses of action required to attain goals (Bandura, 1997). More specifically, leadership self-efficacy (LSE) is confidence in one's knowledge, skills and ability to lead others effectively (Hannah et al., 2008). Leadership self-efficacy has been shown to predict others' ratings of leaders' effectiveness, although cause and effect are not well established (Anderson et al., 2008).

Self-sabotage can result from a type of 'underconfidence', in which people's lack of faith in their own leadership capabilities can deter them from taking on leadership roles or undermine their effectiveness within those roles. Conversely, leaders can self-sabotage because of self-efficacy that is unrealistically high: overconfidence in their decision-making abilities, for instance, such that inappropriate intuitions or instincts interfere with valid and useful analysis, or the mistaken belief that past successes or having skills relevant to one leadership context, such as in a turnaround/cost-cutting situation, necessarily generalize to other situations that require different strategies and tactics.

One solution to inappropriate levels of leadership self-efficacy is realistic optimism, a combination of confidence that things can be made to work out, along with recognizing the current facts and challenges (Schneider, 2001). For those with leadership self-efficacy beliefs that are simply too low, several general approaches to increase self-efficacy have been well-validated in other domains. These include learning through observing role models, hearing persuasive arguments about what can be accomplished, and practice (Bandura, 1997).

Also crucial is to recognize that leadership involves many skills, in many domains and contexts, and that the skills that apply to one may be less relevant to the next. High self-efficacy can be general ('Thankfully, I really am a good leader'), but really should be domain-specific ('Honestly, I have some relevant skills, but have never faced this type of challenge before and may need some coaching.'). Self-directed leaders should strive to develop appropriate levels of self-efficacy for each of the leader competencies he or she is striving to develop, be it the behaviors described above in the context of traditional leadership theories, those described next, or those discussed in other chapters of this volume.

Positive Psychology

Martin Seligman, then-president of the American Psychological Association, observed a decade ago that the field historically had fixated on fixing people's problems (trying to bring them to 'normalcy') but had neglected the huge upside potential of moving people from average to extraordinary. The field of psychology made an important turn. Since then, psychologists have attempted to identify important human virtues and personal strengths, and management scholars have similarly offered new perspectives on organizational behavior – with the common theme of identifying opportunities, strategies and tactics for pursuing and achieving excellence.

Paralleling the positive psychology perspective, much of management traditionally has concerned itself with solving problems: dealing with difficult subordinates, responding to performance shortfalls, coping with crises, and managing by exception (dedicating time and resources to the salient exception, as defined by falling below expectation or standard, or taking action only when mistakes have occurred). Managing by exception is concerned primarily with deviations and shortfalls, and intervening when something goes wrong (Bass, 1990).

This distinction – management by exception vs. pursuing excellence – pertains to leaders throughout organizations, from supervisory levels to the strategic apex inhabited by top management teams. At strategic levels, but potentially pertinent at all levels, Das (2004) suggests reorienting strategy so it is more opportunity-focused, not merely problem-focused.

A common self-sabotage default option is problem-focused thinking. A solution is to adopt an opportunity lens. Every MBA student knows the classroom mantra of turning problem into opportunity, and many managers would benefit from applying this principle. Executives are typically unlikely to see opportunity in crisis, but Brockner and James (2008) suggest some strategies for perceiving opportunity: applying a learning orientation, having high self-efficacy in dealing with difficult challenges, considering long-term change rather than just short-term damage control, attempting to treat causes rather than merely symptoms, and inviting creative solutions.

The self-directed leader can assess not just weaknesses but also her own strengths as well as the strengths of her people. Whereas so much leader training concentrates on fixing shortcomings (say, the low scores from multi-rater feedback), a positive psychology perspective would focus on how to leverage a leader's strengths to full advantage. Further, it suggests creating the conditions necessary for people to leverage their strengths in ways that benefit (satisfy, develop, strengthen) both them and the organization. This is a far cry from management or leadership by exception. One place to start is by conducting personal strengths assessments (for example, at www.authentichappiness.org). The real starting point, though, is to set a personal goal and make a conscious decision to play from strength, not just to correct weakness.

Proactive and Transcendent Behavior

Leadership is about more than occupying a role that includes having authority over other people. Leading, as distinguished from managing, includes the activity of creating change (e.g., Kotter, 1999). In contrast to behavior that is determined by circumstance, in which people are passive respondents to environmental demands (including rewards and punishments), proactive behavior is that which creates constructive change in environments, in others, or in oneself (Bateman and Crant, 1993). As a special category, transcendent behavior creates major and positive change with major impact (Bateman and Porath, 2003). Thus, whereas people so often merely meet expectations, put up with constraints, allow problems to persist, and watch windows of opportunity slam shut, those exhibiting proactive and transcendent behaviors exceed expectations, overcome constraints, fix problems, and seize or create opportunities.

These behaviors have obvious potential utility for leadership. Proactive behavior has been widely studied (Crant, 2000; Grant and Ashford, 2008), not much with respect to leadership but enough to indicate that managers who exhibit more proactive behavior are rated as more charismatic leaders by their bosses (Crant and Bateman, 2000). They have not been studied in conjunction with mainstream leadership theories or with objective leader effectiveness, although predictions and relationships should be straightforward because effective leadership is distinguished in part by acts of change. Short of extreme levels or attempts that violate laws, ethics or important norms, proactive and transcendent behaviors by leaders potentially will increase leaders' impact. The self-directed leader can make a point of self-assessing or seeking feedback from others ('am I more passive and reactive, or proactive in making things happen around here?' 'am I a true leader of change, or a maintenance manager/bureaucrat?') and take action as desired.

One self-sabotaging trap is to engage in proactive behaviors that are inappropriate; another is to not engage in them much at all. A helpful metaphor provides a solution. Imagine your job as an inverse donut: a center made of cake, surrounded by air space, which in turn is surrounded by a solid. The cake at the center is the core of your job: the crucial activities and performance that you are expected to deliver. This is not the small stuff of the job; it is the crucial performance that you must deliver at a high level. The airspace around the essential core is where you have autonomy, or the freedom to innovate, experiment, change things, and expand your responsibilities. The surrounding solid is the out-of-bounds, where you dare not tread: illegalities, unethical actions, and actions that violate corporate strategy or the culture in ways that will not be tolerated.

For the self-directed leader, this metaphor provides a framework for personal assessment, guidance for decisions, and even a vision for both your leadership and your work unit (team, division, organization). Specifically, you should be able to identify your core responsibilities, separating the top priorities that require excellence from the many other routine responsibilities that are less important. You could check with your boss to learn whether you are in agreement, and negotiate to mutual understanding. Do the same with the out-of-bounds – articulate the list, and confirm or negotiate with your boss. What's left over, the things yet undiscussed, comprise the air space, representing possible opportunities for new leadership initiatives and change.

Be clear about priorities and out-of-bounds, and get on the same page as your boss. For more proactive, transcendent, impactful leadership, work the air space – create plenty of room to operate. Identify problems to tackle, scan for opportunities to pursue, and consider how to create new opportunities that serve your organization well. And by the way, you can engage in similar exercises with your direct reports, making sure that they are on the same donut-page with you.

Enacted Problem-Solving

When appraising leaders, people sometimes distinguish between style and substance. As noted in the discussion of charisma, it may be that style gets the most attention, even in academic research. But substance, of course, matters most, in the long run.

Where does substance, in the eye of followers and other leader behold-ers, come from? Expertise and competence provide substance; adding trustworthiness to the equation creates a formula for leader credibility (Kim et al., 2009). Actual performance in the form of results delivered by and attributed to the leader will enhance these perceptions. Self-directed leadership does not let a focus on style drive out the required focus on delivering results.

How to deliver results? One perspective focuses on enacted problem-solving (Bateman, 2010), which consists of the cognitive and behavioral activities of problem solving in the service of performance. An example is the classic phase model of problem solving that so many managers know but don't mindfully implement: defining the problem, establish-ing goals, generating and evaluating an array of alternative solutions, choosing or combining solutions, planning implementation, implement-ing, and following up by assessing progress and adapting as needed. Effective leadership also includes motivating enacted problem solving by followers, thus distributing leadership and generating better results throughout the group, unit or organization for which the leader is responsible.

One related form of self-sabotage, already noted, is to care more about style than results. Another is to care solely about results to the neglect of people; this includes the taskmaster style that creates pushback and burnout, or a focus on short-term results at the expense of the longer term. Another is to define performance inappropriately, such as by sheer quantity of output to the neglect of quality, productivity to the neglect of creativity, and managing by exception rather than also seeking, creating and seizing new opportunities. Yet another is to try to do everything your-self, rather than distributing to others some responsibilities for problem solving and opportunity-pursuit.

The solutions are to supplement these single-minded goals with addi-tional needed goals: establish the dual goals of attending to both people and to results, to the long term as well as the short run, quality as well as quantity, the core of the donut as well as the air space, opportunities as well as problems. These dual goals can be established and pursued by followers as well via distributed leadership throughout the system. See Collins and Porras (1996) for descriptions of how companies, and by extension leaders, can pursue the genius of the 'and' (dual goals pursued strategically and successfully) rather than limit themselves via the tyranny of the 'or' – same dual goals, but viewed as dueling or mutually exclusive rather than complementary.

Strategic Leadership and Cognitive/Behavioral Complexity

Strategic leadership refers to the leadership 'of' organizations rather than 'in' organizations (Hunt, 1991). Strategic leadership is exercised by the people in the upper echelon (Hambrick and Mason, 1984) or top manage-ment team (TMT) with overall responsibility for the organization. Boal and Hooijberg (2000) integrate several literatures into a view of strategic leadership that has important implications for the capabilities that stra-tegic leaders need to develop in their organizations and in themselves. Their model is potentially relevant as well to self-directed leaders without top-level strategic responsibilities.

In the Boal and Hooijberg (2000) integrative model – for our purposes here, viewed as not limited to strategic leadership but rather as a strategic perspective for SDLs of all levels – leaders must create and maintain (1) the ability to learn (absorptive capacity; Cohen and Levinthal, 1990), (2) the ability to change (adaptive capacity), and (3) managerial wisdom. All three of these leadership cornerstones derive (partly in conjunc-tion with charisma and transformational leadership) from three leader competencies: cognitive complexity, behavioral complexity and social intelligence.

As summarized by Boal and Hooijberg (2000), cognitive complexity refers to how a person thinks, and includes the ability, when processing information, to distinguish more rather than fewer categories and to see both differences and commonalities among them. Behavioral complexity means having both a large repertoire of behaviors and the ability to perceive and select the most appropriate behaviors to use in a given situation. Social intelligence is the ability to both understand one's social environment and to act appropriately on that understanding. The self-directed leader (as always) self-assesses and decides his or her developmental needs, with the key options here lying with these three competencies as pathways to developing the ability to learn, to change, and to act with wisdom.

An obvious trap but perhaps the most pervasive form of self-sabotage is simply rigidity. Leaders sometimes are rigid in their thinking, or rigid in their actions, or both. A broad solution is to increase one's repertoire of thinking patterns and behaviors, as described by the theory. Then, engage in flexible tenacity (Gollwitzer et al., 2008): steadfast pursuit of the strategic goal, exploring for the most effective tactics, keeping some tactics and abandoning and replacing others as required. As a related example, political scientist Gil Troy (2008) advises US presidents to engage in tactical fluidity, to be principled plus accommodating, and to be flexible plus anchored.

Components of the Boal and Hooijberg (2000) model have been studied empirically, although not with a focus on self-development as it might apply to leaders at different levels or in different contexts. The model offers a strategic perspective on leadership that the self-directed leader can use to great advantage by considering which aspects are most relevant to self and situation. It also offers high potential and good opportunity for future empirical work on self-directed leader development.

Critical Thinking and Wisdom

School textbooks bombard students with 'critical thinking' exercises and questions for discussion. How much and how often do you truly engage in critical thinking, in life broadly or with respect to leadership in particular? Reminder: this chapter is choosing goals and pursuing them – moving into action in your personal development as a leader. Here, the goal is to become a better thinker, or to engage in more critical thinking on important issues.

Many perspectives on wisdom have been offered over the millennia. Recently, Sternberg (1998) offered a theory describing wisdom as a process of attaining the common good through balancing the interests of multiple entities – oneself, others and surroundings – over short- and long-term time horizons. In the business context, at least five balancing acts characterize wisdom: (1) knowing all/knowing little, in which executives must have extensive knowledge but also acknowledge the limits of their knowledge; (2) diving deep/flying high, in which executives interact closely with relevant stakeholders, but also stand apart and develop transcendent solutions; (3) now/not now, characterized by a decisive action orientation but also patience or inaction when appropriate; (4) complexify/simplify, seeing interdependencies and complexities but also thinking and communicating in clear, simple and thematic ways; and (5) only me/no me, taking on the responsibility but suppressing the ego (Mick et al., 2009).

As always, a pervasive self-sabotage trap is mindlessness, including making leadership-related decisions – strategic, interpersonal and other kinds – unreflectively, on a mindless or default basis. Of course, time sometimes is scarce, and/or intuition serves us well. Often, though, leaders mindlessly engage in business as usual, or apply their default options, when they should be stepping back and thinking things through before deciding and acting.

Greater self-command comes from consciously injecting mindfulness into your leadership processes, creating time and space to think, by executing the strategies and tactics of critical thinking and problem solving, inviting others to participate in and provide feedback on your decision-making processes and the effectiveness thereof, and reflecting on past decisions and performances to draw lessons pertinent to future decisions and leadership challenges. Evidence-based management is a disciplined approach to making decisions based on the best available scientific evidence rather than on personal preference and unsystematic experience (Rousseau, 2006), and offers an effective antidote for mindlessness that can elevate the quality of leaders' critical thinking, wisdom and effectiveness.

Some self-sabotaging traps are to equate wisdom with intelligence, to consider it something that only a few possess and the rest of us never will, and to assume that it will develop naturally but only over time. Self-directed leaders can identify wisdom as a personal development goal, and consider wisdom not an attribute, but a process of how to think. Consider also that it doesn't come naturally with time, but is a function of both leadership-related experiences and reflection on those experiences. Wise leaders develop a more expansive set of perspectives than others via their thinking habits, including reflecting more deeply than the rest on their experiences and on events. 'Leadership is made in large part based on what you take the time to go back and learn, and then apply forward' (Avolio, 2005, p. 110).

Long-Termism

One important aspect of wisdom is thinking and behaving with an eye toward the long term. Whether doing academic research on leadership or leading in the real world, we tend to focus on short-term rather than long-term results. In conducting research, performance data tend to be collected contemporaneously with data gathered about the leader, or with only a short time lag. Business leaders are (with only occasional exception) rewarded and punished based on the results they generate quarterly and annually, rather than on the results that they might generate a few years down the road. It's a short-term world, when it comes to performance evaluation, but a long-term world when it comes to careers, organizational survival, and ultimate impact on society and the planet.

The tragedy of the commons – the scenario in which herders benefit as their animals graze a tract of communal land until overuse leads to its destruction (Hardin, 1968) – is perhaps the best-known example across scientific disciplines of how short-term thinking and behavior sabotage long-term outcomes. The book title *Short-term America* (Jacobs, 1991) captures the United States' obsession with immediate results, as contrasted with Asia's 'psychology of long-termism' (Hampden-Turner and Trompenaars, 2001). But even among Westerners, researchers have documented individual differences in future orientation (Zimbardo and Boyd, 1999) and temporal depth (Bluedorn, 2002).

The importance of learning how to think long-term (and of acting on that basis) seems self-evident, although long-term thinking has gone virtually unexamined by management scholars. It may be possible to train people to become long-term thinkers. El Sawy (1983) increased business managers' future time horizons by asking them first to think about history. Furthermore, an interview study of people pursuing extraordinarily long-term goals – goals that might not be achieved in their own lifetimes – identified the psychological factors that maintained their long-term goal focus and persistence (Bateman and Barry, 2010). The various factors included envisioned possible futures and possible selves; an appreciation of history, future what-ifs, and sustainability goals; work characterized by fun, surprises, puzzle-solving and interesting challenges and tools; various forms of learning and progress; and other factors. Long-term goal pursuit appears to entail both hot and cold (emotional and cognitive) processes sustained by a combination of short-term gratifications and anticipated long-term impact.

Goal Hierarchies

People have many goals, and their goals can be arranged in a hierarchy, from long-term and abstract goals residing at the top, to lower-level, short-term and more concrete goals that serve as stepping stones to the higher goals. Wadsworth and Ford (1983) helped people identify their goals in a number of life domains (work, family, social life, leisure and so on) at four goal levels: short-term (specific), medium-term (broad), medium-long-term (more broad), and long-term (very broad). The long-term goals were more general than the short-term goals, and the short-term goals served as means to long-term ends. People in this study said that the process of verbalizing these various types of goals heightened their consciousness, clarified direction, and raised their motivation levels.

In the business world, the goals of top executives can be arranged into a hierarchy from highest-level personal and sometimes societal goals (which the business can serve) downward through goals for the enterprise, strategic goals that are means to achieving enterprise goals, and project and process goals that serve strategic and higher-level goals (Bateman et al., 2002). High-level goals for the enterprise can include such things as organizational performance (growth, revenues, survival and other success indicators) or other accomplishments (cashing out profitably, going public, avoiding bankruptcy, avoiding a hostile takeover). Strategic goals help achieve enterprise goals, and are defined as the bases for allocating resources, differentiating the firm, and achieving strategic objectives; they often take the form of deliverables to the customer. Project goals are discrete and time-bound objectives, and process goals are more continuous, ongoing, and tactical ways of operating. Examples of project goals are opening a new plant, hiring a new executive, and introducing a new product; process goals include thinking strategically, listening to customers, and communicating with employees.

In terms of content, the executives' goals resided in nine primary categories: personal, financial, customer, market, operations, product, organizational, people, competitive, and strategy-making goals. Determining goal hierarchies can be used to determine content areas on which they focus too much or too little, reveal tendencies toward too many abstract high-level goals to the neglect of concrete lower-level goals (and vice versa), and identify goals that are most instrumental toward multiple higher-level goals, thereby offering the highest leverage and deserving or requiring the most attention.

The interested self-directed leader can create such a goal hierarchy with a focus on leadership development, perhaps fitting together the most personally important ideas in this chapter and in this book. Benefits could come from sharing your goal hierarchy with your boss, direct reports and peers. Build feedback around it. Use it as a roadmap to reaching your loftiest goals, and as a vision of your future self.

Possible Selves

Everyone now seems to know that leaders are supposed to develop and communicate a compelling vision of what they want to accomplish, or what they want their team or organization to 'look like'. The vision can be strategic (as in identifying the businesses we want to compete in or the ways in which we will rewrite the rules of the industry), or they can be cultural (as in the values we strive to uphold and the kind of place we want to work in). A vision is a goal to strive for, a source of motivation for followers, and a guideline for making decisions when it otherwise would not be clear what to do.

For the self-directed leader, this obviously indicates the need to create a compelling vision, learn how to communicate it effectively, and make it a point to convey it often, to all stakeholders. But another type of vision is potentially of great importance here: one's vision for oneself as a leader. Psychologists introduced 'possible selves' as an imagined future self-image (Markus and Nurius, 1986). A compelling possible self can motivate people to make decisions and take action in ways that further their own development toward their desired self-image. In domains other than that of leadership, possible selves are known to provide direction and impetus for decisions and actions, provide standards for evaluating oneself and one's progress, and motivate change (Higgins and Pittman, 2008).

To my knowledge, possible selves have not been studied in the leadership literature as a source of motivation, although Killeen et al. (2006) studied gender effects of envisioned leadership. But as a concluding point to this chapter, I highlight the potential not only of setting personal goals with respect to the specific theories and concepts described herein – chosen based on self-assessment and potential impact – but also of building a richly-textured goal describing a personal vision of the ideal leader you want to become.

It is not uncommon for workshop facilitators to ask audiences to write their own obituaries, and for instructors to require students to write papers describing the leader they want to be. These are useful exercises, probably not used to their full potential either in leadership research or leader development. You can paint a detailed picture of the thinking habits and behaviors of the leader you want to become, or of the goal hierarchy you want to pursue. At a minimum, you can break the constraining self-image of being a non-leader or a maintenance manager, and establish a personal vision of becoming a true leader. And that self-designed leader can and probably should be of a certain well-visualized type: one who actively pursues the right goals.

CONCLUSION: BACK TO GOAL PURSUIT

To help cross the bridge from goals to action, here are some final suggestions. *First*, and repeating, make sure to consciously choose some personal goals worth pursuing; make a decision to act. *Second*, specify (at least mentally, but ideally in writing) the circumstances that create opportunities to try your newly-established leadership efforts. This tactic, called implementation intentions (Gollwitzer et al., 2008), significantly increases the likelihood that you will move from goal to action.

Third, set a 'style-goal' of flexible tenacity: persevere in goal pursuit (including after setbacks; see King and Rothstein, Chapter 13 in this volume), but keep learning, and adapt or adopt new tactics in new circumstances or with different people. And *fourth*, throughout all of your self-development efforts, establish an outlook of realistic optimism (Schneider, 2001). Realism is usually better than naïveté, and optimism is usually better than pessimism – unless it includes self-deception. Realistic optimism means that you do not expect that positive outcomes, such as improved leadership, will come to you with little or no effort. You appreciate the positive aspects of your current situation including your leadership-related strengths and skills, and also understand what you need to develop and want to improve. You are conducting appropriate reality checks and not deceiving yourself – you perform regular progress assessments, fine-tune your tactics, and adjust as necessary. You understand the magnitude of the task, focus on possible opportunities to develop, and frame your goal as an opportunity, not as a problem or an ordeal that you must survive in order to avoid failure. Framing your leadership development goals positively – as high-potential opportunities rather than as chores – encourages mindfulness rather than mindlessness, active goal pursuit, learning from setbacks, perseverance and enjoyment en route.

Moving forward, consider the following quotes:

> If we did all the things we are capable of doing, we would literally astound ourselves.
>
> (Thomas Edison)

> Jump into the pool.
>
> (Erich Fromm)

> The difference between will and might rests with us.
>
> (Mihalyi Cziksentmihalyi)

REFERENCES

Anderson, D., Krajewski, H., Goffin, R. and Jackson, D. (2008), 'A leadership self-efficacy taxonomy and its relation to effective leadership', *Leadership Quarterly*, **19**, 595–608.

Argyris, C. (1993), *Knowledge for Action: A Guide to Overcoming Barriers to Organizational Change*, San Francisco, CA: Jossey–Bass.

Avolio, B. (2005), *Leadership Development in Balance*, Mahwah, NJ: Lawrence Erlbaum.

Banaji, M., Bazerman, M. and Chugh, D. (2003), 'How (un)ethical are you?', *Harvard Business Review*, **81** (12), 56–64.

Bandura, A. (1997), *Self-efficacy: The Exercise of Control*, New York: W.H. Freeman.

Baron, J. (1998), *Judgment Misguided: Intuition and Error in Public Decision Making*, New York: Oxford University Press.

Bass, B. (1985), *Leadership and Performance Beyond Expectations,* New York: Free Press.

Bass, B. (1990), *Bass & Stogdill's Handbook of Leadership: Theory, Research & Managerial Applications*, 3rd edn, New York: Free Press.

Bateman, T. (2010), 'Enacted problem solving by leaders and followers', unpublished manuscript.

Bateman, T. and Barry, B. (2010), 'Masters of the long haul: the pursuit of (very) long-term goals', unpublished manuscript.

Bateman, T. and Crant, J.M. (1993), 'The proactive component of organizational behavior: a measure and correlates', *Journal of Organizational Behavior*, **14**, 103–18.

Bateman, T. and Porath, C. (2003), 'Transcendent behavior', in K. Cameron, J. Dutton and R. Quinn (eds), *Positive Organizational Scholarship: Foundations of a New Discipline*, San Francisco, CA: Berrett-Koehler, pp. 122–37.

Bateman, T., O'Neill, H. and Kenworthy-U'Ren, A. (2002), 'A hierarchical taxonomy of top managers' goals', *Journal of Applied Psychology*, **87**, 1134–48.

Bluedorn, A. (2002), *The Human Organization of Time*, Palo Alto, CA: Stanford University Press.

Boal, K. and Hooijberg, R. (2000), 'Strategic leadership research: moving on', *Leadership Quarterly*, **11**, 515–49.

Brockner, J. and James, E. (2008), 'Toward an understanding of when executives see crisis as opportunity', *Journal of Applied Behavioral Science*, **44**, 94–115.

Cohen, W. and Levinthal, D. (1990), 'Absorptive capacity: a new perspective on learning and innovation', *Administrative Science Quarterly*, **35**, 128–52.

Collins, J. and Porras, J. (1996), *Built to Last*, London: Century.

Conger, J. and Kanungo, R. (1998), *Charismatic Leadership in Organizations*, Thousand Oaks, CA: Sage.

Crant, J.M. (2000), 'Proactive behavior in organizations', *Journal of Management*, **26**, 435–62.

Crant, J.M. and Bateman, T. (2000), 'Charismatic leadership viewed from above: the impact of proactive personality', *Journal of Organizational Behavior*, **21**, 63–75.

Das, T.K. (2004), 'Strategy and time: really recognizing the future', in H. Tsoukas and J. Shepherd (eds), *Managing the Future: Foresight in the Knowledge Economy*, Oxford, UK: Blackwell.

Dubrin, A. (1992), *Your Own Worst Enemy: How to Overcome Career Self-sabotage,* New York: Amacom.

Eisenhardt, K.M. (1989), 'Making fast strategic decisions in high-velocity environments', *Academy of Management Journal*, **32**, 543–76.

El Sawy, O. (1983), 'Temporal perspective and managerial attention: a study of chief executive strategic behavior', *Dissertation Abstracts International*, **44**(05A), 1556–7.

Gollwitzer, P., Parks-Stamm, E., Jaudas, A. and Sheeran, P. (2008), 'Flexible tenacity in goal pursuit', in J. Shah and W. Gardner (eds), *Handbook of Motivation Science,* New York: Guilford Press.

Grant, A. and Ashford, S. (2008), 'The dynamics of proactivity at work', *Research in Organizational Behavior*, **28**, 3–34.

Hambrick, D. and Mason, P. (1984), 'Upper echelons: the organization as a reflection of its top managers', *Academy of Management Review*, **9**, 193–206.

Hampden-Turner, C. and Trompenaars, F. (2001), *Mastering the Infinite Game: How Asian Values are Transforming Business Practices*, Oxford, UK: Capstone.

Hannah, S., Avolio, B., Luthans, F. and Harms, P.D. (2008), 'Leadership efficacy: review and future directions', *Leadership Quarterly*, **19**, 669–92.

Hardin, G. (1968), 'The tragedy of the commons', *Science*, **162**, 1243–8.

Higgins, E.T. and Pittman, T. (2008), 'Motives of the human animal: comprehending, managing, and sharing inner states', *Annual Review of Psychology*, **59**, 361–85.

House, R. and Shamir, B. (1993), 'Toward the integration of transformational, charismatic and visionary theories', in M. Chemers and R. Ayman (eds), *Leadership Theory and Research: Perspectives and Directions*, San Diego, CA: Academic Press, pp. 81–107.

Hunt, J.G. (1991), *Leadership: A New Synthesis*, Newbury Park, CA: Sage.

Jacobs, M.T. (1991), *Short-term America: The Causes and Cures of our Business Myopia*, Boston, MA: Harvard Business School Press.

Judge, T., Piccolo, R. and Ilies, R. (2004), 'The forgotten ones? The validity of consideration and initiating structure in leadership research', *Journal of Applied Psychology*, **89**, 36–51.

Kerr, S. (1975), 'On the folly of rewarding A, while hoping for B', *Academy of Management Journal*, **18**, 769–83.

Killeen, L., Lopez-Zafra, E. and Eagly, A. (2006), 'Envisioning oneself as a leader: comparisons of women and men in Spain and the United States', *Psychology of Women Quarterly*, **30**, 312–22.

Kim, T., Bateman, T., Andersson, L. and Gilbreath, J. (2009), 'Employee cynicism and top management credibility: a comprehensive model', *Human Relations*, **62**(10), 1435–58.

Klein, H., Austin, J. and Cooper, J. (2008), 'Goal choice and decision processes', in R. Kanfer, G. Chen and R. Pritchard (eds), *Work Motivation: Past, Present, and Future*, New York: Routledge, pp. 101–50.

Kotter, J. (1999), *John Kotter on What Leaders Really Do*, Cambridge, MA: Harvard Business School Press.

Latham, G. and Locke, E. (1991), 'Self-regulation through goal setting', *Organizational Behavior and Human Decision Processes*, **50**, 212–47.

Locke, E. and Latham, G. (1990), *A Theory of Goal Setting and Task Performance*, Englewood Cliffs, NJ: Prentice-Hall.

Markus, H. and Nurius, P. (1986), 'Possible selves', *American Psychologist*, **41**, 954–69.

Mick, D., Bateman, T. and Lutz, R. (2009), 'Wisdom: exploring the pinnacle of human virtue as a central link from micromarketing to macromarketing', *Journal of Macromarketing*, **24**(1), 31–43.

Miner, J.B. (2005), *Organizational Behavior I: Essential Theories of Motivation and Leadership*, New York: M.E. Sharpe.

Pfeffer, J. and Sutton, R. (2000), *The Knowing–Doing gap: How Smart Companies Turn Knowledge into Action*, Boston, MA: Harvard University Press.

Rousseau, D. (2006), 'Is there such a thing as 'evidence-based management'?', *Academy of Management Review*, **31**, 256–69.

Schneider, S. (2001), 'In search of realistic optimism', *American Psychologist*, **56**, 25–63.

Sternberg, R.J. (1998), 'A balance theory of wisdom', *Review of General Psychology*, **2** (4), 347–65.

Tannenbaum, R. and Schmidt, W. (1958), 'How to choose a leadership pattern', *Harvard Business Review*, **36**(2), 95–101.

Trevino, L. and Brown, M. (2004), 'Managing to be ethical: debunking five business ethics myths', *Academy of Management Executive*, May, 69–81.

Troy, G. (2008), *Leading from the Center: Why Moderates make the Best Presidents*, New York: Basic Books.

Vroom, V. and Jago, A. (1988), *The New Leadership: Managing Participation in Organizations*, Englewood Cliffs, NJ: Prentice-Hall.

Wadsworth, M. and Ford, D. (1983), 'Assessment of personal goal hierarchies', *Journal of Counseling Psychology*, **30**, 514–26.

Yukl, G. (2006), 'An evaluation of conceptual weaknesses in transformational and charismatic leadership theories', *Leadership Quarterly*, **12**, 451–83.

Zimbardo, P. and Boyd, J. (1999), 'Putting time in perspective: a valid, reliable individual-differences metric', *Journal of Personality and Social Psychology*, **77**, 1271–88.

Zimmerman, B. (2000), 'Attaining self-regulation: a social cognitive perspective', in M. Boekaerts, P.R. Pintrich and M. Zeidner (eds), *Handbook of Self-regulation*, San Diego, CA: Academic Press, pp. 13–39.

10. Self-directed work teams: best practices for leadership development

Wendy L. Bedwell, Marissa L. Shuffler, Jessica L. Wildman and Eduardo Salas

Human resource departments are increasingly interested in developing effective employees (Garavan and McGuire, 2001) for future leadership positions. This effort is largely driven by the desire for greater productivity and flexibility, as well as a reduction in operating costs (Garavan et al., 1999; Hodgetts et al., 1999; Losey, 1999). To achieve this goal, organizations are turning toward a competency-based approach to learning which provides solid linkages and alignment between organizational strategy and leader development efforts. By focusing on the competencies required in complex, dynamic conditions, employees are more flexible, mobile and employable (Garavan and McGuire, 2001). Furthermore, this competency approach assists organizations in meeting the training demands of emerging leaders who expect continuous individual learning opportunities designed to develop their skills, especially those working in dynamic and less rigid team environments such as self-directed work teams.

While the competency approach to developing leader skills can provide the content for effective self-development, it is important to also consider the context in which such development can occur. Much is known about individual learning, which can occur socially through observation and interaction with others, and leads directly to the development of new behaviors (Anderson, 2000; London et al., 2005; Vygotsky, 1978). Wilson and colleagues (2007) suggest that individuals can learn in the context of groups or teams, which can improve team performance and, ultimately, organizational performance. Marsick and Watkins (1990) propose three specific types of individual-level learning that can occur within the context of an organization: (1) formal learning or organizationally sponsored training interventions; (2) informal learning such as interactions with colleagues or supervisors throughout normal work activities; and (3) incidental learning which is a by-product of work interactions not initially intended to 'teach' anything. We focus on the latter two: those informal and incidental opportunities that occur within normal work conditions (in the presence of work action as well as reflection, according to Watkins and Marsick, 1992) that provide rich, meaningful individual knowledge, skill or attitude development. Organizations are beginning to see the value of informal learning (e.g., Enos et al., 2003; Lohman, 2000; Skule, 2004) and several studies have reported that employees attribute most of their learning to activities other than formal training (e.g., Tannenbaum, 1997; Flynn et al., 2005).

Drawing upon this notion of self-managed, informal learning, the purpose of this chapter is to discuss how individuals who are engaged in self-directed work teams can manage their own leadership development through the use of a competency-based approach. Specifically, we present three sections to address our goal. First, we define our constructs. Secondly, we identify the problem, noting why such self-development is important to team effectiveness, highlighting how leadership functions are intertwined with team processes as well as how the exhibition of leadership functions may vary across self-directed work teams. Finally, we suggest potential remedies to this problem by presenting best practices that can be used not only to enhance self-directed work team success, but provide a meaningful opportunity for emerging leaders to manage their own leadership development.

SECTION 1: DEFINING THE CONSTRUCTS

Informal Learning

A central focus of this effort revolves around informal learning opportunities. A relatively recent interest in this topic has prompted researchers to focus on defining this construct. Some suggest that in addition to being non-institutional, key tenets of informal learning include the unstructured nature of the events that prompt learning as well as the fact that it is driven by individual preferences and intentions (Marsick and Volpe, 1999). Others suggest that there does not have to be an intent to learn (Ellinger, 2004) and that it is a result of naturally occurring work opportunities (Ellinger, 2005). For our purposes, we agree with the definition espoused by Tannenbaum et al. (2010) that informal learning (a) is learner-directed and self-guided; (b) reflects some intent for personal development; (c) involves some form of active engagement; (d) occurs outside formal learning/training settings; and (e) is dynamic, and less structured than formal training.

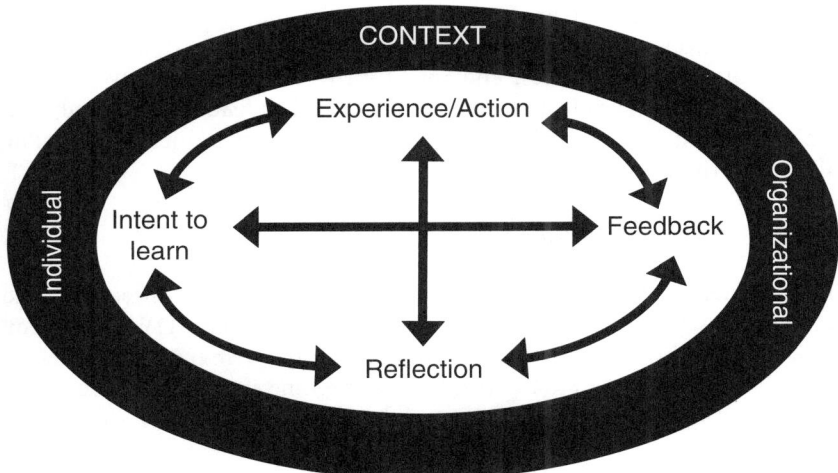

Source: Tannenbaum et al. (2010).

Figure 10.1 Dynamic model of informal learning

Tannenbaum and colleagues suggest that informal learning is comprised of four specific components: intent to learn/develop, experience/action, feedback, and reflection (refer to Figure10.1). They postulate that an individual enters the informal learning process at any given point in the model. An individual may experience several components multiple times. As an example, an individual (Sue) has intent – specifically, she decides she needs additional experience in writing reports (that is, a skill that requires improvement). Therefore, she seeks feedback from her colleague (Dale) who also writes reports and whom Sue perceives has demonstrated greater skill at report-writing. She gets tips from Dale on report-writing and thinks about the differences between how she writes reports and how Dale writes reports (reflection). After thinking about the differences, she integrates some of the tips from Dale into her own report-writing (experience/action).

The four components are integral to the effectiveness of informal learning. Specifically, Tannenbaum and colleagues (2010) note specific problems that can occur if any one of the components is missing. Without intent, individuals may miss key opportunities for learning. Without experience or action, individuals do not practice what has been learned, and practice is an important component of training if transfer is to occur. If feedback is not included in the learning process, individuals may fail to correctly interpret a situation or miss a cue, which could cause poor development of a skill or development of an incorrectly learned skill. Finally, without reflection individuals may not fully understand the implications of their experiences, and therefore would be less likely to learn from them and internalize the experience. This can lead to an incomplete understanding of the learning. There are ample opportunities to engage in all four of these components in self-directed work teams.

Self-Directed Work Teams

To fully understand the role of leader development in self-directed work teams (SDWTs), it is necessary to first understand what SDWTs are and their purpose in the workplace. As organizational demands increase and tasks become more complex, teams have become increasingly prevalent in the workplace (Kozlowski et al., 1999). Furthermore, the flattening of leadership hierarchies has driven the advancement of work teams that do not have a designated leader.

Such teams, often referred to as self-directed work teams, are instead responsible for their own management of leadership functions and team processes in order to accomplish desired goals (Kauffeld, 2006; Manz and Sims, 1993). SDWTs are differentiated from other teams because of this inherent responsibility, which comes with the authority to make decisions regarding their work (Orsburn et al., 1990; Manz and Sims, 1993) – a role traditionally carried out by a manager or team leader. Therefore, SDWTs can be conceptualized as a team that is characterized by high levels of autonomy and control over how team members will execute required tasks (Kozlowski and Bell, 2003). Additionally, the management responsibilities of such teams (functions traditionally assigned to one team leader) are distributed among team members – although the degree and type of distribution may vary, given team composition and other situation factors, as discussed later. While SDWTs may have some type of external leader (Morgeson, 2005), these leaders primarily serve to enable the self-direction and management of the team itself.

Self-directed work team effectiveness
Research on SDWTs has provided some important contributions to the understanding of their functionality and effectiveness. Empirical evidence speaks to the benefits of such teams, including improved quality of work life for employees, as well as decreased levels of absenteeism and turnover (Cohen and Ledford, 1994; Lawler, 1986; Manz and Sims, 1987). While such teams have shown some degree of success in the workplace (Kozlowski and Bell, 2003), there are many instances of failure. For many SDWTs, leadership is an area full of pitfalls. For example, SDWTs with

overly active leaders tend to lose their autonomy (a key defining characteristic) and therefore experience decreased effectiveness (Stewart and Manz, 1995). To be effective, however, SDWTs do demand some degree of functional leadership, which is usually distributed and shared across multiple team members. If team members cannot manage to fulfill these roles, either through emergent leadership or through the capacity of the team to lead as a whole, they will also fail (Day et al., 2004).

While leadership is clearly important to SDWTs, it is highly likely that such teams will not always be prepared to manage leadership functions and balance them with team processes that must also be executed for team effectiveness. While these teams may receive training designed to foster their development as a functional, cohesive team unit, the nature of their complex and challenging tasks combined with the lack of a clearly delineated leadership role may limit this development. Therefore, it is critical for self-directed work team members to be prepared to self-develop leadership abilities in order to improve team effectiveness and add value to their organizations. In order to understand more fully how teams can do this, we turn to the literature on team effectiveness to understand what exactly leads to effective team performance.

Team Effectiveness

For over 50 years, researchers have focused on team effectiveness in response to major restructuring of work processes around teams. The goal of this research effort continues to be the determination of what constitutes effective team performance. This body of literature has provided a substantial foundation of information on the individual, team and organizational inputs as well as the affective, behavioral and cognitive processes that allow individuals to pool their resources in order to engage effectively in teamwork and taskwork demands required for effective team performance (e.g., Mathieu et al., 2008).

Team performance is a bottom-up emergent process that stems from individual team members' behavioral or cognitive actions (Salas et al., 2007b). Team effectiveness is the evaluation of the output resulting from the team's behavioral or cognitive actions (Salas et al., 2007b). Cohen suggests that team effectiveness is clustered into three categories: (1) team performance; (2) team members' attitudes about quality of work life; and (3) withdrawal behaviors. While there is disagreement as to what factors exactly constitute effectiveness, there is general agreement that team effectiveness is not the same as individual effectiveness. Salas and colleagues (2005b) suggest that effective team performance is facilitated by constructs such as leadership, coordination, cooperation and communication. A brief review of some of the more infamous team failures reveals that several of these variables do indeed impact team performance: consider the ascent of Mt Everest as described by Krakauer (1997). Several international teams, led by renowned mountaineers, decided to tackle Everest. Despite the support of these mountaineers, this was one of the most disastrous expedition seasons ever. All but one member, including the veteran leader, perished after reaching the peak. Throughout the rest of the month, 16 additional climbers died attempting to conquer Everest. Clearly the environmental factors played a role; however, many feel the dangerous environmental conditions were exacerbated by failures in team leadership, coordination and communication failures (Krakauer, 1997). Impaired communication was also noted as a major contributor in both the Challenger and Columbia shuttle accidents (NASA, 2008). Team leadership, communication and coordination failures have also been implicated as root causes of major aviation accidents, medical errors, industrial disasters, and several well-documented military failures such as the shooting of a civilian airliner by the USS Vincennes (Kozlowski and Ilgen, 2006). Clearly these variables play an important practical role in team performance.

Team performance is only as effective as the team processes underlying it. There are numerous functions of leadership that are critical to team effectiveness. Extensive research has addressed the team processes and dynamics that comprise effective team performance (Kozlowski and Bell, 2003). Team processes, broadly defined, involve the mechanisms by which team inputs, such as team composition and individual differences, are transformed into outcomes, such as effectiveness and performance (Mathieu et al., 2008). Such processes, compiled with the states that emerge from the interaction of team members as well as the development of the team, comprise the interaction dynamics that leadership functions are designed to influence. These interaction dynamics occur in all teams, but are of particular interest in SDWTs in terms of their relationship to leadership.

Team Processes and Emergent States

Team processes are perhaps best understood through the use of Marks and colleagues' (2001) temporally based taxonomy. This taxonomy of team processes presents three types of core team interaction processes: transition, action and interpersonal. Presented in Table 10.1 as team goal processes, these three phases are tied to performance episodes (Zaccaro et al., 2009). Transition processes entail the information and strategy processes that must occur in order for a team to develop a plan that can be put into action. These processes are followed by action processes, in which

Table 10.1   Team leadership functions and team interaction dynamics

Team leadership functions	Team interaction dynamics

Direction setting
• Environmental scanning
• Sense-making
• Planning
• Sense-giving
	Team goal processes
	• Transition
	  – Mission analysis
	  – Goal specification
	  – Strategy formulation
	• Action

Managing team operations
• Staffing the team
• Calibrating member roles to task requirements
• Facilitating the development of team communication structures, norms, roles, and performance expectations
• Monitoring team actions and providing feedback
• Aligning team actions with environmental contingencies
• Procuring team resources
• Communicating information about the team to external constituencies
• Acting as a communication buffer between external constituencies and team members
	– Monitoring progress toward goals
	  – Systems monitoring
	  – Back-up behaviors
	  – Coordination
	• Interpersonal
	  – Conflict management
	  – Motivation and confidence building
	  – Affect management
	
	Team emergent states
	• Cognitive
	  – Shared mental models
	• Motivational
	  – Cohesion
	  – Trust
	  – Collective efficacy
	• Affective

Developing team's leadership capacity • Developing member leader expertise • Coaching shared direction-setting • Coaching team planning and role assignment • Coaching collective information processing	Team development • Emergence of collective identity • Norm development • Member skill acquisition • Growth in self-management skills and leader expertise

Source: Zaccaro et al. (2009).

team members must back up, monitor and coordinate with one another in order to execute the aforementioned plan successfully. Such processes are supported by interpersonal processes, which are executed to ensure minimal process loss during performance periods. Certainly, effective team processes are critical in SDWTs to promote success, particularly due to the complex and challenging nature of their tasks (Kauffeld, 2006).

Also critical to the success of SDWTs is the emergence of particular team states over time. Emergent states are the team-level factors that materialize as teams begin to interact and perform (Kozlowski and Bell, 2003). Emergent states can be motivational, cognitive or affective in nature, and dynamically impact future team interactions (Marks et al., 2001). Furthermore, as teams develop over time, these emergent states may change and grow. In successful teams, such development will reflect increases in cohesion, cooperation and positive efficacy regarding the team's ability to perform.

Another important aspect of team effectiveness, as noted above, is the leader (e.g., Burke et al., 2006b; Salas et al., 2005a). Effective leaders impact team performance by engaging in required team processes necessary to address noted performance gaps (Burke et al., 2006b). Below we present conceptualizations of leadership functions necessary for effective team performance.

Team Leadership

Leadership is a complex construct that has been studied extensively throughout history in a variety of forms, and has been found to be vital for effective organizational and societal functioning (Yukl, 2006). Due to the expansive study of leadership, numerous definitions have been provided for this construct and for how it is different from team leadership. While leadership is easy to identify in situ, it is difficult to define precisely from a theoretical perspective (Antonakis et al., 2004). Below we discuss several of the most widely accepted and relevant definitions.

Leadership defined

According to Yukl (2006), leadership is defined as 'the process of influencing others to understand and agree about what needs to be done and how to do it, and the process of facilitating individual and collective efforts to accomplish shared objectives' (p. 8). Katz and Kahn (1978) find leadership to be 'the influential increment over and above mechanical compliance with a routine directives of organization' (p. 528). Fleishman and colleagues (1991) define leadership as discretionary problem solving in ill-defined domains. The term 'discretionary' refers to the choices that leaders must make, while problem solving involves understanding the nature of the issues faced by the team or unit and setting directions for collective action. 'Ill-defined domain' refers to the fact that nothing in leadership is truly predetermined, but that leaders have to determine components and make choices. A similar definition would be to define leadership as social problem solving. Social problem solving involves identifying a problem through information acquisition; constructing the problem by making sense of the information acquired; generating solutions by thinking through alternatives and developing a plan; and implementing the solution through sense giving and monitoring of progress.

Team leadership defined

Team leadership can be defined as the 'ability to direct and coordinate the activities of other team members, assess team performance, assign tasks, develop team knowledge, skills and abilities, motivate team members, plan and organize and establish a positive atmosphere' (Salas, 2005a: p. 560). In other words, while leadership is defined more generally as a form of influence of others, team leadership as defined by Salas and colleagues (2005a) is focused on the functional aspects of influencing others in the context of a team setting. Team leadership has also been used synonymously with distributed leadership, which refers to the sharing of leadership functions among team members (Burke et al., 2004). However, using team leadership as a synonym for distributed leadership is not ideal because it implies that all leadership within a team is distributed or shared, which is not necessarily the case. Thus, for our efforts, we accept the conceptualization set forth by Salas and colleagues (2005a) of team leadership as a variety of functional activities focused on influencing team members and performance in a team setting. We specifically focus on team leadership in terms of the various leadership functions and roles that should be fulfilled within a team, such as influencing team direction, managing team operations, and developing the team's problem-solving capacity (Zaccaro et al., 2009), which will be discussed in more detail in the following section.

Team leadership components and roles

Numerous other definitions of leadership exist, but there are several components which tend to remain constant no matter the wording. First, the fundamental role of team leadership is to influence team direction but also to help influence the emergence of direction (Zaccaro and Klimoski, 2001). Direction will vary on different levels of complexity, and is effective when leaders think through consequences of direction-setting. Another primary component of leadership is the creation or influence of organization, also known as operations management. Leaders must establish and facilitate the development of patterned activities considered to be organization. If leaders cannot communicate and cooperate with subordinates, they will be unable to establish these patterned activities (Yukl, 2006). As captured by Katz and Kahn's (1978) definition of leadership, the role of the leader is not simply to create organization but also to maintain the system that is developed because of organization. A third component which combines operations management and direction-setting involves the creation of a vision. Leaders have to create a vision and make sense of information for followers in order to accomplish goals and set directions effectively (Shamir et al., 1993; Jacobs and Jacques, 1987). However, in order to maintain this vision, leaders must also create motivation and 'buy-in' for followers. There has to be some sense given to followers in order for them to act, as well as a purpose in order to keep them motivated.

There have been many attempts to theoretically capture exactly what leadership is in terms of tangible behaviors, characteristics or contextual aspects. Of the existing theories, perhaps the most relevant to SDWTs is functional leadership. From this approach, a leader's primary job in a team is to do whatever is not being adequately addressed by the team members (Zaccaro et al., 2001). This offers unique distinctions from other leadership theories with regard to team leadership, as it posits that the leader is responsible for linking teams to the broader environment, interpreting and defining environment events for the team, and addressing team problems in which multiple solutions are available.

In the functional approach, team leaders hold three primary responsibilities: (1) setting the direction for team action; (2) managing team operations; and (3) developing the team's capacity to manage their own problem-solving processes (Zaccaro et al., 2009; Burke et al., 2006b). Table 10.1 (adapted from Zaccaro et al., 2009) presents an overview of these three functions and their subcomponents. Specifically, team direction-setting involves scanning the environment, sense-giving and sense-making, and developing a plan for team action. Managing team operations involves the actual execution of this plan, and has multiple functions, including team staffing, monitoring team actions, and providing feedback to team members. Finally, leaders are responsible for developing the team's leadership capacity, including developing member leader expertise and coaching team members in direction-setting, planning and role assignment.

Essentially, there are multiple aspects of leadership that must be considered in respect to SDWTs. The functional leadership approach is of most relevance to these types of teams, as this theory puts less emphasis on the leader as an individual and the characteristics of a particular leader, instead focusing upon the specific behaviors that must be performed – by any single team member or set of team members – in order to attain effective team performance. Further, this theoretical approach lends itself well to development of the KSAs underlying these key behaviors within SDWT members, given that this perspective emphasizes functional leadership as social problem solving based on skills that can be developed through training and other learning opportunities, as opposed to personality traits that are less flexible.

Summary

SDWTs are a particular type of team that have the power to make decisions, assign goals, and set their own schedules (Yukl, 1998). As with all teams, SDWTs require effective enactment of both team processes and leadership in order to be successful. However, given the nature of these teams, necessary leadership functions must be assumed by the team. Below we discuss issues that arise with leadership and team processes, especially within the context of a SDWT.

SECTION 2: IDENTIFYING THE PROBLEM

Team Leadership Functions and Team Process: A Blurred Line?

The enactment of leadership functions relates to the success of teams as leaders address gaps in performance and meet unfulfilled needs of the team (Burke et al., 2006b). However, it is important to note that there is a fine line between leadership functions and team process, especially for SDWTs. Traditionally researchers have parsed the functions leaders serve in a team as separate from the processes enacted in teams (Zaccaro et al., 2009); however, for SDWTs with no set leader, the boundaries between leadership and team processes are blurred. Upon closer analysis of leader functions and team processes, there is a noticeable intertwining of the two (Zaccaro and Klimoski, 2002). While many models of team development disregard leadership, it is important to note that for SDWTs, leadership processes can often overlap and contribute significantly to the success of team processes and effectiveness. Indeed, for SDWTs, some leadership functions may in fact be subsumed within team processes as team members must take responsibility to fulfill the leadership capacity of the team (Day et al., 2004).

This is particularly noticeable when presenting team processes and leadership functions side by side as in Table 10.1. A detailed look at this side-by-side layout of leadership functions and team processes reveals that many functions considered to be a part of direction-setting at the leader level actually overlap with team transition processes. For example, the difference between the leadership function of planning and the team goal process of strategy formulation may in fact be one and the same for SDWTs that utilize a combination of team members to fulfill the leadership role. Essentially, for SDWTs, when leader functions are brought from an individual level to a team level, the delineation between what constitutes a team process versus a leader function becomes nearly indistinguishable.

Self-Managed Leadership Development Opportunity

One key implication of this blurring of constructs for SDWTs is that even greater emphasis must be placed upon the capabilities of team members for completing leadership functions. While traditional teams have a leader to depend upon when team processes go awry, SDWTs have no such fallback. For example, in traditional teams, if the strategy formulation process is not as effective as it should be, the leader can step in as needed to aid in planning, sense-making, and sense-giving. Furthermore, the leadership processes which typically facilitate team processes may not be so clear in SDWTs when there is no designated leader to promote such facilitation.

Therefore, it is critical that SDWTs possess the capabilities to balance both team processes and leader functions effectively, as by definition, the only guiding external leadership SDWTs tend to have is focused primarily upon promoting their autonomy as a self-directed agent (Kozlowski and Bell, 2003). Given the blurred line between the two constructs in SDWTs, these types of teams provide unique opportunities for individuals who are interested in taking advantage of informal learning opportunities to increase their own KSAs (Knowledge, Skills and Abilities) on effective leadership and teamwork. Below we present a discussion of what effective leadership should look like in SDWTs to provide guidance for what leaderless groups should strive to achieve.

Effective team leadership in self-directed work teams

As discussed previously, SDWTs are, by their very nature, given the power to make their own decisions, assign their own goals, and set their own schedules (Yukl, 1998). However, just because a self-directed team does not require a formal leader does not mean that leadership functions do not need to be fulfilled. It is precisely because a self-directed team has the freedom to set its own direction and guide its own work that leadership is even more critical to their success. Indeed, a lack of effective leadership has been identified as the root cause of many self-directed team failures (e.g., Cummings, 1978; Manz and Sims, 1987). Research has shown time after time that effective leadership is critical for team performance (cf. Burke et al., 2006b), and SDWTs are no exception.

Much of the research looking at leadership in SDWTs has focused on the role of external leaders or managers in developing the team's ability to lead itself (e.g., Manz and Sims, 1987; Morgeson, 2005). More recent research has shifted focus toward the internal leadership processes that occur in SDWTs. For example, Solanksy (2008) found that self-managed teams who utilize shared leadership have motivational and cognitive advantages over teams that only used a single leader to provide all of the leadership functions. In fact, their results indicated that teams with shared leadership developed a stronger sense of team efficacy and a stronger transactive memory system compared to teams which adopted a single leader structure. However, there is more than one way in which to 'share' leadership in SDWTs; therefore, it is necessary to look at more specific approaches for distributed or shared leadership when a self-directed team is faced with the decision of how to structure and develop leadership.

Types of Team Leadership: Structures and Functions

Leadership structure can generally be divided into five core configurations: external manager, designated team leader, temporary designated team leader, task-based team leader, and distributed team leadership. When there is an external team manager, someone outside the team who does not participate in team tasks performs all of the leadership roles (e.g., Morgeson, 2005). This type of leadership structure is clearly not very applicable to SDWTs, given that by definition, the external leader of an SDWT does not enact many of the leadership functions required for effective team performance. However, the other four leadership structures represent possible options for how a self-directed work team can structure leadership functions. We describe these in detail below.

When one member of the team performs all or a majority of the leadership functions and this member remains the leader across time and tasks, the leadership structure can be considered a designated team leader. In a temporary designated leadership structure, the enactment of leadership functions rotates among team members across time such that one member may be the leader at one time and a different member may be the leader later (e.g., Erez et al., 2002). It is important to note, however, that at any given point only one member is enacting all of the required leadership functions. A task-based leadership structure is similar to the temporary designated leadership structure, but rather than based on time, rotation of leadership functions is based on the task at hand. For example, the expert member of the team for each task may assume the leadership role during that corresponding task. Finally, team leadership can be distributed across the team (Barry, 1991; Gronn, 2002). In other words, the numerous leadership functions are split among multiple members of the team simultaneously. For example, one team member may be responsible for motivating the team, while another team member is responsible for spanning boundaries with other teams and external sources.

Not only are there various ways in which to structure leadership within a team, there are also a variety of leadership functions and roles that can be assumed. The distributed leadership model, developed by Barry (1991), maps four different leadership styles on four team phases. The four leadership roles are (1) envisioning; (2) organizing; (3) spanning; and (4) social. Envisioning is the act of creating new ideas and conveying a compelling vision to the team. Organizing is focused on the task-related aspects of leadership, such as setting and enforcing deadlines, or creating a structure for the work. Spanning leadership behaviors includes networking, presentation management, and other forms of relationship maintenance that occurs outside the team. Finally social leadership is focused on developing and maintaining the interpersonal relationships within the team as well as taking care of any other socio-emotional issues that occur within the team (for example, conflict, frustration).

Carson (2006) developed a similar taxonomy describing four general leadership roles that can be assumed by team members in a self-directed work team: navigator, engineer, social integrator and liaison. The navigator is responsible for establishing the team's primary purpose and direction, as well as keeping the team focused and headed in the right direction. The engineer is more focused on the task-related aspects of leadership, and is therefore in charge of structuring the team and the task in the most effective way possible in order achieve the team's goals. The social integrator is the relationship focused role, responsible for helping with team socialization, development, and conflict resolution. In other words, the social integrator manages the interpersonal aspects of the team. Finally, the liaison is essentially the boundary spanner for the team, serving as a representative for the team when external sources (customers, stakeholders, and so on.) must be contacted.

Finally, Carson (2006) discusses three potential ways in which team members can structure or manage the various leadership roles within a shared leadership approach: role overlap, role switching, and role sharing. In role overlap, team members engage in more than one leadership role simultaneously. For example, one team member may perform both the engineer and liaison roles at the same time. In role switching, the different roles may shift from one person to another over time. In other words, team member A may assume the role of navigator for the first part of the team's task, and then team member B takes over as navigator as the task changes. Finally, team members may share roles simultaneously with others. In this situation, several, or even all, of the team members engage in the same leadership role such as navigation or social integration.

Leadership capacity
In fully self-directed teams, the team members have the unusual advantage, and simultaneous disadvantage, of behavioral discretion. In other words, self-directed teams can decide for themselves how to approach the three previously mentioned issues regarding leadership – specifically, how leadership will be structured, what leadership functions need to be enacted, and who is going to enact them. On one hand, this provides the team with the unique ability to structure and divide leadership in any way they choose, matching specific leadership functions to team members based on ability and expertise. Even more importantly, self-directed teams have the opportunity to develop the necessary leadership competencies within their team members and continually improve team member leadership capabilities. Day et al. (2004) refer to the development of leadership capabilities within a team as the development of leadership capacity. Simply stated, this perspective on team leadership views leadership as an outcome of team processes. As the team engages in activities such as teamwork and team learning, the individual members of the team gain new leadership skills and capabilities, thereby improving the team's leadership capacity for leadership as a whole. The behavioral discretion afforded to self-directed work teams provides a distinct advantage in terms of developing leadership capacity since the team can deliberately choose to focus on leveraging team processes toward the development of new leadership skills.

On the other hand, this behavioral discretion can just as easily leave the team in a position to neglect the enactment of leadership functions, and neglect the development of the team members' leadership capabilities, which could be detrimental to team performance. Therefore, it is critical for SDWTs to ensure that the team is fully aware of the importance of the various leadership functions necessary for success (that is, relational and functional) as well as their own individual strengths and weaknesses and how they map onto the required leadership functions. Members of the self-directed team can then focus on developing the competencies and skills necessary to become effective leaders which will ultimately contribute most effectively to team performance.

One particular strategy for developing the leadership capacity of self-directed work team members is known as self-management. Manz and Sims (1980) suggested self-management as an alternative to formal leadership structures. In this approach, the members of the team set their own standards, evaluate their own performance, and administer their own consequences based on those evaluations. Self-management is one of the most basic forms of behavioral discretion – it is the self-control a person displays even in the absence of external constraints (Manz and Sims,

1980). There are several ways that self-management can be facilitated. Self-observation is the process of observing one's own behavior which will then be used to evaluate one's own behavior. Specifying goals is a mechanism for motivating oneself by setting personal goals that are challenging and attainable (Locke and Latham, 2002). Cueing strategies are ways in which the team members can avoid engaging in non-productive behaviors while encouraging productive behaviors. For example, if a team member has the tendency to gossip a lot, he may close the office door in order to deter any unproductive side chatter. Incentive modification is basically self-reward and self-punishment imposed by the team member to encourage proper behaviors. Finally, rehearsal is the practice of a desired skill (that is, how a self-managing team member would develop new skills and knowledge).

Leadership and SDWTs: a brief empirical review
Research is just beginning to fill the gaps in literature regarding internal team leadership in SDWTs. In a study examining the three different ways self-directed teams can structure leadership roles, Carson (2006) found several interesting findings. First, role overlap was negatively related to role conflict, which is contrary to logic. In other words, the more that a team member's roles overlap with others, the less role conflict she experiences. Role switching, however, was positively related to role conflict. It was suggested this may be due to the fact that frequent switching of leadership roles could lead to inconsistent and confused expectations from the other team members. Overall, the findings of the study suggest that role switching is not a useful strategy for structuring a team's leadership, as there is no positive outcome associated with role switching. Conversely, Erez et al. (2002) found that teams that rotated leadership among members were more cooperative and had better performance. They theorized that rotating leadership would be beneficial to self-directed teams because it would promote a feeling that everyone was playing an important part in the team, and therefore translate into an increase in workload-sharing. They also suggested that rotating leadership would clarify roles and responsibilities for each team member.

Often within self-directed teams, one or more team members step forward to assume the role of leader informally (Carte et al., 2006). Carte and colleagues (2006) found that teams who communicated more frequently about leadership functions had higher performance. In particular, monitoring and producing behaviors were significantly higher among the high performing teams. Monitoring behavior includes collecting and distributing information and checking up on other team members' performance. Producing behaviors are focused on motivating the team to complete their tasks and seeking closure on goals. Others have specifically studied this concept of shared leadership (that is, multiple members engaging in leadership behaviors) and have found that shared leadership has a positive relationship with self-reported effectiveness (Avolio et al., 1996), is a better predictor of change management team effectiveness than vertical leadership of an appointed team leader (Pearce and Sims, 2002), and finally, has a positive relationship with both team performance and potency over a period of time (Sivasubramaniam et al., 2002).

Wolff and colleagues (2002) proposed and tested a model of leadership in SDWTs focused on the role of emotional intelligence in leader emergence. In an empirical test of this model they found that skills in pattern recognition and perspective-taking led to being able to support and develop others, which in turn supported skills in coordinating the group. Additionally, they found that these skills were formed from the foundation of empathy. These findings suggest that empathy helps emergent leaders understand, coordinate and motivate the other members of their team.

Summary

As noted above, the lack of a formal leader in SDWTs presents a specific issue for the team to address – specifically how to incorporate and distribute necessary leadership roles effectively within the team. When looking at leadership functions and team functions side by side (refer to Table 10.1), this problem can become even more confusing, given the blurred line between leadership and team processes. Below we suggest a potential mechanism for dealing with this dilemma by integrating two approaches to team effectiveness – successful completion of team phases and team effectiveness competencies. Through the combination of these approaches to team effectiveness, we present best practices designed not only to improve the effectiveness of SDWTs but also to provide opportunities for emerging leaders to take control of their own learning and practice effective leadership skills.

SECTION 3: A POTENTIAL SOLUTION

Informal Learning in Self-Directed Work Teams

While the leadership divisions and roles mentioned are useful approaches for encouraging productive behaviors in general, in terms of SDWTs, they are not sufficient to replace the full range of leadership functions necessary for optimal performance. For example, there is no technique describing how team members in a self-directed work team should motivate each other or set direction for the team. We extend the idea of personal self-management as an alternative to formal team leadership by applying it specifically to the development of transportable leadership competencies within SDWTs. In other words, we suggest that the members of SDWTs can use self-management techniques to develop and improve a variety of leadership competencies and skills, while improving team performance. In the following section, we provide a set of research-based best practices regarding which leadership competencies are the most critical for SDWTs, and how members of these teams can most effectively develop these skills.

To advance a competency approach towards self-development of leadership functions and team processes required for effective team performance in SDWTs, we first look at the literature on team development, focusing on a phase-based approach. We then discuss team competencies geared towards effective team performance and merge the two literatures to provide a framework to provide context for our discussion of self-managed learning of leadership competencies.

Phases of Team Development in SDWTs

One key to success in SDWTs is the development towards self-direction, regardless of team type; yet there seems to be little agreement in the literature about what exactly constitutes development in SDWTs (Kuipers and Stoker, 2009). Although there are many models of team development (that is, Tuckman, 1965; Gersick, 1988; 1989; Van Amelsvoort and Benders, 1996), there is little empirical support for any of them. In reviewing the literature, Dunphy and Bryant (1996) suggest that there are three team attributes required for team development, including (1) technical expertise (multiple skills required for task accomplishment); (2) self-management (operational responsibilities typically required of a team manager); and (3) self-leadership (cooperation and continuous improvement components of team performance). The premise of these attributes is that once teams have sufficiently developed to the point of the third phase, they are truly self-directed, strategically contributing to organizational performance through reduced costs and increased value and innovation. Based on their lack of empirical support for linear patterns of development, Kuipers and De Witte (2005) incorporated this idea with the notion that teams are engaging in development through simultaneous processes that normally occur throughout their life cycle.

Building on this idea, Kuipers and Stoker (2009) proposed a phase-based, empirically tested model of SDWT development that combines linear approaches such as Tuckman (1965) with recursive models of

*Table 10.2   Team processes included in Kuipers and Stoker's (2009)
            phases of team development*

Internal relations	Task management	External relations and improvement
● Goal orientation ● Planning activities ● Feedback ● Conflict management	● Multifunctionality ● Delegated management and support tasks ● Work communication ● Decision making and control ● Performance management	● Improvement activities ● Customer and supplier relations ● Advanced management and support activities

Source: Kuipers and Stoker (2009).

development such as the Marks, Mathieu and Zaccaro (2001) model. They suggest that team development can be conceptualized as a series of management functions, including (1) internal relations; (2) task management; and (3) external relations and improvement. Internal relations concerns cooperation issues within the team, such as team member accountability, goal orientation, planning activities and conflict management. Task Management includes team multifunctionality and leadership capabilities regarding responsibilities and control. This specifically refers to the processes necessary for accomplishing the specific tasks required of the team, such as decision making, basic work communication, and performance management. Finally, external management and improvement includes activities such as boundary spanning – moving beyond just boundary spanning to actually exploring and developing boundaries and engaging in boundary management as well as improvement issues like team learning (see Table 10.2).

Team Competencies

From the military, to aviation, to healthcare and business, team training has had a large impact in many organizations. This success has been due in large part to the systematic organization of the knowledge, skills and attitudes that underlie effective team performance: team competencies. Key features of these team competency frameworks can provide guidance for aspiring leaders in SDWTs. There have been several frameworks of team competencies advanced. Below we describe two that together provide a framework for discussion of competencies that can be practiced by emergent leaders in SDWTs.

Cannon-Bowers and colleagues proposed a framework based upon the idea that required KSAs differ depending on the type of team. According to this framework, there are two dimensions for delineating team competencies: (a) the nature of the task; and (b) the nature of the team (Cannon-Bowers et al., 1995; Cannon-Bowers and Salas, 1997). This aligns closely with the work of Devine and colleagues (1999) which identifies two types of general categories of tasks performed by teams – behavioral and information processing (that is, production and project teams), and two categories of temporal nature – ad hoc and ongoing. These characteristics were combined to create a parsimonious taxonomy of four team types: (1) ad hoc project teams (finite duration, novel problem-solving taskwork); (2) ongoing project teams (long-term duration, novel problem-solving taskwork); (3) ad hoc production teams (finite duration, more typical taskwork); and (4) ongoing production teams (long-term duration, more typical taskwork). While this taxonomy does not cover all of the critical team differences, it highlights important issues given our purpose, specifically the notion that teams are not all the same. Some are together for extended periods of time working on the same types of tasks, while other long-term or short-term teams change tasks frequently. One general set of competencies cannot apply equally to all teams, given that these teams have very different taskwork and teamwork requirements.

The Cannon-Bowers and Salas framework (1997) conceptualizes competencies based on the task focus (specific or generic) as well as the team familiarity (specific or generic). Required teamwork competencies for any given team depend on whether the required KSAs are task-specific or task-generic, or team-specific or team-generic. Competencies can therefore be defined within this framework as transportable (team-generic/task-generic), team-contingent (team-specific/task-generic), task-contingent (team-generic/task-specific) or context-driven (team-specific/task-specific) as depicted in Table 10.3. Cannon-Bowers and Salas (1997) utilized this framework to organize specific teamwork KSAs required in each scenario. For example, in team-specific/task-generic situations, they propose that knowledge of team-mate characteristics and interpersonal relations are required. Yet in situations that are both team and task-generic, accurate problem models are critical, since the team members are not familiar with one another. Therefore knowledge of team-mate characteristics is not likely to be critical for effective performance in a short term, ad hoc team, while knowledge of problem models would definitely impact team performance in such a case. Research supports the notion that teams with different life-spans and different levels of task stability will have different

Table 10.3   *Cannon-Bowers and Salas' (1997) team competency model
            definitions*

	TEAM SPECIFIC	TEAM GENERIC
TASK SPECIFIC	*Context-Driven Competencies:* Competencies that are dependent both on a particular task and team configuration; these vary as either the task or team members change	*Task-Contingent Competencies:* Competencies that are related to a specific task, but that hold across different team member configurations
TASK GENERIC	*Team-Contingent Competencies:* Competencies that are specific to a particular configuration of team members, but not to any particular task situation	*Transportable Competencies:* Generic competencies that generalize to many tasks and team situations

Source: Cannon-Bowers and Salas (1997).

competency requirements for effective performance (e.g., Druskat and Kayes, 2000). The list of competencies was later updated by Salas and colleagues (2009) to focus on the attitudes, behaviors and cognitions required for effective teamwork (see Table 10.4).

Stevens and Campion (1994) delineated a set of 14 specific competencies divided among five general categories, each of which is labeled as either an Interpersonal or Self-Management KSA (see Table 10.5). The purpose was to generate a list of general competencies that team members should know in order to work in a team successfully. Interpersonal KSAs are grouped under three broad categories, which include conflict resolution, collaborative problem-solving, and communication. Competencies related to goal-setting/performance management and planning and task coordination are considered Self-Management KSAs.

Teamwork Competencies for Leadership Self-Development

Taking a phase-based approach to SDWT development as defined by Kuipers and Stoker (2009), we combine the competency-based approach suggested by Stevens and Campion (1994), Cannon-Bowers et al. (1995) Cannon-Boweres and Salas (1997) and Salas and colleagues (2009) to create a list of required generic competencies for SDWTs (see Table 10.6). Specifically, we focus on those competencies that can generalize to any team context (that is, team generic) – what Cannon-Bowers and Salas

Table 10.4   Team competencies: the ABCs

KSAs	Definition
Attitudes	
● Team/Collective Orientation	● 'A preference for working with others and the tendency to enhance individual performance through the coordination, evaluation, and utilization of task inputs from other group members while performing group tasks' (Salas et al., 2005b: p. 200)
● Team/Collective Efficacy	● 'A sense of collective competence shared among individuals when allocating, coordinating, and integrating their resources in a successful concerted response to specific situational demands' (Zaccaro et al., 1995: p. 309)
● Psychological Safety	● 'A shared belief that the team is safe for interpersonal risk taking' (Edmondson, 1999, p. 354)
● Team Learning Orientation	● 'A shared perception of team goals related to the learning and competence development; goals that guide the extent, scope, and magnitude of learning behaviors pursued within a team' (Bunderson and Sutcliffe, 2003, p. 553)
● Team Cohesion	● The degree to which team members exhibit interpersonal attraction, group pride, and commitment to the task
● Mutual Trust	● 'The shared belief that team members will perform their roles and protect the interests of their teammates' (Salas et al., 2005a: p. 561)
● Team Empowerment	● 'Team members' collective belief that they have the authority to control their proximal work environment and are responsible for their team's functioning' (Mathieu et al., 2006: p. 98)
● Team Reward Attitude	● 'An individual's general evaluation of receiving rewards based on the performance of the team' (Shaw et al., 2001: p. 904)
● Team Goal Commitment/ Team Conscientiousness	● The degree to which team members feel an attachment to the team-level goal and the degree to which they are determined to reach this goal
Behaviors	
● Mutual Performance Monitoring	● The ability of team members to 'keep track of fellow team members' work while carrying out their own . . . to ensure that everything is running as expected' (McIntyre and Salas, 1995: p. 23)

Table 10.4   (continued)

KSAs	Definition
● Adaptability	● 'Ability to adjust strategies based on information gathered from the environment through the use of backup behavior and reallocation of intrateam resources. Altering a course of action or team repertoire in response to changing conditions (internal or external)' (Salas et al., 2005a: p. 560)
● Backup/ Supportive Behavior	● 'Ability to anticipate other team members' needs through accurate knowledge about their responsibilities. This includes the ability to shift workload among members to achieve balance during high periods of workload or pressure' (Salas et al., 2005a: p. 560)
● Implicit Coordination Strategies	● 'Synchronization of member actions based on unspoken assumptions about what others in the group are likely to do' (Wittenbaum and Strasser, 1996: p. 23)
● Shared/ Distributed Leadership	● 'The transference of the leadership function among team members in order to take advantage of member strengths (e.g., knowledge, skills, attitudes, perspectives, contacts, and time available) as dictated by either environmental demands or the development stage of the team' (Burke et al., 2004: p. 105)
● Mission Analysis	● 'The interpretation and evaluation of the team's mission, including identification of its main tasks as well as the operative environmental conditions and team resources available for mission execution' (Marks et al., 2001: p. 365)
● Problem Detection	● An initial sensing that a problem requiring attention exists or will soon exist
● Conflict Resolution/ Management	● 'Preemptive conflict management involved establishing conditions to prevent, control, or guide team conflict before it occurs. Reactive conflict management involved working through task and interpersonal disagreements among team members' (Marks et al., 2001: p. 363)
● Motivation of Others	● Generating and maintaining goal-directed effort toward completion of a team's mission
● Intra-team Feedback	● The provision of information about the team or individual performance either before, during, or after a performance episode

Table 10.4 (continued)

KSAs	Definition
● Task-related Assertiveness	● 'The capacity to effectively communicate in interpersonal encounters by sharing ideas clearly and directly' (Pearsall and Ellis, 2006: p. 577)
● Planning	● The generation of a proposed sequence of actions intended to accomplish a set goal
● Coordination	● 'The process of orchestrating the sequence and timing of interdependent actions' (Marks et al., 2001: pp. 367–8)
● Team Leadership	● 'Ability to direct and coordinate the activities of other team members; assess team performance; assign tasks; develop team knowledge, skills, and abilities; motivate team members; plan and organize; and establish a positive atmosphere' (Salas et al., 2005a: p. 560)
● Problem Solving	● The process of (1) identifying and representing a discrepancy between the present and desired state of the environment and (2) discovering a means to close this gap
● Closed-loop Communication / Information Exchange	● A pattern of communication characterized by (1) a message being initiated by the sender; (2) the message being received by the receiver; and (3) a follow-up by the sender ensuring that the message was received and appropriately interpreted
Cognitions	
● Cue Strategy Associations (Rules for matching a situation with an appropriate action)	● Team members have a repertoire of performance strategies and courses of action associated with frequently occurring situations and problems
● Accurate Problem Models	● 'Shared understanding of the situation, the nature of the problem, the cause of the problem, the meaning of available cues, what is likely to happen in the future, with or without action by the team members, shared understanding of the goal or desired outcome, and a shared understanding of the solution strategy' (Orasanu, 1994, p. 259)
● Accurate and Shared Mental Models	● 'An organized knowledge structure of the relationships among the task the team is engaged in and how the team members interact' (Salas et al., 2005a: p. 561)

Table 10.4   (continued)

KSAs	Definition
(Transactive Memory and Team Situational Awareness)	
• Team Mission, Objectives, Norms, Resources	• An understanding of the purpose, vision, and means available to the team for reaching the team objectives and completing the mission as well as 'the shared expectations that constrain and drive the action of group members' (Graham, 2003: p. 323)
• Understanding Multiteam Systems (MTS) Couplings	• An understanding in the team of how their performance (inputs, processes and outcomes) is tied to the larger organizational structure, including other teams

Source: Adapted from Salas et al. (2009).

(1997) referred to as transportable skills or task-contingent competencies. These key knowledge, skills and attitudes are important for success in team performance, regardless of the context. The ability of an individual to perform required tasks effectively while encouraging the team to do the same, regardless of who the other members are or what the specific goal is, sets emergent leaders apart from the rest. Given the overlap between team process and leadership function described above, especially in SDWTs, individuals who wish to gain opportunities for self-development in team leadership, and thus gain from those informal learning opportunities, need to have a clear understanding of generalizable teamwork and taskwork competencies as well as how they influence team effectiveness.

Internal Relations

Competencies related to internal relations focus on exchanging information effectively, being assertive and flexible, understanding cultural differences, valuing teamwork attitudes, motivating others and engaging in effective conflict management strategies. Mathieu et al., (2008) reviewed team effectiveness literature over the past decade. They discuss how Marks and colleagues (2001) built upon the teamwork and taskwork delineation by McIntyre and Salas (1995) through the taxonomy of team process which includes an interpersonal phase. In the phase, teams engage in conflict management, motivation, confidence building, and affect management

*Table 10.5   Knowledge, Skills and Ability (KSA) requirements for
                teamwork*

INTERPERSONAL KSAs		
Conflict Resolution KSAs	Collaborative Problem Solving KSAs	Communication KSAs
• To recognize and encourage desirable, but discourage undesirable team conflict. • To recognize the type and source of conflict confronting the team and to implement an appropriate conflict resolution strategy • To employ an integrative (win/ win) negotiation strategy rather than the traditional distributive (win/lose) strategy	• To identify situations requiring participative group problem solving and to utilize the proper degree and type of participation • To recognize the obstacles to collaborative problem solving and implement appropriate corrective action	• To understand communication networks, and to utilize decentralized networks to enhance communication where possible • To communicate openly and supportively by sending messages which are: (1) behavior- or event-oriented; (2) congruent; (3) validating; (4) conjunctive; and (5) owned. • To listen non-evaluatively and to use active listening techniques appropriately • To maximize consonance between non-verbal and verbal messages • To engage in ritual greetings and small talk, and to recognize their importance

SELF-MANAGEMENT KSAs	
Goal Setting and Performance Management KSAs	Planning and Task Coordination KSAs
• To help establish specific, challenging, and accepted team goals. • To monitor, evaluate, and provide feedback on both overall team performance and individual team member performance.	• To coordinate and synchronize activities, information and task interdependencies between team members • To help establish task and role expectations of individual team members, and to ensure proper balancing of workload in the teams.

Source: Adapted from Stevens and Campion (1994).

Table 10.6   Transportable competencies based on development phase of SDWT

Internal relations competencies	Task management competencies	External relations and improvement competencies

• Information Exchange (Internal) *(Cannon-Bowers and Salas, 1997)*
 • Assertiveness *(Cannon-Bowers and Salas, 1997)*
 • Flexibility *(Cannon-Bowers and Salas, 1997)*
 • Engage in ritual greetings and small talk, and recognize their importance *(Stevens and Campion, 1994)*
 • Task Motivation *(Cannon-Bowers and Salas, 1997)*
 • Motivation of Others *(Salas et al., 2009)*
 • Psychological Safety *(Salas et al., 2009)*
 • Mutual Trust *(Salas et al., 2009)*
 • Intra-team Feedback *(Salas et al., 2009)*
 • Understand and Value Teamwork *(Cannon-Bowers and Salas, 1997)*
   – Morale Building *(Cannon-Bowers and Salas, 1997)*
	• Team Empowerment *(Salas et al., 2009)*
	 • Task-related Assertiveness *(Salas et al., 2009)*
	 • Information Exchange (Internal and External) *(Cannon-Bowers and Salas, 1997; Salas et al., 2009)*
	   – Understand communication networks, and utilize decentralized networks to enhance communication where possible *(Stevens and Campion, 1994)*
	   – Communicate openly and supportively by sending messages which are:
	   (1) behavior- or event-oriented;
	   (2) congruent;
	   (3) validating;
	   (4) conjunctive; and
	   (5) owned.
	   (Stevens and Campion, 1994)
		• Consulting with Others *(Cannon-Bowers and Salas, 1997)*
		   – Information Exchange (External) *(Cannon-Bowers and Salas, 1997)*
		   – Engage in ritual greetings and small talk, and recognize their importance *(Stevens and Campion, 1994)*
		 • Knowledge of Boundary Spanning Role *(Cannon-Bowers and Salas, 1997)*
		 • Employ an integrative (win/win) negotiation strategy rather than the traditional distributive (win/lose) strategy *(Stevens and Campion, 1994)*
		 • Team Learning Orientation *(Salas et al., 2009)*

Table 10.6 (continued)

Internal relations competencies	Task management competencies	External relations and improvement competencies
– Cooperation (*Cannon-Bowers and Salas, 1997*) – Collective Orientation (*Cannon-Bowers and Salas, 1997; Salas et al., 2009*) – Collective Efficacy (*Salas et al., 2009*) – Cohesion (*Salas et al., 2009*) – Team Reward Attitude (*Salas et al., 2009*) ● Conflict Management (*Salas et al., 2009*) – Recognize and encourage desirable, but discourage undesirable team conflict. (*Stevens and Campion, 1994*) – Recognize the type and source of conflict confronting the team and implement an appropriate conflict resolution strategy (*Stevens and Campion, 1994*)	– Listen non-evaluatively and use active listening techniques appropriately (*Stevens and Campion, 1994*) ● Sense-making Activities – Mission Analysis (*Cannon-Bowers and Salas, 1997*) – Planning (*Salas et al., 2009*) – Problem Detection (*Salas et al., 2009*) – Problem Solving (*Salas et al., 2009*) – Adaptability (*Salas et al., 2009*) – Coordination (*Salas et al., 2009*) – Task-specific role responsibilities (*Cannon-Bowers and Salas, 1997*) – Task Sequencing (*Cannon-Bowers and Salas, 1997*)	

278

- Employ an integrative (win/win) negotiation strategy rather than the traditional distributive (win/lose) strategy
  (Stevens and Campion, 1994)
- Maximize consonance between non-verbal and verbal messages
  (Stevens and Campion, 1994)

- Procedures for Task Accomplishment
  (Cannon-Bowers and Salas, 1997)
- Accurate Task Models
  (Cannon-Bowers and Salas, 1997; Salas et al., 2009)
- Task Interaction(s)
  (Cannon-Bowers and Salas, 1997)
- Situation Awareness
  (Cannon-Bowers and Salas, 1997; Stevens and Campion, 1994)
- Cue/Strategy Associations
  (Cannon-Bowers and Salas, 1997)
- Task Structuring
  (Cannon-Bowers and Salas, 1997)
- Mutual Support Monitoring
  (Cannon-Bowers and Salas, 1997; Salas et al., 2009)
- Back-up / Supportive Behavior
  (Salas et al., 2009)
- Compensatory Behavior
  (Cannon-Bowers and Salas, 1997)
- Team Goal Commitment / Team Conscientiousness
  (Salas et al., 2009)

activities. The competencies we listed within this first phase all directly relate to one or more of these activities. There is empirical support for these KSAs as being effective for successful team performance. A meta-analysis by De Dreu and Weingart (2003) found that task and relationship conflict are negatively correlated with team performance. Therefore, effective management of conflict through pre-emptive planning can help improve team performance (Burke et al., 2006a). Additionally, research has found positive relationships between interpersonal activities and team performance (Mathieu and Schulze, 2006). Still others have suggested that flexibility or adaptability is a key component to team effectiveness (Salas et al., 2005a).

Task Management

Competencies important to effective task management involve both internal and external task-related communication and what we have labeled sense-making activities, which include such KSAs as mission analysis, task sequencing, situation awareness, and mutual support monitoring. This phase most closely resembles the transition process phase outlined by Marks and colleagues (2001). In the team effectiveness review, Mathieu et al. (2008) noted support for transition processes as helpful to team performance. Several studies found support for planning activities as leading to the creation of team norms (Janicik and Bartel, 2003) and as being predictive of performance ratings (Hiller et al., 2006). Others have postulated that mutual support monitoring and situation awareness are critical to team success (Burke et al., 2006a; Salas et al., 2005a). Porter (2005) empirically supported the role of back-up behavior in decision-making performance. Coordination and communication have long been considered critical to team performance (e.g., Salas et al., 1992; Marks et al., 2001). In a recent meta-analysis, LePine et al. (2008) found that various teamwork processes included as competencies within this phase (such as mission analysis, mutual performance monitoring and coordination) are positively related to team performance.

External Relations and Improvement

Competencies important for external relations and improvement focus on effective consultation with others, including boundary-spanning activities, information exchange with those outside the team, and, especially in today's global economy, an understanding of cultural differences coupled with the ability to respond accordingly, like engaging in small talk and ritual greetings. Additionally, team members who are working with other teams (that is, multi-team systems) need to be able to employ effective negotiation strategies. Boundary spanning has recently received more attention in terms of its importance in team performance (Ancona et al., 2002). Effective boundary spanning has been shown to directly benefit team effectiveness in addition to increasing knowledge transfer between and within organizations (Argote et al., 2003), increase organizational innovation (Hargadon, 1998), and increase organizational learning and effectiveness (Carlisle, 2004; Edmondson, 1999). This latter point is important for continued successful team performance. Team learning is critical if teams are to continue to improve.

Self-Managed Leadership Development: Best Practices for Emergent Leaders

In the preceding sections, we described the integration of several lines of research into a list of required competencies that focus on both team process and leadership function. The aim is to provide an overview of issues that SDWTs face (that is, a lack of leadership and discretionary behavior) that could potentially lead to failure, but also to provide opportunities for informal learning and practice of skills to enhance one's own development. We conclude this effort by presenting several guidelines of team leadership, drawing heavily upon previous work by Tannenbaum et al. (1998), who created eight recommended behaviors for team leaders during briefing and debriefs, core components of effective team communication. While their focus was on leader facilitation of team learning, these eight behaviors can be synthesized and adapted to help individuals grow from their experiences in SDWTs. We therefore provide the following five guidelines aimed at providing opportunities for individuals to self-develop through various observation or practice opportunities with teamwork and leadership function competencies (refer to Box 10.1).

Best Practice 1: Engage in a self-critique throughout the team performance process, focusing both on what you did (taskwork) and how you acted (teamwork).

We suggest that emerging leaders in SDWTs should focus on the general competencies outlined above – those that focus on transportable skills since they lend themselves to individual learning. Individuals need to conceptualize the competencies that would enable them to be effective team members regardless of who they are working with. In order to do this, emergent leaders must engage in a self-critique process to determine exactly what competencies they are utilizing effectively and which ones

BOX 10.1   TEN BEST PRACTICES FOR EMERGENT LEADERS IN SELF-DIRECTED WORK TEAMS

Best Practice 1:   Engage in a self-critique throughout the team performance process, focusing both on what you did (taskwork) and how you acted (teamwork).

Best Practice 2:   Seek ideas and feedback from others, reflect on them, and determine how best to integrate them in order to improve personal performance.

Best Practice 3:   Provide specific, constructive feedback that is task-focused, rather than person-oriented, when others request feedback from you.

Best Practice 4:   Encourage active team member participation throughout the life cycle of the team.

Best Practice 5:   Actively strive to understand the role of cultural similarity/differences on team performance and reflect this understanding in actions, cognitions and emotions.

Best Practice 6:   Facilitate and encourage the regular exchange of situation updates between team members.

Best Practice 7:   Facilitate regular debrief sessions following every performance episode within the team, focusing on team learning.

Best Practice 8:   Employ self-correction techniques as required throughout the duration of taskwork and teamwork activities.

Best Practice 9:   Monitor the performance and workload of fellow team-mates and engage in back-up behavior as needed to avoid disruptions in workload synchronization.

Best Practice 10:   Be aware of arising inter-team conflict and manage it as quickly as possible using mediating techniques.

need further development. By looking at both taskwork competencies (that is, sense-making activities) and teamwork competencies (that is, conflict management), team members interested in self-development can critically examine their own strengths and weaknesses. By understanding one's strengths and weaknesses, employees are better able to utilize informal learning opportunities such as working in SDWTs to gain the competencies needed through observation of others who are employing those competencies effectively, or though practice.

Best Practice 2: Seek ideas and feedback from others, reflect on them, and determine how to best integrate them in order to improve personal performance.

Emergent leaders must be able to accept constructive criticism from fellow team members as well as be open to the ideas of others. Research has suggested that feedback-seeking is positively related to adaptation, a key for continued team performance (Kirkman et al., 2004). This will not only help the individuals understand areas needing improvement, but also provide opportunities to practice necessary communication competencies outlined in the task management phase. Specifically, Stevens and Campion (1994) discussed the importance of active listening. When receiving feedback regarding performance or simply listening to ideas presented by others on the team, emergent leaders can utilize active listening techniques to sharpen their own transportable teamwork and leadership skills, while at the same time engaging in an effective team performance behavior.

Best Practice 3: Provide specific, constructive feedback that is task-focused, rather than person-oriented, when others request feedback from you.

In addition to seeking and actively listening to ideas and feedback from others, emergent leaders must be able to provide constructive feedback. This relates to the communication competencies outlined by Stevens and Campion (1994). Specifically, when communicating, provide messages that are behavior- or event-oriented and ensure that your verbal and non-verbal messages are congruent. There is an entire body of literature focused on the importance of providing feedback in many different team contexts, including the findings that feedback is positively related to motivation, interpersonal trust, and performance in virtual teams (Geister et al., 2006). This is not to say, however, that SDWT members who are fulfilling temporary leadership roles in their team should only provide feedback when asked. Given the findings that feedback helps improve team performance, it should be provided as needed. However, in terms of practicing leadership skills that provide benefit to a team, emergent leaders should focus on providing specific, tailored, task-focused feedback.

Best Practice 4: Encourage active team member participation throughout the life cycle of the team.

Competencies outlined by Cannon-Bowers and Salas (1997), such as cooperation, mission analysis, mutual support monitoring and compensatory behavior require team participation to ensure success. Literature has demonstrated the importance of participation for team success (e.g., De Dreu and West, 2001). A key function of a leader is to motivate employees to want to continue to strive towards goals. Motivation has also been shown to be positively related to team performance (LePine et al., 2008). Many argue that goal specification is critical to performance (e.g., Pritchard et al., 1988) and is a key motivational technique (Latham and Locke, 1979). By helping the team set specific goals that are task-focused, members can see what their roles will actively contribute to team success. Emerging leaders should try and help the team focus on setting these goals early during the life cycle of the team in order to ensure maximum team participation.

Best Practice 5: Actively strive to understand the role of cultural similarities/ differences on team performance and reflect this understanding in actions, cognitions and emotions.

Stevens and Campion (1994) noted the value in recognizing the importance of engaging in ritual greetings and small talk. In today's global economic market, this competency is even more important than ever before. In civilian and military organizations alike, individuals from diverse cultural backgrounds are engaging in unparalleled collaborative efforts. Industrial globalization and the widespread use of collaborative technologies that bridge time and distance gaps that were previously barriers to collaboration, have created an environment conducive to the utilization of teams comprised of culturally diverse individuals distributed throughout the globe. Indeed, intercultural collaborations are more common than ever. Therefore, we suggest this competency is crucial to effective team performance. Emergent leaders who wish to be successful in future endeavors need to be culturally competent. Diversity literature to date is inconclusive – demonstrating positive, negative, and no effects at all on team performance (Webber and Donahue, 2001). This indicates the likely presence of moderating variables. While the literature is still in its infancy, given the propensity of organizations to engage in global endeavors, emergent leaders must be culturally sensitive and understand differences that exist in how team members behave in any given performance episode based on their culture.

Best Practice 6: Facilitate and encourage the regular exchange of situation updates between team members.

One of the primary functions of team leadership is to keep the entire team aware of the rest of the team and their work, as well as the situational and environmental context surrounding the team's task. In essence, it is important for the team leader to guide the team in the processes of sense-making and sense-giving described by Zaccaro and colleagues (2009) so that the team has a shared and accurate understanding of their goals and their progress towards them. One effective way to encourage this shared understanding is by regularly performing situations updates, during which the team members provide a brief summary of where they are in terms of their individual taskwork, as well as how that plays into the overall goals of the team. Hart and McLeod (2003) found that engaging in frequent and parsimonious updates helps to maintain strong relationships within teams. Therefore, emerging leaders in SDWTs should practice providing regular and concise situation updates themselves, as this sets an example for other team members, simultaneously developing the emerging leader's skill in giving situation updates while encouraging this same positive behavior in others.

Best Practice 7: Facilitate regular debrief sessions following every performance episode within the team, focusing on team learning.

As described by Zaccaro and colleagues (2009), another critical team leadership function is the development of the team's leadership capacity as a whole. This means that not only should emerging leaders focus on developing their own knowledge, skills and abilities, but an effective leader should also be able to guide and direct the rest of the team in developing their own capabilities. Emerging leaders in SDWTs can use debriefs as a potential strategy for developing the team's capacity for overall leadership and performance. Debriefing is a form of after-action review during which one team member acts as a facilitator and helps to guide the team through a discussion of the team's successes and failures, with a specific focus on learning from past experiences (Smith-Jentsch et al., 2008). Emerging leaders should serve as facilitators for the team in guided debriefs during which the team discusses its successes and failures in terms of taskwork, teamwork and leadership functions, and potential areas of improvement.

This would serve to improve the facilitator's capabilities in guiding teams through the debrief process, as well as to improve the leadership capabilities of the team as a whole.

Best Practice 8: Employ self-correction techniques as required throughout the duration of taskwork and teamwork activities.

Karoly (1993) defined self-regulation as 'those processes . . . that enable an individual to guide his/her goal-directed activities over time and across changing circumstances (contexts). Regulation implies modulation of thought, affect, behavior, or attention' (p. 25). Emergent leaders should engage in self-regulation since, by nature, SDWTs are isolated from individuals who may serve as mediators or external problem-solvers (that is, formal team leaders). Therefore, it is vital that team members be equipped with the means to engage in regulation and, when necessary, self-correction. Guided team self-correction is a debriefing strategy which enables team members to identify and develop solutions for their own team-related problems by providing them with knowledge of what topics they should address, and how to discuss such problems (Smith-Jentsch et al., 2008). Team Dimensional Training is a type of guided team self-correction found to increase teamwork processes and effective outcomes through the development of more accurate shared mental models (Smith-Jentsch et al., 2008). Self-correction is a useful technique in many situations and leads to improved performance (Salas et al., 2007a); therefore, it is a technique that emergent leaders should practice so they can help guide others through the process as well.

Best Practice 9: Monitor the performance and workload of fellow teammates and engage in back-up behavior as needed to avoid disruptions in workload synchronization.

Mutual monitoring refers to the 'team members' ability to keep track of fellow team members' work while carrying out their own . . . to ensure that everything is running as expected and . . . to ensure that they are following procedures correctly' (McIntyre and Salas, 1995: p.23). Mutual monitoring facilitates smooth coordination of actions through the perception and mitigation of performance discrepancies and helps develop awareness of the timing and status of performed actions, which leads to increased situational awareness. Emergent leaders should engage in mutual monitoring in order to perceive when their fellow team members are in need of help. Once a situation is identified where help is warranted (for example, unbalanced workload during high performance periods), an emergent leader should assist the team-mate by engaging in back-up behavior (Salas et al., 2005b). Back-up behavior can take many forms such as providing a team-mate with verbal feedback, assisting a team-mate behaviorally in carrying out actions, or completing a task for a team-mate (Marks et al., 2001). If an emergent leader can recognize that a certain team member is overloaded, work can be shifted to underutilized team members in order to balance the workload and avoid interruptions in workflow.

Best Practice 10: Be aware of arising inter-team conflict and manage it as quickly as possible using mediating techniques.

Research has repeatedly found that conflict between members on a team can have a negative impact on performance (De Dreu and Weingart, 2003). Inter-team conflict can often arise from differences in expertise and specialization between team members, causing them to have differing views regarding how to approach a task, or from cultural differences between team members (Kankanhalli et al., 2007). These differences can lead to interpersonal conflict or misunderstandings, and this friction between team members can be detrimental to performance. Thus, emerging team leaders hoping to be successful in future leadership situations should develop their conflict management skills. In other words, emerging leaders should learn to be sensitive to developing conflict by getting to know their team members and paying attention to changes in behavior that may indicate a developing conflict situation. Furthermore, emerging leaders should practice using mediating techniques (for example, acting as a neutral third party to help disputants find a mutually acceptable settlement; Shin, 2005). By developing the ability to perceive developing conflicts and then successfully mitigate them, SDWT members can effectively improve their own leadership capacity.

CONCLUSION

Teams are not all created equal. SDWTs differ from traditional teams in dramatic ways, specifically a lack of a formally appointed leader and discretion about their own direction. But with the freedom to choose what behaviors to engage in, comes the potential pitfall of not engaging in any effective behaviors. Teams who are self-directed must therefore progress towards their goals and develop in an efficient and effective manner. This requires teams to assume roles and responsibilities typically assumed by a formally appointed leader. This concept of shared leadership requires members who are interested in self-development to understand not only the 'what' and 'how' of *team process*, but the 'what' and 'how' of *team leadership* as well. As demonstrated above, the lines between these two constructs can become muddled, especially in SDWTs. Therefore, team members interested in developing their own leadership capabilities must understand these blurred lines as well as both the specific and generic competencies required to engage in both of these activities successfully.

We have attempted to synthesize the literature on teamwork competencies and team leadership using a phase-based approach to team development. Our list of competencies is by no means exhaustive. We wish to provide the research community with a guiding framework under which to continue development of this important line of research. We hope our best practices provide meaningful avenues to pursue further empirical investigation, and spur continued dialog regarding the role of leadership in SDWTs as well as how emerging leaders can drive their own learning goals in informal learning contexts such as those presented in SDWTs.

REFERENCES

Ancona, D., Bresman, H. and Kaeufer, K. (2002), 'The comparative advantage of X-teams', *MIT Sloan Management Review*, **43**(3), 33–9.

Anderson, J.R. (2000), *Learning and Memory: An Integrated Approach*, 2nd edn. New York: John Wiley.

Antonakis, J., Cianciolo, A.T. and Sternberg, R.J. (2004), 'Leadership: past, present, and future', in J. Antonakis, A.T. Cianciolo and R.J. Sternberg (eds), *The Nature of Leadership*, Thousand Oaks, CA: Sage Publications, pp. 3–15.

Argote, L., McEvily, B. and Reagans, R. (2003), 'Managing knowledge in organizations: an integrative framework and review of emerging themes', *Management Science*, **49**(4), 571–82.

Avolio, B.J., Jung, D.I. and Sivasubramaniam, N. (1996), 'Building highly developed teams: focusing on shared leadership processes, efficacy, trust, and performance', in M.M. Beyerlein, D.A. Johnson and S.T. Beyerlein (eds), *Advances in Interdisciplinary Study of Work Teams: Team Leadership*, Vol. 3, Greenwich, CT: JAI Press, pp. 173–209.

Barry, D. (1991), 'Managing the bossless team: lessons in distributed leadership', *Organizational Dynamics*, **20**(1), 31–47.

Bunderson, J.S. and Sutcliffe, K.M. (2003), 'Management team learning orientation and business unit performance', *Journal of Applied Psychology*, **88**(3), 552–60.

Burke, C.S., Fiore, S.M. and Salas, E. (2004), 'The role of shared cognition in enabling shared leadership and team adaptability', in C.L. Pearce and J.A. Conger (eds), *Shared Leadership: Reframing the Hows and Whys of Leadership*, Thousand Oaks, CA: Sage, pp. 103–21.

Burke, C.S., Stagl, K.C., Salas, E., Pierce, L. and Kendall, D.L. (2006a), 'Understanding team adaptation: a conceptual analysis and model', *Journal of Applied Psychology*, **91**, 1189–207.

Burke, C.S., Stagl, K.C., Klein, C., Goodwin, G.F., Salas, E. and Halpin, S.M. (2006b), 'What type of leadership behaviors are functional in teams? A meta-analysis', *The Leadership Quarterly*, **17** (3), 288–307.

Cannon-Bowers, J.A. and Salas, E. (1997), 'Teamwork competencies: the interaction of team member knowledge, skills, and attitudes', in H.F. O'Niel (ed.), *Workforce Readiness: Competencies and Assessment*, Mahwah, NJ: Lawrence Erlbaum, pp. 151–74.

Cannon-Bowers, J.A., Tannenbaum, S.I., Salas, E. and Volpe, C.E. (1995), 'Defining team competencies and establishing team training requirements', in R. Guzzo, E. Salas and Associates (eds), *Team Effectiveness and Decision Making in Organizations*, San Francisco, CA: Jossey-Bass, pp. 333–80.

Carlisle, P. (2004), 'Transferring, translating, and transforming: an integrative framework for managing knowledge across boundaries', *Organization Science*, **15**, 555–69.

Carson, J.B. (2006), 'Internal team leadership: an examination of leadership roles, role structure, and member outcomes', unpublished doctoral dissertation, University of Maryland.

Carte, T., Chidambaram, L. and Becker, A. (2006), 'Emergent leadership in self-managed virtual teams', *Group Decision and Negotiation*, **15**(4), 323–43.

Cohen, S.G., and Ledford, G.E. (1994), 'The effectiveness of self-managing teams: a quasi-experiment', *Human Relations*, **47** (1), 13–43.

Cummings, T.G. (1978), 'Self-regulating work groups: a socio-technical synthesis', *Academy of Management Review*, **3**, 625–34.

Day, D., Gronn, P. and Salas, E. (2004), 'Leadership capacity in teams', *Leadership Quarterly*, **15**, 857–80.

De Dreu, C.K.W. and Weingart, L.R. (2003), 'Task versus relationship conflict: team performance, and team member satisfaction: a meta-analysis', *Journal of Applied Psychology*, **88**, 741–9.

De Dreu, C.K.W. and West, M.A. (2001). 'Minority dissent and team innovation: the importance of participation in decision making', *Journal of Applied Psychology*, **86**, 1191–201.

Devine, D.J., Clayton, L.D., Philips, J.L., Dunford, B.B. and Melner, S.B. (1999), 'Teams in organizations: prevalence, characteristics, and effectiveness', *Small Group Research*, **30**, 678–711.

Druskat, V.U. and Kayes, D.C. (2000), 'Learning versus performance in short-term project teams', *Small Group Research*, **31**, 328–53.

Dunphy, D. and Bryant, B. (1996), 'Teams: panaceas or prescriptions for improved performance?', *Human Relations*, **49**(5), 677–99.

Edmondson, A. (1999), 'Psychological safety and learning behavior in work teams', *Administrative Science Quarterly*, **44** (2), 350–83.

Ellinger, A.D. (2004), 'The concept of self-directed learning and its implications for human resource development', *Advances in Developing Human Resources*, **6** (2), 158–77.

Ellinger, A.D. (2005), 'Contextual factors shaping informal workplace learning in a workplace setting: the case of "Reinventing Itself Company"', *Human Resource Development Quarterly*, **16**(3), 389–415.

Enos, M.D., Kehrhahn, M.T. and Bell, A. (2003), 'Informal learning and the transfer of learning: how managers develop proficiency', *Human Resource Development Quarterly*, **14**, 369–87.

Erez, A., LePine, J.A. and Elms, H. (2002), 'Effects of rotated leadership and peer evaluation on the functioning and effectiveness of self-managed teams: a quasi-experiment', *Personnel Psychology*, **55**, 929–48.

Fleishman, E.A., Mumford, M.D., Zaccaro, S.J., Levin, K.Y., Korotkin, A.L. and Hein, M.B. (1991), 'Taxonomic efforts in the description of leader behavior: a synthesis and functional interpretation', *Leadership Quarterly*, **2**(4), 245–87.

Flynn, D., Eddy, E., and Tannenbaum, S.I. (2005), 'The impact of national culture on the continuous learning environment: exploratory findings from multiple countries', *Journal of East-West Business*, **12**, 85–107.

Garavan, T.N. and McGuire, D. (2001), 'Competencies and workplace learning: some reflections on the rhetoric and the reality', *Journal of Workplace Learning*, **13** (4), 144–64.

Garavan, T.N., Bamicle, B. and O'Sulleabhain, F. (1999), 'Management development: contemporary trends, issues and strategies', *Journal of European Industrial Training*, **23**(4/5), 3–12.

Geister, S., Konradt, U. and Hertel, G. (2006), 'Effects of process feedback on motivation, satisfaction, and performance in virtual teams', *Small Group Research*, **37**, 459–89.

Gersick, C.J.G. (1988), 'Time and transition in work teams: toward a new model of group development', *Academy of Management Journal*, **31**(1), 9–41.

Gersick, C.J.G. (1989), 'Marking time: predictable transitions in task groups', *Academy of Management Journal*, **32**(2), 274–309.

Graham, C.R. (2003), 'A model of norm development for computer-mediated teamwork', *Small Group Research*, **34**(3), 322–52.

Gronn, P. (2002), 'Distributed leadership as a unit of analysis', *The Leadership Quarterly*, **13**(4), 423–51.

Hargadon, A.B. (1998), 'Firms as knowledge brokers: lessons in pursuing continuous innovation', *California Management Review*, **40**(3), 209–27.

Hart, R.K. and McLeod, P.L. (2003), 'Rethinking team building in geographically dispersed teams: one message at a time', *Organizational Dynamics*, **31**(4), 352–61.

Hiller, N.J., Day, D.V. and Vance, R.J. (2006), 'Collective enactment of leadership roles and team effectiveness: a field study', *Leadership Quarterly*, **17**, 387–97.

Hodgetts, R.M., Luthans, F. and Slocum, J.W. (1999), 'Strategy and IHRM initiatives for the 00s environment: redefining roles and boundaries, linking competencies and resources', *Organizational Dynamics*, **28**(2), 7–21.

Jacobs, T.O. and Jaques, E. (1987), 'Leadership in complex systems', in J. Zeidner (ed.), *Human Productivity Enhancement*, New York: Praeger.

Janicik, G.A. and Bartel, C.A. (2003), 'Talking about time: effects of temporal planning and time awareness norms on group coordination and performance', *Group Dynamics: Theory, Research, and Practice*, **7**, 122–34.

Kankanhalli, A., Tan, B.C.Y. and Wei, K.K. (2007), 'Conflict and performance in global virtual teams', *Journal of Management Information Systems*, **23** (3), 237–74.

Karoly, P. (1993), 'Mechanisms of self-regulation: a systems view', *Annual Review of Psychology*, **44**, 23–52.

Katz, D. and Kahn, R.L. (1978), *The Social Psychology of Organizations*, New York: John Wiley, pp. 525–76.

Kauffeld, S. (2006), 'Self-directed work groups and team competence', *Journal of Occupational and Organizational Psychology*, **79**(1), 1–21.

Kirkman, B.L., Rosen, B., Tesluk, P.E. and Gibson, C.B. (2004), 'The impact of team empowerment on virtual team performance: the moderating role of face-to-face interaction', *Academy of Management Journal*, **47**, 175–92.

Kozlowski, S., and Bell, B.S. (2003), 'Work groups and teams in organizations', in W.C. Borman, D.R. Ilgen and R.J. Klimoski (eds), *Handbook of Psychology: Industrial and Organizational Psychology*, Vol. 12, London: John Wiley, pp. 333–75.

Kozlowski, S.W.J. and Ilgen, D.R. (2006), 'Enhancing the effectiveness of work-groups and teams', *Psychological Science in the Public Interest*, **7**(3), 77–124.

Kozlowski, S.W.J., Gully, S.M., Nason, E.R. and Smith, E.M. (1999), 'Developing adaptive teams: a theory of compilation and performance across levels and time', in D.R. Ilgen and E.D. Pulakos (eds), *The Changing Nature of Work Performance: Implications for Staffing, Motivation, and Development*, San Francisco, CA: Jossey-Bass, pp. 240–92.

Krakauer, J. (1997), *Into Thin Air*, New York: Villard.

Kuipers, B.S. and De Witte, M.C. (2005), 'Teamwork: a case study on development and performance', *The International Journal of Human Resource Management*, **16** (2), 185–201.

Kuipers, B.S. and Stoker, J.I. (2009), 'Development and performance of self-managing work teams: a theoretical and empirical examination', *The International Journal of Human Resource Management*, **20**(2), 399–419.

Latham, G. and Locke, E. (1979), 'Goal setting – a motivational technique that works', *Organizational Dynamics*, **8**(2), 68–80.

Lawler, E.E. (1986), *High-involvement Management*, San Francisco, CA: Jossey-Bass.

LePine, J.A., Piccolo, R.F., Jackson, C.L., Mathieu, J.E. and Saul, J.R. (2008), 'A meta-analysis of teamwork processes: tests of a mutidimensional model and relationships with team effectiveness criteria', *Personnel Psychology*, **61**, 273–307.

Locke, E.A. and Latham, G.P. (2002), 'Building a practically useful theory of goal setting and task motivation: a 35-year odyssey', *American Psychologist*, **57**(9), 705–17.

Lohman, M.C. (2000), 'Environmental inhibitors to informal learning in the workplace. A case study of public school teachers', *Adult Education Quarterly*, **50**, 83–101.

London, M., Polzer, J.T. and Omoregie, H. (2005), 'Interpersonal congruence, transactive memory, and feedback processes: an integrative model of group learning', *Human Resource Development Review*, **4**(2), 114–35.

Losey, M.R. (1999), 'Mastering the competencies of HR management', *Human Resource Management*, **38**(2), 99–111.

Manz, C.C. and Sims, H.P. (1980), 'Self-management as a substitute for leadership: a social learning theory perspective', *Academy of Management Review*, **5**(3), 361–7.

Manz, C.C. and Sims, H.P. (1987), 'Leading workers to lead themselves: the external leadership of self-managing work teams', *Administrative Science Quarterly*, **32**, 106–28.

Manz, C.C. and Sims, H.P. (1993), *Business Without Bosses*, New York: John Wiley.

Marks, M.A., Mathieu, J.E. and Zaccaro, S.J. (2001), 'A temporally based framework and taxonomy of team processes', *The Academy of Management Review*, **26**(3), 356–76.

Marsick, V.J. and Volpe, M. (1999), 'The nature and need for informal learning', in V.J. Marsick and M. Volpe (eds), *Informal Learning on the Job*, Baton Rouge, LA: Academy of Human Resource Development, pp. 1–9.

Marsick, V.J. and Watkins, K.E. (1990), *Informal and Incidental Learning in the Workplace*, London: Routledge.

Mathieu, J.E. and Schulze, W. (2006), 'The influence of team knowledge and formal plans on episodic team process–performance relationships', *Academy of Management Journal*, **49**(3), 605–19.

Mathieu, J.E., Gilson, L.L. and Ruddy, T.R. (2006), 'Empowerment and team effectiveness: an empirical test of an integrated model', *Journal of Applied Psychology*, **91**, 97–108.

Mathieu, J.E., Maynard, M.T., Rapp, T. and Gilson, L. (2008). 'Team effectiveness 1997–2007: a review of recent advancements and a glimpse into the future', *Journal of Management*, **34**(3), 410–76.

McIntyre, R.M. and Salas, E. (1995), 'Measuring and managing for team performance: emerging principles from complex environments', in R.A. Guzzo and E. Salas (eds), *Team Effectiveness and Decision Making in Organizations*, San Francisco, CA: Jossey-Bass, pp. 9–45.

Morgeson, F.P. (2005), 'The external leadership of self-managing teams: intervening in the context of novel and disruptive events', *Journal of Applied Psychology*, **90**(3), 497–508.

National Aeronautics and Space Administration (NASA) (2008), 'Risk of performance errors due to poor team cohesion and performance, inadequate selection/team composition, inadequate training and poor psychosocial adaptation' (HRP-47072), Houston, TX: NASA.

Orasanu, J. (1994), 'Shared problem models and flight crew performance', in N. Johnston, N. McDonald and R. Fuller (eds), *Aviation Psychology in Practice*, Brookfield, VT: Ashgate, pp. 255–85.

Orsburn, J.D., Moran, L., Musselwhite, E. and Zenger, J.H. (1990), *Self-directed Work Teams: The New American Challenge*, Homewood, IL: Business One Irwin.

Pearce, C.L. and Sims, H.P., Jr. (2002), 'The relative influence of vertical vs. shared leadership on the longitudinal effectiveness of change management teams', *Group Dynamics: Theory, Research, and Practice*, **6**, 172–97.

Pearsall, M.J. and Ellis, A.P.J. (2006), 'The effects of critical team member assertiveness on team performance and satisfaction', *Journal of Management*, **32**, 575–94.

Porter, C.O.L.H. (2005), 'Goal orientation: effects on backing up behavior, performance, efficacy, and commitment in teams', *Journal of Applied Psychology*, **90**(4), 811–18.

Pritchard, R.D., Jones, S., Roth, P., Stuebing, K. and Ekeberg, S. (1988), 'Effects of group feedback, goal setting, and incentives on organizational productivity', *Journal of Applied Psychology*, **73**, 337–58.

Salas, E., Nichols, D. and Driskell, J.E. (2007a), 'Testing three team training strategies in intact teams: a meta-analysis', *Small Group Research*, **38**, 471–88.

Salas, E., Sims, D.E. and Burke, C.S. (2005a), 'Is there a big five in teamwork?', *Small Group Research*, **36**(5), 555–99.

Salas, E., Dickinson, T.L., Converse, S.A. and Tannenbaum, S.I. (1992), 'Toward an understanding of team performance and training', in R.J. Swezey and E. Salas (eds), *Teams: Their Training and Performance*, Norwood, NJ: Ablex, pp. 3–29.

Salas, E., Rosen, M.A., Burke, C.S. and Goodwin, G.F. (2009), 'The wisdom of the collectives in organizations: an update of the teamwork competencies', in E. Salas, G.F. Goodwin and C.S. Burke (eds), *Team Effectiveness in Complex Organizations: Cross-disciplinary Perspectives and Approaches*, New York: Routledge Academic, pp. 39–79.

Salas, E., Stagl, K.C., Burke, C.S. and Goodwin, G.F. (2007b), 'Fostering team effectiveness in organizations: toward an integrative theoretical framework of team performance', in J.W. Shuart, W. Spaulding and J. Poland (eds), *Modeling Complex Systems: Motivation, Cognition and Social Processes, Nebraska Symposium on Motivation*, 51, Lincoln, NE: University of Nebraska Press, pp. 185–243.

Salas, E., Guthrie, J.W., Wilson-Donnelly, K.A., Priest, H.A. and Burke, C.S. (2005b), 'Modeling team performance: the basic ingredients and research needs', in W.B. Rouse and K.R. Boff (eds), *Organizational Simulation* Hoboken, NJ: Wiley, pp. 185–228.

Shamir, B., House, R. J. and Arthur, M. (1993), 'The motivational effects of charismatic leadership: a self-concept based theory', *Organization Science*, **4**, 577–94.

Shaw, J.D., Duffy, M.K., and Stark, E.M. (2001), 'Team reward attitude: construct development and initial validation', *Journal of Organizational Behavior*, **22**, 903–17.

Shin, Y. (2005), 'Conflict resolution in virtual teams', *Organizational Dynamics*, **34**, 331–45.

Sivasubramaniam, N., Murry, W.D., Avolio, B.J. and Jung, D.I. (2002), 'A longitudinal model of the effects of team leadership and group potency on group performance', *Group and Organization Management*, **27**, 66–96.

Skule, S. (2004), 'Learning conditions at work: a framework to understand and assess informal learning in the workplace', *International Journal of Training and Development*, **8**(1), 8–17.

Smith-Jentsch, K.A., Cannon-Bowers, J.A., Tannenbaum, S.I. and Salas, E. (2008), 'Guided team self-correction: impacts on team mental models, processes, and effectiveness', *Small Group Research*, **39**(3), 303–27.

Solanksy, S.T. (2008), 'Leadership style and team processes in self-managed teams', *Journal of Leadership and Organizational Studies*, **14**(4), 332–41.

Stevens, M. and Campion, M. (1994), 'The knowledge, skill, and ability requirements for teamwork: implications for human resource management', *Journal of Management*, **20**(2), 503–30.

Stewart, G.L. and Manz, C.C. (1995), 'Leadership for self-managing work teams: a typology and integrative model', *Human Relations*, **7**, 747–68.

Tannenbaum, S.I. (1997), 'Enhancing continuous learning: diagnostic findings from multiple companies', *Human Resource Management*, **36**, 437–52.

Tannenbaum, S.I., Smith-Jentsch, K.A. and Behson, S.J. (1998), 'Training team leaders to facilitate team learning and performance', in J.A. Cannon-Bowers and E. Salas (eds), *Making Decisions under Stress*, Washington, DC: American Psychological Association, pp. 247–70.

Tannenbaum, SI., Beard, R.L., McNall, L.A. and Salas, E. (2010), 'Informal learning and development in organizations', in S.W.J. Kozlowski and E. Salas (eds), *Learning, Training, and Development in Organizations*, The SIOP Frontiers Series, Mahwah, NJ: Lawrence Erlbaum.

Tuckman, B.W. (1965), 'Development sequences in small groups', *Psychological Bulletin*, **63**(6), 384–99.

Van Amelsvoort, P. and Benders, J. (1996), 'Team time: a model for developing self-directed work teams', *International Journal of Operations and Production Management*, **16**(2), 159–70.

Vygotsky, L.S. (1978), *Mind in Society: The Development of Higher Psychological Processes*, Cambridge, MA: Harvard University Press.

Watkins, K.E. and Marsick, V.J. (1992), 'Towards a theory of informal and incidental learning in organizations', *International Journal of Lifelong Education*, **11**(4), 287–300.

Webber, S.S. and Donahue, L.M. (2001), 'Impact of highly and less job-related diversity on work group cohesion and performance: a meta-analysis', *Journal of Management*, **27**(2), 141–62.

Wilson, J.M., Goodman, P.S. and Cronin, M.A. (2007), 'Group learning', *Academy of Management Review*, **32**(4), 1041–59.

Wittenbaum, G. and Strasser, G. (1996), 'Management of information in small groups', in J. Nye and M. Brower (eds), *What's Social about Social Cognition? Social Cognition in Small Groups*, Thousand Oaks, CA: Sage, pp. 3–28.

Wolff, S.B., Pescosolido, A.T. and Druskat, V.U. (2002), 'Emotional intelligence as the basis of leader emergence', *Leadership Quarterly*, **13**(5), 505–22.

Yukl, G.A. (1998), *Leadership in Organizations*, 5th edn, Englewood Cliffs, NJ: Prentice-Hall.

Yukl, G. (2006) *Leadership in Organizations*, 6th edn, Englewood Cliffs, NJ: Prentice-Hall.

Zaccaro, S.J. and Klimoski, R.J. (2001), 'The nature of organizational leadership: an introduction', in S.J. Zaccaro and R.J. Klimoski (eds), *The Nature of Organizational Leadership: Understanding the Performance Imperatives Confronting Today's Leaders*, San Francisco, CA: Jossey-Bass, pp. 3–41.

Zaccaro, S.J., and Klimoski, R. (2002), 'The interface of leadership and team processes', *Group and Organization Management*, **27**, 4–13.

Zaccaro, S.J., Heinen, B. and Shuffler, M.L. (2009), 'Team leadership: key issues, models, and developmental prescriptions', in E. Salas, J. Goodwin and C.S. Burke (eds), *Team Effectiveness in Complex Organizations: Cross Disciplinary Perspective and Approaches*, San Francisco, CA: Jossey–Bass.

Zaccaro, S.J., Rittman, A.L. and Marks, M.A. (2001), 'Team leadership', *Leadership Quarterly*, **12**, 451–83.

Zaccaro, S.J., Blair, V., Peterson, C. and Zazanis, M. (1995), 'Collective efficacy', in J.E. Maddux (ed.), *Self-efficacy, Adaptation, and Adjustment: Theory, Research, and Application*, New York: Plenum.

11. Work motivations, job behaviors and flourishing in work and life[1]

Ronald J. Burke

This chapter includes a selective review of research findings related to the central concepts of the chapter – values, motivations, behaviors and flourishing – self-assessment instruments with normative information allowing readers to see how they compare with others, along with indications of scores on each that should provide 'food for thought', and a framework to identify behavioral changes that might enrich one's life and improve one's performance in several life roles, along with a process for bringing about these changes. We encourage you to have a note pad handy as you work your way through the chapter.

LIFE IS FULL OF PROBABILITIES

One often reads about or sees stories on television in which interviews with a person who has reached the age of 100 are reported. The person is asked for his or her (usually a her, but that's a different chapter) secrets to living a long life. The person responds by saying they smoked a pack of cigarettes a day since they were a teenager, had a few scotches at night to relax, and stayed up late carousing. One then hears or reads about a physically fit individual who made all the desirable life style choices dying of a heart attack while jogging.

There are no guarantees in life; there are only probabilities. There is a reasonably high probability that smoking, drinking, eating badly and being overweight will be associated with a shorter lifespan, but there is no guarantee of this. Individuals who are chronically angry, hostile and impatient have a higher risk of having coronary heart disease, but there is no iron-clad guarantee of this either. Some calm individuals develop heart disease as well, but fortunately significantly fewer of them do. Every one will eventually die, and calm individuals are more likely to die from some other cause than coronary heart disease.

The content summarized in this chapter has been shown to be associated with dissatisfaction, derailed leadership and personal distress as well as flourishing in life and work and effective leadership. But these associations still represent only probabilities. It is still up to you, the reader, to look at yourself – your attitudes, values, behaviors and personal outcomes in several domains and determine which of these might be 'risks' for you and potential areas that you would like to change to increase your chances for life and career success. But remember, there are no guarantees.

DEMANDS OF THE LEADERSHIP ROLE

Effective leaders generally work long hours and hold 'extreme jobs'. One executive I knew spoke to one of my classes and indicated that he had worked 100 hours a week at one point in his career.

What is an 'extreme job'? Hewlett and Luce (2006) studied two large samples of men and women holding senior leadership jobs; one sample working in major US corporations, the other in major international organizations. An 'extreme job' involved working 60 hours a week or more in jobs having several of these characteristics: being available to clients 24/7; having a workload that might reasonably comprise two jobs, and frequent traveling.

Respondents in their work stated that they would like to reduce the number of hours they worked in a few years, and some were concerned about the potential effects of their work hours on their well-being and that of their family.

Men and women in 'extreme jobs' were, however, highly satisfied in their jobs, citing the financial rewards, challenge and meaning they obtained from them.

But not all leaders are satisfied with their work and personal situation nor are all leaders emotionally healthy. This chapter focuses on personal goals and beliefs, sources or types of work motivations, and job behaviors associated with distress (or flourishing) among men and women in leadership roles.

It considers the following central questions: why do leaders work hard (their personal beliefs and work motivations)? How do leaders work hard (their job behaviors)?

It will examine the following content:

- Work hours and work intensity
- Personal beliefs and fears
- Motivation for money
- Extrinsic versus intrinsic goals

- Extrinsic versus intrinsic processes
- Work addiction
- Passion versus addiction
- Type A behavior, anger and irritation
- Perfectionism
- Sleep
- Respite or vacations
- Recovery at the end of the workday and on weekends.

WHY DO LEADERS WORK HARD?

There is no doubt that leaders work long and hard hours. They work long hours most weeks, both at the office and at home. Leaders sometimes do not take all vacation time they are entitled to, and on vacation some leaders have a difficult time disengaging from their work and workplace. Some leaders bring work home in the evenings and at weekends.

We will consider the following sources of motivation for working long hours:

- Extrinsic versus intrinsic goals
- Extrinsic versus intrinsic motives
- Personal beliefs and fears
- Motives for money
- Work addiction
- Passion versus addiction.

WHAT GOALS WOULD YOU LIKE TO ACHIEVE IN THE NEXT FEW YEARS?

List five goals (or projects) that you would like to realize or achieve over the next few years, behavior patterns you will try to establish in your daily life, things you will try to accomplish for yourself, or kinds of circumstances you will try to bring about. Examples might be: getting a promotion; getting to know more people; spending more time with your family; or developing your golf game to a higher level. List these five goals or projects on your notepad.

To what extent do the following reasons explain why you are pursuing or would like to achieve each of these goals? Using the following five-point scale, indicate the extent to which each of these four reasons explains why you are pursuing or would like to achieve each of these five goals.

1 = To a small extent.
2
3 = To some extent.
4
5 = To a great extent.

1. Because I really identify with this goal.
2. Because of the enjoyment or stimulation that this goal would provide me.
3. Because somebody else wants me to or because the situation seems to require it.
4. Because I would feel ashamed, guilty or anxious if I did not have this goal.

Place a number (either a 1, 2, 3, 4 or 5) beside each reason for each goal you listed in your note pad following this structure:

Goal 1.   Reason 1
            Reason 2
            Reason 3
            Reason 4.

THE CONTENT OF ONE'S GOALS: THE 'WHAT' ONE PURSUES MATTERS

Consider the following personal goals. Imagine that you were actually pursuing each of these goals in your own life.

- Having many close and caring relationships with others.
- Being fulfilled and having a very meaningful life.
- Helping to make the world a better place.
- Being known and/or admired by many people.
- Looking good and appearing attractive to others.
- Getting a job that pays very well and having a lot of nice possessions.

The first three goals represent intrinsic goals (emotional intimacy, personal growth, community contribution); the next three goals represent extrinsic goals (fame/popularity, attractive image, financial success).

Extrinsic goals, such as financial success, depend on the contingent reactions of others; they are engaged in as a means to an end (for example, the esteem of others). Intrinsic goals, such as helping others or self-acceptance, express a desire for personal growth and satisfy basic psychological needs possessed by everyone. Extrinsic goals do not provide satisfaction in and of themselves. Others determine whether or not the individual should be deemed worthy.

Attaching a high value to extrinsic goals, or believing that one will achieve these extrinsic goals, has been found to be associated with lower levels of psychological well-being in numerous studies (Kasser and Ryan, 1993, 1996). Why should valuing or achieving extrinsic goals be associated with lower levels of well-being?

Several reasons have been offered and supported by research findings.

- Valuing or pursuing extrinsic goals reflects a general type of neuroticism and emotional insecurity in individuals.
- Extrinsic goals lead individuals to engage in controlling, ego-involving and driven behaviors and have fewer growth, self-actualizing experiences
- Individuals are less likely to successfully achieve extrinsic goals. Yet even when these goals are achieved, they have been found to be associated with reduced psychological health.
- Intrinsic goals are inherently rewarding to pursue because they satisfy basic (human) psychological needs (growth, belonging, agency).
- Extrinsic goals are less directly satisfying of psychological needs.

THE MOTIVES FOR ONE'S GOALS: THE 'WHY' ONE PURSUES SOMETHING ALSO MATTERS

The 'why' behind the pursuit of one's goals has also been found to have important well-being consequences (Deci and Ryan, 2000; Sheldon et al., 2004; Ryan and Deci, 2000; 2001). Two types of motives have been considered:

- *Autonomy motives*: people act in an autonomous and freely chosen manner.
- *Controlled motives*: people feel pressured to think, feel and act in particular ways.

Individuals who act from autonomy motives have been shown to report higher levels of psychological well-being. Controlled or negative motives may be associated with lower levels of psychological well-being for a number of reasons:

- Individuals emphasizing extrinsic goals are more competitive, more Machiavellian and have lower quality personal relationships.
- Individuals pursuing extrinsic goals make their self-worth dependent on the views and opinions of others.
- Focusing on extrinsic goals forces individuals to make more social comparisons in which they may fall short.
- Pursuing (and achieving) extrinsic goals leaves less time available to satisfy intrinsic goals.

The currently available evidence supports the following conclusions. First, valuing and/or pursuing extrinsic goals is associated with lower psychological health. Second, valuing and/or pursuing extrinsic goals is associated with higher levels of controlled motives. Third, controlled motives are associated with lower levels of psychological well-being.

Now go back to your personal goals and your reasons for pursuing them that you listed on your notepad.

1. Are your goals extrinsic, intrinsic or do they contain some of both?
2. Are your motives for pursuing these goals autonomous (mainly the first two reasons) or controlled (mainly the second two reasons)? Add your scores for each of the first two motives for each of the five goals that you provided; this is your autonomy motives score. Then add up your scores for each of the last two motives for each of the five goals that you provided; this is your controlled motives score. Which is higher?

Summarize what you have learned about your goals and your motives for pursuing these goals on your notepad.

WHAT MAKES SAMMY – OR SAMANTHA – RUN?

We will now examine some of the factors that are associated with leaders' over-commitment to work, sometimes at the expense of other important and satisfying life domains. Although some of these factors have a long developmental history starting in one's early upbringing and early life experiences, an examination of them will shed light on your behaviors today.

Beliefs and Fears

Friedman and Rosenman (1974), based on observations of their coronary heart disease (CHD) patients, proposed that the Type A Behavior Pattern

(TABP), comprising attitudes, emotions, behavior and actions were a major contributor to CHD. Research evidence, though sometimes inconsistent as to which TABP components were lethal, have supported such an association, and efforts to reduce levels of one's TABP have reduced levels of CHD. Recent efforts have focused on the development of TABP to better understand both the sources of TABP as well as the causes of CHD.

Price (1982; 1988), a clinician working with Friedman's research team on efforts to reduce TABP, developed a cognitive-social learning model to understand TABP. She suggested that cognitions, or personal beliefs and fears, lie at the core of TABP. TABP represents a striving for social approval and material possessions, reflecting deeper beliefs and fears acquired through social learning in a largely materialistic capitalistic society. TABP is associated with ambitiousness, aggressiveness, competitiveness, alertness, impatience, time urgency, irritability and anger.

She identified three primary beliefs, each associated with accompanying fears, that support the development and maintenance of TABP. We have found that these beliefs and fears also predict specific work addiction components (for example, feeling driven to work because of inner pressures), and we (and others) have found that TABP is also associated directly with these work addiction components.

Her three beliefs and fears are as follows:

1. One must constantly prove oneself through achievements or risk being seen as unsuccessful or lacking in worth. Thus one must constantly achieve to gain the approval of others (high performance standards, achieve a lot, work hard and long).
2. No universal moral principles exist so there are no guarantees that 'good' will prevail. Thus one must take action to ensure personal justice (anger, irritability, hostility).
3. Resources (things worth having) are in limited supply so the individual may fall short in acquiring these. Thus they must act to ensure that they get what they need so that others will value them as people of worth so they can then value themselves (hard driving, competitive).

Several studies have shown a relationship between scores on measurers of these beliefs and fears and both TABP and CHD-related indicators (Burke, 1984; Lee et al., 1996; Watkins et al., 1989; Watkins et al., 1987). In addition, research findings have shown a relationship between scores on these beliefs and fears, components of work addiction, and indicators of psychological well-being.

Box 11.1 presents a questionnaire that assesses these three beliefs and

BOX 11.1   BELIEFS AND FEARS

To what extent does each of the following items describe you? Circle one number by each item.

1 = Extremely non-descriptive.
5 = Neither descriptive nor non-descriptive.
9 = Extremely descriptive.

Must Constantly Prove Oneself Or Else Be Judged Worthless

1. The opinion of others has a lot to do with how I feel about myself.   1   2   3   4   5   6   7   8   9
2. I worry a great deal about what others think of me.   1   2   3   4   5   6   7   8   9
3. How I feel about myself is largely based on what others think of me.   1   2   3   4   5   6   7   8   9
4. I often worry that I'll appear foolish in front of others.   1   2   3   4   5   6   7   8   9
5. I must achieve a lot so others will think well of me.   1   2   3   4   5   6   7   8   9
6. I think others are constantly judging my actions and accomplishments.   1   2   3   4   5   6   7   8   9
7. I feel like I must continually prove myself.   1   2   3   4   5   6   7   8   9
8. I often worry about losing my self-worth.   1   2   3   4   5   6   7   8   9
9. I worry that others will somehow discover my vulnerabilities.   1   2   3   4   5   6   7   8   9

No Moral Principles Exist So Fear That Good May Not Prevail

10.	I believe that unscrupulous actions can produce rewarding consequences.	1	2	3	4	5	6	7	8	9
11.	I think most people would screw you over given half the chance.	1	2	3	4	5	6	7	8	9
12.	Being nice to your peers doesn't pay when it comes to getting ahead.	1	2	3	4	5	6	7	8	9
13.	I think most people are more interested in getting ahead of me than being my friend.	1	2	3	4	5	6	7	8	9
14.	I think that nice guys finish last.	1	2	3	4	5	6	7	8	9
15.	If I don't use people, someone else surely will.	1	2	3	4	5	6	7	8	9

Must Strive Against Others to Win or Gain

16.	I feel another person's loss is my gain and vice versa.	1	2	3	4	5	6	7	8	9
17.	There can be only one winner in any situation.	1	2	3	4	5	6	7	8	9
18.	I think it's healthy to put your needs ahead of those of other people.	1	2	3	4	5	6	7	8	9
19.	I must strive against others to get what I need.	1	2	3	4	5	6	7	8	9
20.	Being second best is practically worthless.	1	2	3	4	5	6	7	8	9
21.	I think it's extremely important to look out for yourself and let other people take care of their own problems.	1	2	3	4	5	6	7	8	9

fears. Take a few minutes to complete it now. Compute your scores as follows:

1. 'I must constantly prove myself or else be judged worthless.'
    Sum your scores on the first 9 items. Then divide this number by 9.
2. 'No moral principles exist so I fear that good may not prevail.'
    Sum your scores on the next 6 items. Then divide this number by 6.
3. 'I must strive against others to win or gain.'
    Sum your scores on the final 6 items. Then divide this number by 6.

You can now compare your scores on these three measures of beliefs and fears with a few other groups.

	Mean	Standard Deviation
Prove oneself	4.3	1.46
No moral principles	3.6	1.29
Striving against others	3.9	1.32

The mean refers to the average score across the total sample. Standard Deviation (SD) is a measure of spread or dispersion of scores. A score of one SD above the mean is obtained by only 32 percent of the sample; a score of two SDs above the mean is obtained by less than 5 percent of the sample. Here are the scores on the three personal beliefs and fears at these two points for each of the three personal beliefs and fears.

	1 SD above	2 SDs above
Prove oneself	5.8	7.3
No moral principles	4.9	6.2
Striving against others	5.2	6.5

This normative group comprised 335 full-time undergraduate college students enrolled in 16 upper division business administration courses in two large US universities. The sample comprised 191 males and 144 females, with a mean age of 21.6 years.

Now consider your scores on these three measures. Did they fall above or below the mean or average score? Did they fall above 1 SD above the average or mean score? Did they fall 2 SDs above the mean score? If they did, they would be very high compared to the normative group. Summarize your responses to these questions on your notepad.

Materialism

We, in the developed world, live in materialistic societies, particularly so in North America. But there is increasing evidence that 'money does not buy happiness' (see Easterlin, 2007; Gowdy, 2007; Kasser et al., 2007; Myers, 2007).

- Kasser and Ryan (1993; 1996) found that placing a high importance on money or financial goals, compared to other goals, was negatively related to psychological well-being.
- Although wealthier people have been found to be happier than poorer people, these differences have been very small.
- Though the standard of living (economic well-being) among North Americans has increased over the past several decades, levels of happiness have remained constant.
- Focusing on extrinsic rewards (for example, money) leaves individuals less time for satisfying intrinsic needs.

Some researchers have suggested that the motives for money may be more important than desiring money itself in determining levels of psychological well-being. Srivastava et al., (2003) conducted three studies in which they first developed a measure for motives for money and then examined the relationship of various motives for money and psychological well-being in samples of business students and entrepreneurs. They identified and measured 10 motives for money including: security, family support, pride, charity and freedom.

Factor analysis of these data indicated three broad categories of motives for money: positive (4 motives), freedom of action (4 motives) and negative (2 motives). They also created a measure of money importance. They reported the following:

1. Positive motives for money were positively related to levels of self-reported psychological well-being.
2. Negative motives for money were negatively related to levels of self-reported psychological well-being.
3. Negative motives for money were the cause of both money importance and psychological well-being.

Now take a few minutes to complete the 30-item survey shown in Box 11.2. There are 10 motives for money, scored as follows:

1. Security: sum of 1, 11 and 21.
2. Family support: sum of 2, 12 and 22.

BOX 11.2   MOTIVES FOR MONEY

Please indicate *how important* each of the following is as a *reason* for you to earn money. Put your importance rating on the line at the end of each reason.

| 1 | 2 | 3 | 4 | 5 | 6 | 7 | 8 | 9 | 10 |

(Totally *un*important)   (Extremely important)

1. To take care of the basic requirements for living such as decent housing. _____
2. To be able to support a family. _____
3. To get just compensation for my work. _____
4. To feel proud of myself. _____
5. To spend time and resources pursuing leisure activities (e.g., poetry, literature, photography, painting, music). _____
6. To donate money to those who need it. _____
7. To implement my ideas by starting my own business. _____
8. To let my mood guide me at times so that I can blow money in shopping just for the thrill of it. _____
9. To prove I am not a failure. _____
10. To show I am better than my friends/brothers/ sisters/relatives. _____
11. To maintain a reasonable bank balance for emergencies. _____
12. To take care of the college education of my children. _____
13. To get what I earned as a result of my thinking and effort. _____
14. To know that I earned my way in life. _____
15. To spend time and money on my hobbies. _____
16. To start a charitable trust dedicated to a cause that I value. _____
17. To not be accountable to anyone for what I do or how I do things. _____
18. To play exciting games in casinos (gamble). _____

19. To prove that I am not as incompetent as some people have claimed. _____
20. To have a house and cars that are better than those of my neighbors. _____
21. To have a feeling of security. _____
22. To leave behind enough money for my spouse and kids when I die. _____
23. To be paid fairly for my work achievements. _____
24. To know that I can deal with life's challenges. _____
25. To get personal pleasure from luxuries (e.g., cars, houses, art). _____
26. To have enough spare time that could be devoted to volunteer activities. _____
27. To direct my own life with no interference from anyone else. _____
28. To spend money on impulse. _____
29. To prove that I am not as dumb as some people assumed. _____
30. To attract the attention and admiration of others. _____

3. Market worth: sum of 3, 13 and 23.
4. Pride: sum of 4, 14 and 24.
5. Leisure, including luxury: sum of 5, 15 and 25.
6. Charity: sum of 6, 16 and 26.
7. Freedom: sum of 7, 17 and 27.
8. Impulse: sum of 8, 18 and 28.
9. Overcoming self-doubt: sum of 9, 19 and 29.
10. Social comparison: sum of 10, 20 and 30.

Then divide your scores on each of the 10 motives for money by 3 to get a mean value. You can compare your scores on each of these 10 motives for money with two groups of respondents: US MBA students and US entrepreneurs.

Now compute your score on positive motives for money by summing your scores on Security, Family support, Market worth and Pride. Then divide this total by 4.

Then compute your score on negative motives for money by summing your scores on Social comparison and Removal of self doubt. Then divide this total by 2.

Finally, compute your score on Freedom of action by summing your scores on Leisure, Freedom, Impulse and Charity. Then divide this total by 4.

You can compare your positive motives for money score, your negative motives for money score, and your freedom of action score with the two US samples as well.

Normative data come from two US samples. One sample involved 266 business students in their fourth and final years of undergraduate study, 118 males and 148 females, with an average age of 23. The second sample involved 145 entrepreneurs, 117 males and 28 females, with an average age of 44 years.

	Students			Entrepreneurs		
	Mean	SD	Rank	Mean	SD	Rank
Security	9.4	.91	1	8.6	1.59	1
Family support	9.1	1.17	2	7.5	2.44	3
Pride	8.8	1.60	3	8.0	1.87	2
Market worth	8.8	1.32	4	7.4	2.24	4
Leisure	7.4	1.74	5	5.3	1.93	7
Freedom	7.0	2.14	6	7.1	2.12	5
Charity	6.5	2.79	7	5.5	2.39	6
Overcoming Self-doubt	5.3	3.08	8	3.0	2.22	8
Impulse	4.6	2.66	9	2.4	1.81	9
Social comparison	3.8	2.41	10	2.0	1.21	10

The mean values for the students and the entrepreneurs were significantly different from each other on all motives but one: Freedom.

Here are the scores on the three composite measures.

	Students		Entrepreneurs	
	Mean	SD	Mean	SD
Positive motives	9.0	.98	7.9	1.43
Negative motives	4.3	2.38	2.5	1.52
Freedom of action	6.6	1.60	5.1	1.44

Students scored higher than entrepreneurs on all three of these composites.

Here are the scores on these three composite measures indicating the mean values at the 1 SD and 2 SD points for the student group and the entrepreneur.

	Students		Entrepreneurs	
	1 SD	2 SDs	1 SD	2 SDs
Positive motives	10.0	11.0	9.3	10.7
Negative motives	6.7	9.1	4.0	5.5
Freedom of action	8.2	9.8	6.5	7.9

Now think about your scores for few minutes. Were they about what you expected? Did you score above or below the means on Positive motives or on Negative motives? Did your scores fall among the highest 32 percent (1 SD above the mean)? The highest 5 percent (2 SDs above the mean)? Summarize this information on your notepad.

Workaholism or Work Addiction

We will now consider workaholism or work addiction; we see these terms as synonymous. Schaufeli et al. (2008) conceptualize workaholism/work addiction as having two dimensions: working excessively (WE) and working compulsively (WC).

Work addicts work hard, working more than is required by their organization. Individuals work long hours for a wide variety of reasons. Work addicts work hard motivated by 'an obsessive internal drive that cannot be resisted'.

Each of their two scales has five items and were found to be highly reliable. These two self-assessment measures are shown in Box 11.3.

In a Dutch data base (N=7594) consisting of 52 percent women and 48 percent men, with a mean age of 36.4, they found the following:

- Men scored higher than women on both: working excessively, men, 2.6; women, 2.5.
- Working compulsively, men, 2.0 and women, 2.0, but though statistically significant given the large sample sizes, the sex differences were very small.
- Work hours were positively correlated with both workaholism components, but slightly stronger with WE than with WC (rs = .43 and .15, respectively).
- Managers, entrepreneurs, executives and medical residents scored high on WE; entrepreneurs, managers and blue and white-collar

BOX 11.3   WORK ADDICTION

The following statements are about how you feel at work. Please read each statement carefully and decide how often you ever feel this way about your job. Please indicate of each statement the alternative that best describes how frequently you felt that way. For instance, if you have never or almost never had this feeling, circle the '1' after the statement. If you have always or almost always had this feeling circle '4'.

1 = (Almost) never.
2 = Sometimes.
3 = Often.
4 = (Almost) always.

Working excessively (WE)

1. I seem to be in a hurry and racing against the clock.   1   2   3   4
2. I find myself continuing to work after my co-workers have called it quits.   1   2   3   4
3. I stay busy and keep many irons in the fire.   1   2   3   4
4. I spend more time working than on socializing with friends, on hobbies or on leisure activities.   1   2   3   4
5. I find myself doing two or three things at one time, such as eating lunch and writing a memo while talking on the telephone.   1   2   3   4

Working compulsively (WC)

1. It's important to me to work hard even when I don't enjoy what I'm doing.   1   2   3   4
2. I feel that there's something inside me that drives me to work hard.   1   2   3   4

3. I feel obliged to work hard, even when it's not enjoyable.	1 2 3 4
4. I feel guilty when I take time off work.	1 2 3 4
5. It is hard for me to relax when I'm not working.	1 2 3 4

workers scored high on WC. Scores on WE were higher than scores on WC in the total sample.

What are the consequences of WE and WC? In a study of 5245 medical residents they reported the following. Medical residents scoring higher on WE also reported more emotional exhaustion, poorer job performance, less life satisfaction and poorer recovery for daily job demands when at home. Work overload was the strongest predictor of WE, followed by work–home conflict and emotional exhaustion. WC was associated with higher levels of emotional exhaustion and more work–home conflict.

Take a few minutes to complete the self-assessment of work addiction, the WC and WE scales, shown in Box 11.3.

Score these scales by summing the scores on the first 5 items (the WC scale) and the next 5 items (the WE scale). Then compare your scores with those in the normative groups shown below.

	Males		Females	
	Mean	SD	Mean	SD
WE	2.6	.60	2.5	.59
WC	2.0	.64	2.0	.62

The comparison group is 7594 Dutch workers, 52 percent males and 48 percent female, with a mean age of 36.4 years (SD=9.5). In a group of Dutch medical residents (N=2115), the WE score was 2.7, and their WC score was 2.1. Males and females scored similarly on WE and WC.

Here are the scores on WE and WC for males and females at the 1 SD (top 32 percent) and 2 SD points (top 5 percent)

Were your scores on WE and WC above or below the mean score? Did they fall above the highest 32 percent (1 SD above the mean), or the highest 1 percent (2 SDs above the mean)? Summarize this information on your notepad.

	Males		Females	
	1 SD	2 SDs	1 SD	2 SDs
WE	3.2	3.8	3.1	3.7
WC	2.6	3.2	2.6	3.2

Passion versus Addiction

The number of hours that managers and professionals work, while a potential cause for concern, is only a modest predictor of their satisfaction and well-being. Both Brett and Stroh (2003) and Hewlett and Luce (2006) have found high levels of satisfaction among managerial and professional women and men working 60 hours a week or more. Brett and Stroh (2003), in a sample of alumni of a prestigious US business school, reported positive reasons among both women and men for working over 60 hours per week. Similarly, Hewlett and Luce (2006), in two samples of women and men holding demanding high-level jobs, reported high levels of satisfaction stemming from high rewards and recognition, and the challenge and meaning provided by their jobs. They were passionate about their work and their jobs. Their respondents, however, did indicate that they hoped to work a few hours less in future and some were concerned about the potential negative effects of their work hours on their health and their personal and family lives.

Burke (2006b), and others (Buelens and Poelmans, 2004; Spence and Robbins, 1992) have found that some workaholic types are more satisfied with their jobs and careers and are psychologically healthier than other types. Healthy types score lower on Feeling driven to work because of inner pressures and higher on Work enjoyment. Vallerand and his colleagues (Vallerand et al., 2003; 2007; Vallerand and Houlfort, 2003) have undertaken a research program on passion, which they see as having two forms. They distinguish between a Harmonious Passion (HP), which is well integrated into one's identity and undertaken freely and willingly and an Obsessive Passion or addiction (OP), which is not well integrated into one's identity and is the result of internal pressure (for example, to increase one's self-esteem). The activity controls the person under OP; the person controls the activity under HP. They hypothesized and found that HP leads to more positive affect, less negative affect and higher levels of flow, while OP produced the opposite effects. Both HP and OP levels were positively associated with commitment to the activities in question.

Burke (2008) has examined the effects of both Passion and Addiction in a series of studies involving different occupations (for example, managers and professionals, psychologists, journalists, manufacturing managers and professionals) in several countries (Australia, Canada, Norway, Turkey). His results have been consistent across these studies. He drew the following conclusions. First individuals indicating higher levels of Passion, and of Addiction, were more involved in their work. Second, scores on Passion were positively but only weakly correlated with scores on Addiction as sources of work motivation. Third, individuals generally reported similar levels of both Passion and Addiction as sources of work motivation. Fourth, individuals scoring higher on Passion were more job and career satisfied, more work engaged, indicated higher levels of flow at work, and reported higher levels of psychological well-being. Fifth, individuals scoring higher on Addiction were less job and career satisfied, less work engaged, indicated lower levels of flow at work and reported lower levels of psychological well-being.

Please complete the measures of both Passion and Addiction shown in Box 11.4.

Then score the Passion scale (the first 10 items in this table) and the Addiction scale (the remaining 7 items in this table). Before scoring the Passion scale, reverse your scores on item 8: 1 now becomes 5, 2 becomes 4, 3 stays at 3, 4 becomes 2, and 5 becomes 1. You can now compare your scores on Passion and Addiction with a normative group shown below.

The normative group involved 530 male and female MBA graduates from a single Canadian business school. The sample contained more males than females.

	Mean	SD
Addiction	23.2	5.59
Passion	35.0	7.06

Here are the scores that fall at the 1 SD and 2 SD points.

	1 SD	2 SD
Addiction	28.8	34.4
Passion	42.1	49.2

Did your scores on Passion and Addiction fit what you expected? Were your scores above or below the mean on Passion or Addiction? Did your scores fall above the highest 68 percent (1 SD or more) or the highest 5 percent (2 SDs or above)? Summarize this information on your notepad.

BOX 11.4 PASSION AND ADDICTION

Passion

5 = Strongly agree.
4 = Somewhat agree.
3 = Neither agree nor disagree.
2 = Somewhat disagree.
1 = Strongly disagree.

1. My job is so interesting that it often doesn't seem like work.	5	4	3	2	1
2. When I get involved in an interesting project, it's hard to describe how exhilarated I feel.	5	4	3	2	1
3. I lose track of time when I'm engaged on a project.	5	4	3	2	1
4. I do more work than is expected of me strictly for the fun of it.	5	4	3	2	1
5. Most of the time my work is very pleasurable.	5	4	3	2	1
6. Sometimes I enjoy my work so much that I have a hard time stopping.	5	4	3	2	1
7. I like my work more than most people do.	5	4	3	2	1
8. I rarely find anything to enjoy about my work.	5	4	3	2	1
9. Sometimes when I get up in the morning I can hardly wait to get to work.	5	4	3	2	1
10. My job is more like fun than work.	5	4	3	2	1

Addiction

1. I seem to have an inner compulsion to work hard, a feeling that it's something I have to do whether I want to or not.	5	4	3	2	1
2. I often feel that there's something inside me that drives me to work hard.	5	4	3	2	1

3.	It's important to me to work hard even when I don't enjoy what I'm doing.	5	4	3	2	1
4.	I often find myself thinking about work even when I want to get away from it for a while.	5	4	3	2	1
5.	I feel guilty when I take time off.	5	4	3	2	1
6.	I feel obligated to work hard, even when it's not enjoyable.	5	4	3	2	1
7.	I often wish I weren't so committed to my work.	5	4	3	2	1

Problematic Job Behaviors

Research evidence has identified particular job behaviors associated with work motives as contributing to leader dissatisfaction, ineffectiveness and psychological distress. Three categories of job behavior will be examined here:

- Perfectionism
- Anger
- Impatience-irritation.

Perfectionism

Several writers have begun to explore the question of why managers fail (Dotlich and Cairo, 2003; Hogan and Hogan, 2001; Kellerman, 2004). Contrary to common beliefs, managers that fail have been shown to be bright, hard-working, possess considerable business skill, and have lots of relevant work experience (Finkelstein, 2003). Instead managers fail because of personality and character flaws and job behaviors that come to undermine their effectiveness and derail their careers (Kaplan, 1991). One such flaw that has been observed to limit the effectiveness of managers is perfectionism (Dotlich and Cairo, 2003; Flett and Hewitt, 2002; 2006; Hogan and Hogan, 2001). Dotlich and Cairo (2003) characterize the perfectionistic manager as one who 'gets the little things right and the big things wrong'. Hogan and Hogan see the perfectionistic mangers as obsessive compulsive, inflexible, over-controlling and rigid.

Initially it was believed that perfectionism had undesirable consequences. More recently it has been suggested that there are different types of perfectionism, some types faring better than others, and some aspects of perfectionism having negative consequences while other aspects have positive consequences. Thus, Stoeber and Otto (2006) identified positive aspects of perfectionism, and Terry-Short et al. (1995) have created measures of positive and negative perfectionism.

Hewitt and Flett (1991) present evidence from four studies confirming three dimensions of perfectionism and show that these can be reliably and validly measured. These three dimensions are:

- Self-oriented perfectionism (SOP) – I expect myself to be perfect;
- Other-oriented perfectionism (OOP) – I expect others to be perfect; and
- Socially-prescribed perfectionism (SPP) – others expect me to be perfect.

Their work has shown a relationship between these perfectionism dimensions and interpersonal stress and personal distress (Flett et al., 1996; Flett et al., 1994). SOP has been found to be associated with depression; OOP was associated with marital and relationship difficulties; and SPP was associated with psychological problems, suicidal ideation, threats and attempts. High perfectionism correlated with a range of adjustment problems such as depression, suicidal ideation, low self-esteem, anxiety and various personality disorders (Flett et al., 1991; Frost et al., 1993; Frost et al., 1990; Hewitt et al., 1992; Flett et al., 2003).

Zhang et al. (2007), in a sample of Chinese undergraduate university students, reported that negative perfectionism (for example doubts about one's actions, concerns over mistakes) was related to burnout, whereas positive perfectionism (for example, high personal standards, being organized) was related to engagement.

Stoeber et al. (2007) made a distinction between striving for perfection (for example, striving to be as perfect as possible) and negative reactions to imperfection (for example, feeling depressed if one is not perfect) and found the latter was related to anxiety. When negative reactions to imperfection were controlled, striving for perfection was associated with lower anxiety and higher self-confidence. Thus striving for perfection and successfully controlling one's negative reactions to imperfection were found to reduce anxiety and increase one's self-confidence.

Finally, Stoeber et al. (2007), in a sample of undergraduate students, compared healthy perfectionists (HPs: high perfectionist strivings, low perfectionist concerns), Unhealthy perfectionists (UPs: high perfectionist strivings, high perfectionist concerns), and Non-perfectionists (NPs: low perfectionist strivings) on a variety of negative feelings. HPs generally indicated lower levels of these negative feelings.

Box 11.5 presents an opportunity for you to assess your own levels of perfectionism and compare your scores with a norm group – more food for thought. Please take some time to complete the survey.

When you have finished the survey merely add up your scores on all 25 items. This measure is called the Perfectionist Cognitions Inventory (PCI). Research by Flett et al. (1998) has showed that scores on the PCI were significantly correlated with various indicators of psychological distress in various samples of university undergraduate students

Here are some normative scores for you to consider.

A large sample of undergraduate students scored as follows:

	Men		Women	
	Mean	SD	Mean	SD
	43.5	22.62	46.4	25.11

Here are their scores shown at the 1 SD and 2 SDs points.

	Men	Women
1 SD	66.1	71.5
2 SDs	88.7	96.6

Did your score on the PCI fall above or below the mean score? Was your PCI score in the highest 32 percent (1 SD)? The highest 5 percent (2 SDs)? Again, summarize this information on your notepad.

One might also argue that striving for perfection (within reason) need not be maladaptive. Stoeber et al. (2007) make a distinction between striving for perfection and negative reactions to imperfection. In a study of high school and university-level athletes, they found that striving for perfection was related to lower levels of anxiety and higher self-confidence, while negative reactions to imperfection were associated with higher levels of anxiety. Thus striving for perfection while controlling one's negative reactions to imperfection may even heighten self-confidence and reduce levels of anxiety.

Striving for perfection included items such as 'I strive to be as perfect as possible'. And 'I am a perfectionist as far as my targets are concerned'. Negative reactions to imperfection included items such as 'I feel depressed if I have not been perfect' and 'I get completely furious if I have made mistakes'.

BOX 11.5　PERFECTIONISM

Listed below are a variety of thoughts about perfectionism that sometimes pop into people's heads. Please read each thought and indicate how frequently, if at all, the thought occurred to you *over the last week*. Please read each item carefully and circle the appropriate number, using the scale below.

0 = Not at all.
1
2
3
4 = All of the time.

1. Why can't I be perfect?	0	1	2	3	4
2. I need to do better.	0	1	2	3	4
3. I should be perfect.	0	1	2	3	4
4. I should never make the same mistake twice.	0	1	2	3	4
5. I've got to keep working on my goals.	0	1	2	3	4
6. I have to be the best.	0	1	2	3	4
7. I should be doing more.	0	1	2	3	4
8. I can't stand making mistakes.	0	1	2	3	4
9. I have to work hard all the time.	0	1	2	3	4
10. No matter how much I do, it's never enough.	0	1	2	3	4
11. People expect me to be perfect.	0	1	2	3	4
12. I must be efficient at all times.	0	1	2	3	4
13. My goals are very high.	0	1	2	3	4
14. I can always do better, even if things are almost perfect.	0	1	2	3	4
15. I expect to be perfect.	0	1	2	3	4
16. Why can't things be perfect?	0	1	2	3	4
17. My work has to be superior.	0	1	2	3	4

18. It would be great if everything in my life were perfect.	0	1	2	3	4
19. My work should be flawless.	0	1	2	3	4
20. Things are seldom ideal.	0	1	2	3	4
21. How well am I doing?	0	1	2	3	4
22. I can't do this perfectly.	0	1	2	3	4
23. I certainly have high standards.	0	1	2	3	4
24. Maybe I should lower my goals.	0	1	2	3	4
25. I am too much of a perfectionist.	0	1	2	3	4

How one reacts to imperfection (for example, mistakes, falling short) may be an important element in understanding the effects of perfectionism on performance and one's emotional state.

Can you identify some of the ways you react to occasions of your own 'imperfection'? Write down a few of your typical reactions on your notepad.

What are the emotional components, if any, in your reactions to imperfection?

Again write down your reflections on your notepad.

Type A Behavior

The Type A behavior pattern (TABP) was identified as an independent risk factor for coronary heart disease (CHD) by Friedman and Rosenman in the late 1960s (Friedman and Rosenman, 1974). TABP was characterized by: high achievement strivings or unbridled ambition, competitiveness, time-urgency, aggressiveness or free-floating hostility, undertaking two or more activities simultaneously (multi-tasking), rapid walking, talking and eating, and the appearance of tension. TABP is learned through socialization (Price, 1982) and is behavior which allows an individual to cope with fears and anxieties generated by particular beliefs individuals develop about their environment (Glass, 1977; Price, 1988). Type B behavior is characterized by the opposite qualities.

Studies involving large samples have shown that:

1. Type As are three times more likely as their Type B counterparts to die from CHD, holding other factors constant;

2. Type As who survive their first heart attack are more likely to have a second than are Type Bs;
3. Type As exhibit a greater severity of coronary arteriosclerosis than do Type Bs;
4. Type A behavior is predictive of CHD but no other disease entity (e.g., ulcers, diabetes, rheumatoid arthritis); and
5. More extreme or highly developed TABP is associated with greater risk of coronary mortality.

Although TABP was first examined as a factor in the incidence and treatment of CHD, later research examined the relationship of TABP and behavior in families and in organizations more broadly. Here is a sample of some of these findings.

1. TABP had a negative impact on marital satisfaction and personal, home and family life of both job incumbents and their spouses;
2. Individuals exhibiting higher levels of TABP worked more hours per week and traveled more days per year in the conduct of their jobs, were more job involved and more identified with their organizations but not more satisfied with their jobs;
3. Individuals exhibiting higher levels of TABP were more likely to report 'career success and personal failure' experiences (Burke and Deszca, 1982; Korman and Korman, 1980) later in their lives because of the career and life trade-offs that they had made earlier; thus
4. Individuals exhibiting higher levels of TABP were more invested in their jobs but less satisfied in their personal lives.

Box 11.6 presents an opportunity to examine your standing on two measures of TABP (Pred et al., 1987; Spence et al., 1987). One, Achievement Striving (AS), is positively related to effective job performance; the other, Impatience-Irritation (II), is positively related to interpersonal difficulties and less positive work attitudes.

Scoring the two TABP scales: the first 7 items are the AS dimension, with higher scores being associated with greater work engagement and more positive job and career satisfactions. The last items represent the II dimension, with higher scores being associated with less job and career satisfaction and more negative attitudes and psychological well-being. Thus higher scores on AS are desirable, whereas high scores on II are potentially troublesome.

The normative group comprised full-time undergraduate college students enrolled in 16 upper division business administration courses in two

BOX 11.6   TYPE A BEHAVIOR

Read each item and circle the alternative for each that comes closest to what you believe is your approach to work and life.

Your Approach to Work

1. How much does your work 'stir you into action?'

5	4	3	2	1
Much more than others	More than others	Neutral	Less than others	Much less than others

2. Nowadays, do you consider yourself to be:

5	4	3	2	1
Very hard driven	Hard driven	Neutral	Relaxed	Very relaxed, easy going

3. How would your best friends or others who know you well rate your general level of activity?

1	2	3	4	5
Too slow	Slow	Active	Too active	Very active: should slow down

4. How seriously do you take your work?

5	4	3	2	1
Much more seriously than most	More seriously	Neither more seriously nor less seriously	Less seriously	Much less seriously

5. How often do you set deadlines or quotas for yourself in work or other activities?

5	4	3	2	1
Very often	Frequently	Sometimes	Occasionally	Almost never

6. Compared with other people, the amount of effort I put forth is:

5	4	3	2	1
Much more	More	Neither more nor less	Less	Much less

7. Compared with other people, I approach life in general:

5	4	3	2	1
Much more seriously	More seriously	Neither more nor less seriously	Less seriously	Much less seriously

8. When a person is talking and takes too long to come to the point, how often do you feel like hurrying the person along?

5	4	3	2	1
Very frequently	Frequently	Sometimes	Occasionally	Almost never

9. Typically, how easily do you get irritated?

5	4	3	2	1
Extremely easily	Easily	Neither easy nor not easily	Not easily	Not at all easily

10. Do you tend to do most things in a hurry?

5	4	3	2	1
Definitely true	True	Neither true nor false	Not true	Not at all true

11. How is your 'temper' these days?

5	4	3	2	1
Very hard to control	Hard to control	Neither easy nor hard	Occasionally get angry	Seldom get angry

12. When you have to wait in a queue such as at a restaurant, the cinema, or the post office, how do you usually feel?

1	2	3	4	5
Accept very calmly	Accept calmly	Neither calm nor impatient	Impatient	Very impatient

	Mean	SD
Achievement Striving	3.6	.64
Impatience-Irritation	3.1	.98

large US universities. The sample included 191 males and 144 females, with a mean age of 21.6 years.

Here are the scores on AS and II at the 1 SD and 2 SD points.

	1 SD	2 SDs
Achievement Striving	4.2	4.8
Impatience-Irritation	4.1	5.1

How did your scores compare to the normative group? Did you score above the mean on AS or II? Did your scores on AS or II fall above the highest 32 percent (1 SD) or the highest 5 percent (2 SDs)? Again, write down your reflections on your notepad.

Your sense of and use of time

Those who rush arrive first at the grave.

(Spanish proverb)

Time urgency   Time urgency, an element in the original view of TABP, has received research attention. Time urgent individuals are concerned with the passage of time and how they can fill that time with productive activity. Time urgency has been shown to have subcomponents such as general hurry, task hurry, speech patterns and eating behaviors. Sample items include:

● General hurry: pressed for time, in a hurry, and in a rush
● Task hurry: work fast, work quickly and energetically

- Speech patterns: put words in others' mouths
- Eating behaviors: eat too fast, eat rapidly, told by others to eat less quickly
- Competitive-hard driving, ambitious, go all out

Conte and his colleagues (2001), in a study of 393 travel agents in the US, found that some of these components were related to positive outcomes (competition and personal accomplishment, job involvement, organizational commitment) while others were related to negative outcomes (general hurry and burnout due to emotional exhaustion, speech pattern related to burnout due to emotional exhaustion). Landy et al. (1991) found, in a small sample of employees from two organizations, that some of the time urgency measures were significantly and positively related to the II dimension of TABP. Finally, Conte et al. (1995), in a sample of university students, reported correlations of some time urgency measures and self-reported health problems.

Polychronicity   Polychronicity is a fancy word to describe the extent to which people prefer to be involved in more than one activity at the same time (akin to multi-tasking). Polychronicity is measured by such items as 'I like to juggle several activities at the same time', 'I believe people should try to do many things at once', 'I believe people do their best work when they have several tasks to complete', and 'I believe it is best for people to be given several tasks and assignments to complete' (see Bluedorn et al., 1999).

In a study involving college students, polychronicity was positively associated with two TABP components, AS and II, identified by Pred et al. (1987). Polychronicity was not correlated with self-reported stress or student performance (Grade point average) in this study. Conte and his colleagues (1999) also found polychronicity to be negatively correlated with time awareness, scheduling and a preference for organization.

In a second study of university students, Conte et al. (1999) reported that polychronicity was positively correlated with time urgency (the general hurry measure).

In a study of 181 train operators, Conte and Jacobs (2003) found that polychronicity was positively correlated with both frequency of absence and lateness and negatively correlated with supervisor's ratings of job performance. Absence and lateness measures were obtained from objective company records.

Bluedorn and his colleagues (1999), in a combination of three samples (dentists, employees of two hospitals), found that polychronicity was negatively correlated with punctuality and a schedule and deadline emphasis.

On a scale of 1 to 5, 1 being 'Not at all time urgent', 3 being 'Somewhat time urgent', and 5 being 'Very time urgent', rate your own time urgency. Write this number on your notepad using the following sentence.

'My time urgency self-rating is—.'

Now on a scale of 1 to 5, 1 being a very low level of polychronicity, 3 being a moderate level of polychronicity, and 5 being a very high level of polychronicity, rate your own level of polychronicity. Write this number on your notepad by completing the following sentence.

'My polychronicity self-rating is—.'

YOUR TIME AND ENERGY INVESTMENT IN YOUR WORK

This section asks you to think about your time investment (hours spent in work-related activities) and your emotional energy expended in your job and work. There is research evidence that hours spent in work-related activities are associated with less satisfaction and diminished psychological well-being (see Burke, 2006b; Burke and Cooper, 2008; Dembe et al., 2005; Sparks et al., 1997; van der Hulst, 2003). In addition there is evidence that working in more intense jobs also has both reduced satisfaction and psychological well-being consequences (Green, 2008).

Please write your responses to the following questions on your notepad.

Work Hours

1.   How many hours do you work in the typical week?
2.   Do you work through your lunch on a regular basis? Occasionally?
3.   How often do you have drinks with colleagues, clients at the end of the work day?
4.   How often do you have business breakfasts? Business dinners?
5.   How often do you have to undertake overnight travel as part of your job?
6.   Do you work on at nights when at home?
7.   Do you work during weekends when at home?
8.   Do you get phone calls or emails at home at night?
9.   Do you get calls or emails at home at weekends?
10. How long is your commute to and from work each day?
11. How do you feel about the number of hours each week that you devote to your work and related activities? Want to do more hours? Fewer hours? The same hours?

Job Demands

1. As reflected in the work intensity measure, how intense is your work?
2. How stressful do you find your job today? What are the major sources of work stress that you are experiencing? Compared to a year or two ago, has your job become more, or less stressful, or is the level of stress the same?

Job Demands and Personal Well-Being

Research findings accumulated over the past 40 years have shown that work stressors or demands are fairly consistently associated with lower levels of job satisfaction and psychological well-being (see Barling et al., 2005; Schabracq et al., 2003, for reviews). A more recent body of work has indicated that the inability to rest and recover from these stressors or demands had negative effects on both satisfaction and well-being (Meijman and Mulder, 1998; Sonnentag and Zijlstra, 2006). Thus the experiencing of these work stressors or demands over time wears the body down (mental and physical fatigue). The experience of workplace stressors entails a process in which these demands are associated with fatigue, distress and related emotional and physiological responses. Recovery and respite experiences, then, are opportunities to reverse the stressor–strain process. It is important then for individuals to reverse the negative psychological and physiological processes cased by job stressors or demands for them to respond fully to their work and life challenges.

Reversing the Job Demands-Wear and Tear Process

What can individuals do to recover from the stressors or demands experienced during their jobs? How can they replenish themselves? Research has emphasized three possibilities: hours of sleep, vacations or respite from work, and recovery during evenings and weekends.

Czeisler (2006) highlights the negative consequences of sleep deficits. Not getting enough sleep is associated with automobile accidents resulting from driver fatigue. Medical residents, noted for working long hours – laws in the US were recently passed limiting their weekly work hours to only 80 – have been known to fall asleep during staff meetings, consultations with patients and while performing surgery. Sleep deprivation, staying awake longer than 18 consecutive hours, interferes with reaction speed, short and long-term memory, ability to focus, decision-making capacity, mathematical processing, cognitive speed and spatial orientation. Sleeping only five–six hours a night for several consecutive days increases these negative effects. Sleep deprivation also has health consequences such as high blood pressure and obesity.

Yet organizations equate working long hours – with associated costs of sleep deprivation – with commitment and performance. Czeisler believes that a major way to improve individual performance and well-being is to ensure that one gets adequate sleep. He advocates getting at least eight hours of sleep a night. And individuals need a few hours of 'down time' before going to sleep if they are to sleep well. Sleeping only four to five hours a night for four or five consecutive days creates the same level of cognitive impairment as being legally drunk. And as individuals age, it becomes even harder to get a good night's sleep.

Benefits to both work and well-being from adequate recovery, whether during a long vacation period or respite (Eden, 2001; Sonnentag and Fritz, 2007; Westman and Eden, 1997, Westman and Etzion, 2001; Etzion et al., 1998) or during time after work or at weekends (Sonnentag, 2001; Sonnentag and Kruel, 2006) have been observed. Research on the benefits of vacation time or respite has shown, however, that the benefits of time away from work are relatively short-lived; they quickly fade (Binneweis and Sonnentag, 2008; Westman and Eden, 1997). It would seem that both the amount of time available for recovery and respite as well as the nature and quality of this time are both important for the recovery process.

We can summarize the following conclusions about the recovery process.

First, individuals need between seven to eight hours of high quality sleep each day in order to perform at their highest levels.

Second, individuals should take all of their vacation time and participate in activities that include detachment from work, relaxation, mastery experiences, and control over what one does and when one does it. The benefits of thoroughly enjoying one's vacation are tangible but short-lived.

Third, as a result, efforts need to be made to engage in recovery experiences each night and at weekends. These activities also need to include psychological detachment from work, undertaking activities that are relaxing, taking part in activities that support learning, growth and development, and exercising discretion and control over what one does and when one does it.

The following questions examine your current use of sleep, your vacation time, and your daily recovery activities.

Sleep

1. How long does it usually take you to fall asleep? (minutes)
2. How many hours of sleep do you get in the typical night? (hours)

3. How many times do you wake up during the night and don't fall asleep easily?
4. How would you rate the quality of your sleep?

Vacations or respite

1. How many days of vacation did you get this year?
2. How many days of vacation did you actually take? Your full allotment?
3. On vacations, do you still do the work of your organization?
4. On vacations, do you receive emails and/or phone calls from your employer?
5. On your vacations, do you still call or email your workplace?
6. How do you spend your vacations? What do you do while on vacation? How do you feel about how you have spent your recent vacations?

Recovery at home at night and at weekends

1. Psychological detachment – to what extent are you able to spend your nights and weekends at home not thinking about your work or your organization?
2. Relaxation – to what extent are you able to just relax, kick back, and do things that you find relaxing at nights and on weekends?
3. Mastery – to what extent to you engage in activities that increase your knowledge, learning, and skill when at home at night or at the weekends (reading books, taking courses)?
4. Control – to what extent are you able to control what you do and when you do things when at home at nights and at the weekends?
5. What specific activities do you engage in at home (away from work) at nights and at weekends to restore your energy and calm? Jot these down on your notepad.

ARE WE HAVING FUN YET?

This section asks you to think about how satisfied you are with your life today, all domains of it – self, family, work and community. Nash and Stevenson (2004a; 2004b) highlight the need to consider all of your life domains in your assessments. How satisfied are you with your life today? If you had it to do over again, would you change some things?

On a scale from 1 to 5, 1 being 'Not very satisfied with my life right now',

3 being 'Somewhat satisfied with my life right now', and 5 being 'Extremely satisfied with my life right now', rate your overall life satisfaction.

Complete the following sentence on your notepad.

My life satisfaction right now rating is—.

Psychological Well-Being

How often do you feel engaged, vigorous and joyous in your work and in your life as a whole? Or do you also feel down, depressed, tired, burned out much of the time?

Write your reflections on these questions on your notepad.

Physical Health

1. How do you feel about your current weight?
2. Do you exercise on a regular basis?
3. Do you smoke on a regular basis?
4. Do you have any current health problems?
5. How would your rate your physical health?
6. How would your doctor rate your level of physical health?
7. Are you currently taking any medication for physical health problems?
8. Has a doctor indicated that you have one or more physical conditions that you need to be concerned about (high blood pressure, hypertension, depression, anxiety)?
9. How would you rate your current level of physical fitness? Circle one number.
   - (1) I am not very physically fit.
   - (2) I am fairly physically fit.
   - (3) I am very physically fit.
   - (4) I am exceptionally physically fit.
10. Considering your physical health overall, do you have any current concerns about it?

Again jot down your reflections on your physical health on your notepad.

The 'Death Bed' Question

I remember seeing a quote attributed to the late Senator Paul Tsongas, the former Democratic senator from Massachusetts, on learning that he had an incurable form of cancer. Upon hearing this news, Tsongas immediately resigned his senate job. He was quoted as saying 'I've never heard of anyone on their death bed saying "I regret not spending enough time with my business"'.

Pausch (2008), who died from an incurable cancer at the age of 47 in late July 2008, also observed that people on their deathbeds were more likely to regret the things that they had not done than the things that they had done.

The last self-assessment activity is for you to put the 'food for thought' afforded you in this chapter to use in looking at the past, the present and the future and identifying some things that you would like to change. Take some time to reflect on your notepad on what you have thought about as you worked your way through this chapter, what felt right and what seemed 'off kilter' for you.

Then identify five specific, concrete activities you would like to start doing or do more of. List them on your notepad.

Who might be involved in helping you undertake these? How will you know if progress is being made? Jot your thoughts on this on your notepad. Then identify five specific, concrete activities you would like to stop doing or do less of. List them on your notepad. Who might be involved in helping you work on these? How will you know if progress is being made? Identify these sources of help on your notepad.

CONCLUSION

The goal of this chapter was to help women and men currently in leadership positions or aspiring to leadership positions, flourish in their work and extra-work lives. Work and extra-work roles and experiences generally go hand-in-hand (Friedman, 2008a; 2008b). That is, individuals who are productive and satisfied at work are more than likely productive and satisfied in their activities and roles outside the workplace. We believe individuals can exhibit positive feelings and positive relationships in both work and in life more broadly, particularly if they know themselves, determine what is important to them, and set priorities to achieve these valued goals.

Flourishing (Keyes, 2002) includes both personal psychological well-being and social well-being. The former includes positive feelings, optimism and resilience. The latter includes social integration, social acceptance and social contribution. Individuals exhibiting high levels of social well-being will feel accepted by others, experience being connected to society, and see themselves making contributions to society. This chapter has the potential to contribute to both.

NOTE

1. Preparation of this chapter was supported in part by York University. I would like to thank the following colleagues for permission to use some of their materials: Arnold Bakker, Wilmar Schaufeli, Patti Watkins, Abs Srinivastava, Gordon Flett, Paul Hewitt, Robert Helmreich and Janet Spence.

REFERENCES

Barling, J., Kelloway, E.K. and Frone, M.R. (2005), *Handbook of Work Stress*, Thousand Oaks, CA: Sage Publications.

Binneweis, C. and Sonnentag, S. (2008), 'Recovery after work: unwinding from daily job stress', in R.J. Burke and C.L. Cooper (eds), *The Long Work Hours Culture: Causes, Consequences and Choices*, Bingley, UK: Emerald Publishing, pp. 275–94.

Bluedorn, A.C., Kalliath, T.J., Strube, M.J. and Martin, G.D. (1999), 'Polychronicity and the Inventory of Polychronic Values (IPV): the development of an instrument to measure a fundamental dimension of organizational culture', *Journal of Managerial Psychology*, **14**, 205–30.

Brett, J.M. and Stroh, L.K. (2003), 'Working 61 plus hours a week: why do managers do it?', *Journal of Applied Psychology*, **58**, 67–78.

Buelens, M. and Poelmans, S.A.Y. (2004), 'Enriching the Spence and Robbins' typology of workaholism: demographic, motivational and organizational correlates', *Journal of Organizational Change Management*, **17**, 459–70.

Burke, R.J. (1984), 'Beliefs and fears underlying Type A behavior: what makes Sammy run – so fast and aggressively?', *Journal of Human Stress*, Winter, 1174–82.

Burke, R.J. (2006a), *Research Companion to Working Hours and Work Addiction*, Cheltenham, UK and Northampton, MA, USA: Edward Elgar.

Burke, R.J. (2006b), 'Workaholism types, satisfaction and well-being: it's not how hard you work but why and how you work hard', in R.J. Burke and C. L. Cooper (eds), *Inspiring Leaders* Oxford, UK: Routledge, pp. 273–90.

Burke, R.J. (2008), 'Work motivations, satisfactions, and health: passion versus addiction', in R.J. Burke and C.L. Cooper (eds), *The Long Work Hours Culture: Causes, Consequences and Choices*, Bingley, UK: Emerald Publishing, pp. 227–51.

Burke, R.J. and Cooper, C.L. (2008), *The Long Work Hours Culture: Causes, Consequences, and Choices*, Bingley, UK: Emerald Publishing.

Burke, R.J. and Deszca, E. (1982), 'Career success and personal failure experiences and Type A behavior', *Journal of Organizational Behavior*, **3**, 161–70.

Conte, J.M. and Jacobs, R.R. (2003), 'Validity evidence linking polychronicity and Big Five personality dimensions to absence, lateness, and supervisory performance ratings', *Human Performance*, **16**, 106–29.

Conte, J.M., Landy, F.J. and Mathieu, J.E. (1995), 'Time urgency: Conceptual and construct development', *Journal of Applied Psychology*, **80**, 178–85.

Conte, J.M., Rizzuto, T.E. and Steiner, D.D. (1999), 'A construct-oriented analysis of individual-level polychronicity', *Journal of Managerial Psychology*, **1**, 269–87.

Conte, J.M., Ringenbach, K.I., Moran, S.K. and Landy, F.J. (2001), 'Criterion validity evidence for time urgency: associations with burnout, organizational commitment, and job involvement in travel agents', *Applied Human Resource Management Research*, **6**, 129–34.

Czeisler, C.A. (2006), 'Sleep deficit: the performance killer', *Harvard Business Review*, October, 53–9.

Deci, E.L. and Ryan, R.M. (2000), 'The "what" and "why" of goal pursuits: human needs and the self determination of behavior', *Psychological Inquiry*, **11**, 227–68.

Dembe, A.E., Erickson, J.B., Delbos, R.G. and Banks, S.M. (2005), 'The impact of overtime and long work hours on occupational injuries and illnesses: new evidence from the United States', *Occupational and Environmental Medicine*, **62**, 588–97.

Dotlich, S.L. and Cairo, T. (2003), *Why CEOs Fail: The 11 Behaviors that Can Derail Your Climb to the Top and How to Manage Them*, San Francisco, CA: Jossey-Bass.

Easterlin, R.A. (2007), 'The escalation of material goals: fingering the wrong culprit', *Psychological Inquiry*, **18**, 31–3.

Eden, D. (2001), 'Vacations and other respites: studying stress on and off the job', in C.L. Cooper and I.T. Robertson (eds), *International Review of Industrial and Organizational Psychology*, Chichester, UK: John Wiley, pp. 121–46.

Etzion, D., Eden, D. and Lapidot, Y. (1998), 'Relief from job stressors and burnout: reserve service as a respite', *Journal of Applied Psychology*, **83**, 577–85.

Finkelstein, S. (2003), *Why Smart Executives Fail and What we can Learn from their Mistakes*, New York: Portfolio.

Flett, G.L. and Hewitt, P.L. (2002), *Perfectionism: Theory and Research*, Washington, DC: American Psychological Association.

Flett, G.L. and Hewitt, P.L. (2006), 'Perfectionism as a detrimental factor in leadership: a multi-dimensional analysis', in R.J. Burke and C.L. Cooper (eds), *Inspiring Leaders*, Oxford, UK: Routledge, pp. 247–72.

Flett, G.L., Hewitt, P.L. and DeRosa, T. (1996), 'Dimensions of perfectionism, psychosocial adjustment, and social skills', *Personality and Individual Differences*, **20**, 143–50.

Flett, G.L., Besser, A., Davis, R.A. and Hewitt, P.L. (2003), 'Dimensions of perfectionism, unconditional self-acceptance, and depression', *Journal of Rational-Emotive and Cognitive Therapy*, **21**, 119–38.

Flett, G.L., Hewitt, P.L., Blankstein, K.R. and Gray, L. (1998), 'Psychological distress and the frequency of perfectionistic thinking', *Journal of Personality and Social Psychology*, **75**, 1336–81.

Flett, G.L., Hewitt, P.L., Blankstein, K.R. and Mosher, S.W. (1991), 'Perfectionism, self-actualization, and personal adjustment', *Journal of Social Behavior and Personality*, **6**, 147–60.

Flett, G.L., Hewitt, P.L., Endler, N.S. and Tassone, G. (1994), 'Perfectionism and components of state and trait anxiety', *Current Psychology*, **13**, 326–35.

Friedman, M. and Rosenman, R.H. (1974), *Type A Behavior and Your Heart*, New York: Alfred Knopf.

Friedman, S.D. (2008a), 'Be a better leader, have a richer life', *Harvard Business Review*, April, 112–18.

Friedman, S.D. (2008b), *Be a Better Leader, Have a Richer Life*, Boston, MA: Harvard Business School Press.

Frost, R.O., Marten P., Lahart, C. and Rosenblate, R. (1990), 'The dimensions of perfectionism', *Cognitive Therapy and Research*, **14**, 449–68.

Frost, R.O., Heimberg, R.G., Holt, C.S., Mattia, J.L. and Neubauer, A.L. (1993), 'A comparison of two measures of perfectionism', *Personality and Individual Differences*, **14**, 119–26.

Glass, D.C. (1977), *Behavioral Patterns, Stress, and Coronary Disease*, Hillsdale, NJ: Erlbaum.

Gowdy, J. (2007), 'Can economic theory stop being a cheerleader for corporate capitalism?', *Psychological Inquiry*, **18**, 33–5.

Green, F. (2008), 'Work effort and worker well-being in the age of affluence', in R.J. Burke and C.L. Cooper (eds), *The Long Work Hours Culture: Causes, Consequences and Choices*, Bingley, UK: Emerald Publishing, pp. 115–36.

Hewitt, P.L. and Flett, G.L. (1991), 'Perfectionism in the self and social contexts: conceptualization, assessment and association with psychopathology', *Journal of Personality and Social Psychology*, **60**, 456–70.

Hewitt, P.L., Flett, G.L. and Turnbull, W. (1992), 'Perfectionism and Multiphasic Personality Inventory (MMPI) indices of personality disorder', *Journal of Psychopathology and Behavioral Assessment*, **14**, 3223–335.

Hewlett, S.A. and Luce, C.B. (2006), 'Extreme jobs: the dangerous allure of the 70-hour work week', *Harvard Business Review*, December 49–59.

Hogan, R. and Hogan, J. (2001), 'Assessing leadership: a view of the dark side', *International Journal of Evaluation and Assessment*, **9**, 40–51.

Kaplan, R.E. (1991), *Beyond Ambition: How Driven Managers can Lead Better and Live Better*, San Francisco, CA: Jossey-Bass.

Kasser, T. and Ryan, R.M. (1993), 'A dark side of the American dream: correlates of financial success as a central life aspiration', *Journal of Personality and Social Psychology*, **65**, 410–22.

Kasser, T. and Ryan, R.M. (1996), 'Further examining the American dream: differential correlates of intrinsic and extrinsic goals', *Personality and Social Psychology Bulletin*, **22**, 280–87.

Kasser, T., Cohn, S., Kanner, A.D. and Ryan, R.M. (2007), 'Some costs of American corporate capitalism: a psychological exploration of value and goal conflicts', *Psychological Inquiry*, **18**, 1–22.

Kellerman, B. (2004), *Bad Leadership*, Boston, MA: Harvard Business School Press.

Keyes, C.L.M. (2002), 'The mental health continuum: from languishing to flourishing in life', *Journal of Health and Social Behavior*, **43**, 207–22.

Korman, A.K. and Korman, R. (1980), *Career Success and Personal Failure*, Englewood Cliffs, NJ: Prentice Hall.

Landy, F.J., Rastegary, H., Thayer, J. and Colvin, C. (1991), 'Time urgency: the construct and its measurement', *Journal of Applied Psychology*, **6**, 644–65.

Lee, C., Jamieson, L.F. and Earley, P.C. (1996), 'Beliefs and fears and Type A behavior: implications for academic performance and psychiatric health disorder symptoms', *Journal of Organizational Behavior*, **17**, 151–77.

Meijman, T.F. and Mulder, G. (1998), 'Psychological aspects of workload', in P.J.D. Drenth and H. Thierry (eds), *Handbook of Work and Organizational Psychology* Vol. 2, Hove, UK: Psychology Press, pp. 5–33.

Myers, D.G. (2007), 'Costs and benefits of American corporate capitalism', *Psychological Inquiry*, **18**, 43–7.

Nash, L. and Stevenson, H. (2004a), 'Success that lasts', *Harvard Business Review*, February, 102–9.

Nash, L. and Stevenson, H. (2004b), *Just Enough: Tools for Creating Success in Your Work and Life*, New York: John Wiley.

Pausch, R. (2008), *The Last Lecture*, New York: Hyperion.

Pred, R.S., Helmreich, R.L. and Spence, J.T. (1987), 'The development of new scales for the Jenkins Activity Survey measure of the TABP construct', *Social and Behavioral Science Documents*, **16**, 51–2.

Price, V.A. (1982), *The Type A Behavior Pattern: A Model for Theory and Practice*, New York: Academic Press.

Price, V.A. (1988), 'Research and clinical issues in treating Type A behavior', in B.K. Houston and C. R. Snyder (eds), *Type A Behavior: Research, Theory, and Intervention*, New York: John Wiley, pp. 275–311.

Ryan, R.M. and Deci, E.L. (2000), 'Self-determination theory and the facilitation of intrinsic motivation, social development, and well-being', *American Psychologist*, **55**, 68–78.

Ryan, R.M. and Deci, E.L. (2001), 'On happiness and human potentials: a review of research on hedonic and eudemonic well-being', in S. Fiske (ed.), *Annual Review of Psychology*, **52**, 141–66.

Schabracq, M.J., Winnubst, J.A.M. and Cooper, C.L. (2003), *The Handbook of Work and Health Psychology*, Chichester, UK: John Wiley.

Schaufeli, W.B., Taris, T. and Bakker, A.B. (2008), 'It takes two to tango: workaholism is working excessively and working compulsively', in R.J. Burke and C.L. Cooper (eds), *The Long Work Hours Culture: Causes, Consequences and Choices*, Bingley, UK: Emerald Publishing.

Sheldon, K.M., Ryan, R.M., Deci, E.L. and Kasser, T. (2004), 'The independent effects of goal contents and motives on well-being: It's both what you pursue and why you pursue it', *Personality and Social Psychology Bulletin*, **30**, 475–86.

Sonnentag, S. (2001), 'Work, recovery activities, and individual well-being: a diary study', *Journal of Occupational Health Psychology*, **6**, 196–210.

Sonnentag, S. and Fritz, C. (2007), 'The Recovery Experiences Questionnaire: Development and validation of a measure for assessing recuperation and unwinding from work', *Journal of Occupational Health Psychology*, **12**, 204–21.

Sonnentag, S. and Kruel, U. (2006), 'Psychological detachment from work during off-job time: the role of job stressors, job involvement, and recovery-related self-efficacy', *European Journal of Work and Organizational Psychology*, **15**, 197–217.

Sonnentag, S. and Zijlstra, F.R.H. (2006), 'Job characteristics and off-job activities as predictors of need for recovery and well-being', *Journal of Applied Psychology*, **91**, 330–50.

Sparks, K., Cooper, C.L., Fried, Y. and Shirom, A. (1997), 'The effects of hours of work on health: a meta-analytic review', *Journal of Occupational and Organizational Psychology*, **70**, 391–409.

Spence, J.T. and Robbins, A.S. (1992), 'Workaholism: definition, measurement, and preliminary results', *Journal of Personality Assessment*, **58**, 160–78.

Spence, J.T., Helmreich, R.L. and Pred, R.S. (1987), 'Impatience versus achievement strivings in the Type A pattern: differential effects on students' health and academic achievement', *Journal of Applied Psychology*, **72**, 522–28.

Srivastava, A., Locke, E.A. and Bartol, K.M. (2003), 'Money and subjective well-being: It's not the money, it's the motives', *Journal of Social and Personality Psychology*, **80**, 959–71.

Stoeber, J., and Otto, K. (2006), 'Positive conceptions of perfectionism: approaches, evidence, challenges', *Personality and Social Psychology Review*, **10**, 295–319.

Stoeber, J., Harris, R.A. and Moon, P.S. (2007), 'Perfectionism and the experience of pride, shame, and guilt: comparing healthy perfectionists, unhealthy perfectionists, and non-perfectionists', *Personality and Individual Differences*, **43**, 131–41.

Stoeber, J., Otto, K., Pescheck, E., Becker, C. and Stoll, O. (2007), 'Perfectionism and competitive anxiety in athletes: differentiating string for perfection and negative reactions to imperfection', *Personality and Individual Differences*, **42**, 959–69.

Terry-Short, L.A., Owens, R.G., Slade, P.D. and Dewey, M.E. (1995), 'Positive and negative perfectionism', *Personality and Individual Differences*, **18**, 663–8.

Vallerand, R.J. and Houlfort, N. (2003), 'Passion at work: toward a new conceptualization', in D. Skarlicki, S. Gilland and D. Steiner (eds), *Social Issues in Management* Vol. 3, Greenwich, CT: Information Age Publishing, pp. 175–204.

Vallerand, R.J., Blanchard, C.M., Mageau, G.A., Koestner, R., Ratelle, C., Leonard, M. and Gagne, M. (2003), 'Les passions de l'âme: on obsessive and harmonious passion', *Journal of Personality and Social Psychology*, **85**, 756–67.

Vallerand, R.J., Salvy, S.J., Mageau, G.A., Elliot, A.J., Denis, P.L., Grouzet, F.M.E. and Blanchard, C. (2007), 'On the role of passion in performance', *Journal of Personality*, **75**, 505–33.

Van der Hulst, M. (2003), 'Long work hours and health', *Scandinavian Journal of Work, Environment and Health*, **29**, 171–88.

Watkins, P.L., Ward, C.H. and Southard, D.R. (1987), 'Empirical support for a Type A belief system', *Journal of Psychopathology and Behavioral Assessment*, **9**, 119–34.

Watkins, P.L., Fisher, E.B., Southard, D.R., Ward, C.H. and Schechtman, K.B. (1989), 'Assessing the relationship of Type A beliefs to cardiovascular disease risk and psychosocial distress', *Journal of Psychopathology and Behavioral Assessment*, **11**, 113–25.

Westman, M. and Eden, D. (1997), 'Effects of a respite from work on burnout: vacation relief and fade-out', *Journal of Applied Psychology*, **82**, 516–27.

Westman, M. and Etzion, D. (2001), 'The impact of vacation and job stress on burnout and absenteeism', *Psychology and Health*, **16**, 595–606.

Zhang, Y., Gan, Y. and Cham, H. (2007), 'Perfectionism, academic burnout and engagement among Chinese college students: a structural equation modeling analysis', *Personality and Individual Differences*, **43**, 1529–40.

12. Enlisting others in your development as a leader

Dawn E. Chandler and Kathy E. Kram

INTRODUCTION

> You learn more quickly under the guidance of experienced teachers. You waste
> a lot of time going down blind alleys if you have no one to lead you.
>
> (W. Somerset Maugham, The Razor's Edge, 1944)

John Lee and Joe Anderson mutually left Joe's yearly performance review discussion frustrated. Joe had been hired by XYZ Corporation two years prior. At the time, he had been identified as a high-potential candidate who John envisioned taking on a key leadership role in the fourth year of his employment. Unfortunately, John mused, Joe had not yet developed the competencies that were critical to success in the role for which he was targeted. While John needed to have an in-depth conversation with Joe about Joe's efforts to develop his leadership capability over the past two years, his intuition hinted at the key reason for Joe's slow progress. One of Joe's comments in particular suggested the reason: when John asked why Joe didn't try to seek him out with any degree of frequency for advice, Joe stated, 'I've always prided myself on my self-sufficiency and I felt that I would be signaling incompetence if I asked for your help with anything'.

By comparison, Joe's counterpart, Ben Levine, who had seemed to have less natural leadership capability when he was hired in the same role as Joe two years prior, had impressed John and other senior leaders alike; he would be going up for promotion within the next six months. Contrary to Joe, Ben had sought John out on a number of occasions for best practices in his and Joe's position. Why has Ben, a person who seemed to have less natural leadership capability than Joe, excelled in his position while Joe has stagnated? This chapter seeks to explain the difference, specifically by highlighting the importance of engaging others in one's leadership development.

Leadership is implicitly a relational process. Typically, when people think of leadership, they think about the relationships a leader has with his or her followers. Scholars and practitioners have focused much attention on this feature of leadership. Within the scholarly world, for example, studies have shown that leaders articulate challenging goals, foster team-work, and inspire followers to achieve established goals (Podsakoff et al., 1990; Schaubroeck et al., 2007). Practitioners regularly note that leaders transform organizations and achieve outstanding performance by mobilizing individuals and teams to work toward a shared vision (Kouzes and Posner, 2007; George, 2007).

Less attention, however, has been paid to the role that relationships play in enhancing a person's ability to lead. In fact, relationships are integral to the process of a person's development as a leader, as evidenced, for example, by studies on the value of 360-degree feedback (Atwater et al., 2000; Smither et al., 2003). A person who fails to engage relationships to foster his or her growth misses significant learning opportunities. To help fill this gap in our understanding of leadership development through relationships, this chapter will highlight and explain how growth-enhancing relationships can accelerate leadership learning. In addition, when individuals make an effort to assess what they need to learn as well as who might be available to assist in that learning, there is an opportunity to create a 'portfolio' of growth-enhancing relationships, which scholars now refer to as a 'developmental network' (Higgins and Kram, 2001). Whereas a mentor was once considered essential to realizing one's leadership potential, it is now clear that a single mentor relationship is not as effective in fostering leadership development as a small group of developers who are responsive to an individual's current development needs (Kram, 1996; Higgins, 2000; Ragins and Kram, 2007).

In their ground-breaking study of senior executives, Morgan McCall and his colleagues discovered that relationships with others were critical to these individuals learning what they needed to learn to advance to positions of greater responsibility and authority (McCall et al., 1988). They illustrated with their sample of 166 senior executives from private, public and non-profit organizations that without exception, relationships with mentors and peers at critical points in their careers were essential to learning from their experiences in challenging assignments. Without people who invited these individuals to reflect on these challenges, individuals were much less likely to learn the lessons that would enable them to be successful and to advance their careers. Concurrently and since then, many researchers have delineated how such relationships actually enhance learning and development (Ragins and Kram, 2007). Perhaps most noteworthy is the reconceptualization of mentoring from a single dyadic relationship that is focused on the junior person's development to a network of developers who are enlisted by the individual to enhance his or her learning and development (Higgins and Kram, 2001; Higgins et al., 2007; de Janasz and Sullivan, 2004).

The mentoring literature is now ripe with types of developmental relationships that offer career and psychosocial functional support – including hierarchical mentoring, peer mentoring, peer coaching, boss-subordinate, and outside work relationships based in family and community settings. Career functional support includes the provision of visibility within an organization, challenging assignments, coaching and protection. Psychosocial support includes the provision of counseling, acceptance and confirmation, and friendship (Kram, 1985). The literature abounds with studies supporting positive protégé outcomes associated with participation in a developmental relationship (see Allen et al., 2004 for a fairly recent meta-analysis on protégé benefits of mentoring).

In this chapter, we draw on the mentoring and leadership literature to understand how a person can foster a responsive network and guide his or her 'developers' (Higgins and Kram, 2001) to aid his/her leadership growth. In particular, we draw on two areas of recent mentoring research – a contingency theory of developmental networks (Higgins, 2007) and Relational Savvy (Chandler, 2009; Chandler et al., 2009) – to explain how an individual can self-manage his or her leadership development.

We present a three-phase process through which individuals can proactively engage relationships that can guide their development as leaders. As a starting point, we apply prior work on the career competency 'Knowing Why', which refers to understanding one's career motivations, strengths and weaknesses and career goals (DeFillippi and Arthur, 1994; Eby et al., 2003; London, 1993) and how these shape an individual's actions and preferences in the work context. Self-awareness around needed leadership competencies and goals, as well as strengths and weaknesses around one's leadership capability enable an individual to achieve alignment with professional opportunities as they are presented. Self-awareness acts as a catalyst for self-initiation and management of a responsive network that can heighten leadership capabilities (see Figure 12.1 for the model). This phase is marked by careful consideration of who one is and what one wants as the pillars of the second and third phases. It is consistent with research on career self-management, which in part involves collecting information about one's interests and existing capabilities (or lack thereof) and identification of a career goal (e.g., Noe, 1996).

Prior research shows that the career competency, 'Knowing How', which refers to career- and job-related knowledge that one gains over time, aids one's career success (for example, it helps one's internal and external marketability). Here, we apply this idea to the notion of 'Relational Know How' to refer to one's capability to initiate and nurture a response developmental network. Once a person is equipped with self-knowledge gained from the first phase, a person must consider his relative 'Relational Savvy'

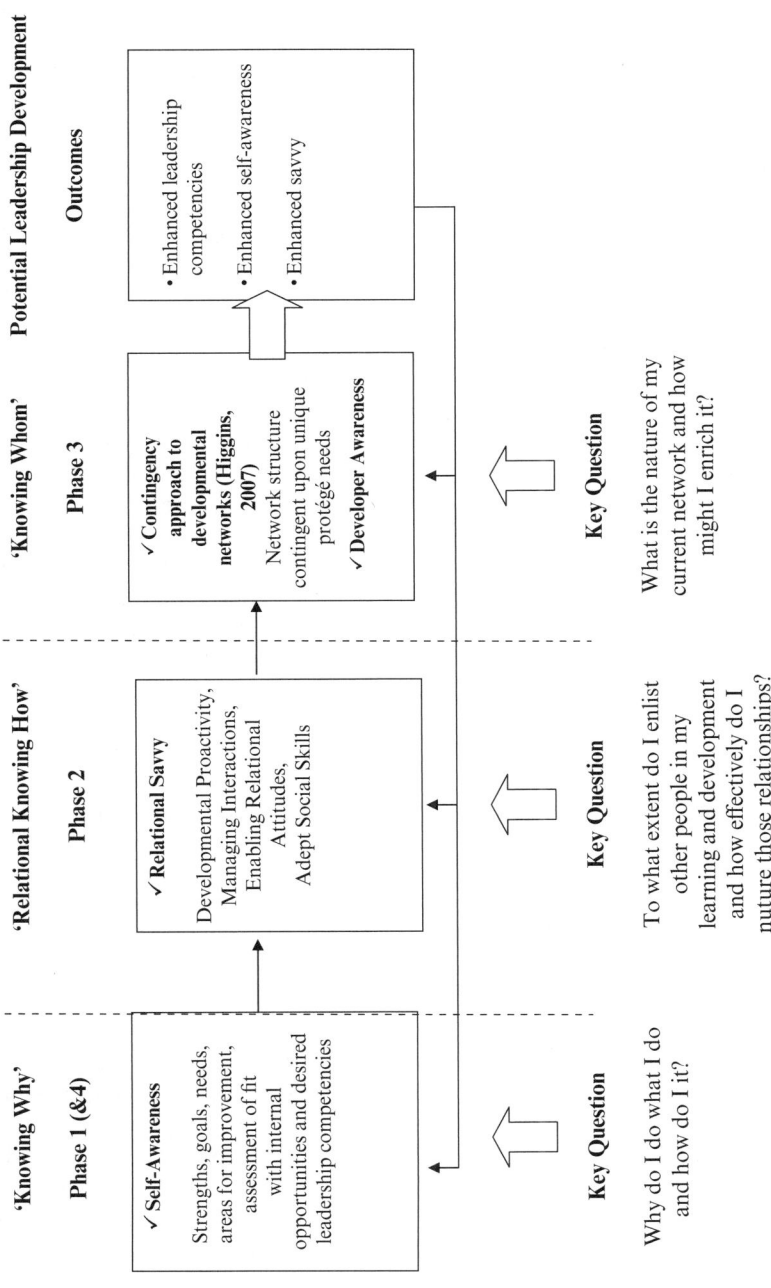

Figure 12.1 A self-managed approach to enlisting others in one's leadership development

– Developmental Proactivity, Managing Others, Enabling Relational Attitudes, Adept Social Skills.

A third career competency, 'Knowing Whom', which relates to investments in career contacts and networks, has also been explored as relevant to career success: (DeFillippi and Arthur, 1994; Eby et al., 2003). In this chapter, we focus on developmental networks, a personal board of directors who take an action to help a focal person's career, as critical to one's leadership development (e.g., Higgins, 2000). During the third phase, a person considers their current developmental network and whether they are well positioned through their network to receive the types of support needed to uniquely aid their leadership development. If relationships are to be a vehicle for a person's leadership development, they must be aware of their relative ability to foster a network that can assist them. The ideal developmental network for that person should be based on their developmental needs and could be comprised of senior, lateral and junior individuals in the person's employing organization as well as individuals outside of the organization, including from their community, family and friend network (Higgins and Kram, 2001). Taken together, these three phases help one prepare to enlist others effectively in their development. At the end of the third phase, they are ready to begin taking action to foster relationships that enhance their developmental network, and to readily engage their developers to facilitate ongoing learning and growth. Figure 12.1 shows the phases and a key question/s that one needs to consider at each of them.[1]

Throughout the remainder of the chapter, we elaborate on each of these phases of self-managed leadership development through developmental networks and we elaborate on the case study of Joe and Ben to enrich the discussion.

PHASE 1: 'KNOWING WHY': DEVELOPING SELF-AWARENESS

Individuals who effectively lead others have an accurate understanding of their personal values. Commitment to a set of clear values enables them to articulate and tirelessly work toward a compelling vision that others want to follow. Leadership research has demonstrated that understanding one's personal drivers and how these shape one's behaviors is critical to effectively setting direction, inspiring others and enabling others to work towards valued ends (Kouzes and Posner, 2007; Goleman, 1998; Goleman et al., 2002; Boyatzis and McKee, 2005). In addition, only with an accurate understanding of one's strengths and weaknesses, can individuals proactively develop the leadership competencies that they may lack. Without this self-awareness, critical blind spots could result in derailment (McCall et al., 1988; Bunker et al., 2002).

This discussion suggests that a starting point for enlisting others in one's leadership development is gaining a better understanding of oneself. In essence, one needs to 'Know Why'; one needs to take stock of the personal values that are the cornerstone of one's leadership philosophy and style, and of one's existing strengths and weaknesses in relation to his ability to lead.

An excellent example of the importance of having *both* the clarity of personal values as well as an accurate assessment of one's strengths and weaknesses is found in examining the founder and CEO of the now extinct airline, People's Express. Don Burr had a compelling and exciting vision for a new airline that would change the way business is done in the industry. Indeed, his principles were adapted by several airlines that followed his. However, within three years of its launch, Burr lost sight of his vision and a lack of self-awareness led him to expand the firm too rapidly into areas that diluted the organization's primary focus. Because he was not reassessing his strengths and weaknesses regularly, he failed to see that his needs for power and his (later) self-described hubris led him to grow the firm without adequate infrastructure, and to ignore attempts to give him feedback regarding his strategic mistakes along the way. Ultimately, the fledgling airline was purchased by a former competitor, many loyal employees left as soon as they could, and the once spirited and enterprising organization was no longer.

Both Joe and Ben, introduced at the outset of this chapter, were fortunate to have been given opportunities to develop their self-awareness. The organization they work for is known for its developmental culture; learning and self-development is valued and encouraged, and a variety of tools are accessible to those who want to make use of them. In fact, their boss, John, has insisted that all of his direct reports participate in leadership assessment activities periodically because he knows from experience how these foster both motivation and direction for self-development. It appears that leaders who embrace this kind of reflective work for themselves are inclined to encourage it in their employees. They appreciate how enabling others to develop themselves will enhance the organization's performance as well.

How does one go about developing accurate self-awareness? There are a variety of assessment instruments that are now regularly offered to professionals and managers to help individuals enhance their self-knowledge. These are accessible through HR departments within organizations, offered by external training organizations (such as the Center for Creative

Leadership, Greensboro, North Carolina), and in graduate and under-graduate management schools. Simply put, systematic reflection with the guidance of structured instruments and/or a professional coach or teacher can lead individuals to understand what they value and how their preferences translate to an appropriate role at work (McKee et al., 2008).

Similarly, with the aid of 360-feedback instruments (e.g., Atwater et al., 2000), individuals receive data on how others perceive them at work. This provides an opportunity to develop an accurate picture of one's strengths and weaknesses as they relate to critical leadership competencies. Without this self-awareness, there is little foundation and rationale for improving one's leadership capability. While there are a number of frameworks available for this kind of feedback process, the key is to make use of a validated instrument and to seize opportunities for coaching from others to develop a thorough understanding of what the data suggest as appropriate next steps in one's development.

Finally, performance appraisal discussions can enhance self-awareness when the relationship is such that feedback is provided honestly and constructively. A manager can contribute to the self-awareness of an employee by providing examples of instances where the employee's behavior was not effective or optimal, and also be helpful in identifying alternative approaches and encouraging new behavior going forward.

Given that Joe and Ben worked for the same individual, it is likely that they have had similar opportunities to make use of an array of assessment tools in order to identify their strengths and weaknesses. John suspects that Joe's self-sufficiency has got in the way of Joe's learning and ongoing development. Indeed, while Joe can recite on which leadership skills he scored high and low, his recitation seems devoid of a recognition that he possesses some skills but lacks others. Further, it seems that he has not figured out how to develop new approaches that would make him more skillful in his current role at work. Nor does he seem motivated to take action to address these limitations in his effectiveness. He may be lacking in adaptability and learning tactics that would enable him to benefit from the feedback that he has received (Hall, 2002).

In contrast, Ben actively solicited additional feedback and coaching from John when he learned that he was perceived as being too autocratic in the way he managed his subordinates. His style was perceived as thwarting creativity and innovation, and this had caused several individuals to take positions in other parts of the organization. During the initial 360-degree feedback discussion, Ben asked probing questions about his strengths and weaknesses that suggested he was earnestly attempting to understand himself and how to improve. He also expressed an enthusiasm for having gained a better understanding of his leadership capability. As a result of his response to the process, John arranged a follow-up assessment six months later that suggested that his subordinates were noticing a welcomed change and enjoying their work significantly more as a result of being given more autonomy and room to tackle new challenges. At the same time, Ben experienced the benefits of delegating effectively; he now had more time to think strategically and to work on other aspects of leading his department to yet better performance.

In the end, clarity of personal values and accurate self-assessment of leadership strengths and weaknesses are necessary for self-development, but not sufficient. Without the establishment of clear, realistic and consistent goals, efforts to enhance one's capabilities will be, at best, undermined by trying to do too much at once, other demands at work, or simply a lack of focus and necessary encouragement to experiment with new behaviors at work. Joe did not establish development goals at all, while Ben decided with input and support from John, that he would practice new behaviors that would enable his direct reports to take more responsibility for the design and outcomes of their efforts, and that he would invite feedback from his department and his boss on a regular basis to assess his own progress. See Table 12.1 for a comparison between Joe and Ben in terms of their effectiveness with the process of enlisting others in their leadership development.

There are many supervisors and organizations that do not encourage the kind of self-inquiry that is essential to developing one's leadership capability. What can be done to foster self-awareness of the sort we are advocating in such a context? In addition to seeking outside opportunities as mentioned earlier, there is also the opportunity to seek feedback from subordinates and peers as well as internal HR practitioners who are willing to provide feedback and coaching (Kram et al., 2002). Indeed, we now know that relationships at work characterized by trust, open communication, mutual learning and caring can be sources of self-insight, skill development and enhanced performance (Dutton and Ragins, 2007). In addition, individuals who have strong developmental networks – comprised of supportive mentors and peers – are likely to experience greater career success and satisfaction than those who do not (e.g., Ragins and Kram, 2007; Higgins, 2002).

PHASE 2: 'KNOWING HOW': DETERMINING YOUR RELATIONAL KNOW-HOW

The process of 'Knowing Why' is a critical starting point in the process of becoming an effective leader because it provides a basic roadmap of an

Table 12.1   Joe and Ben: a comparison of two strategies for enlisting others in one's development

	Joe	Ben
Step 1: Knowing Why	*Low Knowing Why* • Does not use assessment tools or performance appraisals as an opportunity to 'know why' • Lacks clarity about his goals, needs, strengths and weaknesses	*High Knowing Why* • Uses assessment tools and performance appraisals as an opportunity to 'know why' • Has relative clarity about his goals, needs, strengths and weaknesses
Step 2: Relational Knowing How	*Average to Low Relational Savvy* **D1: Developmental Proactivity** • Not highly proactive • Seeks opportunities for support primarily within his immediate work environment • Misses opportunities when solicited by potential developers (e.g., Joe and John) **D2: Managing Interactions** • Prepared • Uses traditional self-disclosure • Low follow-up **D3: Hindering Attitudes** **D4: Average Social Skills**	*High Relational Savvy* **D1: Developmental Proactivity** • Highly proactive • Seeks opportunities for support within *and beyond* his immediate work environment • Responds to opportunities when solicited by potential developers (e.g., Ben and John) **D2: Managing Interactions** • Prepared • Uses strategic self-disclosure • High follow-up **D3: Enabling Attitudes** **D4: Adept Social Skills**
Step 3: Knowing Whom	**Current Developmental Network:** Not well positioned to help **Developer Awareness**: Low	**Current Developmental Network:** Moderately positioned to help **Developer Awareness**: Moderate

individual's current reasons for pursuing a particular job or career (values and interests) as well as the capabilities and developmental needs that will shape the journey ahead. With this self-awareness in place, meaningful goals can be established which will serve as key landmarks and guide their progress in moving towards enhanced effectiveness at work. Without the process of 'Knowing Why', an individual might well try to proceed proactively without any clearly articulated intent, thus following on a journey in which they are vaguely attempting to become 'a leader'. This lack of knowledge and direction will predictably dilute any efforts to enlist others in one's development since such requests are likely to be unfocused and difficult to respond to,

Once 'Knowing Why' knowledge is attained in phase 1, the next task is to consider one's ability to initiate and foster a responsive developmental network to aid leadership development. That is, in order to enlist others in one's development, an individual must now take stock of his or her Relational Savvy, or 'relational knowhow'. Specifically, there are four key skills sets that represent one's savvy: Developmental Proactivity; Managing Interactions; Enabling Relational Attitudes; and Adept Social Skills, each of which will be discussed in turn.

Relational Savvy Dimension 1: Developmental Proactivity (DP)

Some questions that one needs to ask in relation to one's DP are: (1) to what extent do I tend to seek out others to support my career growth? (2) Do I seek out support broadly, for example, with senior employees beyond my immediate boss, with industry professionals outside of my organization, with friends and family, or do I focus on people with whom I immediately interact? (3) To what extent do I initiate developmental relationships with others?

Relationally savvy people are proactive in initiating developmental relationships with a wide range of people and in gaining support from others, whether by asking for feedback, help, advice or information (Chandler, 2009; Chandler et al., 2009). The notion of Developmental Proactivity is consistent with research on self-initiation and career self-management that shows that individuals who make greater efforts to enact development-seeking behaviors and networking reap greater amounts and types of support (e.g., Higgins et al., 2007; Blickle et al., 2009). Compared with individuals who are not developmentally proactive, they are responsive to others' interest in helping them. Their efforts to work with other people to aid their development do not necessarily result in significant time spent on the part of their developers. In fact, they have a tendency to routinely seek out 'mentoring episodes' (Fletcher and Ragins, 2007), which could be even single conversations with people that enable them to better handle their responsibilities, create effective work routines, motivate others, and/ or create a vision for an organizational unit.

Based on his interactions with Joe and Ben, John, their supervisor, had a sense that Joe was not as high on Developmental Proactivity as was Ben. An additional conversation with Joe confirmed that Joe typically relied on himself for leadership challenges and growth rather than reaching out to others, even for minor issues. The few people whom Joe identified as 'developers' were peers in the organization, and Joe didn't have in-depth conversations with them but rather would have occasional 'water cooler chats' about relatively minor issues he confronted. Those relationships had developed naturally over time rather through intentional efforts by Joe to deepen them. Interestingly, John could remember having told Joe at the time of his hire that he was available as Joe's supervisor to be a sounding board and a mentor; Joe had not taken him up on this offer. In essence, Joe was unresponsive to an opportunity for leadership development.

Ben, on the other hand, had intentionally initiated several developmental relationships both within his immediate environment and beyond it. For example, he joined a professional industry group that met on a quarterly basis and took it upon himself to form a group of five peers that met informally every two months to discuss professional and leadership challenges and opportunities. He became particularly close with two members, both of whom had previously been in positions similar to Ben's current one. When Ben felt his subordinate team's motivation slipping, the two developers were instrumental in helping Ben strategize a plan to reignite their engagement.

By way of comparison to Joe, Ben sought out John's assistance on an appropriately regular basis. For example, about six months after having been hired, Ben asked John to lunch and 'picked his brain' about John's leadership development over time. John mentioned that early on, a subordinate told him that it seemed that while he heard his subordinates, he didn't truly listen to them. Thus, subordinates found his attempts to demonstrate empathy for their concerns and his interest in their ideas to be disingenuous. Armed with the knowledge that he needed to work on his emotional intelligence (e.g., Goleman, 1995), John made efforts to improve, and his 360-degree feedback suggested that indeed he had. Ben, taking this information to heart, began to meet informally with each of his subordinates to ensure that he built trusting, respectful relationships with them. Ben had been responsive to John's offer to act as an advisor.

While Joe had occasionally reached out to a few peers, thus showing lackluster Developmental Proactivity, Ben frequently sought out leadership and career-enhancing support from a wide range of people, demonstrating that he was more Developmentally Proactive by comparison. In order to better enlist others in his development as a leader, Joe needs to recognize that his level of Developmental Proactivity is hindering his development. His unexamined commitment to self-sufficiency and total self-reliance is preventing him from using a key vehicle for growth: relationships.

Relational Savvy Dimension 2: Managing Interactions

Some questions that a person needs to ask about their relative ability to 'manage interactions' with current and potential developers include: when I ask someone to help me, am I 'prepared' (Preparedness) to best help that person help me? Do I self-disclose information about myself – vulnerable information or otherwise – haphazardly or with an intent to further the relationship (Strategic Self-Disclosure)? Do I follow up with developers on a regular basis (Follow Up)? Do I find ways to make a relationship mutually beneficial (Mutuality Behaviors)?

Managing interactions with potential and current developers is critical in that the way a person behaves with another person influences the level of interpersonal comfort, liking and trust between them (Dutton and Ragins, 2007). Above are four features of how one manages interactions that a focal person needs to consider in initiating and nurturing developmental relationships.

Whether one is prepared for a meeting in which one seeks to gain developmental support is important because it signals that one cares about that person's time and investment, and it also allows the interaction to go smoothly. To show the downside of being unprepared, imagine a meeting in which a person who needs support with deciphering sophisticated financial data arrives without all of the relevant data. Not only will they not be able to gain all the needed assistance, they have also signaled a lack of conscientiousness and care for that potential or existing developer's time. Being prepared goes beyond having all relevant materials present for a meeting; it also involves having analyzed a situation well enough that a person has both a sense of the challenge at hand and some possible solutions generated. To liken this to Developmental Proactivity, highly savvy people seek out help, but they do so after they have attempted to solve problems and gain as much information as possible prior to doing so. Having generated their own solutions, the focal person can be a partner with their developer.

It turns out that both Joe and Ben are highly prepared for meetings with potential and existing developers. The key difference between them is that Ben has more meetings/mentoring episodes than Joe does (that is, Ben is more proactive in making those meetings happen). Because Joe prides himself on self-sufficiency, he tends to analyze situations carefully and tries to solve his own leadership problems with self-designed solutions. Ben does too, but more because he wants to have collaborative meetings rather than one in which he defers to another person.

Savvy people recognize that relationships are formed and nurtured on the basis of trust, authenticity and liking (Dutton and Ragins, 2007).

Consequently, they are aware of the value of disclosing information to others as a signal of trust, a way to find common ground, and a means to provide a deeper understanding of who they are. They are willing to allow themselves to be vulnerable for the purpose of creating a bond with someone else. Conveying information about oneself as a means to deepen a relationship is called 'Strategic Self-Disclosure'. That information need not be a deep, dark secret, but rather just information about oneself that is not readily available during a 'water cooler' or other type of polite conversation. As a comparison, people who aren't as Savvy either fail to disclose any information that would deepen a relationship or do so without any recognition of or intent to foster a more meaningful relationship.

Joe tends to discuss subjects like the outcome of a football game or a political event that may be interesting conversationally but don't serve to allow people to really get to know him in any way beyond a superficial one. Ben, on the other hand, had the following to say about connecting with others: 'Well, I don't think it's necessary to give someone my whole life story, but I really believe that it's important to allow yourself to be vulnerable with another human being if you want a valuable relationship to flourish. So there have been times when I've disclosed something about myself that involves information about me that matters.'

As an example of this, Ben experienced a naturally-developed, informal peer relationship with a person who was in a similar position within the organization when, at a casual lunch, Ben mentioned that he found himself struggling to celebrate the achievements of his team in a meaningful way (in leadership parlance, this situation involves a leader's ability to 'encourage the heart') (Kouzes and Posner, 2007). The peer appreciated his disclosure of sensitive, meaningful information, offered some solutions, and mentioned having difficulty affecting change in her group. Ben's strategic self-disclosure suggested that he trusted her and she likewise disclosed sensitive information signaling that she, too, was interested in a deeper professional relationship.

When people help others, they want to know that their assistance was valuable. In particular, many senior-ranking individuals, having reached a stage in their adult development in which they want to give back (e.g., Levinson et al., 1978; Levinson and Levinson, 1996; Erikson, 1950), will be interested in remaining abreast of how their advice has benefited someone. Savvy people are excellent at following up with those who have helped them, existing developer or otherwise. Following up with someone may involve a quick note to convey that the focal person did heed that person's advice and it had the intended effect. The follow-up could be a simple thank you and an update about one's current situation in light of the advice, information or feedback. Less Savvy people, on the other hand, may act on others' advice/assistance and then fail to loop back with the latter, leaving the latter with a sense of wonder about whether their help mattered.

Because Joe's 'water cooler' mentoring episodes (Fletcher and Ragins, 2007) have sprung up informally, he hasn't felt the need to go out of his way to keep others 'in the loop' about his leadership development progress. Rather, he may or may not remember to mention his peers' assistance and how it has helped him when he sees them at the water cooler again. While his peers don't seem to mind now, they may be bothered if they offer him assistance of real value at some point and he fails to follow up with them about how he used the assistance to his benefit. Ben, however, is conscientious about emailing or calling developers or others who have helped him.

Finally, an important component of managing interactions with others involves acting in ways that benefit the other party in the relationship. In this way, a relationship involves 'co-learning' or is generally mutually beneficial for both people (Kram and Hall, 1996). Savvy people are highly proactive about helping others in general and they also take action to assist their existing developers. They don't consider relationships one-sided in which one person gives while the other person takes. They realize that they, too, can offer someone assistance, even in relationships in which they are the relative junior person.

One might ask, how can I help someone who is senior to myself given they've already progressed beyond my career path to date? If nothing else, that senior person may actually be interested in helping others or in leaving a legacy (e.g., Levinson et al., 1978; Levinson and Levinson, 1996; Kram, 1985); thus, by virtue of helping someone else, that person's needs are fulfilled. At times, there are creative ways that a person can help someone senior. Let's use Ben as an example. When Ben started with XYZ company, he recognized that some of his seniors lacked computer proficiency (e.g., PowerPoint, Access; Project) in several programs in which he was particularly adept. Therefore, he offered to help fine-tune their work completed on those programs and to teach them some lesser-known tools in the programs. They were both impressed and pleased that he benefited them. Thus, while they were already providing developmental support due to his Developmental Proactivity, they were more willing to help him gain visibility and sponsor him for challenging leadership assignments. By realizing that he had something to offer, Ben made the relationships two-way streets. Joe has assisted some of his peers in various ways, but he's so focused on completing his existing responsibilities and managing his leadership development through his own means – for example, crafting a honed vision for his group and reading about leadership – that he tends to be more isolated.

Relational Savvy Dimension 3: Enabling Relational Attitudes

Here, one should ask whether one's beliefs, attitudes and assumptions about people's interest in providing assistance as well as one's relative preference for working with others are hindering or enabling one to reach out to others for development. One specific question a person should ask is: do I believe that others want to help me? Savvy people tend to hold 'enabling attitudes'; these perceptions involve a sense that others want to and are willing to help, as well as a preference for working with others rather than alone. For example, a Savvy person typically has an attitude that people are willing to help as long as it doesn't consume too much of their time. Less Savvy people often hold at least some hindering attitudes, which entail thinking that others are bothered or annoyed when asked for help, and/or a preference for working together. As one can probably intuit, enabling attitudes are likely to be correlated with greater Developmental Proactivity – if one believes that others are receptive to helping, then one is more likely to ask for it. Conversely, hindering attitudes are likely to be correlated with less DP.

Interestingly, Joe's comment at the end of his performance evaluation session with John – 'I've always prided myself on my self-sufficiency and I felt that I would be signaling incompetence if I asked for your help with anything' – belies a hindering attitude that John holds: reaching out to others for help signals incompetence. Joe may actually recognize the need for others' assistance and be interested in pursuing it, but he hesitates out of concern that doing so will reflect poorly on his ability. Joe does tend, however, to prefer to work alone, which may prevent him from naturally gravitating towards others in his developmental efforts. Ben, by comparison, believes that asking for help flatters the other person and gives them an opportunity to demonstrate competence in a particular arena. Likewise, Ben enjoys working with others; therefore, he seeks out social support for his development.

Relational Savvy Dimension 4: Adept Social Skills

People with outstanding social skills are 'Savvier' because people are attracted to being around them and providing them with support. John's (the supervisor's) earlier admission about his lack of listening skills during his early career with XYZ reflects his social skills. One's ability to empathize, listen, communicate with others, and read others' emotional cues (e.g., Kram, 1996; Goleman, 1995; Cherniss, 2007; Mayer and Salovey, 1997; Salovey and Mayer, 1990) are all key social skills that influence whether others are attracted to and want to interact with a focal person.

While Joe possesses good listening skills and can empathize with others, he has difficulty understanding his subordinates' emotional cues, or expressions. During a recent team meeting, Joe unveiled his vision for a key project and, in hearing no overt resistance when he asked for their feedback and input about it, assumed that everyone was firmly behind it. What he failed to notice was that one longtime XYZ employee and his most skilled subordinate demonstrated facial and bodily cues that signaled she was not wholeheartedly in support of the vision. Later, Joe became angry when he heard that this employee has spoken with others about what she perceived to be the vision's weaknesses. Had Joe been more attuned to his subordinate's cues in the moment, he could have encouraged an open discussion about areas in which she perceived the vision as needing refinement. If Joe had been able to detect these cues, he would have been better able to inspire others around his vision, a key leadership behavior (Kouzes and Posner, 1995). Ben, by comparison, possesses all of the above social skills and can be considered adept.

Taking stock of one's relational savvy is important because it reflects one's 'Relational Knowing How', or know-how related to initiating and cultivating rich developmental relationships. One needs to consider areas where one may be 'low' in Savvy so that one can enhance those skills – or in the case of Enabling Relational Attitudes, reconsider one's attitudes, beliefs and/or assumptions – or at least be aware of them as obstacles.

PHASE 3: KNOWING WHOM: CONSIDERING WHO SHOULD BE IN YOUR DEVELOPMENTAL NETWORK

As noted earlier in the chapter, it used to be that people could rely heavily on a single, omniscient mentor to provide all of the support needed for leadership and career development; this is no longer the case (e.g., Higgins and Kram, 2001). Now, people rely on developmental networks, potentially comprised of individuals from various spheres – for example, family, the community, a professional organization – who provide varying types and amounts of developmental support (Higgins and Kram, 2001). This evolution occurred due to a confluence of trends including globalization, demographic shifts and organizational downsizing. At the heart of the shift is the fact that people no longer stay in a single organization for extended periods but rather transition between organizations over their careers.

The third phase of the process of enlisting others in one's leadership development centers on identifying what one's developmental network should look like in order to attain the desired future. Notice that this phase, Knowing Whom, builds upon one's level of Knowing Why because one's network considerations are based on where one wants to be in terms of a leadership 'destination' (in keeping with the roadmap metaphor). One can think of a developmental network as one's personal board of directors who aid career and leadership growth (e.g., Higgins, 2000; 2007). As goals and skills evolve over time, one's developmental network will necessarily have to be reassessed and modified to be most responsive to new goals and/or new development needs. To provide the reader with an understanding of how to conceive of what one's developmental network looks like, they are 'measured' on two main dimensions: *strength of tie* and *diversity* (e.g., Higgins and Kram, 2001; Granovetter, 1973). In layman's terms, the strength of tie refers to how strong a relationship between a protégé and a developer is in terms of closeness and interpersonal liking. While not introduced as a means to demonstrate stronger and weaker ties, Higgins (2007) and Thomas and Kram (1988) identified four types of developmental relationships offering various amounts and types of support: an ally (low amounts of career and psychosocial support); a sponsor (high amount of career support, low amount of psychosocial support); a friend (high amount of psychosocial support, low amount of career support); and a mentor (high amounts of both career and psychosocial support). An ally, by comparison with the other three types, is the 'weakest' tie relatively; the mentor is the strongest among them. Given that research suggests that motivation to assist a protégé is associated with how strong the tie is (stronger ties involving greater motivation to help), individuals should consider how strong their ties are.

The diversity of a network refers to the extent to which the information a focal person receives is redundant or non-redundant (e.g., Higgins and Kram, 2001). Developmental networks have measured diversity in two ways, the first of which is to consider the types of social spheres from which the relationships stem; as noted earlier, some of the spheres include one's network of family or friends, the organization (from various ranks), the local community, or a professional industry group. The second way to measure diversity is to consider the extent to which one's developers know each other. A 'denser' network occurs when developers in one's network tend to know each other; one that is not as dense involves developers who don't know each other. Diversity matters because research suggests that highly diverse – 'differentiated' – networks carry greater access to a wide range of information (e.g., Brass, 1995) than those that are less diverse by comparison.

Some studies have been conducted that examine outcomes associated with particular aspects of a focal individual's network. For example, diverse networks have been shown to be associated with greater likelihood of career change (e.g., Higgins, 2001); high-status networks have been found to be associated with enhanced likelihood of career advancement and with job commitment (Higgins and Thomas, 2001); and 'entrepreneurial networks' (those with strong ties and diversity) are associated with self-efficacy and clarity of identity (Higgins, 2002).

While a reader's initial response to the above information may be to assume that the best network to initiate and cultivate is a highly-differentiated, strong-tie network, research suggests that a 'one size fits all' approach is not appropriate; rather, the best network for any given person is contingent upon his or her developmental needs and the context in which he or she works (Higgins, 2007).

To highlight why this is the case, consider a person who wants to keep his professional and personal worlds as distinct entities. While he may have a positive, nurturing relationship with his supervisor that involves a high amount of career assistance but a low amount of psychosocial assistance (a developer who provides this combination of support is considered a 'sponsor'), he may not want the relationship to involve discussions about his personal affairs leading to higher psychosocial support and thus evolving that relationship to the strongest tie, that of a mentor status (a mentor, the 'strongest' tie, involves the provision of high amounts of psychosocial and career support). This example above, first offered by Higgins (2007), highlights that a network comprised of developers who are all mentors is not necessarily the most appropriate structure for everyone. Rather the structure of the network should vary based on that particular person's needs and the context in which he or she works. This approach is consistent with a needs-based perspective on mentoring (e.g., Mezias and Scandura, 2005), which emphasizes the notion that an individual should be central to enacting a self-authored, 'protean' career (Hall, 1996).

The above discussion suggests that a person starts with his or her needs and goals (providing further rationale for addressing the 'Knowing Why' phase early in the process) and considers whether his or her existing network can meet the desired destination. They should start by asking who is taking an active interest in and action to advance their career (Higgins and Kram, 2001) as a means to identify their developers. They should evaluate the network's relative overall structure as a way to understand what kind of support they are receiving and then assess whether the support they are receiving is of the right type and amount. It may be that their existing network is not currently assisting them in the right way in light of their leadership goals, but only because they are not interacting with their developers to allow additional support.

Crucial to the process of 'Knowing Why' is an awareness of one's existing developers and potential developers; we term this 'Developer Awareness'. Consistent with the notion of managing one's boss (Gabarro and Kotter, 1980 [1993]), one needs to recognize the importance of a current or potential developer's needs, motivations, goals, strengths and weaknesses. By being aware, a focal person is better positioned to help the targeted others – current developers or potential ones – and interact with them more effectively. For example, a person should look for cues from others that they are motivated to help people – potentially by virtue of their adult development stage (e.g., Levinson et al., 1978) – and thus a potential developer. People can consider their broader social network and assess relationships that can evolve into developmental ones. In both cases, people should consider whether that person can provide the type and/or amount of support someone needs to develop toward desirable ends. Through Developer Awareness and an assessment of one's existing network, one can begin considering what actions would be most likely to foster a responsive, appropriate relationship.

To return to the case of Joe and Ben, Joe had a dense, homogeneous, weak tie network. Essentially, his few developers were peers at his level in the organization who knew each other (and therefore provided redundant support) and were allies (providing low levels of career and psychosocial support). While Joe lacked a clear understanding of himself in numerous ways in relation to leadership, he was aware that he wanted to climb XYZ's hierarchy. At XYZ, however, it was important to have the support of high-status individuals in order to provide the visibility and exposure to challenging assignments. His network did not contain a single high-ranking or high-status individual, thus undermining his potential to secure his goal for career advancement.

Ben had a network that was moderately positioned to aid his leadership development. His network was relatively diverse in that it spanned hierarchical levels within the organization – he identified a strong peer developer (a friend), John (a sponsor), and a senior ranking executive (a sponsor) – as well as outside of it. He also had two peer developmental relationships (friends) with the professional association. While he had a fairly broad network, it did not fully meet his particular needs. For one, Ben was considering making a career change. XYZ company was underperforming vis-à-vis other companies in the industry and it wasn't known for its strength in leadership development. Unfortunately, neither of his two industry peers had significant ties to help him learn more about career opportunities beyond XYZ, nor could he confide in his internal developers about opportunities. Also, interestingly, while Ben had a fairly diverse developmental network, he failed to realize that his father, who had significant executive experience, could potentially be a mentor to him. Their interactions usually centered on sports discussions and never moved into the career realm.

Interestingly, neither employee identified a subordinate developer in their networks. While it may initially seem counterintuitive that a junior employee could aid a senior employee's leadership capability, consider how valuable information about the impact that either one of them is having on their subordinates would be. For example, Ben could receive meaningful feedback from a candid discussion with a subordinate that could help him understand whether his vision for the group was supported, whether he was indeed inspiring and motivating his employees, as well as whether he was serving as a coach and mentor to others; the last two points both affect whether this subordinates would perceive him as an effective leader.

WHAT HAPPENS NEXT?

After someone has sequenced through the three phases, what comes next? At this point, they are ready to take action. The three phases enable them to have the knowledge they need to begin to enlist others in their development. Each phase is important because it offers a different lens through which to view one's current ability to do so. In the event that one does not 'know why', one cannot self-author one's leadership development; rather, one will probably take action toward no specific, relevant end, if one takes action at all. This is consistent with Hall's work (1996, 2002) on the meta-competencies of self-awareness and adaptability; without self-awareness, adaptation is aimless. With respect to the chapter's focal characters, Joe needs to begin the process of considering who he is and what he wants. Until then, he will be unable to enlist people in his development in a meaningful way. Ben, on the other hand, is well-positioned in his 'knowing why' to move forward.

If one is lacking on one of the Relational Savvy dimensions, they are less capable of initiating and nurturing developmental relationships. Thus, as they gain an understanding of their respective Relational Savvy, they can either take action to enhance their Savvy or act with greater awareness of their strengths and relative limitations in enlisting others. Interestingly, one's current developers can probably help strengthen one's Relational Savvy, either by providing role modeling, one of the key mentoring functions, or coaching, another career-related function (Kram, 1985).

Joe's biggest challenge at this point may be in moving beyond his beliefs and attitudes about whether others are willing to assist him. Until he revisits the belief, for example, that enlisting others in his development suggests a lack of competence, it seems unlikely that he will be developmentally proactive. Here again, on the other hand, Ben is well equipped to foster a well-positioned network given he possesses the requisite skills and attitudes.

As a final phase, 'Knowing Whom' is critical to locating the right people for one's network and positioning oneself to gain the right support overall. Someone who undertakes the first two phases yet neglects the third will know where they want to go and have the know-how to enlist others to aid them but won't have an appropriate understanding of who in their environment is willing and able to be a developer (Developer Awareness) or have a deep sense of how their network is currently assisting them. It's important to realize who is in one's personal board of directors and what that board should look like if it is to help move oneself from 'point A to point B'.

At this point, as a starting point, Joe needs to reach out to senior-ranking or high-status individuals in his organization to ensure that he's visible within the organization. He may also determine that he needs leadership coaching (career-related functional support) and thus consider any number of individuals inside (for example, a peer or senior) or outside (for example, someone who teaches a leadership training seminar; an industry support group) the organization. Given Joe's reticence about reaching out for assistance due to his belief that it makes him seem incompetent, he may be most comfortable looking beyond the organization. Not only can this person provide key career-related functional support, he or she can also help Joe gain clarity about his career goals, strengths and weaknesses (interestingly, the Knowing Why component); of course, that is if Joe determines that this person is appropriate to helping him in this way.

Perhaps Ben could take graduate courses at night while maintaining his full-time job at XYZ as a means to locate developers beyond his existing ones who could help him learn about industry opportunities. Should Ben choose to foster a developmental relationship with his father, he will have another source of interpersonal learning. The key for both Ben and Joe is that they closely consider what the existing network offers and whether they are well positioned to receive the support they need to reach their desired leadership ends. If they aren't well positioned via their existing network, they need to scan their social network and the environment to locate potential developers who are suited to help them. As a reminder, it is important for them to consistently keep in mind what they can do to help others, both their current developers and people more generally. Given that growth-enhancing relationships are often characterized by greater levels of closeness, liking and mutuality (Fletcher and Ragins, 2007), it is particularly important for a protégé to ensure that he or she assists others, lest the latter feel that the relationship is a 'one-way street'.

We have presented this model in a linear fashion, suggesting that an individual who wants to enlist a board of directors (Higgins, 2000) should begin at phase one and proceed through each of the second and third stages, respectively. We offered this model to introduce readers to a critical aspect of self-leadership – that of enlisting others in one's development. This model necessarily oversimplifies what actually occurs in practice. In reality, these phases may occur simultaneously, particularly in the event that a person initially enacts all three of them; going forward, that person is sufficiently knowledgeable to consider all of them concurrently. Thus, they can continually evaluate their goals, strengths and weaknesses, consider how to sharpen their Relational Savvy skills and attitudes, and assess whether their developmental network is positioned to help.

We assume that individuals will act on knowledge gained by virtue of cycling through these phases. Thus, at the tail end of the third phase, it is reasonable to assume that they will enlist others in their development by better utilizing the developers in their existing network – toward the ends identified in the 'Knowing Why' phase – and/or by fostering new relationships that offer unique sources of developmental support.

Figure 12.1 shows three outcomes that can occur as the result of enacting this process: enhanced self-awareness, Relational Savvy, and leadership competencies. In fact, it is important to note that enlisting others in one's development can heighten one's 'knowing why' and 'relational know how' in addition to improving one's leadership ability. Developers can act as sounding boards and ask pertinent questions that help someone understand his or her values and goals. Furthermore, as suggested in the early discussion on 'Knowing Why', developers are often part of one's 360-degree feedback and a supervisor is inevitably involved with one's formal performance evaluation, both of which serve as opportunities to gain clarity about the 'why factor'. Developers can heighten one's Relational Savvy in a number of ways, including by providing coaching and feedback about one's capability and by serving as Savvy role models that a focal person can emulate. Finally, by fostering a responsive, contingency-appropriate developmental network, one can gain functional support that actually enables leadership development. As Figure 12.1 shows, there are feedback loops in the process such that 'success begets success': by successfully enacting the three phases, there are positive outcomes that loop back to positively influence later efforts through the phases. Again, in actuality, all three 'phases' may occur simultaneously.

To return to Maugham's quote offered at the beginning of this chapter, this chapter proposes that enlisting teachers to aid one's leadership development will prevent one from wandering aimlessly down blind alleys. Rather than engaging on an isolated journey, we encourage those who aspire to self-managed leadership development to gain the support of a network of developers to help them along the way.

NOTE

1. We acknowledge at the onset that our model oversimplifies reality; we chose to do so to provide a sequence of actions showing a clear path of action. However, in fact, these stages are likely to be conducted simultaneously rather than linearly. Our model indicates this fact by noting a stage 4 in which a person continues the process after sequencing through it. Thus, we assert that a person who opts to conduct all three phases concurrently will experience the same outcomes as someone who does so sequentially.

REFERENCES

Allen, T.D., Eby, L.T., Poteet, M.L. and Lentz, E. (2004), 'Career benefits associated with mentoring for protégés: a meta-analysis', *Journal of Applied Psychology*, **89**(1), 127–36.

Atwater, L.A., Waldman, D., Atwater, D. and Cartier, P. (2000), 'An upward feedback field experiment: supervisors' cynicism, follow-up, and commitment to subordinates', *Personnel Psychology*, **53**, 275–97.

Blickle, G., Witzki, A.H. and Schneider, P.B. (2009), 'Mentoring support and power: a three year predictive field study on protégé networking and career success', *Journal of Vocational Behavior*, **74**, 181–9.

Boyatzis, R.E. and McKee, A. (2005), *Resonant Leadership: Renewing Yourself and Connecting with Others Through Mindfulness, Hope, and Compassion*, Boston, MA: Harvard Business School Press.

Brass, D.J. (1995), 'A social network perspective on human resources management', in G.R. Ferris (ed.), *Research in Personnel and Human Resources Management*, Greenwich, CT: JAI Press, pp. 39–79.

Bunker, K.A., Kram, K.E. and Ting, S. (2002), 'The young and the clueless', *Harvard Business Review*, December, 80–87.

Chandler, D.E. (2009), 'Relational savvy: why some individuals are more adept with developmental relationships', unpublished dissertation, Boston University.

Chandler, D.E., Hall, D.T. and Kram, K.E. (2009), 'Relational learning and talent development: leveraging developmental networks, relational savvy, and HRD practices', unpublished manuscript.

Cherniss, C. (2007), 'The role of emotional intelligence in the mentoring process', in B.R. Ragins and K.E. Kram (eds), *The Handbook of Mentoring at Work: Theory, Research, and Practice*, Thousand Oaks, CA: Sage Publications, pp. 427–46.

DeFillippi, R.J. and Arthur, M.B. (1994), 'The boundaryless career: a competency-based perspective', *Journal of Organizational Behavior*, **15**(4), 304–24.

De Janasz, S.C. and Sullivan, S.E. (2004), 'Multiple mentoring in academe: developing the professorial network', *Journal of Vocational Behavior*, **64**(2), 263–83.

Dutton, J.E. and Ragins, B.R. (eds) (2007), *Exploring Positive Relationships at Work: Building Theoretical and Research Foundations*, Mahwah, NJ: Lawrence Erlbaum.

Eby, L.T., Butts, M. and Lockwood, A. (2003), 'Predictors of success in the era of the boundaryless career', *Journal of Organizational Behavior*, **24**(6), 689–708.

Erikson, E.H. (1950), *Childhood and Society*, New York: W.W. Norton.

Fletcher, J.K. and Ragins, B.R. (2007), 'Stone center relational cultural theory: a window on relational mentoring', in B.R. Ragins and K.E. Kram (eds), *The Handbook of Mentoring at Work: Research, Theory, and Practice*, Thousand Oaks, CA: Sage Publications, pp. 373–400.

Gabarro, J.J. and Kotter, J.P. (1980 [1993]), 'Managing your boss', *Harvard Business Review*, **71**(3), 150–57.

George, W. (2007), *True North: Discover your Authentic Leadership*, San Francisco, CA: Jossey-Bass.

Goleman, D. (1995), *Emotional Intelligence*, New York: Bantam Books.

Goleman, D. (1998), 'What makes a leader?', *Harvard Business Review*, **76**(6), 93–102.

Goleman, D., Boyatzis, R. and McKee, A. (2002), 'The emotional reality of teams', *Journal of Organizational Excellence*, **21**(2), 55–65.

Granovetter, M.S. (1973), 'The strength of weak ties', *American Journal of Sociology*, **78**, 1360–80.

Hall, D.T. (1996), 'Protean careers of the 21st century', *Academy of Management Executive*, **10**(4), 9–16.

Hall, D.T. (2002), *Careers In and Out of Organizations*, Thousand Oaks, CA: Sage Publications.

Higgins, M.C. (2000), 'The more, the merrier? Multiple developmental relationships and work satisfaction', *Journal of Management Development*, **19**, 277–96.

Higgins, M.C. (2001), 'Changing careers: the effects of social context', *Journal of Organizational Behavior*, **22**(6), 595–618.

Higgins, M.C. (2002), 'Career consequences of developmental networks', paper presented at the Academy of Management annual meeting, August, Denver, CO.

Higgins, M.C. (2007), 'A contingency perspective on developmental networks', in J.E. Dutton and B.R. Ragins (eds), *Exploring Positive Relationships at Work: Building a Theoretical and Research Foundation*, London: Erlbaum Associates, pp. 207–24.

Higgins, M.C. and Kram, K.E. (2001), 'Reconceptualizing mentoring at work: a developmental network perspective', *Academy of Management Review*, **26**, 264–88.

Higgins, M.C. and Thomas, D.A. (2001), 'Constellations and careers: toward understanding the effects of multiple developmental relationships', *Journal of Organizational Behavior*, **22**(3), 223–47.

Higgins, M.C., Chandler, D.E. and Kram, K.E. (2007), 'Developmental initiation and developmental networks', in B.R. Ragins and K.E. Kram (eds), *The Handbook of Mentoring at Work: Research, Theory, and Practice*, Thousand Oaks, CA: Sage Publications, pp. 349–72.

Kouzes, J.M. and Posner, B.Z. (1995), *The Leadership Challenge*, San Francisco, CA: Jossey-Bass.

Kouzes, J.M. and Posner, B.Z. (2007), *The Leadership Challenge* 4th edn, San Francisco, CA: Jossey-Bass.

Kram, K.E. (1985), *Mentoring at Work: Developmental Relationships in Organizational Life*, Glenview, IL: Scott, Foresman and Company.

Kram, K.E. (1996), 'A relational approach to career development', in D.T. Hall et al. (eds), *The Career is Dead: Long Live the Career*, San Francisco, CA: Jossey-Bass, pp.132–57.

Kram, K.E. and Hall, D.T. (1996), 'Mentoring in a context of diversity and turbulence', in E.E. Kossek and S.A. Label (eds), *Managing Diversity: Human resource Strategies for Transforming the Workplace*, Cambridge, MA: Blackwell Business, pp. 108–36.

Kram, K.E., Bunker, K.A. and Ting, S. (2002), 'The young and the clueless', *Harvard Business Review*, **80**(12), 80–87.

Levinson, D.J., with Levinson, J.D. (1996), '*Seasons of a Woman's Life*', New York: Alfred A. Knopf.

Levinson, D.J., Darrow, C.M., Klein, E.G., Levinson, M.H. and McKee, B. (1978), *The Seasons of a Man's Life*, New York: Alfred A. Knopf.

London, M. (1993), 'Relationships between career motivation, empowerment, and support for career development', *Journal of Occupational and Organizational Psychology*, **66**, 55–69.

Maughman, W.S. (1944), *The Razor's Edge*, Garden City, NY: Doubleday, Doran and Company.

Mayer, J.D. and Salovey, P. (1997), 'What is emotional intelligence?', in P. Salovey and D. Sluyter (eds), *Emotional Development and Emotional Intelligence: Implications for Educators*, New York: Basic Books, pp. 3–31.

McCall, M., Lombardo, M. and Morrison, A. (1988), *Lessons of Experience: How Successful Executives Develop On the Job*, Boston, MA: Lexington Books.

McKee, A., Boyatzis, R.E. and Johnston, F. (2008), *Becoming a Resonant Leader: Develop Your Emotional Intelligence, Renew Your Relationships, Sustain Your Effectiveness*, Boston, MA: Harvard Business School Press.

Mezias, J.M. and Scandura, T.A. (2005), 'A needs-driven approach to expatriate adjustment and career development: a multiple mentoring perspective', *Journal of International Business Studies*, **36**, 519–38.

Noe, R. (1996), 'Is career management related to employee development and performance?', *Journal of Organizational Behavior*, **17**, 119–33.

Podsakoff, P.M., MacKenzie, S.B., Moorman, R.H. and Fetter, R. (1990), 'Transformational leader behaviors and their effects on followers' trust in leader, satisfaction, and organizational citizenship behaviors', *The Leadership Quarterly*, **1**, 107–42.

Ragins, B.R. and Kram, K.E. (eds) (2007), *The Handbook of Mentoring at Work: Theory, Research, and Practice*, Thousand Oaks, CA: Sage Publications.

Salovey, P. and Mayer, J.D. (1990), 'Emotional intelligence', *Imagination, Cognition, and Personality*, **9**, 185–211.

Schaubroeck, J., Lam, S.K. and Cha, S.E. (2007), 'Embracing transformational leadership: team values and the impact of leader behavior on team performance', *Journal of Applied Psychology*, **92**(4), 1020–30.

Smither, J., London, M., Flautt, R., Vargas, Y. and Kucine, I. (2003), 'Can working with an executive coach improve multisource feedback ratings over time? A quasi-experimental field study', *Personnel Psychology*, **56**, 23–44.

Thomas, D.A. and Kram, K.E. (1988, 'Promoting career-enhancing relationships in organizations: the role of the human resource professional', in M. London and E.More (eds), *The Human Resource Professional and Employee Career Development*, New York: Greenwood Press, pp. 49–66.

13. Resilience and leadership: the self-management of failure

Gillian A. King and Mitchell G. Rothstein

SITUATIONS WHERE MANAGERS EXPERIENCE DISTRESS

Matt couldn't believe what had happened. After 21 years of delivering results, receiving regular promotions, and displaying loyalty to his company, Henry, who was the CEO and Matt's boss and mentor for all these years, had called Matt out of a meeting with his management team and fired him with no warning. Matt had never received any negative performance feedback from Henry – only praise for achieving results, more responsibility, more money and more promotions. Henry would not give a specific reason for Matt's dismissal, only that there was no longer a good fit for Matt and the company. Matt had been led to believe he was the next CEO, but in an instant his career and ambitions were shattered. He was filled with emotions – anger, resentment, suspicion and confusion; what was he going to do now (Mikalachki, 1994)?

There are many reasons why leaders' careers derail. The most common reasons include problems with interpersonal relationships, failure to meet business objectives, failure to build and lead a team, and inability to change or adapt during a transition (e.g., Van Velsor and Leslie, 1995). Matt's experience is not uncommon in the career of a leader. Leaders often experience a variety of adverse events that they may interpret as failure or inadequacy. In addition to getting fired, leaders may be passed over for promotion by a rival, be held responsible for the loss of a major customer to the competition, be unable to resolve a conflict with a powerful mentor, or experience extreme anxiety and turmoil when faced with major ethical dilemmas and value conflicts. What happens when these difficulties occur? How can leaders prepare themselves for the adverse situations they are almost certain to encounter? After extreme work-related distress, what skills, attitudes, and supports are needed to thrive and find meaning in the workplace and in life?

ADVERSITY IN THE WORKPLACE AND THE IMPORTANCE OF PERSONAL RESILIENCE

This chapter addresses one of the most typical and difficult challenges faced by leaders in the course of their careers. At some point or other, it is likely that shame, disappointment or disillusionment will occur as a result of a major failure or loss – a major career setback, job loss, loss of a mentoring relationship, or loss of belief in an organization and its mission. The loss may be large enough to threaten self-esteem, fundamental values and personal identity, and motivation to succeed. A leader may lose self-confidence after experiencing failure or being laid off, become depressed when passed over for promotion, or become bitterly disillusioned and feel exploited by workplace events. Because leaders are required to make decisions involving some degree of risk, they are more likely to experience failure; consequently, personal resilience is a critical leadership competency.

Increased competition on a global scale, technological advances and constant change in business organizations are creating adverse experiences for all individuals in leadership positions. An accelerating pace of change in the workplace is also demanding an accelerated pace of personal change and professional development. New and different challenges are increasingly common (Van Velsor and Leslie, 1995), and continuous growth and transformation are required to adapt and succeed. The personal characteristic of resilience is particularly relevant to organizational leaders' personal growth and transformation (Luthans, 2002). Leaders need to understand what failure means and how to deal with it – how to bounce back from adversity. Developing a capacity for resilience is a vital and largely ignored component of leadership development (Luthans and Avolio, 2003).

A variety of adverse managerial and leadership experiences can result in profound negative emotions, including shame over failure, disappointment and disillusionment, along with feelings of deep sadness and anger. Traumatic workplace experiences can also lead to loss of self-esteem, identity and self-confidence, with subsequent implications for future behavior and desire to succeed. In cases of personal failure, leaders may feel greater shame because their loss of self-esteem, influence and self-reliance is highly public (Sonnenfeld and Ward, 2008).

When we think of adverse workplace experiences, we typically think about career setbacks and performance issues leading to shame over personal failure. It is important to realize, however, that because authentic leaders invest and engage wholeheartedly in an organization, they can experience profound disappointment and disillusionment. What all these experiences have in common is a major work-related loss of some kind.

Disappointment arises when someone does not receive what is expected or promised to them, such as a new position, support for their decisions and initiatives, or sufficient resources to accomplish their goals. Being passed over for promotion can be a major disappointment that makes a person re-evaluate his or her career. Having one's belief in an organizational vision, workplace boss, mentor or colleagues shattered under difficult circumstances can result in a profound sense of disillusionment and loss of a sense of meaning in life. Disillusionment is perhaps most devastating for visionary and charismatic leaders, who hold optimistic and perhaps idealistic views of the future; it can be particularly challenging because it affects leaders' fundamental sense of themselves or their assumptions about the world.

> The person who really thinks learns quite as much from his failures as from his successes.
>
> (John Dewey)

There is truth to the adage that failure is one of the best ways to learn. Strong negative experiences such as shame, disappointment and disillusionment break down preconceived ideas and open the mind to new ways of looking at things and new ways of acting. Failure can be a unique opportunity to make significant personal and career changes, through capitalization on resilience-related processes that lead to new directions in life.

Resilience is a critical issue in leadership. In addition to rapid changes in the business environment, changes in social, political and economic conditions such as terrorism, war and recession, make understanding resilience more important than ever (Coutu, 2002). Resiliency is considered important both to continuing success in a career and career recovery. Although exceptional leaders are considered to be highly resilient (Gardner, 1997; Sonnenfeld and Ward, 2008), resilience is not just a characteristic of exceptional people. Rather, resilience is a characteristic that may exist in all human beings – a general human capacity that reflects how each of us adapts to hardships in life (Bonanno, 2004; Masten, 2001). Resilience occurs through ordinary, not extraordinary, processes underlying human development and adaptation (Masten, 2001).

Much has been written on how organizations can develop leaders by identifying strengths and performance gaps, offering developmental challenges, and providing support (e.g., Spreitzer, 2006). Organizations can provide a variety of interventions and programs, such as career and succession planning, 360-degree feedback, and mentoring programs. Increasingly, however, organizations are not taking responsibility to help individuals succeed. Faced with fierce competition, globalization and demands from shareholders to maintain profits, organizations have responded primarily through mergers and acquisitions, restructuring and downsizing, outsourcing, and cutting costs in every area that does not directly support the core business. Ironically, human resource training and leadership development programs are typically among the first targets of cost-cutting in most organizations, despite the need for leadership talent to carry out the restructuring of the business and rebuild for the future. But faced with dramatic shortfalls in revenue, organizations are forced into survival mode, preserving their cash and drastically cutting expenses. As Moses (1997) and many others have articulated, organizations are no longer willing to commit resources to leadership development because of other short-term needs and the belief that if individuals want to develop, it is up to them to figure out how to do it. The need for individuals to take direct personal responsibility for their leadership development has never been greater.

This chapter considers the protective factors, processes and ways in which people develop resilient attitudes, construct sense and meaning in the workplace, and create personal change. The aim is to create an explicit picture of what it takes to be a resilient leader. We begin by considering what is known about resilience in general, and particularly as it applies to the workplace. We then consider how people bounce back from adversity – how resiliency works – and introduce an affective, cognitive and behavioral model of resiliency in the workplace. The characteristics and actions of resilient people are then considered, using this model as a guide. The final sections address taking instrumental responsibility for self-development of resiliency, and propose directions for research on the role of resilience in self- and career development.

RESILIENCE TO FAILURE AND LOSS IN THE WORKPLACE

> You always pass failure on your way to success.
>
> (Mickey Rooney)

In recent years there has been increasing interest in understanding the characteristics and processes that allow people to withstand and recover from adversity (often referred to as showing 'resilience'). Resilience involves 'bouncing back' from significant adversity (Masten et al., 1990; Rutter, 1990). It is a dynamic process (Luthar et al., 2000) involving resources found in basic human adaptational systems, including self-regulation of emotions, attachment to others, and effectance motivation or desire to master aspects of the environment (Masten, 2001). There is extensive evidence that personal characteristics and aspects of the environment promote adaptation and enable individuals to do well in life despite many types of adversity, including illness and disability (Bonanno, 2004; Curtis and Cicchetti, 2003; King et al., 2003a; Luthar et al., 2000; Maddi, 2005; Rutter, 1985). The characteristics that promote resilience are referred to as protective factors.

Resilience is not the same as thriving at work (Spreitzer et al., 2005). Both resilience and thriving refer to an individual's capacity for adaptability and positive adjustment (Carver, 1998; Sutcliffe and Vogus, 2003); however, thriving can occur with or without adversity. Thriving reflects gains in skills, knowledge, confidence, or a sense of security in personal relationships that do not depend on the occurrence of a traumatic event or longer-term adverse experience (Carver, 1998). Similarly, resilience is not the same thing as coping with a less than ideal work situation. Coping occurs in response to stress rather than traumatic, emotionally compelling events or accumulated experiences.

> More than education, more than experience, more than training, a person's level of resilience will determine who succeeds and who fails.
>
> (Coutu, 2002: p. 47)

As shown in this quote, the management literature considers resilience to be a personal characteristic or outcome, with implications for qualities sought after in hiring. It may, however, be more useful to consider resilience as a process of learning or self-development occurring over a period of time. Resilience in face of workplace adversity is about ultimate success despite immediate strife or discord. Resilience is about *how* a person weathers a storm and the learning that results, *how* he or she deals with a major loss, and the *processes* that lead to personal choices, career recovery, and personal growth and integrity. New personal visions and missions can be born out of the opportunity to step back and reflect on what is important (Sonnenfeld and Ward, 2008). Rather than a personal characteristic or outcome per se, resilience is therefore a process that, if effective, leads to positive life outcomes such as high job performance, successful careers, adjustment, and the like.

There is an extensive literature on resilience, most of it outside the management field. Resilience research has focused primarily on individual and environmental factors that influence the social and personal success of children experiencing various types of adversity (Richardson, 2002), including children with disabilities (Hechtman, 1991) and children living in poverty or who have been abused. As well, there is literature on resilient families (Walsh, 2003; Walsh and Walsh, 1998) and resilience accompanying the process of aging (e.g., Brandtstadter, 1999). The classic work on resilience, by Emmy Werner (Werner and Smith, 1992; Werner, 1982), examined resilience in a group of disadvantaged children in Hawaii. The aim was to determine personal qualities and life events that distinguished children who had better life success over time. The important characteristics included an ability to obtain positive attention from others; a tendency to view experiences constructively and use faith to maintain a positive vision of a meaningful life; and an active approach to solving life's problems.

Organizational and Personal Resilience

Inspired by the positive psychology movement (Seligman and Csikszentmihalyi, 2000), there has been recent interest in the study of positive organizational scholarship, including studies of how individuals in organizations develop strength, resiliency and virtuous qualities (Cameron and Caza, 2002; Cameron et al., 2003; Luthans, 2002). Constructs such as confidence, hope, perseverance, virtue and resiliency are being given increasing attention (Luthans, 2002; Seligman and Csikszentmihalyi, 2000) due to this interest in enhancing wellness, personal adjustment and positive life outcomes.

However, a review of the management literature, using 'resilience', 'protective factors', and 'protective processes' as search terms, uncovered very few articles explicitly dealing with resilience, with most of these examining organizational or corporate resilience (Earvolino-Ramirez, 2007). According to Luthans (2002), there have been few attempts to directly apply the concept of resilience to the workplace, and these largely consider organizational resilience (e.g., Doe, 1994; Hamel and Valikangas, 2003; Mallak, 1998; Sutcliffe and Vogus, 2003). According to Hamel and Valikangas (2003), continued organizational success is dependent on strategic resilience, which is defined as the ability to dynamically reinvent business models and strategies as circumstances change.

Some work in the management literature has considered resilience to be a personal characteristic or quality. Coutu (2002) views resilience as a trait and is interested in why some people bounce back from hardships while others despair. She proposes three crucial ingredients of personal resilience: a staunch acceptance of reality, a deep belief that life is meaningful, and an uncanny ability to improvise, characteristics that exemplify affective, cognitive and behavioral aspects of resilience. These aspects of resilience correspond to the model of resiliency that is proposed in this chapter (see below), in which resilience is considered to be comprised of three domains of protective factors: affective (emotional regulation factors), cognitive (coherence-generating factors), and behavioral (agency-generating factors). However, the major difference between our model and the important resilience factors discussed by Coutu and others is that we do not consider these aspects or domains of resilience solely as characteristics of individuals. Rather, we propose that these domains define processes in which personal characteristics and the environmental context combine to produce resilience-related outcomes. Such a model is relevant to the development of resilience and, therefore, the self-management of this critical component of leadership.

HOW PEOPLE BOUNCE BACK: THE PROCESSES OF RESILIENCE

> Notice the difference between what happens when a man says to himself, 'I have failed three times', and what happens when he says, 'I am a failure'.
>
> (S.I. Hayakawa)

Understanding Resilience

There is current debate about the usefulness of 'resilience' as a construct (Luthar et al., 2000). Some of this debate centers on whether 'resilience' has predictive rather than explanatory worth and how it can be best operationalized and measured. The debate has centered on differences in definitions and conceptual approaches. Many questions remain unanswered such as whether and how the many facets of resilience hang together, and whether they add predictive power over and above constructs such as coping, adaptation, self-efficacy and self-determination. Unfortunately, to date there is almost no research evidence available to answer these questions. In addition, no attempt has been made to integrate differences in definitions and conceptualizations of resilience to build a comprehensive model that captures multiple perspectives on this phenomenon.

In our view, in order to integrate these multiple perspectives, it is most useful to consider resiliency to be an interdisciplinary field of study, comprised of multiple concepts, theories and processes, rather than a single yet multifaceted concept. We therefore use the term 'resiliency' when discussing our proposed model, to stress the process viewpoint – the idea that affective, cognitive and behavioral protective factors interact over time, in accordance with fundamental adaptive processes involving self-regulation, to produce outcomes considered to reflect bouncing back, recovery from, or adaptation to significant hardships.

In addition to being thought of as a characteristic of an individual (Masten et al., 1990), resilience has been considered a process of successful adaptation to stressful events or conditions (Rutter, 1985; Steinhauer, 1997). In fact, resilience has been viewed variously as a personal characteristic, outcome, state and process (Richardson, 2002). In the management literature, Luthans (2002) adopts a state-like view, seeing resilience as something that can be learned or acquired. In a process or state view, resilience is considered to be a capability that changes over time, enhanced by protective factors in the individual or environment (Stewart et al., 1997).

According to Richardson (2002), resilience is a fundamental force or motivation that drives a person to grow through adversity and disruptions. Richardson focuses on the process of biopsychospiritual homeostasis, by which individuals have the opportunity to make choices, leading to a reintegrative or coping process that results in growth, knowledge, self-understanding and resilient qualities. This work reflects a cognitive view of resilience. An affective view of resilience is proposed by Frederickson (2001) in this theory of positive emotions. According to this theory, positive emotions contribute to resilience by broadening thought-action repertoires and building enduring personal resources.

In the present chapter, we view resilience as an 'umbrella term' comprised of multiple personal, interpersonal and environmental factors and adaptational processes, much the same way as the experience of 'disability' is comprised of personal features (bodily impairment), interpersonal aspects (day-to-day functioning in activities), and environmental aspects (societal influences such as support and stigma) (De Kleijn-de Vrankrijker et al., 1998). Similarly, 'social support' is a multifaceted and multifunctional umbrella term that encompasses various types of support (Hupcey, 1998), and 'thriving' is considered to be a work-related outcome dependent on personality variables such as optimism, contextual variables such as social support, and situational variables such as coping reactions elicited by an adverse event (Carver, 1998). All of these phenomena (that is, resilience, disability, social support, thriving) are best understood as multidimensional constructs comprised of personal, interpersonal and environmental factors, as well as processes describing how these factors interact and combine to produce specific outcomes. With respect to outcomes, we expect that resilient leaders will display affective, cognitive and behavioral indicators of resilience in the workplace (that is, resilience-related outcomes), such as acceptance and adjustment to failure or disappointment, high performance (or recovery from poor performance), successful careers, and other positive life outcomes.

Resilience is a super-ordinate construct – a class of phenomena – representing or characterized by positive adaptation despite adversity (Bonanno, 2004; Luthar, 2006; Masten, 2001). The central objective of resilience researchers is to identify factors that modify the negative effects of adverse life circumstances, and the mechanisms or processes that underlie recovery, adaptation or new directions in life (Luthar, 2006).

Resilience can be thought of as a characteristic of individuals, but also as a group of neurobiological and psychosocial processes by which individuals are able to reduce the potential negative impact of adversity. Masten (2001), for example, discusses the importance of systems underlying adaptive processes, such as brain development and cognition, regulation of emotion and behavior, and motivation for learning and engaging in the environment.

In summary, resilience involves the complex and dynamic interplay between characteristics of individuals and the broader environment (Reid et al., 1996). In our model of resiliency in the workplace (discussed below), resilience is considered to reflect the interplay between a set of affective, cognitive and behavioral protective factors and processes.

How Resilience Works: Turning Point Processes

> This thing we call 'failure' is not the falling down, but the staying down.
>
> (Mary Pickford)

An ideal way to understand how protective factors and processes operate in people's lives is to examine what have been called 'turning points' (Rutter, 1990). These significant life events, experiences or realizations are also called critical junctures (Mandelbaum, 1973) and epiphanies (Denzin, 1989). Opportunities and choices at crucial turning points play an important role in the life course of resilient individuals, who may find new mentors, leave toxic workplace environments, start new business ventures, embrace a new or deeper faith, or otherwise take actions that have positive consequences for their life course (Masten, 2001).

Turning points are triggered by adverse events, characterized by high levels of emotion, and resolved when a person makes a decision or reappraises their situation (King et al., 2003b). Turning points are emotionally compelling experiences and realizations that involve meaning acquired through the routes of belonging, doing, or understanding the self or the world (King et al., 2003b). Thus, highly emotional and adverse work experiences can be considered turning points.

A good example of a turning point that illustrates resilience processes may be drawn from a real life case written by one of us (Rothstein, 1995).

James Reed (not his real name) was an extremely successful management consultant on the verge of being made a partner, a goal he believed he very much wanted. As he strived to achieve this goal, he maintained long work hours (80 to 100 hours per week) and travelled away from home and his young family almost every week. He was under tremendous pressure to demonstrate his worth to the firm and experiencing increasing levels of stress as he attempted to meet the demands of his career while managing growing alienation and conflict with the needs of his family. A particularly adverse event, in which James explicitly put the needs of his career over those of his family, triggered the real possibility that he would lose his family. This personal crisis filled with emotional turmoil caused James to reappraise his values and goals, come to an understanding of what was truly important to him, and led him to resolve the crisis by deciding to make a change in his career. This situation is a good illustration of a turning point in which an adverse event, the conflict between family values and career aspirations, is resolved through a process that leads James to reinvent his career in a way that is consistent with other goals and values in his life.

> Keep on beginning and failing. Each time you fail, start all over again, and you will grow stronger until you have accomplished a purpose – not the one you began with perhaps, but one you'll be glad to remember.
>
> (Anne Sullivan)

There is sparse literature on the mechanisms underlying resilience. Rutter (1990) discusses several turning point processes, including the development of steeling qualities, stopping a negative chain of events, developing self-efficacy, and the opening up of new opportunities. These mechanisms focus on instrumental actions and personal transformation through changes in or affirmation of identity. As part of the resolution to turning points, people often become clearer about their goals and what they value in life (Bruner, 1994).

The case of James Reed illustrates these processes. James got through his emotional crisis by engaging a process to deal with the stress of his job while he worked on a plan to resolve the problem (leading to the development of steeling qualities). He made a critical decision to change his career (stopping a negative chain of events), and he was able to discover new possibilities for his career that resolved his inner conflict on who he was and what he was able to accomplish (developing self-efficacy and opening new opportunities) (for a full description of these processes see Rothstein, 1995).

Rutter's (1990) protective processes are primarily instrumental in nature. Less attention has been given to the 'coming to terms' or meaning-making aspect of resilience. Understanding the meaning of adverse experiences is an essential aspect of coming out the other side of a deeply distressing event or situation. When sense is restored, individuals are able to comprehend and explain experiences in ways that give meaning, purpose and direction to action (Weick, 1995). Meaning-making is the way resilient people build bridges from present hardships to future better-constructed lives (Coutu, 2002).

In the briefly summarized case that opened this chapter, subsequent events revealed that Matt struggled to make sense out of getting fired. For a long time, he attributed the event to a mistake or 'politics', and could not or would not take any personal responsibility for this adverse experience. After more than a year working with an outplacement counselor and failing to obtain a new position, Matt finally started to come to terms with what happened and why, including his personal responsibility for the situation. It was only when Matt reached this full understanding of his experience that he was able to take appropriate actions that led to his re-employment and a new career.

Several cognitive mechanisms of resilience have been proposed, including replacing a loss with a gain (transcending), recognizing new things about oneself (self-understanding), and making decisions about relinquishing something in life (accommodating) (King et al., 2003b). These processes reflect contextual reframing strategies, in which events are placed into a larger perspective or goals are adjusted to reflect situational constraints. In contextual reframing, the risk-causing experience is still there, but a new understanding has emerged – a new way of seeing the self or the world. These mechanisms are similar to coping stances such as optimism and seeing failure as the best way to learn, but occur within the context of significant adversity. They reflect resilience as a process of conceptual change brought about by significant events and experiences (Dole and Sinatra, 1998). The case of James Reed is an excellent example of these cognitive mechanisms. James was able to recognize core values around family that were threatened, transcend the loss of his goal to become a partner in the consulting firm by establishing a new career goal, and accept this accommodation as a net gain in his leadership development.

The instrumental and cognitive mechanisms of resilience correspond to two basic ways in which individuals adapt to life events. One (assimilation) is primarily action-oriented and involves striving to create change or to achieve one's goals (Brandtstadter, 1998). The other (accommodation) is primarily cognitive and involves self-regulative and self-reflective loops (stimulus control, milieu selection, attentional resource allocation, emotion or motivation control). The self is adjusted to fit the environment through cognitive re-appraisal and reframing strategies (Brandtstadter, 1998).

One of the important lessons from studies on aging is the delicate balance that exists between accommodation and assimilation. Sometimes it is better to relinquish a goal rather than to continue to strive vainly in its pursuit (Brandtstadter and Renner, 1990). Coming to accept limitations or irreversible loss is not a tragedy. On the contrary, disengaging from an unrealistic or blocked goal is adaptive. Accommodating to the situation by rescaling goals or changing one's self-definition allows a person to reinvest energy in another direction. A balance between tenacious goal pursuit (pushing the limits) and flexible goal adjustment (accepting or redefining the limits) is what is needed to be resilient in life (Brandtstadter, 1999). Similarly, in leadership development, leaders must find the balance between unrelenting pursuit of their goals and learning to accept their limitations and relinquishing unrealistic or unobtainable goals. In leadership, it is wise to pick one's battles – making good decisions about what is worth fighting for.

Faced with continuous challenges and the risks inherent in deciding on the most appropriate course of action, leaders frequently experience loss or failure. Leaders who grow and develop in their careers must learn from their losses and failures, and bounce back. They make the best of the situation, develop enhanced self-understanding, recognize whatever their responsibility was in the situation and what they must do differently in the future, and make the appropriate compromises or accommodations in order to move forward in their jobs and careers. Leaders who miss out on a desired promotion, or experience a major setback by losing an important customer to a competitor, must quickly come to terms with what has happened and replace these losses with a new and perhaps quite different goal that will re-focus and motivate them.

In summary, although much has been written about the nature of resilience as a characteristic of all individuals and as a set of fundamental processes by which people adapt to changing environments, little empirical research has been conducted on resilience in management. To provide coherence to the disparate literature and provide guidance for future research, we propose a model of resiliency in the workplace, which is then linked to the self-management of failure and loss. Models help people see the big picture, draw attention to things that matter, and allow them to intervene more effectively in the world (Morrison and Morgan, 1999).

AN AFFECTIVE, COGNITIVE AND BEHAVIORAL SELF-REGULATORY MODEL OF RESILIENCY IN THE WORKPLACE

We propose that the protective factors and processes involved in resilience can be conceptualized in terms of affective, cognitive and behavioral domains (see Figure 13.1). This model was developed based on a comprehensive review of the literature on protective factors for young people at risk due to chronic physical illness or adverse personal circumstances (Masten and Coatsworth, 1998), psychological adaptation across the lifespan (Csikszentmihalyi and Rathunde, 1998), traumatic experience (Janoff-Bulman, 1992), and more general models of resilience (Garmezy, 1983; Luthar, 2006; Rutter, 1987; Wyman et al., 2000). It was necessary to develop our model on the basis of this literature because there has been very little empirical research or theoretical formulations on resilience in the management literature

In the literature, the most commonly identified protective factors are emotional regulation, a sense of agency or self-efficacy, social support or connection to others, positive views of self, engagement in meaningful activity or motivation to be effective in the environment, and a sense of meaning in life and of life (Earvolino-Ramirez, 2007; King et al., 2003b; Masten, 2001). These factors can be grouped into *affective* factors (for example, emotional regulation), *cognitive* or coherence-generating factors (for example, sense of meaning), and *behavioral* or agency-generating factors (for example, self-efficacy). To illustrate, Benard (1991) has identified the attributes of resilience to be social competence (affective), sense of purpose and future (cognitive), and problem-solving skills and autonomy (behavioral). Similarly, Earvolino-Ramirez (2007) proposed the defining attributes of resilience to be positive relationships/social support, sense of humor, easy temperament/flexibility (affective); self-esteem and high expectancy (cognitive); and self-efficacy and self-determination (behavioral).

To pull together the many features and processes involved in resilience, we therefore propose an integrated affective, cognitive and behavioral model of resiliency in the workplace (see Figure 13.1). This model outlines key components of resilience, draws attention to three major types of protective factors, and illuminates the major types of resilience mechanisms.

The visual model illustrates three domains of protective factors: the affective domain (self-regulatory factors), the cognitive domain (coherence-generating factors), and the behavioral domain (agency-generating factors). Each of these protective factors can be understood at the personal, environmental and physiological levels (Curtis and Cicchetti, 2003; Luthar et al., 2000). (We are primarily interested in the personal and environmental levels with respect to leadership resilience and do not include physiological phenomena in the current model.) For example, at the personal level, self-regulatory capacities reflect the affective domain of resiliency; beliefs, worldviews and expectations reflect the cognitive domain; and demonstrated self-efficacy reflects the behavioral domain. At the environmental

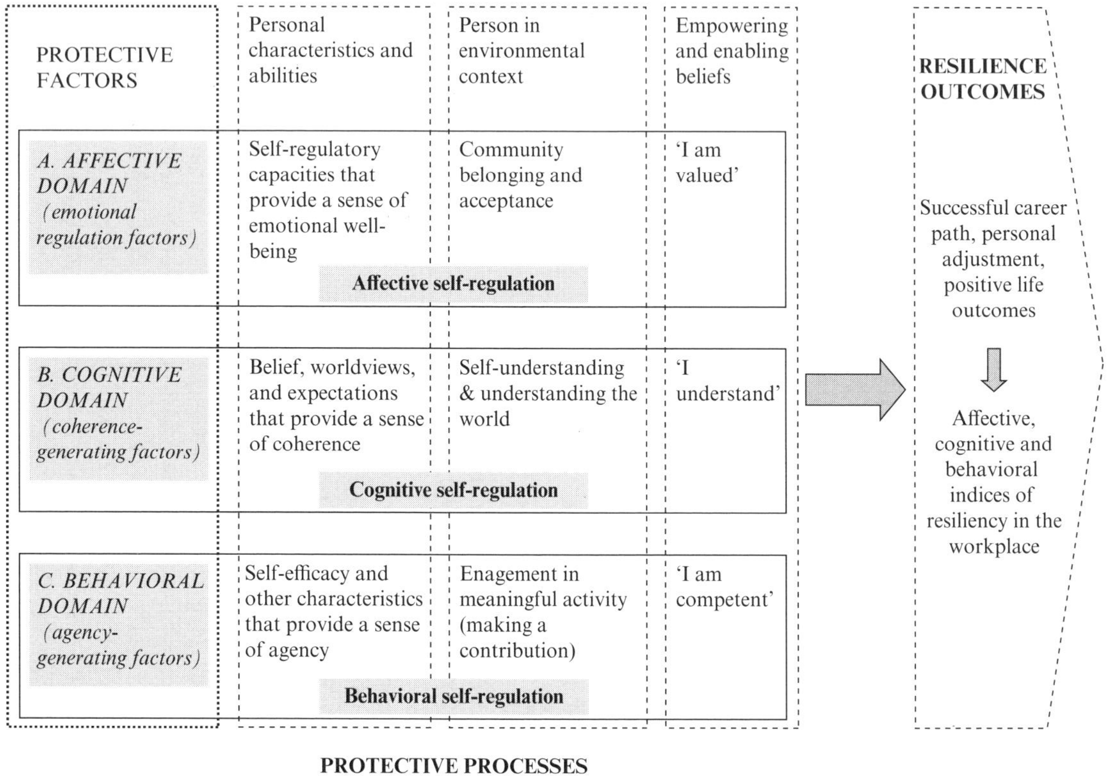

Figure 13.1   An affective, cognitive and behavioral self-regulatory model of resiliency in the workplace

level, a sense of belonging and acceptance reflect the affective domain; self-understanding and understanding the world reflect the cognitive domain; and engagement in meaningful activity reflects in the behavioral domain.

The specific protective processes associated with each domain apply to both the personal and person-in-environment levels. These self-regulatory processes (affective self-regulation, cognitive self-regulation, and behavioral self-regulation) lead to enabling and empowering beliefs ('I am valued', 'I understand' and 'I am competent'), thereby influencing resilience as an outcome. As shown in Figure 13.1, resilience outcomes are defined in terms of successful career paths, personal adjustment and positive life outcomes.

Affective, Cognitive and Behavioral Domains of Resiliency

According to the model, feelings, thoughts and actions are all implicated in resiliency. The affective domain consists of self-regulatory factors that play out on both the personal and person-in-environment levels, including regulation of emotions and thoughts on the personal level, and, on the person-in-environment level, caring and emotionally supportive relationships that lead to a sense of community belonging and acceptance. Personal characteristics in the affective domain include the ability to regulate emotions (Murphy and Moriarty, 1976), emotional stability, and having a sense of humor (Wolin and Wolin, 1993). Positive affect enhances openness and personal capability, and relationships with others provide social support and inspiration (Roberts et al., 2005).

The cognitive domain consists of coherence-generating factors (that is, belief systems, including worldviews, beliefs and expectations) resulting in self-understanding and understanding of the world. Belief systems are considered to be the heart and soul of resilience (Walsh and Walsh, 1998). On the personal level, these cognitive factors include spiritual beliefs (Stinnett and DeFrain, 1985) and sense of coherence (Antonovsky and Sourani, 1989).

The behavioral domain consists of agency-generating factors such as sense of self-efficacy (Garmezy, 1983), problem-solving ability, mastery and the ability to set and persevere at goals. These factors facilitate engagement in meaningful activity.

In our model, we have distinguished among the three components or domains to facilitate a greater understanding of how each domain contributes to empowering beliefs, which in turn influence resilience outcomes. Although resilience, as an outcome, may depend on self-regulation in all three domains, it is useful to consider the contribution of each domain separately, since protective processes associated with each domain are different and have different implications for the self-management of resiliency in leaders.

Self-Regulatory Processes

According to our model, resiliency (or 'bouncing back') is achieved through self-regulatory processes that operate with respect to emotions, thoughts and behaviors. The importance of self-regulation and the existence of affective, cognitive and behavioral self-regulatory processes is supported by theory and research in a number of fields. In optimal human development, individuals develop a flexible repertoire of self-regulative strategies that allow them to adapt to unforeseen conditions (Lerner, 1984). According to Masten (2001), resilience involves a set of basic adaptational processes that include regulation of emotion and behavior, connections to others (attachment), and motivation for learning and engaging in the environment. These processes protect people from stressful emotional and cognitive effects of adversity, and promote mastery (Wyman et al., 2000). In motivational theory, three innate psychological needs are commonly proposed, namely interpersonal relatedness, self-determination and competence (Connell and Wellborn, 1990; Deci and Ryan, 1985). Similarly, Maslow (1970) has discussed three basic human needs – the need for affiliation (belonging), the need for self-actualization (understanding), and the need for achievement (doing). Researchers often emphasize a subset of these processes. For instance Luthar (2006) has stressed the affective functions of interpersonal relationships.

Self-regulation of attention, emotion and behavior is an essential characteristic of successful individuals. Self-regulatory capacities enable individuals to control negative emotions and thoughts, allowing them to move forward from shame, disappointment and disillusionment. Self-regulative and accommodative processes lead to the flexible adjustment of goals, preferences or standards to the situational constraints of the workplace, and to engagement and disengagement in different activities across the life span (Brandtstadter and Renner, 1990). It is important to know when to fight and when to step back, and when to go around an obstacle rather than through it. Flexibility is crucial to resilience (Earvolino-Ramirez, 2007).

CHARACTERISTICS AND ACTIONS OF RESILIENT PEOPLE

In this section we consider in more detail the self-regulatory, coherence-generating and agency-generating protective factors associated with resilience. As noted previously, there is limited work on personal resilience in the management literature. The term 'resilience' has been used broadly, and defined and used differently by each author. Very little of this literature has an empirical base, and there have been no attempts to develop a comprehensive theory of resilience. However, a major theme in the existing literature is the importance of coherence in dealing with career-related losses, including restoration of meaning and redefining the self. Some of the literature also discusses self-regulatory factors, such as the ability to manage one's thoughts and reactions, and the importance of self-awareness. For example, Coutu (2002) discusses the importance of the capacity to accept and face down reality, and Doe (1994) considers the ability to be flexible and quickly adapt to changes in the work environment.

In the following sections, we consider each of the three major types of factors in the resiliency model. We then integrate what is known in the management literature with this broader view of resilience, and provide workplace examples of the characteristics and actions of resilient people.

Emotional Regulation Factors

> When we begin to take our failures non-seriously, it means we are ceasing to be afraid of them. It is of immense importance to learn to laugh at ourselves.
>
> (Katherine Mansfield)

These factors include the ability to engage in self-reflection and develop a high awareness of one's feelings and thoughts (Hauser, 1999). The effective self-regulation of feelings and affective responses is critical to attaining resilience outcomes. Major setbacks in personal or organizational performance may cause intense anxiety due to their career implications. In the previously discussed case of Matt, the leader who was fired for reasons he could not at first understand, an analysis of the case reveals that Matt had commonly expressed emotional outbursts to his superiors when his ideas or decisions were challenged. Despite Matt's objectively assessed high performance, his boss eventually lost patience with Matt's immaturity and self-centeredness, and this contributed substantially to the decision that Matt could no longer remain on the senior management team. In this case, Matt's resilience was shown in how he dealt with the major disappointment and shame he felt about his job loss. Over time, he came to accept the role played by his failure to regulate his emotions and, through this enhanced self-understanding, was able to develop strategies to deal with this area of weakness and to put aside the turmoil created by the whole situation, and move on with his career.

Coherence-Generating Factors

> There are no failures – just experiences and your reactions to them.
>
> (Tom Krause)

Belief systems enable individuals to regain a sense of meaning after workplace failure or loss. Belief systems encompass such things as dreams and goals, religious faith, beliefs about what is important in life, fundamental values, ways of seeing or knowing the world, the existential meaning of life, and beliefs about the self (Glantz and Johnson, 1999; Urbanowski and Vargo, 1994). Values, in particular, are a critical component of a leader's self-awareness because values influence people's preferences, perceptions of problems, and choice of behavior (Yukl, 1998).

Belief systems are important to resilience for several interrelated reasons. They provide a sense of meaning in life, a sense of purpose or direction, and a sense of hope or optimism in the face of life's adversities. People who have a strong sense of meaningfulness in life have a pervasive and enduring feeling of confidence. They view activities and events as challenging and as worthy of emotional investment and commitment (Antonovsky, 1984). In addition, belief systems motivate people and create a direction for their efforts by providing anchorage and stability (Glantz and Johnson, 1999). Belief systems can also generate hopefulness and thereby lead to perseverance and determination (Glantz and Johnson, 1999).

Belief systems – particularly values – are implicated in two of the major theories of leadership, transformational leadership (Bass and Avolio, 1990) and charismatic leadership (Shamir et al., 1993). The inspirational motivation component of transformational leadership includes communicating a vision of what can be achieved and influencing followers to value the goals of the organization or team over their own self-interest. Burns (1978) describes transformational leaders as those who appeal to positive moral values and higher order needs of followers. Similarly, charismatic leaders seek to build commitment to the ideals of an organization and emphasize internalizing organizational values over personal self-interest (House and Howell, 1992; Howell, 1988; Shamir et al., 1993). Although we are not aware of any research that has linked transformational or charismatic leadership to personal resilience, conceptually these leadership values are very consistent with belief systems linked to resilience. These leadership values reflect a sense of what is really important and what provides meaning in life, and project a vision of optimism and hopefulness. Values can carry a person through adversity and often become clearer after a period of hardship.

The ability to make sense of events and experiences – to understand them and then 'let them go' – is fundamental to resilience (Earvolino-Ramirez, 2007; King et al., 2003b). Turning points come to an end when there is a sense of coming to terms, acceptance or resolution. This does not mean passive acceptance or admission of culpability but rather a sense of dismissal or reduction of the experience in importance. The experience is reframed and put into another perspective. James Reed once again provides an excellent example of reframing a negative experience and resolving to change career directions, based on his identification with and acceptance of core values around family. He became clearer about his need to live in accordance with his values, which included the importance of family life.

Coherence-generating factors include self-complexity in recognizing multiple facets to different situations (Hauser, 1999) and spirituality, which refers to the basic human need to experience meaning, purpose and connectedness. Spirituality is a critical component of life, inclusive of all faiths and beliefs, including beliefs expressed within and outside of a religious framework (McColl, 2000). Spiritual beliefs have long been implicated in resilience.

Agency-Related Factors

Never confuse a single defeat with a final defeat.

(F. Scott Fitzgerald)

Agency-related factors are those implicated in regaining a sense of control after workplace failure or loss. These factors operate through adaptational processes that meet basic human needs for control. Individuals come out the other side of adverse experiences when they regain a sense of control over a new direction in life – a renewed sense of self-determination involving realistic goals.

Characteristics such as perseverance, determination and self-efficacy have repeatedly been found to be of importance in studies of resiliency (Hauser, 1999; King et al., 2003b), and effectance motivation is considered to be a fundamental adaptational process underlying resilience (Masten, 2001). Persistence and ambition in careers is also considered to be a major protective attribute (Hauser, 1999). Once again, there is no empirical research that we are aware of in the leadership literature that specifically links these characteristics to leader resilience. However, the characteristics of perseverance, ambition, determination and the like have been associated with managerial leadership (e.g., Hogan, 1991; Howard and Bray, 1988) and it is logically consistent to assume that, as with the literature cited above, these characteristics would contribute to resilience in the process of leadership as well. Certainly, in the two case studies we have been considering, these characteristics contributed to resilience-related outcomes. In the case of Matt, it took more than a year of getting over his resistance to accepting what had happened and coming to terms with his own responsibility for getting fired, but he was determined to get back into a senior management position and his persistence and ambition (along with an equally persistent relocation counselor) eventually led to success. James Reed also experienced a very difficult period in which he had to come to the realization that his career goal was not attainable unless he was willing to sacrifice his family. But along with the other factors discussed earlier, James was determined to resolve this internal conflict and his strong sense of self-efficacy helped him to adapt and move into his next career.

Resilience in the Management Literature

In this section, we consider how resilience has been discussed in the management literature, showing how the focus has been on resilience as a personal quality and outcome, rather than as an ongoing adaptational process involving self-regulation of emotion, thought and behavior.

Sonnenfeld and Ward (2008) recently discussed how great leaders rebound after career disasters. Some individuals are energized by their losses (the notion of 'steeling qualities'), while others are defeated. Great leaders are considered to possess powerful skills in three areas: ability to candidly self-assess strengths and weaknesses, ability to analyze situations appropriately, and capacity to reframe their setbacks or losses (Gardner, 1997; Sonnenfeld and Ward, 2008). These characteristics reflect aspects of the three general factors and processes in our resiliency model: emotional self-regulation (ability to self-assess – which includes awareness of feelings) coherence (capacity to reframe), and agency (capacity to act based on appropriate analysis of situations). Of the three characteristics of great leaders, the ability to construe losses in ways that are enabling and empowering appears most conducive to resiliency (Sonnenfeld and Ward, 2008). Sonnenfeld and Ward's (2008) focus is on great leaders, but it is important to realize that all individuals may display resiliency (Bonanno, 2004).

Sonnenfeld and Ward (2008) also discuss the use of personal networks in recovery from setbacks, and silver linings arising from losses brought on by career disasters. These silver linings include discovering what we truly value, who we can really trust, and new dimensions of our own character. These silver linings reflect one of the cognitive processes involved in resiliency – 'transcending' or replacing a loss with a gain (King et al., 2003b). Although discussing thriving at work rather than resilience, Spreitzer et al. (2005) state that positive meaning resources enable individuals to reappraise an event as an opportunity for growth rather than a loss.

Coutu (2002) also views resilience as a set of personal qualities. She considers three main aspects of resilience: the capacity to accept and face down reality, the ability to find meaning in some aspect of life, and the ability to improvise. Accepting and facing down reality reflects a resilient outlook or grounded approach to life, and ability to find meaning is a fundamental coherence-generating aspect of resiliency. The notion that resilient individuals have an ability to innovate seems specific to leadership and managerial success, but is similar to the notion of 'flexibility' or adaptability as an essential marker of resilience.

There is limited literature on resilience in the management literature, and it is not linked to a broad conceptual framework outlining important resiliency-related factors and processes. A limited number of characteristics of resilience have been the focus of attention and there has been no attempt to develop a taxonomy, model or theory of resilience in management or leadership. To address this need, we have taken initial steps to develop a comprehensive model of resiliency. Since very little management-related literature explicitly discusses resilience, we considered related concepts in the management literature in order to extract insights about dealing with workplace adversity. Work on career derailment (Van Velsor and Leslie, 1995) indicates several characteristics critical to success at higher levels. These include the ability to adapt one's thinking to changes in the marketplace and develop multiple perspectives, the ability to deal with change and complexity, and use of a relational management style (Van Velsor and Leslie, 1995). These characteristics essentially deal with ability to adapt to evolving job demands. They deal with general coping and adaptation rather than resiliency-related characteristics that help individuals weather bad times. However, since resilience is a process of adaptation – adaptation to failure and loss – one would expect similar characteristics to assist individuals in bouncing back from hardship in the workplace.

One of the characteristics emphasized by Van Velsor and Leslie (1995) is the ability to use a more relational orientation, to strike a balance between 'mastery over' and 'connection to'. In addition to the ability to connect with or engage with others, a relational management style involves the ability to adapt thinking to changes in the workplace and to develop multiple perspectives. Thus, a relational orientation is similar to the view that resiliency involves finding a balance between accommodation and assimilation in life – knowing when to keep striving (mastery) and when to let go (adaptation to change). Wisdom, a characteristic of great leaders, involves this superlative sense of judgment. Wise individuals have exceptional insight; they make good judgments based on consideration of the broader context (Baltes and Staudinger, 1993, 2000). Wisdom is considered to be a state of mind and behavior reflecting the coordinated and balanced interplay of affective, cognitive and behavioral or motivational aspects of human functioning (Baltes and Staudinger, 2000). As leaders develop wisdom, we also expect them to develop resilience.

Recently, Roberts et al. (2005) have discussed the idea of 'reflected best-self portraits' as pathways for excelling in work organizations. These self-knowledge structures are thought to change as a result of 'jolts' experienced in the workplace. Jolts are similar to turning points, but can be positive or negative in nature and are 'aha' experiences rather than traumatic events. According to Roberts et al. (2005), revisions to individuals' reflected best-self portraits are most likely to occur in the presence of three socially embedded resources (positive affect, positive relationships and personal agency), which enable individuals to respond to jolts in constructive ways. Feelings, thoughts and actions are considered to generate resources that enable individuals to advance along the trajectory of becoming extraordinary. Although this work focuses on excellence, extraordinary achievement and flourishing rather than resilience to failure, the emotional, relational and agentic resources discussed by Roberts et al. (2005) are highly similar to the self-regulatory processes and emotional regulation, coherence-generating and agency-generating protective factors of the broader resiliency model presented here.

Aspects of resiliency not yet considered in the management literature, or which deserve more attention, include the role of supportive mentorship in fostering belief in oneself, the roles of values and integrity, and the use of assimilation strategies such as adapting goals and adopting attitudes of optimism and appreciation. A comprehensive model of resiliency in the workplace must include all the factors identified in the literature across disciplines and apply them to the context of leadership. Such a comprehensive understanding of resiliency will enable researchers to test empirical relationships suggested by the model, which will contribute to our knowledge of the development of resilience in leadership.

TAKING INSTRUMENTAL RESPONSIBILITY FOR PREPARING FOR WORKPLACE ADVERSITY

Aspiring leaders have the personal responsibility to influence and manage their own development. According to Roberts and colleagues (2005), individuals are active participants in constructing their organizational experience and career development, through how they take initiative, seek information about themselves and their performance, and draw from relationships with others. The authors in the current volume share the view that leaders must take more responsibility for their own development, and they provide many specific recommendations on the self-management of leadership development. Resilience-related capacities such as emotional regulation, construction of personal meaning, and a sense of agency and control can be self-developed (Luthans, 2002). As an illustration, research on resiliency in children raised in adverse conditions has led to prevention and intervention approaches focusing on promotion of competence and enhancement of assets (Masten, 2001). The implication is that resiliency can be acquired or learned through self-directed activities and reflection, cultivated mindsets, and supportive environments.

Self-adaptation is a process by which individuals guide goal-directed activities over time and across changing circumstances (Kanfer, 1990). The literature on thriving in the workplace suggests that thriving occurs when individuals are open to challenges and have opportunities to grow (Spreitzer et al., 2005). However, organizations tend to provide generic opportunities rather than ones designed to meet the developmental needs of specific individuals (McCall et al., 1988). Individuals will benefit from setting their own individually-tailored paths to self-development, guided by an integrated framework of their strengths and weaknesses that drives their pursuit of new learning opportunities and experiences. To develop self-integration, leaders need to process their experiences (reflection) and then seek out experiences and settings that provide opportunities for development, all the while integrating this information into a broader view of themselves as a person and leader. A key component of this self-integration is obtaining accurate data on strengths and weaknesses. An excellent source of such data are 360-degree feedback programs. These programs facilitate increased self-awareness, identify development needs, and result in improved leadership performance when appropriate developmental activity is engaged (Waldman and Atwater, 1998).

Leaders must continuously grow, develop and improve their performance capabilities to meet the new and complex challenges they face. In the remainder of this section, we discuss how individuals can take direct personal responsibility for developing resilience-related characteristics, such as emotional regulation, construction of personal meaning, and a sense of agency and control, and for ensuring that they have adequate organizational supports and personal networks, which function as protective factors in times of adversity. We also discuss ways to cultivate self-awareness and self-regulation, and ways to cultivate self-efficacy and a resilient outlook. By highlighting the importance of these factors/processes in achieving a successful career path, personal adjustment and positive life outcomes, the resiliency model (Figure 13.1) indicates how individuals can take responsibility for managing their own development. When individuals realize the importance of positive attitudes, broad perspectives, and the nature of new knowledge or additional skills required to succeed, they can seek out direct experiences, supports and resources to facilitate personal growth (King, 2009). Taking the initiative to target and seek out particular experiences based on identified development needs, such as project work or 'stretch assignments', provides individuals with transformational opportunities for personal growth (Hamel and Valikangas, 2003; Roberts et al., 2005). Feedback from others is a crucial component in developing self-awareness and identifying appropriate development needs, and ultimately self-development (London et al., 1999).

Cultivating Self-Awareness and Affective Self-Regulation

Experiences of positive affect can interrupt the rumination that often occurs in the midst of stressful situations (Folkman and Moskowitz, 2000). This is why activities that bring the self into the body, including physical exercise and laughter, are effective in interrupting worrisome thought patterns and cultivating a sense of appreciation for the present.

A sense of humor – even dark humor – provides a critical sense of perspective (Coutu, 2002) that plays an important role in the ability to make light of adversity (Earvolino-Ramirez, 2007). In addition, it is important to keep expectations of oneself and others low enough to prevent disappointment, yet high enough to provide hope, motivation and goal attainment. The considerable body of research on goal-setting informs this process of identifying realistic expectations. Setting specific challenging, yet realistic goals, has been consistently shown to increase motivation and performance (Locke and Latham, 1990). When faced with failure or disappointment, self-directed goal-setting provides an effective means for leaders to identify a course of action to lead them out of this experience and into the next stage of their leadership careers.

The concept of 'broaden and build' (Frederickson, 2001) is highly relevant to regulating one's emotions and self-development. Frederickson proposes that positive emotions fuel resiliency. Individuals can cultivate experiences of positive emotions in times of adversity, in order to cope with negative emotions. According to this theory, positive emotions broaden people's thought-action repertoires and build enduring personal resources. Again, the self-directed goal-setting process is helpful here. Having a plan for a concrete course of action based on specific challenging, yet realistic goals, provides a means for coping with the negative emotions of shame, disappointment and disillusionment. As the plan is implemented and actions are taken to achieve these goals, the sense of moving on contributes to more positive emotions and resilient outcomes. We do not mean to suggest that this is a quick or easy process. It took Matt well over a year to deal with his anger and resentment at being fired. Moreover, his first goal, to attain a position as president of a major firm, was unrealistic, given that he had been a vice-president in his former job. His continual failure to attain this goal did nothing to dispel his negative emotions. Only when Matt was able to accept what had happened by coming to see the role played by his emotional outbursts, was he able to use this self-understanding to refocus on a more realistic goal, become more positive, and attain resilient outcomes of adjustment and a new career path.

Based on self-awareness and self-knowledge, people can come to understand the particular contexts in which they thrive (Spreitzer et al., 2005). They can then seek out the niches or milieu that are the best fit with their personality and skills. 'Niche seeking' refers to finding healthy contexts that provide opportunities for personally-defined success, desired achievements and mentorship (Scarr and McCartney, 1983). 'Milieu selection' is an accommodative strategy that maximizes the fit between the individual and the environment (Brandtstadter, 1998). 'Social architecting' refers to individuals' proactive selection of settings, people and tasks that draw on their strengths (Roberts et al., 2005). All of these concepts reflect the idea of finding suitable workplace environments, and they help to explain the experience of James Reed. Faced with the anxiety-filled dilemma of choosing between a highly desirable career goal versus a deeply felt personal goal involving his family, James sought a new career direction that fitted better with his values and yet still provided him with opportunities for career achievement.

Cultivating Self-Efficacy and a Resilient Outlook

I have not failed. I've just found 10 000 ways that won't work.
(Thomas Alva Edison)

According to Weick and Sutcliffe (2001), it is important to cultivate the processes of resilience in order to manage the unexpected in the workplace. Organizational leaders require mindsets that allow them to deal with unexpected and rapid change (Daft, 2004). These mindsets include the ability to embrace failure as a fresh opportunity to meet challenges (Sonnenfeld and Ward, 2008). Although leadership training regarding change management almost invariably focuses on managing others in the organization (e.g., Kotter, 1996), rather than the self, the principles and mindsets required to manage crisis and change at the organizational level have much in common with self-management of these issues. For example, understanding and dealing with resistance to change is a major component of efforts to develop change management skills in leaders, and resisting change is also a considerable problem for individuals who experience failure and disappointment and are unable to engage the protective processes necessary for resilience. It took Matt and James Reed considerable time and cognitive effort to come to terms with the reality they were facing. Leaders need to develop mindsets that help them to deal effectively with their own resistance to change, if they are to display resilience in the face of failure.

> Only those who dare to fail greatly can ever achieve greatly.
>
> (Robert F. Kennedy)

Having a sense of purpose in life is a defining characteristic of resilience that can be cultivated. An increased sense of self-determination may result from looking forward to what the future holds, not living in fear of future events, and perceiving experiences constructively, as opportunities for growth (Coutu, 2002; Mallak, 1998). James Reed discovered his sense of purpose when he engaged in a self-assessment process in which he clarified his fundamental values and goals in life. He reconstructed his career and his future in ways that incorporated both his work experience and personal values.

> Fortune favors the prepared mind.
>
> (Louis Pasteur)

Contingency planning and advance preparation provide jumping off points when faced with crucial changes in the workplace. Wise individuals are knowledgeable about alternative back-up strategies to use when development does not proceed as expected (Baltes and Staudinger, 2000). It is unrealistic for leaders to plan their careers as a linear path to some ultimate goal; career planning should include contingencies for failure. Cognitive preparation can build the protective factors and supports that lead to self-regulatory processes, allowing recovery from failure and loss in the workplace.

Social Support: A Relational View of Self-Development

Personal relationships in a leader's social network are one of the most important sources of support for self-development. The supportive benefits of interpersonal networks for the career development of managers have a strong theoretical basis (e.g., Ibarra, 1993) and considerable empirical support (e.g., Rothstein et al., 2001). Furthermore, according to a relational view of self-development, learning occurs from social interaction, and knowledge is gained from discussing challenges with others (Spreitzer et al., 2005). Social support is provided by interpersonal relationships that involve the expression of positive affect, the affirmation or endorsement of a person's beliefs, and the provision of tangible assistance (Kahn and Antonucci, 1980).

Jacobson (1986) defined social support in terms of three types of resources that meet fundamental needs: emotional support (establishing a sense of rapport or belonging), cognitive support (information, knowledge and advice to enable the individual to understand his or her world and adjust to changes), and material support (goods and services to enable doing). Social support makes people feel good about themselves (emotional support), helps them to feel not alone in their situations and experiences (cognitive support), and gives them tools and strategies to address their issues (instrumental support) (King et al., 2006). In other words, support systems and networks improve adaptive competence by providing emotional support and guidance, providing feedback on identity and the accuracy of performance, and promoting mastery (Caplan and Killilea, 1976). Social support therefore facilitates self-regulation of emotion, thought, and behavior. It promotes and encourages the development of empowering and enabling beliefs such as 'I am valued' (self-esteem), 'I am understood' (self-concept), and 'I am competent' (self-efficacy).

Interpersonal relationships and the support they provide play an important role in the development of resilience. Resilient individuals work to ensure they have adequate external resources, including advice, emotional support and practical help (Mallak, 1998), and they use personal networks in their recovery from career setbacks (Sonnenfeld and Ward, 2008). Networks provide inspiration, opportunities and a sense of belonging and connection. It is extremely important to build quality relationships with professional colleagues, even over the internet (Rousseau, 2007).

Seeking a mentor is another important social support strategy. Mentor relationships have been identified as contributing to resilience in high-risk young people (Rhodes, 1994). The role of a mentor can include providing feedback on observed performance, serving as a role model (Benner, 1984), providing one-on-one instruction and encouraging reflection through guided discussion (Heath, 1998), and providing emotional support (Rees and Hays, 1996). Mentors can provide emotional support to help protégés integrate identities through acceptance and confirmation, and can provide knowledge of the workplace context that helps protégés make sense of a traumatic experience (Kram, 1985).

Much more can be said about the supportive role of networks and

Table 13.1   Actions that can be taken to promote personal resilience

Self-understanding and awareness	Approach to life and experiences	Goal-setting and actions
Understand: Your strengths and weaknesses, through reflection and by seeking information and feedback from others	*Cultivate:* A sense of humor, positive emotions, and positive experiences	*Engage in:* Self-directed goal-setting, which will allow you to pursue relevant opportunities and experiences
What is realistic for you to achieve (set realistic expectations for yourself)	A mindset that allows you to deal with the unexpected, be open to change, accept and appreciate reality, and perceive difficult events as opportunities for growth	Networking and mentoring
The particular contexts in which you thrive and then seek out these milieus or workplace environments	A sense of purpose, a larger perspective on what is important, and hope for the future	Contingency planning

mentors in the development of leadership potential generally, and specifically with respect to resiliency. The interested reader is directed to two other chapters in the current volume that are devoted to this critical activity of developing leaders (Chandler and Kram, Chapter 12; Langkamer Ratwani et al., Chapter 14).

In summary, the self-directed actions in Table 13.1 are recommended for the effective self-management of failure and development of resilience. They are based on our review of the literature and our conceptual model of resiliency in the workplace.

DIRECTIONS FOR RESEARCH ON THE ROLE OF PERSONAL RESILIENCE IN SELF- AND CAREER DEVELOPMENT

The study of resilience in the workplace is in its infancy. This chapter has reviewed the literature on resilience in the workplace and compared it to the broader resilience literature. As well, a model of workplace resiliency was proposed, which provides insights into areas where future research is needed. The areas requiring research include detailed examination of the roles and combinations of factors that constrain or enable individuals to be resilient and thrive in the workplace. How does resiliency, as a capacity, affect performance in the workplace (Luthans, 2002)? How crucial are the roles of social networks and mentorship? Which challenging organizational experiences undermine personal growth and which experiences are most likely to promote growth, development, and personally defined success? Which protective processes work best and how do they operate as a whole in contributing to workplace resiliency? What role is played by accommodative processes in achieving resilience-related outcomes (Brandtstadter, 1999)? Finally, there is a need for longitudinal studies examining adaptation and development in response to highly challenging adverse experiences over the career course.

In times of personal hardship, it is important to consider the lessons shared by others about resilience and transcendence of failure and loss in the workplace. Failure and loss are times of opportunity to grow personally and as a leader. Knowing one's needs and what one truly values, employing self-regulatory strategies, and understanding the necessity of support from others, lead to self-integration, strong values and a principled approach to moving successfully through the experience of failure or disappointment. When leaders demonstrate resiliency, they inspire and motivate others in addition to enhancing their own positive life outcomes.

REFERENCES

Antonovsky, A. (1984), 'A call for a new question – salutogenesis – and a proposed answer – the sense of coherence', *Journal of Preventative Psychiatry*, **2**(1), 1–13.

Antonovsky, A. and Sourani, T. (1989), 'Family sense of coherence and family adaptation', *Journal of Marriage and the Family*, **50**, 79–92.

Baltes, P.B. and Staudinger, U.M. (1993), 'The search for a psychology of wisdom', *Current Directions in Psychological Science*, **2**, 1–6.

Baltes, P.B., and Staudinger, U.M. (2000), 'Wisdom: a metaheuristic (pragmatic) to orchestrate mind and virtue toward excellence', *American Psychologist*, **55**(1), 122–36.

Bass, B.M., and Avolio, B.J. (1990), 'The implications of transactional and transformational leadership for individual, team, and organizational development', in W. Pasmore and R.W. Woodman (eds), *Research in Organizational Change and Development*, Vol. 4, Greenwich, CT: JAI Press, pp. 231–72.

Benard, B. (1991), *Fostering Resiliency in Kids: Protective Factors in the Family, School and Community*, Portland, OR: Northwest Regional Educational Laboratory.

Benner, P. (1984), *From Novice to Expert: Excellence and Power in Clinical Nursing Practice*, Menlo Park, CA: Addison-Wesley.

Bonanno, G.A. (2004), 'Loss, trauma, and human resilience: have we underestimated the human capacity to thrive after extremely aversive events?', *American Psychologist*, **59**(1), 20–28.

Brandtstadter, J. (1998), 'Action perspectives on human development', in R.M. Lerner (ed.), *Handbook of Child Psychology. Theoretical Models of Human Development*, 5th edn, Vol. 1, New York: John Wiley, pp. 807–70.

Brandtstadter, J. (1999), 'Sources of resilience in the aging self: toward integrating perspectives', in T.M. Hess and F. Blanchard-Fields (eds), *Social Cognition and Aging*, San Diego, CA: Academic Press, pp. 123–41.

Brandtstadter, J. and Renner, G. (1990), 'Tenacious goal pursuit and flexible goal adjustment: explication and age-related analysis of assimilative and accommodative strategies of coping', *Psychology and Aging*, **5**(1), 58–67.

Bruner, J. (1994), 'The "remembered" self', in U. Neisser and R. Fivush (eds), *The Remembering Self: Construction and Accuracy in the Self-Narrative*, Cambridge, MA: Cambridge University Press, pp. 41–54.

Burns, J.M. (1978), *Leadership*, New York: Harper and Row.

Cameron, K. and Caza, A. (2002), 'Organizational and leadership virtues and the role of forgiveness', *Journal of Leadership and Organizational Studies*, **9**(1), 33.

Cameron, K.S., Dutton, J.E., and Quinn, R.E. (eds) (2003), *Positive Organizational Scholarship*, San Francisco, CA: Berrett-Koehler.

Caplan, G. and Killilea, M. (1976), *Support Systems and Mutual Help*, New York: Grune and Stratton.

Carver, C.S. (1998), 'Resilience and thriving: issues, models, and linkages', *Journal of Social Issues*, **54**, 245–66.

Chandler, D. and Kram, K.E. (in press), 'Enlisting others in your development as a leader', in M.G. Rothstein and R.J. Burke (eds), *Self-management and Leadership Development*, Cheltenham, UK and Northampton, MA, USA: Edward Elgar.

Connell, J.P. and Wellborn, J.G. (1990), 'Competence, autonomy, and relatedness: a motivational analysis of self-system processes', in M. Gunnar and L.A. Sroufe (eds), *Minnesota Symposium on Child Psychology*, Vol. 22, Minneapolis, MN: University of Minnesota Press, pp. 43–77.

Coutu, D.L. (2002), 'How resilience works', *Harvard Business Review*, **80**(5), 46–55.

Csikszentmihalyi, M. and Rathunde, K. (1998), 'The development of the person: an experiential perspective on the ontogenesis of psychological complexity', in R.M. Lerner (ed.), *Handbook of Child Psychology. Theoretical Models of Human Development*, 5th edn, Vol. 1, New York: John Wiley, pp. 635–84.

Curtis, W.J. and Cicchetti, D. (2003), 'Moving research on resilience into the 21st century: theoretical and methodological considerations in examining the biological contributors to resilience', *Developmental Psychopathology*, **15**(3), 773–810.

Daft, R. (2004), *Organization Theory and Design*, 8th edn, Mason, OH: Thomson.

Deci, E.L. and Ryan, R.M. (1985), *Intrinsic Motivation and Self-determination in Human Behavior*, New York: Plenum.

De Kleijn-de Vrankrijker, M.C., Heerkens, Y.F. and van Ravensberg, C.D. (1998), 'Defining disability', in M.A. McColl and J. E. Bickenbach (eds), *Introduction to Disability*, London: W.B. Saunders, pp. 11–18.

Denzin, N.K. (1989), *Interpretive Interactionism*, Newbury Park, CA: Sage.

Doe, P.J. (1994), 'Creating a resilient organization', *Canadian Business Review*, **21**, 22–26.

Dole, J.A. and Sinatra, G.M. (1998), 'Reconceptualizing change in the cognitive construction of knowledge', *Educational Psychologist*, **33**, 109–28.

Earvolino-Ramirez, M. (2007), 'Resilience: a concept analysis', *Nursing Forum*, **42**(2), 73–82.

Folkman, S. and Moskowitz, J.T. (2000), 'Positive affect and the other side of coping', *American Psychologist*, **55**(6), 647–54.

Frederickson, B.L. (2001), 'The role of positive emotions in positive psychology: the broaden-and-build theory of positive emotions', *American Psychologist*, **56**, 218–26.

Gardner, H. (1997), *Extraordinary Minds: Portraits of Four Exceptional Individuals and an Examination of Our Own Extraordinariness*, New York: Basic Books.

Garmezy, N. (1983), 'Stressors of childhood', in N. Garmezy and M. Rutter (eds), *Stress, Coping, and Development in Children*, New York: McGraw-Hill, pp. 43–84.

Glantz, M.D. and Johnson, J.L. (1999), *Resilience and Development: Positive Life Adaptations*, New York: Kluwer.

Hamel, G. and Valikangas, L. (2003), 'The quest for resilience', *Harvard Business Review*, **81**(9), 52–63.

Hauser, S.T. (1999), 'Understanding resilient outcomes: adolescent lives across time and generations', *Journal of Research on Adolescence*, **9**(1), 1–24.

Heath, H. (1998), 'Reflection and patterns of knowing in nursing', *Journal of Advanced Nursing*, **27**, 1054–9.

Hechtman, L. (1991), 'Resilience and vulnerability in long term outcome of attention deficit hyperactive disorder', *Canadian Journal of Psychiatry*, **36**, 415–21.

Hogan, R.T. (1991), 'Personality and personality measurement', in M.D. Dunnette and L.M. Hough (eds), *Handbook of Industrial and Organizational Psychology*, Vol. 2, Palo Alto, CA: Consulting Psychologist Press, pp. 873–919.

House, R.J. and Howell, J.M. (1992), 'Personality and charismatic leadership', *Leadership Quarterly*, **3**(2), 81–108.

Howard, A. and Bray, D.W. (1988), *Managerial Lives in Transition*, New York: Guilford Press.

Howell, J.M. (1988), 'Two faces of charisma: socialized and personalized leadership in organizations', in J.A. Conger and R.N. Kanungo (eds), *Charismatic Leadership: The Elusive Factor in Organizational Effectiveness*, San Francisco, CA: Jossey-Bass, pp. 213–36.

Hupcey, J.E. (1998), 'Social support: assessing conceptual coherence', *Qualitative Health Research*, **8**(3), 304–18.

Ibarra, H. (1993), 'Personal networks of women and minorities in management: a conceptual framework', *Academy of Management Review*, **18**, 56–87.

Jacobson, D.E. (1986), 'Types and timing of social support', *Journal of Health and Social Behavior*, **27**(3), 250–64.

Janoff-Bulman, R. (1992), *Shattered Assumptions: Towards a New Psychology of Trauma*, New York: MacMillan.

Kahn, R.L. and Antonucci, T. (1980), 'Convoys over the life course: attachment, roles, and social support', in P.B. Baltes and O. Brim (eds), *Life-span Development and Behavior*, Vol. 3, Boston: Lexington Press, pp. 254–86.

Kanfer, R. (1990), 'Motivation and individual differences in learning: an integration of developmental, differential and cognitive perspectives', *Learning Individual Differences*, **2**, 221–39.

King, G. (2009), 'A framework of personal and environmental learning-based strategies to foster therapist expertise', *Learning in Health and Social Care*, **8**(3), 185–99.

King, G.A. Brown, E.G. and Smith, L.K. (2003a), *Resilience: Learning from People with Disabilities and the Turning Points in their Lives*, Westport, CT: Praeger.

King, G., Willoughby, C., Specht, J. and Brown, E. (2006), 'Social support processes and the adaptation of individuals with chronic disabilities', *Qualitative Health Research*, **16**(7), 1–24.

King, G., Cathers, T., Brown, E., Specht, J.A., Willoughby, C., Miller Polgar, J. et al. (2003b), 'Turning points and protective processes in the lives of people with chronic disabilities', *Qualitative Health Research*, **13**(2), 184–206.

Kotter, J.P. (1996), *Leading Change*, Boston, MA: Harvard Business School Press.

Kram, K.E. (1985), *Mentoring at Work: Developmental Relationships in Organizational Life*, Glenview, IL: Scott Foresman.

Langkamer, L.K., Zaccaro, S.J., Garven, S. and Geller, D.S. (in press), 'The role of developmental social networks in effective leader self-learning processes', in M.G. Rothstein and R.J. Burke (eds), *Self-management and Leadership Development*, Cheltenham, UK and Northampton, MA, USA: Edward Elgar.

Lerner, R.M. (1984), *On the Nature of Human Plasticity*, New York: Cambridge University Press.

Locke, E.A. and Latham, G.P. (1990), *A Theory of Goal Setting and Task Performance*, Englewood Cliffs, NJ: Prentice Hall.

London, M., Larsen, H.H., and Thisted, L.N. (1999), 'Relationships between feedback and self-development', *Group and Organization Management*, **24**(1), 5–27.

Luthans, F. (2002), 'The need for and meaning of positive organizational behavior', *Journal of Organizational Behavior*, **23**(6), 695–706.

Luthans, F. and Avolio, B. (2003), 'Authentic leadership development', in K.S. Cameron, J.E. Dutton and R.E. Quinn (eds), *Positive Organizational Scholarship: Foundations of a New Discipline* San Francisco, CA: Berrett-Koehler, pp. 241–58.

Luthar, S.S. (2006), 'Resilience in development: a synthesis of research across five decades', in D. Cicchetti and D.J. Cohen (eds), *Developmental Psychopathology: Risk, Disorder, and Adaptation*, 2nd edn, New York: Wiley, pp. 739–95.

Luthar, S.S., Cicchetti, D. and Becker, B. (2000), 'The construct of resilience: a critical evaluation and guidelines for future work', *Child Development*, **71**(3), 543–62.

Maddi, S.R. (2005), 'On hardiness and other pathways to resilience', *American Psychologist*, **60**(3), 261–2, 265–7.

Mallak, L. (1998), 'Putting organizational resilience to work', *Industrial Management*, **40**(6).

Mandelbaum, D.G. (1973), 'The study of life history: Gandhi', *Current Anthropology*, **14**, 177–206.

Maslow, A.H. (1970), *Motivation and Personality*, 2nd edn, New York: Harper and Row.

Masten, A.S. (2001), 'Ordinary magic: resilience processes in development', *American Psychologist*, **56**(3), 227–38.

Masten, A.S. and Coatsworth, J.D. (1998), 'The development of competence in favorable and unfavorable environments: lessons from research on successful children', *American Psychologist*, **53**(2), 205–20.

Masten, A.S., Best, K.M. and Garmezy, N. (1990), 'Resilience and development: contributions from the study of children who overcome adversity', *Development and Psychopathology*, **2**, 425–44.

McCall, M.W., Lombardo, M.M. and Morrison, A.M. (1988), *The Lessons of Experience: How Successful Executives Develop on the Job*, Lexington, MA: Lexington Books.

McColl, M.A. (2000), 'Spirit, occupation and disability', *Canadian Journal of Occupational Therapy*, **67**(4), 217–28.

Mikalachki, A. (1994), *Kapco (A,B,C,D) (Case Nos. 993D105, 993D016, 993D017, 993D018)*, London, Canada: Richard Ivey School of Business, The University of Western Ontario.

Morrison, M. and Morgan, M.S. (1999), 'Models as mediating instruments', in M.S. Morgan and M. Morrison (eds), *Models as Mediators: Perspectives on Natural and Social Sciences*, Cambridge: Cambridge University Press, pp. 10–37.

Moses, B. (1997), *Career Intelligence*, Toronto, Canada: Stoddart.

Murphy, L.B. and Moriarty, A. (1976), *Vulnerability, Coping, and Growth: From Infancy to Adolescence*, New Haven, CT: Yale University Press.

Rees, P.G. and Hays, B.J. (1996), 'Fostering expertise in occupational health nursing: levels of skill development', *Journal of the American Association of Occupational Health Nursing*, **44**(2), 67–72.

Reid, G.J., Stewart, M., Mangham, C., and McGrath, P.J. (1996), 'Resiliency: relevance to health promotion', *Health and Canadian Society*, **4**(1), 83–116.

Rhodes, J.E. (1994) 'Older and wiser: mentoring relationships in childhood and adolescence', *The Journal of Primary Prevention*, **14**(3), 187–96.

Richardson, G. (2002), 'The metatheory of resilience and resiliency', *Journal of Clinical Psychology*, **58**, 307–21.

Roberts, L.M., Dutton, J., Spreitzer, G., Heaphy, E. and Quinn, R. (2005), 'Composing the reflected best-self portrait: pathways for becoming extraordinary in work organizations', *Academy of Management Review*, **30**(4), 712–36.

Rothstein, M.G. (1995), *James Reed (A,B) (Case Nos. 9A95C023, 9A98C018)*, London, Canada: Richard Ivey School of Business, The University of Western Ontario.

Rothstein, M.G., Burke, R.J. and Bristor, J. M. (2001), 'Structural characteristics and support benefits in the interpersonal networks of women and men in management', *International Journal of Organizational Analysis*, **9**, 4–25.

Rousseau, D.M. (2007), 'Standing out in the fields of organization science', *Journal of Organizational Behavior*, **28**, 849–57.

Rutter, M. (1985), 'Resilience in the face of adversity: protective factors and resistance to psychiatric disorder', *British Journal of Psychiatry*, **147**, 598–611.

Rutter, M. (1987), 'Psychosocial resilience and protective mechanisms', *American Journal of Orthopsychiatry*, **57**(3), 316–31.

Rutter, M. (1990), 'Psychosocial resilience and protective mechanisms', in J. Rolf, A.S. Masten, D. Cicchetti, K.H. Neuchterlein and S. Weintraub (eds), *Risk and Protective Factors in the Development of Psychopathology*, Cambridge, UK: Cambridge University Press, pp. 181–214.

Scarr, S. and McCartney, K. (1983), 'How people make their own environments: a theory of genotype-environment effects', *Child Development*, **54**, 424–35.

Seligman, M.E.P. and Csikszentmihalyi, M. (2000), 'Positive psychology: an introduction', *American Psychologist*, **55**(1), 5–14.

Shamir, B., House, R.J. and Arthur, M.B. (1993), 'The motivational effects of charismatic leadership: a self-concept based theory', *Organizational Science*, **4**, 1–17.

Sonnenfeld, J. and Ward, A. (2008), 'How great leaders rebound after career disasters', *Organizational Dynamics*, **37**(1), 1–20.

Spreitzer, G., Sutcliffe, K., Dutton, J., Sonenshein, S. and Grant, A.M. (2005), 'A socially embedded model of thriving at work', *Organization Science*, **16**(5), 537–49.

Spreitzer, G.M. (2006), 'Leading to grow and growing to lead: leadership development lessons from positive organizational studies', *Organizational Dynamics*, **35**(4), 305–15.

Steinhauer, P.D. (1997), 'Developing resiliency in children from disadvantaged populations', in *Canada Health Action: Building on the Legacy. Determinants of Health: Children and Youth*, Sainte-Foy, QC: Editions MultiMondes, pp. 51–102.

Stewart, M., Reid, G. and Mangham, C. (1997), 'Fostering children's resilience', *Journal of Pediatric Nursing*, **12**, 21–31.

Stinnett, N. and DeFrain, J. (1985), 'Spiritual wellness', in *Secrets of Strong Families*, Boston, MA: Little, Brown and Company, pp. 100–121.

Sutcliffe, K.M. and Vogus, T.J. (2003), 'Organizing for resilience', in K.S. Cameron, J.E. Dutton and R.E. Quinn (eds), *Positive Organizational Scholarship: Foundations of a New Discipline*, San Francisco, CA: Berrett-Koehler, pp. 94–121.

Urbanowski, R. and Vargo, J. (1994), 'Spirituality, daily practice, and the occupational performance model', *Canadian Journal of Occupational Therapy*, **61**(2), 88–94.

Van Velsor, E. and Leslie, J.B. (1995), 'Why executives derail: perspectives across time and cultures', *Academy of Management Executive*, **9**(4), 62–72.

Waldman, D.A. and Atwater, L.E. (1998), *The Power of 360 Feedback*, Houston, TX: Gulf Publishing.

Walsh, F. (2003), 'Family resilience: a framework for clinical practice', *Family Process*, **42**(1), 1–18.

Walsh, F. and Walsh, F. (1998), 'Belief systems: the heart and soul of resilience', in *Strengthening Family Resilience*, New York: Guilford Press, pp. 45–78.

Weick, K.E. (1995), *Sensemaking in Organizations*, Thousand Oaks, CA: Sage.

Weick, K.E. and Sutcliffe, K.M. (2001), *Managing the Unexpected: Assuring High Performance in an Age of Complexity*, San Francisco, CA: Jossey-Bass.

Werner, E. and Smith, R. (1992), *Overcoming the Odds: High Risk Children from Birth to Adulthood*, Ithaca, NY: Cornell University Press.

Werner, E.E. (1982), *Vulnerable but Invincible: A Longitudinal Study of Resilient Children and Youth*, New York: McGraw-Hill.

Wolin, S.J. and Wolin, S. (1993), *The Resilient Self*. New York: Villard.

Wyman, P.A., Sandler, I., Wolchik, S., Nelson, K., Cicchetti, D., Rappaport, J. et al. (2000), 'Resilience as cumulative competence promotion and stress protection: theory and intervention', in *The Promotion of Wellness in Children and Adolescents*, Washington, DC: Child Welfare League of American Press, pp. 133–84.

Yukl, G. (1998), *Leadership in Organizations*, Upper Saddle River, NJ: Prentice-Hall.

14. The role of developmental social networks in effective leader self-learning processes

Krista Langkamer Ratwani, Stephen J. Zaccaro, Sena Garven and David S. Geller

Today's dynamic, post-industrial work environment demands continuous employee development. The rapid pace of change, however, does not allow for the efficient delivery of formal organizational training on each and every skill-domain combination that shifting environmental contingencies may require for success. Accordingly, for organizations to maintain (and, indeed, enhance) their competitive advantage, their employees need to be engaged in continuous learning (Sessa and London, 2006), primarily through the learning mechanisms of self-development. Self-development is a fully learner-constructed process that individuals undertake in order to gain knowledge or strengthen a skill-set (Confessore and Kops, 1998). Specifically, the focus of this chapter is on *leader* self-development. Constantly changing work demands make identifying particular skills that leaders need in the near and far future extremely difficult (Hall, 1986). The idiosyncratic nature of these shifting skill requirements often means that employees need to take some of the responsibility for their own leader development. However, understanding this development process itself, as well as the means to more effectively facilitate it, is an area in need of more research.

The leader self-development process requires a number of specific preparatory and supporting actions to maximize potential learning gains for the leader. Preparatory actions concern those activities in which leaders engage to establish an effective foundation for pending self-development activities. Such activities can include an analysis of what entails effective leadership, a self appraisal of one's own strengths and developmental needs as a leader, and a general inventory of learning resources available to the self developer. Supporting actions refer to those activities that foster and nurture the ongoing process of self-development. These activities can include use of specific learning tools directly tied to self-development goals, ongoing assessment of learning gains, and use of self-motivators to encourage adherence to self-development curricula. Both sets of activities are vital to effective self-development; in this chapter, we integrate them into a *self-instructional system* that is specifically patterned on classic training models (Goldstein and Ford, 2002). A foundational thesis of our chapter is that self-learners need to use the same procedures and processes that define formal training systems, including a needs assessment, definition of learning objectives, construction of an instructional curriculum, assessment of progress through the curriculum, and evaluation of total learning gains, including transfer of such gains to performance environments (Cortina et al., 2004; Goldstein and Ford, 2002). Accordingly, self-developers need particular resources and skills in self-appraisal, self-regulation, and in the development of self-learning curricula. Yet, self-learners generally do not have the full range of these skills, nor are they typically effective in understanding how to use available resources to accomplish these self-training activities.

To accomplish both the preparatory and supportive activities of self-development, individuals need to find and utilize a variety of resources that (a) provide a means for actual learning and development to occur, and (b) help them stay motivated by and throughout the self-development process. One key set of resources refers to the advisors, mentors, coaches, peers, instructors, supervisors and subordinates that can potentially help the self-developer prepare an effective self-learning curriculum and also work through this curriculum to a successful completion. These connections can be defined as constituting a *social network* (Brass et al., 2004; Tichy et al., 1979) that leaders can use to facilitate their self-development. The primary focus of this chapter is on how a leader's social network can serve as a learning resource within a self-instructional system. Each individual occupying a node in the self-learner's social network fulfills a different role that can have varying effects on the development process. Together, these individuals comprise a system that we label a *developmental social network* (cf. McCauley and Douglas, 2004, on 'developmental relationships'). We describe in this chapter ways a developmental social network can facilitate specific preparatory and supportive self-development activities.

This approach to understanding leader growth through social networks presents a unique perspective on the self-development process. Previous research on self-development has focused on dyadic relationships and how such relationships aid in self-development. For example, research has studied the impact of perceived leader support on intention to engage in self-development activities (Boyce, 2004; Maurer and Tarulli, 1994), and the impact of leader modeling behaviors on the quality of leader self-development activities (Langkamer, 2008). The ideas presented in this chapter go beyond past research, however, by using the concept that a leader's relationships are part of a system or network that exerts an integrated influence on that leader's self-learning processes. As leaders engage in the self-development process, the relationships in their networks interact in unique ways to provide recommendations, help and support. Further, the combination of different relationships, and therefore perspectives, can help leaders derive a more integrated understanding of leadership; they also benefit from a more comprehensive and more effective self-development process. In addition, the unique aspects of each leader's developmental social network (for example, density, nature of ties) may serve as predictors of self-learning outcomes. We will explore these ideas further in this chapter.

The ideas presented in this chapter align with research that discusses mentoring and the importance of developmental networks (e.g., Higgins and Kram, 2001). The original work by Kram (1985) in this area asserts that individuals do not just rely on select mentors to provide developmental support, but instead, have a 'relationship constellation' that comprises a network of individuals who are all developmentally supportive. Drawing on this work to make assertions about how social networks can aid in leader self-development is useful. However, our work differs in several important ways from the work on mentoring. First, our work expands how we think about the use of networks to a wider focus. Leader self-development is a large process, of which only one component is mentoring. Examining the function of networks from this larger perspective requires thinking about multiple ways such connections can be developmental. Second, our work here attempts to delve more deeply into how leaders' social networks can foster each of the processes within the self-instructional system.

Although researchers (e.g., McCauley and Douglas, 2004) have extolled the developmental functions that others play in leader development, the exact process of how these individuals may best provide developmental benefits is not clear. For example, the different roles various learning partners play can trigger comparison processes for the self-learner that assist at multiple points in a self-instructional system; our use of social psychological theory to make these assertions provides an alternative perspective on the use of social networks as developmental entities. Also, different types of learning partners (for example, mentor, boss, peers, coaches) can present alternative perspectives on the self-learner's role in the organization, helping that leader derive a more integrated and complex understanding of leadership. Our emphasis on an accurate self-appraisal and the specification of appropriate self-learning objectives within the self-instructional systems rests on self-developers having this understanding.

In the next section, we detail the process of self-development and the steps involved in effectively engaging in leader self-development activities. Then, we describe the nature of developmental social networks and the individuals who are part of this network. Finally, we discuss the role that each of these individuals plays at various stages of the leader self-development process and the unique contribution each makes to the self-learner's growth as a leader.

THE PROCESS OF LEADER SELF-DEVELOPMENT

Leader self-development is defined as 'a process in which leaders take personal responsibility for initiating, sustaining, and evaluating growth in their own leadership capacities and in their conceptual frames about the conduct of leadership' (Boyce et al., in press). Self-development represents a form of continuous self-learning. Therefore, it must follow a formalized learning process in order to be effective. We propose that the self-development learning process should follow the instructional systems model put forth by Goldstein and Ford (2002) which calls for both preparatory and supportive actions. This process contains five steps that, if followed, will help leader self-developers increase their leadership capacity: 1) assessment of learning and development needs; 2) identification and development of learning objectives; 3) development of a learning curriculum; 4) development of learning criteria to monitor goal progress; and 5) evaluation of learning gains. The first two steps can be considered preparatory actions in that they provide a strong foundation for the remaining steps in the process. Steps 3 to 5 reflect supporting actions that help the leader maintain the continuous process of self-development.

Even though these steps were put forth in regard to more traditional training systems, they still apply to self-development. A key difference, though, is that in a self-training system, the individual learner is obviously in control of, and responsible for, each of the steps to a much greater extent than in a traditional training system. Typically, self-development efforts are often unsystematic and not tied coherently to skill and knowledge deficits (Cortina et al., 2004). Leaders who engage the prescribed steps in the self-instructional system are more likely to confront the challenges associated with self-development successfully, and perhaps ensure that skill growth or development is actually occurring. The remainder of this section will discuss each of these steps, and why each one is necessary for effective leader self-development.

1.   Assessment of Learning and Development Needs

One's ability to assess one's developmental needs provides the cornerstone to successful leader self-development activities. Without carefully identifying and understanding what skills need to be developed, leaders are likely to target the wrong skill-set, ensuring that the self-development activities will not increase one's leader capacity. Thus, in order to assess developmental needs appropriately, individuals need to develop *self-awareness* about their strengths and weaknesses. Self-awareness is 'a measure of the person's ability to be truly conscious of the components of the self and to observe it accurately and objectively' (Hall, 2004: p. 154). The development of self-awareness has been highlighted several times in the leader development arena as one of the keys to engaging in effective development (cf. Cortina et al., 2004; London, 1995; 2002).

This process of self-awareness is analogous to the needs assessment phase in more traditional instructional design systems (Goldstein and Ford, 2002). Also, self-awareness derives from self-regulation processes, particularly the subprocess of self-evaluation. Self-regulation is the mechanism by which individuals direct their goals over time by modifying thoughts, affect and behavior in comparison with some set standard (Carver and Scheier, 1982; Porath and Bateman, 2006). This process begins with a self-evaluation that may produce a self-assessed gap in skills or discrepancy between current skill-sets and skills needed in the future (for example, for a future or desired leadership position). According to self-regulation theory, individuals will then allocate attention and resources toward these self-discrepancies in order to bring about change (Kanfer and Ackerman, 1989). Also, the observed gap between current and desired leadership states serves as a motivator for a leader to engage in self-development activities.

Another perspective on this self-appraisal process derives from social comparison theory (Festinger, 1950), as well as from the concepts of actual, possible/ideal, and feared selves (Higgins, 1987; Markus and Nurius, 1986). An individual's assessment of his or her actual self defines the self in the present and includes current leadership roles and current strengths and weaknesses. In contrast, the possible or ideal self is future-oriented and defines what the self would like to be. Finally, a feared self represents what an individual does not want to become. Each of these 'selves' can foster a comparison process and provide motivation for skill development that moves the self-learner toward the ideal self and away from the feared self. Murphy (2002) specifically applied these concepts to the leader by indicating that leaders possess ideas about an ideal leader-self, or an ideal set of skills and abilities that they believe an effective leader possesses. This ideal leader-self provides a powerful basis for the self-appraisal aspects of the leader's self-instructional system. Cortina et al. (2004, p. 5) posited several steps in this appraisal, including the following:

- Assessment of one's own leader role requirements and the nature of effective leadership;
- Specification of one's ideal leader self within the context of current and anticipated leader roles;
- Assessment of one's actual leader self;
- Perceived discrepancy between one's ideal and actual leader self;
- Perceived capability to reduce this discrepancy.

The two core processes in these five steps are (a) the comparison of one's ideal and actual leader selves, and (b) the self-learner's felt efficacy in reducing any observed discrepancies. These two processes should help the self-learner construct definable learning goals and objectives (Goldstein and Ford, 2002).

2.   Identification and Development of Learning Objectives

After conducting a needs assessment or self-evaluation to determine strengths and weaknesses, self-learners should set learning goals and objectives based on any gaps noted during the self-appraisal process. Goal choice is one of the main components of the self-regulation process (Chen et al., 2005). Goal choice is important because it dictates the direction in which self-learners will expend effort. Goals also serve as the anchors for evaluation of learning progress, and for potential decisions to alter the learning curriculum if learning objectives are not being met.

Learning goals and objectives that are likely to be effective in a self-instructional system have several key properties. First, they are challenging but realistic (Locke and Latham, 1990; Ting and Hart, 2004). Challenging or difficult goals motivate learners and achievers; easy goals do not (Locke, 1968; 1982). Second, goals must be specific enough to promote effective goal planning and the development of goal implementation strategies (Earley and Perry, 1987; Locke and Latham, 1990). Third, goals and learning objectives should be stated in behavioral terms that promote later assessment of learning gains (Ting and Hart, 2004). Indeed, some training researchers argue that learning objectives should be stated in terms of what the learner will accrue from successfully completing the training effort (Gagne et al., 1992; Goldstein and Ford, 2002; Mager, 1984). These attributes of learning goals and objectives feed directly into the subsequent steps in the self-instructional system (Goldstein and Ford, 2002).

Unless facilitated by a coach (Ting and Hart, 2004), self developers rarely think systematically about what their developmental objectives and goals relative to their strengths and developmental needs should be; nor do they define their objectives and goals with the aforementioned level of detail. The result can be a self-development effort that short-circuits to failure.

3. Development of Learning Curriculum

Following the appraisal and awareness of one's ideal and actual leader self, and the setting of goals to reduce perceived discrepancies between the two, the next step in the leader self-development process is determining how learning goals will be met – what activities will be completed to achieve stated goals? Goals dictate *what* needs to be done, and the learning curriculum spells out *how* it will be done. The learning curriculum should be as detailed a course of action as necessary for goal completion. For example, it should contain information about the type of self-development activity the leader will complete for each goal (for example, read a specific book, attend a specific seminar), any resources to be utilized, the timeframe for completing that goal or each step involved in reaching the goal (Ting and Hart, 2004). An especially useful tool to utilize when developing a learning curriculum is a *learning contract* (also called a 'learning agenda' by Ting and Hart, 2004). Learning or behavioral contracts are agreements about the goals that individuals have and the detailed steps they will take to reach stated goals in specified amounts of time. Learning contracts are beneficial because they provide the level of structure that allows learners to have more control over their actual learning (Ellinger, 2004).

4. Development of Learning Criteria to Monitor Goal Progress

After designing a learning curriculum, a self-developer also needs to establish criteria to monitor his or her progress toward set goals. Criteria cannot be ill-defined, but instead must represent very precise ways of deriving where one stands in relation to one's learning objectives. In other words, the learning criteria must assess the specific skills and abilities that a leader targets in self-development (Goldstein and Ford, 2002). Each learning objective can be assessed on multiple levels, including, for example, results of the self-training system in relation to organizational objectives, performance on the job, amount of knowledge accrued from self-instructional activities, and reactions to the learning experience itself (Kirkpatrick, 1994). Because of the individual nature of the self-development process, leaders are better served if they establish multiple criteria to assess their own development from a variety of angles. Each of these criteria can provide a different piece of information about one's development. Also, as will be discussed later in the chapter, a leader should utilize others to ensure that various types of criteria are assessed.

5.   Evaluation of Learning Gains

Finally, leaders engaging in self-development should assess overall learning gains (Goldstein and Ford, 2002). Evaluation is important because it can provide important information about what changes need to be made to the training program. If leaders evaluate their learning gains and realize that they did not, to a large extent, develop targeted skills, they will need to return to the different steps in the self-instructional system and make necessary revisions. Perhaps the leader conducted a biased needs assessment and did not adequately depict his or her developmental needs. Or perhaps the learning objectives set did not accurately fulfill the developmental needs. A third cause may be a deficient learning curriculum. Good evaluation data can provide important clues that can help ameliorate insufficient self-development.

For several reasons the evaluation of a self-training system may be one of the most challenging components to the self-development process. First, self-learners may simply not think to conduct such an evaluation, often using enjoyment of the learning activity itself as a marker for learning success. Second, they may not know how to assess learning gains accurately. Measurement of learning gains is a skill rooted in the application of scientific and psychometric theory. Because self-development inherently places learning evaluation in the hands of the learner, he or she needs to attain some level of this skill for a successful self-learning process. However, although self-development requires that individuals take ownership of the evaluation process, multiple resources can be utilized. Again, the self/social comparison that the leader conducts during the self-appraisal step of the self-instructional system can provide a basis for evaluation by raising the question of whether perceived gap between the actual and ideal leader selves has been narrowed. The specification of the ideal leader self can serve as the measurable standard against which to evaluate gains. Here is a significant point of intervention for learning partners and the developmental social network – we will discuss this in more detail in later sections.

Leaders need to be motivated to engage in self-development activities and specifically to utilize the process just described to expand their leadership capacity. The utilization of social resources can be particularly helpful to a leader's successful application of the self-development process. This idea is consistent with a relational approach to development (McCauley and Douglas, 2004). This type of approach emphasizes interaction with a network of learning partners as a prime developmental resource (Hall and Associates, 1996).

THE NATURE OF DEVELOPMENTAL SOCIAL NETWORKS

Background on Social Networks

A network can be defined as 'a set of nodes and the set of ties representing some relationship, or lack of relationship, between the nodes' (Brass et al., 2004, p. 795). Nodes reflect the actors or individuals in the network, while ties refer to the relationships among them (Borgatti and Foster, 2003). A leader's social network can contain a number of different types of people that represent a variety of relationships. For example, a social network can contain individuals at all levels of the organizational hierarchy – supervisors, peers and subordinates. It can include individuals within the same organization, individuals in different organizations, and individuals tied by friendship or other social functions. The main principles of social network theory are based on the interactions and relationships among the actors in the network (Granovetter, 1985; Tichy et al., 1979). Another guiding principle is that these relationships provide social capital to the leader (Borgatti and Foster, 2003; Brass, 2001). Social capital can be defined as 'the social relationships that can potentially confer benefits to individuals and groups' (Brass, 2001: p. 133). The amount of social capital a leader can accrue will depend in part on the number and variety of individuals in that leader's social network, as well as the nature of the relationships among the actors (Balkundi and Kilduff, 2005; Brass, 2001). For example, as leaders expand their network to include friends and colleagues at other companies, they can potentially gain greater knowledge about the general or strategic operating environment of their organizations.

Much of the research on social networks has focused on understanding the antecedents to certain connections formed among nodes or actors in the network, as well as on the consequences of those relationships. For example, there has been research on how individual level factors such as similarity between individuals (e.g., Ibarra, 1992) and personality (e.g., Klein et al., 2004) influence social network formation and the connections within that network. Research has also demonstrated relationships between higher-level antecedents, such as organizational structure and workflow (e.g., Borgatti and Cross, 2003), and social networks. Regarding important consequences of these interpersonal networks, past research has found linkages to such outcomes as performance (e.g., Cross and

Cummings, 2004) and job satisfaction (e.g., Shaw, 1964). This past research demonstrates that not only are the formation of social networks influenced by a number of different variables, but the characteristics of networks have the potential to facilitate important individual, team and organizational outcomes.

A stream of research on social networks has focused on the structural features of those networks. For example, much research has been devoted to the property of centrality, which refers to how directly connected an individual is to others in his or her network (Balkundi and Harrison, 2006). An individual who has a direct tie to many other actors in a social network has more centrality than an individual linked only to a few actors in the same network. This property of centrality has been related to positive outcomes such as power (e.g., Brass, 1984), and individual job performance in certain types of networks (e.g., Sparrowe et al., 2001). The prime benefits of centrality lie in (a) the greater amount of information available to the centrally-located actors; (b) the greater levels of social support available to such actors; and (c) the greater potential for social impact and social influence (Adler and Kwon, 2002; Balkundi and Harrison, 2006).

Another critical and widely researched aspect of social networks refers to the nature of the ties among nodes. Brass (2001) distinguished between strong and weak ties in social networks, with strong ties reflecting relationships of greater intensity, intimacy, reciprocity and duration than weak ties. He noted that 'strong tie relationships involve actors who may be more credible and trusted sources of information (or other resources), more motivated to provide the resources in a timely fashion, and more readily available than weak tie relationships' (p. 136). The benefits of social capital defined in social networks, as well as the benefits of occupying a central position within those networks, rest in part on the strength of ties linking the central individual to the other actors. Also, Balkundi and Harrison (2006; see also Lincoln and Miller, 1979) distinguish between instrumental and expressive ties. Instrumental ties refer to more work-related linkages that provide 'information resources or knowledge that is relevant to completing one's job within a unit' (Balkundi and Harrison, 2006: p. 51). Expressive ties refer to friendship linkages that transcend work-related domains. According to Balkundi and Harrsion, such ties are more likely to provide social and value support to the individual.

Social Networks and Leader Development

As discussed above, social networks and the individuals that are contained within them can influence leaders in several different ways. What about the impact of social networks on leader development? Brass et al.

(2004) theorized that social networks can facilitate leaders' effectiveness by fostering more successful exertions of social influence (a central tenet of leadership theories). We also suggest that social networks can influence leaders' effectiveness by serving as developmental resource to them, aiding them particularly in the process of self-development. When constellations of relationships are used to facilitate self-development, they become developmental social networks. Expanding upon the definition of networks offered by Brass et al. (2004: p. 795), we define developmental social networks as *a set of nodes, and a set of ties representing the quality of relationships among the nodes, that provide leaders with the opportunity to assess, compare and receive information and feedback relative to the development and the expansion of their leader capacity.*

There has been some research that provides ideas about how social networks can be useful to leaders engaged in self-development processes. For example, Ibarra (1995) discusses three specific types of network that are important to individuals in positions of management or leadership: task networks, friendship/support networks, and career networks. According to Ibarra, task networks facilitate information exchanges that may include expertise and materials. Friendship/social support networks are important for leaders because they provide a degree of nurturance that can facilitate work accomplishments. These two types of network can respectively (a) provide new types of knowledge to self-developers engaged in different kinds of learning activities; and (b) provide support and motivation to engage in such activities. Career networks, the last type mentioned by Ibarra, are more directly related to self-development because they offer the leader information about career growth and progression. Accordingly, they can be instrumental in helping the leader determine the most effective developmental assignments and learning activities for career-related skill acquisition.

McCauley and Douglas (2004) also describe how social networks can be developmental. They argue that social network relationships can serve three different major developmental functions: (a) providing assessment (acting as a feedback provider, sounding board, and point of comparison); (b) providing challenging assignments, and helping learners handle them (for example, by acting as a dialogue partner, role model, and helping to monitor goal progress); and (c) offering support (acting as a counselor and cheerleader). They also note the Corporate Leadership Council's 2001 Leadership Survey as finding that leader development activities were rated as more effective if they were grounded in feedback and relationships such as mentoring and peer interaction.

Bartol and Zhang (2007) integrated ideas and concepts from both McCauley and Douglas (2004) and from Ibarra (1995) to describe how developmental networks can be used as resources for leaders who are engaging in the self-learning process. We use their notions along with some from Balkundi and Harrsion (2006) to summarize several ways developmental social networks facilitate leader self-development. First, obtaining relevant feedback is a huge part of the self-development process (Orvis, 2007), and individuals occupying different nodes in a developmental social network can provide feedback about strengths, developmental needs, and learning goal progress from different perspectives. When the ties connecting them to the leader self-developer are highly expressive (that is, high in friendship and personal affection; Balkundi and Harrison, 2006), these individuals can also provide to the leader a particularly trusted source for targeted and honest feedback. Second, when certain individuals in the developmental social network are bound to the leader by strong instrumental ties (for example, boss, mentor, coach), they may be able to offer developmental assignments that are particularly pertinent in helping to advance a self-learner's career. Finally, individuals having either (or both) strong instrumental and expressive ties to the leader self-developer can provide motivational support to that person. Self-development is often an activity that needs to happen in addition to the leader's typically heavy work load and is generally relegated to the leader's 'spare time'. Organizations may support the leader by providing developmental 'time-off' (e.g., Boyce, 2004), but most leaders will need to engage in self-learning offline. This extra effort means that motivation for such activity needs to be particularly strong. Also, to be effective, such activities need to be challenging and have substantial experiential variety (Langkamer and Zaccaro, 2009). These characteristics make such assignments more difficult to complete and therefore increase the need for the kinds of motivational support and encouragement that can be provided by developmental social networks.

We have noted that the structural features of networks have been the subject of considerable research on social networks. These features can have interesting implications in developmental social networks, and particularly in how such networks can be useful to leader development. In our discussion here, we briefly note the influence of several network attributes, including *network size*, *node diversity*, *network density*, the *aggregate nature of ties*, and the *position of the leader self-developer within the network*.

Size refers to the total number of actors that compose the nodes within a network. Leader self-developers need to choose the size of their networks carefully. Granovetter (1973; see also Balkundi and Kilduff, 2005) suggests that a large number of weak ties in a network can be useful because such a network fosters a greater flow of information to an individual. In addition, these types of network expose the leader to varying perspectives

(Brass and Krackhardt, 1999). The exploration of a variety of perspectives in learning assignments can lead to the development of more complex and adaptive frames of reference (Horn, 2008; Langkamer, 2008; McCauley and Douglas, 2004).

Node diversity can also provide such breadth of perspectives. We define node diversity as the degree of qualitative and demographic differences among the actors composing nodes in a developmental social network. A network composed of individuals from demographically and culturally different backgrounds, from different positions within and outside of the organization, and from different types of occupations and careers will provide a greater variety of different ideas and frames of reference than more homogeneous networks. We note, though, that while greater node diversity can provide a greater range of perspectives, they also can increase the cognitive load on self-learners, specifically, the need to integrate these different frames of reference into a more complex mental model (cf. Horn, 2008). Self-learners who do not have the conceptual capacity to handle such complexity (Jacobs and Jaques, 1987) may not be as well served by higher levels of node diversity.

Social networks can vary in terms of their degree of *density*. Balkundi and Harrison (2006) defined density as reflecting the total interconnectedness of the network, or the ratio between the actual number of ties among nodes to the total possible number of ties. The density of a developmental social network can have some interesting implications for the self-developer. Balkundi and Harrison examined density among team members and the 'viability' of the team (defined as 'a team's potential to retain its members through their attachment to the team and their willingness to stay together as a team', 2006, p. 52). They found that greater density of both instrumental and expressive ties with the team's network was positively associated with team viability. Other researchers have suggested that greater attachment to the team makes team norms more powerful regulators of member behaviors (Festinger, 1950). Extrapolating these findings and ideas to developmental social networks suggests that dense networks situated within a learning organization that allows for a systematic integration of learning values and norms into organizational policies, practices and processes (Sessa and London, 2006) will be likely to have network members who are more centered on learning and development. Network density is also related to greater levels of shared attitudes and values (Balkundi and Kilduff, 2005; Brass and Krackhardt, 1999). Accordingly, denser developmental social networks may provide stronger, more integrated and systematic sources of learning support to self-developers.

The *aggregate nature of the ties* in a developmental network refers to whether ties are predominantly instrumental, predominantly expressive, or a relatively even mix of the two. Our focus in relating this property to developmental social networks combines the aggregate nature of ties with density. Therefore, we focus on the ratio of the number of a type of tie to the total number of ties in the network (density refers to the ratio of actual number of ties to total possible ties). Thus, a predominantly instrumental network is one in which more than half of the ties are instrumental in nature, while in an expressive network, more than half the ties are expressive. Each type of developmental network, along with one with an even mix of the two tie types is likely to provide different types of information and support to the self-developer. Because they are more task-focused, instrumental networks will be likely to offer more information that can be useful in defining performance standards and the most appropriate developmental assignments. Because expressive networks will be more friendship-based, they may provide more sources of motivation and support for the self-developer's learning efficacy. We suspect the most useful developmental networks may be those containing a relatively even aggregation of instrumental and expressive ties.

We have assumed that the self-developer would occupy a *central position in the developmental social network*, where there are direct ties from him or her to many of the nodes. We have noted that higher centrality can be related to greater amounts of information and social support available to the centrally-located actors. However, the self-developer may be tied only to a few nodes (for example, boss, mentor) that in turn may have higher centrality – that is, the self-developer may occupy a position of lower centrality within the developmental network. Such a position would be likely to dilute the developmental advantages of such networks by filtering information through the perspectives of central actors. For example, self-developers with less centrality in their networks are likely to receive assessment and feedback information only through their ties to centrally located individuals. Likewise, peripheral location may reduce available social support to the self-developer. For these reasons, we suspect that the benefits that accrue from developmental social networks will be larger for self-developers who have greater centrality. This premise would put a premium on the self-developer's ability to construct a large network of learning partners, where he or she had direct ties to many of these partners.

Learning Partners

We have argued that node diversity within a leader's developmental social network can provide substantial learning benefits. More specifically, these benefits occur when a self-developer's network contains a variety of different learning partners, including bosses, mentors, coaches, peers, friends and subordinates. A learning partner is an individual who can facilitate one or more of the steps outlined earlier in this chapter as part of the self-development instructional system. As McCauley and Douglas (2004) discuss, different individuals serve different developmental roles that help in the development process by providing an element of assessment, challenge and/or support. This chapter discusses how learning partners can help with each of these elements but within the context of a self-instructional system and the training steps described at the beginning of this chapter.

Importantly, each learning partner may facilitate a social comparison process within the leader to help him or her understand and assess current strengths and weaknesses more accurately. According to Cortina et al. (2004), this process of having an accurate appraisal of one's working self is one of the hallmarks of successful leader self-development. Cortina et al. describe the self-appraisal process in self-development as grounded in ideas of a prototypical or ideal leader (c.f., Murphy, 2002). Leaders compare their current self within their leader role to the ideal leader self to make assessments about strengths and weaknesses; these assessments then serve as the basis for leader self-development activities. We assert that particular individuals in a leader's social network can facilitate idea generation about one's ideal leader self, and thus, collectively they can serve as comparison points. Note that each of the individuals in a leader's developmental social network does not have to be an 'ideal' leader to be of help in the social comparison process. Rather, these individuals can provide different kinds of information to the self-learner about the type of leader he/she wants to be. Therefore, the network as a whole allows the learner to gain many different perspectives on leadership and leader prototypes that can serve as one basis for self-development goals.

We describe several learning partner roles that can be filled by various individuals in a leader's social network, including: (a) mentor; (b) coach; (c) supervisors (multiple levels); (d) peers inside the organization; (e) peers outside the organization; and (f) subordinates. A mentor is traditionally defined as a more senior person in an organization who provides both career and personal support and assistance (Thomas and Kram, 1988). The focus of mentoring is typically on the overall career growth and career trajectory of the protégé. Coaches are more behaviorally-focused and are utilized by individuals to help create learning goals and development plans to improve their leadership performance (Kilburg, 2000; Ting and Hart, 2004; Ting and Riddle, 2006). A supervisor is a person higher in the organizational hierarchy than the self-developer, with direct (or indirect) responsibility for his or her work assignments. The supervisor's focus would include the career path or promotion prospects of the self-developer within the organization. A responsibility of the supervisor is to provide feedback on job-related tasks and performance in relation to organizational objectives. An individual may have supervisors at multiple levels of the organization, with each providing different perspectives on intra-organization prospects and job-related performance.

Peers also serve as important learning partners. Parker et al. (2008) argued that peers may perhaps be a more valuable resource than senior mentors because peers are engaged in, and must perform within, the same work environment as the self-learner. Thus, they are likely to have a perspective that is most congruent with that of the self-developer. Alternatively, peers can offer a different perspective on a common problem, and engage with self-learners in a 'shared sense-making of each other's worldview' (Parker et al., 2008: p. 491). Peers are likely to draw on more current experiences when helping a colleague with his or her development, while senior mentors may be providing advice based on experiences that are no longer as directly applicable to the self-developer's immediate and changing operating environment.

We specify two different types of peer that may serve as learning partners. Inside peers are those from the self-developer's same organization. Such peers are likely to be engaging in similar tasks and facing common organization-driven challenges. Thus, they can provide perhaps the most direct points of social comparison (Festinger, 1950). Outside peers are those individuals who occupy similar jobs, roles or functions in other organizations. These peers can provide information about a common job but from an operationally, and even strategically, different perspective. Thus, such outside peers can help the self-developing leader to envision the knowledge and skills that would be needed from a longer-term strategic picture.

Finally, subordinates are individuals for whom the leader self-developer is responsible for directing and managing work activities. Leaders can have direct or indirect responsibility for these individuals (Jacobs and Jaques, 1987; Zaccaro, 2001). Subordinates may not be intuitively perceived by the leader self-developer as learning partners. However, subordinates can provide valuable data as part of a 360-degree assessment regimen. They also serve as sources of data for evaluating learning gains by the leader – improvements in the self-developer's leadership skill may surface first in the activities and performance of his or her subordinates.

We assert that each of these learning partners can serve the self-developer at multiple points of the self-instructional system. We articulate these kinds of service more fully in the next section of this chapter.

LEARNING PARTNERS AND THE LEADER SELF-DEVELOPMENT PROCESS

Each of the learning partners described above are useful in similar and different ways at similar and different phases of the self-instructional system. Table 14.1 presents a mapping of different learning partners and their potential influences at each of the five steps of the self-development process. In general, across the five steps of the self-development process, each learning partner provides the following unique contributions (McCauley and Douglas, 2004): *mentors* provide ideas about how to develop oneself in alignment with professional and career goals; *supervisors* are instrumental in helping the leader align the skills to be targeted in self-development with the anticipated needs of the current organization, and with the likely performance requirements of the leader's next anticipated position; *coaches* serve as a source of support and motivation while providing an unbiased assessment of one's leadership skills, including helping the self-developer construct a viable development plan (Ting and Hart, 2004; Ting and Riddle, 2006). Coaches can also provide general advice and expertise on how to make the most of the information provided by other learning partners; *inside peers* are a direct source of comparison within the self-learner's organization and can serve as thought partners; *outside peers* serve to promote a more global and integrated view of leadership and of the self-learner's larger operating environment; *subordinates* can provide a direct measure of self-developers' leadership skills, and provide feedback throughout the self-learning process. The sections below will describe the role of each of the learning partners in regard to each of the steps of the self-training system. It is important to note that (a) one person may fill multiple roles, and (b) more than one learning partner may fulfill the same function at any given step in the process.

Step 1: Assessment of Learning Needs

The first step in the leader self-development process is assessing one's learning and development needs. Learning partners can be an integral component to this step by providing both comparison points and different kinds of feedback. McCauley and Douglas (2004) note that there are two different types of comparison points – comparing oneself against an expert or role model and asking 'how do I compare to someone who is doing what I want to be doing?', and comparing oneself to individuals at equivalent levels (asking 'Am I doing as well as others?') (p. 88). We also assert that leaders could make downward comparisons (Wills, 1981), and ask 'Am I doing better than other people at lower organizational levels, or other peer

Table 14.1 *The role of learning partners in each step of a self-instructional training system*

	Mentors	Supervisors	Coaches
Assessment of Learning Needs	• Provide feedback on strengths and developmental needs relative to career goals • Provide norms and standards of professional excellence for use in self-assessment • Provide information on 'ideal leader' and career-related performance dimensions for self-appraisal	• Provide work opportunities that provide self-assessment information • Provide feedback on strengths and developmental needs based on knowledge about the leader's current and possible future positions • Provide information on 'ideal leader' and job-related performance dimensions for self-appraisal	• Provide psychometrically sound self-assessment tools • Provide an unbiased assessment of current self: help self-developer interpret assessment data • Counter/challenge any appraisal biases by the self-developer
Identification of Learning Objectives	• Provide motivation and support for setting challenging professional goals • Help align learning objectives with current career trajectory	• Serve as a source of normative organizational support when setting learning goals • Help align learning objectives with current position trajectory	• Facilitate idea generation by the self-learner and encourage them to identify areas for growth • Provide motivation and outside support in setting challenging goals
Development of Learning Curriculum	• Provide guidance on the types of assignments that would promote career trajectory	• Provide ideas about self-development activities that may be offered 'in-house'	• Provide expert ideas about the self-development activities that may best target the leader's goals

Table 14.1 (continued)

	Mentors	Supervisors	Coaches
	• Provide ideas and feedback on how to best complete particular self-development activities (mentor may have personally engaged in these activities in his/her self-learning)	• Provide specific support mechanisms (release time for specific activities, funding for self-learning activities)	• Help self-developer identify most appropriate activities for learning goals • Help self-developer construct development action plan with appropriate tasks and time lines
Development of Learning Criteria	• Provide benchmarks against professional standards that denote successful learning gains	• Provide benchmarks against unit and organizational standards that denote successful learning gains	• Provide feedback and input on how to develop clear criteria that are understandable and measurable
Evaluation of Learning Gains	• Serve as a source of informal assessment; assessment feedback provided should be directly related to learning curriculum	• Serve as a source of formal assessment and performance evaluation; feedback may be directly or indirectly related to learning curriculum	• Provide an unbiased assessment of current self directly related to learning curriculum

Table 14.1   (continued)

	Inside Peers	Outside Peers	Subordinates
Assessment of Learning Needs	• Provide a point of organization-based social comparison for current self • Provide a check on self appraisal biases	• Provide opportunities to view current self from a perspective that does not focus solely on current position in current organization • Provide a point of professional or career-based social comparison	• Provide information about a feared self and also current leader self • Feedback, actions and performance provide a baseline assessment of strengths and developmental needs
Identification of Learning Objectives	• Serve as a partner to generate goals • Serve as a check to make sure that goal level and difficulty is appropriate	• Provide ideas about how learning objectives can include skills needed to operate strategically	• May serve as focal points for learning objectives
Development of Learning Curriculum	• Provide ideas about self-development activities derived through own experiences	• Provide ideas about new self-development opportunities outside the leader's 'inner circle'	• May serve as conduits of development activities
Development of Learning Criteria	• Provide ideas based on current experiences about realistic criteria	• Provide ideas about useful criteria outside the leader's	• Changes in subordinate behavior and performance may serve as one

Table 14.1   (continued)

	Inside Peers	Outside Peers	Subordinates
		current organization	criterion for gains in leadership skills
Evaluation of Learning Gains	● Serve as a source of both formal and informal feedback; formal feedback could be provided in a 360 appraisal; informal feedback may be direct comparisons to peers	● Serve as a source of informal feedback to think about how gains correspond to the 'bigger picture'	● Serve as a source of both formal and informal feedback; formal feedback could be provided in a 360 appraisal; informal feedback may be provided based on subordinate performance

leaders who do not presumably have my skills?' These questions are each tied to a different learning partner and can help a self-learner define current and future performance requirements against which to evaluate gaps.

Mentors
Mentors serve as a valuable learning resource to a leader by providing both comparison standards and feedback. In general, the role of the mentor is to help self-developers assess themselves from a wider perspective that focuses not just on their current job, but on their career goals and possible career trajectory. A mentor provides clarity in professional identity for a leader (Kram, 1985). In terms of comparison standards, we assert that mentors can offer a comparison for an 'ideal' leader and provide career-related performance dimensions. In addition to perhaps possessing desirable leader characteristics themselves (and thereby serving as the ideal leader self), they can provide ideas about norms and standards of professional excellence. Leaders can use information about these standards to draw comparisons against their current leader selves. Finally, a mentor can also help a leader assess his or her current leader self through the provision of feedback on strengths and developmental needs. A mentor should be familiar with a leader's career goals and is therefore in a position to understand any areas in the leader's current skill-set that may not be adequate to reach those career goals.

Supervisors

The role of a supervisor in this first step of a self-training system is to provide job-related information so that the leader can assess him or herself in regard to current and future positions within the same organization. Supervisors provide leaders with information about job-related performance dimensions (in contrast to the career-oriented dimensions provided by the mentor), thus giving the self-learner an idea of the ideal leader self within the organization. Also, given a supervisor's intimate knowledge about both the leader's current and possible future organizational positions, he/she is in a good place to assess the self-learner's strengths and developmental needs according to future position requirements. Finally, the supervisor is also in a unique role to provide the leader with work opportunities and assignments that can provide self-assessment information. By giving the leader challenging work assignments that stretch him or her beyond current skill-sets (Ohlott, 2004), the leader learns the limitations of current skills sets, and gains a better understanding of developmental needs.

Coaches

Generally speaking, one role of coaches in the needs assessment step is to help the leader develop an unbiased and valid self-assessment (Ting and Hart, 2004; Ting and Riddle, 2006). There are at least three ways in which a coach can help a leader do this. First, coaches typically have at their disposal scientifically validated metrics and measures to help leaders self-assess their current leadership capacities. Second, coaches should help leaders interpret any assessment data that comes from using the tools, providing an unbiased perspective of the results. Finally, self-developers will often be biased in how they perceive causes of their own performance (Fiske and Taylor, 1991); it is the job of a coach to help leaders see through these biases.

Inside peers

Peers inside an organization serve as one of the main points of social comparisons. By definition, a peer is someone on the same position or organizational level, having similar types of work experiences. When performance comparisons to comparable peers are made, a leader may gain better understanding of his or her own strengths and developmental needs, especially if the comparison other is superior to the self-learner on some performance dimensions (Festinger, 1950). This direct comparison point may also be useful in mitigating some of the leader's self-appraisal biases. In addition, by knowing that someone on his/her same leadership level has different skill-sets that are necessary for effective leadership, the leader may also be more motivated to try and grow those skills.

Outside peers

Peers outside a leader's organization also serve as a direct comparison point. However, instead of the comparison being in relation to someone in the same organizational position (as is the case with inside peers), leaders can utilize outside peers to make comparisons along career performance dimensions. This perspective is a bit larger in scope and will allow the leader to make assessments about current strengths and developmental needs within the larger professional community. A self-assessment against inside peers versus outside peers is likely to yield different findings, and provide the leader with a more global, integrated perspective on how to be an effective leader. For example, through a comparison to inside peers, a leader may realize that he or she needs to work on project management skills in order to be able to manage a significant project successfully. A comparison with outside peers may yield the assessment that he or she needs to attend more conferences to improve one's professional knowledge and remain on the cutting edge of one's discipline or vocation.

Subordinates

Finally, subordinates facilitate self-learning needs assessment by serving as a source of direct feedback on a leader's strengths and developmental needs. Subordinates may operate as a source of information for the 'feared leader-self' (that is, the type of leader the self-learner does *not* want to be). Such a comparison may indicate qualities and traits that the leader/self-learner should have mastered before reaching current positions. Also, because subordinates are in the direct line of influence from the leader, their feedback, actions and performance provide a baseline of information to the leader about strengths and developmental needs. If subordinates are not performing well, such data may offer clues that the leader possesses some undesirable leadership attributes. For example, if a leader sees that many of their subordinates are consistently absent from work, they may assess that they need to do a better job at motivating the subordinates. Or, subordinates not 'performing beyond expectations' (Bass, 1985) may suggest that the leader/self-learner may be micromanaging (or not delegating enough), or not giving sufficient feedback and/or task responsibility to his/her charges; these assessments would imply deficiencies – and therefore development needs – related to skills in delegation, feedback provision and participative management. Thus, based on comparison with subordinates and information about subordinate performance levels, leaders may set specific goals to make sure that they develop certain essential skills that move them away from the feared leader-self and toward the ideal leader-self.

Steps 2 and 3: Identifying Learning Objectives and Development of Learning Curriculum

The second step in the leader self-development process is to identify learning objectives based on the information gathered during the self-appraisal process. This identification of learning objectives is followed by the development of a learning curriculum. In these steps of the self-instructional system, leaders set learning goals, deciding what skills will be the target of development, and then develop a plan that specifies how to meet those goals. The role of each learning partner is similar across the two steps, and therefore they will be discussed as a set.

Mentors

Because mentors are often viewed as 'teachers', their role in this goal-setting step of the self-development process should be one of providing professional support and oversight. Self-learners may experience difficulty in setting learning objectives that are simultaneously challenging yet reasonable. Mentors should encourage leaders to develop learning goals that will stretch them professionally, but be achievable with an appropriate learning timeframe. Mentors can also help by offering suggestions for developmental activities that would be most helpful for the attainment of particular targeted skills; doing so may help learners understand better how to reach challenging learning goals and in turn, foster greater learning efficacy. When the leader self-developer sees the mentor as an ideal leader, his or her ideas have even greater credibility, providing additional sources of motivation for the leader/self-learner.

Mentors can also help ensure that the learning objectives developed are aligned with a leader's current career trajectory. Growth along this trajectory should reflect the self-learner's ideas about what skills are reflected in their ideal leader self; mentors can reinforce these ideas and provide feedback and suggestions on goal activities that will mostly likely result in attainment of these skills. The self-learner benefits from the mentor's knowledge of his/her own career progression and the developmental activities that were most efficacious for professional career growth.

Supervisors

We assert that one of the ways supervisors are most helpful during the self-development process is in the generation of learning objectives, particularly ones that will help the leader gain skills for future positions within the organization. Also, the learner's supervisor can provide developmental support in several ways. First, he/she may convey strong norms for learning and development within the organizational climate; leaders are often the most powerful purveyors of organizational norms to their subordinates (Schein, 1992). Thus, when such norms reflect learning-oriented behaviors, supervisors can convey messages that the setting of challenging learning goals will likely be endorsed within the organization. Second, to help learners develop an effective and comprehensive learning curriculum, supervisors can provide ideas about available 'in-house' self-development activities that were previously unfamiliar to the leader. They can also suggest the activities that in their experience and knowledge of the organization are most effective in attaining set learning goals. Also, the supervisor can offer support in terms of resources that should be helpful for the achievement of the learning curriculum (for example, release time, funding for specific activities).

Coaches

During the identification and development of learning objectives and curriculum, the role of a coach is first to serve as a thought partner for the leader and help prioritize the leadership areas that are most in need of development. Because a coach is not the leader's direct supervisor, a self-developer may feel more comfortable discussing developmental needs; with an outside coach they need not be concerned that this information will be a detriment to career advancement. While helping to generate goals, the coach can also provide expert advice on self-development activities that may best target the leader's goals. Also, during these steps, coaches operate much in the same way that mentors do by providing motivation and support to set challenging goals (McCauley and Douglas, 2004; Ting and Hart, 2004). Like mentors, a coach should help a leader assess appropriate developmental professional activities for each of the goals. The leader works collaboratively with his/her coach to generate a specific learning curriculum that reflects not only action steps, but also necessary resources, means of measuring learning progress (see below), and achievable timelines for each step (Ting and Riddle, 2006).

Inside peers

A leader's peers within an organization can also be an excellent source for identifying and clarifying learning objectives. Because peers within the organization are sharing the same experiences and may even be on the same career trajectory, they may possess novel and more specific ideas about particular learning objectives. For example, from their experiences, peers may know what skills are necessary in more specific leadership contexts. For example, peers who have had to provide periodic briefings to particular executives within the organization, or to client groups, may identify presentation skills as an important skill for leaders at their level.

They may also be able to provide ideas and feedback about particular self-development activities, based on their own experiences in completing them. For example, if the self-learner identifies as a learning activity a particular formal leadership development program, peers who have previously participated in this program can provide helpful information regarding its suitability and value. A caveat, of course, is that inside peers may be competitors for future positions, making them possibly reluctant partners. The climate within the organization (that is, whether it operates as a learning culture; Sessa and London, 2006) is instrumental in resolving such potential issues.

Outside peers
Information from peers outside a leader's organization may assist in setting learning objectives and defining developmental activities that reach beyond the scope of his/her current organization or job. For example, if a leader's self-assessment indicates a developmental need for greater strategic awareness and knowledge of the industry environment, outside peers can provide access to resources (for example, regular community meetings of local professionals, insight into how other companies are handling the same industry-level issues; new techniques for confronting these challenges) that may offer such information. Also, outside peers who have the skills a self-learner is targeting can provide suggestions on the kinds of learning activities and experiences that helped them gain and nurture these skills. Because these peers are not in the self-developer's same organization, they are less likely to be considered competitors for the same positions, and therefore may be more willing to act as learning partners. One caveat, though, pertains to situations where peers come from strongly competing companies – there will be obvious constraints on them acting as learning partners for one another. Thus, in such situations, leader self-developers need to be particularly judicious in what ties they form with certain outside peers and how they use these relationships.

Subordinates
Setting learning objectives and designing a learning curriculum are developmental steps that are less likely to benefit from the direct input of subordinates. Subordinates provide assessment data that contribute to the definition of learning goals (see step 1), and they may be instrumental as conduits of developmental activities (for example, when the self-developer wants to work on skills in giving feedback to subordinates). Because they typically lack the kinds of skills sought by the leader self-developer, however, they may not be in the best position to define the particular goals and contents of the leader's learning curriculum.

Step 4: Development of Learning Criteria

This step in a self-instructional system is the initial process in evaluating possible learning gains. Here, leaders develop the criteria by which they will judge their progress through their self-learning curriculum. The various learning partners available to the leader can provide these types of criteria. By seeking data on learning gains from many different learning partners, the leader is likely to gain multiple perspectives on goal progression. Therefore, the role of learning partners in this step involves providing benchmarks and feedback on the types of learning criteria that a leader can utilize. Because of the similarity across what these learning partners can provide, we do not consider them separately in this section.

In order to develop a comprehensive learning criterion list, leaders should incorporate several different standards into their assessment. The valuable contribution of a coach can be to provide the leader with input and suggestions on learning criteria that are both understandable and measureable (Ting and Riddle, 2006). A mentor can help the leader derive criteria to evaluate his or her goal progress against professional standards. In comparison, a more narrow view may be offered by the supervisor, who provides benchmarks that denote unit and organizational standards. Inside peers can help a leader in this step by drawing on their own current experiences to provide ideas about realistic criteria within the organization's operating environment. Outside peers can help provide useful criteria about targeted skills that reach outside the learner's immediate work environment. For example, if self-learners are focusing on growing presentation skills, then talks before professional groups of peers offer a forum for testing skill attainment. Finally, subordinates also act as sources of learning criteria. As leaders engage in self-development activities to improve certain leadership skills (for example, feedback-giving, developing others), skill attainment can be defined in terms of improvements in subordinate actions and performance.

Step 5: Evaluation of Learning Gains

The last step of the self-development process is to evaluate and understand what gains were accrued by the self-learner's completion of the learning curriculum and transferred to his or her leadership context. This step entails a re-evaluation of strengths and weaknesses after sufficient time has lapsed to determine if developmental needs were fulfilled. All types of learning partners can help provide feedback during this re-evaluation. For example, a 360-degree assessment from inside peers, subordinates and supervisors, which includes as performance dimensions the skills targeted in the completed learning curriculum, makes excellent use of three types of learning partners to evaluate developmental gains. Such assessments do not have to be limited, however, to the three aforementioned groups – they can also include mentors, outside peers and coaches, as well as customers and clients of the leader's work. The focus of any feedback and evaluation should be on helping self-learners determine if they have gained both knowledge and skilled behavior in ways that bear desired results for themselves and for their organization (Kirkpatrick, 1994).

CONCLUSIONS

Engaging in leader self-development is a useful way for individuals to grow their leadership skills in an individualized manner that works best for them. However, leaders do not typically make use of the appropriate skills and resources to conduct *effective* self-development. It is the thesis of this chapter that individuals must treat self-development as a self-instructional system, and implement the following necessary preparatory and supportive actions when deciding to embark on a self-learning program of self-development: (1) assessment of learning and development needs; (2) identification and development of learning objectives; (3) development of a learning curriculum; (4) development of learning criteria to monitor goal progress; and (5) evaluation of learning gains. In order to make use of this process effectively (and thus, effectively engage in self-development activities), leaders should utilize learning partners as key resources. We have defined these partners as composing the leader developmental social network. Each learning partner in the social network is instrumental at every step of the process, hence the whole network can operate collaboratively and in coordination to provide leaders with the comprehensive information needed to proceed through the aforementioned steps effectively.

There are several advantages to examining the connections between effective use of a self-instructional system and developmental social networks. First, using social networks as a developmental resource helps to mitigate some of the inherent challenges associated with the self-development process – namely low motivation and a lack of support for self-development activities. Learning partners can be extremely helpful in motivating the self-learner, if for no other reason than they provide self-developers with a check on goal progress. Also, learning partners can help set challenging goals, motivate the leader to meet these goals and also serve as a means of evaluation and feedback.

Second, social networks provide analysis tools that can be utilized to explore relationships between network attributes and the processes and outcomes of a self-instructional system. We have offered some hypotheses in this chapter suggesting that the density of the developmental social networks, the dominant types of ties, the diversity of nodes, and the leader self-developer's location within the network can influence self-learning outcomes. We have not offered more specific propositions linking particular network attributes to the outcomes of each step in the self-instructional system. We think a fruitful avenue for future research is to develop and test a more comprehensive model of developmental social networks and their effects on specific aspects of the self-learning process.

This chapter argues that self-development needs to be structured to include the same processes and steps that are most effective in formal training interventions. We have also asserted that the use of social networks as a developmental resource can help leaders progress through this system. By using the ideas in this chapter, we hope that leaders can engage in more effective self-development to help them remain up-to-date and grow adaptive skill-sets that respond to dynamic operating environments. The result should be greater competitive advantages both for the leader self-developer and for his or her organization.

REFERENCES

Adler, P.S. and Kwon, S. (2002), 'Social capital: prospects for a new concept', *Academy of Management Review*, **27**(1), 17–40.

Balkundi, P. and Harrison, D.A. (2006), 'Ties, leaders, and time in teams: strong inference about network structure's effects on team viability and performance', *Academy of Management Journal*, **49**, 49–68.

Balkundi, P. and Kilduff, M. (2005), 'The ties that lead: a social network approach to leadership', *Leadership Quarterly*, **16**, 941–61.

Bartol, K.M. and Zhang, X. (2007), 'Networks and leadership development: building linkages for capacity acquisition and capital accrual', *Human Resource Management Review*, **17**, 388–401.

Bass, B.M. (1985), *Leadership and Performance Beyond Expectations*, New York: Free Press.

Borgatti, S.P. and Cross, R. (2003), 'A relational view of information seeking and learning in social networks', *Management Science*, **49**, 432–45.

Borgatti, S.P. and Foster, P.C. (2003), 'The network paradigm in organizational research: a review and typology', *Journal of Management*, **29**, 991–1013.

Boyce, L.A. (2004), 'Propensity for self-development of leadership attributes: understanding, predicting, and supporting leader self-development performance', unpublished doctoral dissertation, George Mason University.

Boyce, L.A., Zaccaro, S.J. and Wisecarver, M. (in press), 'Propensity for self-development of leadership attributes: understanding, predicting, and supporting performance of leader self-development', *Leadership Quarterly*.

Brass, D.J. (1984), 'Being in the right place: a structural analysis of individual influence in an organization', *Administrative Science Quarterly*, **29**, 518–39.

Brass, D.J. (2001), 'Social capital and organizational leadership', in S.J. Zaccaro and R. Klimoski (eds), *The Nature of Organizational Leadership*, San Francisco, CA: SIOP Frontiers Series, Jossey-Bass, pp. 132–52.

Brass, D.J. and Krackhardt, D. (1999), 'The social capital of 21st century leaders', in J.G. Hunt, G.E. Dodge and L. Wong (eds), *Out-of-the-box Leadership* Stamford, CT: JAI Press, pp.179–94.

Brass, D.J., Galaskiewicz, J., Greve, H.R. and Tsai, W. (2004), 'Taking stock of networks and organizations: a multilevel perspective', *Academy of Management Journal*, **47**(6), 795–817.

Carver, C.S. and Scheier, M.F. (1982), 'Control theory: a useful conceptual framework for personality-social, clinical, and health psychology', *Psychological Bulletin*, **92**(1), 111–35.

Chen, G., Thomas, B., and Wallace, J.C. (2005), 'A multilevel examination of the relationships among training outcomes, mediating regulatory processes, and adaptive performance', *Journal of Applied Psychology*, **90**(5), 827–41.

Confessore, S.J. and Kops, W.J. (1998), 'Self-directed learning and the learning organization: examining the connection between the individual and the learning environment', *Human Resource Development Quarterly*, **9**(4), 365–75.

Cortina, J., Zaccaro, S.J., McFarland, L., Baughman, K., Wood, G. and Odin, E. (2004), 'Promoting realistic self-assessment as the basis for effective leader self-development', ARI Research Note 2004-05, Alexandria, VA.

Cross, R. and Cummings, J.N. (2004), 'Ties and network correlates of individual performance in knowledge-intensive work', *Academy of Management Journal*, **47**, 928–37.

Earley, P.C. and Perry, B.C. (1987), 'Work plan availability and performance: an assessment of task strategy priming on subsequent task completion', *Organizational Behavior and Human Decision Processes*, **39**, 279–302.

Ellinger, A.D. (2004), 'The concept of self-directed learning and its implications for human resource development', *Advances in Developing Human Resources*, **6**(2), 158–77.

Festinger, L. (1950), 'Informal social communication', *Psychological Review*, **57**, 271–82.

Fiske, S. and Taylor, S. (1991), *Social Cognition,* New York: McGraw Hill.

Gagne, R.M., Briggs, L.J. and Wager, W.W. (1992), *Principles of Instructional Design*, 4th edn, Fort Worth, TX: Harcourt Brace Jovanovich College Publishers.

Goldstein, I.L. and Ford, J.K. (2002), *Training in Organizations*, 4th edn, Belmont, CA: Wadsworth.

Granovetter, M. (1973), 'The strength of weak ties', *American Journal of Sociology*, **78**, 1360–80.

Granovetter, M. (1985), 'Economic action and social structure: the problem of embeddedness', *American Journal of Sociology*, **91**, 481–510.

Hall, D.T. (1986), 'Dilemmas in linking succession planning to individual executive learning', *Human Resource Management*, **25**(2), 235–65.

Hall, D.T. (2004), 'Self-awareness, identity, and leader development', in D.V. Day, S.J. Zaccaro and S.M. Halpin (eds), *Leader development for transforming organizations: Growing leaders for tomorrow*, Mahwah, NJ: Lawrence Erlbaum, pp. 153–76.

Hall, D.T. and Associates (1996), *The Career is Dead – Long Live the Career: A Relational Approach to Careers*, San Francisco, CA: Jossey-Bass.

Higgins, E.T. (1987), 'Self-discrepancy: a theory relating self and affect', *Psychological Review*, **94**, 319–40.

Higgins, M.C. and Kram, K.E. (2001), 'Reconceptualizing mentoring at work: a developmental network perspective', *Academy of Management Review*, **26**(2), 264–88.

Horn, Z.N.J. (2008), 'Explaining the influence of stretch assignments on adaptive outcomes: the importance of developing complex frames of reference', unpublished doctoral dissertation, George Mason University.

Ibarra, H. (1992), 'Homophily and differential returns: sex differences in network structure and access to an advertising firm', *Administrative Science Quarterly*, **37**, 422–47.

Ibarra, H. (1995), 'Managerial networks', *Harvard Business School Cases*, **1**, March 1–5.

Jacobs, T.O. and Jaques, E. (1987), 'Leadership in complex systems', in J. Zeidner (ed.), *Human Productivity Enhancement: Organizations, Personnel, and Decision-making*, Vol. 2, New York: Praeger, pp. 7–65.

Kanfer, R. and Ackerman, P.L. (1989), 'Motivation and cognitive abilities: an integrative/aptitude-treatment approach to skill acquisition', *Journal of Applied Psychology*, **74**, 657–90.

Kilburg, R.R. (2000), *Executive Coaching: Developing Managerial Wisdom in a World of Chaos*, Washington, DC: American Psychological Association.

Kirkpatrick, D.L. (1994), *Evaluating Training Programs: The Four Levels*, San Francisco, CA: Berrett-Koehler.

Klein, K.J., Lim, B.C., Saltz, J.L. and Mayer, D.M. (2004), 'How do they get there? An examination of the antecedents of centrality in team networks', *Academy of Management Journal*, **47**, 952–63.

Kram, K.E. (1985), *Mentoring at Work: Developmental Relationships in Organizational Life*, Glenview, IL: Scott, Foresman.

Langkamer, K.L. (2008), 'The development of a nomological net surrounding leader self-development', unpublished doctoral dissertation, George Mason University.

Langkamer, K.L. and Zaccaro, S.J. (2009), 'The self-development of adaptive outcomes', unpublished manuscript.

Lincoln, J.R. and Miller, J. (1979), 'Work and friendship ties in organizations: a comparative analysis of relational networks', *Administrative Science Quarterly*, **24**, 181–99.

Locke, E.A. (1968), 'Toward a theory of task motivation and incentives', *Organizational Behavior and Human Performance*, **3**, 157–89.

Locke, E.A. (1982), 'Relation of goal level to performance with a short work period and multiple goal levels', *Journal of Applied Psychology*, **67**, 512–14.

Locke, E.A. and Latham, G.P. (1990), *A Theory of Goal Setting and Task Performance*, Upper Saddle River, NJ: Prentice-Hall.

London, M. (1995), *Self and Interpersonal Insight: How People Gain Understanding of Themselves and Others in Organizations*, New York: Oxford University Press.

London, M. (2002), *Leadership Development: Paths to Self-insight and Professional Growth*, Mahwah, NJ: Lawrence Erlbaum Associates.

Mager, R.F. (1984), *Preparing Instructional Objectives* 2nd edn, Belmont, CA: Pitman Learning.

Markus, H. and Nurius, P. (1986), 'Possible selves' *American Psychologist*, **41**, 954–69.

Maurer, T.J. and Tarulli, B.A. (1994), 'Investigation of perceived environment, perceived outcome, and person variables in relationship to voluntary development activity by employees', *Journal of Applied Psychology*, **79**(1), 3–14.

McCauley, C.D. and Douglas, C.A. (2004), 'Developmental relationships', in C.D. McCauley and E. Van Velsor (eds), *The Center for Creative Leadership Handbook of Leadership Development*, 2nd edn, San Francisco, CA: Jossey-Bass, pp. 85–115.

Murphy, S.E. (2002), 'Leader self-regulation: the role of self-efficacy and multiple intelligences', in R. Riggio (ed.), *Multiple Intelligences and Leadership*, Mahwah, NJ: Lawrence Erlbaum.

Ohlott, P.J. (2004), 'Job assignments', in C.D. McCauley and E. Van Velsor (eds), *The Center for Creative Leadership Handbook of Leadership Development*, 2nd edn, San Francisco, CA: John Wiley, pp. 151–82.

Orvis, K.A. (2007), 'Supervisory performance feedback as a catalyst for high quality employee self-development', unpublished doctoral dissertation, George Mason University.

Parker, P., Hall, D.T. and Kram, K.E. (2008), 'Peer coaching: a relational process for accelerating career learning', *Academy of Management Learning and Education*, **7**(4), 487–503.

Porath, C.L. and Bateman, T.S. (2006), 'Self-regulation: from goal orientation to job performance', *Journal of Applied Psychology*, **91**(1), 185–92.

Schein, E.H. (1992), *Organizational Culture and Leadership*, 2nd edn, San Francisco, CA: Jossey-Bass.

Sessa, V. and London, M. (2006), *Continuous Learning in Organizations: Individual, Group, and Organizational Perspectives*, Mahwah, NJ: Lawrence Erlbaum.

Shaw, M.E. (1964), 'Communication networks', in L. Berkowitz (ed.), *Advances in Experimental Social Psychology*, Vol. 1, New York: Academic Press, pp. 111–47.

Sparrowe, R.T., Linden, R.C., Wayne, S.J. and Kraimer, M.L. (2001), 'Social networks and the performance of individuals and groups', *Academy of Management Journal*, **44**, 316–25.

Thomas, D.A. and Kram, K.E. (1988), 'Promoting career enhancing relationships in organizations: the role of the human resource professional', in M. London and E. Mone (eds), *The Human Resource Professional and Employee Career Development*, New York: Greenwood, pp. 49–66.

Tichy, N.M., Tushman, M.L. and Fombrun, C. (1979), 'Social network analysis for organizations', *Academy of Management Review*, **4**, 507–19.

Ting, S. and Hart, E. (2004), 'Formal coaching', in C.D. McCauley and E. Van Velsor (eds), *The Center for Creative Leadership Handbook of Leadership Development*, 2nd edn, San Francisco, CA: Jossey-Bass, pp. 116–50.

Ting, S. and Riddle, D. (2006), 'A framework for leadership development coaching', in S. Ting and P. Scisco (eds) *The Center for Creative Leadership Handbook of Coaching*, San Francisco, CA: John Wiley, pp. 34–62.

Wills, T.A. (1981), 'Downward comparison principles in social psychology', *Psychological Bulletin*, **90**, 245–71.

Zaccaro, S.J. (2001) *The Nature of Executive Leadership*, Washington, DC: American Psychological Association.

PART III

Self-Management and Unique Leadership
Challenges

15. Self-assessment and self-development of global leaders

Paula Caligiuri and Ruchi Sinha

Developing one's own career is important in today's labor market where the guarantee of lifetime employment with a single organization is obsolete. As individuals manage their careers, they become personally responsible for identifying their strengths and developmental needs for the target area profession. In our interconnected world, many individuals would like to expand their positions to include global leadership roles. For some, their organizations provide the training and development. However, for many others, this development for global leadership competencies needs to be self-initiated.

The backdrop for developing one's global leadership competencies is the global economy. Today's global economy has created a more complex and dynamic environment in which most firms compete effectively to achieve sustainable growth. With the inception of internet-based business, cross-border trade agreements, the ease of international travel and the like, domestic firms with solely domestic operations serving exclusively domestic client bases are becoming increasingly more difficult to find. Firms, both large and small, have increased the number of their foreign suppliers, partners, employees, shareholders and customers. Relevant for global leaders (or those who wish to become global leaders), this global environment has not only changed the competitive landscape of business, it has also changed the way in which people must conduct business and the competencies they need to compete successfully.

Clearly globalization and this new business reality have also created a demand for global business leaders who can operate successfully across borders and in multicultural situations. Global leaders, defined as executives who are in jobs with some international scope (cf. Spreitzer et al., 1997), must effectively manage through the complex, changing, and often ambiguous global environment (Bartlett and Ghoshal, 2003; Caligiuri and Di Santo, 2001). The following ten tasks or activities are found to be common among those in global leadership positions (Caligiuri, 2006).

1. Global leaders work with colleagues from other countries.
2. Global leaders interact with external clients from other countries.
3. Global leaders interact with internal clients from other countries.
4. Global leaders will often speak another language (other than their mother tongue) at work.
5. Global leaders supervise employees who are of different nationalities.
6. Global leaders develop a strategic business plan on a worldwide basis.
7. Global leaders manage a budget on a worldwide basis.
8. Global leaders negotiate in other countries or with people from other countries.
9. Global leaders manage foreign suppliers or vendors.
10. Global leaders manage risk on a worldwide basis for your unit.

To complete these ten tasks successfully, global leaders must learn to be culturally agile as they adapt across multicultural contexts. Cultural agility is an ability of both individuals and organizations to move quickly, comfortably and successfully from one cultural context to another (Caligiuri, 2007; Caligiuri and Tarique, 2008). Cultural agility is the capability that helps managers succeed in multicultural environments by enabling them to vary their behavioral responses to the needs of the cultural environment. Culturally agile managers are able to accurately assess the differences in behaviors, attitudes, and values between themselves and others and know how and when to use cultural knowledge and behaviors appropriately (Caligiuri and Tarique, 2008).

Global leaders who understand a diversity of foreign markets and cultures are able to interact with people from other countries, and can live and work effectively outside their own countries, are a premium human resource for global firms (Adler and Bartholomew, 1992; Black and Gregersen, 1991). Globally competent leaders have cultural agility and have the ability to create cultural synergy because they are able to integrate the best of their own business practices with the practices of other cultures (Adler and Bartholomew, 1992; Adler and Ghadar, 1990; Harris and Moran, 1987). Effective global leaders, as one can imagine, are in high demand for firms operating across national borders. The concern for many businesses, however, is that there may not be enough culturally agile individuals filling their leadership pipelines today. When over 1000 CEOs in more than 50 countries were polled in PriceWaterhouseCoopers' 10th Annual Global CEO Survey (2007), 'managing diverse cultures' was one of the top concerns they cited for the future. Most CEOs in the PriceWaterhouseCoopers survey indicated that their organizations are challenged by cultural barriers such as cultural issues/conflicts, conflicting regulatory requirements, unexpected costs, stakeholder opposition, and – most central for this chapter – inadequate leadership to manage this increasingly complex environment.

To address this demand, companies are using a variety of developmental activities including formalized global leadership developmental programs. The typical global leadership development program is designed to give individuals exposure to working in (at least) one foreign subsidiary (Rhinesmith, 1996; Thaler-Carter, 2000). These global leadership developmental programs often have a rotational component, where, for the duration of the assignment, the individual will spend between 12 and 24+ months in any given location, before moving to the next location (Rhinesmith, 1996; Thaler-Carter, 2000). These global leadership development programs are both expensive and somewhat limited given the low number of associates who can go through a given program in any given year.

The rising need for future global leaders and the inability for firms to keep pace with the demand provide an opportunity for those wishing to take control of their careers themselves and self-develop their global leadership competencies. Organization-initiated global leadership development programs alone cannot keep pace with the increasing demand. The good news for individuals and organizations alike is that, even without the formal intervention of organizations' global leadership development program, people can increase their global leadership competence through self-initiated activities. From the organizations' perspective, self-initiated development can increase the talent pipeline without any additional burden on the resources of the organization. From the individuals' perspective, self-initiated global leadership development can increase future professional marketability and enhance their current careers.

While the demand is high, global leadership is not right for everyone and not everyone will benefit from developmental global experiences. This chapter encourages a high level of self-awareness among individuals wishing to self-initiate activities for global leadership, as the most effective global leadership development occurs among those who are predisposed to learn from multicultural and cross-cultural experiences. This aptitude–treatment–interaction approach (Snow, 1991) suggests that people will benefit differentially from a given developmental experience depending on their individual aptitudes (for example, knowledge, skills, abilities, other personality characteristics, or KSAOs). When the right people (those with the requisite KSAOs) engage in the right developmental opportunities the result will be an increase in performance in global leadership tasks and activities. As such, this chapter will delve into both the individual differences and *self-assessment* of those differences and the *self-development* opportunities in which individuals can engage in order to increase their global leadership competencies.

SELF-ASSESSMENT FOR GLOBAL LEADERSHIP DEVELOPMENT

There are some underlying knowledge, skills, abilities and personality characteristics (KSAOs) necessary for successful performance of these aforementioned tasks. In the global leadership development context, individuals' KSAOs can affect the extent to which self-initiated training or developmental experiences will be effective. For this reason, individuals should have a self-awareness of their level of KSAOs which may affect them as global leaders.

Culture and Language Knowledge, Skills and Abilities

Great global leaders are not great in only one or two countries; they are culturally agile across many countries and cultures. Knowledge in a second language and culture is not the end goal of global leadership but helpful in the process of becoming an effective global leader given that the best global leadership development occurs in circumstances where one is living and working outside of one's home country. This is an important distinction. Many believe that if they learn another language or live in another country they have developed cultural agility. This is not true and warrants repeating; speaking another language and living in another culture are the mechanisms through which global leadership development can occur.

With the understanding that language fluency and cultural knowledge are the vehicles for development, it follows that someone with knowledge of a given country's culture and fluency in the given country's national language would have the ability to develop more quickly in a given country compared to someone without knowledge of either the culture or the language. The person without the cultural knowledge or language fluency could, presumably, gain both over time given the right developmental opportunities; the rate of change, however, would be different.

It is important for individuals to better understand their level of language fluency and cultural knowledge to better understand their potential rate of development when experiencing a different cultural context. In the self-development context, one might want to consider learning the basics of a second language or have a basic understanding of a host culture before working in a country with a different first language or with people from that host culture.

Personality

Research suggests that individuals with the requisite personality characteristics will benefit differentially from global leadership development activities such as cross-cultural training and international assignments (Caligiuri and Tarique, 2009; Leiba-O'Sullivan, 1999). Personality characteristics are relatively stable and predispose humans to behave in certain ways, given particular situations, to accomplish certain goals, and so on. (e.g., Buss, 1989; Costa and McCrae, 1992).

While improving language and cultural knowledge, skills and abilities is a reasonable expectation as a precursor to a developmental experience, altering one's basic underlying personality characteristics is far less likely to occur, as personality is relatively immutable. Illustrating this order effect, Caligiuri and Di Santo (2001) found that personality characteristics did not change as the result of participating in a global leadership development program, while knowledge and abilities did change. Given that certain personality characteristics may be necessary for global leadership development to occur, and that personality characteristics are not likely to change from the training and development aimed at improving global leadership competence, it is important for individuals who are self-initiating global leadership development to be honest with themselves about their own personalities. Thus, individuals should be realistic about their personality characteristics in the context of developing their global leadership competence.

Considering personality characteristics more closely, research has found that five factors provide a useful typology or taxonomy for classifying them (Digman, 1990; Goldberg, 1992; 1993; McCrae and Costa, 1987; 1989; McCrae and John, 1992). These five factors have been found repeatedly through factor analyses and confirmatory factor analyses across, time, contexts and cultures (Buss, 1991; Digman, 1990; Goldberg, 1992, 1993; McCrae and Costa, 1987; 1997; McCrae and John, 1992) and are labeled 'the Big Five'. The Big Five personality factors are: (1) extroversion; (2) agreeableness; (3) conscientiousness; (4) emotional stability; and (5) openness or intellect. Each of the Big Five personality characteristics has some relationship to success of people who live and work internationally (Ones and Viswesvaran, 1997; 1999; Caligiuri, 2000a; 2000b) and are likely to underlie, to some extent, the ability to complete some of the global leadership tasks successfully and develop through global leadership experiences, such as international assignments.

Self-awareness of these five personality characteristics may also be particularly important given that some traits are reflected in given countries' cultural norms and values. For example, researchers at Personnel Decisions International (PDI) conducted a five-year study exploring the personality traits that characterize managers and executives around the globe. The study was attempting to better understand the personality differences that exist across cultures which may, at times, lead to miscommunication and misperceptions among associates working in a multicultural setting. Data were collected from 12000 managers and executives from 12 countries: the United States, Canada, China, France, Germany, Hong Kong, India, Japan, Mexico, Saudi Arabia, The Netherlands and the United Kingdom (Lewis, 2006). Their findings suggest that certain traits are more prevalent in given cultures. The knowledge of one's personality match (or mismatch) in a given country may also affect one's ability to be an effective global leader in that country or with people from that country. As before, the cultural match does not, on its own, make one an effective global leader, as culturally agile leaders need to be great in many countries and with people from many cultures (even when there is a mismatch). However, given that cultural experiences are the mechanisms through which global leadership development can occur, these cultural matches may affect the outcome of development, especially in the initial stages of development.

Based on the research related to cultural differences and the research on predicting who will do well completing global leadership tasks, self-awareness of one's personality characteristics is important. The following will consider each characteristic in turn to better understand why each of the Big Five will influence one's global leadership effectiveness.

Extroversion
Many of the global leadership tasks have a social component (for example, working with colleagues from other countries, supervising employees who are of different nationalities). Extroverts have a greater natural ease with social demands and may be more willing to put forth the effort necessary to interact effectively with people from different countries. These extroverted individuals can successfully assert themselves and navigate through the hierarchy of their social environment to achieve personal success (for example, learn 'who is who', who has influence, who can be trusted). As extroverts enjoy being with people, they try to seek out the company of others, which allows them to mix well with the host nationals despite the cultural differences.

In the context of living and working in another country (the most common developmental activity), international assignees who assert themselves to establish relationships with both host nationals and other expatriates can effectively learn the social culture of the host country (Abe and Wiseman, 1983; Black, 1990; Dinges, 1983; Mendenhall and Oddou, 1985; 1988; Searle and Ward, 1990). Thus, extroversion is particularly important to learn the work and non-work social culture in the host country.

Self-awareness of this personality characteristic may be particularly important given that in some cultures the trait of extroversion reflects cultural norms which may change the rate of development at the onset. In the study conducted by PDI, some cultures have a tendency to seek out others' input and insights in problem-solving, such as brainstorming, while people from other cultures have a preference for working independently on an assignment (Lewis, 2006).

Agreeableness

The ability to form reciprocal social alliances is achieved through the personality characteristic of agreeableness (Buss, 1991). Leaders who are more agreeable (that is, deal with conflict collaboratively, strive for mutual understanding, and are less competitive) report greater cross-cultural adjustment while living and working internationally (Caligiuri, 2000a; 2000b; Ones and Viswesvaran, 1997; Black, 1990; Tung, 1981) and are likely to have greater success with global leadership tasks involving collaboration (for example, working with colleagues from other countries). They tend to be empathetic, considerate, friendly, generous, helpful, and value getting along with others. For self-development of global leadership competence to be effective, it is important to understand whether one possesses the personality characteristic of agreeableness given that much of how culture is learned is through peer-to-peer interactions with people from diverse cultures.

Self-awareness of this personality characteristic may be particularly important given that in some cultures the trait of agreeableness or harmony reflects cultural norms. In the study conducted by PDI, participants from Japan and Saudi Arabia scored highest on agreeableness. Individuals within this cultural context will put their own emotions aside for the sake of the group (Lewis, 2006). For individuals experiencing these cultures in the context of development, this self-awareness may be very important because it will affect the nature of the experience, making it more or less challenging depending on the cultural match.

Conscientiousness

Individuals who are conscientious demonstrate greater effort and task commitment. Given the higher level of complexity, global leadership tasks (for example, managing foreign suppliers or vendors) are likely to require more effort than comparable tasks in the domestic context (for example, managing domestically-based suppliers or vendors). In the case of developing global leadership skills through international assignments, Ones and Viswesvaran (1997) suggest that those who are conscientious will feel a greater sense of commitment to their tasks, which may be especially important when the assignment is particularly challenging (as they often are). Self-awareness about one's level of conscientiousness is also important given the higher level of complexity embedded in global leadership tasks (for example, managing foreign suppliers or vendors) which will often require more effort than comparable tasks in the domestic context (Caligiuri, 2006). For self-development of global leadership competence to be effective, it is important to understand one's level of conscientiousness given that much of how culture is learned is through significant work experiences in diverse countries and with people from other cultures. These developmental experiences, in general, can be more complex given cultural bounds of one's knowledge, and may require a higher level of determination and conscientiousness.

Emotional stability
Emotional stability is a universal adaptive mechanism enabling humans to cope with stress in their environment (Buss, 1991). Given that great stress is often associated with leadership in ambiguous and unfamiliar environments, emotional stability is an important personality characteristic for those interested in working as global leaders (Caligiuri, 2006). For self-development of global leadership competence to be effective, it is important to understand whether one possesses the personality characteristic of emotional stability. This is important given that much of how culture is learned is through significant experiences in diverse cultures, experiences which will test one's assumptions and allow one to see the cultural bounds of one's values and knowledge. Being pushed to this realization can be stressful.

Related to emotional stability, Mendenhall and Oddou (1985) proposed that having self-orientation was important for the cross-cultural adjustment of global assignees and, by extension (given that many developmental opportunities involve living internationally), for developing global leaders. Self-orientation encompasses characteristics 'that enable the expatriate to maintain mental health, psychological well-being, and effective stress management' (Mendenhall and Oddou, 1985). Both self-efficacy and self-confidence refer to one's belief regarding one's own competence or ability to overcome obstacles and succeed in a given situation (Bandura, 1982; Rosenberg, 1979).

Having self-confidence and a healthy emotional strength while working internationally may be especially important because verbal and non-verbal signs of encouragement or support may be un-interpretable in host countries due to cultural or language differences. Further research suggests that confidence is linked with encouragement-seeking and training-seeking behaviors (Tharenou et al., 1994), both of which are likely to facilitate the likelihood of self-initiating global leadership development. In self-initiated development, encouragement will not originate from an outside source, such as one's supervisor. Instead, in self-initiated development, individuals will need to enhance their performance by inspiring confidence from within themselves.

Self-awareness of this personality characteristic may also be particularly important in self-development given that in some cultures the trait of emotional stability may reflect their cultural norms, affecting one's experience in a given cultural context or with people from that culture. In the PDI study, for example, it was found that the Netherlands and Germany scored highest on the emotional balance scale, which reflects a preference for control and predictability over extreme overt expressions of feelings or emotionality (Lewis, 2006).

Openness
The self-awareness about one's openness is important given that success in global business activities requires a non-judgmental and open-minded approach toward the attitudes and behaviors of people from other cultures. Individuals with greater openness will have fewer rigid views of right and wrong, appropriate and inappropriate, and so on, and are more likely to be accepting of diverse cultures (e.g., Abe and Wiseman, 1983; Black, 1990; Cui and van den Berg, 1991; Hammer et al., 1978). Having non-judgmental attitudes enables global professionals to respect cultural differences; they believe that the values, norms and behaviors are as justified as their own – even when they are vastly different. People who are open to the differences in others are less likely to treat people from different cultures as inferior. For self-development of global leadership competence to be effective, it would be important to honestly assess whether one possesses the personality characteristic of openness, given that much of how culture is learned is experiential through interactions with people from diverse cultures. Openness, therefore, is critical for development to occur.

AN EXAMPLE OF A SELF-INITIATED TOOL FOR GAINING SELF-AWARENESS OF KSAOS

There are self-assessment tools available to help individuals better understand whether they are predisposed for global leadership activities.

One example is The Self-Assessment for Global Endeavors for Global Business Leaders (The SAGE for Global Business Leaders; Caligiuri, 2007). The SAGE for Global Business Leaders was designed to self-assess an individual's dispositional characteristics, experiential background and cultural orientations that will influence his or her ability to be successful as a global business professional. The SAGE for Global Business Leaders takes about 20 minutes to complete and offers a detailed feedback report. This tool was designed for self-awareness, as a guide to illustrate individuals' strengths and potential opportunities for personal and professional development (Caligiuri, 2007).

If an individual opts to self-initiate an international assignment, there is another related tool called The Self-Assessment for Global Endeavors (The SAGE) which has been used for over a decade by organizations sending people on international assignments (Caligiuri, 1998). In this tool, The SAGE is a decision-making guide designed for individuals who are contemplating whether to pursue an international assignment. The exercises in The SAGE encourage individuals to critically evaluate their personality characteristics relative to those needed for an international assignment. The SAGE also encourages individuals to explore their career development and career motivation for a global assignment. Moreover, The SAGE prompts individuals to engage their family members in the decision-making process – and offers structured exercises to facilitate this. The SAGE is intended for individuals to do privately (or with his or her family) – either self-initiated or as a part of a career counseling or decision counseling session. If self-development will involve an international assignment, it is critical for individuals to consider the readiness of their family members.

SELF-INITIATED GLOBAL LEADERSHIP DEVELOPMENT ACTIVITIES

There are different self-initiated methods for individuals to acquire information and gain knowledge and improve their global leadership competence. Assuming the requisite immutable attributes are present, self-initiated training and development will increase one's effectiveness on global leadership tasks. Self-initiated training and development interventions can include taking formal education programs, seeking a cultural coach or mentor, engaging in immersion programs, and self-initiating developmental international assignments (Caligiuri et al., 2005).

There is a variety of cross-cultural training and developmental activities in which individuals can self-initiate to improve their cultural knowledge and their performance on global leadership activities and increase their cultural agility. According to Caligiuri and Tarique (2006), international training activities tend to have a present (or near-future) time frame. They address particular deficiencies in individuals' intercultural competencies, develop specific competencies, focus on more tangible aspects of improving performance, and help individuals gain knowledge in a certain area. Training is the easiest to self-initiate because much of this learning can come from independent acts such as reading books, watching documentaries, taking an on-line course, and the like.

While individuals can read about cultures, study cultural artifacts in a museum and watch documentaries, the deepest level of global leadership development will happen when individuals experience culture for themselves, learning from their experiences in different countries and with people from different cultures (Caligiuri and Tarique, 2008). Development, unlike training, involves interaction with others and may be somewhat more challenging to self-initiate. The following two sections of this chapter will focus on both self-initiated training activities and self-initiated development activities.

Self-Initiated Global Leadership Training Activities

Cross-cultural training and language training are two areas in which individuals can self-initiate opportunities to readily increase their knowledge, which will be helpful in their self-development of global leadership competence (Caligiuri and Tarique, 2006). By definition, cross-cultural training can help individuals to behave in a more culturally appropriate manner and help managers identify suitable ways of performing their tasks with people from a given culture or in a given country (Black and Mendenhall, 1990; Kealy and Protheroe, 1996). Cross-cultural training may also help individuals develop methods of coping with the uncertainty when working with people from different cultures or in foreign countries (Earley, 1987) and may help individuals form realistic expectations for their cross-national interactions and experiences (Black and Mendenhall, 1990; Black et al., 1991; Caligiuri et al., 2001). It warrants repeating that speaking another language and living comfortably in another culture are not the goals of global leadership development; they are the mechanisms through which global leadership development can occur.

Individuals can self-initiate cross-cultural training in a variety of ways as there are many different ways to readily acquire information and gain knowledge; one can learn by taking a trip and exploring a new culture, by reading a non-fiction book about another culture, or by attending a lecture or class on a different culture. Formal educational training programs can easily be self-initiated; one can enroll to gain foundational knowledge on more tangible topics of international business such as international finance, currency exchange and cross-cultural negotiations. Formal educational training programs include self-study courses offered electronically or in the traditional paper and pencil distance education format, off-site courses offered by academic institutions, and in-house or on-site company seminars offered by subject matter experts (Noe, 2004; Gupta and Govindarajan, 2002).

Individuals can self-initiate formal education by applying to the academic degree program of their choice. There are formal educational programs specifically designed to build competence in global business leadership. For example, the university currently ranked number 1 for their MBA in International Business is the Thunderbird School of Global Management in Arizona (USA). Thunderbird specializes in international management and global business and the university's programs facilitate the development of global competencies. As the www.thunderbird.edu website offers, the students will receive:

> an unmatched global business education with international and cross-cultural studies to ensure you're fluent in the language of international business, no matter where in the world you choose to go. Imagine a global macro-environment that provides you with the cultural, political, regulatory, legal, and economic knowledge you need for the micro-management of business, in specific regional and local business environments.

It would seem that an individual who would like to self-initiate global leadership development and who does not yet possess some of the basics of international business, would benefit from enrolling in international business courses from well-regarded universities.

Increasing in popularity, there are various online cross-cultural training tools available to help individuals to self-assess and gain cultural knowledge. RW-3's Culture Wizard is one such web-based tool that helps in providing valuable insight on ways to work successfully with people and teams from different cultures. RW-3 tools are stand-alone, self-guided learning experiences that are designed to create an awareness of the importance of culture in everyday business interaction and illustrate the impact that culture has on people's values, beliefs and behaviors. The online facility allows learners to assess their needs, evaluate their life experiences and develop programs that are tailored to their individual information requirements. For example, the tools range from assessments for global business professionals and international assignees to a full cross-cultural course and business applications such as managing global teams and collaborating across styles and cultures.

Like cultural training, self-initiated language training will also help individuals who are interested in increasing their global leadership competence given that interactions with people from diverse countries are the mechanisms through which global leadership development can occur. Language training enhances individuals' language skills necessary for communication in a given target foreign language. Also, like cultural training, language training can be gained more informally through self-directed audio courses or formally in a classroom setting or in formal immersion programs.

Language training enhances individuals' language skills necessary for communication in a given target foreign language. Language training aids in communications, demonstrates an attitude of attempting to learn about the host culture, enables one to be polite, permits understanding not otherwise available and is an intrinsic part of the culture. Language training exposes the trainee to words that are not easily translated, yet captures important values unique to the culture. When combined, the linguistic learning blended with the social psychological learning is a comprehensive way to learn much about a target culture (Oberg, 1960). Like cultural training, language training can be gained more informally through self-directed audio courses or formally in a classroom setting or in immersion programs.

In the self-initiated context (often also self-funded), self-directed audio courses are comprehensive, affordable and convenient learning solutions. They enable individuals to learn at their own pace and at the time and place most convenient for them. Examples are the 'eBerlitz Self Study' (Berlitz Publishing) and 'Teach Yourself' (NTC Publishing). Language training provides an interactive online or audio learning for language skills training. Individuals can develop their language skills at their own pace and probably in their own time after work. Like cultural training, self-initiated language training will also help individuals who are interested in increasing their global leadership competence.

Language immersion programs are more structured and usually involve some classroom and some natural interaction in given host countries. Anyone who has traveled abroad on their own will attest to the fact that language learning is quickest when there is no alternative. A total immersion experience means that the student is isolated from his or her native language and must use the new target language for communication. For example, the Foreign Language Study Abroad Service in Miami, Florida arranges home-stay instruction of a week or longer during which time the student stays with a family living in another culture (Zhan, 1999).

Many language immersion programs involve some classroom and some natural interaction in given host countries. An example is 'Lingua Service

Worldwide, Ltd', a language study abroad agency which specializes in full immersion intensive language program opportunities in different countries. These experiences give individuals opportunities to learn new languages within the country where the target language is the first language. Apart from the classroom training, this type of an immersion experience allows participants to interact with host nationals (and practice language skills) and learn more about the host culture.

Self-Initiated Global Leadership Development Activities

The deepest level of cultural development happens when individuals experience culture for themselves. Experientially, individuals learn from every cross-cultural encounter as they seek opportunities for peer-to-peer contact with people from diverse cultures and seek opportunities to question their own assumptions to realize the limits of their own knowledge base (Caligiuri and Tarique, 2009). There are many types of developmental experiences which can be self-initiated but for them to be effective they would need both elements: peer-to-peer contact and opportunities to realize the limits of one's knowledge.

As Caligiuri and Tarique (2009) found, greater participation in high-contact cross-cultural leadership development experiences allows individuals to improve their ability to reproduce culturally-appropriate skills and behaviors. The more exposure an individual has with high-contact cross-cultural leadership development experiences, the more opportunity he or she has to practice the modeled behavior and to refine the ability to reproduce the modeled behavior at a later time in the appropriate situation. Several studies have used the basic principle of contact hypothesis to examine the relationships and interactions between individuals from different cultures (e.g., Church, 1982; Caligiuri, 2000b).

Self-initiated international assignments are an example of a high-contact developmental opportunity as they provide an opportunity to live in different countries and develop an extensive understanding of the local culture by interacting with host nationals and participating in local traditions and customs. International assignments increase cultural agility through high-level contact with people from different cultures. Those on international assignments report that they develop an appreciation for new things, become culturally sensitive, and learn to respect the values and customs different from their own (Osland, 1995). Many also report to have developed valuable skills through their international experience (Tung, 1998) and that these newly developed skills greatly enhance their expertise both in the domestic and the international context (Adler, 1981; 2001; Baughn, 1995; Black et al., 1992; Napier and Peterson, 1991). The ability for individuals to understand the extent to which their skills and abilities are culturally bound is one of the most powerful lessons learned on international assignments related to global leadership competence (Caligiuri and Di Santo, 2001).

There are various international internship opportunities available which allow individuals to gain hands-on experience in their preferred field; these can last from one month to one year. For example, Masters of Human Resource Management (MHRM) students at Rutgers University can apply for the Chelius International Internship. The goal of this internship is to expand cross-cultural understanding for students who are interested in furthering their careers in the area of global human resources, and who may need international experience to achieve this goal. Each year, the internships are awarded to students identified as excellent scholars in the MHRM program with an expressed interest in international human resource management issues. As the first author is also one of the administrators of this program, she can report that the students who have participated in the program enthusiastically describe the experience as being highly developmental.

CONCLUSION

This chapter explored the various self-initiated global leadership activities which can help individuals to become culturally agile and build their global leadership competencies. To be effective global leaders, individuals should initiate cross-cultural training and development opportunities, such as taking language training and cultural training and self-initiating an international assignment. We hope that those who are predisposed and motivated to become global leaders will invest in themselves as they self-initiate and engage in high-contact global leadership developmental opportunities. The need for future global leaders will remain high and it is not likely that firms will be able to keep pace with the demand for future leaders. The opportunity is ripe for individuals who wish to take control of their careers and self-develop their global leadership competencies.

REFERENCES

Abe, H. and Wiseman, R. (1983), 'A cross-culture confirmation of the dimensions of intercultural effectiveness', *International Journal of Intercultural Relations*, **7**, 5–67.

Adler, N.J. (1981), 'Re-entry: managing cross-cultural transitions', *Group and Organizational Studies*, **6**, 341–56.

Adler, N.J. (2001), *International Dimensions of Organizational Behavior*, 4th edn, Cincinnati, OH: South-Western.

Adler, N.J. and Bartholomew, S. (1992), 'Managing globally competent people', *Academy of Management Executive*, **6**, 52–65.

Adler, N.J. and Ghadar, F. (1990), 'Strategic human resource management: a global perspective', in R. Pieper (ed.), *Human Resource Management in International Comparison*, Berlin: Walter de Gruyter, pp. 235–60.

Bandura, A. (1982), 'Self efficacy mechanism in human agency', *American Psychologist*, **37**, 122–47.

Bartlett, C. and Ghoshal, S. (2003), 'What is a global manager?', *Harvard Business Review*, August, pp. 101–8.

Baughn, C. (1995), 'Personal and organizational factors associated with effective repatriation', in J. Selmer (ed.), Expatriate Management: New Ideas for International Business, Westport, CT: Quorum Books, pp. 215–30.

Black, J. (1990), 'The relationship of personal characteristics with adjustment of Japanese expatriate managers', *Management International Review*, **30**, 119–34.

Black, J.S. and Gregersen, H.B. (1991), 'Antecedents to cross-cultural adjustment for expatriates in Pacific Rim assignments', *Human Relations*, **44**, 497–515.

Black. J. and Mendenhall, M. (1990), 'Cross-cultural training effectiveness: a review and a theoretical framework for future research', *Academy of Management Review*, **15**, 113–36.

Black, J.S., Gregersen, H.B. and Mendenhall, M.E. (1992), *Global Assignments*, San Francisco, CA: Jossey-Bass.

Black, J., Mendenhall, M. and Oddou, G. (1991), 'Toward a comprehensive model of international adjustment: an integration of multiple theoretical perspectives', *Academy of Management Review*, **16**, 291–317.

Buss, A. (1989), 'Personality as traits', *American Psychologist*, **44**, 1378–85.

Buss, D.M. (1991), 'Evolutionary personality psychology', in M. Rosenzweig and L. Porter (eds), *Annual Review of Psychology*, **42**, 459–92, Palo Alto, CA: Annual Reviews Inc.

Caligiuri, P. (1998), *The Self-Assessment for Global Endeavors (The SAGE)*, New York: RW-3.

Caligiuri, P.M. (2000a), 'The Big Five personality characteristics as predictors of expatriate success', *Personnel Psychology*, **53**, 67–88.

Caligiuri, P. (2000b), 'Selecting expatriates for personality characteristics: a moderating effect of personality on the relationship between host national contact and cross-cultural adjustment', *Management International Review*, **40**, 61–80.

Caligiuri, P.M. (2006), 'Developing global leaders', *Human Resource Management Review*, **16**, 219–28.

Caligiuri, P. (2007), *The Self-Assessment for Global Endeavors – Global Business Leaders* (The SAGE-GBL), New York: RW-3.

Caligiuri, P.M. and Di Santo, V. (2001), 'Global competence: what is it, and can it be developed through global assignments?', *Human Resource Planning*, **3**, 27–35.

Caligiuri, P.M. and Tarique, I. (2006), 'International assignee selection and cross-cultural training and development', in J. Björkrnan and G. Stahl (eds), *Handbook of Research in International Human Resource Management*, Cheltenham, UK and Northampton, MA, USA: Edward Elgar Publishing, pp. 302–21.

Caligiuri, P. and Tarique, I. (2008), 'Developing managerial and organizational cross-cultural capabilities', in C. Cooper and R. Burke (eds), *The Peak Performing Organization*, Abington, UK: Routledge Publishers, pp. 234–51.

Caligiuri, P. and Tarique, I. (2009), 'Predicting effectiveness in global leadership activities', *Journal of World Business*, **44**(3), 336–46.

Caligiuri, P.M., Lazarova, M. and Tarique, I. (2005), 'Training, learning and development in multinational organizations', in H. Scullion and M. Linehan (eds), *International Human Resource Management: A Critical Text*, Basingstoke, UK: Palgrave Macmillan, pp. 71–90.

Caligiuri, P.M., Phillips, J., Lazarova, M., Tarique, I. and Burgi, O. (2001), 'Expectations produced in cross-cultural training programs as a predictor of expatriate adjustment', *International Journal of Human Resource Management*, **12**(3), 357–72.

Church, A. (1982), 'Sojourner adjustment', *Psychological Bulletin*, **9**, 540–72.

Costa, P. and McCrae, R. (1992), 'Four ways five factors are basic', *Personality and Individual Differences*, **13**, 653–65.

Cui, G. and van den Berg, S. (1991), 'Testing the construct validity of intercultural effectiveness', *International Journal of Intercultural Relations*, **15**, 227–41.

Digman, J.M. (1990), Personality structure: emergence of the five-factor model. *Annual Review of Psychology*, **41**, 417–40.

Dinges, N. (1983), 'Intercultural competence', in D. Landis and R.W. Brislin (eds), *Handbook of Intercultural Training: Issues in Theory and Design: Vol.1*, New York: Pergamon Press, pp. 176–202.

Earley, P.A. (1987), Intercultural training for managers: a comparison of documentary and interpersonal methods', *Academy of Management Review*, **39**, 685–98.

Goldberg, L. (1992), 'The development of markers for the big-five factor structure', *Psychological Assessment*, **4**, 26–42.

Goldberg, L. (1993), 'The structure of phenotypic personality traits', *American Psychologist*, **48**, 26–34.

Gupta, A. and Govindarajan, V. (2002), 'Cultivating a global mindset', *The Academy of Management Executive*, **16**, 116–26.

Hammer, M.R., Gudykunst, W.B. and Wiseman, R.L. (1978), 'Dimensions of intercultural effectiveness: an exploratory study', *International Journal of Intercultural Relations*, **2**, 382–93.

Harris, P.R. and Moran, R.T. (1987), *Managing Cultural Differences*, 2nd edn, Houston, TX: Gulf.

Kealy, D. and Protheroe, D. (1996), 'The effectiveness of cross culture training for expatriates: an assessment of the literature on the issue', *International Journal of Intercultural Relations*, **20**, 141–65.

Leiba-O'Sullivan, S. (1999), 'The distinction between stable and dynamic cross cultural competencies: implications for expatriate trainability', *Journal of International Business Studies*, **30**, 709–25.

Lewis, Bob (2006), 'Managing across borders', available at www.talentmgt.com/departments/dashboard/2006/November/166/index.php?pt=a&aid=166&start=3284&page=2, accessed 31 March 2009.

McCrae, R. and Costa, P. (1987), 'Validation of the five-factor model of personality across instruments and observers', *Journal of Personality and Social Psychology*, **52**, 81–90.

McCrae, R. and Costa, P. (1989), 'More reasons to adopt the five-factor model', *American Psychologist*, **44**, 451–2.

McCrae, R. and Costa, P. (1997), 'Personality trait structure as a human universal', *American Psychologist*, **52**, 509–16.

McCrae, R. and John, O. (1992), 'An introduction to the five factor model and its applications', *Journal of Personality*, **60**, 175–216.

Mendenhall, M.E. and Oddou, G. (1985), 'The dimensions of expatriate acculturation', *Academy of Management Review*, **10**, 39–47.

Mendenhall, M.E. and Oddou, G. (1988), 'The overseas assignment: a practical look', *Business Horizons*, **31**, 78–84

Napier, N. and Peterson, R. (1991), 'Expatriate re-entry: what do expatriates have to say?', *Human Resource Planning*, **14**, 19–28.

Noe, R. (2004), *Employee Training and Development*, Boston, MA: McGraw-Hill.

Oberg, K. (1960), 'Cultural shock: adjustment to new cultural environments', *Practical Anthropology*, **7**, 177–82.

Ones, D. and Viswesvaran, C. (1997), 'Personality determinants in the prediction of aspects of expatriate job success', in Z. Aycan (ed.), *Expatriate Management: Theory and Practice*, Greenwich, CT: JAI Press, pp. 63–92.

Ones, D. and Viswesvaran, C. (1999), 'Relative importance of personality dimensions for international assignee selection: a policy capturing study', *Human Performance*, **12**, 275–94.

Osland, J. (1995), *The Adventure of Working Abroad: Hero Tales from the Global Frontier*, San Francisco, CA: Jossey-Bass.

PriceWaterhouseCoopers (2007), '10th annual global CEO survey', available at http://www.pwc.com/extweb/insights.nsf/docid/46BC27700D2C1D18852572 600015D61B.

Rhinesmith, S. (1996), *A Manager's Guide to Globalization*, 2nd edn, New York: McGraw-Hill.

Rosenberg, M. (1979), *Conceiving the Self*, New York: Basic Books.

Searle, W. and Ward, C. (1990), 'The prediction of psychological and socio-cultural adjustment during cross-cultural transitions', *International Journal of Intercultural Relations*, **14**, 449–64.

Snow, R.E. (1991), 'Aptitude-treatment interaction as a framework for research on individual differences in psychotherapy', *Journal of Consulting and Clinical Psychology*, **59**, 205–16.

Spreitzer, G., McCall, M., Jr. and Mahoney, J. (1997), 'Early identification of international executive potential', *Journal of Applied Psychology*, **82**, 6–29.

Thaler-Carter, R.E. (2000), 'Whither global leaders?', *HR Magazine*, **45**(5), 83–8.

Tharenou, P., Latimer, S. and Conroy, D. (1994), 'How do you make it to the top? An examination of influences on women's and men's managerial advancement', *Academy of Management Journal*, **37**, 899–931.

Tung, R.L. (1981), 'Selection and training of personnel for overseas assignments', *Columbia Journal of World Business*, **16**, 21–5.

Tung, R.L. (1998), 'American expatriates abroad: from neophytes to cosmopolitans', *Journal of World Business*, **33**, 125–44.

Zhan, E.S. (1999), 'Becoming bilingual: caught in conversation – or out of it', *World Trade*, **12**, 68–9.

16. Learning from life experiences: a study of female academic leaders in Australia

Linley Lord and Susan Vinnicombe

There has been an increased representation of women within Australian universities. This is due in part to structural changes in the system and in part to equal opportunity and affirmative action legislation, policy and practices. However, gender equality has not been reached and universities continue to operate as highly gendered organizations (Currie et al., 2002; Eveline, 2004; Fogelberg et al., 1999). For women in academic roles some gains have been made. Their participation rate has risen from one-fifth of all academic staff in the mid-1980s to two-fifths of all academic staff nearly two decades later. Women, however, remain under-represented at senior levels with men accounting for more than 80 per cent of the most senior academic positions in Australian universities (Carrington and Pratt, 2003).

Overall women make up 30 per cent of university management positions. Women remain concentrated in discipline areas that are considered traditionally female so that there are both horizontal and vertical gender differences in the academic workforce in Australia (Carrington and Pratt, 2003). During the period 1996 to 2003 the number and proportion of women vice-chancellors in Australia increased from 2 (5 per cent) to 10 (27 per cent) of all vice-chancellors. At the deputy vice-chancellor/pro vice-chancellor and dean position level, however, the gains are considerably lower. There were 19 (19 per cent) women in 1996 at these levels and by 2003 there were 27 (21 per cent) (Chesterman et al., 2005). In 2004 only 16 per cent of professors were women (Winchester et al., 2005). It is common in many Australian universities for academic leadership roles such as head of school appointments to be offered on a 'contract' basis. That is, the leadership position is offered for a fixed term, usually three to five years. At the completion of the contract the position is usually readvertised. Thus the incumbent can potentially return to their previous school/department role at the end of the contract, either through their own choice or as a result of an unsuccessful application for a further term in the leadership role.

447

RESEARCH APPROACH

The research took a phenomenological approach informed by feminist perspectives to contribute to our understanding of the lived experience of academic women leaders in Australian universities. Thirty-five in-depth semi-structured interviews were conducted and led to the development of a model of engagement and enactment of leadership. Insight was also gained regarding the context within which this engagement and enactment occurred. All of the women interviewed were in positions that the institutions regarded as leadership positions, that is, they had responsibility for financial and human resources. The data collection process was adapted from Creswell's (1998) cycle of data collection. A purposeful sampling approach was used to identify academic women who held formal organizational positions that included responsibility for human and financial resources. The research took place within the context of being an academic woman within an Australian university at a time when universities were under increasing pressure resulting from globalisation and national agendas for reform.

A set of interview questions acted as a guide for the interview process. The questions focused on how the women experienced leadership, seeking information on events such as a typical day, how they saw their gender impacting on their career and in their current role, and how they gave and received support as leaders.

ENGAGING IN AND ENACTING LEADERSHIP

The leadership experiences of the 35 women leaders were framed as a four-step model of engaging in and enacting leadership shown in Figure 16.1. 'Stepping' explained the process by which women entered leadership positions; 'settling' focused on doing the job and recognized the integral aspects of being a woman; 'strengthening' focused on the particular aspects the women saw as important to their enactment of leadership; and finally 'sustaining' focused on how the women were supported and given support in their role as leaders. In this chapter we explore how the women responded to the challenges at each of the four stages through lessons learned from personal life experiences.

Stepping

A key factor that prompted these women's decisions to enter leadership was the impact of role models. Overwhelmingly when role models

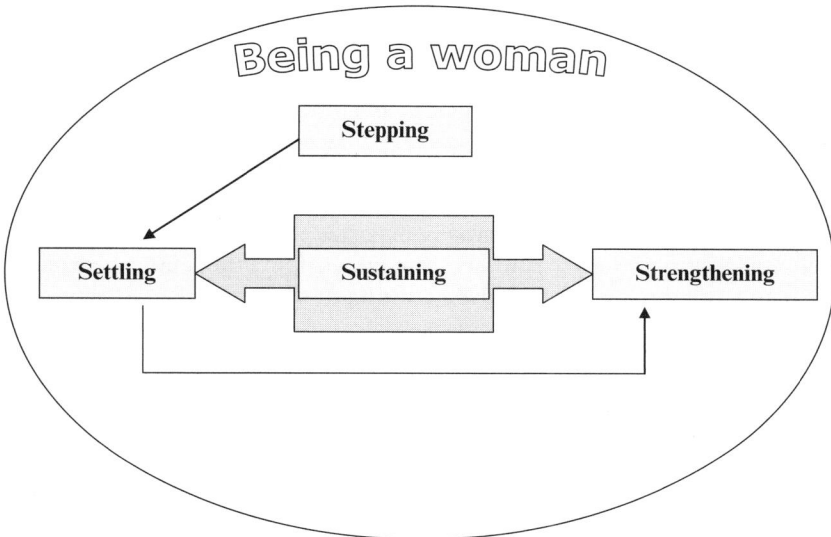

Figure 16.1   Engaging in and enactment of leadership

were discussed, they were male role models. This is not surprising given the relative under-representation of women in senior roles in Australian universities (Commonwealth Higher Education Management Services, 1998; Currie et al., 2002; Eveline, 2004). Moreover, it was the negative aspect rather than the positive aspect of male role models that was most often raised. For example, one woman's decision to enter leadership was the result of her experience of the then current incumbent who she saw as having 'no management skills whatsoever; less vision and was a bully'. This not only led to her decision to apply for the role but made her determined to be a very different type of leader. Another noted that she had:

> watched these guys in positions and how they keep their positions of authority when they see people, you know, coming up because they feel threatened, and I'm thinking, and I've seen them do it and they do it in this sarcastic cynical, like put down way and I don't want to do that.

The absence of positive role models may explain why many of the women in this study had not considered taking up a leadership role until they were 'pushed', encouraged or told by others more senior to themselves to apply for a specific position. Senior staff, peers and friends played an important role in encouraging or 'forcing' women to step into leadership. This included being asked by peers who recognized their leadership potential or in some cases told they were needed by the dean or vice-chancellor, often in response to an organizational crisis. Friends who were external to the organization had encouraged some. Thus for most of the women it was a sense of being needed, either by the organization or by others, or their frustration they had experienced with current leaders that lead them to consider a leadership role. They felt pressured to accept the 'invitation' or had a sense of obligation to their peers. They spoke about their move into leadership roles as unexpected, unplanned and often accidental. Throughout their paid and unpaid work life they had consistently chosen work that was for them interesting and where they felt that they could make a difference. Being prepared to volunteer, 'whenever a volunteer is called for I put my hand up . . . it doesn't matter what it is . . . I think it is a new learning experience, probably won't do any harm on my cv' or for some to be volunteered, 'well it wasn't my choice it was a crisis situation' shaped their development as a leader. Their community work often provided the opportunity to develop their leadership skills further, 'I join something socially in the community, and I think, first thing you know I am going to be the President of something in the community. I know I can do that because I have organizational skills and I tend to speak up.'

Some had taken the steps to develop themselves professionally including being prepared to gain international experience that wasn't available in Australia at the time. This meant that for one woman she had:

> educated myself or exposed myself to things that I thought I needed to know or know more about. Quite early on for example in my working life as a young professional, I needed a certain sort of work experience and I knew I couldn't get it in Australia at that time so I worked in the UK for a couple of years.

Thus leadership for most was shaped by the absence of positive role models and their ability to draw together the learning from various roles they had undertaken in paid and unpaid roles. Key characteristics of these previous roles were that they were interesting, had intrinsic value, and offered incumbents the opportunity to make a difference. In summary, these women's moves into leadership were rarely triggered through a desire to take on a leadership role but rather by the need for change or by others' encouragement or pressure to take on a particular role.

Settling

Once they had 'stepped' into leadership the women had to establish themselves in the new role. They were faced with a number of choices. They had to determine their goals and what style they would adopt and/or develop as a leader. Many didn't see themselves as leaders although their early experiences would suggest that others had seen their leadership potential and had encouraged them to undertake leadership roles: 'I suppose in a way I've always sort of had a bit of a leadership personality. I've been pushed into these positions right from the time I was in school into being captain of the hockey team.'

Others, regardless of their earlier experiences, found that:

> leadership was a concept that is utterly alien to me in that until sort of recent years and it has been my own reading on it that has developed my concepts of it but there is nothing in my career anywhere that I would consider even informed me or encouraged me to develop concepts of what is leadership.

Thus, for some, sport provided the opportunity to begin to develop their leadership skills and style. For others, leadership remained a somewhat 'alien' concept and it wasn't until they were in a leadership role that they reconsidered their conceptions of leadership and what it might mean for them as a leader.

A number of women commented on the lack of training provided, which meant that they felt unprepared for the role and faced a steep and often lonely learning curve. For most, learning the job and developing their style as a leader were concurrent activities coupled with the unrelenting pressure of the role, the hard grind that impacted on their energy levels and their feeling of being able to meet or attempting to meet the demands of the role. This added stress, particularly for those who were entering their first formal leadership role in the organization. However, there was for some a sense of surprise that, despite their feelings of unpreparedness, they were enjoying the role more than they had expected, and this helped them to continue making things happen and to meet the demands of the role.

Being a woman impacted on the way they did the job and how others saw them. Even if they tried to ignore their gender they were reminded by others of the impact that being a woman in a leadership role had and how it impacted on their being accepted as a leader in their own right. Early experiences of not being heard or taken seriously impacted on the type of leader women wanted to be.

> I would say things at these meetings and it was like I hadn't spoken . . . I got a very much feminist awakening of things. And then twenty minutes later a male would say the same thing and it would be jumped on as a marvellous idea. This idea, 'Am I invisible? What's wrong with me?' It took me a while to figure out that you are female and you're young.

This meant that they took active steps to ensure everyone's voice was both heard and acknowledged and became active mentors to more junior members of staff who were invariably women.

Gender impacted on the way many of the women developed their operating style as leaders. For some it meant that their choices were often constrained by the views that others held about appropriate operating styles for women. However, for some it was the combination of being a women and an immigrant that really shaped their leadership development.

> One that I was a woman, two I was an immigrant so I had a double situation. When I arrived I didn't speak any English . . . I had a long tortuous road. So in other words, my start and my finish of what I was doing was so delayed and it was the combination of being a woman and an immigrant I believe. It is not just one or the other. So when I was here I was absolutely dedicated, I locked everything out, just to educate myself. So I didn't marry, I didn't do anything, just to do that and I had to do that as a woman because if I had married or anything else I would have never got to this position.

Being an outsider in many situations meant that she became good at reading body language and observing what was going on around her. In her leadership role it meant that she was able to 'read' the situation more accurately and therefore was able to respond to situations more effectively, both with her staff and engaging with those more senior in the institution.

Most women, as noted above, felt unprepared for the roles they had taken on and this had the potential to impact on the way that they wanted to develop themselves as leaders. One of the ways many responded to this was to use their networks to make the job somewhat easier, 'I am quite instrumental. I know that you can build up a network and people will help you if you help them.'

Their networks provided a space that enabled them to test their ideas, get support and to get advice on a range of issues that they were confronting. For some, especially those who were at more senior levels, an external network was seen as particularly important for many of the issues they wanted to discuss.

Settling into the role meant that women drew on the networks that they had established as an important means of both learning the job and providing them with some support. Through the experience of being either invisible or highly visible because of their gender, many had become skilled at effectively reading the situation they were in and had actively taken steps to ensure that their and others' voices were heard and acknowledged.

Strengthening

Being in a leadership role was more complex than just developing a style of leadership and undertaking a range of tasks that the particular university saw as appropriate for the role. Being transparent and consistent in their decision making was seen as an important demonstration of their integrity, and a signal to others about how they intended to do the job regardless of the toughness of the circumstances. How they went about managing change and making decisions was driven by their values. For some, early experiences of isolation followed by success in sport helped shaped the way they 'did' leadership.

> I grew up in total isolation. I went to a one-teacher school and I had to start school when I was 4 because the school was going to close down and virtually I knew very few people until I went to boarding school. So I didn't have the opportunity to be socialized into thinking whether some things were appropriate for girls or boys to do and I guess I've always been a high achiever and I got, I suppose I got most of the feedback from that from being very good at sport. So my father for instance used to drive me all over the state for tennis because I was a state junior champion. And I suppose that sort of achievement gives you a lot of confidence about yourself which then prevents you from being – feeling like other people are threats to you or something.

The women willingly tackled long-standing issues and problems that included, in some cases, significant budget deficits, under-performing staff (even at a more senior rank), the quality and relevance of some teaching programs and under-performing research centers. A typical response was that they were committed to carrying out their roles properly, 'I suppose that's always been my approach, that if this is worth doing, I'll get in and do it 100 per cent'. In these various difficult situations some of the women realised that they were prepared to take risks, 'what I have discovered which is amazing, I would have described myself as a coward but compared to most of the boys I'm a risk taker'. For some it was the discipline of their doctoral studies that they believed had helped prepare them for demands of their role. As one noted, 'Ph.D. was the thing that prepared me for this. Like the training and the application and making you read . . . the rigor of the Ph.D. I wouldn't be here today without that.'

The women expressed a strong focus on equity. They wanted to ensure that there was internal equity within the school or faculty and that staff and students were treated fairly by the systems that were in place or that they put in place. They wanted to act in ways that made sure that staff were not exploited, particularly junior academic staff who were more likely to be women. For some it was their earlier experience of sexual harassment or discrimination that had resulted in the strong focus on gender equity. Earlier experience of ongoing short-term contracts or insecure employment resulted in a determination that their experience should not be repeated, and as a leader they would do whatever they could to ensure others weren't treated in the same way. They did this even when this put them at odds with the university or when the expectation was clearly not to 'rock the boat'.

Sustaining

Having adequate support sustained the women, making the job of leadership easier. The women identified five main areas where they received support; the organization, a supportive boss, peers, family and friends. The organization was discussed in terms of the presence or absence of structural support such as adequate policies and procedural frameworks or appropriate levels of administrative support. Peers were divided into two groups. First, there are those that are at the same organizational level either within the institution or external to it and secondly, where the women were head of a school, they spoke about staff members of the school as peers.

Support from senior staff was available for some women and problematic for others. The lack of support ranged from a level of indifference through to bullying situations. Some had experienced what had at first appeared to be support:

> The benevolent man is very dangerous because you don't pick it up for years. The person who tries to put you down and hold you down . . . in my early career I worked under two benevolent men . . . and they supported and encouraged me, they were really pleased to take on my ideas, to take on whatever I had created, whatever new policy, whatever new processes.

Nearly all of the women commented on the lack of support they received from other senior women, something they found surprising and disappointing, 'I have been mentored by senior male colleagues at crucial times, no women.' Most had used peer networks for their support and some established their own support groups to ensure an effective support base, 'I am very good at networking and running my own support groups and I get all my support from below and support from across.'

Interestingly very few women spoke about receiving support from their family and/or partner. There were some who stated that they had been really well supported but for others, when they spoke about their partner, it was in relation to the support they gave in order to get or keep the support they were given, 'he's immensely supportive but I'm keenly aware that there is a sort of constant pay-off and the pay-off is that I have to watch his ego.'

The demands of children presented a range of challenges for women who felt the burden of trying to be there for the university and for their children, my private life and my family life are incredibly important to me . . . I have two teenagers and that complicates my life significantly . . . I mean its not at all uncommon to be cooking dinner, listening to someone reading, talking to someone else about their school project having a phone call and trying to write an article.

However, having children meant developing certain skills, including the ability 'to do five things at once, it doesn't matter if the floor is filthy. . . it kind of grounds you' and not to worry as much about some of the things that don't get done.

Women received support from a range of people, both internal and external to the university and will build support networks if none are available. The support, however, was often conditional. It relied on them continuing to fulfill gender role expectations such as caring for others or taking major responsibility for running the home. A number of the women have also experienced lack of support from senior managers, peers and subordinates. It made their role more difficult and challenging as well as disappointing. Of particular surprise has been the lack of support they have received from other senior women and as a result they were more conscious, having moved into a leadership role, of the need to provide support to the women who reported to them.

DISCUSSION

Getting to a leadership position and determining how to be a woman leader continues to be challenging (Burke, 2005). For women there is the additional stress of being highly visible and often without the support structures of their male colleagues (Gardiner and Tiggemann, 1999; Kanter, 1977; Kerman, 1995).

In universities academic staff can move into leadership positions without having had managerial or supervisory experience. A strong research record is often viewed as a major requirement for leadership. However, being a good researcher doesn't necessarily provide opportunities for leadership development or relevant experience for roles that are increasingly managerial and driven by audit cultures in tight financial times (for Australian universities). Taking on a leadership role in such circumstances can be daunting.

Indvik (2004: pp. 292–3) suggests that women need 'resilience, perseverance, and initiative' to overcome the barriers and challenges they will face in organizations. For women, awareness of their gender, coupled with the lack of female role models, can act as limiting factors as far as developing their own leadership capacities, capabilities and styles is concerned

(Ruderman and Ohlott, 2004). Little attention has been paid to the career experiences of women, how women overcome barriers to career advancement and that to understand women's careers requires acknowledging that women have fundamentally different career development situations (Hamel, 2009).

In her study on career transition and leader development, Gibson (2008) identified five themes relating to leader development. These were 'validation of self'; the power of shared experiences; direct feedback from those who know you; guidance freely given – modelling the way; and opening the doors – new learning (p. 658), and although each theme was seen as an essential aspect it was their combination that impacted on career development (p. 661). These themes resonate with the women's experiences. Despite rarely planning for leadership, key personal experiences helped the women to determine the type of leader they wanted to be and to develop skills that they found useful. Gender, negative male role models, personal networks and a supportive family all contributed to shaping the type of leaders they wanted to be and helped them to develop their own particular leadership identities.

Role Models

Role models have long been recognized as playing an important part in women's career development, as has the lack of women in senior roles who are available as role models (Eriksson-Zetterquist, 2008; Gibson and Cordova, 1999; Quimby and DeSantis, 2006). People tend to seek role models who are similar to them in some identifiable way such as gender or race (Quimby and DeSantis, 2006). Given women's relative absence from senior roles, Eriksson-Zetterquist (2008) found that men were often mentioned as role models by both women and men, but women were seldom mentioned as role models, and when they were mentioned it was only by females.

The female role models available in the public arena tend to be presented as polar opposites (Sinclair, 2004) which can be unhelpful for women trying to establish themselves as leaders. The models tend to be the 'iron lady' Margaret Thatcher mode, or the leadership 'saint' such as Mother Teresa who is seen as being 'all-collaborative, conflict avoiding, and endlessly empathic' (Sinclair, 2004: p. 14). Sinclair notes that these idealized types of women do little to reflect the reality of the complexity and multifaceted nature of women's leadership.

Role models are defined by Gibson and Cordova (1999: p. 123) as 'cognitive constructs created by observers . . . with whom the observer seeks to enhance similarity based on his or her ideals, goals and needs'. Importantly they go on to point out that role models provide 'positive lessons of how to act' as well as 'negative lessons' of how not to act and have been seen as important in leadership development, particularly for women (Gibson and Cordova, 1999). Thus people focus on the traits or behaviors they wish to emulate as well as identifying the behaviors they wish to avoid (Eriksson-Zetterquist, 2008). In an earlier study regarding factors that facilitate career success, Vinnicombe et al., (2000) found that women directors had used role models to define both positive and negative behaviors.

Negative role models can be considered either as those who are seen as generally positive but they possess some traits that are seen as being negative, or those who possessed a majority of negative traits (Gibson, 2003). Gibson (2003: p. 598) identifies three aspects relating to negative traits, perceived dissimilarity, actions perceived to have a negative impact for the team or firm, and disidentification with the role model in that they wanted to differentiate themselves clearly from the negative role model. Eriksson-Zetterquist (2008: p. 268), in her study of role modelling in Sweden, noted that for women the construction of 'a role model was never complete: either the gender was wrong, . . . or the traits were not enough (childless women); or else negative actions made traits uncertain.' As a result women constructed proto-models on which to model their behavior.

In the absence of positive role models the women academics used the role models that were available to them, most of whom they characterized as negative role models, to create proto models that were useful to them. They disidentified with negative role models although they did see value in observing their behavior. It became their reference point for how not to act. They articulated a strong desire and took specific action to ensure that they would not be perceived as behaving in the same way. It was as Gibson (2003: p. 598) has noted that 'negative role models, though frequently disliked, were nonetheless considered useful for learning'. Ibarra has conducted research into how individuals in professional service firms make various career transitions, including from senior manager to leader. Most participants described how role models displayed the role identity they wished to emulate. This they saw as 'a possible self'. As with Gibson's studies Ibarra found participants who used role models to define negative behaviors – 'an improbable self'. This indicates the value of senior role models even if they are not attractive. She points out, however, that 'the benefits of modelling styles and behaviors that do not feel very self congruent have not received much empirical attention' (Ibarra, 1999: p. 785).

Gender

In Kanter's seminal work *Men and Women of the Corporation* (1977), Kanter observed how the majority (men) dominate and marginalize the minority (women). In the book Kanter shows how women become tokens when in a numerical minority of less than 15 per cent – similar to the percentage of women professors in Australia. Even where the percentage hits a tipping point of 35 per cent, women continue to encounter discrimination at work.

Ely, in her study in 1994, looked at the impact of women's proportional representation at the top of organizations and what effect it had on relationships with other women in those organizations. She found that in organizations with few senior women, women were 'less likely to experience gender as a positive basis for identification with women, less likely to perceive senior women as role models with legitimate authority, more likely to perceive competition in relationships with women peers, and less likely to find support in these relationships' (Ely, 1994).

Notwithstanding the problems facing women who are in the minority at executive levels, such experiences can make these women better leaders. Often these women emerge as leaders who are open, caring and nurturing of their team members. Their own experiences of being marginalized encourage them to be inclusive and ensure that everyone is treated equally in terms of rewards and promotion (Vinnicombe and Bank, 2003: pp. 273–80).

Networks

A key function of networks is that they provide support for career development (Mavin and Bryans, 2002). Tharenou (2005) has provided empirical support that shows that women are likely to face more barriers than men to managerial career advancement. The barriers include gender discrimination, existing male hierarchies and the lack of informal networks that promote and assist career advancement. The lack of access to informal organizational networks results in women's exclusion from knowledge-sharing and alliance-building which impacts on their career progression (Ibarra, 1993). Women also have less opportunity for networking because of their additional caring responsibilities (Linehan and Scullion, 2008). Networks are seen as important because of the social capital they build by increasing access to a range of potentially influential people and their social resources which can lead to greater career success (Ismail and Rasdi, 2007; Metz, 2009).

Women are less likely to follow age-related linear career expectations (Morley, 1999), to have moved as much as their male counterparts in order to gain promotion (Chesterman et al., 2005) or to have had access to mentoring (Lord and Pike, 1998). Cross and Armstrong (2008) suggest that exclusion from men's networks leads women to form other networks, both internal and external to the organization, to develop their own communities of support where stories can be shared, identity formed and learning shared. Quinlan has also noted that in the absence of appropriate mentors or networks, women actively seek career supportive relationships with other women. Such relationships provide emotional, psychological and social support (Quinlan, 1999).

Female networks can be a safe place for women to test with other women the meaning of their experiences and to develop their identity as leaders. They can be both internal, that is they occur within the organization, or external to the organization (Gibson, 2008; Metz, 2009). Despite their lack of access to formal and informal organizational networks, the women had developed effective networks, some of which were internal. These provided a means of 'collective learning' (Cross and Armstrong, 2008), and were a safe space for testing ideas, sharing career advice and challenging assumptions about the way leadership can be done (Metz, 2009). 'Collective learning' provided support for career development through increasing access to mentors and through the sharing of tacit knowledge (Cross and Armstrong, 2008: pp. 606–8). However, there can be an additional cost for women in having to maintain more extended and differentiated networks than their male counterparts (Hopkins and O'Neil, 2007) but as Marcinkus et al. (2007: p. 91) note, 'supportive relationships make career advancement and success more likely for women'.

Work and Family

There are continued and increasing tensions between the demands of family, however broadly or narrowly defined, friends and the organization (Winslow, 2005) and for women, who carry the major responsibility for families, the psychological conflict between these competing demands is often internalized and individualized (Belle, 2002). Tower and Alkadry (2008: p. 161) suggest that women face an unfair choice in that they are asked to choose between 'embracing work at the expense of family, or embracing family at the expense of career success'. Working women continue to face a greater challenge in trying to balance work and family commitments than their male counterparts (Grady and McCarthy, 2008; King, 2008).

Emslie and Hunt's (2009: p. 166) study of work–life balance in mid-life found that 'gender remains interwoven in the business of negotiating home and work life'. Despite evidence that men and women are increasingly defining career success in terms of work–life balance (Smith-Ruig, 2008), women remain caught in the double bind of social expectations regarding family responsibility and organizational expectations of devotion to work

(Tower and Alkadry, 2008). Additionally women face pressure to also demonstrate leadership abilities whilst fulfilling gender expectations with respect to caring responsibilities (Tower and Alkadry, 2008).

Much has been written about the challenges for women of balancing work and family (see for example Pocock, 2003; 2005). Schwartz (1989) proposed the idea of two career tracks in organizations, one for those who were focused only on a career and one for those seeking to find some balance between their career and family demands. This second track was dubbed the 'mommy track' and being on this track impacted on career advancement. Some twenty years later some changes have occurred in the work–life balance debate, particularly in relation to men's roles as carers of family members (Galinsky et al., 2008). In their introduction to a special issue of the journal *Gender Work and Organization* focusing on work–life balance, Gregory and Milner (2009: p. 3) note that the existing literature focuses on three core issues, 'time management; inter-role conflict (role overload and interference) and care arrangements for dependents'. They also note, however, that even when work–life balance arrangements are in place in organizations, they are not extensively used. The mommy track has morphed into the parent track, and both women and men are reluctant to risk career progression in order to gain greater balance between the competing demand of family and the organization.

The research emphasis has been on women with young children (Emslie and Hunt, 2009) and on the negative impact that caring responsibilities have on women's careers. There has been less focus on how the demands of balancing work and family may help women develop skills that are usefully transferred to later leadership roles in the organization. Ruderman and Ohlott's (2004) study with alumni from the Centre for Creative Leadership's Women's Leadership Programme illustrates a positive association between women's varied life roles and effective leadership performance. They show how community roles, family roles and multiple tasking can offer rich lessons in how to handle the challenges of leadership. The authors suggest three important ways in which private life encourages and enhances leadership development. Firstly, it provides psychological strength. Secondly it provides the support of family and close friends who can offer encouragement and advice. Finally, out-of-work roles 'can be your laboratory for mastering management skills'. Ruderman and Ohlott conclude that drawing on all life experiences enhances and enlivens individuals and the way they carry out their leadership roles. Similarly the academic women in this study were able to point to the benefits to themselves as well as to their career that they felt they had derived from finding ways to balance competing demands.

CONCLUSION

To engage in and enact leadership, these Australian women leaders draw on their organizational experience, formal qualifications, and for some, formal leadership development opportunities. Overwhelmingly, however, they self-managed applying their life experiences. Although leadership for most was an accidental destination, they ensured that they personally accessed the resources required for the journey.

REFERENCES

Belle, F. (2002), 'Women managers and organisational power', *Women in Management Review*, **17**(3/4), 151–6.

Burke, R.J. (2005), 'High-achieving women: progress and challenges', in R.J. Burke and M.C. Mattis (eds.), *Supporting Women's Career Advancement*, Cheltenham, UK and Northampton, MA, USA: Edward Elgar, pp. 13–30.

Carrington, K. and Pratt, A. (2003), 'How far have we come? Gender disparities in the Australian higher education system', available at from www.avcc.edu.au/policies_activities/university_management/uni_women_action_plan/gender_disparities_%20report_jun03.pdf, accessed 18 November, 2003.

Chesterman, C., Ross-Smith, A. and Peters, M. (2005), '"Not doable jobs!" Exploring senior women's attitudes to academic leadership roles', *Women's Studies International Forum*, **28**, 163–80.

Commonwealth Higher Education Management Services (1998), *A Single Sex Profession: Female Staff Numbers in Commonwealth Universities*, London: Association of Commonwealth Universities.

Creswell, J.W. (1998), *Qualitative Inquiry and Research Design Choosing among Five Traditions*, Thousand Oaks, CA: Sage.

Cross, C. and Armstrong, C. (2008), 'Understanding the role of networks in collective learning processes: the experiences of women', *Advances in Developing Human Resources*, **10**(4), 600–613.

Currie, J., Thiele, B. and Harris, P. (2002), *Gendered Universities in Globalized Economies*, Lanham, MD: Lexington Books.

Ely, R.J. (1994), 'The effects of organisational demographics and social identity on relationships among professional women', *Administrative Science Quarterly*, **39**, 203–39.

Emslie, C. and Hunt, K. (2009), '"Live to work" or "work to live"? A qualitative study of gender and work–life balance among men and women in mid-life', *Gender, Work and Organisation*, **16**(1), 151–71.

Eriksson-Zetterquist, U. (2008), 'Gendered role modelling – A paradoxical construction process', *Scandinavian Journal of Management*, **24**(3), 259–70.

Eveline, J. (2004), *Ivory Basement Leadership*, Crawley: University of Western Australia Press.

Fogelberg, P., Hearn, J., Husu, L. and Mankkinen, T. (1999), 'Hard work in the academy', in P. Fogelberg, J. Hearn, L. Husu and T. Mankkinen (eds), *Hard Work in the Academy*, Helsinki: Helsinki University Press, pp. 11–19.

Galinsky, E., Aumann, K. and Bond, J. (2008), 'Times are changing gender and generation at work and home', available at http://familiesandwork.org/site/research/reports/Times_Are_Changing.pdf.

Gardiner, M. and Tiggemann, M. (1999), 'Gender differences in leadership style, job stress and mental health in male- and female dominated industries', *Journal of Occupational and Organizational Psychology*, **72**, 301–15.

Gibson, D. (2003), 'Developing the professional self-concept: role model construals in early, middle, and late career stages', *Organization Science*, **14**(5), 591–610.

Gibson, D. and Cordova, D. (1999), 'Women's and men's role models: the importance of exemplars', in A.J. Murrell, F.J. Crosby and R.J. Ely (eds), *Mentoring Dilemmas: Developmental Relationships Within Multicultural Organisations*, Mahwah, NJ: Lawrence Erlbaum, pp. 121–42.

Gibson, S. (2008), 'The developmental relationships of women leaders in career transition: implications for leader development', *Advances in Developing Human Resources*, **10**(5), 651–70.

Grady, G. and McCarthy, A. (2008), 'Work–life integration: experiences of mid-career professional working mothers', *Journal of Managerial Psychology*, **23**(5), 599–622.

Gregory, A. and Milner, S. (2009), 'Editorial: work–life balance: a matter of choice?', *Gender, Work and Organization*, **16**(1), 1–13.

Hamel, S. (2009), 'Exit, voice, and sensemaking following psychological contract violations: women's responses to career advancement barriers', *Journal of Business Communication*, **46**(2), 234–61.

Hopkins, M. and O'Neil, D. (2007), 'Women and success: dilemmas and opportunities', in D. Bilimoria and S. Piderit (eds), *Handbook on Women in Business and Management*, Cheltenham, UK and Northampton, MA, USA: Edward Elgar, pp. 132–54.

Ibarra, H. (1993), 'Personal networks of women and minorities in management: a conceptual framework', *Academy of Management Review*, **18**(1), 56–87.

Ibarra, H. (1999), 'Professional selves: experimenting with image and identity in professional adaptation', *Administrative Science Quarterly*, **44**, 764–79.

Indvik, J. (2004), 'Women and leadership', in P.G. Northouse (ed.), *Leadership Theory and Practice*, 3rd edn, Thousand Oaks, CA: Sage Publications, pp. 265–300.

Ismail, M. and Rasdi, R. (2007), 'Impact of networking on career development: experience of high-flying women academics in Malaysia', *Human Resource Development International*, **10**(2), 153–68.

Kanter, R.M. (1977), *Men and Women of the Corporation*, New York: Basic Books.

Kerman, L. (1995), 'The good witch: advice to women in management', in L. Morley and V. Walsh (eds), *Feminist Academics*, London: Taylor and Francis, pp. 131–44.

King, E. (2008), 'The effect of bias on the advancement of working mothers: disentangling legitimate concerns from inaccurate stereotypes as predictors of advancement in academe', *Human Relations*, **61**(12), 1677–711.

Linehan, M. and Scullion, H. (2008), 'The development of female global managers: the role of mentoring and networking', *Journal of Business Ethics*, **83**, 29–40.

Lord, L. and Pike, L. (1998), 'Not in our master's image: mentoring for change at Edith Cowan University; applications of the women in leadership model', paper presented at the Winds of Change Women and The Culture of Universities, Sydney.

Marcinkus, W., Whelan-Berry, K. and Gordon, J. (2007), 'The relationship of social support to the work–family balance and work outcomes of midlife women', *Women in Management Review*, **22**(2), 86–111.

Mavin, S. and Bryans, P. (2002), 'Academic women in the UK: mainstreaming our experiences and networking for action', *Gender and Education*, **14**(3), 235–50.

Metz, I. (2009), 'Organisational factors, social factors, and women's advancement', *Applied Psychology: An International Review*, **58**(2), 193–213.

Morley, L. (1999), *Organising Feminisms: the Micropolitics of the Academy*, New York: St Martin's Press.

Pocock, B. (2003), *The Work/Life Collision: What Work is doing to Austalians and what to do about it*, Annandale, NSW: Federation Press.

Pocock, B. (2005), *The Impact of The Workplace Relations Amendment (Work Choices) Bill 2005 on Australian Working Families*, Adelaide: University of Adelaide.

Quimby, J. and DeSantis, A. (2006), 'The influence of role models on women's career choices', *The Career Development Quarterly*, **54**, June, 297–306.

Quinlan, K. (1999), 'Enhancing mentoring and networking of junior academic women: What, why and how?', *Journal of Higher Education Policy and Management*, **21**(1), 31–42.

Ruderman, M. and Ohlott, P. (2004), 'What women leaders want', *Leader to Leader*, **31**, 41–7.

Schwartz, F. (1989), 'Management women and the new facts of life', *Harvard Business Review*, **67**(1), 67–77.

Sinclair, A. (2004), 'Journey around leadership', *Discourse: Studies in the Cultural Politics of Education*, **25**(1), 7–18.

Smith-Ruig, T. (2008), 'Making sense of careers through the lens of a path metaphor', *Career Development International*, **13**(1), 20–32.

Tharenou, P. (2005), 'Women's advancement in management: what is known and future areas to address', in R.J. Burke and M.C. Mattis (eds), *Supporting Women's Career Advancement*, Cheltenham, UK and Northampton, MA, USA: Edward Elgar, pp. 31–57.

Tower, L. and Alkadry, M. (2008), 'The social costs of career success for women', *Review of Public Personnel Administration*, **28**(2), 144–65.

Vinnicombe, S. and Bank, J. (2003), *Women with Attitude*, London: Routledge.

Vinnicombe, S., Singh, V. and Sturges, J. (2000), 'Making it to the top in Britain', in R.J. Burke and M.C. Mattis (eds), *Women on Corporate Boards of Directors: International Challenges and Opportunities*, Dordrecht, Netherlands: Kluwer Academic Press.

Winchester, H., Chesterman, C., Lorenzo, S. and Browning, L. (2005), *The Great Barrier Myth: An Investigation of Promotions Policy and Practice in Australian Universities*, Australian Vice-Chancellors' Committee.

Winslow, S. (2005), 'Work–family conflict, gender, and parenthood, 1977–1997', *Journal of Family Issues*, **26**(6), 727–55.

17. Preparing next generation business leaders

Philip Mirvis, Kevin Thompson and Chris Marquis

As in past economic transformations, major institutions of society are being redesigned. The recent surge in global integration has brought millions of people into the expanding web of global commerce. Countries formerly considered on the financial fringe are now participants in the modern marketplace. Empowered consumers, angered by business misconduct, are demanding more regulation, and interests of all kinds, including the next generation of people moving toward executive ranks, are calling for socially responsible business behavior (cf. Googins et al., 2006). Meanwhile, increasing numbers of people and devices are linked via the internet, extending companies' and people's reach and providing opportunities to make more of what we do smarter.

Dynamic systems underlying this epochal change have altered the way businesses work, and the skills executives need to lead their people and organizations forward. Here we will describe how changes in the traditional office environment, work team composition, reporting structures, corporate control and authority systems, as well as increases in the numbers and types of stakeholders making claims on companies, and the shift in developed countries from making products to providing solutions have together added significant complexity to the next generation leaders' work. Amidst all these changes, business leaders still have to do what they've always had to do: produce growth, deliver results, develop their people, and innovate to meet marketplace needs and beat competitors.

What will it take for next generation leaders to be successful in the redesigned business world of the twenty-first century? The curriculum proffered by business schools and the executive classroom promotes 'hard' skills to gain financial acumen and technology literacy and 'soft' ones to develop emotional intelligence and manage diversity. Who could disagree? But, valuable as these might be, these skills don't fully prepare tomorrow's leaders to operate in a faster-paced, globally connected, stakeholder-driven marketplace where uncertainty is the norm, knowledge is rapidly outdated, relationships regularly morph, and demands on time and personal stamina multiply.

Here we consider some of the competencies needed by the next generation of business leaders and take a close look at how one global company, IBM, helps to cultivate them through its global service program, the Citizen's Service Corps. To begin, let's look at the changing contours of the corporation and its environment and how 'self-management' has emerged as a vital executive competency.

THE RISE OF 'SELF-MANAGEMENT'

Two decades ago, scholars began to map a landscape where companies routinely reshape and resize themselves, regularly buy and sell off businesses, outsource non-strategic functions, and partner periodically with other institutions to do their work. Handy (1989), as one example, described a federalist organization design featuring three layers of activity from core to non-core tasks. These layers would be populated, respectively, by core full-time personnel, independent contractors, and contingent workers. The underlying logic is that this enables an organization to reconfigure its human systems quickly and efficiently in response to environmental demands, such as new market openings, competitors' responses, and supply chain costs and reach, while preserving its core competencies.

More generally, what has come to be called the post-bureaucratic structure – whether depicted as a boundaryless organization, flex-firm, or virtual corporation – features less vertical hierarchy, more lateral interaction, and constant exchange between the firm and its environment at every level and in every part of the organization (cf. Kates and Galbraith, 2007). The work of the business, in turn, is handled by more or less self-contained units where teams, whether on a temporary or ongoing basis, 'self-manage' their projects, production or service delivery.

Specialists in organization design contend that these configurations give a firm sufficient variety in structure and skill to sense and react better to complexity in its markets and operating environments (cf. Emery and Trist, 1973; Cohen and March, 1986). In turn, the minimal specification of job duties, coupled with self-managing work units, allows companies to respond flexibly and fully to new circumstances. Finally, and key to the success of the post-bureaucratic organization, is its capacity to self-design for new circumstances. This means moving people quickly into new assignments, forming them into new structures, and having them hit the ground running.

Extrapolating from these structural trends and design principles, Hall and Mirvis (1994) have argued that working people, too, need to be able to reshape and retool themselves to operate effectively in their companies and, indeed, to remain employable. Practically, this means giving people more varied work experiences and assignments so that they learn to cope with constant changes in their task and reporting environments. Companies also need to provide practice and resources to help people self-manage in their jobs. What does it mean for their training and development? Not much in early formulations, because people have had to embark on lifelong learning and self-design much of their personal and career development.

Building on the work of Hall (1976), Hall and Mirvis (1996) described the career implications of this future as 'protean'. They write:

> The term is taken from the name of the Greek god Proteus who could change shape at will, from fire to a wild boar to a tree, and so forth. The protean career is a process which the person, not the organization, is managing. It consists of . . . varied experiences in education, training, perhaps work in several organizations, changes in occupational field, etc. The protean person's own personal career choices and search for self-fulfillment are the unifying or integrative elements in his or her life.

This writing on the protean career emphasized how people would have to 'learn a living' to achieve 'psychological success' throughout their work lives. Mirvis and Hall (1994) identified two meta-competencies required for success: identity development (to gain a clearer sense of self amidst changes in roles and responsibilities) and adaptability (to adjust to a shifting task and reporting environment). Here we extend this thinking and contend that as companies themselves, and the rhythms of work therein, now routinely shape-shift, these meta-skills (and several more) seem equally applicable to corporate professionals cum leaders as they learn to self-manage through ever more complex jobs and responsibilities.

SHAPE-SHIFTING AT WORK

Consider, as a starter list, some 'open ended' questions raised by the constantly changing work world:

What happened to my office? For many, going to work used to mean a commute to a building where most of the people that you worked with were located. Offices were in commercial centers of developed countries. There were morning greetings, in-person meetings and easy access to the marketing, finance and human resources people supporting your business. Teams were co-located. The traditional office of the old system has changed. New global commercial centers such as Bangalore, Beijing and Sao Paulo are mentioned as frequently as New York, London and Tokyo. Telecommuters and placement full-time at client sites and business partners means the traditional office experience is a distant memory for many business professionals.

Who is on my team? As teams become more global, who you share an office with may not be who you work with. Advanced communication and social networking technologies allow virtual teams to self-organize from multiple time zones and business units, work collaboratively, and an hour later pivot to a different team and project with different people from another part of the world. The physical office has become less important. Teams gather virtually.

Who do I work for? Multinational corporations succeeded in the old system by developing hierarchical, functional organizations with defined, linear reporting structures. Authority and control were top-down. Leaders set direction by speaking and directing. This worked well until the system changed. When global teams assemble around client projects based on their skills, the center of gravity is distributed to wherever the work is being delivered. Flatter organizations that work effectively across silos, where work flows to where it can be done best at the lowest cost, are replacing the old organizational system. This new system does not have clear reporting structures, and modern incentive schemes have yet to effectively quantify the value of bottom-up and horizontal collaboration.

What am I supposed to do? As more of the global economy shifts to services, the work businesses do creates solutions instead of products. Solutions may vary from customer to customer, leaving behind the old system's defined processes for creating and delivering products and replacing them with a need to problem solve in an ambiguous setting. Add to this the cultural complexity of working globally where people and business partners may have different values and norms and operate in different regulatory contexts.

What do I do with all this information? Computational power is being put into things no one would recognize as computers – phones, cameras, cars, appliances, roadways, power lines and clothes. All of this is being connected through the internet, which has come of age. The result is massive amounts of data and information – 350 times more every day than is contained in all the university research libraries in the United States. Making sense of the world's digital knowledge and pulse places new intellectual and time demands on executives who operate 24/7.

To whom am I responsible? In the old system the stakeholders universally engaged by business were customers, shareholders and employees. These are not going away. But their expectations are growing and changing.

Customers want confirmation that your supply chain does not violate human rights and environmental standards because your supply chain becomes your customer's supply chain. Investors want a clear picture of and more certainty that firms are handling social and environmental risks. Young talent are prioritizing how potential employers' values align with their own, and in some instances forgo higher-paying job offers for an opportunity to work at a company they believe is responsible. More broadly, there are now increased demands by society worldwide for greater transparency, sustainable business practices, and responsible leadership.

Governments are playing an increased role in defining corporate behavior through legislation and regulation while also serving as gatekeepers for market entry. Governments are the primary spenders for major infrastructure projects in key emerging markets. The social sector, powered by increasingly sophisticated non-governmental organizations (NGOs) and activists, influences public opinion through the use of new media and consumer campaigns. This threatens business-as-usual models but also provides new engagement and partnership opportunities for a range of activities.

There are no easy or reliable answers to these questions about how to operate in the new world of work. They have to be invented by professionals and business leaders in context of their everyday jobs, and often co-created in relationship to peers, partners and a network on stakeholders. Meta-skills such as those aimed at refreshing one's identity and increasing one's adaptability are crucial not only to psychological but also commercial success. A more detailed consideration of what else is needed focuses attention on four domains for developing the next generation of leadership: self-leadership, leading others, leading systems and leading enterprises. Let's look briefly at each of them.

DEVELOPMENTAL CHALLENGES FOR BUSINESS LEADERS

Given the kinds of challenges that executives face in this new world of work, consider four next generation meta-skills that are needed for success.

1. *Self-Leadership.* At the individual level, the need for heightened self-awareness and emotional intelligence already inform the developmental agenda of executives in leading companies. But in addition to developing these intra-personal skills, future leaders also need to develop their cognitive sophistication and emotional maturity to

cope with the mental complexity and multi-tasking requirements of globalized work and deal with the ups-and-downs of doing business globally.

2. *Leading Others.* As top-down, hierarchical management systems reinforced by centralized control are being replaced by more bottom-up, globally distributed management systems, leaders need to expand their inter-personal, group and social integration skills. Learning how to operate in and exert authority in fluid, loosely-structured teams and task groupings is a crucial part of the leader's new work. In turn, leading by listening, eliciting and catalyzing could be more effective than by speaking, persuading and directing.

3. *Leading Systems.* Within the firm, traditional divisions by hierarchy and function are giving way to multilevel and cross-functional forms of collaboration that span countries and cultures. Populating these new structures is a multigenerational and multicultural workforce. In this context, leaderly visions and direction may be less relevant than skills at pattern recognition, improvisation, and meaning making. In turn, learning how to best form, align and leverage these multipurpose structures is a skill that needs development.

4. *Leading the Enterprise.* Meanwhile, across firms, collaboration encompasses the extended enterprise – from supply chain to customers – as well as multisector partnerships, multibusiness ventures and alliances, and of course M&A. Partnerships between government, business, community groups, and multiple NGOs can create 'sector blur' which conflicts with previously established business understandings and roles. Gaining experience in and a comfort level with navigating across so many boundaries is integral to the development of twenty-first century executives and organizations.

DEFINING THE DEVELOPMENTAL AGENDA

To build capacity in these domains requires identification of key competencies for next generation leaders. Consider some examples of what is on the developmental agenda.

Domain 1: Self-Leadership

With the breakdown in the traditional corporate career and its promise of lifetime job security, success depends deeply on self-reliance and self-assurance. But this is not the same as the rugged individualism celebrated in cowboy pictures or manager-as-hero myths that pervade the popular business press and business school cases. Rather, the message here is that a manager's self-reliance grows from having confronted and tested 'Who I am' – strengths *and* weaknesses – along the course of a career. And self-assurance grows from facing and mastering situations involving uncertainty, change, emotional challenge, and, yes, even and especially personal failure. What are the requisite skills?

- *Self-awareness.* There is increased emphasis today on self-awareness in leadership development (Rooke and Torbert, 2005). The injunction to 'know thyself' is received wisdom from Socrates in ancient Greece and from spiritual and martial teachings in Asia. Most branches of modern psychology see self-knowledge as integral to human development and essential to being a healthy, functioning adult (Goleman et al., 2002). Leadership development programs typically encourage people to cultivate this through personality assessments, 360-degree feedback, coaching and the like. And, while these all have their place in personal development, the research is clear that self-knowledge is best gained through the crucible of action.
- *Learn How – Reflection.* Action itself is not a teacher; it is through reflecting on action that leaders come to know themselves better (Schön, 1983). 'How am I reacting to this situation? To this person? What do my dealings tell me about my own assumptions and how I handle a situation or people?' Schein (1990) calls this reflective discipline 'listening to ourselves'.
- *Cognitive Complexity/Tolerance for Ambiguity.* What's to be learned? Self-appraisal, even when aided by peer feedback, can signal predilections and tendencies, strengths and weaknesses. Digging deeper, a reflective leader will notice how 'mental models' are used to construct situations and how anxious moments can spur ill-considered actions. This takes the motivated leader on a journey to 'know more of what I don't know' to enrich ways of thinking about and modeling a more complex world. Reflection on action also calls attention to one's tolerance for ambiguity and the psychic tension between hanging-on versus letting-go of favored ways to respond to the world.
- *Adaptability.* The capacity to read a complex situation and respond thoughtfully, often in real time, is a feature of survival. This is fundamentally a practiced skill, developed by regular exposure to novel and demanding stimuli that stretch a leader's understandings of the world and how to navigate it (Calarco and Gurvis, 2006). The key, however, is to act, then take stock of how things work out, and then act again – with a smarter, better calibrated response. Adaptability

often means relying on others with different skills or another point of view to get the job done. Adaptable leaders know their limits and when to let others do their thing (Heifetz, 2004).

- *Emotional Resilience.* Not every action, no matter how sensible or nimbly executed, yields positive results in a complex world. Know-how ups the odds for success. Learn-how eliminates prior mistakes and can point to a better course of action. But, ultimately, it is the courage to move forward in an uncertain situation and to forgive oneself for past failings that propels a leader forward. Needless to say, risk aversion or punishment for failure can send a leader backward, sideways or underwater.

Domain 2: Leading Others

None of us is as smart as all of us. No matter the brainpower of managers today, there is simply too much information in too many places for any one person or even a co-located team to access and digest it when formulating action strategies. Action, in turn, is guided by distributed intelligence, whereby local managers take locally appropriate decisions mindful of the 'whole'. In many situations, the guiding principles of the 'whole' are the core values of the organization, and from the organizational values flow high-level direction for local managers to make decisions beyond the reach of senior managers who are, at times, thousands of miles away (Mirvis, 2002).

Among American managers, American football was once the sporting metaphor for managing: a well-devised game plan, special teams for offense and defense, top-down play calling from men in a booth sitting way off the ground, and lots of meetings. On the global playing field, the better metaphor is basketball or soccer, where strategy is emergent, action is fluid and spontaneous, leadership moves around the team and meetings are unscheduled and largely unscripted.

The success of these informing and performing activities hinges on truly engaging people and relies on selfless teamwork. Emotional intelligence is important to understanding and gaining a feel for others. But today's managers also need the capacity to size up and relate to groups of people which, often unpredictably, change their composition, contours and roles. The idea of someone being 'in charge' in this game surrenders to models of collaborative action and collective responsibility where all the players share a vision and have an informed sense of what it takes to win. The manager's job is to promote social networking, influence the field of play through talk and decisions, and get everyone engaged in the flow of events. What are the key skills here?

- *Social Intelligence.* Business leaders today are advised to develop their interpersonal sensitivities and skills and to move beyond simply understanding others to empathizing with and connecting to them deeply. But Goleman (2006) notes that the next generation skill is social intelligence. This encompasses 'group mindedness' – capacities to read group development and guide interdependent action. Knowing what's going on in a group is more than textbook identification of group forming, storming and norming stages. It is also the ability to lift these dynamics up for collective consideration so a group can work through them and move forward.
- *Group Process/Engagement.* This process-oriented skill helps a team to confront its dynamics and dysfunctions and 'see itself as a group'. Of course, motivational speeches and chalkboard talks have their place in group engagement. But so does providing process observations and insights, and cultivating interaction and conflict management skills that facilitate group dialogue (Schein, 1999).
- *Influencing without Authority.* It's hard for a leader to get a work group smarter about its social operations and rhythms. It's harder still when the leader is not the 'boss' and lacks formal authority. Still, this is the structure in many cross-functional, cross-national project teams common in the modern marketplace. Personal smarts, emotional centering, and social intelligence are of course sources of authority for a leader. So is mastering the leaderly arts of demonstrating respect, tact, building on others' contribution, and confronting people in face-saving ways.
- *Communication Skills.* Influence with and especially without authority is dependent on a leader's power of communication. This is a practiced skill not only of speechmaking and personal presentation but also of active listening, synthesizing and summarizing. Leaders today often operate in a world of multitasking, asynchronous communication, electronic interaction, and virtual teaming. Not everyone on a global team speaks the same language at the same level. Add distance and time zones while removing face-to-face interaction by phone and email and the challenges magnify.
- *Sense-Making Skills.* In a world where projects change shape and team members morph, a leader's skills at making sense of things have also to be cultivated by a work group. Here the leader's new job is to help a group make sense of itself and its efforts – while in motion. This is what Weick (1995) calls enacting the situation. To teach a group how to adapt its roles, modus operandi, and identity through its work, the leader has to be able to step back to see what's

going in and then step in with observations and imagery that define 'where we are' and detail 'where we are going'.

Domain 3: Leading Systems

Even as leaders are tasked to apply their business, personal and group management acumen to the scramble of fast-paced changes in the world around them, they also have to attend to diverse stakeholders' interests and to the moral, social and environmental impact of their own and their team's doings. This is further complicated by the 'sector blur' taking place across previously defined barriers between the public, social, civil, academic and private sectors.

Cognitive complexity and group engagement skills help a leader and team to see a bigger picture and calibrate smarter moves. But, without a better sense of what stakeholders want and about the social-and-environmental challenges to business in an interconnected world, there is a risk that the plans developed will be inadequate, at best, and harmful at worst. More reading and reflection, participation in diverse networks, and study of the best practices of other leaders can help a leader get better informed about the new operating environment and what it takes to negotiate it. But these information bites simply go into mental storage files without an organizing framework to connect them and bring them into action.

Management sage Drucker (1994) argues that leaders need to define, articulate and test their 'theory of the business'. This is a map of causes-and-effects that organizes and connects perceptions of a situation and arrays the potential results of different courses of action. This kind of messy mapping opens up possibilities, promotes creativity, and stimulates innovation. It necessarily precedes tactical plans and charts that map the way to action.

Diverse inputs enrich these maps and yield different points of view about how actions might unfold. But getting everyone on the same page intellectually, or into the same space emotionally, may sound ideal but is not necessary for successful action to result. In the case of simple problems, alignment helps to speed simple solutions. But for complex problems, where cause–effect linkages are not fully known and lockstep coordination is impossible or costly, a little friction can be useful, and high energy can make up for missteps. More broadly, knowing how to lead a 'motley crew' is a requisite for leaders of diverse teams populated by talented and ambitious people. What are the key skills here?

- *Systems thinking – pattern recognition.* Senge (1990) popularized the idea of systems thinking and embedded it in logic of organizational learning. The next skill is pattern recognition whereby consequential causal loops move to the foreground, and the noise in a system moves to the background. Here a theory of a business is formalized, added to, and comes to life. The thinking required is not just analytical and rational. Pattern recognition also calls for the incorporation of values in action frames and for an aesthetic appreciation of how things look and could be put together differently.

- *Cultural intelligence – appreciating diversity.* The global leader needs cultural intelligence to get 'inside' how different people think and feel and to understand how societal cultures are built on different foundations of philosophy and history (Earley and Peterson, 2004). Living in a different culture, and deeply engaging with people from a different culture, helps to reveal the more tacit dimensions of life outside one's own skin and society.
- *Social Responsibility/Sustainability.* Tomorrow's leaders need up-to-date knowledge about changing expectations concerning corporate social responsibility, good governance, and environmental sustainability. Systems thinking is a start, but it needs to extend to social and natural systems outside the boundaries outside the firm. Comfort in dealing with diverse stakeholders, including critics, understanding the myriad risks and opportunities in a firm's engagement with society, and knowing how to translate all of this into corporate strategy are requisites to leading in the new economy.
- *Foresight.* Most would agree that deeply understanding a situation is crucial toward changing it. But many business innovations are based also on seeing the new, and from this creating a new pattern of possibilities. It's arguable whether or not intuition can be cultivated and personal creativity can be taught. But it's undeniable that a leader can stimulate creativity in a group by seeding it with fresh information and ideas, promoting free thinking and brainstorming, and giving people the time, space and resources to experiment, design and prototype new options. These leadership skills, both attitudinal and behavioral, are learned by watching, experiencing and then doing.
- *Conducting/Aesthetic Intelligence.* Learning how to stage, sequence and manage the flow of energy and resources in a system is integral to a leader's success in taking actions that engage multiple actors, that span units and boundaries, and that extend around the globe. Planning and problem-solving are certainly a part of this. But a leader also needs aesthetic intelligence to transform action into a story, with a plot, characters, and dramatization much like a conductor transforms music with varied instrumentation, dialogues,

tension and release (Mirvis et al., 2003). If leading is truly an art, as most would say, then learning the art of performance humanizes action and brings the best out of people.

Domain 4: Leading the Enterprise

The skills of leading the self, others and systems are building blocks that prepare a leader to get to the scale of leading an enterprise. This is an action field that grows from multiple projects, to multiple businesses, to a global stage and includes a full range of local and global stakeholders. Most important, it also means leading other leaders.

- *Global Mindset.* Cultural intelligence and skills in stakeholder engagement yields a cornucopia of global action possibilities and local adaptations for an enterprise. A global mindset synthesizes these into a holistic picture that enables leaders inside a company and stakeholders outside it to understand what an enterprise is and is not, what it stands for, and what responsibilities it assumes on a global scale (Gosling and Mintzberg, 2003).
- *Purposing the Whole.* Seeing the whole is not the same as leading people holistically. And having a well formed action theory for the business is not the same as leading an enterprise into action. Skills here concern the leaderly work of crafting and articulating a vision and infusing action with values that mean something to people. Vaill (1982) uses the term 'purposing' to combine vision and values into a deep sense of personal and collective purpose for people.
- *Orchestrating/Strategizing.* Taking performance to scale involves orchestrating a wide range of actions over time and across space. It means attending to the forest and simultaneously to the trees. Strategic plans and business reviews are a part of this. But leaders also need to devise strategy in action in light of successful experiments within a firm and rapidly changing circumstances outside it. This is emergent strategy and it is like the soccer metaphor mentioned earlier (Mintzberg and Waters, 1985).
- *Judgment.* The leader's work is judged by his or her judgments made to continue in a current way or take a new course of action, to hire or fire others, particularly powerful ones, and especially how one deals with crisis. Judgment relies on vision, principles, and, in the end, on practicality and the politics of getting things done. This necessarily engages a leader's moral compass and sense for doing the right thing. On this count, Tichy (1997) stresses the importance for the leader of developing a 'point of view' that links vision and values

to actions that can engage the emotional energies of those who are led (Tichy and Bennis, 2007). In applying these, leaders need 'edge' – the capacity to make yes/no decisions. Sometimes you have to have an opinion.

- *Responsible Leadership.* Finally, tomorrow calls for responsible leadership. Being true to oneself (authentic), serving as a positive example to others (role model), and purposing, judging well, and so forth are all part of this. At core, however, this means acting with integrity in one's business and personal life and, with the power and authority of enterprise leadership, leading in a way that enables people, the business, and the world we live in to flourish.

DEVELOPING FUTURE LEADERS

The current economic transformation demands a re-engineered twenty-first century leadership development experience that provides for a new foundation across the four leadership domains. An MBA is still a valuable learning experience, but the curriculum and student experience are not evolving at the same rate of change experienced in the business world. As for 'in-house' development, rotational assignments are increasingly less common as enterprises distribute work globally, creating centers of excellence for individual functional areas that are so geographically dispersed that rotating requires costly moves. International assignments are prohibitively expensive, focused on employees in later stages of their career and based in developed countries. These development options are not wrong. They just are not enough.

As the leader's new work moves to a global stage under the banner of commercial and social development, what could an optimal development experience include?

- Opportunities to work independently in unstructured environments;
- Chance to manage across an organization, not just up a management chain;
- Tasks that require comfort with ambiguity and unstructured problem solving;
- Co-learning with peers in a 'leaderless' group;
- Global experiences requiring cultural adaptability;
- Exposure to emerging markets;
- Utilizing modern technology including data analytics and social networking tools;

- Exposure to new demands of customers, shareholders, employees, governments and the social sector.

One program incorporating these features is the IBM Corporate Service Corps, which embodies the idealism and spirit of international service of the US Peace Corps and the pragmatism and global business capability of information technology giant IBM. The idea is to send top talent in the business world on twenty-first century experiences that merge global teams, immersion in strategic emerging markets and 'out of the office' pro bono assignments with organizations and institutions addressing core societal, educational and environmental challenges.

THE CORPORATE SERVICE CORPS

The IBM Corporate Service Corps (CSC) was launched in 2008. Kevin Thompson, a Peace Corps alumnus and later the program manager for the corps, had discussions with representatives of two NGOs that placed volunteers in international assignments. He wondered, at the time, whether a Peace Corps program would work for corporations and set about contacting NGOs specializing in global volunteering, benchmarked the few corporate programs featuring the same, and gathered intelligence within IBM about program interest and possible parameters, including type of participants, the length of an assignment, and the work that IBMers would do and with whom (see Marquis and Kanter, 2009, for background).

Launching the Corporate Service Corps involved many program design decisions, from how to find the right implementation partners to how many people to assign to each team. Ultimately, it was decided that the program would span six months – three months of 'pre-work' preparation, one month working in-country, and two months of 'post-work.' Employees would be placed with in-country NGOs or community groups where they could utilize their specific skills. In a case study on CSC, Thompson described,

> We laid out the type of experience we were looking for. On one end of the continuum is the mud hut in the bush with no electricity experience; on the other end of the continuum are the three- or four-star business-travel hotels in the capital city with high security walls, cheeseburgers and CNN. We were looking for an experience in the middle. We wanted to avoid capital cities. We wanted to be in secondary metro markets.

By mid-March, the CSC members had been selected, assigned to countries, and notified. The pre-work program encompassed 40–60 hours of additional work, as participants were expected to continue to perform their regular duties during these three months. The curriculum focused on four areas: team development, skills development, logistics and assignment-related tasks. Learning modules covered topics such as IBM's corporate social responsibility strategy, cross-cultural management, knowledge of the destination country, and information about health and travel safety. Teams organized conference calls, utilized online social networking platforms, shared expectations and figured out how to work together.

In July of 2008, the first 11 teams were in the field. They engaged in a variety of projects.

- In Romania, for example, they helped the Center for Entrepreneurship and Executive Development improve their ability to serve as a regional business network hub and increase regional market access.
- In Ghana, teams worked to improve business processes and provide training for a network of small and medium enterprises that are part of the Association of Ghanaian Industries (AGI). As a result of this project, the organization is now able to access financing through an AGI partnership, and also conduct a supply chain assessment of the handicraft sector and provide training on business fundamentals and the use of ICT to a local NGO.
- In Tanzania the IBM teams collaborated with KickStart, a non-profit that develops and markets new technologies in Africa to develop modular training courses in marketing, sales and supply chains. Others worked with communities in and around three wildlife management areas to develop tourism in the area that combined conservation with livelihood enhancement. A team worked with the Tanzania Association of Tour Operators to update their website and provide a search capability that enabled tourists to identify reliable tour operators.
- In the Philippines, the team assisted the Davao City Chamber of Commerce in the development of an online marketing service facility and an investment opportunity database. As described by one of the local partners in the Philippines:

> We already had a Directory for sources of funds. The Corporate Services Corps organized this into what they termed e-fund tool, an electronic version of what we have done. They also organized the way we interact with enterprises into another tool they called the CAT (client assessment tool), which again electronically made it possible for us to assess our clients. The CSC not only gave us strategic direction, but outlined things we could do to improve our organization in the short term, the medium term and the long term.

- In Vietnam, the teams supported the rapid development of small and medium enterprises by conducting stakeholder engagement and consultation with Chamber of Commerce members as well as government and regulatory bodies.

CONTENT VERSUS COMPETENCIES

Comparing the leadership competencies needed by next generation leaders with what the CSC had to offer as a developmental experience shows a good match in many domains (see Box 17.1). In cultivating self-leadership, for example, the CSC experience provides exposure to a broader array of stimuli and situations that can stretch and deepen a leader's world view. Hall and Mirvis (1996) contend that this adds 'requisite variety' to the idea-and-experience pool that executives draw on when faced with complex problems. It can also continuously challenge and inform their self-picture as leaders. The combination of an ill-structured task, undertaken with an unfamiliar emerging market context, with a minimum of resources at hand all served to develop the participants' adaptability and resilience. The same was true of their living arrangements. A survey of the participants showed that members of each team reported increases in their resilience comparing pre- to post-assignment ratings (see Figure 17.1).

In the area of leading others, the on-the-ground curriculum was a constant goad to developing participants' social intelligence and group process skills. Connecting with others of a different background can also yield leadership lessons on diversity. The IBMers lacked formal authority in their assignments, both within the client system and in drawing on resources from the parent company, its regional offices and fellow team members. In this sense, they had to talk their way to action through communication and continuous social construction of their project, the task and social system supporting it, and the delivery of results. This developed both their technical and project management skills.

It also demanded, up to a point, that they enhance their skills at leading systems. The strategic skills of systems thinking, foresight and conducting were needed in almost every case to align a client system around a project, think through its organization and flow, and prepare for and respond to contingencies. To complicate this, the CSC leaders were also tasked to work more sensitively and effectively with people of different ethnic, racial, and socio-economic backgrounds and from different cultures. The post-assignment survey showed increases in their cultural intelligence as well (see Figure 17.2).

BOX 17.1   LEADERSHIP SKILLS AND IBM CSC LEARNING COMPONENTS

Self-Leadership

- Self-awareness begins with program application covering why the participant wants to join CSC and how it connects to personal and career goals. Continues through pre-work via self-assessment exercises and throughout six months of program.
- Reflection may involve personal journaling, blogging and video publication about in-country insights. Post-work has intensive focus on 'internalizing' the experience.
- Cognitive complexity/tolerance for ambiguity are both stimulated by in-country assignment that has to be conceptualized in advance and modified throughout by changing circumstances of client's needs and situation and by the facts on the ground.
- Adaptability is engaged from the get-go through interview process and selection. Builds in context of client assignment and living in emerging market where housing, food and transport all have to be self-managed.
- Emotional resilience as above and needed to cope with enormity of social/commercial tasks versus limited resources of time, money, skills at client site.

Leading Others

- Social intelligence activated at every phase in context of virtual coordination, team dynamics, engaging unfamiliar client system, and delivering on contract.
- Group process skills are developed throughout in context of client assignment (often working with local team) and in daily living circumstances (with fellow CSC members in country).
- Influence without authority is developed when working as an advisor to client and interacting with client system, absent formal authority or much in the way of financial resources. Also needed when engaging IBM resources, sponsoring NGOs, and fellow team members.
- Communication skills are cultivated through face-to-face interaction, project briefings and reports, and virtually across various social networking platforms.

- Sense-making/enactment skills evolve given ambiguity of project goals, processes, resource requirements, and communication across different languages and cultures.

Leading Systems

- Systems thinking expands in context of project diagnosis and definition of deliverables and extends into post-work through definitions of next steps for the client organization and implications of the assignment for IBM's business.
- Cultural intelligence/diversity skills grow through client interaction, engagement with client system, and dealings with diverse IBM team in everyday living.
- Corporate responsibility/sustainability knowledge covered in pre-work and in real-time in country. The CSC is itself an example of innovation in this arena.
- Foresight refined in context of project work and in projecting implications of this assignment for IBM and one's own career.
- Conducting is cultivated through leadership of the project and delivery of results for client. Aesthetic intelligence may be developed in peer leadership of in-country team events and learning experiences.

Leading the Enterprise

- Global mindset develops in pre-work studies of global IBM and local conditions in country assignment. Post-work calls for global positioning of IBM based on in-country learnings.
- Purposing the whole seems a stretch given CSC structure but may be activated in post-assignment conversations and presentations to IBM leadership.
- Judgment is activated throughout in-country projects and in calibrating next steps in one's own career.
- Strategizing/orchestrating skills germinate in context of in-country engagement and in hand-off of the project for final delivery.
- Responsible leadership is an ongoing subject of inquiry for participants and teams.

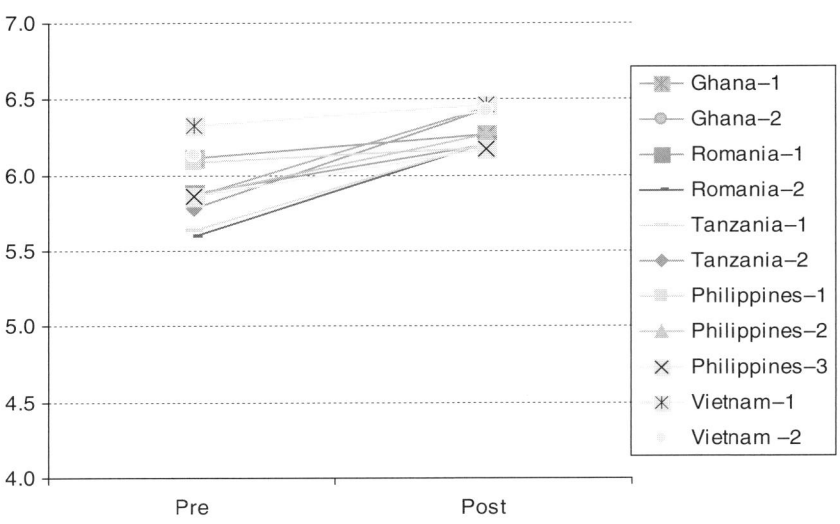

Figure 17.1   Changes in resilience for CSC participants (pre-versus post-participation ratings by country teams)

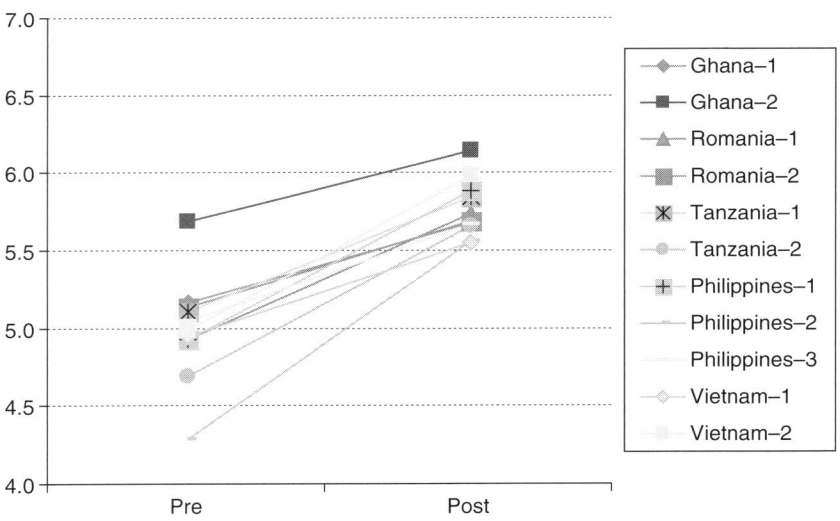

Figure 17.2   Changes in cultural intelligence for CSC participants (pre-versus post-participation ratings by country teams)

Finally, the CSC program also stimulated, a bit, the participants' skills at leading an enterprise. Pre-work gave them a glimpse into the global environment of business, and the in-country assignment gave them first-hand experience of doing business in an emerging market. The scale of assignments gave many exposure to local and national government officials, community groups and NGOs. At the end, many also had to report to senior managers about IBM concerning not only their own learnings but the implications for the business. Media coverage, conferences, and such also put several on public platforms – an arena that challenges many senior leaders.

PARTICIPANT EXPERIENCES

IBM is not the only company offering enriching international volunteer experiences for its next generation leaders. Ernst and Young, Accenture, Pfizer and others offer some variant of the same. There are also firms that take whole classes of future leaders abroad for developmental experiences (AMD, Unilever) and a few that take current and future leaders together on global journeys (cf. Mirvis, 2008).

Certainly the projects were a prime vehicle for developing next generation leadership skills. Volumes attest to the benefits of global project learning (cf. Wankel and DeFillippi, 2005). In reflecting on the experience, however, many CSC participants believed that teaming was the crucial aspect to the experience. Noted one who served in Tanzania: 'Teaming is absolutely one of the best parts of the experience – we found that the intra-team cultural experience was perhaps even more valuable than the cultural experience of living in another country.' A Filipino Romanian reflected similarly: 'The best part of the experience was getting to know each other. Discussing project progress at meals. Sharing experiences. I believe it does not matter how many people are in the team and they definitely should share the same accommodations. As a whole that helped create the team spirit.'

In addition to living in close quarters with a diverse group of other IBM employees, experiencing the different cultures of the assignment generated significant self-reflection and intra-personal change. A key learning cited by participants was how to work in different business climates and cultures, particularly the importance of emerging markets. For example, a Vietnam participant described the one thing that he learned is 'that the USA is not the center of the universe; in fact the center of the universe may be Danang, Vietnam. What a fantastic city!' Upon reflection, participants described how they had gained a new perspective on the world, on other cultures, and on themselves. A Philippines participant described that they learned to 'be a better global citizen and have better appreciation of the differences in upbringing, actual physical environment, physical dangers (i.e., terrorism) and how that can shape an individual's approach.' By being in a range of situations, participants felt they had developed as a leader during the project, specifically citing cross-cultural networking skills and the ability to work with others through language and cultural differences. Furthermore, many expressed a new sense of confidence in their own abilities after being in the program.

An independent evaluation by Harvard Business School confirmed improvements in the areas of global leadership skills, cultural intelligence and global awareness, employee retention and commitment to IBM, new knowledge and skills contribution to IBM, and interpersonal growth. Local organizations with which CSC participants worked identified four impact areas: improvements in their internal business processes, impact on local organizational staff, expanded internal and external networks, and perception of IBM.

TOWARD NEXT GENERATION EXECUTIVE DEVELOPMENT

The primary vehicles for leadership development have evolved incrementally over decades. But today's options are not dramatically different from what was available twenty or thirty years ago. Business schools have grown in number, class size, and importance to career advancement. This is in addition to the numerous executive education and targeted learning workshops attended by active professionals. Curriculum is still primarily focused on the 'blocking and tackling' fundamentals of finance, marketing, strategy and operations. An impediment to large-scale change in business schools are entrenched interests, notably deans and tenured faculty, and ranking systems that fail to reward innovation in the student experience, instead focusing on what can be easily measured such as entrance exam scores and salary upon graduation.

GE transformed corporate leadership development training in the 1980s at its Crotonville Leadership Development Institute. But today corporate education is still primarily a gathering of managers at approximately the same stage in their careers at a corporate facility for 3–5-day workshops with company leadership and outside experts. There is a shift towards virtually delivered online courses that target tactical competencies. Funding is at risk during down cycles and the recent economic situation has led to dramatic cuts in employee education.

International experiences have also remained fairly consistent in their objectives and structure over recent years. Long considered the last resort for firms trying to fix a problem that remains unresolved by local staff, international assignments often made the development experience a secondary consideration. Further, when an international assignment is principally a development experience it is targeted at late career senior leaders. The ensuing high costs limit the number of executives who can have these experiences.

What the CSC program offers is an up-to-date 'curriculum' that cultivates the next generation of business leaders. It teaches them how to 'self-manage' their work and careers. At the same time, it also makes them more valuable to their current companies and prepares them, should circumstances dictate, to manage their boundaryless career wherever it takes them.

REFERENCES

Calarco, A. and Gurvis, J. (2006) *Adaptability: Responding Effectively to Change*, Greensboro, NC: CCL Press.

Cohen, M.D. and March, J.G. (1986) *Leadership and Ambiguity*, 2nd edn, Boston: Harvard Business School Press.

Drucker, P.F. (1994), 'The theory of the business', *Harvard Business Review*, September–October.

Earley, P.C. and Peterson, R.S. (2004), 'The elusive cultural chameleon: cultural intelligence as a new approach to intercultural training for the global manager', *Academy of Management Learning and Education*, 3(1), 100–115.

Emery, F.E. and Trist, E.L. (1973), *Toward a Social Ecology*, London: Tavistock.

Goleman, D. (2006), *Social Intelligence: The New Science of Human Relationships*, New York, Bantam.

Goleman, D., Boyatzis, R. and McKee, A. (2002), *Primal Leadership*, Boston, MA: Harvard Business School Press.

Googins, B., Mirvis, P.H. and Rochlin, S. (2006), *Beyond Good Company: Next Generation Corporate Citizenship*, New York: Palgrave-McMillan.

Gosling, J. and Mintzberg, H. (2003), 'The five minds of a manager', *Harvard Business Review*, November, 1–9.

Hall, D.T. (1976), *Careers in Organizations*, Glenview, IL: Scott, Foresman.

Hall, D.T. and Mirvis, P.H. (1994), 'Careers as lifelong learning', in A. Howard (ed.), *The Changing Nature of Work*, San Francisco, CA: Jossey-Bass.

Hall, D.T. and Mirvis, P.H. (1996), 'The new protean career: psychological success and the path with a heart', in D.T. Hall and Associates (eds), *The Career is Dead – Long Live the Career*, San Francisco, CA: Jossey-Bass.

Handy, C. (1989), *The Age of Unreason*, Boston, MA: Harvard Business School Press.

Heifetz, R. (2004), *Leadership Without Easy Answers*, Boston, MA: Harvard University Press.

Kates, A. and Galbraith, J.R. (2007), *Designing your Organization: Using the STAR Model to Solve 5 Critical Design Challenges*, San Francisco, CA: Jossey-Bass.

Marquis, C. and Kanter, R.M. (2009), *IBM: The Corporate Service Corps*, Cambridge, MA: Harvard Business School.

Mintzberg, H. and Waters, J.A. (1985), 'Of strategies, deliberate and emergent', *Strategic Management Journal*, **6**, 257–72.

Mirvis, P.H. (2002), 'Community building in business', *Reflections*, **3**, 45–51.

Mirvis, P.H. (2008), 'Executive development through consciousness raising experiences', *Academy of Management Learning and Education*, **7**(2), 173–88.

Mirvis, P.H. and Hall, D.T. (1994), 'Psychological success and the boundaryless career', *Journal of Organizational Behavior*, **15**, 365–80.

Mirvis, P.H., Ayas, K. and Roth, G. (2003), *To the Desert and Back: The Story of One of the Most Dramatic Business Transformations on Record*, San Francisco, CA: Jossey-Bass.

Rooke, D. and Torbert, W. (2005, April), 'Seven transformations of leadership', *Harvard Business Review*, reprint, pp. 1–7.

Schein, E.H. (1990), *Discovering your Real Values*, San Diego, CA: Pfeiffer.

Schein, E.H. (1999), *Process Consultation Revisited*, Reading, MA: Addison-Wesley.

Schön, D. (1983), *The Reflective Practitioner*, New York: Basic Books.

Senge, P. (1990), 'The leader's new work: building learning organizations', *Sloan Management Review*, Autumn, 7–23.

Tichy, N. and Bennis, W. (2007), *Judgment: How Winning Leaders Make Great Calls*, New York: Penguin.

Tichy, N. (with Cohen, E.) (1997), *The Leadership Engine: How Winning Companies Build Leaders at every Level*, New York: HarperInformation.

Vaill, P.B. (1982), 'The purposing of high performing systems', *Organizational Dynamics*, Autumn, 23–39.

Wankel, C. and DeFillippi, R. (eds) (2005), *Educating Managers Through Real-world Projects*, Greenwich, CT: IAP.

Weick, K.E. (1995), *Sensemaking in Organizations*, Thousand Oaks, CA: Sage.

18. And leadership development for all

Lyndon Rego, David G. Altman and Steadman D. Harrison III

INTRODUCTION

Say the word 'leadership' and it often generates an image of 'people in charge' or those who sit 'at the top of organizations' or in the 'C-suite'. Leadership development too has been highly geared towards senior-level people in formal organizations or those being groomed for these roles. Yet, if we unpack what leadership development *does* rather than who receives it, it has a great deal of relevance to enhancing the effectiveness, satisfaction and productivity of all people in all roles. This chapter is about the democratizing leadership development and Center for Creative Leadership's (CCL) effort to make it more affordable and accessible in our world.

To begin, we would like to take you to a class that took place in a Mumbai, India slum on a weekend. When we visited, we saw on the walls pictures of Indian movie stars and models along with a solitary picture of Mahatma Gandhi over to the side. The juxtaposition of these pictures caused us to reflect on the underlying meaning. The class is filled with young women and men, most under the age of 20 and all visibly excited about the chance to learn something new. The women are dressed in traditional *salwar kameez*, the men in Western attire; one of them is even sporting a black heavy-metal t-shirt. They are there by choice and eager to learn. An enthusiastic young trainer stands in front of the class beaming at the group and radiating energy and optimism. He invites the class to introduce themselves in English. After a brief pause, a young woman in the front stands up first to make her introduction. In halting English, she says her name and why she is present. Each introduction is followed by applause from the group. The class is meant to teach the young people English and social skills and to help them gain self-confidence. The prize is a job in India's booming retail industry, as a store clerk, a barista, or a cashier. Once employed, these young people will earn more than their parents ever did from tedious, underpaid work as laborers, street vendors and household servants. The classroom is run by an NGO. The students are there because they want these upwardly mobile jobs. Employers want soft skills. And the young people know it. This 'training' is a potential pathway for a better life for themselves and their families. The creative tension in the room is palpable. After a successful few hours together, we leave, sadly realizing once again that the field of leadership development, which has so much to offer, ignores most of the world's population with its high cost, non-scalable intervention models.

Leaving the Mumbai slum, we make our way to Pantaloon, one of the fast-growing retail companies in India. Developing leadership skills is what Pantaloon focuses on with new hires, most of whom are from lower socioeconomic strata. The head of Pantaloon's training arm began building the organization's development program with a key insight from the street. This began by watching beggars at a traffic intersection. He noticed that some beggars did better than others, and the difference he observed was that the more effective beggars displayed a greater sense of self-efficacy and self-esteem. If efficacy and esteem could make a difference to beggars, he wondered, what could it do for motivated young people wanting to work at Pantaloon? The program he implemented at Pantaloon was ultimately very successful in strengthening employee engagement and organizational results (personal communication, January 2008).

Our encounter with Pantaloon triggered the question: if leadership skills can influence individual and organizational effectiveness, might they be even more important to those who are not formally employed? Indeed, the vast majority of people in the world are young, reside in developing countries, and live on less than $2 a day. Most of these individuals live in rural areas, have had limited access to formal education, and do not work in formal organizations. For these individuals, much of their well-being depends on their own ability to make a living and take care of their families. Their ability to envision and enact change, motivate themselves and influence others, and deal with conflict and difference has profound implications for their lives. Leadership skills are relevant. Thus, developing their capacity can have a significant impact on themselves and society.

This rang true to us when we visited Uganda. At the close of one of the first leadership programs we ran on the continent, an individual who had formerly been part of a vicious guerrilla organization shared with us the following:

> This training is very important. And you need to understand why we say to you, 'You need to come back.' You hear us saying, come back soon. And it's for a reason. Where you come from, this leadership training may result in better management and better business practices. But here, here in Uganda, this teaching has the potential to save lives. This region, these governments have been at

war for many years. If they heard today what you were teaching us, I believe we could end many of these conflicts. We could see an end to these wars.

He was right. So much of formal leadership development is focused on improving the skills of high-functioning managers and leaders in resource-rich organizations. Rarely do professionals in leadership development organizations talk about their work ending wars. In reality, leadership development can have an impact on the health and well-being of people who live and work in slums and poor villages. In a program we delivered in Kenya, people traveled as far as 14 hours and slept in their cars to attend. In their eyes, we saw as deep a hunger for learning as we have ever seen in the eyes of corporate executives. In large African cities, street vendors offer an abundance of leadership titles and self-help books that are snapped up by young people. These young people are looking for resources to help them navigate the life challenges they are facing. One young man we met in Kampala, Uganda, for example, told us that the reason he and his peers were turning to popular books for answers was to make up for mentorship lost through war and disease. 'We have lost a generation. Where do you turn when your fathers and mothers are gone? Who will teach us the life lessons we so desperately need to know?' The traditional African proverb has never been more applicable: 'When an elder dies, a library is burned.' Young people around the world are hungry for development and mentoring.

This is a thread that extends to youth in the US. At a prominent high school for high-achieving and affluent kids, we found a common desire to learn and grow and perhaps a different idea of good leadership than one might find in academia and business tomes. We prepared a deck of images of people, from political and business leaders to community organizers and people from everyday walks of life. The cards that surfaced at the top of the list were the 'soccer mom' and social change leaders. Bill Gates made the cut not for his role as mega-billionaire but for his role as mega-philanthropist and social activist. Young people told us in repeated encounters that they were interested in leadership as a force to create greater social good rather than a vehicle for money and power. This is exactly the message that Bill Gates has conveyed on creative capitalism:

Capitalism has improved the lives of billions of people – something that's easy to forget at a time of great economic uncertainty. But it has left out billions more. They have great needs, but they can't express those needs in ways that matter to markets. So they are stuck in poverty, suffer from preventable diseases and never have a chance to make the most of their lives. Governments and non-profit groups have an irreplaceable role in helping them, but it will take too long if they try to do it alone. It is mainly corporations that have the skills to make technological innovations work for the poor. To make the most of those skills, we need a more creative capitalism: an attempt to stretch the reach of market forces so that more companies can benefit from doing work that makes more people better off . . . As I see it, there are two great forces of human nature: self-interest and caring for others. Capitalism harnesses self-interest in a helpful and sustainable way but only on behalf of those who can pay. Government aid and philanthropy channel our caring for those who can't pay. And the world will make lasting progress on the big inequities that remain – problems like AIDS, poverty, and education – only if governments and nonprofits do their part by giving more aid and more effective aid. But the improvements will happen faster and last longer if we can channel market forces, including innovation that's tailored to the needs of the poorest, to complement what governments and nonprofits do. We need a system that draws in innovators and businesses in a far better way than we do today (Gates, 2008).

It may surprise some that leadership skills matter a great deal to those who have little money or power. Mohammed Yunus, 2006 Nobel Peace Prize winner and father of the microfinance movement, likens a poor person to a seed of a tree that is planted in a tiny pot with little room to grow. The same seed planted in open ground has the opportunity to develop to become a great tree (Knowledge@Wharton, 2005). Ela Bhatt, founder of SEWA, observes that self-employment develops all aspects of the person – social, economic and political. She writes in her book, *We Are Poor But So Many*, that self-employment creates a virtuous cycle:

> When the poor come together on the basis of their work and build organizations that decentralize production and distribution and promote asset formation and ownership, build people's capacities, and provide social security, and allow for active participation and a voice, they are dynamic and healthy. . .We need policies that encourage self-help, support local cooperative economic initiatives, and emphasize sharing and pooling of resources at every level. This strengthens the community and stops migration; it prevents alienation and exploitation, and it stems the freefall into poverty (Bhatt, 2006: p. 217).

The challenge, then, is not the lack of need or interest in learning and growth in the populations not served by leadership development providers, but rather the affordability and access of options. If we decouple our thinking about leadership development from the limited context of executive education and organizational effectiveness, it brings into focus the vast open space of human potential. Here there are two expansive areas to which the field of leadership development can extend. First, there is a need to reach out to young people and to the environments in which they learn and develop. And second, there are opportunities to engage with the poor and self-employed and the contexts in which they work and live. In this chapter, we explore these domains and some of the practices being used to pour leadership development into new molds and models. Before we do that, let's examine some key mechanisms that connect development to positive outcomes.

LEADERSHIP DEVELOPMENT IN A NEW LIGHT

The field of training and development mostly targets the behaviors of individuals in formal organizations in the developed world. There is strong evidence in the literature that education and training is beneficial to both individuals and organizations across a variety of outcomes (Aguinis and Kraiger, 2009). While the literature on leadership development is still predominantly focused on studying individuals and organizations at higher levels of socioeconomic status, there are a small, but growing number of studies that examine leadership across the spectrum of public, private and government organizations in different parts of the world (Avolio et al., 2009). The effects of the organizational and community context and culture on individual behavior, a focus of community psychology (Trickett, 2009) and of the intervention work described in this chapter, speaks to the importance of moving beyond intrapsychic processes when studying leadership. Indeed, in research on twins, where genetics are obviously controlled, it has been found that the context in which leaders operate is more important in influencing subsequent leadership capability than genetic factors; genetics account for only about 30 percent of the variability in leadership effectiveness. Thus, while there are many genetically gifted individuals who become great leaders, the environments in which individuals live and work are more important predictors of success and thus should be the target of intervention (Avolio et al., 2009).

There is a debate in the leadership development literature around whether the focus should be predominantly on enhancing existing strengths and/ or on shoring up weaknesses (Kaiser, 2009; McCall, 2009; White, 2009). Our approach, to focus on both strengths and weaknesses in a balanced fashion, is consistent with those presented by Kaiser (2009). When working with underserved populations who often reside at the bottom of society's socioeconomic pyramid, the debate about focusing on strengths vs. weaknesses is largely irrelevant. We have found that people who have not had access to developmental interventions and who struggle to improve their basic status and the status of their families and communities (for example, food, housing, health), afford themselves of every opportunity to become more effective, whether it is to build on strengths or to reduce the negative impact of weaknesses. As noted throughout the cases presented in this chapter, we focus on growth rather than on strengths and weaknesses per se. Our approach is resonant with the work on the growth mindset by Carol Dweck and colleagues at Stanford University (Dweck, 2006). Modern day experts on personality and intelligence point out that while intelligence, or other fixed abilities, play a role in individual effectiveness, effectiveness is much more heavily influenced by perceptions that people have of themselves, actions that they take, life experiences and context (Dweck, 2006; McAdams, 2008). Dweck introduced the powerful concept of a growth mindset, or the belief that your skills and effectiveness are not pre-determined but rather influenced by cultivation, practice and re-do loops. People with a growth mindset 'believe that a person's true potential is unknown (and unknowable); that it's impossible to foresee what can be accomplished with years of passion, toil, and training' (Dweck, 2006: p. 7). Dweck has shown that people can be trained to have a growth mindset and that managers who have a growth mindset appreciate talent in their workforce but do not rely on talent alone to ensure that their workforce is effective. Dweck has found that growth mindset managers invest in developmental conversations, coaching, mentoring and other interventions to ensure that their employees become more effective and not just stuck in place with the same skill sets.

In our work with leaders around the world, we implicitly take a growth mindset and assume in our interventions that everyone, regardless of their status in society or their prior effectiveness (or lack thereof), have the potential to learn, to be more effective in the leadership roles that they play, and to help others grow as well. Other research supports our unabashed and egalitarian focus on growth and development. Bandura has written extensively on the central role that perceived self-efficacy takes in human behavior (Bandura, 1986; 1997; 2001). He wrote:

> Among the mechanisms of personal agency, none is more central or pervasive than people's beliefs in their capability to exercise some measure of control over their own functioning and over environmental events. Efficacy beliefs are the foundation of human agency. Unless people believe they can provide desired results and forestall detrimental ones by their actions, they have little incentive to act or to persevere in the face of difficulties (Bandura, 2001: p. 10).

Bandura (2001) has also suggested that to navigate a world of opportunity, challenge and complexity successfully, individuals must have self-awareness of their capabilities, an ability to estimate probable cause and effect of actions they take, an understanding of the context in which they operate, and an ability to regulate their behavior. Bandura further argues that human agency (that is, the ability to connect one's actions to outcomes) is comprised of four key dimensions: (a) intentionality, or the ability to develop plans of action for a specific purpose; (b) forethought, or the ability to establish goals and to understand the relationship between one's behavior and goals accomplished; (c) self-reactiveness, or the ability to self-regulate one's motivation, emotion and behavior; and (d) self-reflectiveness, or the ability to evaluate one's cognitions, values and actions. As noted throughout this chapter, our work to scale leadership development by bringing it to people living in all walks of society illustrates vividly these four concepts in practice.

While much of Bandura's writings have focused on individual perceptions of efficacy, he has extended these concepts from the individual to the collective. He posited that if a group of individuals have a shared belief (or confidence) that they can effectively engage in action to produce a desired outcome, the likelihood that they will engage in a behavior is enhanced. If, as Bandura suggests and empirical studies support, self- and collective efficacy is a central influence on whether one is optimistic or pessimistic, takes on a challenge, perseveres in the faces of obstacles, expends or conserves energy on a task, or participates in a social setting or not, then it stands to reason that increasing perceptions of efficacy should be a keen focus of leadership development. Obviously, individuals cannot control all aspects of their environment or of the outcomes of their lives. But through personal and collective agency, they can exert influence on key factors that affect their lives. But can self-efficacy be increased among people living in poverty and in contexts which on the surface lack resources? The work described in this chapter shows that it can.

CCL's own work has focused on creating overarching frameworks for leadership and leadership development that extend beyond the context of the workplace to encompass how people work together and grow as leaders.

A Framework for Leadership

CCL has developed a framework for leadership that is comprised of *Direction, Alignment and Commitment* (DAC) (Drath et al., 2008). This framework suggests that leadership does not exist unless: (1) there is a shared understanding of where the collective is headed with respect to its vision, goals and objectives (i.e., *Direction*); (2) effective communication, coordination and collaboration occur within the collective (i.e., *Alignment*); and (3) individuals pursue collective goals over and above individual goals (i.e., *Commitment*). In cases where DAC are not adequately in place, there is a lack of leadership and the inability of people to work together effectively. While the Center itself is in the early stages of considering societal level leadership challenges, we believe that individual leader development is foundational to the actions of groups, whether they reside in a multinational corporation or a rural village. Leader development is about building self-awareness and the skills of individuals to be more effective in working with others.

The Center's model of *Assessment, Challenge and Support* (ACS) is at the heart of the leader development process (McCauley and Van Velsor, 2004). *Assessment* provides formal and informal data that helps increase understanding of oneself and others; *challenge* identifies the growth experiences that lead to development; and *support* provides the means and assistance to achieve milestones along the developmental journey. It is possible to see the pattern of ACS present in most forms of development. We need to understand where we are and where we want to go. We need to have support to achieve goals that extend beyond our existing abilities. Support includes access to knowledge and skills but also mentors and well-wishers who can help us get through transitions with encouragement and feedback.

What Develops in Leader Development

Leader development produces greater individual and collective efficacy. Increased leadership capacity entails a greater ability to achieve change. At the individual level, this extends from self-awareness, interpersonal skills and a learning orientation. A learning orientation is a personal commitment to constantly assess and challenge oneself to acquire needed new knowledge and skills, and make course corrections as needed. This flow is illustrated in Figure 18.1.

- *Self-Awareness.* Understanding self is to be aware of what one does well and not so well, what one is comfortable with and uncomfortable with. It is to be aware of which situations bring out one's best and which are difficult to handle. It is to recognize when one has appropriate knowledge to draw on and when one needs to look to other sources. Self-awareness also entails understanding the impact that personal strengths and weaknesses have on others.
- *Interpersonal Skills.* In enacting leadership, the ability to develop positive relationships with other people is particularly important. The foundation of this ability is the capacity to respect people from differing backgrounds and to understand the perspectives that they bring. A key interpersonal skill is being able to communicate information and ideas clearly and to work to understand what others are saying, thinking and feeling.
- *Learning Orientation.* When an individual has a propensity to learn, the person recognizes when new behaviors, skills, or attitudes are

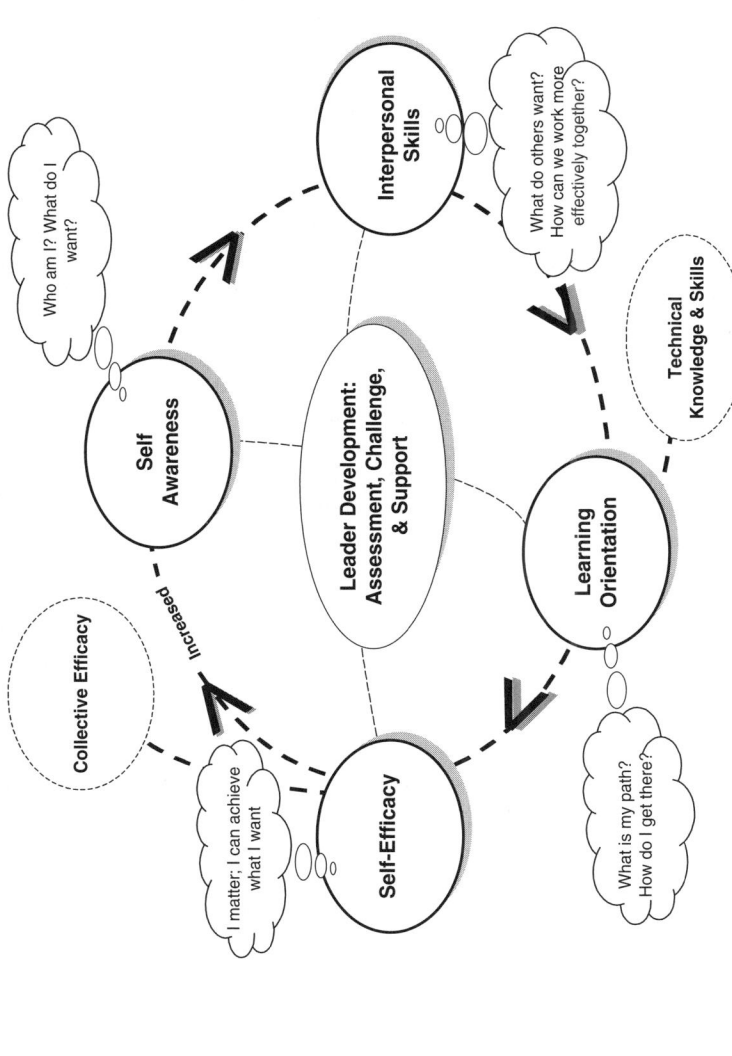

Note: *Handbook of Leadership Development* offers explanations of many of these core leadership concepts (McCauley and Van Velsor, 2004, pp. 12–15).

Figure 18.1   Leader development: from self-awareness to self-efficacy

495

needed, and accepts responsibility for developing these skills and knowledge. The individual understands and acknowledges current personal strengths and weaknesses, and engages in activities that provide the opportunity to learn or test new skills and behaviors.

As noted previously, Bandura (1986) has written extensively about self-efficacy:

- *Self-efficacy.* The ability to be effective is a product of skills, knowledge and belief in one self. Bandura (1986) wrote that self-efficacy is: 'The belief in one's capabilities to organize and execute the sources of action required to manage prospective situations.'

Collective-efficacy, another term introduced by Bandura, is the product of individual action and their ability to act together effectively – to achieve direction, alignment and commitment. Effective action does not take place at the exclusion of knowledge, of course. A plumber, farmer or lawyer must have technical knowledge related to their field. Yet there are also so-called soft skills that are an essential corollary to achieving outcomes. These self-management and interpersonal skills are often not formally developed but are expected to emerge from life. While it is true that we can learn to lead from life, we can do more to develop these abilities with conscious and consistent effort.

In his article, 'Everybody a changemaker', Ashoka founder Bill Drayton (2006), voiced the need to help young people gain 'applied empathy, teamwork, and leadership' skills. This is especially important for those who have been subject to the kind of education that leaves out inspiration and empowerment:

> The children of elite families grow up at home and usually in school being expected to take initiative and being rewarded for doing so. This confident ability to master new situations and initiate whatever changes or actions are needed is in essence what defines the elite. Entering adult life with confidence and mastery of empathy, teamwork, and leadership skills is what ultimately has given this small group control of the initiative and therefore of power and resources for millennia. However, the other 97 percent grow up getting very little such experience with taking initiative. Adults control the classroom, work setting, and even sports and extra-curricular activities. And this situation, coupled with society's attitudes, drums home the message to this majority: 'You're not competent or perhaps even responsible. Please don't try to start things; we can do it far better.' (Drayton, 2006: pp. 10–11).

Fortunately there are a number of educational and community institutions that reject the notion that leadership is just for the elite. These institutions are building viable models to unlock human potential for the young and the poor.

Creating Self-Awareness: PRADAN

Established in Delhi in 1983, Professional Assistance for Development Action (PRADAN) is an Indian NGO that operates in some of the poorest and least developed districts in India where basic government and economic infrastructure is lacking and accessibility to markets and services are severely constrained (Noponen, 2002). The people at PRADAN believe that overcoming economic poverty requires that the poor must be enabled to break free from their past, develop an alternative vision of their future and set achievable goals. The organization is a pioneer of the self-help group (SHG) practice that enables women to gain increased access to and control over the economic resources of their families.

PRADAN (2009) describes the Self-Help Group as:

> an informal association of 10 to 20 poor women belonging to the same village and sharing a common socio-economic background. The group enables its members to gain their identity as individuals, while realizing – and utilizing – the immense power of mutual aid. It provides them with a platform from where they can access banks and public services, and spearhead changes that affect them as poor women.

Women belonging to a particular SHG contribute 25 to 50 cents each week to build a collective fund. The seed money is used to provide members with low-interest loans that they can easily repay, freeing them from village moneylenders. Earned income goes into investments in land and agriculture, purchase of livestock and is used for medical expenses and children's education.

D. Narendranath, a program officer at PRADAN, states in *Beyond Microcredit* that the SHG has a bigger role besides creating financial benefit for the poor:

> It is an institution based on the concept of 'peer learning' as against learning that is externally controlled. This is a powerful process that enables growth and progress in the community. Members learn from each other in a group and SHGs learn from other SHGs, which leads to collective progress. The cohesion that SHGs foster enables them to address issues such as health and education . . . SHGs are also a forum for solidarity and empowerment of women, providing them the space and voice to negotiate and participate as equals within the family and society in general (Fisher and Sriram, 2002).

The key variable in changing a person's well-being is changing the person's view of themselves. The path PRADAN takes includes helping people envision the future they wish for themselves and to start taking small steps based on what they are able to do. This is accomplished with methods PRADAN has developed such as the Seven Rivers model. In this exercise, a woman first reflects on her living conditions and material welfare and ranks her position on a scale of seven rivers of being. The seventh river represents her ultimate state of well-being with all that life includes – such as adequate food, clothing, shelter, safety, healthcare and education. She is then asked to identify which river represents her present life. Often, a woman will offer that her life is only at the first or second river and mired with hardship and stagnation. She is then challenged to think about what it would take to traverse the rivers to get closer to her desired state of being. She is asked to consider changes she may need to enact, such as savings. A livelihood module then systematically guides her through her total available resources. An important element that sustains the model is support, which is provided by peers in the group of women who provide mutual encouragement and shared resources. Furthermore, leader roles in the group rotate so that they are shared by the group – this enables the less vocal or confident individuals to discover that they too can lead (personal communication, February 2009).

The PRADAN example illustrates that the assessment–challenge–support process can be accomplished with simple resources such as the Seven River method. It also indicates that creating self-awareness of the gap between present state and aspirations can be a powerful driver to stimulate change.

Developing Interpersonal Skills: Foundation for the Alleviation of Poverty

The Foundation for the Alleviation of Poverty in Chile is a not-for-profit institution that is dedicated to serving people at the margins of society. Across its social programs, the Foundation works in ways that enable the poor to develop the skills and processes to raise themselves out of poverty. At the same time that it brings together the poor, social organizations and both public and private institutions co-create solutions. The Foundation's *Servicio Pais* program places young professionals from around the country in areas stricken by poverty to teach skills and assist in development of the community. The Foundation's chairman, Rodrigo Jordan, explains that the service program doubles as a leadership program for the youth who sign up: 'When they go and work for the communities they realize how important social skills, leadership, communication are for the community. They also bring back a lesson that they need their leadership to develop wherever they go and work.' A profound outcome of the program is that half of these professionals return on completion of their service assignment to work in the rural regions they served in rather than stay on in the capital, which is a magnet for those young and educated. In the rural areas, regardless of whether they work for the government, a private company, or a non-profit, they bring a deep understanding of how to engage effectively with the local community. The service program models a way of sitting with the people to gain empathy and understanding, and influence not by power or knowledge but through relationships. States Rodrigo, 'Corporations love these professionals because in addition to the technical skills that they developed at the university they now know how to work in teams, they know how to hear people, how to balance different opinions, and know how to take into account different visions from different groups.'

In another initiative geared to lower-income young people, children as young as 10 or 11 are engaged in a multi-day team project such as building a garden for their school. While the objective isn't the point, they are forced to tackle the challenge together. At the end of the program the children are often transformed. They discover that they are not powerless. They discover that they have resources, perhaps not financial, but their capacities, their interests, their will. They also see leadership as something that is flexible, and a role that multiple people can step into. This learning is their own discovery and they carry the learning into their lives (personal communication, March 2009).

What is abundantly evident is that the Chilean programs create a mental shift for individuals on how they can more effectively engage with others. The strong interpersonal skills they gain from the service programs translate into more successful engagements with groups, organizations and communities. For the poor themselves comes a greater recognition of self-worth and a realization that far more can be achieved when they work together to address their challenges.

Creating a Learning Orientation: Barefoot College

The Barefoot College represents a model of development that honors the knowledge and capabilities of the poor. The College was established by social entrepreneur Bunker Roy in 1972, with a belief that traditional knowledge and sustainable technology can better help the poor. The College professes a profoundly unique orientation to learning:

> The Barefoot College is a place of learning and unlearning. It's a place where the teacher is the learner and the learner is the teacher. It's a place where NO degrees and certificates are given because in development there are no experts-only resource persons. It's a place where people are encouraged to make mistakes so that they can learn humility, curiosity, the courage to take risks, to

innovate, to improvise and to constantly experiment. It's a place where all are treated as equals and there is no hierarchy. (Barefoot College, 2009)

The idea of 'barefoot professionals' brings together the reality of the poor, many of whom walk without shoes, and the idea that professionalism is about competence, confidence and belief in one's knowledge system (Social Edge, 2006). The College's approach is also departure from the typical approach of aid agencies, which focus on enacting ideas created by outside experts and solutions that may not be sustainable. Founder Roy states: 'Tackling poverty requires a fundamentally different approach: one that starts with people themselves and encourages the initiative, creativity and drive from below that must be at the core of any transformation of their lives if it is to be lasting' (Roy, 2007). He emphasizes that when poor communities think at the human level, all their goals are interconnected. In contrast, states Roy, the aid model operates with the absence of communities as equal partners and the goals driven more by the needs of donors and governments than the needs of the poor.

The College's instructors have little formal education and use hands-on practice to transfer learning. Students create illustrated manuals to guide them in their work, which includes solar systems in rural areas, which provide electricity for as little as 10 cents a month. The College also focuses primarily on women who focus on enhancing their family's well-being and tend to stay on in communities, instead of migrating to the cities with their new skills. The Barefoot College model has been exported from India to Africa and Afghanistan. Bunker emphasizes that the need is for South–South transfer rather than the traditional modes of North–South. This is a powerful idea that opens up a new domain of relatively untapped expertise.

Bunker Roy's statement about leveraging the creativity and initiative of the poor provides an articulation of the potential of the poor to solve their own problems. The practices at Barefoot College take a strengths-based perspective rather than the more common deficit mindset applied towards the poor. The head of India's leading social work college emphasized to us that the poor are not without talents and resources. The need is for developing and harnessing these strengths. The 'return on development' can significantly alter the lives of the poor in a way that the aid model has failed to do. As a UN representative in India stated to us, the need is to meet the poor where they are. He quoted the saying, 'If I can't learn the way you teach, teach me the way I can learn.' It is clear that organizations such as PRADAN, the Chilean Foundation and Barefoot College are transforming the lives of the poor because they see the poor as partners – *as leaders* – in solving the challenges of poverty.

Building Self-Efficacy: Boomerang

Boomerang is a YMCA program in Chapel Hill, North Carolina, that was created to provide students who are suspended from middle and high school with a positive environment. These students are typically suspended for between 3–10 days and are sent to Boomerang by school administrators. The vast majority of students are from minority communities and have distressed backgrounds – single-parent homes, poverty, a family history of substance abuse, and physical or emotional abuse. While the suspension from school is meant to serve as a punishment, it often results in students' deepening problem behaviors. The students who are suspended from school are three times more likely to drop out of school and twice as likely to commit a crime during unsupervised time away from school. Furthermore, young people who fail to complete high school earn lower wages and are much more likely to be unemployed long-term than more educated peers.

Boomerang works to change that pattern. The key to Boomerang's approach lies in how they engage the students. The suspended students are recognized for their strengths rather than their problems. This three-day intervention helps the students focus on their potential and change interpersonal dynamics with parents and school officials. A technique Boomerang uses is to have the students draw a 'tree of life'. For the roots, the students are asked to represent their talents and what they are good at – things that nourish and anchor them. They are then asked to draw branches to represent their hopes and dreams. They are asked to consider what would help them grow these dreams. Finally, the students are asked to talk about what obstacles would damage their tree. Students quickly turn to the problem with parents, teachers and the police but they are nudged to think about how their personal behaviors can be stumbling blocks. The tree of life is then presented to a family member and a school representative in a ceremony. This tends to be a powerful encounter. The school representatives gain insight into aspects of the child they have not seen and understand what causes pain and stress. The parent gets to see their child in a light that illuminates positive attributes and aspirations rather than the problem behaviors that are often the focus.

'A miracle doesn't happen every time,' says Tami Pfeifer, Program Director for Boomerang, 'but it happens often enough.' What opens up is a measure of trust. The students gain ways to express things they haven't been able to say out loud. Young people who have been through the program tend to stay out of trouble, and 70 percent avoid being suspended again. A pattern is that students who have been in the Boomerang program tend to come back voluntarily to visit the program office in their free time. This demonstrates, says Pfeifer, how much they crave supportive and affirming environments (personal communication, April 2009).

The Boomerang example illustrates what can be achieved by building self-esteem even in a short intervention with children in trouble. Boomerang's two founders formerly worked in the local county school system and recognized the reoccurring failure of interventions with students who were constantly getting suspended. By engaging the larger system – parents and school representatives – Boomerang is able to turn the collective interactions in a more positive direction.

TAKING LEADERSHIP BEYOND BOUNDARIES: CCL

As a leadership development organization, CCL has begun to work to develop models that can make leadership development more affordable and accessible to all people. The organizations we have profiled above are exceptional in creating new models to unlock the potential of those who are young and poor. Many community and social sector organizations, however, lack leadership development curriculum and tools. Providing them with reliable methods enables them to focus on delivering on their mission rather than designing curriculum. CCL's work centers on a number of methods:

- *Tools and Curriculum development:* developing simplified tools and methods anchored in the assessment–challenge–support framework enables a 'plug-and-play' set of elements that can be adapted to individual contexts and needs.
- *Facilitation training:* leadership development is less about teaching content than enabling individuals to look within and think deeply about their situation and aspirations. This requires creating a safe space where people can open up with a high degree of candor.
- *Using existing platforms:* scaling leadership development requires the collective action of entities that are already engaged in education and empowerment. The millions of schools, community organizations and NGOs are all potential partners in human development.
- *Creating new platforms:* new technologies such as the internet and cellular phones are increasingly available to all people and offer significant potential for scale. Used to provide content and support for learning, they extend learning beyond geographical and time constraints.
- *Coalescing a movement:* extending leadership development to the billions of people who have been left out will require creative and

cascading action motivated by a twin desire to improve the human condition and serve underserved markets.

Over the past year, this CCL effort has extended leadership development to a broad spectrum of populations – from community health leaders in the Caribbean and Africa, to microfinance organizations and women's self-help groups in Asia and Africa, to minority high-school students and high-potential college students in the US, to high school principals and police officers in India, to NGOs and government institutions in the US, Africa and Asia, to orphans and street children in Africa and India, and to social entrepreneurship organizations and programs.

For instance, CCL worked with Mission to the World (MTW), a faith-based NGO operating in the Bole district of Addis Ababa. Over the course of the last four years, MTW has helped transform the quality of life for many of the residents of the slums living in this neighborhood. When they first arrived in Bole, the mission was to help individuals die with dignity. The local residents were dying of AIDS and the many ancillary illnesses to which these HIV-positive patients were susceptible. Through simple process innovations – the introduction of pill boxes and Timex watches with two daily alarms to prompt patients to take their antiretroviral treatments (ARTs) – mortality rates rapidly declined. Instead of helping residents to die a dignified death, the new challenge is helping them live a dignified life. Living with dignity is fundamentally about self-awareness, recognizing human potential, overcoming the boundaries and barriers of stigma and the limits imposed by a lack of vision. CCL has worked with MTW, representatives of their expert patient base in Bole, and members of the Ministry of Health to introduce a leadership program in early 2008. In follow-up conversations with participants six and 12 months post-program, we heard the importance of giving and receiving feedback and the power of simple leadership tools in helping individuals describe complex matters, such as what they wanted to do with their life and how they could improve the life of their children. One participant, Daniel, a year after his participation in the program, confided that he now sees his NGO work through the lens of leadership development – 'At the end of the day, our work with these [community members] is all about helping them see their personal potential, helping them see what is possible for their lives.'

TAPPING THE POTENTIAL FOR TRANSFORMATION

By building self-awareness, interpersonal skills and a learning orientation, we believe that individuals gain the means to transform their lives.

We believe that the methodology of leadership development represents a significant and untapped opportunity to improve the lives of many people around the world, especially those who are not traditionally seen as leaders. The world has already democratized much that was once the exclusive domain of the privileged. Some of what has been democratized – from literacy, to the right to vote, to human rights, to clean water (all prevalent in developed nations) – stems from the actions of social change agents. Other amenities that have been democratized have been delivered by the marketplace which has put many products and services in the hands of the common person – consider the ability to own a home, a watch, or a bank account (all far more prevalent in developed nations than developing countries). We believe it is time too to democratize leadership development. This requires the actions of social change institutions that see leadership development as a lever to enhance the lives of the poor. It also requires the actions of providers of leadership content and methods, which can make these resources more affordable through approaches that favor access over exclusivity.

The pay-off lies in achieving greater individual and common good and higher levels of personal and collective effectiveness. Because once we transform our view of our potential, our greater potential becomes within reach. When we have a learning orientation, we can overcome adversity and find opportunity. Once we understand where we most want to go, we can channel our energies to what matters most. Once we can work more effectively with others, we can leverage the power of many. Indeed, leadership development is a key to unlocking our potential as individuals and communities. Our hope is that this chapter inspires awareness, inspiration and action to take leadership development to those who have traditionally been left out. A world of need and opportunity awaits us.

REFERENCES

Aguinis, H. and Kraiger, K. (2009), 'Benefits of training and development for individuals and teams, organizations, and society', *Annual Review of Psychology*, **52**, 451–74.

Avolio, B.J., Walumbwa, F.O. and Weber, T.J. (2009), 'Leadership: current theories, research and future directions', *Annual Review of Psychology*, **52**, 421–49.

Bandura, A. (1986), *Social Foundations of Thought and Action: a Social Cognitive Theory*, Englewood Cliffs, NJ: Prentice Hall.

Bandura, A. (1997), '*Self-efficacy. The Exercise of Control*, New York: W.H. Freeman and Company.

Bandura, A. (2001), 'Social cognitive theory: an agentic perspective', *Annual Review of Psychology*, **52**, 1–26.

Barefoot College (2009), 'What is the Barefoot College?', available at http://barefootcollege.org/enroll1.htm, accessed 16 April 2009.

Bhatt, E. (2006), *We Are Poor But So Many: The Story of Self-employed Women in India*, New York: Oxford University Press.

Drath, W.H., McCauley, C.D., Palus, C.J., Van Velsor, E., O'Connor, P.M.G. and McGuire, J.B. (2008), 'Direction, alignment, commitment: toward a more integrative ontology of leadership', *Leadership Quarterly*, **19**, 635–53.

Drayton, B. (2006), 'Everyone a changemaker social entrepreneurships ultimate goal', *Innovation*, **1** (1), 10–11.

Dweck, C.S. (2006), *Mindset: The New Psychology of Success*, New York: Ballentine Books.

Fisher, T. and Sriram, M.S. (2002), *Beyond Micro-credit: Putting Development Back into Micro-finance*, Oxford, UK: Oxfam Publishing.

Gates, B. (2008), 'Making capitalism more creative', *TIME Magazine*, 31 July.

Kaiser, R.B. (2009), 'The rest of what you need to know about strengths-based development', in R.B. Kaiser (ed.), *The Perils of Accentuating the Positive*, Tulsa, OK: Hogan Press, pp. 1–9.

Knowledge@Wharton (2005), 'Muhammad Yunus, banker to the world's poorest citizens, makes his case', available at http://knowledge.wharton.upenn.edu/article.cfm?articleid=1147, accessed 5 April, 2009.

McAdams, D.P. (2008), *The Person: An Introduction to the Science of Personality Psychology*, 5th edn, Hoboken, NJ: John Wiley.

McCall, M.W., Jr. (2009), 'Every strength a weakness and other caveats', in R.B. Kaiser (ed.), *The Perils of Accentuating the Positive*, Tulsa, OK: Hogan Press, pp. 41–56.

McCauley, C. and Van Velsor, E. (eds) (2004), *The Center for Creative Leadership Handbook of Leadership Development*, 2nd edn, Hoboken, NJ: John Wiley.

Noponen, H. (2002), 'The Internal Learning System (ILS) – A tool for participant and program learning in micro-finance and livelihoods interventions', *Development Bulletin*, February, no. 57.

PRADAN (2009), 'Promotion of SHGs', available at http://www.pradan.net/index.php?option=com_content&task=view&id=33&Itemid=19, accessed 16 April 2009.

Roy, B. (2007), 'Ending poverty, but only on paper', available at http://www.american.com/archive/2007/july-0707/ending-poverty-but-only-on-paper, accessed 16 April, 2009.

Social Edge (2006), 'Story of Tilonia – Abode of Sanjit "Bunker" Roy', available at http://www.socialedge.org/blogs/not-to-be-missed/skoll-scholars/topics/Barefoot%20College, accessed 16 April, 2009.

Trickett, E.J. (2009), 'Community psychology: individuals and interventions in community context', *Annual Review of Psychology*, **52**, 395–419.

White, R.P. (2009), 'Strengths-based development in perspective', in R.B. Kaiser (ed.), *The Perils of Accentuating the Positive*, Tulsa, OK: Hogan Press, pp. 159–70.

Index

accelerate stage of personal growth
    model 124
Adams-Ender, Clara 187
adaptability 470–71
addiction to work 309–12
    passion versus addiction 312–15
adversity in the workplace 362–4
    failure and loss 364–7
    instrumental responsibility in
        preparing for 382–4
        cultivating self-awareness and
            affective self-regulation
            384–5
        cultivating self-efficacy and
            resilient outlook 385–6
        social support 386–8
    turning point processes 369–72
aesthetic intelligence 474–5
affective self-regulation 384–5
agreeableness, global leaders and 435
align stage of personal growth model
    118–24
Allen, S.J. 174
Amazon.com 1
ambiguity 470
Argyris, Chris 93, 112, 228
Arthur, M.B. 207, 209
assessment 108–9
    assessment and development centres
        202
    development of emotional and
        interpersonal competencies and
        171–2
    feedback from, see feedback
    five-phase individual feedback
        development and change model
        33–55
        assessment and feedback phase
            40–44
        initiation phase 34–9
        measuring change phase 52–5

planning for development phase
    44–9
taking action phase 49–52
learning and development needs
    398–400, 411–17
model for driving personal growth
    109
    accelerate stage 124
    align stage 118–24
    awaken stage 109–18
    case study 124–8
    self-assessment, see self-assessment
    types of 40–41
Athos, Tony 103
Augustine, St 108
Australia
    study of female academic leaders
        447, 455–6, 461
    engaging in and enacting
        leadership 448–55
    gender issues 457–8
    networks 458–9
    research approach 448
    role models 456–7
    work and family 459–60
Avolio, Bruce 172, 173–4
awaken stage of personal growth model
    109–18

Balkundi, P. 4–7, 404, 406
Ballou, R. 70
Bandura, A. 492, 496
Bank of America 49
Barefoot College 499–500
Bar-On, R. 175
Barry, D. 264
Bartol, K.M. 405–6
Baruch, Y. 166, 217
Beckham, David 218
Beckhard, R. 32
begrudging adopters 31

beliefs 300–304, 378
Bhatt, Ela 490
Bluedorn, A.C. 324
Boal, K. 241, 242
Boomerang programme 501–2
Boyatzis, R.E. 63, 71, 75, 82, 164, 171
Brass, D.J. 404, 405
Brett, J.M. 312
Brousseau, Ken 102
Buckingham, M. 8, 12
Buffett, Warren 187
Burke, R.J. 312
Burleson, B.R. 176
Burr, Don 341
buy-in scale 96

Caligiuri, P. 439, 442
Cameron, K.S. 3
Campion, M. 271, 283, 284
Camus, Albert 128
Canada 313
Cannon-Bowers, J.A. 270, 271, 284
careers 197, 221–2
    career entrepreneurs 216–19
    career success and personal failure syndrome 10
    changing context 197–9
    coping with careers 210–14
    emerging trends 219–21
    human/social capital and successful self-managed careers 208–10
    ignorance of career concepts 101–2
    leadership or managerial careers 199–200
    organizational support for career development 200–201
        assessment and development centres 202
        career information 203
        career workshops 204–5
        common career paths 205–6
        education and training 202
        high-flyer programmes 205
        induction 201–2
        internal recruitment 201
        lateral moves to create cross-functional experience 202–3

    mentoring, coaching and counselling 204
    performance appraisal 205
    secondments 203
    unemployment and 214–16
    who owns and manages your career 206–8
Carnegie, Dale 165
Carson, J.B. 264
Center for Creative Leadership (CCL) 3, 142, 487, 493, 502–3
    framework for leadership 493–500
challenges 144–9, 296
change management 3, 140
    competency development through intentional change in MBA program 70–71
    five-phase individual feedback development and change model 33–55
        assessment and feedback phase 40–44
        initiation phase 34–9
        measuring change phase 52–5
        planning for development phase 44–9
        taking action phase 49–52
    measuring change 52–5
        methods 53–4
        problems 54–5
    resistance to change 52–3
character, *see* personality
charismatic leadership 378
    goals and 233–4
Chatman, J. 200
Chile
    Foundation for the Alleviation of Poverty 498–9
China 316
Church, A.H. 36, 39
Ciarrochi, J. 174
Clawson, J.G. 7
Clifton, D.O. 8
coaching 49, 204, 411, 416, 419
cognitive intelligence 63, 72, 83
Collin, A. 197, 198
Colvin, Geoffrey 188
commitment 140–41
commons, tragedy of 244
communication 472

competencies 38, 62, 251
  assessing competency development
      outcomes 71–2
    discussion 80–84
    instruments 73–5
    methods 72
    results of study 75–6
  competency development through
      intentional change in MBA
      program 70–71
  emotional competencies of leaders
      160–65
    best practices for development
        169–70
    developmental readiness and
        motivation 170–76
  as focus of self-managed
      development 62–4
  interpersonal competencies 165–7
    best practices for development
        169–70
    developmental readiness and
        motivation 170–76
    gap between research and training
        167–9
  work teams 269–75
complexity theory 69
confidentiality 110
conflict management 76, 82
  work teams 287
conscientiousness, global leaders and
    435–6
Conte, J.M. 324
Cordova, D. 455
Corporate Service Corps, *see* IBM
    Corporate Service Corps
    (CSC)
Cortina, J. 399, 409
counselling 204
Coutu, D.L. 365, 366, 377, 381
Coyle, Daniel 190
credit crunch 220
Creswell, J.W. 448
critical thinking, goals and 242–3
culture
  appreciating diversity 474
  feedback and 112
  self-assessment and 27
    cultural and language skills and
        abilities 432–3

training in 440
work teams and 284–5
Currie, G. 202
Czeisler, C.A. 326, 327
Cziksentmihalyi, Mihalyi 247

Das, T.K. 238
Davids, Kenneth 189
Day, David 169, 265
De Dreu, C.K.W. 280
De Janasz, S.C. 175
death bed question 329–30
decisiveness 141–2
DeFillippi, R.J. 209
demands of leadership role 296–7, 326
  reversing wear and tear process
      326–7
Derr, C. 205
development, *see* leadership
    development
Devine, D.J. 270
Dewey, John 363
dictators 95
distress 361
Doe, P.J. 377
'doormats' 95
Douglas, C.A. 405, 409
Drayton, Bill 496
Driver, Mike 102
Drucker, P. 5, 473
Dubrin, A. 227
Dweck, Carol 492

Eby, L.T. 209
Edison, Thomas 247, 385
education 202, 440
El Sawy, O. 244
Elias, M.J. 175
emotional intelligence 63, 72, 74, 76,
    80, 83, 176–7, 471
  emotional competencies of leaders
      160–65
    best practices for development
        169–70
    developmental readiness and
        motivation 170–76
    gap between research and training
        167–9
  global leaders and emotional
      stability 436–7

emotional regulation 377
employees 251
    development 140
    employee–customer–profit chain
        model 46–7
    leadership self-development and 417,
        420
    teams, *see* work teams
Emslie, C. 459
enacted problem-solving, goals and
    240–41
Enron 33, 200
entrepreneurship 216–19
Ericsson, K. Anders 188
ethics, goals and 235–6
Ethiopia
    Mission to the World (MTW) 503
ethnic minorities, feedback and 112
experience
    development and 143–4
    learning from 152–5
    reflection on 155–6
experiential learning 172
experimentation 67–8
extroversion, global leaders and
    434–5

failure, resilience and 364–7
fears 300–304
feedback 108–9, 109–10, 118–19
    case study 124–8
    delivery mechanisms 41–2
    development of emotional and
        interpersonal competencies and
        171–2
    engagement with direct reports
        123–4
    engagement with manager 121–2
    engagement with peers 122–3
    exploring context 120–21
    five-phase individual feedback
        development and change model
        33–55
        assessment and feedback phase
            40–44
        initiation phase 34–9
        measuring change phase 52–5
        planning for development phase
            44–9
        taking action phase 49–52

making sense of 118
    ongoing 156
    personal reflection 119–20
    preparation for receiving
        110–12
    reactions to 43–4
    tying results to company or
        industry 114, 117
    understanding psychological
        inventories 113–14, 115–16
    work teams 283–4
feedback junkies 31
Feldman, D.C. 212
Feldman, M.S. 204
Field, Sally 186
first timers 31
Fitzgerald, F. Scott 379
Fleishman, E.A. 258
Flett, G.L. 316, 317
Ford, D. 245
foresight 474
Foundation for the Alleviation of
    Poverty 498–9
Franklin, Benjamin 109
Frederickson, B.L. 384
free time 328
Friedman, M. 300, 319
Friedman, S.D. 5, 8
Fritz, Robert 101
Fritz, S.M. 175
Fromm, Erich 247
future leaders, *see* next generation
    business leaders

Gallup Organization 8
Gates, Bill 489–90
General Electric (GE) 484
Ghana 478
Gibson, D. 455, 457
Gibson, S. 455
Gladwell, Malcolm 102, 188, 189
Glanz, L. 212
globalization 131, 475
    self-development and self-assessment
        for global leaders 429–32,
        438–9, 443
    cultural and language skills and
        abilities 432–3
    development activities 442–3
    personality 433–7

tool for gaining self-awareness
    437–8
  training activities 439–42
goals 124, 191–2, 226–7, 297–8
  choice of 228
  content of goals 298–9
  critical thinking and wisdom 242–3
  development of learning criteria to
    monitor goal progress 401–2,
    421
  enacted problem-solving 240–41
  ethics and 235–6
  hierarchies of 244–5
  identification and development of
    learning objectives 400–401,
    418–20
  leadership self-efficacy and 236–7
  leadership theories and 230
    attending to people and to task
      performance 230–31
    charismatic leadership 233–4
    participative leadership 231–2
    transactional leadership 232–3
    transformational leadership 234–5
  long-termism 243–4
  motivation for 299–300
  positive psychology and 237–8
  possible selves 246
  proactive and transcendent
    behaviour 238–40
  pursuit of 228–30, 247
  self-sabotage 227, 231, 233, 236–7,
    238, 239, 240–41, 242, 243
  strategic leadership and cognitive/
    behavioural complexity 241–2
Goleman, Daniel 93, 160, 168, 171, 472
good soldiers 31
Gosling, J. 91
government 468
Granovetter, M. 406
Greene, J.O. 176
Grey, C. 211
Gunz, H.P. 199

habit 93–4
Hall, D.T. 198, 355, 466, 479
Handy, C. 465
Harris, P. 200
Harris, R.T. 32
Harrison, D.A. 4–7, 404, 406

Hart, R.K. 285
Hayakawa, S.I. 367
health 329
  job demands and 326
Hewlett, S.A. 296, 312, 316
high-flyer programmes 205
Hoffer, Eric 93
holidays 328
Hooijberg, R. 241, 242
Hughes, E.C. 198
Hughes, M. 174
Hull, R. 101
human capital, careers and 208–10
Hunt, J.W. 166
Hunt, K. 459

Ibarra, H. 405
IBM 49
IBM Corporate Service Corps (CSC)
    477–9, 485
  content versus competencies 479–83
  participant experiences 483–4
iceberg model 47
India 487–8
  Barefoot College 499–500
  Professional Assistance for
    Development Action
    (PRADAN) 497–8
  shortage of leaders 134–8
induction 201–2
inductive thinking 105
Industrial-Organizational (I/O)
    Psychology 37
Indvik, J. 455
Inference, Ladder of 112, 113
informal learning 251, 252–4
  self-directed work teams 267–8
integration frameworks 46–7
Intentional Change Theory (ICT) 62,
    64–70
interactions 347–9
  work teams 275–80
internal recruitment 201
interpersonal competencies 165–7
  best practices for development
    169–70
  developmental readiness and
    motivation 170–76
  gap between research and training
    167–9

interpersonal skills 494
inventories, psychological 113–14,
    115–16

Jacobs, R.R. 324
Jacobson, D.E. 387
Jago, A. 231
Jobs, Steve 187
Johari's Window 92
Joyce, James 95
judgement 475–6

Kahn, R.L. 258
Kaiser, R.B. 491
Kanter, R.M. 217, 457, 458
Kaplan, R.E. 9
Karoly, P. 286
Katz, D. 258
Keller, Thomas 189
Kennedy, John F. 386
Kenya 489
Killeen, L. 246
Kirkpatrick, D.L. 53
knowledge
    acquisition of 63
    knowing–doing gap 228–9
    relational know-how 343–51
    self-assessment of cultural and
        language knowledge 432–3
Korman, A.K. 10, 11
Korman, R.W. 10, 11
Kotter, J.P. 3, 5
Krause, Tom 378
Kubler-Ross, E. 43
Kuipers, B.S. 268, 271

Ladder of Inference 112, 113
Landy, F.J. 324
languages
    self-assessment of cultural and
        language skills and abilities
        432–3
    training in 441–2
lateral moves to create cross-
    functional experience
    202–3
Lavelle, M. 200
Lawrence, P. 101
Lay, Kenneth 200
Lazarus, R.S. 213

leadership 1–3, 258–9; *see also*
    individual topics
leadership development 3–4, 20–21,
    57
for all 487–91
    Barefoot College 499–500
    Boomerang programme 501–2
    Foundation for the Alleviation of
        Poverty 498–9
    framework for leadership 493–500
    leadership development in new
        light 491–3
    Professional Assistance for
        Development Action
        (PRADAN) 497–8
    taking leadership beyond
        boundaries 502–3
    tapping potential for
        transformation 503–4
development of emotional and
    interpersonal competencies
    169–70
developmental readiness and
    motivation 170–76
enlisting others into your
    development as leader 336–40
    next steps 355–8
    phase 1: developing self-awareness
        340–43
    phase 2: determining relational
        know-how 343–51
    phase 3: considering who should
        be in your developmental
        network 351–5
establishing developmental
    relationship 149–52
next generation business leaders
    468–9
    Corporate Service Corps, *see* IBM
        Corporate Service Corps
        (CSC)
    defining developmental agenda
        469–76
    developing future leaders 476–7
    executive development 484–5
objectives and scope of book 4–5
personal responsibility 84–7
principles 142–4
self-assessment and self-awareness
    and 5–9

self-development, *see* self-
  development
structure of book 13–20
using this book 11–13
work teams 281–7
learning 30, 138–40
  agenda 67
  assessment of learning and
    development needs 398–400,
    411–17
  development of learning criteria to
    monitor goal progress 401–2,
    421
  development of learning curriculum
    401, 418–20
  evaluation of learning gains 402–3,
    421–2
  from experience 152–5
  experiential 172
  identification and development of
    learning objectives 400–401,
    418–20
  informal 251, 252–4
    self-directed work teams 267–8
  learning partners 408–10, 411–22
  measurement 53
  organizational 494, 496
  typology of leader learners 30–31
Leavitt, Hal 101
Leslie, J.B. 381
Lewin, Kurt 32, 33
long-termism, goals and 243–4
loss, resilience and 364–7
Luce, C.B. 296, 312
Luthans, F. 368

McCall, Morgan 337
McCauley, C.D. 173, 405, 409
McGill, Mick 93
McIntyre, R.M. 275
McKibbin, L.E. 71, 166
McLeod, P.L. 285
managerial careers 199–200
Mansfield, Katherine 377
Manz, Charles 92, 265
Maree, J.G. 175
Marks, M.A. 256, 275, 280
Marshall, J. 212
Marsick, V.J. 251, 252
Masten, A.S. 376

materialism as motivation 305–9
Mathieu, J.E. 280
mattering 183–4
  goals 191–2
  how to matter 184–6
  love it or lose 186–91
  mindset matters 191
Maugham, W. Somerset 336
Mayer, J.D. 160, 161, 174
MBA programs, competency
  development through intentional
  change in 70–71
mediation 287
mentoring 204, 337–8, 351, 387, 411,
  415, 418
mindset matters 191
Mintzberg, Henry 91, 103, 166
Mirvis, P.H. 466, 479
Mission to the World (MTW) 503
Molinaro, D. 129
Moses, B. 364
motivation 30, 299–300, 402
  beliefs and fears 300–304
  materialism 305–9
  passion versus addiction 312–15
  workaholism/work addiction
    309–12
multi-tasking 324–5
Myers–Briggs Type Inventory 233

Nash, L. 5, 328
negative emotional attractors (NEAs)
  69
Netherlands 309, 311
networking 210, 216, 403–4
  considering who should be in your
    developmental network 351–5
  leadership self-development and
    395–8, 404–8, 422–3
  learning partners 408–10, 411–22
  preparing for adversity in the
    workplace 386–8
  resilience and 380
  study of female academic leaders in
    Australia 458–9
Newburg, Doug 97
next generation business leaders 464–5
  defining developmental agenda
    469–76
  developing future leaders 476–7

developmental challenges for
business leaders 468–9
executive development 484–5
IBM Corporate Service Corps (CSC)
477–9, 485
content versus competencies
479–83
participant experiences 483–4
rise of self-management 465–6
shape-shifting at work 466–8
Nicholson, Nigel 99
Nohria, N. 101

objectives, *see* goals
obligation 96–7
Ohlott, P.J. 145, 460
openness
global leaders and emotional
stability 437
organization development 32–3
organizational culture, *see* culture
organizational learning 494, 496
organizational resilience 366–7
organizational structures 131
organizational support for career
development 200–201
assessment and development centres
202
career information 203
career workshops 204–5
common career paths 205–6
education and training 202
high-flyer programmes 205
induction 201–2
internal recruitment 201
lateral moves to create cross-
functional experience 202–3
mentoring, coaching and counselling
204
performance appraisal 205
secondments 203
outside-in-ness 94–6
overreaction 9

Parker, P. 410
participative leadership, goals and
231–2
passion versus addiction 312–15
Pasteur, Louis 386
Patterson, L.B. 174

Pausch, R. 330
Penhoet, Ed 184–5
PepsiCo 35, 38, 47, 48, 49, 52
perfectionism 315–19
performance
appraisal 6, 205
attending to 230–31
underperformance 1
work teams 286–7
personal growth model 109
awaken stage 109–18
case study 124–8
personal life 141
personal reflection 119–20
personal resilience, *see* resilience
personality
iceberg model 47
measures 37–8
overestimation of concept of
character 99–100
self-assessment of 28–30, 433–4
Peter, L.J. 101
Peters, Tom 216
Pfeffer, J. 228
Pfeifer, Tami 501
Philippines 478
Pickford, Mary 369
polychronicity 324–5
Porter, L.W. 71, 166
positive emotional attractors (PEAs)
69
positive psychology
goals and 237–8
Price, V.A. 301
proactive behaviour
developmental proactivity 345–6
goals and 238–40
probabilities 295–6
problem-solving 100–101
enacted problem-solving 240–41
Professional Assistance for
Development Action (PRADAN)
497–8
psychological inventories 113–14,
115–16
psychological well-being 329

recruitment 201
rejection, fear of 94
relational know-how 343–51

relational theories 68
relationships, *see* networking
renegades 31
resilience
  characteristics and actions of
    resilient people 376–7
    agency-related factors 379–80
    coherence-generating factors
      378–9
    emotional regulation factors 377
  cultivating self-efficacy and resilient
    outlook 385–6
  directions for research on 388–9
  failure and loss in workplace and
    364–7
  importance of 362–4
  in management literature 380–82
  self-regulatory model 372–6
  turning point processes 369–72
  understanding 367–9
resisters 31
responsibility 476
  instrumental responsibility in
    preparing for adversity in the
    workplace 382–4
    cultivating self-awareness and
      affective self-regulation 384–5
    cultivating self-efficacy and
      resilient outlook 385–6
    social support 386–8
  personal responsibility for leadership
    development 84–7
  social responsibility 474
reward systems 232
  materialism as motivation 305–9
Rhee, K. 82
Richardson, G. 368
Robbins, S.P. 175
Roberts, L.M. 382
Romania 478
Rooney, Michel 364
Rosenman, R.H. 300, 319
Rouse, Jeff 97
Roy, Bunker 499–500
Ruderman, M. 460
Rutter, M. 370

Saatcioglu, A. 75, 82
Salas, E. 259, 270, 271, 275, 284
Salovey, P. 160, 161

SARAH model 43, 56
satisfaction 328–9
Schaufeli, W.B. 309
secondments 203
self-adaptation 383
self-assessment 6–9, 12, 25–7, 55–6, 57,
    103–6
  context of organization development
    32–3
  critical nature of 39
  factors impacting on effectiveness of
    27–30
    individual characteristics 28–30
    organizational cultural orientation
      27
    supporting tools and processes
      27–8
  five-phase individual feedback
    development and change model
    33–55
    assessment and feedback phase
      40–44
    initiation phase 34–9
    measuring change phase 52–5
    planning for development phase
      44–9
    taking action phase 49–52
  global leaders 429–32, 443
    cultural and language skills and
      abilities 432–3
    personality 433–7
    tool for gaining self-awareness
      437–8
  Intentional Change Theory (ICT)
    as model for self-directed
      competency development 64–70
  problems in management of process
    91–2
    focus on problem-solving rather
      than creation 100–101
    ignorance of career concepts
      101–2
    inattention to habituality 93–4
    invisible self-deception 92
    lack of desire to be self-aware 92
    obligation over choice 96–7
    outside-in-ness 94–6
    overestimation of concept of
      character 99–100
    type I and type II leaders 98–9

underestimation of energy and
     feel 97–8
  wrong kind of intelligence 93
  typology of leader learners 30–31
self-awareness 5–6, 7, 172, 340–43,
     384–5, 399, 434, 435, 437, 470,
     494
  tool for gaining self-awareness
     437–8
self-correction techniques 286
self-deception 92
self-development 9–11, 173
  competencies as focus of self-
     managed development 62–4
  global leaders 429–32, 438–9, 443
     development activities 442–3
     tool for gaining self-awareness
        437–8
     training activities 439–42
  networking and 395–8, 404–8,
     422–3
     learning partners 408–10
  process of leader self-development
     398
     assessment of learning and
        development needs 398–400,
        411–17
     development of learning criteria
        to monitor goal progress
        401–2, 421
     development of learning
        curriculum 401, 418–20
     evaluation of learning gains
        402–3, 421–2
     identification and development of
        learning objectives 400–401,
        418–20
     learning partners 408–10, 411–22
  teamwork competencies for
     leadership self-development
     271–5
self-efficacy 496
  cultivating self-efficacy and resilient
     outlook 385–6
  goals and 236–7
self-image 66
self-management 4, 9–11, 20, 226
  careers 206–10
  competencies as focus of self-
     managed development 62–4

next generation business leaders
     468–71
  rise of 465–6
  self-regulatory model of resilience
     372–6
  teams 265–6
self-regulation
  affective 384–5
  model of resilience and 372–6
self-sabotage 227, 231, 233, 236–7, 238,
     239, 240–41, 242, 243
self-training system 402
Seligman, Martin 237
Senge, P. 473
sense-making skills 472–3
Shankman, M.L. 174
shape-shifting at work 466–8
shortage of leaders (leadership gap)
     129–30
  closing leadership gap 138–56
  data 134–8
  trends contributing to 130–33
short-termism 244
Sims, H.P. 265
Singapore 134–8
skills 38–9, 102
  interpersonal skills 494
  self-assessment of cultural and
     language skills 432–3
  shortages 131
  social skills 350–51
sleep 327–8
smart coaching 49
social capital, careers and 208–10
social identity groups 68
social intelligence 63, 72, 74, 76, 80,
     93, 472
social networks, *see* networking
social responsibility 474
social skills 350–51
Socrates 91
Sokol, M. 71
Sonnenfeld, J. 214, 380
Spreitzer, G. 380
staff, *see* employees
Sternberg, R.J. 242
Stevens, M. 271, 283, 284
Stevenson, H. 5, 328
Stoeber, J. 316, 317
Stoker, J.I. 268, 271

strategic leadership
  goals and 241–2
strategic planning 140
strengths inventory 8, 12
Stroh, L.K. 312
Sturges, J. 207
Sullivan, Anne 370
supervision 416, 418–19
Sutcliffe, K.M. 385
Sutton, R. 228
systems thinking 473–4

Tannenbaum, S.I. 253, 281
Tanzania 478
targets, *see* goals
Tarique, I. 439, 442
teams, *see* work teams
technology, career management and
  220–21
Terrell, J.B. 174
Thompson, Kevin 477
Thunderbird School of Global
  Management 440
Tichy, N.M. 5
time sense 323–5
Tolstoy, Leo 118
total leadership development 5, 8
training 173, 202
  self-development leadership for
    global leaders 439–42
  self-training system 402
transactional leadership 232–3
transcendent behaviour 238–40
transformational leadership
  234–5
Troy, Gil 242
Tsongas, Paul 329
Tuckman, B.W. 268
turning point processes 369–72
Twain, Mark 198
type A behaviour pattern 319–23
type I and type II leaders 98–9

Uganda 488, 489
underperformance 1
underreaction 9
unemployment, careers and 214–16
United Kingdom 198
United States of America
  Boomerang programme 501–2

career development in 198
leadership for all 489–90
passion for work versus addiction
  312
shortage of leaders 134–8
short-termism in 244
universities
  study of female academic leaders in
    Australia 447, 455–6, 461
  engaging in and enacting
    leadership 448–55
  gender issues 457–8
  research approach 448
  role models 456–7
  work and family 459–60
Useem, M. 3

vacation 328
Vaill, Peter 33
values 378
Van Velsor, E. 173, 381
Vietnam 479
Vroom, V. 231

Wadsworth, M. 245
Ward, A. 214, 380
Waters, Alice 185
Watkins, K.E. 251, 252
Watkins, Sherron 200
Watson, T.J. 200
Watts, A.G. 91, 197, 198
Weick, K.E. 198, 385, 472
Weingart, L.R. 280
Weiss, D. 129
Wheeler, J.V. 68
Whetten, D.A. 3
wisdom
  goals and 242–3
  resilience and 381–2
women
  self-management and 10
  study of female academic leaders in
    Australia 447, 455–6, 461
  engaging in and enacting
    leadership 448–55
  gender issues 457–8
  networks 458–9
  research approach 448
  role models 456–7
  work and family 459–60

work
    addiction to 309–12
        passion versus addiction 312–15
    hours of 296–7, 325
    shape-shifting and 466–8
    workaholism 309–12
    work–life balance 141, 220
work teams 287–8, 466–7
    competencies 269–75
    conflict 287
    culture and 284–5
    debrief sessions 285–6
    effectiveness 254–6
    external relations and improvement
        280–81
    informal learning in 267–8
    internal relations 275–80
    leadership 258, 261
        best practices for emergent leaders
            281–7
        blurred line between leadership
            functions and team process
            261–2
        capacity 265–6
        components and roles 259–61
        definition 259
        empirical review 266–7

    in self-directed work teams 262–3,
        266–7
    self-managed leadership
        development opportunity
        262
    teamwork competencies for
        leadership self-development
        271–5
    types 263–4
member participation 284
performance monitoring 286–7
phases of team development 268–9
self-correction techniques 286
situation updates 285
task management 280
team processes and emergent states
    256–8
    blurred line between leadership
        functions and team process
        261–2

Yukl, G. 2, 258
Yunus, Mohammed 490

Zaccaro, S.J. 285
Zhang, X. 405–6
Zhang, Y. 316